A Practitioner's Guide to Directors' Duties and Responsibilities

Sixth Edition

A Practitioner's Guide to Directors' Duties and Responsibilities

Sixth Edition

Consultant Editor
Tim Boxell
Slaughter and May

SWEET & MAXWELL

THOMSON REUTERS

First Edition	2000	by Glen James
Second Edition	2003	by Glen James
Third Edition	2007	by Tim Boxell
Fourth Edition	2010	by Tim Boxell
Fifth Edition	2013	by Tim Boxell

Published in 2019 by Thomson Reuters, trading as Sweet & Maxwell. Registered in England & Wales, Company No.1679046. Registered Office and address for service: 5 Canada Square, Canary Wharf, London, E14 5AQ.

For further information on our products and services, visit *www.sweetandmaxwell.co.uk*

Typeset by Letterpart Limited, Caterham on the Hill, Surrey, CR3 5XL.

Printed and bound in Great Britain by CPI Group (UK) Ltd, Croydon, CR0 4YY.

No natural forests were destroyed to make this product: only farmed timber was used and re-planted.

A CIP catalogue record of this book is available from the British Library.

ISBN: 978-0-414-05699-2

Biographies

Tim Boxell is a partner at Slaughter and May. Tim's practice mainly involves corporate, corporate finance, mergers and acquisitions and private equity work. A substantial part of his practice is of a cross-border nature. He has extensive experience of international transactions involving a number of overseas jurisdictions in a variety of business sectors. He was, until 2018, a member of the Law Society's Company Law Committee and is a member of the Policy & Technical Advisory Committee of the Association of Corporate Treasurers.

Chris Hale is the senior partner of Travers Smith LLP. For the last 25 years he has specialised in UK and international buyout work, acting for both institutional investors and management teams on investments and divestments, as well as private equity-backed companies on mergers and acquisitions and other corporate matters. He writes and lectures regularly on company law and private equity in particular.

Rachel Woodburn joined Travers Smith in 1995, having qualified as a solicitor in 1991 at McKenna & Co (now part of CMS). Rachel became a partner in the Corporate Department at Travers Smith in 1999, specialising in private M&A, private equity and general company law. She moved to a professional support role in 2000 and now leads Travers Smith's Knowledge and Learning teams. Rachel is a regular contributor to company law publications.

Phillip Becker is a professional support lawyer in the Private Equity and Financial Sponsors Group at Travers Smith. He specialises in private M&A, private equity and general company law.

Ben Koehne is a Corporate partner at Addleshaw Goddard LLP. Ben's experience includes advising on a wide range of corporate and strategic transactions including UK and cross-border mergers and acquisitions (including acquisitions under the UK Banking Act 2009), disposals, joint ventures and intragroup restructurings. He also advises the boards of companies, building societies, co-operatives and other entities on directors' duties and constitutional, corporate governance, strategic and regulatory driven matters and projects. Ben's clients include banks, building societies, mutuals, asset managers, brokers and stock exchanges, amongst others. Ben closely monitors regulatory developments and advises clients on compliance and the strategic importance of regulatory change.

Michelle de Kluyver is a partner in Addleshaw Goddard LLP's Corporate Crime and Regulatory Investigations group. Michelle has broad and deep experience in complex, cross-border financial crime investigations relating to bribery and corruption, financial sanctions, money laundering, fraud and related issues. Michelle's investigation experience covers the UK, the US, Europe, the Middle East, Asia, Africa, South America and offshore jurisdictions. Michelle is an expert on directors' duties and also advises clients on compliance, remediation and governance: "In my area of practice, compliance, investigation, enforcement and the management of collateral risks come together as a discipline".

Elliot Shear is managing director of W Legal Ltd. Elliot specialises in mergers and acquisitions for public and private companies and undertakes a full range of transactional and advisory work for corporate clients, financial institutions and Ultra HNWs. His experience includes advising on mainstream corporate law and corporate governance—as well as joint ventures, private equity investments and general commercial matters. Elliot's sector expertise is particularly in the Defence industry—and also Financial Services. The strength of Elliot's reputation was recognised through his inclusion in *The Lawyer's* "Hot 100" lawyers.

Stephen Hewes is a partner at Freshfields Bruckhaus Deringer LLP. His practice includes public and private M&A (in particular cross-border), minority investments and joint ventures, and corporate governance and general company law advice. He is a member of the Law Society's Company Law Committee.

Andrew Taggart leads Herbert Smith Freehills LLP's UK and EMEA employment team and advises clients in various business sectors on a wide range of employment issues. He has been involved in many cases in the Employment Tribunal and the Employment Appeal Tribunal, as well as in the High Court, the Court of Appeal and the Supreme Court. He is regularly involved in board-level reorganisations, corporate governance matters and internal investigations, in particular for listed companies and for firms in the financial services sector.

Jemima Coleman is an experienced employment lawyer and member of the Corporate Governance Advisory Team at Herbert Smith Freehills LLP. She has advised on cross-border transactions, equalities law, and High Court and Tribunal litigation. She has particular expertise in relation to directors' remuneration and women in the workplace, and has published widely on employment law developments. Jemima has chaired various working parties of the Employment Lawyers Association's Legislative and Policy Committee. She speaks at in-house client seminars and provides tailored client training on recent and forthcoming legislation. Jemima is a non-executive board member of the Legal Services Board and a non-executive director of Creative Access.

Paul Lester is a partner in the Corporate Department of Cripps LLP. He specialises in corporate finance, stock exchange issues, public company takeovers, mergers and acquisitions, joint ventures, partnerships and LLPs, structured property transactions, and property investments and funds. Paul has extensive experience of advising corporate and institutional clients on the full range of corporate transactions both in the UK and internationally.

Crowley Woodford is a partner in the London office of Ashurst LLP where he leads the European employment practice. He specialises in all aspects of contentious and non-contentious employment law and has extensive experience in the employment aspects of corporate transactions, corporate governance matters and executive arrivals and departures. Crowley is a regular speaker and commentator on employment law matters and is often quoted in industry publications and the national press.

Nick Williamson is a partner in the Corporate team at Ashurst LLP. He focuses primarily on the energy/natural resources sectors. He specialises in M&A and ECM/corporate finance, advising companies (both listed and private) and investment banks/brokers (as sponsors, brokers, nomads and underwriters). He regularly advises on complex cross-border M&A matters, including reverse takeovers and acquisitions funded by equity. In addition to M&A matters, he is well-versed in corporate matters, and regularly advises boards of directors and GCs on complex strategic and governance matters.

Jonathan Marks has been a partner at Slaughter and May since 1997. He has a corporate and corporate finance practice and has been involved in a wide range of domestic and cross-border transactions including demutualisations, fund-raisings such as IPOs and placings, joint ventures, private and public acquisitions and shareholder disputes. Jonathan has advised a number of listed and other clients on accounting, constitutional, corporate governance and regulatory matters. He also has experience of advising on the corporate aspects of banking, capital markets and other financing transactions, and outsourcing and other commercial agreements.

Michael Hatchard established the English law practice at Skadden Arps Slate Meagher & Flom LLP and was a partner from 1994 until his retirement from the practice of law in December 2017. He was previously a partner at Theodore Goddard where he began his career in law in 1978. Michael had particular responsibility for mergers and acquisitions and corporate governance, with broad ranging complementary experience in corporate finance and restructuring, covering transactions governed by the UK or other European takeover and governance regimes. Michael has broad experience advising companies, boards and individual directors on their duties, liability and protection, and continues to provide consulting services on corporate governance.

Michael Todd QC is head of Erskine Chambers. He specialises in litigation and transactional advice on company law, corporate finance, capital markets and corporate insolvency, in the UK and internationally. He is a principal contributor to FromCounsel. Michael was Chairman of the Bar of England & Wales in 2012 and Chairman of the Chancery Bar Association from 2008–2011.

Hamish Anderson is a consultant (and former partner) in the banking department at Norton Rose Fulbright LLP, specialising in insolvency. Hamish qualified as a solicitor in 1973. He is a past president and former council member of the Insolvency Lawyers' Association and a former council member of the Association of Business Recovery Professionals (R3). Hamish is a member (and former chairman) of the City of London Law Society Insolvency Committee. He is also an Honorary Professor at Nottingham Trent University and a regular speaker and writer on insolvency matters. Amongst other publications, he is the author of *The Framework of Corporate Insolvency Law* (OUP, 2017) and one of the editors of *Lightman & Moss on the Law of Administrators and Receivers of Companies*, 6th edn (Sweet & Maxwell, 2017).

Rob Dedman is a partner in the Special Matters practice of King & Spalding's London office. Between 2007 and 2017, Rob spent a decade as a regulator in a variety of senior positions. He led the team that created the FCA and PRA, and from April 2013 established and led the Bank of England/PRA's enforcement division, where he was responsible for enforcement investigations into banks, insurers and their directors. Rob defends corporate and individual clients under investigation by regulatory authorities, and carries out internal investigations for clients. He also advises clients on compliance matters, including helping them determine the extent to which their policies, procedures, systems and controls comply with regulatory expectations and industry best practice.

Gareth Rees QC is a partner in the King & Spalding Special Matters and Government Investigations team. He was called to the Bar in 1981 and was appointed Queens Counsel in 2003. At the Bar, he represented many company directors in criminal and regulatory matters, and as Director of Enforcement at the Financial Reporting Council between 2012 and 2017 was responsible for investigations and prosecutions of accountant directors and auditors' conduct in the preparation and audit of financial statements. He now acts for corporates and directors in regulatory and criminal investigations and advises on a range of directors' duties.

Aaron Stephens is a partner in the London office of King & Spalding LLP, and an English and US (California) qualified lawyer and solicitor-advocate with 17+ years' experience practicing in the London and international market. He has acted in a wide variety of internal and/or government investigations (involving FCA, PRA, SFO, NCA, Lloyd's of London and The Takeover Panel), and has cross-border experience with US and other international investigations and matters involving over 20 countries. He also regularly advises financial institutions and other corporates in connection with their financial crime compliance programmes. His recent cases include LIBOR, FX, SSA bonds, precious metals, "spoofing" and other FCA and/or SFO matters involving alleged market abuse, bribery, money laundering and fraud.

Stephen Robins is a barrister at South Square Chambers. He was called to the Bar in 2001. He has a general commercial practice with a focus on insolvency, banking and company law. Recent cases include *Heritable Bank Plc v Landsbanki Islands HF* [2013] 1 W.L.R. 725 (Supreme Court), *Rubin v Eurofinance SA* [2013] 1 A.C. 236 (Supreme Court), *Leisure (Norwich) II Ltd v Luminar Lava Ignite Ltd* [2012] 4 All E.R. 894, *Lomas v JFB Firth Rixson Inc* [2012] 2 All E.R. (Comm) 1076 (Court of Appeal) and *Tambrook Jersey Ltd, Re* [2013] EWCA Civ 576.

Contents

3   Directors' Duties

Ben Koehne
Partner
Addleshaw Goddard LLP

Michelle de Kluyver
Partner
Addleshaw Goddard LLP

4   Potential Liabilities

Elliot Shear
Managing Director
W Legal Limited

5   Fair Dealing and Connected Persons

Stephen Hewes

6   Service Contracts and Remuneration

Andrew Taggart, Partner and Jemima Coleman, Professional
Support Lawyer
Herbert Smith Freehills LLP

7   Share Dealing by Directors and Connected Persons

Paul Lester, Partner
Cripps LLP

8 Directors' Powers and Proceedings

Crowley Woodford, Employment Partner and Nick Williamson, Corporate Partner

Ashurst LLP

9 Corporate Governance

Jonathan Marks, Partner

Slaughter and May

10 Directors Facing Disputes

Michael Hatchard, Retired Partner

Skadden, Arps, Slate, Meagher & Flom (UK) LLP

Michael Todd QC

Erskine Chambers

11   Duties of Directors Facing Insolvency

Hamish Anderson
Consultant
Norton Rose Fulbright LLP

12   Regulatory Investigations

Rob Dedman, Gareth Rees QC, Aaron Stephens
Partners, King & Spalding

13   Disqualification of Directors

Stephen Robins
South Square, Gray's Inn

Chapter 1

Introduction

Tim Boxell

Partner

Slaughter and May

This Guide for practitioners—company directors and their professional advisers—is now in its sixth edition. Practitioners are only too aware that there is no simple model role for the company director. This is partly because of the way in which company law and the codes of corporate governance have developed in the UK, but also because of the diverse nature of the purposes and interests which corporate structures serve. Practitioners will want to master all aspects of the regulatory regime, both legal and voluntary, which prescribe the conduct expected of directors, as the consequences of breach can be serious. Further, practitioners need to be aware of, and must be in a position to react to, changes which occur in the regulatory regime.

Directors face different responsibilities and duties according to the type of company they serve, the level of regulation to which they are subject and, to some extent, the nature of their position. As a preliminary question, directors may therefore ask whether there is any underlying framework to which they may refer for guidance and from which they may infer what is expected of them.

The Companies Act 2006 (CA 2006 or the Act) is the principal legislation governing companies in the UK. It applies to all UK companies, small or large, private or public. When enacted, the CA 2006 consisted of 1,300 sections and 16 Schedules, with a view to meeting the Labour Government's promise to simplify company law and deregulate small businesses.[1] Some of the provisions simply restated the existing law, but many brought about a fundamental change in how companies would need to be governed in the future. Notably, it codified directors' duties for the first time.

Since the fifth edition of this book, the legislative and regulatory landscape for companies and directors has continued to evolve. On 5 April 2017, the House of Commons Business, Energy and Industrial Strategy (BEIS) Committee published a report on corporate governance after failures were exposed at BHS and Sports Direct. This recognised a need for greater

---

[1] Subsequent amendments have been made by statute and statutory instruments including the Small Business, Enterprise and Employment Act 2015.

transparency, stronger mechanisms to enforce the CA 2006 and increased stakeholder engagement on pay, together with initiatives to increase gender and ethnic diversity at the executive level.[2] In August 2017, the Government published its response to a green paper consultation on corporate governance reform which largely agreed with the BEIS Committee's recommendations. It therefore appears that executive remuneration, stakeholder engagement and boardroom diversity will be important themes going forward.

In June 2018, the Financial Reporting Council (FRC) published an updated version of the UK Corporate Governance Code (the Governance Code). The Governance Code sets out the principles that underlie an effective board and emphasises the value of good corporate governance to long-term sustainable success.[3] Premium listed companies are required to report against this latest incarnation of the Governance Code on a "comply or explain" basis for accounting periods beginning on or after 1 January 2019, though other companies may choose to apply the Governance Code (or at least any applicable provisions thereof). The FRC expects to publish the third version of its Stewardship Code, which aims to promote transparency and engagement between institutional investors and the boards of listed companies, in the summer of 2019. The Stewardship Code and the Governance Code are complementary and both should be considered by directors when performing their roles.

Companies involved in wholesale and retail finance remain subject to a tripartite system of regulation comprising the Financial Policy Committee (a macro-prudential regulator), the Prudential Regulation Authority (PRA) (a micro-prudential regulator, responsible for systemically important banks, building societies and insurers) and the Financial Conduct Authority (FCA) (a micro-prudential regulator of firms not regulated by the PRA, including asset managers). The introduction of the tripartite system on 1 April 2013 was intended to create "more intense supervision" as part of the Coalition Government's promise to enhance the UK's reputation for transparency and efficiency in business and position as one of the world's leading financial centres.[4] The PRA and FCA have implemented a number of corporate governance initiatives, including the senior managers and certification regime (SMCR), which banks became subject to in March 2016 and which is scheduled to be extended to financial services firms solely regulated by the FCA in December 2019. The SMCR aims to increase the personal accountability of senior people in the financial services industry, with persons performing designated senior management functions requiring (i)

---

2   Ethnic diversity and gender diversity in boardrooms have also been considered by (respectively) the Parker Review, which reported in October 2017, and the Hampton-Alexander Review, which was first published in November 2016 and has had annual updates every November since—most recently in November 2018.
3   FRC, UK Corporate Governance Code, July 2018.
4   Speech at the Lord Mayor's Dinner for Bankers and Merchants of the City of London by the Chairman of the FSA, Lord Turner, 16 June 2010.

approval to take up such positions; (ii) to be in ongoing compliance with certain standards of fitness and propriety; and (iii) to comply with two tiers of conduct rules.

Excessive executive remuneration continues to attract scrutiny from the government, media, investing public and other stakeholder groups. Both the Companies (Miscellaneous Reporting) Regulations 2018 and the updated Governance Code have introduced additional requirements in relation to the setting of and reporting on executive remuneration, in each case applicable to accounting periods beginning on or after 1 January 2019. These new requirements seek to arrest a perceived tendency in recent years for executive pay to increase at a rate neither justified by performance nor consistent with the pay increases offered to rank-and-file employees. Consistent with these concerns, the BEIS Committee launched an inquiry on fair pay in March 2018 and is currently preparing a report on executive rewards for publication.

At the time of publication, the method and date by which the UK will leave the EU is uncertain. Although matters of corporate governance are to some extent harmonised on a European level—for example, through Directive (EU) 2017/828 amending Directive 2007/36/EC as regards the encouragement of long-term shareholder engagement—it is unlikely that "Brexit", to the extent it occurs, will have an immediate effect on the area of directors' duties and responsibilities. The long-term impact is unknown.

1.1   CA 2006 reforms

The CA 2006 is a complex piece of legislation, much of which falls outside the scope of this Guide. The following chapters, however, pick out and examine a number of areas of particular relevance to directors' duties and responsibilities, a few of which are highlighted in this introduction. Since its enactment, the CA 2006 has been interpreted by a steady stream of cases testing the new sections. These cases, combined with the useful practical guidance that has been published by industry groups, should give a degree of comfort to practitioners when applying the CA 2006 in practice.

1.1.1   *Codification of directors' duties*

Before the CA 2006 was enacted, the general duties owed by directors of UK companies had not been placed on a statutory footing. Instead, directors had specific duties built up over many years by case law. In 2001, the Company Law Review (CLR)—commissioned in 1998 and comprising an independent group of experts, practitioners and business people—reported that there was a need to make the law in this area more consistent, certain, accessible and comprehensible, and recommended that the general duties

3

owed by directors should be codified.[5] The Law Commission and the Scottish Law Commission had, in 1999, also recommended the codification of a director's main fiduciary duties and the common law duty of care and skill.[6] The CLR proposed that any statutory statement should largely reproduce the existing regime without hindering the development of the law by the courts.

The Labour Government accepted these recommendations and thereby set itself a challenge. As acknowledged in the Explanatory Notes to the CA 2006, codification is not just a matter of transposing wording taken from judgments into legislative propositions. This is because judgments are directed at particular cases and therefore even when they appear to state general principles such principles will rarely be exhaustive. Moreover, company law principles are frequently taken from other areas of the law, such as trusts and agency, with the Labour Government recognising the importance of maintaining a linkage between the principles underlying directors' duties once codified and the development of other related legal principles through the common law, in order that the law relating to directors' duties could continue to reflect important developments elsewhere. Simply put, the challenge was to balance precision against the need for continued flexibility and development.

Sections 171 to 177 of the Act codify the general duties that a director owes to his or her company. These duties are considered in more detail in Section 1.2 below. As for the interrelationship between directors' duties, as codified, and the old common law regime, the Act provides:

> "(3)   The general duties are based on certain common law rules and equitable principles as they apply in relation to directors and have effect in place of those rules and principles as regards the duties owed to a company by a director.
>
> (4)   The general duties shall be interpreted and applied in the same way as common law rules or equitable principles, and regard shall be had to the corresponding common law rules and equitable principles in interpreting and applying the general duties."[7]

The fact that the general duties must be interpreted and applied in the same way as the common law rules and equitable principles causes some difficulties, as the statutory language introduced to replace such common law rules and equitable principles does not always mirror how the duties, as codified, were previously expressed or understood under the hitherto prevailing common law regime.

---

[5]   The Company Law Review Steering Group presented its Final Report (Company *Law Reforms: Modern Company Law for a Competitive Economy*) to the Secretary of State for Trade and Industry on 26 July 2001.

[6]   Joint report Company Directors: Regulatory Conflicts of Interest and Formulating a Statement of Duties, September 1999 (Law Com. No.261, Scot Law Com. No.173).

[7]   CA 2006 s.170.

The majority of the sections of the CA 2006 imposing the general duties came into force on 1 October 2007, but the duty to avoid conflicts of interest did not become effective until 1 October 2008. This was to give companies more time to amend their articles of association to reflect the new provisions.

Of course, the specified general duties do not cover all the duties that a director may owe to the company. They are the general duties for a director to have in mind in carrying out his duties but there are other specific duties imposed (such as the duty to file accounts and reports with the registrar of companies).[8]

The CA 2006 made changes to the manner in which a breach, or possible breach, of a director's duty may be sanctioned. The Act abolished a director's right to ratify his or her own breach of duty by providing that the necessary majority of votes in favour of ratification at a shareholders' meeting must be obtained disregarding any votes cast in favour of ratification by the director and any member connected with him or her.[9] Curiously though, it did not abolish the right of directors to vote, in their capacity as shareholders, to authorise in advance acts which may otherwise be in breach of their duties. Helpfully, the CA 2006 confirms that a substantial property transaction between the company and a director may be entered into provided either: (i) prior shareholder approval has been received; or (ii) completion of the substantial property transaction in question is conditional upon receipt of shareholder approval. Previously, there had been some doubt as to whether this was permitted, or whether the approval had to be obtained before the transaction could be entered into.[10] The Act also allows loans to be made by a company to its directors, provided that they are first approved by shareholder resolution.[11]

1.1.2 Derivative claims

The codification of directors' duties was closely linked the introduction of CA 2006 s.260, which put derivative claims by shareholders onto a statutory footing. A derivative claim is a claim by a member in respect of a cause of action vested in the company and seeking relief on behalf of the company.

Derivative claims may be brought only in respect of a cause of action arising from an actual or proposed act or omission involving negligence, default, breach of duty or breach of trust by a director of the company (including the duty to exercise reasonable care, skill and diligence). Once a shareholder has commenced a derivative claim, he or she must apply to the court for permission to continue the action. If it appears to the court that the

---

[8] CA 2006 s.441.
[9] CA 2006 s.239.
[10] CA 2006 s.190.
[11] CA 2006 s.197.

application and the evidence filed in support of it do not disclose a prima facie case for giving permission to continue the action, the court must dismiss the application and may make any consequential order that it considers appropriate.[12] Permission must be refused if the court is satisfied that:

(a) a person acting in accordance with CA 2006 s.172 (duty to promote the interests of the company) would not seek to continue the claim;
(b) the act or omission has not yet occurred and has been authorised by the company; or
(c) the act or omission has occurred, but was authorised before it occurred or has since been ratified by the company.[13]

The court must also consider further factors before deciding whether or not to grant permission, including whether the member is acting in good faith in seeking to continue the claim and whether the relevant act or omission could be authorised or ratified by the company. The court is required to have particular regard to any evidence before it as to the views of members of the company who have no personal interest in the matter.

Prior to the introduction of the Act, there had been some concern that the advent of explicitly codified directors' duties combined with further new provisions placing a means of challenging directors for breach of those duties on a statutory footing for the first time would encourage activist shareholders to commence (or at least to threaten to commence) derivative proceedings more readily. However, since the Act has come into force, there has not been any appreciable increase in the number of derivative claims (which remain rare) being brought. This can most likely be explained by the extent of judicial control exercised by the courts in their general reluctance to grant permission to continue, a reluctance which is well documented across various cases.[14] That said, there are a limited number of cases in which permission to continue was granted which demonstrate what is needed to make out the prima facie case required to be allowed permission to continue.[15]

---

[12] CA 2006 s.261.
[13] CA 2006 s.263(2).
[14] *Mission Capital Plc v Sinclair* [2008] EWHC 1339 (Ch); [2008] B.C.C. 866; [2010] 1 B.C.L.C. 304; *Franbar Holdings Ltd v Patel* [2008] EWHC 1534 (Ch); [2008] B.C.C. 885; [2009] 1 B.C.L.C. 1; *Stimpson v Southern Landlords Assoc* [2009] EWHC 2072 (Ch); [2010] B.C.C. 387; *Kleanthous v Paphitis* [2011] EWHC 2287 (Ch); [2012] B.C.C. 676; (2011) 108(36) L.S.G. 19; *Langley Ward Ltd v Trevor* [2011] EWHC 1893 (Ch); [2011] All E.R. (D) 78 (Jul); *Zavahir v Shankleman* [2016] EWHC 2772 (Ch); [2017] B.C.C. 500; and *Brannigan v Style* [2016] EWHC 512 (Ch).
[15] *Kiani v Cooper* [2010] EWHC 577 (Ch); [2010] B.C.C. 463; [2010] 2 B.C.L.C. 427; *Stainer v Lee* [2010] EWHC 1539 (Ch); [2011] B.C.C. 134; *Kleanthous v Paphitis* [2011] EWHC 2287 (Ch); [2012] B.C.C. 676; (2011) 108(36) L.S.G. 19; *Parry v Bartlett* [2011] EWHC 3146 (Ch); [2012] B.C.C. 700; *Phillips v Fryer* [2012] EWHC 1611 (Ch); [2013] B.C.C. 176; *Hughes v Weiss* [2012] EWHC 2363 (Ch) and *Hook v Sumner* [2015] EWHC 3820 (Ch); [2016] B.C.C. 220.

In *Fort Gilkicker Ltd, Re*,[16] the court considered whether the statutory claim had wholly replaced the common law claim; specifically, whether it was still possible to bring a "multiple" derivative claim as was available under the common law.[17] It was held that the Act had not abolished the whole of the common law in relation to shareholder actions and that, as a result, a "multiple" derivative claim could still be brought.

1.1.3 Directors' reports

Some years ago, the Labour Government announced that quoted companies would be required to prepare and publicise an "operating and financial review". However, this proposal was dropped in November 2005 as part of that Government's drive to stop "gold plating" European legislation. Instead, until 1 October 2013, the now repealed CA 2006 s.417 simply required the directors' reports of large and medium sized companies to contain a "business review". Now, under CA 2006 Pt 15 Ch.4A, companies formerly required to include a "business review" in their directors' reports must instead produce a standalone "strategic report" separate from their directors' report. Furthermore, since 1 January 2017, certain large entities with over 500 employees are additionally required to include a "non-financial information" statement in their strategic reports providing information on environmental, social and employee matters to the extent necessary for an understanding of the company's development, performance and position and the impact of its activities. This "non-financial information" statement also mandates such disclosure in respect of human rights and anti-corruption and anti-bribery matters. The legislation also obliges quoted companies not required to make a "non-financial information" statement to nevertheless make certain further related disclosures. Additionally, in relation to financial years beginning on or after 1 January 2019, large companies must include in their strategic reports a statement describing how the directors have had regard to the matters set out in s.172(1)(a)–(f) when performing their duty under that section. The introduction of this last obligation is symptomatic of a wider drive to encourage companies to engage non-shareholder stakeholders more frequently and effectively. For more details on the precise content requirements of the strategic report, as determined by the nature of the entity in question, see Section 9.6.6 of Chapter 9.

In terms of content requirements in respect of the directors' report, CA 2006 s.416 provides that the directors' report must state the names of the persons who, at any time during the financial year, were directors of the company, while directors' reports (other than those prepared by small companies)

---

[16] *Fort Gilkicker Ltd, Re* [2013] EWHC 348 (Ch); [2013] 3 W.L.R. 164; [2013] B.C.C. 365.
[17] A multiple derivative claim is the name given to a claim when the court recognises the conferral of locus standi upon one or more members of a holding company, who are attempting to bring a derivative claim for and on behalf of a subsidiary of that holding company.

must also state the amount, if any, that the directors recommend should be paid by way of dividend. Regulations made under CA 2006 s.416(4) prescribe further matters that, depending on the company's size, must be included in the directors' report.[18] Listed companies subject to the Disclosure Guidance and Transparency Rules are required to include a corporate governance statement either: (i) in the directors' report; (ii) in a separate report published together with and in the same manner as its annual report; or (iii) in a document publicly available on the company website to which reference is made in the directors' report.[19]

Directors of quoted companies are undoubtedly aware that CA 2006 s.420 requires them to prepare a directors' remuneration report in respect of each financial year, given they will commit an offence if they fail to do so. The Enterprise and Regulatory Reform Act 2013 amended the CA 2006 to require the directors' remuneration report to contain a forward-looking remuneration policy, such policy to be subject to a binding shareholder vote at least every three years.[20] Payments to directors are permitted only to the extent they are consistent with such approved policy.[21] Recently, more detailed reporting requirements in relation to remuneration have been introduced via secondary legislation, applicable to financial years beginning on or after 1 January 2019. Such legislation requires quoted companies with more than 250 employees to include the ratio of the total pay of their chief executive to the median, 25th and 75th percentile remuneration of their UK employees, along with an explanation of year-on-year changes to those ratios. Additionally, in order to better align the extent of executive rewards with company performance, new reporting obligations require companies to make disclosures linking the payment of discretionary remuneration to executives with share price performance.[22] There has also been a recent focus on disparities in pay driven by factors other than straightforward seniority differentials—gender pay gap reporting has been mandatory for most companies (listed or unlisted) with over 250 employees since 6 April 2017, and BEIS concluded a consultation on the introduction of a statutory ethnicity pay reporting regime in January 2019.[23]

Shareholder rebellions over executive pay have been a fixture of the AGM season since the "shareholder spring" of April and May 2012. The 2018 season proved particularly awkward for FTSE 100 companies, with 18

---

[18] Large and Medium-sized Companies and Groups (Accounts and Reports) Regulations 2008 (SI 2008/410); Small Companies and Groups (Accounts and Directors' Report) Regulations 2008 (SI 2008/409); Companies Act 2006 (Strategic Report and Directors' Report) Regulations 2013 (SI 2013/1970) and Companies (Miscellaneous Reporting) Regulations 2018 (SI 2018/860).

[19] DTR 7.2.

[20] CA 2006 s.226B.

[21] CA 2006 s.439A.

[22] See Large and Medium-sized Companies and Groups (Accounts and Reports) Regulations 2008 (SI 2008/410) Sch.8, as amended by Companies (Miscellaneous Reporting) Regulations 2018 (SI 2018/860).

[23] Equality Act 2010 (Gender Pay Gap Information) Regulations 2017 (SI 2017/172).

pay-related resolutions facing shareholder dissent levels above 20%—twice the figure for the corresponding period in the previous year. Responding to an invitation in the Government's response to BEIS' 2016 green paper on corporate governance reform, the Investment Association now maintains a publicly searchable register of listed companies who have experienced significant protest votes (defined as 20% or more) against pay-related resolutions. This development is supplemented by the inclusion in the latest version of the Governance Code of provisions requiring companies to engage in additional consultation and communication with shareholders in the event they receive such significant protest votes.

It is imperative that directors pay careful attention when compiling their reports, as the Act provides that a director is liable to compensate the company for any loss suffered by it as a result of any untrue or misleading statement in, or omission from, the directors' report, the strategic report, the directors' remuneration report or any separate corporate governance statement. However, a director will only be held so liable if he or she knew the statement to be untrue or misleading or was reckless as to whether the statement was untrue or misleading or knew the omission to be dishonest concealment of a material fact. Moreover, a director is not liable under the Act to compensate any person other than the company as a result of that person's reliance on a false or misleading statement, although this does not affect potential liability for a civil penalty or for a criminal offence.[24] On this basis, therefore, it is prudent to bring as much of a company's narrative reporting as possible within the ambit of the above-mentioned company reports. The FRC has established a "Financial Reporting Lab" that brings together investors and companies in order to test new reporting formats.

The defence provided in CA 2006 s.463 operates as a matter of English law and may not be effective to exclude liability for a claim brought outside the UK—for instance, where the claimant has received company reports containing misleading information outside the UK. For this reason, many companies now disclaim liability (aside from that arising under English law) in their reports. Although this approach is not necessarily effective it is unlikely to be prejudicial. Market practice increasingly supports the inclusion of an additional disclaimer stating that any "forward looking statements" contained in a report are not guarantees of future performance and that there is no assurance given that such statements will prove to be accurate.

Directors of companies with listed securities should also note the separate liability under the Financial Services and Markets Act 2000 (FSMA) s.90A and Sch.10A to pay compensation to persons who have suffered loss as a result of a misleading statement or dishonest omission in certain published information relating to those securities. This is provided such securities are listed on a market situated or operating in the UK, or the UK is the

---

[24] CA 2006 s.463.

company's home state. While this liability attaches to the company itself, para.7(4) of Sch.10A provides that the liability of individual directors pursuant to a court order for restitution or a FCA/PRA-issued requirement to make restitution is not precluded.[25] The possibility of individual directors being held liable under various civil causes of action (including breach of contract and misrepresentation) or receiving a civil or criminal penalty is similarly not precluded.[26] Since 1 October 2010, the liability under FSMA s.90A and Sch.10A has extended to all information in respect of the relevant listed securities which is published, or the availability of which is announced, by means of a recognised information service.[27]

1.1.4 Shadow directors

A shadow director is any person in accordance with whose directions or instructions the directors of a company are accustomed to act, although a person is not deemed to be a shadow director on the sole basis that the directors act on advice given by him or her in a professional capacity.[28] The Act applies the general directors' duties to shadow directors where and to the extent that such duties are capable of so applying.[29] This means that the precise extent of shadow directors' duties is not conclusively defined by the Act and practitioners are instead forced to rely on the previous, uncertain case law in this area.

In *Smithton Ltd v Naggar*,[30] which applied the leading case of *Revenue and Customs Commissioners v Holland*,[31] the Court of Appeal found that the question of whether a person is a shadow director is a question of fact and degree, and that it is not necessary for a person's role to extend over the whole range of a company's activities in order for that person to be determined to be a shadow director.

1.1.5 Register of directors' addresses

Previously, directors who were subject to the risk of violence or intimidation were permitted to keep their home addresses confidential. The CA 2006 contains broader protections for all directors. The Act permits a director to provide a service address for the public record (which may be the company's registered office) rather than his or her home address. However, each director must also provide his or her usual residential address to the company for inclusion in a register which is not subject to public inspection.

---

[25] See 384 FSMA ss.382 and 384.
[26] FMSA Sch.10A para.3.
[27] FSMA Sch.10A para.2.
[28] CA 2006 s.251.
[29] CA 2006 s.170(5).
[30] *Smithton Ltd v Naggar* [2014] EWCA Civ 939; [2015] 1 W.L.R. 189; [2014] B.C.C. 482.
[31] *Revenue and Customs Commissioners v Holland* [2010] UKSC 51; [2010] 1 W.L.R. 2793; [2011] B.C.C. 1.

The Act imposes an obligation on the Registrar of Companies not to disclose directors' usual residential addresses for public inspection.[32]

1.2 Duties and responsibilities

Prior to the introduction of the CA 2006 this area of the law was fragmented and difficult to navigate. This situation was in large part due to the fact that the law pertaining to directors' duties was comprised of a number of statutory provisions superimposed onto pre-existing common law principles. The CA 2006 now provides a list of the general duties of directors, which are:

(a)　to act in accordance with the company's constitution and only exercise powers for the purposes which they are conferred[33];

(b)　to promote the success of the company[34];

(c)　to exercise independent judgment[35];

(d)　to use reasonable care, skill and diligence[36];

(e)　to avoid conflicts of interest[37];

(f)　not to accept benefits from third parties[38]; and

(g)　to declare an interest in a proposed transaction or arrangement.[39]

As mentioned above, these general duties are based on, and apply in place of, certain common law rules and equitable principles.[40] However, the general duties must be interpreted and applied in the same way as those common law rules and equitable principles.[41] Hence, the extent to which the statutory regime has actually increased clarity is debatable, though there is an obvious benefit to directors in having a list of their general duties available in one place. Furthermore, practical guidance offered by institutional bodies such as the Institute of Chartered Secretaries and Administrators (ICSA) has helped to elucidate the statutory regime under the CA 2006.[42] Although the general duties will be examined in more detail in other chapters, it is worth touching briefly on some aspects.

---

[32]　CA 2006 s.242.

[33]　CA 2006 s.171.

[34]　CA 2006 s.172.

[35]　CA 2006 s.173.

[36]　CA 2006 s.174.

[37]　CA 2006 s.175.

[38]　CA 2006 s.176.

[39]　CA 2006 s.177.

[40]　CA 2006 s.170(3).

[41]　CA 2006 s.170(4).

[42]　ICSA, *Guidance Note on Directors' General Duties*, June 2015. The guidance is intended primarily for public and listed companies, but much of it can be applied to private companies as well.

1.2.1 The duty to promote the success of the company

This requires a director to "act in the way he considers, in good faith, would be most likely to promote the success of the company for the benefit of its members as a whole".[43]

The concept of "members as a whole" is discussed in more detail later in this chapter. A useful starting point for determining the meaning of "success" is the Attorney-General's consideration of this point in the House of Lords during the Company Law Review:

> "... [W]hat is success? The starting point is that it is essentially for the members of the company to define the objectives that they wish to achieve. Success means what the members collectively want the company to achieve. For a commercial company, success will usually mean long-term increase in value. For certain companies, such as charities and community interest companies, it will mean the attainment of the objectives for which the company has been established. But one can be more refined than that. A company's constitution and the decisions that a company makes can also go on to be more specific about what is the appropriate success model for the company. I have indicated that usually for a company it will be a long-term increase in value, but I can imagine commercial companies that would have a different objective as to their success."[44]

1.2.2 The duty to avoid conflicts of interest

A director of a company must avoid a situation in which he or she has, or can have, a direct or indirect interest that conflicts with the interests of the company. This duty also applies to former directors, as regards the exploitation of any property, information or opportunity of which he or she became aware at a time when he or she was a director.[45] The duty to avoid conflicts of interest has been controversial, as it raises the question of whether directors can hold multiple directorships.

For both current and former directors, the duty will not be breached if the relevant situation cannot reasonably be regarded as likely to give rise to a conflict of interest.[46] The duty will also not be infringed if the matter has been authorised by the directors.[47] There is an argument that it is sufficient to obtain authorisation ahead of a director's appointment in respect of possible future conflicts, but the better view is that a specific authorisation is required in respect of each matter arising after the appointment.

---

[43] CA 2006 s.172(1).
[44] House of Lords, *Hansard*, 6 February 2006.
[45] CA 2006 s.170(2).
[46] CA 2006 s.175(4)(a).
[47] CA 2006 s.175(4)(b).

For a private company whose constitution does not prevent it, authorisation may be given by directors who have no interest in the matter giving rise to the conflict.[48] This represents a departure from the previous law, which required that any potential conflict of interest had to be authorised instead by the members of the company. A public company's constitution must include a provision enabling the directors to authorise the matter and the authorisation must also be given by directors who have no interest in the matter.[49]

According to the GC100—an industry body of general counsels and company secretaries—most companies (including public companies) should include in their articles of association a general power for directors to authorise conflicts of interest.[50] The GC100 guidance, among other things, highlights potential conflict situations and provides suggested procedures for authorising these and reviewing authorisations.

1.2.3 *The level of reasonable care, skill and diligence*

Directors are required to exercise reasonable care, skill and diligence.[51] Traditionally, it was thought that the level of care, skill and diligence required to be a director was fairly minimal. Directors need no qualification to hold their post, and so the test appeared to be a subjective one against each individual director's own level of knowledge and skill. This approach found less favour with time and has now been completely replaced by a dual standard of care, skill and diligence, containing both an objective and a subjective limb, in the CA 2006. The Act expressly provides that reasonable care, skill and diligence:

> "means the care, skill and diligence that would be exercised by a reasonably diligent person with—
>
> (a)   the general knowledge, skill and experience that may reasonably be expected of a person carrying out the functions carried out by the director in relation to the company, and
> (b)   the general knowledge, skill and experience that the director has."[52]

This replicates the test set out in the Insolvency Act 1986 (IA 1986) s.214 for the purpose of determining the standard against which a director's actions will be evaluated in a wrongful trading context. Therefore, the case law in relation to that provision has been of great importance in setting the scope of the general duty of care. Indeed, prior to the introduction of the CA 2006, Hoffmann LJ held that the duty of care to which a director is subject under IA 1986 s.214 accurately reflected the wider position at common law and

---

[48]   CA 2006 s.175(5)(a).
[49]   CA 2006 s.175(5)(b).
[50]   GC100, *Companies Act 2006—Directors' Conflicts of Interests*, 18 January 2008.
[51]   CA 2006 s.174.
[52]   CA 2006 s.174(2).

was therefore applicable more broadly, including in relation to directors' duties.[53] Cases under the Company Directors Disqualification Act 1986 may also be helpful in determining whether a director is in breach of his or her standard of reasonable care, skill and diligence under the CA 2006. One such case is *Continental Assurance Co of London Plc (In Liquidation), Re,*[54] in which a non-executive director was disqualified even though he was unaware of the wrongful conduct in question. It was held that any competent director in his position would have been aware of such conduct. Therefore, it seems the non-executive director's unawareness of that conduct would lead to a breach of his duty of reasonable care, skill and diligence under the CA 2006.

In *Secretary of State for Trade and Industry v Baker,*[55] it was established that there is a continuing obligation on directors to acquire and maintain a sufficient knowledge and understanding of the company's business for the proper discharge of their duties. It is therefore critical that a person accepting the office of director is aware not only of the nature of the duties that he or she owes to the company and its members, but also regularly updates and refreshes his or her knowledge and understanding of the company's business in order to be capable of discharging those duties.[56] Exact parameters will vary according to the nature of the company and the individual experience and skill that the director in question possesses.

1.3 Further regulation

Although the codification of directors' duties in the CA 2006 is helpful in bringing certain duties together, it should be remembered that those sections do not constitute an exhaustive list of such duties. As well as the specific duties and obligations imposed elsewhere in the CA 2006—for example, the duty to file accounts and reports[57]— there are numerous other regulatory requirements applicable to directors. Thus, for example, directors of certain listed companies are subject to the Listing Rules, the Takeover Code, the Disclosure Guidance and Transparency Rules and the Governance Code (on a "comply-or-explain" basis). The latest version of the Governance Code was published in June 2018 and is applicable to accounting periods beginning on or after 1 January 2019. Directors of companies listed on the Alternative Investment Market (AIM) are subject to the AIM Rules for Companies, which were last amended in October 2018.

---

[53] *D'Jan of London Ltd, Re* [1993] B.C.C. 646; [1994] 1 B.C.L.C. 561.
[54] *Continental Assurance Co of London Plc (In Liquidation), Re* [1996] B.C.C. 888; [1997] 1 B.C.L.C. 48.
[55] *Secretary of State for Trade and Industry v Baker* [1999] 1 B.C.L.C. 433.
[56] Development was previously a main principle of the UK Corporate Governance Code, but this was removed from the July 2018 version.
[57] CA 2006 s.441.

Such rules and codes seek to improve standards of transparency and accountability, and are increasingly being put on a statutory footing in order to make them more effective at doing so. For example, the Takeover Panel has statutory authority pursuant to CA 2006 Pt 28 to make rules and regulations in relation to takeovers and mergers of listed companies, as well as authority to demand information from companies and to impose sanctions for non-compliance.

The FCA operates an approved persons regime, under which people wishing to be directors or controllers of regulated companies are required to apply to either or both of the PRA and FCA for approval. In order to attain such approval applicants have to demonstrate the necessary skills, expertise and integrity to undertake such a role. The application of the SMCR to FCA solo-regulated firms, currently scheduled for December 2019, will essentially mark the end of the approved persons regime.

In response to criticism received in the aftermath of the banking crisis, the PRA and FCA have become more pro-active on corporate governance matters, seeking to exert tighter control over the conduct of directors in the regulated sector. This trend is evidenced by the introduction of the SMCR in March 2016—a regime designed to reduce consumer harm and strengthen market integrity by combining systems of FCA authorisation and self-certification with new conduct rules setting minimum standards of individual behaviour in financial services. The SMCR initially replaced the approved persons regime for banks, building societies and dual (FCA and PRA) regulated investment firms, and was subsequently extended to insurers in December 2018. From 9 December 2019, the SMCR will apply to firms solely regulated by the FCA.

In the first enforcement action brought under the SMCR, the FCA and the PRA jointly fined James "Jes" Staley, Chief Executive Officer of the Barclays Group, a total of £642,430 for having failed to act with due skill, care and diligence in attempting to identify an anonymous whistle-blower.[58] The FCA and the PRA also imposed special reporting requirements on Barclays. Mr Staley's case demonstrates the willingness of the UK regulators to penalise individual directors for wrongful conduct, even where it is not alleged that the director in question acted without integrity.

Directors should note that the PRA and the FCA have the power to penalise any person found to have been performing controlled functions without approval.[59]

---

[58] FCA Final Notice JXS02208, 11 May 2018.
[59] FSMA s.63A.

1.4 The company's interests

The common law provided that directors owe their duties to their companies. There was much debate at the beginning of the Company Law Review process as to whether directors should continue to owe their duties solely to the company, except in limited cases, or whether directors should be required as a matter of law to account directly to third parties (such as suppliers, local communities and employees, etc). While the CA 2006 codified the existing position that directors' general duties are owed solely to the company,[60] it also introduced a requirement for directors to have regard to what the then Labour Government termed "enlightened shareholder value" when discharging their duty under CA 2006 s.172. In order to fulfil that duty, a director must act in the way that he or she considers, in good faith, would be most likely to promote the success of the company for the benefit of its members as a whole, and in doing so have regard (amongst other matters) to:

(a)   the likely long-term consequences of any decision;
(b)   the interests of the company's employees;
(c)   the need to foster business relationships with suppliers, customers and others;
(d)   the impact of the company's operations on the community and the environment;
(e)   the desirability of the company maintaining a reputation for high standards of business conduct; and
(f)   the need to act fairly as between members of the company.[61]

The requirement for directors to "have regard" to the above-mentioned factors was controversial on its introduction, especially given the Government's stance that a merely tokenistic engagement with such factors would not be permitted—directors must give each factor due and careful consideration when making decisions. Critics argued that this would make decision-making more onerous and serve as an additional source of litigation and bureaucracy, leading directors to become unnecessarily risk-averse to the potential detriment of their companies' interests.

However, the argument that directors of well-run companies already had regard to a wide variety of factors in their decision-making, meaning that the codification of such factors would not be a significant new imposition, received considerable support. When pressed as to why a list of relevant factors was to be included in the CA 2006, the Attorney-General, Lord Goldsmith, stated:

---

[60]   CA 2006 s.170(1).
[61]   CA 2006 s.172.

"If there are people at the moment who do not have regard to these factors then—on the basis of the best business practices that we have had explained to us by some of the best business leaders in this country—they should."[62]

Further, directors are only required to *have regard* to the s.172 factors. This means a director is entitled to take a decision that would, for example, inevitably have an adverse reputational impact provided that he or she has regard to such impact and gives it due consideration in the decision making process. A director will not breach his or her duty under s.172 unless he or she fails to consider such an impact entirely. Indeed, given that the directors' general duties are ultimately owed solely to the company it is quite possible that a situation could arise where s.172 actually requires a director to take a decision to promote the success of the company where that decision might, for example, negatively impact the effect of the company's operations on the community. The most prudent means of ensuring compliance with s.172 is for directors to ensure that their decisions are appropriately documented, with that documentation reflecting the due regard paid to the factors listed above. Establishing a paper trail demonstrating this due regard may be appropriate in cases where very significant decisions are made, while circulating an aide-memoire on directors' duties may suffice in respect of decisions of lesser importance.

That said, it is important to guard against reducing compliance with s.172 to a "box-ticking" exercise that fails to adequately engage with the stated factors, particularly in light of the raft of new legislative measures intended to improve the quality of corporate engagement with stakeholders. In respect of accounting periods beginning on or after 1 January 2019, large companies must make a statement in their strategic reports describing how their directors have had regard to the matters set out in the CA 2006 s.172(1)(a)–(f). Similarly applicable are new requirements obliging directors' reports to contain statements summarising the nature and impact of their engagement with employees and other stakeholders (such as customers and suppliers). Greater substantive engagement with employees in particular, is likely to arise as a consequence of provisions in the most recently published version of the Governance Code requiring boards to engage with the workforce using one or more of a variety of possible methods—one such method being the appointment of a director from the workforce. For more information on these provisions see Section 9.4.9 of Chapter 9.

Fortunately, there are now multiple resources available to directors seeking to ensure compliance with their stakeholder engagement obligations under the CA 2006. In September 2017, ICSA and the Investment Association published joint guidance concerned with ensuring that the stakeholder voice is heard sufficiently loudly and clearly in board decision making. The guidance is intended to "help company boards think about how to ensure they understand and weigh up the interests of their key stakeholders when

---

[62] House of Lords, *Hansard*, 9 May 2006.

taking strategic decisions".[63] It sets out ten core principles to achieve this end, most notably advocating that boards should regularly review who they consider their key stakeholders to be and why. In October 2018, the GC100 published practical guidance for directors which suggests potential means of fulfilling their s.172 duties with regards to stakeholders. This guidance identifies the creation of a culture sensitive to stakeholder concerns as the best route to achieving this and consequently recommends certain specific steps for embedding stakeholder considerations in the "habits and behaviours of board, management and employees".[64]

It is worth emphasising that the general duty owed by a director to the company is to act in the way he or she considers, in good faith, would be most likely to promote the success of the company *for the benefit of its members as a whole*. The concept of "success" pertinent here will generally be conceived in terms of maximising value for shareholders over the long term, but it is possible for the constitution of a company to provide that the company should have different aims, such as achieving a particular goal (e.g. completing a construction project), or even maximising dividend income received by shareholders over the short term. Ultimately, it is for the members of the company to define a company's purpose(s) on incorporation and to subsequently avail themselves (if required) of their ability to amend such purpose(s) by way of a special resolution passed at an annual general meeting or a general meeting. Where or to the extent that the purposes of the company consist of or include purposes other than the benefit of its members, the reference to promoting the success of the company for the benefit of its members should be taken as a reference to achieving such purposes.[65]

Certain situations may test these general principles. For example, on a takeover offer, the primary concern of the current board of directors of the target company will normally be to achieve the best price available for the current shareholders in the target company. While the relationship between target directors and target shareholders does not of itself involve direct responsibility on the part of the target directors to the target shareholders, the directors may assume a responsibility to shareholders directly when the circumstances require. An example would be where a director makes a personal representation to shareholders to induce them to transfer shares in the company and the director has a high degree of inside knowledge in relation to the shareholders.[66]

The duty to promote the success of the company is expressly stated to have effect subject to any enactment or rule of law requiring directors, in certain

---

[63] ICSA and the Investment Association, *The Stakeholder Voice in Board Decision Making, Strengthening the business, promoting long-term success*, September 2017, p.4.
[64] GC100, *Guidance on Directors' Duties: Section 172 and stakeholder considerations*, October 2018, p.6.
[65] CA 2006 s.172(2).
[66] This was the situation in *Platt v Platt* [1999] 2 B.C.L.C. 745.

circumstances, to consider or act in the best interests of the company's creditors.[67] This means that when a company is in financial difficulties the interests of creditors become paramount, although directors still need to have regard to the stakeholder and other matters listed at the CA 2006 s.172(1)(a)–(f).

It will not always be easy for directors to appreciate precisely when the "tipping point"—where a company can no longer hope to continue trading and must instead prepare for the onset of insolvency—has been reached. Following the banking crisis, which saw many companies in financial distress benefitting from insolvency and debt restructuring tools such as pre-pack administrations and company voluntary arrangements, the need for directors to give due attention to creditors' interests has come into sharper focus. In practice, directors of companies of doubtful solvency are faced with some very difficult decisions in order to attempt to minimise the loss to creditors whilst still acting to promote the success of the company as a whole.

Financially distressed situations are particularly fraught for directors because insolvency is a sphere in which there are various risks of incurring personal liability. Not only may a director commit the civil offence of wrongful trading or the criminal offence of fraudulent trading, he or she may be disqualified by the court from holding a company directorship for a specified period of time pursuant to the Company Directors Disqualification Act 1986. Indeed, s.6 of that Act provides that the court *must* disqualify the director (or former director) of an insolvent company if his or her conduct as a director of that insolvent company makes him or her "unfit to be concerned in the management of a company". The act also provides for the making of disqualification orders in other circumstances, such as conviction for certain indictable offences, persistent breaches of companies legislation, or fraud on a winding up.

1.5 Nature of companies

The general duties provide a good framework for practitioners seeking to determine the duties and responsibilities of directors. However, it has always been important to apply these general duties in context, taking into account of both the type of company and particular role of the director concerned.

The majority of companies in the UK are private limited companies. Many are owner managed, with some such companies effectively housing a sole trader while others operate more like partnerships. For many of these companies, there will be little practical need to distinguish between the interests of directors and the interests of shareholders. However, there

---

[67] CA 2006 s.172(3).

remains a need for legal safeguards to be in place should things go wrong. The luxury of limited liability enjoyed by the owners of these companies requires the prescription (chiefly in the CA 2006 and insolvency legislation) of minimum standards of behaviour, if only for the benefit of third parties.

In companies in which there are numerous shareholders, especially those that are listed, there is a much greater distinction between management and shareholders. This means there is also much greater potential for the respective interests of those two groups to diverge, given that the duties and responsibilities of directors are not blurred by the coincidence of ownership. Directors of such companies will likely be granted substantial freedom to carry on the day-to-day business of the company, but should be aware that this freedom is subject to compliance with various regulatory and legislative regimes. The SMCR, as applicable to the regulated sector, is a good example of this while the CA 2006 imposes personal liability on directors in relation to the veracity of certain reports. The directors of listed companies in particular must comply with very high standards of disclosure and transparency in their dealings with the public.

1.6 The particular role of non-executive directors

The role of non-executive directors remains the subject of much discussion and debate, particularly in relation to listed and regulated entities. The CA 2006 retained the position existing prior to its enactment and therefore makes no distinction between the duties owed to a company by its executive directors and its non-executive directors. As mentioned above, developments in the law (through both development of precedent and statutory reform) and corporate governance standards mean that the duties of non-executive directors clearly go far beyond simple attendance of board meetings—indeed, they are subject to the full suite of general directors' duties under the CA 2006.[68]

ICSA published a guidance note in January 2013 designed to help non-executive directors demonstrate that they have fulfilled their duty to exercise reasonable care, skill and diligence.[69] The guidance suggests that persons who have been offered non-executive directorships should undertake due diligence adequate to satisfy themselves that the company is one in which they have confidence, and to which they can make a strong, ongoing contribution before accepting the role. The guidance further suggests that from the time of their appointment non-executive directors should take responsibility for their own ongoing training and continuous development. In order to stay appraised of the company's activities for the

---

[68] CA 2006 s.250 states that "director" includes any person occupying the position of director, by whatever name called.
[69] ICSA, *ICSA Guidance on Liability of Non-Executive Directors: Care, Skill and Diligence*, January 2013.

purpose of making meaningful contributions in board meetings, non-executive directors should routinely insist on receiving high-quality information sufficiently far in advance of such meetings to allow them to review it. In addition, ICSA has also published a revised version of its sample non-executive director's appointment letter. The letter is designed to provide an initial checklist of items a company may wish to set out when appointing a non-executive director, such as the level of time commitment expected and the nature of the non-executive director's anticipated role.[70] This letter should assist in highlighting and confirming from the outset the precise responsibilities and duties owed by the non-executive director to the company.

FRC guidance also provides suggestions as to how non-executive directors may discharge their general duties.[71] This guidance impresses the point that non-executive directors should not operate "exclusively within the confines of the boardroom" but should instead meet with shareholders, key customers and a cross-section of the workforce in order to develop their understanding of the business and the ways in which that business impacts its stakeholders. Executive directors are asked to "welcome constructive challenge from non-executive directors as an essential aspect of good governance".

There has been a tendency for non-executive directors to be assigned responsibility for maintaining corporate governance standards on major company boards. This is evidenced by the latest version of the Governance Code, which provides at Principle H that:

> "Non-executive directors should have sufficient time to meet their board responsibilities. They should provide constructive challenge, strategic guidance, offer specialist advice and hold management to account."

Provision 13 continues:

> "Non-executive directors have a prime role in appointing and removing executive directors. Non-executive directors should scrutinise and hold to account the performance of management and individual executive directors against agreed performance objectives. The chair should hold meetings with the non-executive directors without the executive directors present."

The banking crisis prompted the FCA's predecessor, the Financial Services Authority (FSA), to call for non-executive directors of companies in the regulated sector to become more actively involved in the businesses on whose boards they sit. The Turner Review on the regulatory response to the banking crisis, which published its final report in March 2009, identified skill level and time commitment as two of the key areas of non-executive

---

[70] ICSA, *ICSA Guidance: A Sample Non-Executive Director's Appointment Letter*, February 2019 (updated to reflect the new UK Corporate Governance Code).
[71] FRC, *Guidance on Board Effectiveness*, July 2018.

director performance requiring improvement from a corporate governance perspective. This spurred on the review by Sir David Walker, commissioned by the Labour Government, which re-evaluated the role of non-executive directors of companies performing regulated activities. In May 2009, the FSA's chief executive, Hector Sants, called for "a different calibre of non-executive directors, with a different mindset".[72]

The courts have emphasised that while non-executive directors have a general responsibility to oversee the activities of a company they are not required to overrule specialist directors (for example, finance directors) on matters pertaining to their specialist fields. In other words, a non-executive director is not required "to ensure that the company gets everything right" in order to discharge his or her duty.[73] The precise extent of what is expected of a particular non-executive director will of course generally depend on the facts and circumstances of the matter in hand, but Lord Woolf, in an extrajudicial capacity, offered the general characterisation that the function of the non-executive director is to act like a guard dog that is prepared to bark when necessary.[74]

1.7 Group company directors

Directors of companies which are members of groups of companies often find themselves having to consider their position with great care when intra-group transactions or group interests are in issue—all the more so when they are directors of more than one of the group companies involved. Any director of a company within a group owes a duty to act in the best interests of the company of which he or she is a director, whatever the competing interests of a subsidiary company, parent company, holding company or sister subsidiary. While, in certain circumstances, European legislation is framed so as to hold a group as a single economic entity in relation to creditors, the regulation of competition, employment issues and for capital adequacy purposes, there remains no English law doctrine which permits the directors of one company to take account of the interests of other group companies as such. Given the advantages of limited liability enjoyed by each company within a group, the approach in the UK has been to ensure that the assets of each company are protected for their individual creditors.

The statutory duty to avoid conflicts of interest came into force on 1 October 2008 and led many companies to amend their articles of association to deal with any possible such conflicts and to evaluate the workings of their

---

[72] Speech by Hector Sants, chief executive, FSA Securities & Investment Institute Conference 2009, 7 May 2009.
[73] *Singer v Beckett* [2007] 2 B.C.L.C. 287; [2001] B.P.I.R. 733 at [399].
[74] In response to a question from the audience following the COMBAR Annual Lecture 2008, "Global companies can and should have the highest ethical standards" 21 October 2008.

ratification procedures. Some companies also appointed independent directors to their boards in order to take advantage of the CA 2006 provisions permitting ratification of certain acts by fellow directors.

The issue of group conflicts surfaces most frequently in relation to two situations: financings, where lenders often seek to achieve exposure on a group basis for contractual arrangements through the obtaining of cross-guarantees and the like; and intra-group reorganisations, whether undertaken for taxation or other purposes. In the latter context, transactions at an undervalue and the transfer of assets intra-group for nominal consideration give rise to particular difficulties, notwithstanding the relaxation of the rules prohibiting financial assistance for private companies.[75]

1.8 Conclusion

Despite past steps to simplify the directors' duties regime and better illuminate precisely what is required of directors, this remains a nuanced and complex area of law. For instance, though directors' general duties are codified in the CA 2006 these are not the only duties which a director may owe to a company. Similarly, while the CA 2006 continues to provide that directors owe their duties solely to their companies—except in limited cases, such as insolvency—it provides a statutory basis for shareholders to bring derivative claims on behalf of the company in respect of alleged breaches of such duties. Where the impetus for further reform in this area will come from, however, is clearer, with executive remuneration, stakeholder engagement and boardroom diversity clearly the key concerns of government, regulators, corporate governance organisations and the general public.

The following chapters go into more detail on these and other topics.

---

[75] CA 2006 Pt 18 Ch.2.

Chapter 2

Appointment and Vacation of Office

Chris Hale, Rachel Woodburn and Phillip Becker
Travers Smith LLP

2.1 Introduction

The Companies Act 2006 (CA 2006) is largely silent on the issue of how directors are to be appointed and leaves the shareholders to define their preferred procedures in the company's articles of association and/or in a shareholders' agreement.

The articles of most companies contain provisions along the same lines as those contained in the model articles for private companies and for public companies (i.e. the Regulations made pursuant to CA 2006 s.19)[1] (the Model Articles), which permit the appointment of directors either by an ordinary resolution of the shareholders or by a decision of the board, and provide a standard list of circumstances in which a director's appointment will terminate automatically. Companies incorporated prior to 1 October 2008 (when the CA 2006 Model Articles came into force) under the Companies Act 1985 (CA 1985) or earlier statutes (a pre-CA 2006 company) may still have articles based on Table A,[2] but the provisions of Table A as to the appointment of directors and the circumstances in which a director's appointment will terminate automatically are substantially the same as those in the Model Articles.

In practice, for most companies, decisions relating to the appointment of new directors (after incorporation) will be a matter primarily for the existing directors rather than the shareholders. In this way, the existing directors, acting properly, are able to identify the skills required within the boardroom and find the right personality fit. Section 2.2 below discusses the mechanics for the appointment of directors in more detail and Section 2.3 sets out the qualifications which are required of prospective directors.

However, in larger companies, shareholders will wish to have some control over board composition and to monitor the performance of the directors after their appointment, and institutional shareholders of listed companies

---

[1] Companies (Model Articles) Regulations 2008 (SI 2008/3229).
[2] Companies (Tables A–F) Regulations 1985 (SI 1985/805), as amended by Companies (Tables A–F) (Amendment) Regulations 1985 (SI 1985/1052).

are required by our corporate governance regime to do so. So, for a listed company, board composition and the process for board appointments will be driven by the regime set out in the UK Corporate Governance Code (the Code),[3] which is discussed in more detail in Section 2.4 below.

Section 2.5 investigates the effects of an invalid appointment of a director. This is followed by an overview of how a director can vacate his office (voluntarily, by operation of law or the company's articles or pursuant to a shareholder resolution) in Section 2.6.

Companies are also subject to various filing requirements in respect of their directors. These are set out in Section 2.7.

CA 2006 contains no clear definition of the term "director", merely stating (s.250) that for the purposes of the Act generally a "director" includes any person occupying the position of director, by whatever name called. This means that someone who acts as a director, even though he has never been appointed as such, may be deemed to be a "director" for the purposes of CA 2006 (i.e. a shadow or de facto director—see Section 2.9 below). Modern business practice has given rise to a number of sub-categories of director, not all of which are formally recognised in CA 2006. For example, a director may be executive or non-executive, or he may be acting as a de facto director, shadow director, nominee or alternate. Only the term "shadow director" is defined in CA 2006 (s.251). Sections 2.8, 2.9 and 2.10 below deal with the manner in which such "directorships" are created, and in which they may be terminated.

2.2 Method of appointment of directors

2.2.1 Consent to act

Any person to be appointed as a director, whether on incorporation of the relevant company or subsequently, must not just be qualified to act as a director (see Section 2.3 below for more detail) but must also be willing to be appointed.

Prior to 10 October 2015, the appointee was required to countersign the Companies House form regarding the appointment and evidenced his willingness to act by doing so. From that date, the company or, in the case of an appointment as first director of the company, the subscribers to its

---

[3] At the time of writing, the latest iteration of the Code applies to all accounting periods commencing on or after 1 January 2019. Any corporate reporting related to accounting periods commencing before that date is still governed by the iteration of the Code issued in 2016 (the 2016 Code).

memorandum of association confirm the willingness to act on behalf of the appointee pursuant to CA 2006 ss.167(2) and 12(3)[4] respectively.

The registrar then notifies the director of his appointment as required by CA 2006 s.1079B. Upon receipt of such notice, a person who was appointed without having given his consent can rely on the rectification procedure under CA 2006 s.1095 to have his name removed from the register.

It is best practice for new directors to sign a short form consent letter as part of their appointment to evidence that the company or the subscribers to its memorandum of association, as the case may be, had the appropriate authority to notify Companies House of the appointment.

2.2.2 The first director(s)

In order to effect registration of a new company under the CA 2006, a number of documents need to be delivered to the Registrar of Companies. The application for registration required under CA 2006 s.9 must contain the name(s) of the person(s) who is/are to be the company's first director(s). CA 2006 s.12 sets out the additional particulars of the director(s) which are to be included in the application. These include, in the case of an individual, his name and any former name (i.e. a name by which the individual was formerly known for business purposes), a service address (for more on this, see Section 2.7.3 below) and the country or state (or part of the UK) in which he is usually resident, his nationality, business occupation (if any) and his date of birth.[5] The application must also contain a consent by each person named as a director to his acting as such. When the Registrar of Companies issues the certificate of incorporation, those persons named as directors in the application are deemed to have been appointed as the first directors of the new company (see CA 2006) s.16(6). No separate notice of appointment is needed under CA 2006 s.167.

Companies can be incorporated electronically, that is to say that certain of the documents required to be sent to the Registrar of Companies on incorporation may be submitted electronically, and Companies House has arrangements in place to verify the authenticity of any signatures on such documents. See Section 2.7.2 below for more on electronic filing.

CA 2006 is silent on the procedures for the appointment of further directors following incorporation of the company (other than in certain specific circumstances, such as the appointment of a director to replace one removed by the shareholders under CA 2006 s.168). These procedures are

---

[4]   As amended by Small Business, Enterprise and Employment Act 2015 (SBEEA 2015) ss.100 and 101.
[5]   Pursuant to CA 2006 s.1087B, only the month and the year will be included in the public register provided that the director has been appointed on or after 10 October 2015 and the Company has not consented to the publication of the full register.

left as a matter for shareholders to determine in the company's articles. In every instance when considering the appointment (or removal—see Section 2.6 below) of a director it is, therefore, necessary to check the company's articles and any relevant shareholders' agreement.

2.2.3 Appointment by the board

The most common method of appointment of a director after the company's incorporation is by a decision of the board itself. Regulation 20 of the Model Articles for public companies contains a simple power for the directors to appoint further directors by a decision of the board. There is a similar power in the Model Articles for private companies, at reg.17.

The board will usually appoint a director in accordance with the standard procedure for directors' decision-making as set out in the company's articles. The provisions governing decision-making by directors are slightly different in the Model Articles for public and private companies. The Model Articles for public companies regs 7–19 enable directors to take decisions by a resolution passed either at a board meeting or in writing. Under the Model Articles for private companies regs 7–16, directors' decisions may be taken either at a meeting or more informally, by a unanimous "decision", which may or may not take the form of a written resolution, although it must still be recorded in writing. The articles should be checked for special arrangements relating to directors' decisions and particularly those relating to the appointment of directors. Special provisions apply in the Model Articles where the number of directors has fallen below the requisite quorum for directors' meetings in that the continuing director(s) may still act for the purposes of filling vacancies by appointing additional directors or convening a general meeting to enable shareholders to do so (Model Articles for public companies reg.11(2) and (3) and Model Articles for private companies reg.11(3)).[6] See also Sections 2.2.7 and 2.3.2 below on dealing with a situation where there are insufficient or no continuing directors.

Limited protection for shareholders in all companies is provided by the fact that, in exercising their powers of appointment, the directors must have regard to their general duties under CA 2006 Pt 10 Ch.2. These duties will apply to all aspects of the decision to appoint a new director, including the timing of the appointment, the selection of the candidate and the resulting balance of power which the directors seek to create within the boardroom.

---

[6] If Table A-based articles are relevant, Table A reg.90 fulfils the same purpose.

2.2.4   *Appointment by shareholders—general considerations*

The shareholders, as a whole, have an inherent power to appoint directors by shareholders' resolution unless this power has been restricted in the company's articles.[7] The Model Articles for public companies reg.20 and the Model Articles for private companies reg.17, for example, confirm this power, stating that the company may, by ordinary resolution, appoint a person who is willing to act as a director and is permitted by law to do so.[8]

Where any shareholders' resolution for the appointment of a director is originally proposed by the board, as with any other resolution proposed by the directors, it will be necessary for the directors to include with the notice of that resolution sufficient information to enable shareholders to make a proper judgement as to whether and, if so, how they wish to vote. The nature and amount of information required to discharge this duty will depend upon the circumstances and particular provisions apply for listed companies (see below). It would also probably be a breach of the directors' general duty under s.172 (to promote the success of the company for the benefit of its members as a whole) to propose a candidate for improper purposes. For companies with Table A-based articles, Table A regs 76 and 77 require biographical details of any director who is put forward for appointment or re-appointment by shareholders to be made available to shareholders in advance of the meeting, but the Model Articles do not replicate this requirement.

It was thought, when CA 2006 was passed, that Pt 13 of the Act provided an adequate framework for appointments of directors by shareholders, and the requisition provisions set out in ss.292, 303 and 338 do provide members with the opportunity to propose candidates for the office of director independently of anyone put forward by the company's management. However, the articles of most listed companies still contain provisions similar to regs 76 and 77 since Provision B.7.1 of the 2016 Code also required that the names of directors submitted for election or re-election should be accompanied by sufficient biographical details to enable shareholders to make an informed decision.[9]

A public company in general meeting may not consider a single motion for the appointment of two or more directors (whether a first appointment or

---

[7]   *Worcester Corsetry Ltd v Witting* [1936] Ch.640.

[8]   A similar power is set out in Table A reg.78. Until 1985, earlier versions of Table A provided that the number of directors should be determined by the subscribers to the company's memorandum of association. On that basis, the number of directors was fixed and it is therefore for this historical reason that reg.78 refers to the appointment of new directors as "filling a vacancy" or appointing an additional director". This language has been dropped in the CA 2006 Model Articles.

[9]   In its 2018 iteration, the Code no longer contains this provision but requires that companies publish, for each director being put forward for election, the specific reasons why his contribution is, and continues to be, important to the company's long-term sustainable success (Provision 18). This assessment will also be informed by the relevant director's CV.

re-election), unless it has first been agreed by the meeting, without any vote being cast against the proposal, that a single resolution is acceptable (CA 2006 s.160). In the absence of such unanimous agreement, a separate resolution must be proposed for the appointment of each candidate. Any resolution moved in contravention of the requirement is void, whether or not any objection was raised at the time. Section 160 is designed to ensure that shareholders are given a genuine choice as to the composition of the board and shareholders can vote down the appointment of a particular director without having to reject the entire board.[10] For listed companies, Listing Rule 9.3.7 has the same effect.

Although a resolution moved in contravention of s.160 is void, it may still have some consequences, namely:

(a)   CA 2006 s.161(1)(a) states that the acts of a director are valid notwithstanding any defect that may be discovered in his appointment afterwards[11]; and
(b)   the second part of s.160(2) will prevent the application in these circumstances of any provision which states that, if at the meeting at which a director retires by rotation the company does not fill the vacancy, the retiring director shall (if willing to act) be deemed to have been reappointed. (There was such a provision in reg.75 of Table A, but there is no equivalent in the Model Articles.)

It should be noted that nothing in s.160 prevents a resolution altering the company's articles (see s.160(4)). Accordingly, it would be possible, although highly unusual (and subject to the unfair prejudice protection regime set out in CA 2006 s.994), for the general meeting to pass a special resolution adopting an article providing that two or more named persons be directors of the company without first obtaining uncontested consent to the proposing of such a resolution.

In order to avoid the cumbersome nature of the statutory procedures for calling or requisitioning meetings or resolutions (see Section 2.2.5 below), a company's articles or a shareholders' agreement may contain provisions granting certain shareholders special rights to appoint directors to the company's board. Such provisions are common in a private company context where the structure of the board or the identity of the directors is important to certain shareholders and where it may be important for such shareholders to effect board changes quickly to enable them to take control with a view to protecting their investment in the company. Examples would be where the company is private equity-backed, is the vehicle for a joint venture or is a wholly-owned subsidiary of another company.[12] In such circumstances, the articles will also usually specify a simple procedure for

---

[10]   The requirements of CA 1985 s.292, which were replaced by CA 2006 s.160, were considered in *PNC Telecom Plc v Thomas* [2002] EWHC 2848 (Ch); [2003] B.C.C. 202; [2004] 1 B.C.L.C. 88.
[11]   See Section 2.5 on the effect of invalid appointments.
[12]   See Section 2.10 on nominee directors.

the appointment without the need for a shareholders' resolution, such as the deposit at the registered office of the company of a written notice of appointment and consent to act. Care is required when drafting or interpreting such provisions in order to distinguish between a power to appoint and a power to nominate a candidate to be considered by the directors or by the company in general meeting. If the latter, the candidate may be voted down by the directors or shareholders.

Where a director is appointed by the shareholders, the moment at which he assumes office is determined by the time at which the resolution appointing him is passed. Where the resolution is taken at a meeting and is to be determined by a poll, it will be effective not from the moment that the poll is taken but from the moment that the result of a poll is declared or ascertained.

It is not unusual for resolutions appointing directors to specify that the appointment will take effect at a particular date and time or upon the happening of a specified event (e.g. completion of a transaction whereupon new directors are to be appointed). In an acquisition context, if two parties have entered into a conditional agreement for the sale and purchase of a company, the buyer occasionally requests the right to appoint someone to the board of the target company during the period between exchange of contracts and completion of the sale in order to give the buyer some control over the business it has contracted to acquire. For reasons of commercial sensitivity and confidentiality, the seller may object to such a request and there may instead (or in addition) be a list of matters requiring the consent of the buyer or the buyer's representative during such a period. If this list is very extensive, the buyer's representative may be deemed to be a shadow director of the target company in any event (for more on shadow directors see Section 2.9 below).

2.2.5 Appointment by shareholders—requisitions

CA 2006 ss.292 and 303 enable shareholders either to require circulation of a written resolution (in the case of a private company only), or to require the directors to call a general meeting. In either case, these rights could be used to put forward a resolution to appoint one or more new directors, provided there is sufficient support for the requisition amongst the shareholders. Both ss.292 and 303 require members representing at least 5% of the paid-up voting shares to make the requisition. (In the case of s.303, the percentage was reduced from 10% to 5% by the Shareholders' Rights Regulations.[13]) CA 2006 s.338 also makes provision for shareholders of public companies to require the circulation of a resolution in advance of the AGM provided it is not defamatory or otherwise "frivolous or vexatious", although they can still use the powers in CA 2006 s.303 to requisition a general meeting if they consider that their proposed appointment of a new director cannot wait

---

[13] Companies (Shareholders' Rights) Regulations 2009 (SI 2009/1632).

until the next AGM. Both are useful powers, particularly for a substantial shareholder who does not control the board and who may wish to secure control by appointing additional directors.[14] The requisition route was rarely used under the CA 1985 regime because of the level of formality involved. However, there have recently been a number of high-profile examples of the Companies Act requisition procedures being used by hedge funds and other shareholders seeking to put a representative on the board or replace the incumbent board altogether.

Listed company shareholders are now actively encouraged by the UK Stewardship Code (the Stewardship Code) to take action where they believe that the directors are not managing the company in the best interests of shareholders as a whole. Principle 3 of the Stewardship Code requires institutional investors to monitor their investee companies and, in particular, to satisfy themselves that the company's leadership is effective. Principle 4 requires institutional shareholders to "establish clear guidelines on when and how they will escalate their stewardship activities", and the underlying guidance on Principle 4 suggests that requisitioning a general meeting, possibly to change the board, should be considered if boards do not respond constructively to shareholder intervention. Principle 5, which recommends that institutional investors should be willing to act collectively with other investors where appropriate, is also relevant in this context, since the requisition route requires shareholder co-operation, both in making the requisition (see above) and in getting the relevant resolution(s) passed.

In practice, what may happen is that one or more shareholders could write to, or otherwise enter a dialogue with the company as regards proposed board changes and, if no action is taken by the board, the shareholder may proceed to requisition a general meeting to remove incumbent directors under s.168 (see Section 2.6.5 below) and appoint one or more new directors using the shareholders' power to do so by ordinary resolution under the articles. Few institutional shareholders will be willing to embark on the requisition route without a reasonable chance of success in view of the potential cost and adverse publicity involved in a failed attempt. For this reason it is common for the lead shareholder(s) to appoint proxy solicitation agents to carry out an analysis of the company's shareholder profile and solicit support for the resolutions.

Shareholders considering the requisition route for the appointment of new directors should also take account of: (i) the provisions of CA 2006 on directors' conflicts of interest; (ii) the Code requirements and the shareholder bodies' views on non-executive directors' independence criteria; and (iii) the provisions of the Stewardship Code on investors' conflicts of interest (see Principle 2). There is inherent potential for a conflict of interest where a director is appointed to the board by or on behalf of a shareholder

---

[14] These provisions replaced CA 1985 s.386, which provided for shareholders' rights to requisition an extraordinary general meeting.

or group of shareholders, which is the same issue confronted by a nominee director in a private company context (see Section 2.10 below). In essence, a nominee director is not permitted by company law to prefer the interests of his appointor over the interests of the company as a whole—see CA 2006 ss.172 and 175. Also, a shareholder nominee for a board appointment will automatically give rise to an issue under the independence criteria in Code Provision 10.[15] That provision states that the board should, in the annual report, give reasons for their judgment that a particular director is deemed to be independent notwithstanding the existence of a whole range of relationships or circumstances, one of which is a relationship with a significant shareholder. Both the Pensions and Lifetime Savings Association (PLSA) and Pensions & Investment Research Consultants Ltd (PIRC) take the view that a shareholder nominee will not automatically infringe the independence criteria, but the candidate will have to be able to demonstrate the absence of a prior material link with the relevant shareholder and should be able to satisfy the remaining criteria. Premium Listing Principle 5 of the Listing Rules would also come into play. This requires all holders of the same class of securities to be treated equally, and is designed to ensure a premium listed company is not overly-dominated by a significant shareholder. For more on dealing with conflicts of interest generally see Chapter 3.

If the requisition is made by the shareholders of a public company, the written resolution route is not available, so the incumbent board must respond to the requisition under s.303 by convening a general meeting. Even if the requisition is aimed at replacing board directors, the directors are obliged to act on it under s.304. If they do not, s.305 allows the members to do so at the company's expense and the cost may ultimately be collected from the defaulting directors out of their fees or other sums due to them (s.305(7)).

Occasionally, the requirement for a general meeting gives rise to practical difficulties. If there are no surviving directors or if there is an insufficient number of directors to make up a quorum in order to convene a general meeting under CA 2006 s.302, then the company's articles may enable any director or a certain percentage or number of members to convene the necessary general meeting. The Model Articles for public companies reg.28 deals with such a situation,[16] but there is no equivalent provision in the Model Articles for private companies.

If there is no such provision in the company's articles, or if for any other reason it is impractical to call or hold the necessary general meeting, the shareholders of a private company with at least one director or a company secretary could rely on s.292 to make the appointment by written resolution (although the written resolution could not be used for a resolution to

---

[15]   Provision B.1.1 in the 2016 Code.
[16]   As does Table A reg.37.

remove a director under CA 2006 s.168, which may be proposed at the same time). Alternatively, if the written resolution route is unavailable, any director or member entitled to vote may apply to the court pursuant to CA 2006 s.306 for it to order a meeting to be called, held and conducted in the manner the court sees fit. Section 306 replaced CA 1985 s.371 without substantive amendment, and there were several cases considering the extent to which s.371 could be relied upon in circumstances in which a director or shareholder or body of shareholders was using his or its position to frustrate the holding of a general meeting in order to effect changes at board level.

In *Woven Rugs Ltd, Re*,[17] a director threatened with dismissal refused to attend board meetings convened to call a general meeting to table a resolution to remove him as a director. His presence was required at the meeting to make up a quorum. It was held that a meeting could be ordered under s.371, despite submissions of unfairness by the director. In *Union Music Ltd v Watson*,[18] the Court of Appeal ruled that CA 1985 s.371 was intended to ensure that a company is not frustrated in its affairs by the impracticability of calling a meeting in the manner prescribed by its constitution. In that case, the shareholders' agreement required the prior written consent of both the minority and majority shareholder for the holding of a general meeting. The shareholders were in dispute and when a director resigned, the majority shareholder applied under s.371 for an order that a general meeting be held to appoint a replacement. The Court of Appeal held that where there are unequal shareholdings, the court is under no obligation to assume the parties had intended a veto for either shareholder, and a meeting was ordered to take place. The principles applied in both the *Union Music* and *Woven Rugs* cases were helpfully summarised in the subsequent case of *Vectone Entertainment Holding Ltd v South Entertainment Ltd*,[19] and more recently applied in the cases of *Smith v Butler*[20] and *Schofield v Jones*.[21]

2.2.6   Appointment by third parties

It is fairly unusual for directors to be appointed by third parties (i.e. other than by the board or the shareholders). The board or the nomination committee of the board may, in practice, seek assistance from third parties in identifying potential candidates and this is thought not to be prohibited under the terms of CA 2006 s.173 which requires the directors to exercise independent judgment. It is possible for the company to adopt articles which confer the power to appoint directors on a third party, although the

---

[17]   *Woven Rugs Ltd, Re* [2002] 1 B.C.L.C. 324.
[18]   *Union Music Ltd v Watson* [2003] EWCA Civ 180; [2004] B.C.C. 37; [2003] 1 B.C.L.C. 453.
[19]   *Vectone Entertainment Holding Ltd v South Entertainment Ltd* [2004] EWHC 744 (Ch); [2005] B.C.C. 123; [2004] 2 B.C.L.C. 224.
[20]   *Smith v Butler* [2012] EWCA Civ 314; [2012] Bus. L.R. 1836; [2012] B.C.C. 645.
[21]   *Schofield v Jones* [2019] EWHC 803 (Ch).

Model Articles contain no such provision.[22] Such delegation through the articles could be in favour of, for example, a seller of a company who is to receive consideration based upon the performance of the target business after the completion of the sale and is granted the right to appoint a director of the company during the period of the "earn-out" so as to monitor and/or control the company during that period.

A third party to whom the articles give a right to appoint and remove directors should be aware that it cannot enforce that right against the company. Whilst the provisions of a company's constitution bind the company and its members to the same extent as if there were covenants to observe those provisions on the part of the company and each member (see CA 2006 s.33),[23] they do not have the effect of conferring rights on third parties which are directly enforceable against the company. This is confirmed by the Contracts (Rights of Third Parties) Act 1999 s.6(2), which specifically excludes a company's constitution from the scope of that Act. If a third party wishes to ensure that its right to appoint or remove a director is always respected, that party should seek a direct contractual undertaking from the shareholders in the company to act on its instructions.

The third party should also be aware that there are circumstances in which its appointee could be removed by the shareholders or by the board of the company. The shareholders have a statutory right (in CA 2006 s.168) to remove a director by ordinary resolution and the shareholders (or a particular group or class of shareholders) may have a right in the articles to remove a director without going through the s.168 procedure. The directors may also be entitled to remove a director under a provision in the articles (although there is no such provision in the Model Articles). Again, the third party should consider seeking an undertaking from the shareholders and the directors (as relevant) not to exercise their rights to remove a director nominated by the third party unless the third party has requested or agrees to his removal[24] (see also Sections 2.2.8 and 2.6.5 below).

Aside from contractual arrangements, the Model Articles for private companies reg.17(2) allows the personal representative of the last shareholder of a company to appoint a person to be a director where the death of such shareholder results in the company having no shareholders and no directors.

---

[22] Table A contained no such provision either.

[23] This section replaced CA 1985 s.14 from 1 October 2008 without a change of substance.

[24] Only an undertaking from the relevant shareholders and directors would be enforceable. An undertaking from the company itself would be void for violation of the principle in *Russell v Northern Bank Development Corp Ltd* [1992] 1 W.L.R. 588 which states that a company may not fetter its statutory powers.

2.2.7 Appointment by the court

Theoretically, it is possible, on application by a member to the court pursuant to CA 2006 s.994 (unfair prejudice),[25] that the court may exercise the extremely wide powers granted to it by s.996 to make "such order as it thinks fit" for giving relief in respect of the matters complained of, and order the appointment of one or more directors. In practice, however, in the exercise of their powers under s.996, the courts are reluctant to interfere in the management of a company's affairs in this way, preferring instead to order the acquisition of one party's shares by another and for the resulting shareholders to appoint whomsoever they wish to act as the ongoing directors.

2.2.8 Appointment by the Secretary of State

CA 2006 s.156 enables the Secretary of State to direct the company to appoint one or more directors if it appears that the company is in breach of the statutory requirements as to the number of directors set out in CA 2006 s.154, or that a company should have at least one director who is a natural person, under s.155. CA 2006 s.155, though, is set to be repealed[26] (at a date which is yet to be appointed at the time of writing) and will be replaced by a new s.156A which will require each director to be a natural person. Once this section takes effect, s.156C provides that any existing director who is not a natural person will cease to be appointed as a director unless the Secretary of State has provided for an exception to s.156A under s.156B. Such exceptions will remain subject to the requirement that any company must have at least one director who is a natural person.[27] The direction made by the Secretary of State (who would usually act through Companies House in these circumstances) will specify what the company must do in order to rectify the breach and the period within which it must do so, which must be not less than one month nor more than three months after the date on which the direction is given. If in the meantime the company has rectified the breach, it must give notice of the relevant appointment or appointments under s.167 before the end of the period specified in the direction. There is a criminal penalty for failure to comply with a direction made under s.156 which may be levied on the company and every officer of the company in default (as defined in CA 2006 s.1121). For these purposes, a shadow director is an officer of the company.

2.2.9 Entrenchment

The right to remove a director by way of an ordinary resolution under CA 2006 s.168 applies "notwithstanding anything in any agreement between [the company] and [the director]" and although it is no longer specifically

---

[25] This section replaced CA 1985 s.459 from 1 October 2008 without a change of substance.
[26] Pursuant to SBEEA 2015 s.87.
[27] CA 2006 s.16B(4).

expressed to override any contrary provision in the company's articles,[28] such a provision, or any exclusion of the shareholders' rights under CA 2006 s.168, may still constitute an unlawful fetter on the company's statutory powers (*Russell v Northern Bank Development Corp Ltd*)[29] and therefore be unenforceable against the company. See further Section 2.6.5 below.

The Companies Act 2006 introduced statutory rights of entrenchment for provisions of the articles, ensuring that certain provisions of the articles, including those relating to directors' appointments, can only be amended or repealed if certain conditions are met, or procedures complied with, that are more restrictive than a special resolution (see CA 2006 s.22).[30] There does not appear to be any restriction either on an agreement between shareholders inter se whereby they agree not to exercise their rights to remove a director nominated by a particular shareholder or class of shareholders or indeed a third party, unless the appointor has requested or agreed to his removal. Such an agreement could not bind the company (and could not therefore appear in the articles) without falling foul of the *Russell v Northern Bank* principle. The agreement will, though, bind the shareholders who are party to it. In *Thomas v York Trustees Ltd*[31] a shareholder was prevented from voting its shares in favour of a special resolution to remove directors under CA 1985 s.303, which would have been in breach of a provision of a shareholders' agreement providing another shareholder with the right to appoint a director at all times and until expiry of the agreement. See also Section 2.6.5 below on *Bushell v Faith* clauses and similar weighted voting rights provisions in articles, which are designed to protect a director in the event of a shareholder motion to remove him, and which are not outlawed by CA 2006.

2.3 Qualification

As we have seen, the Act defines a "director" as including any "person" occupying the position of director, by whatever name called. The Interpretation Act 1978 Sch.1 states that a "person" includes a body of persons corporate or unincorporated. Accordingly, any individual (subject to the age limits discussed in Section 2.3.1 below) or corporation is currently eligible to be a director.[32]

---

[28]   Unlike its predecessor, CA 1985 s.303, which contained express wording to this effect.
[29]   *Russell v Northern Bank Development Corp Ltd* [1992] 1 W.L.R. 588; [1992] 3 All E.R. 161; [1992] B.C.C. 578.
[30]   CA 2006 s.22(2) is not yet in force. The implementation of this section was delayed as a result of concern that provisions in companies' articles relating to variation of class rights might be caught by s.22(2) and this was not the intention.
[31]   *Thomas v York Trustees Ltd* [2001] All E.R. (D.) 179.
[32]   Although corporate directors are still permitted under CA 2006, s.155 requires companies to

Although the position of director is one of considerable importance to the effective management of the company, there is no statutory requirement that a director should hold any form of qualification or take any examination in order to enable him to take up his office. Nevertheless, there are certain safeguards designed to reduce the risk that inappropriate persons become directors or, if they do, to ensure that on the occurrence of certain events they should vacate their office automatically or shareholders should have the opportunity to remove them. Apart from those safeguards which are inherent in the mechanism for appointment, for example:

(a)   references above to the general duties of directors contained in CA 2006 Pt 10 Ch.2, when exercising their powers to appoint additional or replacement directors;

(b)   the general duty of directors who propose a resolution for appointment of a director at a general meeting to provide sufficient information about the proposed appointee to shareholders to enable them to make an informed decision;

(c)   the requirement that a separate shareholders' resolution is used for the appointment of each director of a public company; and

(d)   for listed companies, the nomination committee procedure set out in the Code,

there are a number of additional relevant provisions which are summarised in the sections which follow.

For accounting periods beginning on or after 1 January 2019, large private companies[33] will also need to comply with the Wates Corporate Governance Principles for Large Private Companies (the Wates Principles). These operate on an "apply and explain" basis[34] which means that companies will need to set out in their annual report how they have applied the Wates Principles. Principle 2 requires that all directors should collectively demonstrate a high level of competence relevant to the company's business needs and stakeholders and that individual evaluation of directors should demonstrate whether each director continues to contribute effectively.

2.3.1   Age limit

It used to be the case under CA 1985 for a public company (or, a private company which is a subsidiary of a public company or of a body corporate registered as a public company in Northern Ireland) that no person was

---

have at least one director who is a natural person. In addition, there is a pending amendment to CA 2006 which would further restrict the use of corporate directors (see Section 2.2.8 above).

[33]   Larger companies are defined, for this purpose, as any company which has (i) more than 2,000 employees and/or (ii) a turnover of more than £200 million and a balance sheet of more than £2 billion.

[34]   As opposed to the UK Corporate Governance Code which applies on a "comply or explain" basis.

capable of being appointed a director if, at the time of his appointment, he had attained the age of 70. Further, any director of such a company was required to vacate his office at the conclusion of the AGM following his 70th birthday and was not then eligible for automatic reappointment in default of another director being appointed in his place (CA 1985 s.293). CA 1985 s.293 was repealed on 6 April 2007,[35] largely due to concerns that the age limit might infringe the Employment Equality (Age) Regulations 2006.[36] Despite the repeal of CA 1985 s.293, it is worth checking a company's articles for any specific age limitations for directors, although such provisions are no longer common.

CA 2006 s.157 prescribes 16 as the minimum age for a director, although it would be possible to appoint a person younger than 16 as a director provided the appointment did not take effect until that person attains the age of 16 (see s.157(2)). Regulations may in future be made under CA 2006 s.158 providing exceptions to the underage directors rule, but no such regulations have yet been proposed. Assuming therefore that no exceptions apply, any person who was under the age of 16 on 1 October 2008[37] who had been appointed as a director would automatically have ceased to be a director on that date, by virtue of CA 2006 s.159. No notification of the revocation of the appointment was required to be filed at Companies House but any affected companies should have made the necessary arrangements for the appointment of a replacement, if appropriate, and recorded the changes in the company books. The statutory prohibition on underage directors in s.157 will not prevent a person who is younger than 16 but who acts as a shadow or de facto director from incurring liability as such (s.157(5)). There was no equivalent provision to CA 2006 s.157 in the CA 1985. Under Scottish law, however, where Age of Legal Capacity (Scotland) Act 1991 s.1 states that a person under the age of 16 years shall have no capacity to enter into any transaction and the expression "transaction" includes "the giving by a person of any consent having legal effect", it is possible that a person under the age of 16 is incapable of consenting to be appointed a director.

2.3.2 Number of directors

For an analysis of the corporate governance considerations in relation to the number of directors on a listed company board, see Section 2.4.2. This Section focuses on the general company law position as to the size of the board.

CA 2006 does not prescribe the maximum number of directors that a company may have and neither do the Model Articles. A company's articles

---

[35] See Companies Act 2006 (Commencement No.1, Transitional Provisions and Savings) Order 2006 (SI 2006/3428) s.4(2)(c).
[36] Employment Equality (Age) Regulations 2006 (SI 2006/1031).
[37] The date on which CA 2006 s.157 came into force.

may contain some provision on this, although a prescribed maximum would be unusual in a private company context other than, for example, in a joint venture company where it may be important to specify the precise number of directors and who may appoint them to preserve a balance between the joint venture partners. When considering any appointment of a new director it is wise, however, to check if there is any maximum fixed by or under the authority of the relevant articles and, if so, that it will not thereby be exceeded.

With the exception of situations like joint ventures, most private companies maintain maximum flexibility in respect of board appointments. For example, a private equity-backed company will rarely have a maximum limit on the number of directors, so that the private equity house can "flood" the board by appointing such number of additional directors as would give it control of the board in order to safeguard its investment if the company is under-performing.

The Wates Principles also require that size and structure of boards of larger companies should be appropriate to meet the strategic needs and challenges of the organisation and enable effective decision-making.

More commonly, a company's articles may set a minimum number of directors. Table A stated (in reg.64) that, unless otherwise determined by ordinary resolution, the number of directors shall not be less than two. The Model Articles contain no such provision, although CA 2006 itself prescribes a minimum number of directors for both private and public companies (one and two respectively—see CA 2006 s.154).

If, for any reason, a company which should have more than one director ends up with a sole director, the company's articles will usually determine what the sole director can and cannot do until such point as a new director is appointed to comply with the minimum requirement. For example, reg.11 of both the Model Articles for private companies and the Model Articles for public companies state that if there are fewer directors than required for a quorum, the directors can only act to appoint more directors or call a general meeting to enable shareholders to do so.[38]

If a company finds itself with no directors at all, it will be in breach of CA 2006 ss.154 and 155 and could be directed to appoint directors by the Secretary of State under s.156 (see Section 2.2.8 above). To rectify the situation, either before or in response to any such direction, the shareholders should exercise their rights to appoint directors. For a private company, the easiest way to do this, in the absence of directors to call a general meeting, would be by written resolution. The Model Articles for private companies regs 17(2) and (3) also make provision for the situation where there are no directors or shareholders as a result of death, enabling personal

---

[38] Regulation 90 of Table A contains provisions to the same effect.

representatives to appoint directors. A public company, for whom the written resolution procedure is unavailable, will have to rely on the shareholders' right to call a general meeting under CA 2006 s.305, or petition the court to convene a shareholders' meeting under CA 2006 s.306.

2.3.3 *Qualifications specific to certain types of company*

In some instances, legislation specific to particular types of company may contain provisions requiring directors to have certain qualifications or provide that the appointment of a particular individual may result in the company losing the right to conduct certain types of business.

For example, in the case of firms authorised under the Financial Services and Markets Act 2000, persons who are to be appointed to perform certain specified controlled functions must be approved by the Financial Conduct Authority (the FCA) (or, in some cases, by the Prudential Regulation Authority (the PRA), with the FCA's consent) prior to performing those functions. The precise regime that applies to the approval of such individuals varies depending on the type of financial services firm concerned. Firms which are regulated solely by the FCA are currently subject to the Approved Persons Regime, although it is expected that they will transition to a tailored version of the Senior Managers Regime (see below) in December 2019. Under the Approved Persons Regime, board functions that require pre-approval include the CEO and executive and non-executive directors (which will include, where applicable, any non-executive chair of the board).

Banks and insurers (both of which are subject to dual regulation by the FCA and PRA) are subject to the Senior Managers Regime. (In the case of insurers, this has been the case since 10 December 2018, before which they were subject to a modified regime known as the Senior Insurance Managers Regime.) Senior management functions which require pre-approval by the FCA under the Senior Managers Regime include the CEO, executive directors and the chair of the board. Non-executive directors do not need regulatory approval under the Senior Managers Regime, unless they are also performing another senior management function which does require pre-approval (e.g. chair of the board, chairing certain committees of the bank or insurer, such as the risk, audit, remuneration or nomination committees, or acting as senior independent director with responsibility for the assessment of the chair's performance). However, the firm will need to take reasonable steps to satisfy itself that non-executive directors are fit and proper individuals to perform that role prior to their appointment. When the Senior Managers Regime is extended to firms regulated solely by the FCA in December 2019, a modified list of senior management functions will apply to such firms (but the CEO, executive directors and the chair of the board will in any case still require regulatory pre-approval).

If a regulated firm fails to obtain the necessary approval prior to the individual starting to perform the relevant role, the firm may be subject to regulatory enforcement action and appropriate sanctions. In order to obtain approval, there is an application process under which the regulator will assess whether the person is fit and proper, although the firm is also expected to have performed its own assessment of the individual's suitability prior to submitting the application. Would-be board members may be interviewed by the FCA (and/or where applicable for dual-regulated firms, by the PRA), depending on the significance of the firm and the potential degree of risk involved. For dual-regulated firms, the FCA and the PRA will generally try to co-ordinate a single, joint interview if an interview is considered necessary. Once approved, a senior manager is required to observe minimum standards of conduct set out in regulatory rules. The regulators may take direct enforcement action against a senior manager who is found to be guilty of misconduct or who is found not to be a fit and proper person. Regulated firms may also be required to notify the regulators if they become aware of serious misconduct by a senior manager.

Additional requirements may apply under specific legislation covering particular financial services entities. For example, before an investment company with variable capital (otherwise known as an open-ended investment company or OEIC) can be formed, the Open-Ended Investment Companies Regulations 2001 require that the FCA must be satisfied that the proposed directors are fit and proper persons to act as directors of it and, if there are two or more directors, that the combination of their experience and expertise is such as is appropriate for the purposes of carrying on the business of the company.[39] These are ongoing requirements, failure to comply with which is a ground for revocation of the authorisation of the OEIC by the FCA. Another example relates to ring-fenced bodies (i.e. broadly, firms carrying out retail banking operations). The Financial Services (Banking Reform) Act 2013, which implements the reforms recommended by the Independent Commission on Banking chaired by Sir John Vickers, introduced new requirements for the boards of such firms, imposing new rules on board composition and independence and on the overlap of board membership with other group entities.

There have also been various initiatives at an international level which have sought to address the perceived failure in governance leading up to the financial crisis of 2007/2008, and which may therefore be relevant in considering the board structure of a financial institution. These include the recommendations of the OECD (Organisation for Economic Co-operation and Development) in its February 2010 report, *Corporate Governance and the Financial Crisis*, a review of the OECD's own 2004 *Principles of Corporate Governance* in the light of the financial crisis. Further, the *Principles for Enhancing Corporate Governance* published by the Basel Committee on Banking Supervision in October 2010, and finally, the report *Toward Effective*

---

[39] See Open-Ended Investment Companies Regulations 2001 (SI 2001/1228) paras 15(5)–(7).

Governance of Financial Institutions published in April 2012 by the Group of 30 (G30). In general terms, these initiatives have resulted in best practice recommendations as regards the composition, independence, competence, and functioning of the boards of financial institutions, many of which are consistent with the UK's own corporate governance regime.

2.3.4   Shareholding qualification

Neither the CA 2006 nor the Model Articles[40] require a director to hold any shares in the company of which he is a director. It used to be common for a company's articles to require directors to own a minimum amount of shares in the company while in office, to ensure that the director had a personal financial interest in the success of the company beyond his salary. Today this sort of provision is extremely rare.[41] Although not a requirement as such, it is, however, common practice for directors of listed and certain high-growth companies to be awarded shares or options over shares as performance-related remuneration. To ensure such awards are designed to promote the long-term success of the company, the Code requires that shares should not vest and options should not be exercisable within five years of grant, and that shares should only be released for sale on a phased basis (see provision 36 of the Code).[42]

It is also usual for directors of private equity-backed companies to hold shares as a means of incentivising them to manage the company successfully, and for there to be a prohibition (with limited exceptions) in the company's articles on directors transferring shares, to ensure they maintain a stake in the company.

---

[40]   Table A had no such requirement either.

[41]   The provisions of CA 1985 s.291 required a director who was subject to qualification shares provisions to obtain his qualification shares within two months after his appointment (or such shorter time as may be fixed by the relevant articles). Section 291 was repealed with effect from 1 October 2009. If the articles require the director merely to "hold" the qualification shares, this is satisfied by the director being the registered holder and he does not also have to own the shares beneficially. However, the precise wording of the relevant article must be considered carefully.

The articles may provide that the director will cease to hold office automatically if he does not, within the required period, obtain his qualification shares. He may also cease to be a director automatically if at any subsequent date he ceases to hold his qualification shares and will be incapable of being reappointed as a director of that company until he has reacquired the necessary qualification shares. Unless the articles state that a director is required to obtain his qualification shares in the form of new shares issued by the company, he would usually be free to acquire them from any source and on any terms.

[42]   The 2016 Code specified a minimum vesting/exercise period of three years but noted that longer periods may be appropriate (see Sch.A).

2.3.5 Other qualifications contained in the company's articles

It is possible for companies to place further qualifications in their articles on who may act as a director, although care needs to be taken to ensure that any such provisions do not contravene any rules against discrimination contained within UK or EU law (e.g. if qualification was on the grounds of race or religion). Such provisions are not common.

2.3.6 Disqualification

An individual may, from time to time, be disqualified from acting as a director. Such disqualification may arise by virtue of provisions in the relevant company's articles. For example, there are often provisions in articles designed to ensure the removal of an existing director who is disqualified under statute or is made bankrupt or becomes physically or mentally incapable of acting as a director and may remain so for more than three months or suffers some other event which makes his position untenable. Regulations 18 and 22 of the Model Articles for private and public companies (respectively) contain the standard list of such events (see Section 2.6.4 below for more details).[43]

Disqualification may also arise, and this is the sense in which the term "disqualification" is usually employed, as a result of an order made by the court or a disqualification undertaking given by a director under the Company Directors' Disqualification Act 1986[44] (CDDA 1986). The Small Business, Enterprise and Employment Act 2015 (SBEEA 2015) also introduced the possibility of disqualifying individuals who have committed a relevant company law related offence outside of Great Britain.[45]

Any person against whom the court has made a disqualification order or from whom a disqualification undertaking has been accepted under the CDDA 1986 shall not, without the leave of the court, be a director, receiver or manager of a company's property or be in any way, whether directly or indirectly, concerned or take part in the promotion, formation or management of a company and shall not act as an insolvency practitioner[46] for the period specified within the relevant order or undertaking (see also Section

---

[43] The list was amended by SBEEA 2015 s.106 to take into account a wider range of behaviours when considering whether a director should be disqualified. These changes incorporated the proposals made in the BIS consultation "Transparency & Trust: enhancing the transparency of UK company ownership and increasing trust in a UK business".

[44] Note that the regime pursuant to CDDA 1986 only applies in England, Wales and Scotland. Northern Ireland relies on its own regime under the Company Directors Disqualification (Northern Ireland) Order 2002 (NISI 2002/3150). An individual who is subject to a disqualification order under this instrument, will still be treated as disqualified in the other UK jurisdictions unless he has leave from the High Court of Northern Ireland to act as a director despite the order (see CDDA 1986 s.12A).

[45] CDDA 1986 s.5A.

[46] The court has a discretion to grant such person leave to act as an insolvency practitioner during the relevant period.

2.6.4 below). In deciding whether to grant leave, the court will have regard to two factors in particular: the protection of the public[47] and the need for the applicant to be a director.[48] Need in this case refers to the company's practical need for the person to be a director.[49] The use of disqualification orders and undertakings has increased in recent years.

Directors may also be disqualified for breaches of competition law pursuant to certain provisions of the Enterprise Act 2002. Under these provisions, a disqualification order may be made or a disqualification undertaking accepted in respect of a director who is in breach of competition law and whose conduct as a director is considered to make him unfit to be a director of a company. The effect of Competition Disqualification Orders and Competition Disqualification Undertakings are broadly similar to a disqualification order or undertaking made or accepted under the CDDA 1986. The first ever disqualification of a company director for a breach of competition law occurred in December 2016.

The OFT had previously published guidance on the Enterprise Act disqualification provisions[50] but this guidance has been partially withdrawn. A public consultation on changes to the OFT's earlier guidance concluded on 13 September 2018 but, at the time of writing, the revised guidance had not yet been issued.

In March 2018, BEIS published a consultation paper which, among other items, included a proposal to increase the investigative powers of the Insolvency Service. The new powers would allow the Insolvency Service to investigate and, if appropriate, disqualify former directors of companies which have since been dissolved. The Government's response to the consultation was published on 26 August 2018.[51] It confirmed that this proposal will be implemented when legislative time allows and that the disqualification powers will mirror the regime under the CDDA 1986 as far as possible.

---

[47] The question of whether the applicant has shown themselves unlikely to offend again has been described as "highly material" (see *Grayan Building Services Ltd (in liquidation), Re* [1995] Ch. 241).

[48] *Tech Textiles, Re* [1998] 1 B.C.L.C. 259.

[49] A subsequent judgment held that these two tests are not cumulative and that leave can be granted where the applicant failed to demonstrate the requisite need as long as satisfactory safeguards to protect the public have been put in place (see *Barings Plc (No.3), Re* [2000] 1 W.L.R. 634).

[50] This can be found at *http://www.oft.gov.uk/shared_oft/business_leaflets/enterprise_act/oft510.pdf* [Accessed 25 April 2019].

[51] See *https://assets.publishing.service.gov.uk/government/uploads/system/uploads/attachment_data/file/736163/ICG_-_Government_response_doc_-_24_Aug_clean_version__with_Minister_s_photo_and_signature__AC.pdf* [Accessed 25 April 2019].

2.4 Board appointments—public company considerations

For listed companies, further provisions apply in relation to board appointments over and above the basic statutory framework, driven by the need to ensure that high standards of corporate governance and management suitability and competence are imposed upon the directors of companies listed on the London Stock Exchange. The corporate governance regime for UK listed companies is covered in detail in Chapter 9. This section focuses on those elements of our corporate governance regime which are particularly relevant to decisions on board appointments.

When the FRC published the updated Code in July 2018, it also produced updated detailed guidance on board effectiveness[52] as one of a series of guidance notes to assist companies in applying the Code. It replaced the guidance published in 2011.[53] It is not prescriptive and only addresses issues where guidance was thought to be needed. The FRC guidance is referred to where relevant in the sections which follow.

The Code contains the principle (Principle A) that every company should be headed by an effective and entrepreneurial board, which is collectively responsible for the long-term success of the company.[54]

The QCA Corporate Governance Code (the QCA Code), which was published in April 2018 and which replaces the previous QCA Corporate Governance Code for Small and Mid-Size Quoted Companies 2013, contains similar provisions, albeit adapted such that they are proportionate and practicable for smaller quoted companies.[55]

2.4.1 Nomination committee

Code Principle J states that: "Appointments to the board should be subject to a formal, rigorous and transparent procedure". Code Provision 17 requires companies to appoint a nomination committee which should lead the process for board appointments, ensure plans are in place for orderly succession to both the board and senior management positions and oversee the development of a diverse pipeline for succession.[56] In June 2013, the Institute of Chartered Secretaries and Administrators (ICSA) published

---

[52] See https://www.frc.org.uk/getattachment/61232f60-a338-471b-ba5a-bfed25219147/2018-Guidance-on-Board-Effectiveness-FINAL.PDF [Accessed 25 April 2019].

[53] See https://www.frc.org.uk/getattachment/11f9659a-686e-48f0-bd83-36adab5fe930/Guidance-on-board-effectiveness-2011.pdf [Accessed 25 April 2019].

[54] As did Main Principle A and its Supporting Principles in the 2016 Code.

[55] Note that, since April 2018, the AIM Rules for Companies r.26 sets out that companies quoted on AIM are required to apply the provisions of a recognised corporate governance code. This was previously only done on a voluntary basis.

[56] These provisions reflect Main Principle B.2, its Supporting Principles and Provision B.2.1 in the 2016 Code.

updated standard terms of reference for nomination committees[57] which are widely used by listed companies. The list of duties in the ICSA terms of reference is based on existing best practice from a number of sources, including the Code itself and the FRC Guidance on Board Effectiveness (see above) but ICSA acknowledges that some companies may wish to add to the list or modify it in other ways.

Accordingly, for most listed companies, the appointment of a new director by the board involves first a recommendation of a particular candidate by the nomination committee and secondly (unless, unusually, the power of appointment has been delegated to the nomination committee) a resolution of the board itself.

The Code requirement on the composition of the nomination committee is that a majority of its members should be independent non-executive directors.[58] Where the chairman is also the chair of the nomination committee, he should not chair the committee when it is dealing with the appointment of his successor. The ICSA terms of reference suggest that, as a matter of good practice (although not a Code requirement), the company secretary should act as secretary to the committee. The chairman and members of the nomination committee should be identified in the annual report. The Code also requires the committee's terms of reference to be made available to shareholders and others, for example by publishing them on the company's website (Provision 14), and for the work of the committee to be disclosed in the annual report (Provision 23).[59] The committee chairman will be expected to attend the AGM to answer any queries on the activities of the committee.

Although the Code itself requires only a majority of the nomination committee to be independent non-executive directors, in theory permitting even the chief executive to be a member of it, companies should also be aware of the views of the shareholder bodies, some of whose requirements as regards the composition of the nomination committee are even more prescriptive. For example, PIRC's 2019 UK Shareowner Voting Guidelines state that all of the directors on the committee should be independent and the chairman of the board should not be a member of the committee at all, to preserve the independence of his role.

The QCA Code acknowledges that some small and mid-size quoted companies will use the whole board for nomination decisions, whereas others will require board appointments to be made following a recommendation by a dedicated nomination committee.

---

[57] See *https://www.icsa.org.uk/download-resources/downloadt?fileId=3320* [Accessed 25 April 2019].
[58] See Provision 17 in the Code and Provision B.2.1 in the 2016 Code.
[59] The Code no longer expressly requires that this information is disclosed in a separate section of the annual report (as was the case under Provision B.2.4 of the 2016 Code).

The Code also requires that open advertising and/or external search consultancy should generally be used for the appointment of the chairman and the non-executive directors (see Code Provision 20[60]).[61]

2.4.2 Number of directors on a listed company board

The Institutional Shareholders' Committee recommended, in its 2009 *Statement of Best Practice*,[62] that the articles of listed companies should provide for a maximum as well as a minimum number of directors, although not all listed companies' articles prescribe a maximum and if they do, the limit is set at a fairly high level to preserve flexibility. The Code does not prescribe a minimum or maximum board size. It is more concerned with the balance of executive and non-executive directors on the board, and the independence of the chairman and the non-executive directors.[63] For more on this see Sections 2.4.3 and 2.4.4 below.

The QCA Code contains similar provisions to those in the Code as to board balance and independent non-executive directors.

In its 2019 UK Shareowner Voting Guidelines, PIRC observes that the average board size for companies in the All Share Index is seven or eight, and this will be taken by it as the benchmark in assessing compliance with Principle G of the Code.[64]

2.4.3 Board composition

It is no longer the case (since July 2005) that the Listing Rules explicitly require the directors and senior management of an applicant for listing to have appropriate expertise and experience. However, a person's suitability for a listed company board appointment is still a relevant consideration.

A company with a premium listing is subject to the six Premium Listing Principles (see Listing Rule (LR) 7.2.1A).[65] The purpose of the principles is to ensure that such companies pay due regard to the fundamental role they play in maintaining market confidence and, in relation to directors,

---

[60] Provision B.2.4 of the 2016 Code contained similar wording.

[61] This matches a recommendation which had been made in the final report of the Parliamentary Commission on Banking Standards which was released in June 2013. The report had made the recommendation in respect of certain banking bodies but had suggested that it might also be applied to financial services companies in general.

[62] The Role and Duties of Directors—A Statement of Best Practice, available from *http://www.ivis.co.uk* [Accessed 25 April 2019].

[63] One of the Supporting Principles to Main Principle B.1 of the 2016 Code also required that the board should be of sufficient size that the requirements of the business can be met … and should not be so large as to be unwieldy.

[64] Or the Supporting Principles to Main Principle B.1 of the 2016 Code as the case may be.

[65] Until 16 May 2014, a company with a standard listing was subject to the same principles. From this date, only the two more general Listing Principles (see LR 7.2.1) apply to a company with a standard listing.

Principle 1 requires a premium-listed company to take reasonable steps to enable its directors to understand their responsibilities and obligations as directors.

When a company publishes a prospectus, the Prospectus Rules require disclosure of certain information about its directors, their interests, remuneration, management expertise and experience, other directorships and details of any personal bankruptcy, convictions, sanctions or disqualifications and of receiverships or liquidations of any company of which the individual has been a director (see, for example, s.14 of Annex I, Appendix 3 to the Prospectus Rules). The same disclosure requirements apply in relation to admission documents published under the AIM Rules (see AIM r.3).

A premium-listed company's sponsor must also be satisfied, before any application for listing is made, that the directors of the issuer have established procedures which enable the company to comply with the Listing Rules and Disclosure and Transparency Rules on an ongoing basis (LR 8.4.2) and understand the nature and extent of their responsibilities under the Listing Rules and Disclosure and Transparency Rules (LR 8.3.4). The sponsor will be required to confirm that it is satisfied about such matters in its Declaration on an Application for Listing which it makes to the FCA.

In terms of continuing obligations of a listed company as regards an individual's suitability for a board appointment, the Code contains requirements for the requisite skills, experience and independence of judgment among board members. For example, Principle K requires that the board and its committees should have a combination of skills, experience and knowledge to enable them to discharge their duties and responsibilities effectively.[66] Principle G also requires an appropriate combination of both executive and non-executive directors (in particular, independent non-executives), such that no individual or small group of individuals can dominate the board's decision-taking.[67] Code Provision 10 contains detailed independence requirements which are discussed in detail in Chapter 9. Both the PLSA and PIRC are particularly concerned with the criteria for independence of the chairman and non-executive directors. The PLSA highlights length of tenure and links to a significant shareholder as factors which will be seen as compromising independence. PIRC will only assess a director as independent if he can satisfy the additional criteria in PIRC's 2019 UK Shareowner Voting Guidelines over and above those set out in the Code.

---

[66] As was the case under Main Principle B.1 of the 2016 Code.
[67] As was the case under one of the Supporting Principles to Main Principle B.1 of the 2016 Code.

In addition, Code Provision 9 requires that the chairman and chief executive role should not be combined.[68]

The Code is supported by the recommendations in the FRC's guidance on board effectiveness as to board composition and succession planning.

The QCA Code also requires the board to have "the necessary up-to-date experience, skills and capabilities between them".

As noted in Section 2.3.3, there are also special considerations for board appointments to a bank or other financial services institution.

2.4.4 Board diversity

Principle J of the Code states that appointments to the board should be subject to a formal rigorous and transparent procedure made on merit and objective criteria.[69] Appointments should, within this context, promote diversity of gender, social and ethnic background and cognitive and personal strengths. The Code's board diversity provisions, which were the result of the Davies Review carried out in 2011, also require listed companies to include relevant information in their annual reports. Companies will need to report on their policy on diversity and inclusion, its objectives and linkages to company strategy, how it has been implemented and progress on achieving the objectives as well as on the gender balance of those in senior management[70] and their direct reports (see Code Provision 23 and Provision B.2.4 in the 2016 Code).

In September 2018, the FRC published a review of board diversity reporting which found that 88% of FTSE 250 companies reported on their board diversity policies. 74% of FTSE 250 companies had a diversity policy which expressly referred to gender and 30% referred to ethnicity.[71]

Separately, the European Commission is continuing to push for mandatory quotas for women on larger listed company boards. In November 2012, the Commission published a proposal for a European Directive setting a minimum objective of 40% female non-executive directors in listed companies by January 2020.[72] The UK Government continues to favour the non-statutory model espoused by Lord Davies and in the subsequent

---

[68] As was the case under Provision A.2.1 of the 2016 Code.

[69] As was the case under Main Principle B.2 of the 2016 Code and its Supporting Principles.

[70] The executive committee or the first layer of management below board level (including the company secretary).

[71] The latter was in part attributed to the prominence which ethnic diversity has gained through the Parker Review into the ethnic diversity of UK boards; see *https://www.gov.uk/government/publications/ethnic-diversity-of-uk-boards-the-parker-review* [Accessed 25 April 2019] for the final report.

[72] This instrument remains at the proposal stage at the time of writing.

Hampton-Alexander review[73] which increased the target for women in leadership roles across the FTSE 350 to 33%, but has put on record its intention to take tougher measures, in the form of quotas, if the voluntary approach now set out in the Code does not work.

More recently, on 5 April 2017, Parliament's BEIS Select Committee published a report on corporate governance[74] which suggested as an additional target that from May 2020 at least half of all appointments to senior and executive level positions by listed companies should be women.

2.4.5   Board training and evaluation

The latest version of the Code no longer includes an express requirement that all directors should receive induction on joining the board[75] but the FRC Guidance on Board Effectiveness still recommends such induction as part of maintaining an effective board. Paragraph 41 of the guidance also notes that the company's approach to stakeholder engagement will be an important topic in the induction programme for new directors. Code Principle 21 requires the board to undertake a "formal and rigorous annual evaluation of its own performance and that of its committees and individual directors" and, in the case of FTSE 350 companies, that the performance evaluation should be externally facilitated at least every three years.[76] Code Principle 22 requires each director to engage with the process and take appropriate action when development needs have been identified. The 2016 Code contained no such express requirement.

The QCA Code is less prescriptive: performance evaluation should take place "regularly" and "may be carried out internally or, ideally, externally facilitated from time to time" (see Principle 7).

Performance evaluation is a key feature of the FRC's guidance on board effectiveness, which sets out a suggested (but non-prescriptive) scope for a board evaluation exercise.[77] ICSA periodically produces a report on board evaluation procedures and reporting in the top 200 listed companies. The latest report, in relation to the 2011 Financial Year,[78] indicates that companies are, by and large, falling into line on this Code requirement, at least as regards internal evaluations, and most of those who have not yet

---

[73] See   *https://www.gov.uk/government/publications/ftse-women-leaders-hampton-alexander-review* [Accessed 25 April 2019].

[74] See   *https://www.parliament.uk/business/committees/committees-a-z/commons-select/business-energy-industrial-strategy/news-parliament-2015/corporate-governance-report-published-16-17/* [Accessed 25 April 2019].

[75] As was the case under Main Principle B.4 of the 2016 Code.

[76] As was the case under Main Principle B.6 and Provision B.6.2 of the 2016 Code.

[77] See para.113 in the FRC's guidance to the Code and para.5.5 in the guidance to the 2016 Code.

[78] See *https://www.icsaglobal.com/assets/files/pdfs/Publications/top_200_report_2012.pdf* [Accessed 25 April 2019].

commissioned an external evaluation in the three years since the relevant Code provision was introduced are gearing themselves up to do so within the three-year timeframe set out in the Code. ICSA's report also suggests that, despite the still-widespread use of boilerplate language in some company reports, companies are in general reporting more fully and meaningfully on the outcome of board evaluation procedures, and on any action being taken by companies in response to it. Subsequently, the ABI also carried out a board evaluation survey for its December 2012 *Report on Board Effectiveness*,[79] which is broadly in line with the conclusions in the ICSA report.

In 2017, Grant Thornton, the accountancy firm, published a report on board effectiveness[80] which found that 60% of directors who provided feedback for the report were of the opinion that there are adequate processes in place to evaluate the performance of the whole board in their organisation. The feedback did show a strong discrepancy between companies listed on the main market and companies quoted on AIM. Almost 90% of main market directors agreed with this statement while only a third of AIM directors held the same opinion.

The QCA's Corporate Governance Behaviour Review[81] published in December 2018 found that only 42% of AIM quoted companies which have adopted the QCA Code adequately explain their board evaluation process and notes that investors have found this figure disappointing.

The Institute of Directors (IoD), ICSA, some executive search firms and audit firms and a number of other organisations and independent consultants carry out external board evaluations. The ABI report notes that the market for external evaluations is still developing, and some companies are concerned about the lack of experience, credibility and independence of available practitioners. For this reason, the ABI supports the suggestion made in the Walker Review[82] for the formation of a professional grouping of board evaluation consultants in order to provide some quality assurance and consistency, and manage potential conflicts of interest.

In the response to its consultation on Insolvency and Corporate Governance,[83] BEIS announced on 26 August 2018, that it is inviting ICSA to convene a group including representatives from the investment community

---

[79] See *http://www.ivis.co.uk/pdf/abi%20report%20on%20Board%20effectiveness%202012%20-%20 final.pdf* [Accessed 25 April 2019].
[80] See *https://www.grantthornton.co.uk/globalassets/1.-member-firms/united-kingdom/pdf/ publication/board-effectiveness-report-2017.pdf* [Accessed 25 April 2019].
[81] See *https://www.theqca.com/article_assets/articledir_348/174461/Corporate%20Governance%20 Behaviour%20Review%202018.pdf* [Accessed 25 April 2019].
[82] See *http://webarchive.nationalarchives.gov.uk/+/http://www.hm-treasury.gov.uk/d/walker_review_ 261109.pdf* [Accessed 25 April 2019].
[83] See *https://assets.publishing.service.gov.uk/government/uploads/system/uploads/attachment_data/ file/736163/ICG_-_Government_response_doc_-_24_Aug_clean_version__with_Minister_s_photo_ and_signature__AC.pdf* [Accessed 25 April 2019].

and companies to identify further ways of improving the quality and effectiveness of board evaluations including the development of a code of practice for external board evaluations.

An additional outcome of the BEIS consultation on Insolvency and Corporate Governance is that the Government will bring forward further proposals to strengthen access to training and guidance for directors, tailored to different sizes of company, and will consider whether some level of training should be mandatory for directors of large companies.

In response to a desire by some of its members to improve their skills and to provide a solution for outside observers seeking to ensure the presence of certain skills at board level, in 1999 the IoD introduced a voluntary training and assessment programme leading to qualification as a chartered director. The qualification process is a very rigorous one, and those who attain the qualification must also undertake continuing training to maintain and develop their knowledge and skills. A list of those directors who have been chartered since the chartered director qualification was introduced in 1999 is available on the IoD's website, and, as the Code strongly advocates training for all listed company board directors, it seems likely that the use of the qualification will increase. The IoD also runs courses and examinations leading to either a Certificate or Diploma in Company Direction, both of which are effectively preliminary steps towards chartered status.

2.5 Effect of invalid appointment

CA 2006 s.161 provides that the acts of a director are valid, notwithstanding any defect that afterwards may be discovered in his appointment or eligibility to act as a director or that he had ceased to hold office at all, or was not entitled to vote on the matter in question. This would be so even if the appointment had been void under s.160 (appointment of public company directors to be voted on individually). A similar provision was contained in Table A at reg.92 and this provision, or something similar, may still be incorporated in the articles of many companies, although the Model Articles under CA 2006 do not replicate reg.92, relying instead on CA 2006 s.161. All that said, it is likely that the provisions of s.161 and any equivalent provisions in a company's articles relating to defective appointment offer only limited protection to a person dealing with the company because their application appears to be restricted to a procedural defect in the appointment only. See *Morris v Kanssen*[84] at 459 and 471, which is authority for a number of propositions:

(a)   that neither Companies Act 1929 s.143 (and therefore presumably its successors, Companies Act 1948 s.180, CA 1985 s.285 and CA 2006 s.161), nor art.88 Companies Act 1929 Table A (or its successors,

---

[84]   *Morris v Kanssen* [1946] A.C. 459; [1946] 1 All E.R. 586.

reg.105 Companies Act 1948, Table A or reg.92 of Table A) validate an appointment which is contrary to the Companies Acts or the articles of association of the relevant company;

(b) that neither the section nor the articles can assist a party if that party had knowledge of the facts giving rise to the invalidity;

(c) it cannot assist the party if that party is put on enquiry and does not enquire; and

(d) it cannot avail anyone where there is no appointment at all.[85]

The case of *Aidiniantz v Sherlock Holmes International Society Ltd*[86] further qualifies the application CA 2006 s.161 by noting that it will validate unauthorised actions in favour of those dealing with a company but will not validate hostile actions by a company against third parties.

2.6 Vacation of office

Once appointed, there are then a number of ways in which a director's term of office may be brought to an end.

2.6.1 Voluntary resignation

A director may resign his office at any time, despite the fact that he may also be employed by the company and have a service agreement with it which requires him to serve for a fixed term or to give a period of notice of resignation. An executive director's service agreement (and therefore his employment with the company) may continue notwithstanding his resignation from the office of director. If the director terminates his service agreement at the same time and, without giving the notice required by the service agreement, he may be liable to the company in damages for breach of contract. Sometimes a company's articles will specify a procedure to be followed for giving effect to a resignation from the office of director. The Model Articles for private companies reg.18(f) and the Model Articles for public companies reg.22(f),[87] for example, provide that the office of a director shall be vacated upon the company receiving notice that he is resigning or retiring and such notice coming into effect. Any notice to be given by any person pursuant to those provisions will be governed by the notices provisions in the articles (e.g. see the Model Articles for private companies reg.48 and the Model Articles for public companies reg.79). In addition to any such procedural measures in the articles, CA 2006 s.1139 enables a notice of resignation to be served on the company by leaving it at,

---

[85] See also *New Cedos Engineering Co Ltd, Re* [1994] 1 B.C.L.C. 797 but note the Scottish case *Macnabs LLP v Fordlane Ltd* 2014 S.L.T. (Sh Ct) 80 which comments obiter that persons who are acting as de facto directors may, depending on the facts of the individual case, be treated as "appointed" for the purposes of CA 2006 s.161.

[86] *Aidiniantz v Sherlock Holmes International Society Ltd* [2016] EWHC 1392 (Ch).

[87] Regulation 81(d) of Table A contains a similar provision.

or sending it by post to, the company's registered office. A resignation, once made, cannot be withdrawn except with the consent of the company and, unless the articles provide otherwise, it is not necessary for a resignation to be accepted by the board before it becomes effective.

The articles of private equity-backed companies commonly discourage directors from resigning voluntarily by requiring them to sell any shares in the investee company held by them or their family members for a sum which can be well below the full market value if they resign (known as "leaver" provisions). Such provisions are designed to incentivise managers to see the investment through to a successful exit for both the private equity investors and management.

In the unusual circumstances where a share qualification exists (see Section 2.3.4 above), a director may resign voluntarily simply by disposing of his qualification shares.

2.6.2 Retirement by rotation and potential re-election

The Model Articles for private companies do not (unlike Table A) contain retirement by rotation provisions, and even if they are operating with Table A-based articles, many private companies disapply the retirement by rotation provisions because they are considered unnecessary and cumbersome for a small, closely-held company, particularly where there may be a shareholders' or other agreement giving shareholders the right to review directors' appointments. Indeed private companies are not required to have an AGM under CA 2006, and the retirement by rotation provisions generally operate by reference to the AGM cycle.

By contrast, most listed and many other public companies have provisions in their articles requiring a proportion of the directors to retire at each AGM. The rationale behind these retirement by rotation provisions, which are reinforced by the Code (see below), is to ensure that an individual director's appointment as a director is not wholly entrenched and shareholders have an opportunity to review that appointment periodically.

By way of example of the way retirement by rotation works, the Model Articles for public companies[88] contain provisions (at reg.21) to the effect

---

[88] The corresponding provision of Table A is slightly different. Regulation 73 provides that at every AGM subsequent to the first one, one-third of directors subject to retirement by rotation (or if their number is not three or a multiple of three, the number nearest one-third) shall retire from office and may put themselves up for re-election. In order to determine which of the directors are to retire at any particular AGM from amongst those eligible, it is normal for companies to select for retirement those directors who have been in office longest since their last appointment or reappointment. Where more than the required number were last appointed or reappointed at the same time, then those to retire are to be determined by lot, unless they agree amongst themselves who is to stand for re-election in that year (reg.74 of Table A).

that at a company's first AGM all of the directors shall retire from office and, at every subsequent AGM, any director appointed since the last AGM or who was not appointed (or re-elected) at either of the previous two AGMs shall retire from office and may offer himself for reappointment. A director who retires by rotation is normally eligible for reappointment and would (until the recent focus on corporate governance) normally be re-elected as a matter of formality.[89] If the director is not reappointed then he will usually continue to hold office until the end of the meeting at which he is due to retire. For details about persons eligible for appointment in his place see Section 2.3 above.

Any person appointed as a director in place of a person removed from office under s.168 is treated, for the purposes of determining the time at which he or any other director is to retire, as if he had become a director on the day on which the person in whose place he is appointed was last appointed a director (s.168(4)).

If there is provision in a public company's articles to require that a director appointed initially by the board must retire at the first AGM following his appointment (e.g. the Model Articles for public companies reg.21(2)(a)),[90] this provision can, at times, create practical difficulties. For example, if the board appoints a new director after the dispatch of notice of the company's AGM but before the meeting itself takes place, many companies' articles would require (as in the case of the Model Articles reg.21) that the director concerned must, nevertheless, still retire at the AGM and, if not reappointed at that meeting, vacate office at the end of it. In these circumstances, the board will need to consider carefully the other provisions of the company's articles and the precise wording of the notice convening the meeting. Possible courses of action may include:

(a)   proposing a resolution at the AGM to reappoint the relevant director under a provision in the company's articles if they enable such a resolution to be included within the "ordinary business" of the AGM, for which no specific notice is required in the notice of the meeting[91];

(b)   sending a further notice to shareholders including details of the additional resolution and, if necessary, adjourning the AGM to enable the necessary notice period to elapse; or

---

[89]   Table A (reg.75) provided that if the retiring director was willing to continue, he would be deemed to have been reappointed unless, at the meeting, it was resolved not to fill the vacancy, or unless a resolution for his reappointment was put to the meeting and lost, but there is no corresponding provision in the Model Articles under CA 2006.

[90]   See also reg.73 of Table A, Provision B.7.1 of the 2016 Code and Code Provision 18 (referred to in more detail later in this Section).

[91]   If, as is common, the notice of AGM contains full particulars of the directors retiring by rotation and submitting themselves for reappointment, it is doubtful whether the company could rely on the ordinary business provisions to table the resolution for the reappointment of a director who had not been named in the notice.

(c)   allowing the new director's appointment to lapse at the end of the AGM and then reappointing him immediately by further resolution of the board.

In this last situation, the director will have to retire again at the next AGM and proper notice of his proposed re-election should be given.[92]

It is effectively no longer open to listed companies to opt out of retirement by rotation provisions in view of the corporate governance requirements applicable to them. Historically, the Combined Code always imposed retirement by rotation requirements on directors of listed companies. The financial crisis in 2008–2009 triggered widespread reappraisal of the UK corporate governance regime, including the FRC's review of the Combined Code (now the UK Corporate Governance Code). One of the (at the time) most controversial suggestions made by the FRC was that all directors should be subject to annual re-election (rather than every three years), in order to increase accountability to shareholders. Many commentators felt that annual re-election of the entire board would risk uncertainty and short-termism in the company's governance and create the potential to destabilise the board. Nevertheless Provision 18 of the Code requires all directors of listed companies to be subject to annual election by shareholders. Provision B.7.1 of the 2016 Code only required this of directors of FTSE 350 companies and then went on to require directors of all other listed companies to submit themselves for re-election at the first AGM after their appointment and thereafter at intervals of no more than three years.

Provision B.7.1 of the 2016 Code also required that the names of all directors subject to election or re-election should be accompanied by sufficient biographical details and other relevant information to enable shareholders to make informed decisions as to their election. Code Provision 18 instead requires the company to set out, in respect of each director subject to re-election, why his contribution is, and continues to be, important to the company's long-term sustainable success.

Consistent with CA 2006 s.160, which effectively requires a separate resolution for each director, to enable shareholders to cast their vote on each director individually, LR 9.3.7 requires that the proxy form for re-election of retiring directors allows votes to be cast for or against the re-election of each director individually.

---

[92] A further possible solution for a company with Table A-based articles would be for the director to retire at the AGM and for the board then to recommend his appointment to the AGM, thus taking advantage of the provisions of regs 76(a) and 78 of Table A (if they apply). Not less than seven days' notice must be given to all who are entitled to receive notice of the meeting of the intention so to recommend and including details of the relevant director, all as required by reg.77 of Table A (if it applies).

By 2012, annual re-election of the whole board had become standard among FTSE 350 companies.[93] At the time of writing, a significant minority of smaller listed companies has also adopted annual re-election of the whole board on a voluntary basis. It will remain to be seen how soon the remaining smaller listed companies will adopt this approach. Companies quoted on AIM will remain free to adopt the QCA Code instead of the Code to avoid this requirement.

Any departure from the Code's requirements must be highlighted in the next following annual report and accounts, as required under LR 9.8.6(6)(b) but shareholders are unlikely to go along with the removal of, or exemption from, retirement by rotation provisions. PIRC, for example, states that annual re-election is good practice for *all* listed companies. In effect, all of the shareholder bodies regard it as fundamental to good corporate governance that directors are required to seek regular re-election by shareholders, and the retirement by rotation provisions provide shareholders with a powerful weapon since the threat of a negative vote at AGM enables them to express disapproval, and exert control over board composition and performance, without having to go through the potentially costly and cumbersome requisition procedures.

Directors of listed companies can no longer assume that their re-election is a formality, as directors are more accountable than ever to shareholders for their performance. As noted in Section 2.2.5, institutional shareholders are under a positive obligation under the Stewardship Code to monitor the performance of their investee companies and their directors and senior management.

The PLSA Corporate Governance Policy and Voting Guidelines 2017 recommend a vote against the re-election of any non-independent director who compromises the independence balance on the remuneration committee. In the case of severe or persistent infringements of good practice in the company's remuneration arrangements, the chair, as the person deemed responsible for the board's overall corporate governance practices, could be in the firing line.

In 2018, 85 directors of companies included in the FTSE All Share index received a vote in excess of 20% against their re-election and five directors failed to be re-elected. This constitutes a measurable increase against 2017 which saw 58 significant votes against the re-election of a director and four directors who were not re-elected.[94]

---

[93] PLC's review of the 2012 reporting season indicated that 98% of the FTSE 350 put the whole board up for annual re-election in 2012 compared to 79% in 2011. In 2017, only two FTSE 350 companies did not put their whole board up for annual re-election and one of these was a company with a dual listing in Germany which was prevented from complying with this provision of the 2016 Code due to German employee co-determination constraints.

[94] As disclosed in the Investment Association's Public Register which had been last updated on 5 December 2018 at the time of writing.

For more on directors' remuneration see Chapter 6.

2.6.3 Age

CA 1985 s.293, which set a maximum age limit of 70 for directors of public companies, was repealed in April 2007 but, as referred to in Section 2.3.1 above, it may be worth checking a company's articles for age limits which may apply to terminate a director's period of office. For a discussion on the minimum age limit for directors see also Section 2.3.1 above.

2.6.4 Vacation of office pursuant to the company's articles

Most companies' articles contain provisions pursuant to which directors must vacate office automatically. The most common provisions are similar to those contained in the Model Articles for private companies reg.18 and the Model Articles for public companies reg.22, both of which state that a person ceases to be a director as soon as:

(a)   that person ceases to be a director by virtue of any provision of the Companies Act 2006 or is prohibited from being a director by law;

(b)   a bankruptcy order is made against that person;

(c)   a composition is made with that person's creditors generally in satisfaction of that person's debts;

(d)   a registered medical practitioner who is treating that person gives a written opinion to the company stating that that person has become physically or mentally incapable of acting as a director and may remain so for more than three months; or

(e)   notification is received by the company from the director that the director is resigning from office as a director and such resignation has taken effect in accordance with its terms.

These provisions largely replicate the corresponding ones in reg.81 of Table A,[95] although there is no longer a provision in the Model Articles which

---

[95]   Regulation 81 of Table A states that the office of a director shall be vacated if:
(a) he ceases to be a director by virtue of any provision of CA 1985 or becomes prohibited by law from being a director;
(b) he becomes bankrupt or makes any arrangement or composition with his creditors generally;
(c) he is, or may be, suffering from mental disorder and either:
(i) he is admitted to hospital in pursuance of an application for admission for treatment under the Mental Health Act 1983 or, in Scotland, an application for admission under the Mental Health (Scotland) Act 1960; or
(ii) an order is made by a court having jurisdiction (whether in the UK or elsewhere) in matters concerning mental disorder for his detention or for the appointment of a receiver, curator bonis or other person to exercise powers with respect to his property or affairs;
(d) he resigns his office by notice to the company; or
(e) for more than six consecutive months he shall have been absent without the permission of the directors from meetings of directors held during that period and the directors resolve that his office be vacated.

would automatically trigger the termination of a director's appointment in the event of mental illness resulting in a court order. The relevant provision (what used to be the Model Articles for private companies para.18(e) and the Model Articles for public companies para.22(e)) was repealed with effect from 28 April 2013 as being discriminatory, under the Mental Health (Discrimination) Act 2013. There is no requirement for companies whose articles contain a provision similar to those paras 18(e) and 22(e) to amend them, but some may wish to do so. Mental health problems may still trigger the termination of a director's office though, if a director is "signed off" by a doctor as being incapable of acting as a director for mental health reasons, under the Model Articles for private companies para.18(d), or the Model Articles for public companies para.22(d).

A director's failure to attend directors' meetings for a certain period was also treated as a termination event under Table A, whereas there is no corresponding provision in the Model Articles. Early drafts of the Model Articles had a more general provision under which the director's appointment would terminate when all the other directors decided that a director should be removed from office, providing greater flexibility as to the circumstances in which non-attendance may arise. However, that provision gave rise to concern that the directors could use it to overturn the appointment of a director by shareholders, so it was dropped. That said, there are often provisions in a company's articles enabling the board to remove a director by resolution of a particular majority or by unanimous resolution of the directors (excluding the director concerned). Such provisions are usually designed to enable the board to deal with a disruptive director without the publicity and procedural difficulties of CA 2006 s.168 in circumstances where a director, who no longer has the support of his fellow directors, refuses to resign.

The Model Articles provisions incorporate the consequences of the CDDA 1986 and the Enterprise Act 2002, pursuant to which a director may be prohibited by court order or pursuant to a disqualification undertaking from being a director for a specified period, unless he first obtains leave of the court. Such orders may be granted (or undertakings given) following general misconduct in connection with companies (such as conviction for indictable offences, persistent breaches of companies legislation or fraud); or for reasons of unfitness to hold the office of director (if the court is satisfied that the individual has been a director of a company which has, at any time, become insolvent and his conduct as a director of that company makes him unfit to be concerned in the management of a company); or, in the case of disqualification under the Enterprise Act 2002, for breach by the company of which the individual is a director of EU or UK competition law. (See also Section 2.3.6 and Chapter 13.)

In addition to these "standard" provisions, specific provisions on termination of a director's appointment may be found in a company's articles or in a shareholders' agreement. For example, where a director has been appointed by a particular interest group, the company's articles may provide for his appointor to remove the director in a similar manner to which the appointment was made (e.g. a private equity investor may be entitled to appoint and/or remove a specified number of directors, or sometimes any and all directors, by depositing a notice to that effect at the company's registered office). Similarly a director's period of office may terminate on some event specified in the articles (e.g. the end of an earn-out period where a particular director was appointed by the vendor and where the appointment was to be limited to the duration of the earn-out period).

2.6.5   Removal pursuant to CA 2006 s.168

As a safeguard for shareholders a company may, pursuant to CA 2006 s.168, by ordinary resolution remove a director before the expiration of his period of office. This provision overrides any agreement or arrangement between the company and the director, although it does not prevent the director from seeking compensation for breach (by reason of the operation of the section) of any contractual rights which he may hold. Section 168 can be helpful if the board is unwilling to operate the provisions (if any) contained in the company's articles (see Section 2.6.4 above) or in the relevant director's service agreement (see Section 2.6.6 below) entitling them to remove a director, provided the director to be removed controls fewer than 50% of the voting rights in issue.

As noted in Section 2.2.5 above, activist shareholders in listed companies have, in recent years, been more inclined to use their powers to propose resolutions at the company's AGM or requisition a general meeting in order to force board changes, removing incumbent directors and putting forward their own nominees. The Stewardship Code does suggest that if boards do not respond constructively to behind-the-scenes intervention on the part of institutional investors, then one of the ways in which shareholders can escalate their action is to requisition a general meeting or resolution to change the board. However, shareholder bodies still mainly focus on voting on re-election at the AGM rather than the more aggressive step of implementing the s.168 procedure.

The s.168 procedure may be used where the directors who are being targeted by the shareholders for removal are not retiring by rotation at the AGM, or the action cannot wait until the AGM. In the well-publicised case of Mitchells & Butlers in January 2010, a shareholder with a 22.8% stake used a combination of all of the statutory powers available to it to replace the board, putting forward resolutions to appoint new directors and remove the former chairman and leading a revolt which resulted in several incumbent directors being voted down on re-election. (That case was the subject of a Takeover Panel investigation into allegations that certain shareholders had acted in concert, but the Panel found that no breach of the Takeover Code had occurred.)[96]

Despite an increase in campaigns by activist investors since then,[97] cases such as this are still relatively rare, and it may be that often companies agree to a behind-the-scenes compromise before the matter comes before a general shareholders' meeting. In a sense, this may be achieving the intention behind successive governments' efforts to make boards more accountable to their shareholders, whilst not putting the company's fortunes at risk by publicising the shareholders' dissatisfaction.

Another reason why the s.168 procedure can be unattractive or impracticable is that special notice of a s.168 resolution is required, essentially to enable the director concerned to protest against his removal. Pursuant to CA 2006 s.312, a s.168 resolution is not effective unless notice of the intention to table it has been given to the company at least 28 days before the meeting at which it is to be considered and the company has given its members notice of any such resolution at the same time and in the same manner as it gives notice of the meeting. If that is not practicable, the company must give members notice, either by advertisement in a newspaper having an appropriate circulation or by any other mode allowed by the company's articles, at least 14 clear days (i.e. 14 days without counting the date on which notice is given and the date of the meeting)[98] before the meeting at which the resolution is to be considered. If, after notice of the intention to table such a resolution has been given to the company, a meeting is called for a date 28 days or less after the notice has been given to the company, the notice is deemed properly given, even though the notice was not actually given within the time required.[99]

On receipt of the notice of an intended resolution to remove a director under s.168 the company must, forthwith, send a copy of the notice to the director concerned. The director is entitled to be heard on the resolution at the meeting at which it is put, whether he is a member of the company or not. The director is also entitled to make written representations to the company (not exceeding a reasonable length) and to request that they be

---

[96] See Panel Notice 2010/1 on the Panel's website at *http://www.thetakeoverpanel.org* [Accessed 25 April 2019].

[97] The Global Shareholder Activism Map published by FTI Consulting in February 2018 lists 51 activist campaigns in the UK for each of 2016 and 2017 compared to 28 campaigns for each of 2014 and 2015. In each case, removing the CEO or another board member was the most popular type of campaign.

[98] Previously the limit was 21 days under CA 1985 s.379. The change was made to bring it into line with CA 2006 s.307, which provides that 14 clear days' notice will be sufficient for all general meetings except an AGM of a public company which still requires at least 21 clear days' notice.

[99] In view of the special arrangements for notice of a resolution to remove a director, under s.288(2)(a), the written resolution procedure available to private companies under CA 2006 s.288 does not apply to s.168 resolutions.

notified to members. The company must then (unless the representations are received by it too late for it to do so):

(a) in any notice of the resolution given to members of the company, state the fact that the representations have been made; and

(b) send a copy of the representations to every member of the company to whom notice of the meeting is sent (whether the notice is sent to members before or after the company receives the director's representations).

If a copy of the representations is not sent as required above because they were received too late or because the company failed to do so, the director may, in addition to being able to speak at the meeting, require that his written representations be read out at the meeting. Copies of the director's representations need not be sent out and they need not be read out at the meeting if, on the application of either the company or any other person who claims to be aggrieved, the court is satisfied that the director's rights to have his statement circulated are being abused.[100] Even if the director is not a party to such an application, the court may order the company's costs on the application to be paid by him.

As to whether it is possible to contract out of these provisions, CA 1985 s.303 applied "notwithstanding anything in [the company's] articles". Although this saving was not carried over into s.168, CA 2006 Explanatory Note 68 states in general terms that a company's articles cannot contain anything that is contrary to the provisions of the Act. In any event, such a provision or exclusion would in all likelihood constitute an unlawful fetter on the company's statutory powers, as outlined in the case of *Russell v Northern Bank Development Corp Ltd*.[101] A company's articles would not, therefore, be able to exclude the ability of a company to remove its directors by ordinary resolution. However, as was the position under the CA 1985, a company should be able to provide in its articles for another removal mechanism, for example removal by the majority shareholder(s) on written notice—a provision which is not uncommon in the articles of private equity-backed companies. Section 168 does not provide that removal by ordinary resolution is the only permissible method but simply that a company may use this method.

It was generally considered that nothing in the CA 1985 prevented the operation of any provision in the articles of the company, pursuant to which the director concerned (or any other person) is granted enhanced voting rights entitling him to defeat any resolution proposed pursuant to s.303

---

[100] CA 1985 s.304 previously required the court to be satisfied that the director's rights were being abused "to secure needless publicity for defamatory matters". It is now sufficient under s.169(5) for the court to be satisfied that the director's rights are being abused.

[101] *Russell v Northern Bank Development Corp Ltd* [1992] 1 W.L.R. 588; [1992] 3 All E.R. 161; [1992] B.C.C. 578.

(*Bushell v Faith*[102]) and there seems no reason why this should not be the case under CA 2006.[103] However, such provisions do need to be drafted carefully if they are to provide effective protection for the director concerned and if they are not to be circumvented. For example, the provisions need to create enhanced voting rights not only in respect of the s.168 resolution itself but also any resolution which may first be proposed to change the articles in order to remove or dilute the article by which his voting rights are enhanced.

The provisions of s.168 and the *Russell v Northern Bank* case should not prevent there being an agreement between a company's shareholders (outside the articles of association), enforceable as between shareholders, that they will not exercise their rights under s.168 to remove a particular director, provided the agreement is not binding on the director or the company. This might be useful to secure the position of a director appointed by a particular shareholder or class of shareholder, for example, a private equity investor (see also Section 2.2.9 above for more on entrenchment). In private equity-backed companies, the appointment and removal of nominee directors of such investors is usually, as mentioned above, within the power of the private equity investor itself acting on its own (see also Section 2.10 below on nominee directors).

Shareholders should, however, consider the risk of a claim for unfair prejudice from a director who is also a shareholder, particularly if such a provision is to be added to a company's articles specifically in order to remove the director in question. There were several cases under the CA 1985 regime considering a petition for relief under CA 1985 ss.459–461 (the predecessors to CA 2006 ss.994–998) as a result of allegations of unfair prejudice in relation to the removal of directors. It appears from the case law on the old CA 1985 s.303 that the circumstances in which a petition under s.994 (CA 1985 s.459) would be most likely to succeed are where the director is a "founder", or the company is a family company, and where the individual would have some reasonable expectation of involvement in management. In a quasi-partnership context the House of Lords decision in *Ebrahimi v Westbourne Galleries Ltd*[104] may be relevant. See also *Brownlow v GH Marshall Ltd*[105] and *Parkinson v Eurofinance Group Ltd*.[106] Conversely, in the case of *Astec (BSR) Plc, Re*,[107] it was held that unfair prejudice could not

---

[102] *Bushell v Faith* [1970] A.C. 1099; [1970] 2 W.L.R. 272; (1970) 114 S.J. 54.

[103] There is some doubt, however, as to whether *Bushell v Faith* provisions would be upheld in the articles of association of a public company, as a result of obiter dicta the judgment of the House of Lords in the *Bushell v Faith* case which indicate that the principle is most appropriate to small, family-owned private companies.

[104] *Ebrahimi v Westbourne Galleries Ltd* [1973] A.C. 360; [1972] 2 W.L.R. 1289; [1972] 2 All E.R. 492.

[105] *Brownlow v GH Marshall Ltd* [2001] B.C.C. 152; [2000] 2 B.C.L.C. 655.

[106] *Parkinson v Eurofinance Group Ltd* [2001] B.C.C. 551; [2001] 1 B.C.L.C. 720; (2000) 97(27) L.S.G. 37.

[107] *Astec (BSR) Plc, Re* [1999] B.C.C. 59; [1998] 2 B.C.L.C. 556.

be established simply because there was no reason for the removal of directors, nor were "legitimate expectations" relevant.[108]

The cases on alteration of the company's articles to the detriment of the minority suggest that the majority shareholders should be particularly careful if a provision entitling them to remove a director summarily on written notice (effectively disapplying the special notice provisions of s.168) is added to the articles after incorporation, where they may be perceived to be acting other than in good faith and in their own interests rather than those of the company as a whole. See, for example, *Allen v Gold Reefs of West Africa Ltd*,[109] *Greenhalgh v Arderne Cinemas Ltd*[110] and, more recently, *Charterhouse Capital Ltd, Re*.[111]

2.6.6 *Vacation of office pursuant to a provision in a service contract*

Provisions are often contained in a director's service contract with the company which require, as a matter of contract, a director to resign his office as director of the company if his employment with the company is terminated. Such provisions would usually also grant a power of attorney[112] in favour of one or more of the remaining directors, enabling such other directors to sign a letter of resignation on his behalf should he fail to do so as required by the terms of the service contract. Care needs to be taken when operating such provisions in a service contract to ensure that the service contract is terminated lawfully and that the events which give rise to the requirement for the director to resign have arisen.

In the case of many private equity-backed companies, it is not unusual to find provisions in the service contract providing for termination of the director's employment (and therefore triggering dismissal as a director) for breach of the director's undertakings (or covenants or warranties), qua shareholder, in any shareholders' agreement or the company's articles of association.

2.6.7 *Vacation by order of the court*

The court's powers on an application under CA 2006 s.994 (unfair prejudice) are, in theory, wide enough for the court to order that a director cease to hold office. In practice, however, the courts are extremely reluctant to interfere in the direct management of a company in this way.

---

[108] See also *Woolwich v Twenty Twenty Productions Ltd* [2003] EWHC 414 (Ch); [2003] All E.R. (D) 211.

[109] *Allen v Gold Reefs of West Africa Ltd* [1900] 1 Ch. 656.

[110] *Greenhalgh v Arderne Cinemas Ltd* [1951] Ch. 286; [1950] 2 All E.R. 1120; (1950) 94 S.J. 855.

[111] *Charterhouse Capital Ltd, Re* [2014] EWHC 1410 (Ch).

[112] To be valid the power of attorney must be properly executed as a deed in accordance with the Law of Property (Miscellaneous Provisions) Act 1986. So, either the power of attorney should be contained in a separate document or the service contract should be executed as a deed.

2.7 Notification obligations and returns to regulators

On a director's appointment to, or removal from, office, and upon any change in the identity or details of a director of a company, in addition to any requirements specific to a particular type of company (see Section 2.3.3 above), a number of notifications must be made and returns filed with regulators, as follows.

2.7.1 Notifications to the company

On the appointment of any director, the company must record, in the register of directors maintained pursuant to CA 2006 s.162, the details of the director specified by CA 2006 s.163 or in the case of a corporate director, CA 2006 s.164. CA 2006 s.162(3) requires that a company's register of directors is open to public inspection. In the case of a director who is an individual, the register of directors will contain details of the director's service address rather than his home address, and the company must also maintain a separate register of directors' residential addresses under s.165, which is not available for public inspection, in order to preserve confidentiality for a director who has chosen to file a service address which is not his usual residential address. CA 2006 s.240 makes the details of a director's home address (or an indication that the director's service address is his home address) "protected information" which means that it may be disclosed only in limited circumstances. For more on this see Section 2.7.3 below.

For the purposes of CA 2006 s.1144, the service address must be a place where service of documents can be effected by physical delivery and delivery of documents is capable of being recorded by the obtaining of an acknowledgement of delivery.[113] For this reason, a PO Box address or similar will not be suitable. Many directors have opted to use the company's registered office or principal place of business as their service address.

Pursuant to CA 2006 s.228, the company must keep a copy of any written service contract between the director and the company (or a subsidiary) or, where it is not in writing, a written memorandum setting out its terms. As a result of the expanded definition of "service contract" set out in s.227, the requirement also now extends to contracts for services and letters of appointment. Such copies must be kept available for inspection at the company's registered office or such other place as may be specified in the Regulations made under CA 2006 s.1136.[114] Those Regulations apply to the company registers and other records, as well as directors' service contracts, which must be available for inspection, and enable a company to designate a single alternative location for inspection of service contracts and other

---

[113] See Companies (Annual Return and Service Addresses) Regulations 2008 (SI 2008/3000) para.10.
[114] Companies (Company Records) Regulations 2008 (SI 2008/3006).

company registers and records, for example, the company's principal place of business. Such documents must be open to inspection by any member of the company without charge under s.229(1). Section 228(3) also requires service contracts to be retained and available for inspection for at least one year after they have expired.

As referred to above, a director's home address is "protected information" under CA 2006 s.240 and the disclosure restrictions will apply equally to a director's home address appearing in a service contract. In practice, a director may consent to his home address appearing in his service contract and therefore becoming publicly available by virtue of s.228, but if he withholds his consent or his consent has not been sought, the company may be obliged under CA 2006 s.241 to remove details of the home address from the relevant service contract, and a service address should instead be used in the service contract. This should be the same service address as appears in the company's register of directors.

CA 1985 s.324, which required a director, on his appointment, to notify his interests (and those of certain connected persons) in the share capital of, and any debentures issued by, the company and any other body corporate and thereafter, while he remained a director, to notify any changes to such interests, was repealed on 6 April 2007. However, directors of listed companies will have obligations under the Disclosure and Transparency Rules to notify the company of dealings in shares and similar obligations apply to directors of AIM companies under the AIM Rules.

2.7.2 Notifications to the Registrar of Companies

As mentioned in Section 2.2.2 above, on the application for the incorporation of a new company under CA 2006, the registration details which are delivered to the Registrar of Companies under CA 2006 s.9 must contain the names and required particulars of the first directors. The same details, including a statement from the company that the relevant person has consented to act as a director, must be delivered to the Registrar of Companies, under CA 2006 s.167, on the appointment thereafter of any new director. Similarly, any vacation of office for whatever reason and any change in the director's registered particulars (including residential address) must be notified to the Registrar of Companies. All such notifications must be made to the Registrar of Companies within 14 days after the relevant event. In addition, any changes must be properly recorded in the next confirmation statement filed under s.853A.

Under CA 2006 s.1068(5), the Registrar of Companies is obliged to ensure that various documents (the full list is set out in s.1078) can be delivered to the Registrar in electronic form. Advice on how documents can be filed electronically with Companies House can be found on the Companies House website.

2.7.3   Disclosure of directors' residential addresses

Following a number of much-publicised cases of harassment of directors of companies involved in particular sectors of commerce or industry (e.g. Huntingdon Life Sciences), CA 1985 was amended in 2002 to permit directors to apply for a confidentiality order whereby their usual residential address would be kept on a confidential register and the public register would contain details of a service address only. Until 1 October 2009, when the relevant provisions of the CA 2006 came into force, these provisions[115] applied only to directors who were threatened with violence or intimidation. Since 1 October 2009, the relevant provisions of the CA 2006 have effectively extended the confidentiality provisions to all directors. So, on first appointment (and thereafter), directors are required to file only a service address for the public register at Companies House, and in the company's register of directors. The company must, though, keep a separate register of directors' residential addresses (s.165). When a director is appointed, Companies House must be notified under s.167 of the particulars of the director, including his residential address, but the residential address is "protected information" for the purposes of CA 2006 ss.240–246. As such, a company must not use or disclose that protected information except:

(a)   in communications with the relevant director;
(b)   to comply with any filing requirements under the Companies Acts; or
(c)   under court order,

unless the director consents to the use or disclosure of his home address details.

Similarly, the address may not be disclosed by Companies House, with limited exceptions (e.g. if the Registrar of Companies is obliged to disclose it to a credit reference agency or under a court order). Under the transitional provisions,[116] for a director of a pre-CA 2006 company, whatever address the company had in the register of directors for that director (usually the home address unless a Confidentiality Order under CA 1985 had been granted) will have been deemed to be the service address. As such the director's home address will not be "protected information"[117] unless and until the director notifies the company that he wishes to use a service address, whereupon the company will be obliged to amend the register of directors and notify Companies House of the change. Some directors of pre-CA 2006 companies will not have filed a service address thus far, either because there is no particular sensitivity surrounding disclosure of their

---

[115] Inserted into CA 1985 by the Companies (Particulars of Usual Residential Address) (Confidentiality Orders) Regulations 2002 (SI 2002/912)).
[116] See Companies Act 2006 (Commencement No.8, Transitional Provisions and Savings) Order 2008 (SI 2008/2860) Sch.2 para.27.
[117] See Companies Act 2006 (Commencement No.8, Transitional Provisions and Savings) Order 2008 (SI 2008/2860) Sch.2. para.33.

home address or possibly because they have taken the view that there is no advantage to be gained from doing so since there is a rather obvious loophole under the CA 2006 regime whereby historic filings which contained the director's home address (e.g. the original CA 1985 Form 288) will still be on the register even if a subsequent change of address notification has been filed. Directors wishing to have these details removed must apply to the Registrar of Companies under the regulations made under CA 2006 s.1088.[118] Following an amendment to these regulations on 26 April 2018, directors making such an application are no longer required to demonstrate that they are at risk of violence or intimidation as a result of their address being publicly available.

2.7.4 Notifications to the UK Listing Authority

For a listed company, LR 9.6.11 requires that the company notifies an RIS[119] of any change to the board as soon as possible and no later than by the end of the business day following the decision or receipt of notice about the change by the company. Such a notification must also be made if there are significant changes to the role, functions or responsibilities of an incumbent director, as well as in the event of directors' appointments and removals. However, no such notification is required where a director retires by rotation and is reappointed at a general meeting. The notification must state the effective date of the change if it is not with immediate effect. If the effective date is not known at the time of the announcement, or has not been determined, the announcement should state that fact and the company must notify an RIS when the effective date has been decided. In the case of the appointment of a new director, the company's notification must state whether the position is executive, non-executive or as chairman and the nature of any specific function or responsibility to be undertaken by the director.

In addition, LR 9.6.13 requires listed companies to notify to an RIS the following information in respect of any new director appointed to the board:

(a) the details of all directorships held by such director in any other publicly quoted company at any time in the previous five years, indicating whether or not the individual is still a director; and

---

[118] Companies (Disclosure of Address) Regulations 2009 (SI 2009/214).
[119] References in the Listing Rules to "RIS" or "Regulatory Information Service", are defined under the Listing Rules as either (i) a person approved by the FCA as a primary information provider under FSMA 2000 s.89P or (ii) an incoming information society service that has its establishment in an EEA state other than the UK and that disseminates regulated information in accordance with the minimum standards set out in Directive 2004/109 on the harmonisation of transparency requirements in relation to information about issuers whose securities are admitted to trading on a regulated market [2004] OJ L390/38 art.12. The RNS is approved as a primary information provider.

(b)   the details of any unspent convictions, relevant insolvencies or public criticisms by regulatory bodies (all as detailed in LR 9.6.13(2)–(6)),

or, if there are no such details to be disclosed, that fact (see LR 9.6.15).

The information required must be notified as soon as possible and in any event within five business days following the decision to appoint the director being made. In addition, under LR 9.6.14, an RIS must be notified as soon as possible if there is any change in any of the information in relation to current directors which has already been notified under LR 9.6.13, as well as any new directorships in another listed company.

2.7.5   Information on company stationery

Regulation 26 of the regulations made under CA 2006 ss.82 and 84[120] requires the names of all directors to be stated on business letters if any director's name is included somewhere on the letter (other than in the text or as a signatory). Therefore, any change in the identity of the directors of the company would also need to be reflected in the company's notepaper if the notepaper sets out the names of the directors. The regulations retain the old CA 1985 prohibition on companies cherry-picking which directors' names appear on the company stationery and the option will be to include all or none.

2.8   Alternate directors

There is nothing in CA 2006 itself in relation to alternate directors, but it is common for companies, in their articles, to make provision for a director to appoint an alternate to stand in his place as a director of the company when he is not available. Table A had standard provisions allowing for the appointment of alternates (regs 65–69) but provision for alternates only appears in the Model Articles for public companies under CA 2006. It was assumed when CA 2006 was enacted that few private companies would want or need a provision for alternates, but there is nothing to prevent a private company adopting articles which allow for alternates.

It is necessary to look carefully at the wording of the particular company's articles to identify the precise detail of any procedures to be followed for the appointment and removal of an alternate.

Where the Model Articles for public companies apply, reg.25 enables a director to appoint any other director or any other person approved by a resolution of the directors as his alternate to exercise his powers and carry

---

[120] The Company, Limited Liability Partnership and Business (Names and Trading Disclosures) Regulations 2015 (SI 2015/17).

out his responsibilities in relation to the taking of decisions by the directors. This provision reflects the narrower view adopted in the Model Articles that it is in relation to formal decision-making processes that alternates are most likely to be useful, as this is probably the only context in which it is critical to have a particular number of directors involved. Regulations 25 and 26(1), therefore, envisage that alternates will only act in relation to formal decision-making rather than exercising all the same rights and responsibilities as the appointors have as directors.

The Model Articles for public companies reg.27 sets out the circumstances in which an alternate's appointment will terminate, for example when the appointor revokes the appointment by notice to the company, upon his appointor ceasing to be a director (unless he retires by rotation and is then reappointed at the same general meeting), upon the death of the appointor or upon the occurrence of any event in relation to the alternate which, had it applied to his appointor, would result in the appointor ceasing to be a director (if, for example, the provisions on termination of a director's appointment set out in the Model Articles for public companies reg.22 apply to the alternate).[121]

The Model Articles for public companies reg.15 deals with alternates' voting powers and provides that an alternate director has an additional vote on behalf of any appointor who is not participating in the meeting and would have been entitled to vote had he participated. Otherwise, if the appointor is present, the alternate is not entitled to vote. The same would normally be true of a directors' written resolution, although there is no explicit provision to this effect in the Model Articles for public companies.

Under the Model Articles for public companies, the alternate is not entitled to receive any remuneration from the company for his services as an alternate except such part of the appointor's remuneration as he shall direct.

---

[121] Where Table A applies, regs 65–69 state that any director may appoint any other director, or any other person approved by a resolution of the directors and willing to act, to be his alternate, and may remove his alternate from office at any time. Appointment and removal are by notice to the company, signed by the director, or by any other manner approved by the board. Under Table A, the board retains control over the identity of the alternate.
Regulation 66 goes on to detail certain administrative provisions. For example, an alternate is entitled to:
(a) receive notice of all meetings of directors and all meetings of committees of directors of which his appointor is a member;
(b) attend and vote at any such meetings at which his appointor is not personally present; and
(c) generally perform all of the functions of the appointor as a director, in his absence.
Regulation 67 provides that a person shall automatically cease to be an alternate if his appointor ceases to be a director. If his appointor retires by rotation or otherwise but is reappointed or deemed to have been reappointed at the meeting at which he retires, any appointment of an alternate made by him which was in force immediately before the retirement of the director continues after his reappointment.

71

Apart from administrative arrangements, the actual status of the alternate is also governed by the company's articles. In the case of the Model Articles for public companies, reg.26 provides that an alternate is deemed for all purposes to be a director of the company and shall alone be responsible for his own acts and omissions. However, an alternate is not deemed to be the agent of or for his appointor.[122] Given that the position of an alternate is defined by the articles of the particular company, great care needs to be taken in drafting and in interpreting the relevant regulations to identify the precise boundaries of an alternate's powers and the nature of his responsibilities.

As a general rule, it is likely that an alternate will be treated as a director for the purposes of CA 2006[123] and the company would, therefore, have to complete and file a return to Companies House under s.167 on his appointment. In those circumstances, his details should also be entered into the Register of Directors and the Register of Directors' Residential Addresses and he will be subject to all of the statutory duties of directors under CA 2006 Pt 10, so far as relevant to the scope of his appointment, including those relating to conflicts of interest.

As regards whether alternates can sign Companies House forms, the Registrar's Rules made under CA 2006 s.1117 do not address alternates specifically. In most cases the form itself will specify by whom the form should be signed, or in the case of a statement of compliance required under CA 2006, by whom the statement should be made. Where the signature of a director is required, Companies House has advised that only an alternate who was on the register at Companies House as a director of the relevant company (see above) would be treated as a director for these purposes. Where a statutory declaration is required of directors, the accepted view is that an alternate can swear a statutory declaration in place of (but not in addition to) his appointor.

It is also thought that an alternate can act as a director for the purposes of signing contracts on behalf of the company, and witness the company seal, if the company has one, and its articles provide that documents to which the company seal is affixed may be signed by a director or a person authorised by the directors (as is the case with the Model Articles for public companies reg.81 and the Model Articles for private companies reg.49).[124] However, in respect of documents executed as a deed without the company seal, under CA 2006 s.44(2), it is less certain that an alternate is entitled to sign as a director because the section seems to envisage personal signature by the directors and/or secretary in question (as did its predecessor, CA 1985 s.36A(4)). If a director is not going to be available to execute a document as a deed under CA 2006 s.44(2), rather than the director

---

[122] Regulation 69 of Table A made similar provision.
[123] This is supported by the definition of director in CA 2006 s.250.
[124] Or see reg.101 of Table A.

appointing an alternate to execute the document in place of the director, the better route would be for the company to appoint an attorney in advance to execute the document as a deed on its behalf. The appointment of either a corporate or individual attorney to act on behalf of the company would be valid, provided the power of attorney itself was validly executed by the company as a deed.

2.9   Shadow directors and de facto directors

Where a person exerts control over a board of directors to the extent that the directors (as a whole) are accustomed to acting in accordance with his directions or instructions then (unless the directors are merely acting (i) on advice given by him in a professional capacity, (ii) in accordance with instructions, a direction, guidance or advice given by that person in the exercise of a function conferred by or under an enactment or (iii) in accordance with guidance or advice given by that person in that person's capacity as a Minister of the Crown)[125] CA 2006 s.251 states that he will be treated as a "shadow director" of the company.[126]

The purpose of the shadow director provisions is to ensure that those persons who seek to control the affairs of a company without accepting a formal appointment as a director of it are, nevertheless, caught by the relevant parts of the legislation. So, by definition there is no question of a person being "appointed" as a shadow director. The appointment as such will happen by default.

Those sections of CA 2006 which expressly apply to shadow directors[127] include the general duties of directors in ss.171–177, the provisions relating to transactions with directors (s.223) and s.231 (contract with sole member who is also a director). However, CA 2006 s.251(3) states that, in relation to these sections, a body corporate is not to be treated as a shadow director of any of its subsidiary companies by reason only that the directors of the subsidiary are accustomed to acting in accordance with its directions or instructions.

The application to shadow directors of the general duties of directors set out in ss.171–177 is subject to s.170(5) which states that they will only apply where and to the extent that they are capable of applying. Previously, this section qualified these duties as applying to shadow directors where and to the extent that the corresponding common law rules or equitable principles

---

[125] Limbs (ii) and (iii) of the exemption were inserted by SBEEA 2015 s.90(3) to clarify that the government will in no circumstances be a shadow director.
[126] Save for limbs (ii) and (iii), the definition was the same under CA 1985 s.741(2).
[127] In the case of *Revenue and Customs Commissioners v Holland* [2010] 1 W.L.R. 2793 the Supreme Court implies, as obiter dicta, that only those statutory provisions which expressly refer to shadow directors will apply to such directors.

applied.[128] The wording was amended to provide greater clarity and to ensure that shadow directors are held to the same standards as properly appointed directors.

In addition, some provisions of other legislation are expressly stated to apply to shadow directors. See CDDA 1986 ss.6–9E (in relation to disqualification for unfitness) and the wrongful trading provisions of Insolvency Act 1986 s.214.

Whether or not a particular person is held to be a shadow director will depend on the precise nature of the relationship and the facts of each individual case.[129] As noted above, because of the very nature of the position, there is no formal appointment or removal process and, therefore, it will be necessary for any person engaged in a relationship with the board of directors of a company to consider very carefully whether he is likely to fall within the definition, and to act accordingly.

A de facto director is a person who acts as a director without having been duly appointed as such, or who continues so to act after his formal appointment has been terminated or expired. This definition of de facto director does not appear in CA 2006, but derives from the common law. In the case of *Smithton Ltd v Naggar*,[130] the Court of Appeal summarised the main principles for determining whether a person is a de facto director. These principles include, among other things, whether the person assumed responsibility as a director and whether he was considered as such by the company and third parties. The court will need to be objective in determining whether a person is a de facto director and must consider what the person actually did and not any job title given to him. The general duties of directors set out in CA 2006 ss.171–177 are owed by a de facto director in the same way and to the same extent as a properly appointed director. In addition, certain provisions of the CDDA 1986 and the Insolvency Act 1986 also apply to de facto directors.

---

[128] This was replaced with the current wording by SBEEA 2015 s.89(1).

[129] In the case of *Secretary of State for Trade and Industry v Deverell* [2001] Ch. 340; [2000] 2 W.L.R. 907; [2000] 2 All E.R. 365, the Court of Appeal gave a broad definition to the term "shadow director". The judgment in that case stressed that the primary purpose of including the concept of shadow directors in legislation is to protect the public and therefore the term should be construed broadly. The statutory definition of the term "shadow director" was further considered in the High Court case of *Ultraframe (UK) Ltd v Fielding* [2005] EWHC 1638 (Ch); [2006] F.S.R. 17; [2007] W.T.L.R. 835 and in that case the court expressed the view that a person at whose direction the board is accustomed to act would be a shadow director, a test which was not satisfied in that case, or in the more recent case of *McKillen v Misland (Cyprus) Investments* [2012] EWHC 2343 (Ch).

[130] *Smithton Ltd v Naggar* [2014] EWCA Civ 939.

2.10   Nominee directors

The term "nominee director" generally means a director appointed by one of the shareholders or a lender to look after the interests of the appointor or some other third party, but again there is no statutory definition of nominee director, or recognition of his role as nominee as distinct from any other director and, for Companies Act purposes, a nominee director is simply a director like any other. A nominee director may be executive or non-executive. However, the role of the nominee director is potentially complex. He represents the interests of his appointor and reports to him on the activities of the company, but he must also bear in mind his general duties as a director to the company itself under CA 2006 ss.171–177, which will be paramount. Except where the interests of his appointor and the company coincide, the nominee director should not identify the interests of the company with those of his appointor (see *Scottish Co-operative Wholesale Society Ltd v Meyer*).[131] This does not mean, though, that the nominee may not pay any attention to the concerns and interests of his appointor, or that he should not, in appropriate cases, have special regard to such interests, as long as he does not subordinate the company's interests to those of his appointor. CA 2006 s.172 states clearly that directors are to act in the interests of the company's members as a whole, which has particular relevance to the position of nominee directors.

In October 2018, the Association of General Counsel and Company Secretaries working in FTSE 100 Companies published Guidance on Directors' Duties—Section 172 and Stakeholder Considerations which contains specific guidelines for directors of joint venture companies. These guidelines will be relevant for nominee directors as well. The relevant recommendations are that nominee directors should (i) be clear as to when they are acting as representatives of their appointor and when they are acting as directors of the company; (ii) take into account processes and goals which have been agreed between the shareholders when considering the best interests of the company; and (iii) have regard to the expectations of the shareholders as to the attributes and perspectives which each director is to bring to the board.

---

[131] *Scottish Co-operative Wholesale Society Ltd v Meyer* [1959] A.C. 324; [1958] 3 W.L.R. 404; 1958 S.C. (H.L.) 40.

Chapter 3

Directors' Duties

Ben Koehne

Partner

Addleshaw Goddard LLP

Michelle de Kluyver

Partner

Addleshaw Goddard LLP[1]

3.1 Introduction

This Chapter focuses on the general duties which directors owe to their company. The Companies Act 2006 (CA 2006) Pt 10 includes a statutory statement (codification) of these general duties. They are set out in CA 2006 ss.171–177 under the following headings:

(a) duty to act within powers;
(b) duty to promote the success of the company;
(c) duty to exercise independent judgment;
(d) duty to exercise reasonable care, skill and diligence;
(e) duty to avoid conflicts of interest;
(f) duty not to accept benefits from third parties; and
(g) duty to declare interest in proposed transaction or arrangement.

These codified general duties do not, however, cover all of the duties that a director will owe to the company.

Many duties are imposed by other provisions in CA 2006 (for example, directors need to take into account the obligations on them that arise as a result of the unfair prejudice regime contained in CA 2006 Pt 30 and the duty to keep accounting records under CA 2006 Pt 15). Other fiduciary and common law duties also remain uncodified, such as the duty of confidentiality which a director owes to the company, the duty to act fairly as between different members and the duty to consider the interests of creditors in appropriate circumstances.

---

[1] Many thanks to Will Chalk, Nicky Higginbottom and David Wigg of Addleshaw Goddard LLP for contributing their valuable insights.

There are also a significant number of other specific obligations and attendant sanctions (including criminal offences and potential grounds for disqualification) imposed upon directors by statute. In addition to those under CA 2006, these include, amongst other things, obligations under legislation relating to matters such as the environment, health and safety, employment, immigration and equality, pensions, financial regulation and other areas of regulatory compliance, competition law, anti-bribery and corruption law and tax evasion. This chapter does not deal with these matters.

This chapter does not seek to address detailed principles of corporate governance (see Chapter 9), the duties of directors in relation to a company facing potential insolvency (see Chapter 11) or the specific requirements imposed upon directors of listed companies (see Chapter 11).

3.2 Continuing relevance of common law and equitable principles applicable prior to CA 2006

When interpreting and applying the general duties of directors, it remains necessary to have regard to corresponding common law and equitable principles (both as applied to directors' duties before codification and as developed in other areas of law on an ongoing basis).

CA 2006 s.170 states that:

> "The general duties are based on certain common law rules and equitable principles as they apply in relation to directors and have effect in place of those rules and principles as regards the duties owed to a company by a director."

It also provides that:

> "The general duties shall be interpreted and applied in the same way as common law rules or equitable principles, and regard shall be had to the corresponding common law rules and equitable principles in interpreting and applying the general duties."

These provisions ensured continuity of law following the transition to the codified duties under CA 2006 from the previous uncodified regime.

CA 2006 s.170 also recognises that common law and equitable principles will continue to develop in other areas (such as those applying to trustees, agents and other fiduciaries). The effect of this is that the courts may continue to have regard to developments in the common law and equitable principles applying to such other types of fiduciary relationships.

The combined effect is that the courts can interpret the statutory general duties in a flexible and an evolving manner, having regard not only to pre-existing common law and equitable principles at the time of enactment, but also to developments in those principles in other fiduciary relationships over time.

In addition, as there has been no codification of the remedies for breach of the general duties, the consequences of a breach (or threatened breach) are the same as they would have been in the case of a breach of the previous corresponding common law rule or equitable principle. Consequences of breach are addressed further in Section 3.3 below.

3.3   To whom do the general duties apply?

3.3.1   *General*

The general duties are owed by a director of a company to the company and a director will not, by virtue of being a director, generally owe a direct duty to the company's members or creditors. It follows that only the company (which in practice generally means the board) can generally enforce the duties. As a practical matter, the company's incentive to enforce the duties owed by directors usually comes to the fore in the context of board disputes and upon changes of ownership or management. There may also be exceptional circumstances where a direct duty to members arises (see Section 3.15 below).

CA 2006 Pt 11 (which is considered in Chapter 10) covers the circumstances where members of the company may be able to enforce the duties on behalf of the company where the board will not take action by way of a derivative claim. CA 2006 Pt 11 does not, however, operate to give shareholders direct rights of recovery against the company for breaches of directors' duties.

3.3.2   *Who is a director?*

A "director" is defined in CA 2006 s.250 to include any person occupying the position of director, by whatever name called. It is accepted that the term "director" is wider than simply including a person who has been validly appointed as a director (de jure) and that the duties of a director may be assumed by a person who acts as a director (de facto director) without having been appointed validly, or at all.

3.3.3 Shadow directors

A "shadow director" is defined in CA 2006 s.251(1) as a person in accordance with whose directions or instructions the directors of the company are accustomed to act. CA 2006 s.251(2) clarifies that a person is not to be regarded as a shadow director by reason only that the directors act on advice given by that person in a professional capacity or in accordance with instructions, a direction, guidance or advice given by that person in the exercise of a function conferred by or under any enactment. For the purposes of the general duties of directors, CA 2006 s.251(3) also expressly exempts a body corporate from being a shadow director of any of its subsidiary companies by reason only that the directors of the subsidiary are accustomed to act in accordance with its directions or instructions.

The position regarding the precise duties owed by shadow directors has been the subject of some debate over the years. Upon its enactment, CA 2006 provided in s.170(5) that: "The general duties apply to shadow directors where, and to the extent that, the corresponding common law rules or equitable principles so apply". The effect of this was that where a common law rule or equitable principle applied to a shadow director prior to CA 2006, the statutory duty replacing the common law rule or equitable principle would apply to the shadow director instead. Where the position was that certain common law rules and equitable principles did not apply to shadow directors, the effect was that the statutory duty replacing those rules or principles would not apply either. This approach was taken because the law prior to CA 2006 was unclear as to the extent to which the common law duties and equitable principles applied to shadow directors.

Case law, culminating in the case of *Ultraframe (UK) Ltd v Fielding*,[2] differed on the extent to which shadow directors were subject to directors' duties. In the *Ultraframe* case, the court concluded that simply falling within the definition of a shadow director was not enough to impose on a person the same fiduciary duties as owed by the company's de jure or de facto directors; this was especially the case where the shadow director did not deal with, or claim the right to deal directly with, the company's assets. However, if the acts of a shadow director went beyond indirect influence, such a person could then be subject to specific fiduciary duties (particularly where they sought to further their own interests, as opposed to those of the company). Given that the position was unclear, the decision to preserve the status quo rather than to attempt to codify the duties applicable to shadow directors gave the courts flexibility to continue to develop the law in this area.

In the case of *Secretary of State for Trade and Industry v Hall*,[3] the question arose as to when a director of a corporate director could be characterised as

---

[2] *Ultraframe (UK) Ltd v Fielding* [2005] EWHC 1638 (Ch); [2006] F.S.R. 17; [2007] W.T.L.R. 835.
[3] *Secretary of State for Trade and Industry v Hall* [2006] EWHC 1995 (Ch); [2009] B.C.C. 190.

a shadow (or alternatively, de facto) director for the purpose of disqualification proceedings under the Company Directors Disqualification Act 1986 (CDDA). The court analysed those issues by applying the principle set out in *Hydrodan (Corby) Ltd (In Liquidation), Re*[4] that a shadow directorship would arise where an individual gave instructions based on which the company (through its directors) was accustomed to act. In *Secretary of State for Trade and Industry v Hall*, a company called Legal Directors Ltd (LDL) was appointed as a corporate director of a company called Mercury Solutions UK Ltd (Mercury), which later went into insolvent liquidation. The Secretary of State sought to have Mr Nuttall, a director of LDL, disqualified under the CDDA on the basis that he was responsible for the inactivity of the corporate director which in turn had contributed to Mercury's failure. Mr Nuttall successfully challenged the proceedings on the basis that he had no role in the management of LDL or LDL's management of Mercury; nor had he held himself out as a de facto director. A director of a corporate director of a company is therefore unlikely to be characterised as a shadow or de facto director of the underlying company unless he exercises the requisite degree of control required by the *Hydrodan* test. Thus, although complete inactivity by a director can constitute unfitness, some activity amounting to sufficient control is required to constitute that person as a shadow director (or indeed de facto director) of a company in the first place.

In *McKillen v Misland (Cyprus) Investments Ltd*,[5] the court held that in order to establish that a person had acted as a shadow director, it is not necessary to show that a person who had a real influence in the corporate affairs of a company exercised that influence over the *whole field* of its corporate activities. The fact that he had only been involved in a narrow range of decisions was not fatal to the allegation.

In *Vivendi SA v Richards*,[6] the court addressed the perceived conflict in the authorities regarding whether a shadow director would owe fiduciary duties to a company at all. After a review of the authorities, the court held that shadow directors will owe fiduciary duties to a company with respect to at least the instructions given to the board. In other words, there must be a connection between the instructions given and the duties imposed.

CA 2006 s.170(5) was subsequently amended with effect from 26 May 2015, with the intention of clarifying the statutory position in relation to the duties of shadow directors, to provide that: "The general duties apply to a shadow director of a company where and to the extent that they are capable of so applying". The section still ultimately leaves room for interpretation, and the proper application of the general duties to shadow directors in the light of relevant case law is likely to remain very fact specific.

---

[4]   *Hydrodan (Corby) Ltd (In Liquidation), Re* [1994] B.C.C. 161; [1994] 2 B.C.L.C. 180.
[5]   *McKillen v Misland (Cyprus) Investments Ltd* [2012] EWHC 521 (Ch).
[6]   *Vivendi SA v Richards* [2013] B.C.C. 771.

3.4 When do a director's duties cease?

In general, a director's duties to the company will come to an end when the director ceases to hold office (whether voluntarily or otherwise).

CA 2006 s.170(2) sets out two specific cases, however, where the general duties will continue to apply after a person ceases to be a director. These are that a person who ceases to be a director will continue to be subject to:

(a) the duty under CA 2006 s.175 to avoid conflicts of interest concerning the exploitation of any property, information or opportunity of which he became aware at a time when he was a director; and

(b) the duty not to accept benefits from third parties relating to things done or permitted by him before he ceased to be a director.

There may be exceptional (and very fact specific) circumstances where the general duties of a director come to an end or are reduced in scope while still in office. Relevant considerations in this regard are likely to include, amongst other things, whether the director is, in effect, prevented from exercising any relevant powers as a director. *In Plus Group Ltd v Pyke*[7] is an example of a case where a director was effectively excluded by the other directors from participating in the company's business and where, based on the relevant facts, the Court of Appeal held that the director no longer owed certain duties to the company.

Resigning from office before a company takes certain substantive actions (for example embarking on a significant corporate re-organisation and/or capital reduction) will not necessarily absolve a director from liability for breach of duty. This may be the case, in particular, where the director in question is closely involved in driving forward the relevant corporate actions to be taken by the company and should have properly assessed the foreseeable consequences of such actions, notwithstanding the director's resignation before those consequences actually came about (*LRH Services Ltd (in liquidation) v Trew*[8]).

3.5 The general duties

Set out below is an analysis of each of the statutory general duties. In respect of each, there is an outline of the duty and consideration of particular issues that arise in interpreting it.

CA 2006 s.179 confirms that, unless otherwise provided, more than one of the general duties may apply in relation to any particular set of facts. The

---

[7] *In Plus Group Ltd v Pyke* [2002] EWCA Civ 370.
[8] *LRH Services Ltd (in liquidation) v Trew* [2018] EWHC 600 (Ch).

duties are cumulative and directors must take care to ensure that they comply with every duty that could apply on any particular set of facts. Thus, for example, taking a bribe from a third party, apart from anything else, would fall within the codified duty not to accept benefits from third parties but could also be a breach of the duty to promote the success of the company or represent a failure to exercise independent judgment. One specific exception to this general proposition about cumulative duties is that the duty to avoid conflicts of interests is expressly stated not to apply to a conflict of interest arising in relation to a transaction or arrangement with the company. In this situation, the duty to declare an interest in a proposed (or an existing) transaction or arrangement will apply instead of the duty to avoid conflicts of interests.

In relation to charitable companies, CA 2006 s.181 modifies certain aspects of the general duty to avoid conflicts of interests and the application of certain exceptions to such general duty and to the duty not to accept benefits from third parties.

3.6 Duty to act within powers

The duty set out in CA 2006 s.171 requires a director to act in accordance with the company's constitution and only to exercise powers for the purposes for which they are conferred. The latter aspect of this duty is often referred to as the "proper purpose test".

3.6.1 Acting in accordance with the company's constitution

The reference to a company's constitution is given a wide meaning. Under CA 2006 s.257, the constitution includes resolutions or decisions arrived at in accordance with the constitution and any decision of the company or a class of members that is treated as equivalent to a decision by the company (under any enactment or rule of law). It also includes the company's articles of association and any resolutions or agreements covered in CA 2006 s.29. These are the specified resolutions and agreements which must be filed with the Registrar of Companies. It may also include shareholders' agreements.[9] Of course, the consequence of the broad definition of the constitution is that directors must ensure that they are aware not only of what is in the company's articles of association, but also of all resolutions, decisions and agreements that comprise the constitution for these purposes to ensure that they act in accordance with this general duty.

The duty to act in accordance with the constitution is likely to extend only to valid provisions of the company's constitution. A director would generally not be expected to comply with a provision in a company's

---

[9] *Jackson v Dear* [2012] EWHC 2060 (Ch).

constitution that was void or unlawful (although in these circumstances the director may be under a duty to take steps to seek to remedy the position as far as possible).

3.6.2 Proper purpose test

In considering whether there has been a breach of the proper purpose test, an important consideration for the court will be to determine the "substantial" or "dominant" purpose for which the relevant power has been exercised (see, for example, *Extrasure Travel Insurances Ltd v Scattergood*[10]).

In *Eclairs Group Ltd v JKX Oil & Gas Plc*,[11] the Supreme Court considered the basis and application of the proper purpose test. Lord Sumption explained that the duty to exercise powers only for their proper purpose derived from the equitable principle of a "fraud on a power". This does not connote fraud in the typical common law sense, but an abuse of a power. The rule is not concerned with actions taken where no power exists, but with the abusive use of a power otherwise rightly exercised.

What constitutes a proper purpose in relation to the exercise of powers must therefore be ascertained in the context of the specific situation under consideration and regard may be had to previous case law. For instance, directors must not exercise their powers to protect their own positions or to make life difficult for particular shareholders or potential shareholders or in order to obtain a particular outcome in a takeover situation. This is the case even if the manner in which they exercise their powers happens to be in the best interests of the company.

The authoritative case on the issue is *Howard Smith Ltd v Ampol Petroleum Ltd*,[12] in which a company (Millers) had two shareholders together holding 55% of the shares. A third shareholder (Howard Smith) announced its intention to make an offer, which the board of Millers wanted to succeed but which the two principal shareholders opposed. The board allotted additional shares to Howard Smith, which diluted the two principal shareholders' interest to a minority interest. The court held that, although the board acted bona fide and the directors believed it was in the best interests of Howard Smith to raise funds by the issue of shares, the substantial purpose of the allotment was to favour one shareholder over others. The allotment was therefore set aside. It was not necessary for the plaintiffs to prove that the directors acted out of self-interest or to preserve

---

[10] *Extrasure Travel Insurances Ltd v Scattergood* [2003] 1 B.C.L.C. 598. See also the Privy Council decision in *Howard Smith Ltd v Ampol Petroleum Ltd* [1974] A.C. 821.
[11] *Eclairs Group Ltd v JKX Oil & Gas Plc* [2015] UKSC 71; [2016] 3 All E.R. 641.
[12] *Howard Smith Ltd v Ampol Petroleum Ltd* [1974] A.C. 821; [1974] 2 W.L.R. 689; 118 S.J.L.B. 330.

their own control of the management. It was sufficient that the directors had exercised their powers for an improper purpose. The court set out the judicial approach as follows:

> "Having ascertained, on a fair view, the nature of this power, and having defined, as can best be done in the light of modern conditions, the, or some, limits within which it may be exercised, it is then necessary for the court, if a particular exercise of it is challenged, to examine the substantial purpose for which it was exercised and to reach a conclusion whether that purpose was proper or not. In doing so it will necessarily give credit to the *bona fide* opinion of the directors, if such is found to exist, and will respect their judgment as to matters of management; having done this, the ultimate conclusion has to be as to the side of a fairly broad line on which the case falls."

The real issue, therefore, relates to the directors' substantial or dominant purpose. It does not matter if a consequence of a particular course of action by the directors is that their own interests are advanced if that was not their principal or substantial purpose (*Hirsche v Sims*,[13] and restated in the case of *CAS (Nominees) Ltd v Nottingham Forest FC Plc*[14]).

The principle could be invoked in relation to any power whose purpose could be clearly discerned from the articles. For example, in *Company (No.00370 of 1987) Ex p. Glossop, Re*,[15] the principle was applied to the directors' power to recommend dividends.

In practice, it can be difficult to establish what the substantial or dominant purpose behind a decision was in reality. This is because it requires a forensic analysis of the impact of a number of considerations on the mind of a director, after the event and in the context of a dispute, when, in reality, it is unlikely that a decision was made with such a conscious weighing of factors in mind. This is particularly so if all factors would have pointed to the same outcome. The difficulty is increased if multiple directors are involved.

In *Eclairs Group Ltd v JKX Oil & Gas Plc*,[16] the Supreme Court considered, in this context, whether a causative "but for" test should instead be determinative of whether a power was properly exercised. In other words, the exercise of the power would be struck down if the action would not have been taken in the absence of the improper purpose. Despite support from two justices, the majority view was that, as argument had not been heard from the parties on the point, no concluded view would be given.

The causative approach brings its own difficulties. A director could have two reasons for making a decision, one proper and one improper. The

---

[13] *Hirsche v Sims* [1894] A.C. 654 at 660.
[14] *CAS (Nominees) Ltd v Nottingham Forest FC Plc* [2002] B.C.C. 145; [2002] 1 B.C.L.C. 613.
[15] *Company (No.00370 of 1987) Ex p. Glossop, Re* [1988] 1 W.L.R. 1068; (1988) 4 B.C.C. 506; [1988] B.C.L.C. 570.
[16] *Eclairs Group Ltd v JKX Oil & Gas Plc* [2015] UKSC 71.

decision would have been made "but for" the improper purpose. But this might fail to give the improper purpose the weight it merits, and which it would have been given under the substantial purpose test. The question is one that is likely to be revisited in future cases.

3.7 Duty to promote the success of the company

CA 2006 s.172 provides that a director "must act in the way he considers, in good faith, would be most likely to promote the success of the company for the benefit of its members as a whole", and in doing so have regard to a non-exhaustive list of factors. The list covers the following:

(a) the likely consequences of any decision in the long term;
(b) the interests of the company's employees;
(c) the need to foster the company's business relationships with suppliers, customers and others;
(d) the impact of the company's operations on the community and the environment;
(e) the desirability of the company maintaining a reputation for high standards of business conduct; and
(f) the need to act fairly as between members of the company.

Subsection (2) of this section provides that, where the purpose of the company is something other than the benefit of its members (for example, in the case of a company with restricted objects in its articles of association), the directors must act in the way they consider, in good faith, would be most likely to achieve that purpose. It is a matter for the good faith judgment of the directors as to how best to satisfy the purposes for which the company has been established, and where the company's purposes are partly for the benefit of its members and partly for other purposes, the extent to which those other purposes apply in place of the benefit of the members.

Subsection (3) recognises (amongst other things) that the duty to promote the success of the company is displaced when the company is insolvent. Rather than specifying the duties that apply in that situation, the subsection leaves the previous law intact with a view to allowing the existing common law to develop in this area. Chapter 11 deals with the duties of directors facing insolvency.

Section 172 enshrined in statute the principle of enlightened shareholder value and brought this firmly onto the boardroom agenda. The reference to directors' good faith judgment is designed to ensure that business decisions on, for example, strategy and tactics are for the directors, and not subject to decision by the courts, provided the directors were acting in good faith.

Prior to the enactment of CA 2006, the Government made a number of important clarificatory remarks when the Bill was debated in Parliament. The Minister for Industry and the Regions made statements to the following effect:

(a)   the words "have regard to" mean "think about" or "give proper consideration to";

(b)   while a director must have regard to the various factors stated, that requirement is subordinate to the overriding duty to promote the success of the company. A director will not be required to consider any of the factors beyond the point at which to do so would conflict with this overriding duty;

(c)   directors are subject to the "good faith business judgment" test and not the reasonableness test;

(d)   "the decisions taken by a director and the weight given to the factors will continue to be a matter for his good faith judgment";

(e)   "there is no particular reason that a director would have to provide written evidence proving that in taking a particular decision he or she had had regard to these factors; that evidence would not be required for him or her to defend themselves against such action";

(f)   the provision "does not impose a requirement on directors to keep records ... in any circumstances in which they would not have to do so now"—"the onus will be on the company to prove that the director has not complied, rather than on the director to show that he has"; and

(g)   "we do not intend a director to be required to do more in having regard to the factors than acting in good faith and in accordance with the duty of care and skill. It will, for example, be for the director to make a judgment on the likely longer-term consequences of his decisions in good faith and in compliance with his duty to exercise reasonable care, skill and judgment".

In the House of Lords, the Attorney-General made the following remarks on the interpretation of certain words and phrases:

(a)   on the meaning of "success", Lord Goldsmith stated "it is essentially for the members of the company to define the objectives that they wish to achieve. Success means what the members collectively want the company to achieve. For a commercial company, success will usually mean long-term increase in value. For certain companies, such as charities and community interest companies, it will mean the attainment of the objectives for which the company has been established";

(b)   "... it is for the directors ... by reference to the objectives of the company ... to judge and to form a good faith judgment about what is to be regarded as success for the benefit of the members as a whole ... and they will need to look at the company's constitution, shareholder decisions and anything else that they consider relevant in helping them reach their judgment"; and

(c)   on the meaning of "members as a whole", Lord Goldsmith stated that this means: "for the members as a collective body—not only to benefit the majority shareholders, or any particular shareholder or section of shareholders ..."

This duty replaced the previous duty to act in the best interests of the company. It has now become clear that the courts are interpreting the codified duty in very much the same way as the old duty. For example, in *West Coast Capital (Lios) Ltd, Re*,[17] Lord Glennie in the Court of Session observed that CA 2006 s.172 did "little more than set out the pre-existing law on the subject". In *Southern Counties Fresh Foods Ltd, Re*,[18] Warren J. expressed the view that the pre- and post-CA 2006 duties "come to the same thing".

When making a decision, a director should give proper consideration to the listed factors, along with any other factors which are relevant to the matter in question. This requirement to have regard to these factors is, however, subordinate to the overriding duty to promote the success of the company.

The list of factors that directors are required to take into account can be seen to reflect wider expectations as to what constitutes responsible business behaviour. In light of a number of high profile examples of poor corporate governance over recent years where there was little evidence that appropriate regard had been had to the needs of a broader range of stakeholders and other s.172 considerations, there has been a much greater focus from a corporate governance perspective on the proper discharge by directors of their duty under CA 2006 s.172 to ensure that boards are taking the steps needed to recognise fully their responsibilities to all stakeholders, including employees, customers, pension scheme beneficiaries, suppliers and to wider society. The rebuilding of trust between companies, their stakeholders and society more generally and the role that stakeholders play in helping companies to achieve long-term success lie at the heart of recent corporate governance reforms.[19] The duty under CA 2006 s.172 is also increasingly viewed as an important factor in seeking to ensure that boards embed the right corporate culture and behaviours within companies in the company's pursuit of success for the benefit of the shareholders as a whole. This is one of the overarching themes to emerge over recent years from both a corporate governance and a regulatory perspective (see Chapter 1).

This approach to business decision-making has already found some recognition in company law. For example, the Court of Appeal made a passing reference to the CA 2006 s.172 duty in the employment case of

---

[17]   *West Coast Capital (Lios) Ltd, Re* [2008] CSOH 72 at [21].
[18]   In *Southern Counties Fresh Foods Ltd, Re* [2008] EWHC 2810 (Ch) at [52].
[19]   See BEIS, *Government response: Corporate Governance Reform*, 29 August 2017. See also, for listed companies, the 2018 UK Corporate Governance Code s.1 published by the Financial Reporting Council and, for private companies, the Wates Corporate Governance Principles for Large Private Companies (December 2018).

Rolls-Royce Plc v Unite the Union[20] where the court referred to the need for an employer to judge a situation from the wider perspective of "enlightened self-interest" rather than his own self-interest. The former included the employer taking into account the interests of the employees as one of the factors in determining the needs of the business. The court indicated that this approach should be compared with the duty of directors in CA 2006 s.172. The use of the term "enlightened self-interest" is almost certainly drawn from and echoes the concept of "enlightened shareholder value" and seems to indicate an acceptance in the court that business decisions based on pure self-interest alone belong to a different time.[21]

In line with the enlightened shareholder value concept, CA 2006 links the duty to promote the success of the company to narrative reporting requirements. CA 2006 s.414(1) provides that: "The purpose of the strategic report is to inform members of the company and help them assess how the directors have performed their duty under s.172 (duty to promote the success of the company)". CA 2006 s.414CZA,[22] which has effect in relation to the financial years of companies beginning on or after 1 January 2019, requires large companies to include in their strategic report[23] "a statement (a 's.172(1) statement') which describes how the directors have had regard to the matters set out in s.172(1)(a) to (f) when performing their duty under section 172". Within certain parameters the decision as to what information is provided in the report and the statement and the level of disclosure is left to the directors' discretion. If directors consider that they have breached their duties or that other directors have done so, the breach would be disclosable under their CA 2006 ss.171–177 duties and, by extension, in the strategic report.[24]

The duty to promote the success of the company also encompasses, to some extent, the previous fiduciary duty to act fairly as between members of the company. This duty was spelt out in *Mutual Life Insurance Co of New York v The Rank Organisation Ltd*,[25] where US shareholders of Rank brought an action on the grounds that the directors had excluded them from participating in a rights issue by Rank. The directors justified the exclusion on the grounds of the cost and effort which would be incurred in meeting US registration requirements if the offer had been extended to all

---

[20] *Rolls-Royce Plc v Unite the Union* [2009] EWCA Civ 387.
[21] One of the members of the Appeal Court was The Rt Hon Lady Justice Arden DBE Court of Appeal, who was a member of the Steering Group for the Company Law Review.
[22] CA 2006 s.414CZA was added by the Companies (Miscellaneous Reporting) Regulations 2018 (SI 2018/860) Pt 2 reg.4 which came into force on 1 January 2019.
[23] The Companies (Miscellaneous Reporting) Regulations 2018 (SI 2018/860) also require certain companies to include a basic level of information in their Directors' Reports on their stakeholder engagement, including in relation to UK employees, customers and suppliers to the extent not disclosed in their s.172(1) CA 2006 statement.
[24] See *Item Software (UK) Ltd v Fassihi* [2004] EWCA Civ 1244; [2004] B.C.C. 994; [2005] 2 B.C.L.C. 91; *Customer Systems Plc v Ranson* [2012] EWCA Civ 841; [2012] I.R.L.R. 769; (2012) 156(26) S.J.L.B. 31; *GHLM Trading v Maroo* [2012] EWHC 61 (Ch); [2012] 2 B.C.L.C. 369.
[25] *Mutual Life Insurance Co of New York v The Rank Organisation Ltd* [1985] B.C.L.C. 11.

shareholders. The action failed as the court held that the directors had exercised their powers in good faith in the interests of the company and that they had, in fact, exercised them fairly as between the different shareholders.

There is a significant body of case law considering CA 2006 s.172 in the context of applications by shareholders for permission to continue derivative claims. This arises because the court has to refuse permission for a derivative claim to proceed if a director acting in accordance with the CA 2006 s.172 duty to promote the success of the company would not continue the derivative claim. In *Iesini v Westrip Holdings Ltd*,[26] the court held that it would only bar a derivative claim on this ground if none of the directors would have continued the derivative claim themselves. Where directors were likely to disagree among themselves, the court would not apply the mandatory bar.

As it is the directors' subjective state of mind when making decisions that is paramount,[27] it is unlikely that the court will interfere with their commercial decisions unless they lacked good faith or were so irrational that an intelligent and honest person could not reasonably have thought the decision was in the company's best interests or would promote the success of the company.

The Association of General Counsel and Company Secretaries of the FTSE 100 (GC100) published guidance on 7 February 2007 setting out some suggested best practice guidelines for compliance with directors' duties under CA 2006 (GC100 Guidance on Directors' Duties). More recently, in response to the Government's request for industry-led solutions to various aspects of its governance reform agenda, in October 2018, the GC100 published "Guidance on Directors' Duties: Section 172 and Stakeholder Considerations" which contains additional guidance on the practical interpretation of the duty under s.172 (GC100 Guidance 2018).

The Institute of Chartered Secretaries and Administrators (ICSA) has also published practical guidance on directors' duties including on the duty under s.172. This includes a guidance note on directors' general duties dated June 2015 (ICSA Guidance) and, more recently, a joint paper published by ICSA and the Investment Association in 2017 on "The Stakeholder Voice in Board Decision Making".

The GC100 Guidance 2018 recommends, amongst other things, the following five practical steps to help embed s.172 in company decision making:

---

[26] *Iesini v Westrip Holdings Ltd* [2009] EWHC 2526 (Ch); [2010] B.C.C. 420; [2011] 1 B.C.L.C. 498.
[27] *Regentcrest Plc (In Liquidation) v Cohen* [2001] B.C.C. 494; [2001] 2 B.C.L.C. 80 at 120. Although the question of whether a decision was made in good faith can be tested by reference to objective considerations.

"•   Strategy: reflect the section 172 duty when you set and update your company's strategy.
 •   Training: establish and attend training courses on induction to the board, with ongoing updates on the section 172 duty in the context of your wider duties and responsibilities.
 •   Information: consider, and arrange to receive, the information you need on appointment and going forward to help you carry out your role and satisfy the duty.
 •   Policies and process: put in place policies and processes appropriate to support your company's operating strategy and to support its goals in the light of the section 172 duty.
 •   Engagement: consider what should be the company's approach to engagement with employees and other stakeholders."

As stated above, while it is mandatory for directors to take into account the various factors set out in the non-exhaustive list in CA 2006 s.172, they are subsidiary to the overall duty under s.172.

Having regard to the list of factors should not be a "box ticking" exercise, and outside of the requirements of CA 2006 s.414 and other company reporting requirements, there is nothing to be gained by a company creating a paper trail simply stating that the directors considered the non-exhaustive list of six factors. Indeed, as the GC100 Guidance 2018 notes "a checklist approach to every single thing … would be unworkable and interfere with good judgment and effective prioritisation".

Equally, directors will not absolve themselves from their duty to take account of the relevant factors simply because management has been tasked with preparing detailed supporting papers referring to the relevant factors. However, in circumstances where one or more of the factors is particularly relevant to a significant decision (or indeed other factors are particularly pertinent), it may be helpful and appropriate to record the relevant considerations within the supporting board or committee papers. The ICSA Guidance notes that "minutes should record decisions taken and do not necessarily need to give detail on how each factor was considered because the board paper should have provided the relevant information". The GC100 Guidance on Directors' Duties similarly states that "board minutes should not be used as the main medium recording the extent to which each of the factors of the Companies Act were discussed". The GC 100 Guidance 2018 recommends, however, "a consistent approach to minute taking, whether brief or detailed and as to when section 172 factors are minuted".

Evidencing consideration of the factors (e.g. in board minutes and/or relevant board or committee papers or contemporaneous notes) may be of particular benefit in circumstances where the directors anticipate a problem or wish to have on record a demonstration that they have carried out their duties.

Directors should, however, be mindful that it may, in some circumstances, not be possible to record a summary of all relevant discussions within board minutes for legal reasons, particularly where reference to legal advice in minutes could result in a loss of legal privilege (for example if the board is considering the effect of a proposal on employees). The GC100 Guidance on Directors' Duties states that directors should not be "forced to evidence their thought processes whether that is with regard to the stated factors or any other matter influencing their thinking. Apart from the unnecessary process and paperwork this would introduce into the boardroom, it would inevitably expose directors to a greater and unacceptable risk of litigation".

3.8 Duty to exercise independent judgment

CA 2006 s.173 provides that a director must exercise independent judgment. This duty will not, however, be infringed by a director acting either:

(a) in accordance with an agreement duly entered into by the company that restricts the future exercise of discretion by its directors; or
(b) in a way authorised by the company's constitution.

This duty codifies the principle that directors must exercise their powers independently and not subordinate their powers to the will of others (either by delegation or otherwise) unless authorised under the constitution. This does not prevent a director from taking proper advice from lawyers, accountants or other professional advisers; it is only the director's judgment that must be independent, in the sense that it must be the judgment of the director, not that of someone else.

A director may also adopt someone else's judgment if the director considers that judgment to be in the best interests of the company. In *Madoff Securities International Ltd (in liquidation) v Raven*,[28] Popplewell J stated that "Directors bring different experience and expertise to the joint exercise of corporate management. Whilst each is required to exercise independent judgment, he may legitimately defer to the views of those with greater experience or expertise than him. Where a director has a record and reputation for outstanding skill and experience in the company's business activity, his fellow directors are entitled to accord a high degree of deference and trust to his views as to what is in the company's best interests". This does not, however, mean that a director can simply defer to a more experienced director without giving the relevant matter proper consideration and challenge. To do so is unlikely to be consistent with the duty to exercise reasonable care, skill and diligence (see Section 3.9 below).

---

[28] *Madoff Securities International Ltd (in liquidation) v Raven* [2013] EWHC 3147 (Comm).

The case of *Stobart Group Ltd v Tinkler*,[29] involved a fractious boardroom dispute in which Stobart Group Ltd (a Guernsey incorporated company listed on the London Stock Exchange) sued its former CEO, Mr Tinkler, following his removal from the board. Whilst the fiduciary duties considered by the court were those under Guernsey common law, the court acknowledged they were the same as the fiduciary duties that a director of an English company owed before the statutory duties enacted by the Companies Act 2006 came into force. The court held that Mr Tinkler had committed a number of serious breaches of his fiduciary and contractual duties when he "briefed against the board" (including, amongst other things, by improperly sharing confidential information, communicating with a number of significant shareholders and employees to criticise the board's management with a view to destablising the board and seeking to orchestrate the removal of the non-executive chair). HHJ Russen QC (sitting as a judge in the High Court) stated that the duty to exercise independent judgment does not allow a director to "go off and do his own thing, independently of the board, in relation to matters that fall within the sphere of management of the company's business". The judge went on to state that any discussions of those matters should be "in the presence of the rest of the board or with the prior approval of the board" and that

> "for so long as a person occupies the office of director, I do not see how the duty to exercise an independent mind can carry with it any entitlement to speak or act as if he were not a member of the board without responsibilities to that collective decision-making body".

A dissenting director should therefore raise their concerns at board level and must not seek to "pick off" particular shareholders in advance of a general meeting by making private approaches and airing their own views on board management matters without the authority of the board or the other board members being present.

The duty to exercise independent judgment is of particular relevance when considering the position of a director of a subsidiary company within a group. Directors must exercise independent judgment in the interests of their own company. This may coincide with the interests of other group companies, or it may not. This may be particularly acute in the case of a ring-fenced entity within a larger group, or where the objects of one group company are not the same as another group company.

The section is silent on the powers of directors to delegate. The powers of delegation will, therefore, need to be clearly set out in the articles of association. Directors may delegate the performance of their functions and the exercise of their powers if the company has given them the power to do so. They may not, however, by delegation absolve themselves of their ultimate responsibilities as directors (see further Section 3.9 below).

---

[29] *Stobart Group Ltd v Tinkler* [2019] EWHC 258 (Comm).

One of the exceptions to the duty to exercise independent judgment is where the directors are authorised by the "constitution". As referred to in Section 3.6 above, the constitution is given an extended meaning for the purposes of CA 2006 Pt 10. This seems to include ordinary resolutions passed by the members of the company. Prior to CA 2006 the position was that only a resolution passed as a special resolution could constitute a direction to the directors, leaving the directors free to exercise their own judgment in matters of management in other circumstances. The consequence is that the directors' powers of management may be subject to more interference from shareholders than was previously the case.

Section 173 permits the status of the nominee director (a concept which is of particular significance in the context of joint ventures and private equity backed businesses) to be enshrined in the company's constitution with the effect that a nominee is able to follow the instructions of the person who appointed him. However, the director must still comply with the other duties, such as promoting the success of the company.

Previous common law principles regarding the extent to which it is proper for directors to cause a company to enter into an agreement which restricts the future exercise of their discretion remain relevant. For example, a director must not bind themselves to vote on board resolutions (or to fulfil other functions as a director) in a particular predetermined way or place themselves in a position where they are unable to, or do not, exercise any discretion in carrying out their duties. When voting (or fulfilling such other functions), a director must consider all the circumstances at the time and decide then what best promotes the success of the company.

Even a director appointed specifically to represent a particular shareholder (a nominee director) must comply with this duty. In the absence of any specific provision in the company's articles of association, a nominee director must exercise independent judgment and cannot blindly follow the instructions of the appointer. Even if the articles seem expressly to allow the director to follow the instructions of their appointer without being in breach of this duty to exercise independent judgment, this remains a difficult area, and the director will still need to reconcile this with other applicable duties (such as the duty to promote the success of the company).

However, this duty does not prevent the directors from causing their company to enter into a contract and undertaking to exercise their powers in such a way as to ensure the proper fulfilment of the contract. If it promotes the success of the company to enter into the contract, it is open to the directors to agree to exercise their powers to ensure that the contract was carried out. This was decided in *Fulham Football Club Ltd v Cabra Estates Plc*,[30] where the Court of Appeal approved a rule established in an Australian case (*Thorby v Goldberg*[31]):

> "If, when a contract is negotiated on behalf of a company, the directors *bona fide* think it in the best interests of the company as a whole that the transaction should be entered into and carried into effect, they may bind themselves by the contract to do whatever is necessary to effectuate it."

Two earlier cases (*Rackham v Peek Foods Ltd*[32] and *John Crowther Group v Carpets International*[33]) held (at first instance) that undertakings by directors to recommend proposed transactions to shareholders for their approval were unenforceable. The court in the *Fulham Football Club* case stated that, whilst these cases may be justified on their particular facts, they should not be read as laying down a general proposition that directors can never bind themselves as to the future exercise of their powers. Each of these cases involved an agreement by a company to sell a subsidiary to a purchaser with the agreement being conditional on the approval of the shareholders; in one case these were the seller's shareholders and in the other case they were the purchaser's shareholders. The directors of the relevant companies agreed with the other side to recommend the transactions to their shareholders, or to use their best endeavours to procure the fulfilment of the condition. Before the meeting of the shareholders other events occurred which caused the sale/purchase to be seriously disadvantageous to the relevant companies, and the directors refused to recommend the relevant transaction to their shareholders. The courts held that the directors were under a fiduciary duty to make full and honest disclosure to their shareholders and not to give bad advice. The courts upheld the directors' actions in each case.

These cases support the principle that directors should not give an unqualified undertaking in advance to recommend a course of action to shareholders in case, at the time of the recommendation, the directors are no longer of the view that the proposed course of action is in the best interests of the company; the recommendation could not then be made honestly. Nor should the directors give an unqualified undertaking to make statements to shareholders in the future which might amount to a misrepresentation, for example as to the supposed merits of a proposal compared with the merits of any available alternative. If pressed to give such undertakings, directors should make it clear that their obligations are subject to the proper fulfilment of their duties to the company and to its shareholders.

---

[30] *Fulham Football Club Ltd v Cabra Estates Plc* [1992] B.C.C. 863; [1994] 1 B.C.L.C. 363; (1993) 65 P. & C.R. 284 at 392.

[31] *Thorby v Goldberg* (1964) 112 C.L.R. 597.

[32] *Rackham v Peek Foods Ltd* [1990] B.C.L.C. 895.

[33] *John Crowther Group v Carpets International* [1990] B.C.L.C. 460.

3.9 Duty to exercise reasonable care, skill and diligence

This duty provides that a director must exercise reasonable care, skill and diligence. CA 2006 s.174(2) states that:

> "This means the care, skill and diligence that would be exercised by a reasonably diligent person with:
>
> (a) the general knowledge, skill and experience that may reasonably be expected of a person carrying out the functions carried out by the director in relation to the company, and
>
> (b) the general knowledge, skill and experience that the director has."

This duty mirrors the test laid down in Insolvency Act 1986 s.214.

The objective test, set out in (a) above, represents the minimum standard required by the duty to be exhibited by all directors. However, if the particular director possesses greater general knowledge, skill or experience than may reasonably be expected of a director carrying out the same functions, the director will have to meet the higher standard of care, skill and diligence appropriate to their general knowledge, skills and experience as a result of the subjective test referred to in (b) above. This does not mean, however, that a professional on the board is expected to use all their skills. So, for example, a lawyer does not have to research a particular point but can rely on external advisers, although the director must use their general knowledge, skill and ability when considering the matter.

For the purposes of the objective test set out in (a) above, the minimum standard of knowledge, skill and experience is to be determined by reference to the particular role carried out by the relevant director in relation to the company. Accordingly, a person carrying out the role of finance director, for example, will reasonably be expected to have a greater level of understanding and experience of financial matters than, say, the human resources director, even though all directors on the board will be expected to act collectively in signing off the annual accounts. The Government has also stated that a non-executive director will not be expected to have all the knowledge about the internal workings of the business that an executive director has, and so the law will take account of individuals' different perspectives. An executive director will often be required to devote significantly more time and attention to the company than a non-executive director and may therefore have a more in-depth understanding of certain aspects of the company (although this will not always be true and the specific circumstances of each company and the actual and expected knowledge and experience of the directors needs to be assessed carefully on a case by case basis).

Given the above, it is dangerous for a person to accept a directorship when they are not sufficiently qualified or experienced to be able to fulfil the functions they are expected to carry out. A director of a rubber company, for example, is unlikely to be able to claim as a defence complete ignorance of the rubber industry, nor will a finance director of a FTSE 100 company be able to claim as a defence that they are innumerate.

On the other hand, whilst a director of a small building firm may not normally be expected to have a sophisticated grasp of the foreign exchange markets, a director would be expected to have such knowledge (and to have exercised it) if they were also a senior employee of a bank engaged in that sphere of activity. This was illustrated by *Continental Assurance Co of London Plc (In Liquidation) (No.1), Re*,[34] where a senior executive of a bank was appointed a non-executive director of the company and its subsidiary. In breach of the financial assistance restrictions contained in the Companies Act 1985, the subsidiary made a loan to the holding company to enable it to service its bank loans. When the subsidiary became insolvent, the director was disqualified—his ignorance about the purpose of the upstream loan was held not to be a defence but evidence of his failure to exercise the appropriate degree of competence, especially in the light of his experience as a banker and his ability to understand the accounts of the holding company.

The moral of the cases is that a person should not accept a directorship where they are out of their depth and, further, that a highly qualified person should remember to continue to exercise their skills even when they are acting as a director in a role where the exercise of such skills would not normally be expected. Equally, given the substantial risk that a person assumes in becoming a director of any company, it is imprudent for a person to take on the role of director without having, as a very minimum, a proper understanding of the functions and duties of directors as a matter of English law and the more fundamental principles of company law, an understanding of the nature of the business of the company, the risks it faces and the regulatory and compliance regime in which it operates and at least a basic knowledge of relevant financial and accounting matters. Directors should also, as a practical matter, ensure that they receive a proper induction and ongoing training once appointed to keep their knowledge, skills and experience up to date. The FRC's Guidance on Board Effectiveness provides that:

> "under the direction of the chair, the company secretary's responsibilities include ensuring good information flows within the board and its committees and between senior management and non-executive directors, as well as facilitating induction, arranging board training and assisting with professional development as required".

Once appointed, directors cannot discharge themselves from their responsibilities by maintaining a negligible actual involvement in the affairs of the

---

[34] *Continental Assurance Co of London Plc (In Liquidation) (No.1), Re* [1996] B.C.C. 888; [1997] 1 B.C.L.C. 48; (1996) 93(28) L.S.G. 29.

company. For example, in *Galeforce Pleating Co Ltd, Re*,[35] it was held that, for as long as an individual continued to hold office as a director, and in particular to receive remuneration from it, it was incumbent on that person to inform themselves as to the financial affairs of the company and to play an appropriate role in the management of its business.

In *Bairstow v Queens Moat Houses Plc*,[36] the court held that an executive director who is paid substantial remuneration is expected to know the requirements that must be satisfied before a payment of dividends may be made.

However, a director is entitled, in the absence of suspicious circumstances, to rely on the experience and expertise of his co-directors and other officers of the company. Directors may also rely on the opinions of outside experts and, indeed, they may be negligent if they do not obtain an outside opinion in appropriate circumstances (*Duomatic Ltd, Re*[37]). Boards do, however, need to exercise care to ensure that they do not permit directors who may have a conflict of interest to instruct the external advisers on whose advice they wish to rely: *Iesini v Westrip Holdings Ltd*.[38]

In seeking advice from professional advisers, directors should also ensure that they request advice from an appropriate specialist who could reasonably be assumed to be competent to give such advice (see, for example, *Coleman Taymar Ltd v Oakes*[39] where advice on a company law issue was not obtained from a company law specialist and therefore could not, in the court's view, be reasonably relied on by the relevant director). Directors must also ensure that they ask suitably precise questions of their professional advisers. In *LRH Services Ltd (in liquidation) v Trew*,[40] a director was found liable for breach of duty even where he had instructed solicitors to act on the relevant transaction as there was no evidence to suggest that the director had instructed the solicitors to advise on the pertinent issue.

Directors cannot absolve themselves entirely of responsibility by delegation to others. In *Bradcrown Ltd, Re*,[41] a finance director who relied solely on professional advice received without making his own independent judgment was found to be unfit. Lawrence Collins J stated that a director is obviously entitled to rely on legal advice, but in this case, he had asked no questions and sought no advice while approving transactions that removed substantially all of the assets from the company. The director had simply

---

[35] *Galeforce Pleating Co Ltd, Re* [1999] 2 B.C.L.C. 704.
[36] *Bairstow v Queens Moat Houses Plc* [2000] B.C.C. 1025; [2000] 1 B.C.L.C. 549.
[37] *Duomatic Ltd, Re* [1969] 2 Ch. 365; [1969] 2 W.L.R. 114; (1968) 112 S.J. 922.
[38] *Iesini v Westrip Holdings Ltd* [2009] EWHC 2526 (Ch); [2010] B.C.C. 420; [2011] 1 B.C.L.C. 498.
[39] *Coleman Taymar Ltd v Oakes* [2001] 2 B.C.L.C. 749.
[40] *LRH Services Ltd (in liquidation) v Trew* [2018] EWHC 600 (Ch).
[41] *Bradcrown Ltd, Re* [2002] B.C.C. 428; [2001] 1 B.C.L.C. 547.

done what he was told and abdicated all responsibility: "In these circumstances he cannot seek refuge in the fact that professional advisers were involved in the transactions".

By contrast, in *Stephenson Cobbold Ltd (In Liquidation), Re*,[42] the court refused to disqualify a non-executive director as, although he was a cheque signatory, he was not involved in deciding which creditors should be paid where preferential treatment had been given. On the evidence, the defendant, an experienced businessman, was not a party to any policy of non-payment of Crown debts as he relied on professional accountants. The fact that he was a cheque signatory did not make him a party. Again, on the facts, his being a signatory did not amount to permitting a breach of fiduciary duties by the managing director in relation to the misuse of the company's funds. He had queried the payment and received assurances from the auditors. He was not disqualified.

The extent to which non-executive directors could be liable for failures within the company will depend on the circumstances, including the part which the director could be reasonably expected to play. There is no difference between the tests to be applied to non-executives and those applied to executives; the difference will lie in the functions they fulfil and the extent of the care and diligence that they can be reasonably expected to exercise. For instance, failure to ensure that proper controls are exercised over management (and by management) could be evidence of breach of duty, though the extent to which directors are expected to investigate whether proper controls are exercised will vary in the circumstances.

Continental Assurance Co of London Plc (In Liquidation), Re[43] involved a trial of an application made by the liquidators against eight former directors (two executive and six non-executive) alleging wrongful trading and misfeasance. The liquidators' case, with respect to the misfeasance, was that the non-executive directors had failed to exercise the requisite skill and care as directors in relying on the management accounts and other financial information as presented to them from time to time. It was held in this case that the non-executive directors had not blindly followed the advice of the finance director and auditors but had been in the habit of probing and testing the financial information provided from time to time, and it had been reasonable and proper for them to have relied on such financial information.

In *Barings Plc (No.5), Re, Secretary of State for Trade and Industry v Baker*,[44] the chief executive of a bank faced disqualification proceedings following the insolvency of the bank caused by unauthorised securities trading of an individual employee. The executive chairman sought (unsuccessfully) to

---

[42] *Stephenson Cobbold Ltd (In Liquidation), Re* [2001] B.C.C. 38; [2000] 2 B.C.L.C. 614.

[43] *Continental Assurance Co of London Plc (In Liquidation), Re* [2007] 2 B.C.L.C. 287; [2001] B.P.I.R. 733 (also referred to as *Singer v Beckett*).

[44] *Barings Plc (No.5), Re, Secretary of State for Trade and Industry v Baker* [1999] 1 B.C.L.C. 433.

defend himself by claiming that his expertise was in the corporate finance side of the business, that he had very little understanding of the activities in which the trader was involved (despite its representing a significant proportion of the bank's reported profits) and that he relied on the internal audit department and external auditors. The judge's summary of the duties of directors includes the following (at [489]):

"(i)   Directors have, both collectively and individually, a continuing duty to acquire and maintain a sufficient knowledge and understanding of the company's business to enable them properly to discharge their duties as directors.

(ii)   Whilst directors are entitled (subject to the articles of association of the company) to delegate particular functions to those below them in the management chain, and to trust their competence and integrity to a reasonable extent, the exercise of the power of delegation does not absolve a director from the duty to supervise the discharge of the delegated functions.

(iii) No rule of universal application can be formulated as to the duty referred to in (ii) above. The extent of the duty, and the question whether it has been discharged, must depend on the facts of each particular case, including the director's role in the management of the company."

The judge also stated (at [488]):

"Where there is an issue as to the extent of a director's duties and responsibilities in any particular case, the level of reward which he is entitled to receive or which he may reasonably have expected to receive from the company may be a relevant factor in resolving that issue."

Although the decision in the *Barings* case was on the question of disqualification, it does not require much imagination to conclude that, if a director has conducted himself in a manner which renders him unfit to be a director, the company may have a claim against him for not exercising proper skill, care or diligence if it has suffered a loss as a result.

A test of the law in this area was the claim brought by the Equitable Life Assurance Society against 15 of its former directors. The proceedings as originally filed sought £3.9 billion in damages, making the claim one of the largest ever brought before the English courts. The Society alleged that its former board had failed to seek legal advice prior to instituting a differential bonus policy which was subsequently found to be unlawful by the House of Lords in *Equitable Life Assurance Society v Hyman*.[45] It alleged further that the board had failed to take precautions against losing the *Hyman* litigation by cutting bonuses and warning policyholders about the risks of losing. The non-executive directors sought to have the claim against

---

[45]   *Equitable Life Assurance Society v Hyman* [2002] 1 A.C. 408; [2000] 3 W.L.R. 529; [2001] Lloyd's Rep. I.R. 99.

them struck out (*Equitable Life Assurance Society v Bowley*[46]), arguing that it was fanciful to contend that no reasonable non-executive director would have failed to challenge the advice of the executive directors in these circumstances. They relied upon the comments of Romer J in *City Equitable Fire Insurance Co Ltd, Re*[47] that a director was entitled, in the absence of grounds for suspicion, to assume that an employee of the company would perform their duties honestly. Langley J in *Bowley* did not accept that this represented the modern law insofar as it was suggested that directors were entitled to place unquestioning reliance on others to do their job. Instead, he indicated that the extent to which a non-executive director may reasonably rely on the executive directors would be fact-sensitive. For this and other reasons he declined to strike out the claim. It should be noted, however, that the claims were eventually withdrawn at the end of a six-month trial, suggesting that the Society had encountered significant difficulties in showing that the directors had actually been negligent.

In *Lexi Holdings Plc (In Administration) v Luqman*,[48] the court found that sibling directors had been in breach of this duty by their total inactivity in relation to notifying anyone that their brother, who was also a director of the company, had a conviction for fraud. The brother had appropriated money from the company. The court found that had advice been sought and the auditors informed, the subsequent misapplications of funds could not have been perpetrated.

3.10   Duty to avoid conflicts of interest

3.10.1   General

This duty covers all conflicts, actual and potential, between the interests of the director and the interests of the company. It includes situations in which the personal interests of a director or the interests of others to whom the director owes duties are, or may possibly be, inconsistent with the duties that a director owes to the company, including, in particular, conflicts relating to the exploitation of the company's property, information or opportunity. The only conflicts not covered by this duty are those relating to transactions or arrangements with the company, which have to be declared and which are covered separately in ss.177 and 182 CA 2006 (see Section 3.12 below). Any reference in s.175 to a conflict of interest includes a conflict of interest and duty and a conflict of duties. CA 2006 s.175(1) states that "A director of a company must avoid a situation in which he has, or can have, a direct or indirect interest that conflicts, or possibly may conflict, with the

---

[46]   *Equitable Life Assurance Society v Bowley* [2003] EWHC 2263 (Comm); [2003] B.C.C. 829; [2004] 1 B.C.L.C. 180.
[47]   *City Equitable Fire Insurance Co Ltd, Re* [1925] Ch. 407; [1924] All E.R. Rep. 485.
[48]   *Lexi Holdings Plc (In Administration) v Luqman* [2009] EWCA Civ 117; [2009] B.C.C. 716; [2009] All E.R. (D) 269 (Feb).

interests of the company". The test is an objective one and does not depend on whether the director is aware that what they are doing is a breach of duty (see *Richmond Pharmacology Ltd v Chester Overseas Ltd*[49]) or is acting in good faith. In *Boardman v Phipps*,[50] Lord Upjohn stated that:

> "The phrase 'possibly may conflict'… means that the reasonable man looking at the relevant facts and circumstances of the particular case would think that there was a real and sensible possibility of conflict; not that you could imagine some situation arising which might, in some conceivable possibility in events not contemplated as real sensible possibilities by any reasonable person, result in a conflict."

Where the conflict involves the exploitation of property, information or opportunity, it is immaterial whether the company could take advantage of the property, information or opportunity. In *Towers v Premier Waste Management Ltd*,[51] a director who accepted a free loan of equipment from a customer without disclosing the transaction or seeking approval for it from the board was found to be in breach of this duty. His conduct had deprived the company of the ability to consider whether it objected to the diversion of an opportunity offered by one of its customers away from the company to the director personally. There was a breach of duty even though the company may not have taken advantage of the opportunity or suffered any loss. This duty will therefore address a situation where the directors could create the (false) impression that the company could not take advantage of the property, information or opportunity, and it is prudent to operate from a working assumption that if a conflict of interest exists (and has not been authorised), the obligation will be breached.[52]

The conflict will arise even where the information is not confidential, although not where the information is part of the director's general knowledge and expertise.[53] The reference to "indirect interest" means that it is likely that interests of anyone connected with a director will be considered in deciding whether or not a director has a conflict. It should be noted that the categories of persons "connected" with a director were broadened under CA 2006 s.252 to include, amongst others, live in partners, parents, adult children and infants of his/her cohabitant.

In addition to the GC100 Guidance on Directors' Duties (referred to in Section 3.7 above), the GC100 has also published separate guidance (dated August 2008) on directors' conflicts of interest, which includes, amongst other things guidance for directors on exercising the power to authorise

---

[49] *Richmond Pharmacology Ltd v Chester Overseas Ltd* [2014] EWHC 2692 at [71].
[50] *Boardman v Phipps* [1967] 2 A.C. 46.
[51] *Towers v Premier Waste Management Ltd* [2011] EWCA Civ 923; [2012] B.C.C. 72; [2012] 1 B.C.L.C. 67.
[52] For a less severe approach in relation to an opportunity that a director took up post his resignation see *Island Export Finance Ltd v Umunna* [1986] B.C.L.C. 460.
[53] *CMS Dolphin Ltd v Simonet* [2002] B.C.C. 600; [2001] 2 B.C.L.C. 704; [2001] Emp. L.R. 895.

conflicts, including suggested procedures for authorising conflict situations and reviewing authorisations, and some illustrative examples of potential conflict situations.

3.10.2 When will the duty not be infringed?

CA 2006 s.175(4) provides that the duty is not infringed:

> "(a)   if the situation cannot reasonably be regarded as likely to give rise to a conflict of interest; or
> (b)   if the matter has been authorised by the directors."

Subsections (5) and (6) provide further detail on authorisation by the directors.

In the case of a private company incorporated on or after 1 October 2008, authorisation may be given by the directors so long as the company's articles do not prohibit this.

In the case of a private company incorporated before 1 October 2008, authorisation may be given by the directors if the company either passes an ordinary resolution permitting this (assuming the articles have not already been amended so as to prohibit it) or if the company amends its articles to expressly allow it.

In the case of a public company, authorisation may be given by the directors only if the company's articles expressly allow this.

In each of the above cases, the authorisation will only be effective if:

(a)   the meeting at which authorisation is given is quorate without counting the director in question or any other interested director; and
(b)   the authorisation was given without any such director voting or would have been agreed to if their votes had not been counted.

It appears that s.175(4)(b), which provides that the duty is not infringed "if the matter *has been* authorised by the directors", requires director authorisations to be given in advance (and not retrospectively) and (when read in the light of the wording in s.175(6)) that the authorisation must relate to a particular conflict of interest facing one or more named directors.

Authorisation by shareholders also remains possible. The powers of shareholders to authorise conflicts and to prevent a breach of duty are preserved by CA 2006 s.180(4) but care is needed to ensure that sufficient information is given to shareholders to enable them to make an informed decision. Although the general duties contained in CA 2006 ss.171–177 have now replaced the common law duties of directors, *Hogg v Cramphorn Ltd*[54] provides authority for the view that the members of the company may, by ordinary resolution, authorise in advance (or subsequently ratify) an action which would otherwise constitute a breach of a directors' general duties. There are, however, some limits to this. In particular:

(a) the members of a company cannot authorise acts of the directors which are unlawful as a matter of law (for example approving an unlawful dividend or capital reduction);

(b) a special resolution would be required to authorise a director to act in a manner which is prohibited by the company's articles of association (and in effect to achieve what would constitute an amendment to the company's articles); and

(c) it would not be open to majority shareholders to exercise their powers in bad faith to authorise actions by the directors that would constitute a "fraud on the minority". This may arise where "the majority are endeavouring directly or indirectly to appropriate to themselves money, property, or advantages which belong to the company, or in which the other shareholders are entitled to participate" (see *Burland v Earle*[55]) or "where what has been done amounts to fraud and the wrongdoers are themselves in control of the company" (see *Prudential Assurance Co Ltd v Newman Industries (No.2)*.[56]

Authorisation and ratification are addressed further in Section 3.14 below.

The duty to avoid conflicts of interest can be particularly pertinent in relation to people holding multiple directorships, and potential conflicts should be identified and authorised in advance.

To ensure an effective authorisation of a conflict of interest, it is necessary for a director to give full disclosure of the scope and nature of the conflict (or potential conflict). In the absence of full disclosure by a director, there is a risk that any resolution authorising the conflict may be viewed as invalid. The precise extent of the disclosure will depend on the relevant facts at the time, but a director should seek to provide as much information as possible about the full extent of the conflict, including the potential advantages that may flow to the director as a result of the conflict and the potential disadvantages that may be incurred by the company in permitting the conflict. Directors also need to ensure that disclosures are kept up to date and a further authority sought if the nature and extent of the conflict has changed.

---

[54] *Hogg v Cramphorn Ltd* [1967] Ch. 254.

[55] *Burland v Earle* [1902] A.C. 83.

[56] *Prudential Assurance Co Ltd v Newman Industries (No.2)* [1982] Ch. 204. See also *Harris v Microfusion 2003-2 LLP* [2016] EWCA Civ 1212 and the judgment of David Richards J in *Abouraya v Sigmund* [2014] EWHC 277 (Ch).

Some use may be made of the safe harbour in CA 2006 s.175(4)(a) (sometimes referred to as the "materiality test"), which applies where the situation cannot reasonably be regarded as likely to give rise to a conflict of interest (but this, in itself, gives rise to some difficulties as to interpretation). In the Parliamentary debate prior to the enactment of CA 2006, the Solicitor-General stated that:

> "For as long as that remains true, the director will not be in breach of the duty… if he [the director] cannot foresee a situation, it cannot reasonably be regarded as being likely to give rise to a conflict of interest. If a person can foresee a situation, the directors or members of the company should be informed about that and can then act accordingly."

The duty to avoid a situation where interests or duties are in conflict will come into play only where there is a real possibility of such conflict. In the Scottish case of *Eastford Ltd v Gilliespie*,[57] two directors asked the board to ratify their prior decision to raise an action in the name of the company alleging a breach of duty against another director. The court accepted that on the facts of the case the directors could exercise their voting power to ratify their own conduct because on the particular facts of the case there was no conflict of interest between them and the company.[58] Where a company is prevented from taking advantage there might not be a breach of the no-conflict rule.[59]

3.10.3 To what extent can the constitution of a company contain provisions to facilitate dealing with conflicts?

CA 2006 s.180(4)(b) provides that the general duties are not infringed by anything done (or omitted) by the directors, or any of them, in accordance with provisions in the company's articles for dealing with conflicts of interest.

CA 2006 s.232(4) (relating to protecting directors from liability) states that: "Nothing in this section prevents a company's articles from making such provision as has previously been lawful for dealing with conflicts of interest". So these provisions clearly envisage that the articles can address dealing with conflicts, although the precise extent to which this is possible is the subject of some debate. It is generally, however, accepted that it is open to a company to adopt a bespoke mechanism for authorising directors' conflicts within the company's articles of association.

---

[57] *Eastford Ltd v Gilliespie* [2009] CSOH 119; 2009 G.W.D. 37-618; on appeal [2011] CSIH 12; 2011 S.C. 501.
[58] The two directors risked being personally liable for commencing an action without the authority of the board but in this case that risk remained as the company was impecunious: ratification did not improve the directors' position in that regard.
[59] *Wilkinson v West Coast Capital* [2005] EWHC 3009 (Ch); [2007] B.C.C. 717.

3.10.4   Consequences of breach of CA 2006 section 175 and remedies

Insofar as remedies are concerned, the position under CA 2006 is discussed below in Section 3.13.

The courts will draw on the remedies which applied to breaches of the no conflict rule in existence prior to CA 2006. Pre-CA 2006 case law established that if there was a conflict between an interest of the company and another interest (or a duty) of the director in any transaction, the director must account to the company for any benefit they received from the transaction (unless, by reason of the company's constitution or an informed approval given by the shareholders, the director was permitted to retain the benefit). For example, in the case of *JJ Harrison (Properties) Ltd v Harrison*,[60] a director of a company acquired some land from the company at a price which reflected the fact that planning permission had been refused to develop the land. At the time of the acquisition, the director was aware that, for various reasons, the prospect of planning permission being granted had improved. This fact was not disclosed to the board at the meeting to approve the transaction. The court found that the director was in breach of his fiduciary duties to the company and held the property upon trust for the company. Accordingly, he was liable to account for the profits he made from the subsequent sale by him of the land.

If the company suffers a loss by virtue of the conflict (e.g. because the director directs a benefit to go to another entity rather than to the company), the director will be liable to account for the loss. This is so even though the director does not derive any benefit personally and is under a duty to that other entity to promote its interests. For example, in *Scottish Co-operative Wholesale Society Ltd v Meyer*,[61] directors of a partly owned subsidiary acquiesced in a policy of its holding company to deprive the subsidiary of business contracts, which were diverted to the parent company. In an action by minority shareholders in the subsidiary, those directors of the subsidiary who were "nominees" of the holding company (and also directors of the holding company) were held to be in breach of their duties to the subsidiary by their inaction in failing to protect that company from the loss of business.

3.11   Duty not to accept benefits from third parties

This duty originated from the fiduciary duty existing prior to CA 2006 prohibiting the exploitation of the position of director for personal benefit (sometimes referred to as the duty not to make secret profits).

---

[60] *JJ Harrison (Properties) Ltd v Harrison* [2001] EWCA Civ 1467; [2002] B.C.C. 729; [2002] 1 B.C.L.C. 162.
[61] *Scottish Co-operative Wholesale Society Ltd v Meyer* [1959] A.C. 324; [1958] 3 W.L.R. 404; 1958 S.C. (H.L.) 40.

CA 2006 s.176 provides that a director must not accept a benefit from a third party conferred by reason of him being a director or his doing (or not doing) anything as a director.

For these purposes a third party is defined as meaning "a person other than the company, an associated body corporate or a person acting on behalf of the company or an associated body corporate" (CA 2006 s.176(2)). Bodies corporate are associated if one is a subsidiary of the other or both are subsidiaries of the same body corporate (which means, for example, that a 50/50 joint venture company will not be an associated body of the joint venture parties). Where a director provides services to the company through another person, benefits received by the director from that person are not regarded as conferred by a third party.

The term benefit is intended to be construed widely. In the Parliamentary debate prior to the enactment of CA 2006, the Solicitor General stated that:

> "A benefit for the purposes of this duty includes benefits of any description, including non-financial benefits. In using the word 'benefit', we intend the ordinary dictionary meaning of the word. The Oxford English Dictionary defines it as 'a favourable or helpful factor, circumstance, advantage or profit'."

This could include, at one end of the scale, corporate hospitality offered to a director and, at the other end of the scale, a financial bribe paid to a director by a supplier or potential supplier.

Although there is no provision for authorisation by independent directors, the duty will not be infringed if the acceptance of the benefit cannot be reasonably regarded as likely to give rise to a conflict of interest. Although it may be possible to do so, it is generally not considered appropriate to attempt to deal with the acceptance of third party benefits in a company's articles (for example, by specifying that de minimis amounts of particular benefits up to a specified level may be accepted); the appropriate test is whether or not acceptance of the benefit can reasonably be regarded as likely to give rise to a conflict.

In practice, the question of whether the acceptance of a particular benefit can reasonably be regarded as likely to give rise to a conflict will be fact specific. It requires an assessment, amongst other things, of the nature of the remuneration or benefits received, the circumstances in which the benefits are conferred (including whether the benefit is a one off benefit of de minimis value or a more significant benefit or one which follows a pattern of events), an understanding of market practice for the type of company concerned and potentially consideration of the expectations (if any) of the donor in providing the benefit to the director.

This duty can be illustrated by the pre-CA 2006 case of *Regal (Hastings) Ltd v Gulliver*.[62] In that case, four directors and Regal's solicitor subscribed for shares in a subsidiary of Regal to give it sufficient additional funds to acquire extra cinema leases. Regal did not have sufficient resources itself to provide the funds to the subsidiary. When the shares in the subsidiary were sold at a profit, Regal (controlled by new owners) claimed the profits from the directors and the solicitor. The court held that, as fiduciaries, the directors were liable to account to the company for the profit that they had made (in fact, the solicitor was held not to be liable). It was held in the House of Lords that:

> "The rule of equity which insists on those who by the use of a fiduciary position make a profit, being liable to account for that profit, in no way depends on fraud or absence of *bona fides*; or upon such questions or considerations as whether the profit would or should otherwise have gone to the plaintiff, or whether he took a risk or acted as he did for the benefit of the plaintiff, or whether the plaintiff has in fact been damaged or benefited from his action."

The directors were liable even though Regal could not have made the profit itself (because of lack of resources) and even though they had acted in the best interests of the company and had not caused it loss. However, the directors could have kept the profit if they had obtained the approval of the company's shareholders in a general meeting.

There is some overlap between this duty not to accept third party benefits and the duty to promote the success of the company. This overlap may give a degree of flexibility to the judges to decide cases upon the merits of the parties in particular factual situations, as was possible in relation to the overlap of the corresponding common law duties before the implementation of CA 2006. For example, the Court of Appeal's judgment in *Bhullar v Bhullar*[63] (concerning the diversion by a director of a business opportunity to himself) considered the test for determining what constitutes an opportunity for the company. The court affirmed that the test would be satisfied if a reasonable man looking at the facts would think there was a real, sensible possibility of conflict between the director's personal interest and the interests of the company. Another example is the case of *Wilkinson v West Coast Capital*,[64] where it was held, on the facts, that directors who discovered an opportunity and pursued it for their own benefit were not in breach of fiduciary duty to their company. A shareholders' agreement (which was expressed to take precedence over the company's articles) required a specified majority consent before the company could buy any business. As the directors were party to the shareholders' agreement and had power to block the company from pursuing the opportunity, they were

---

[62] *Regal (Hastings) Ltd v Gulliver* [1942] 1 All E.R. 378.
[63] *Bhullar v Bhullar* [2003] EWCA Civ 424; [2003] B.C.C. 711; [2003] 2 B.C.L.C. 241.
[64] *Wilkinson v West Coast Capital* [2005] EWHC 3009 (Ch); [2007] B.C.C. 717.

held not to be in breach of the no conflict rule in pursuing the opportunity through another company to their own advantage.

3.12 Duty to declare interest in proposed transaction or arrangement

This general duty (contained in CA 2006 s.177) replaced the equitable rule that directors may not have an interest in transactions with the company unless the interest has been authorised by the members. In practice, the equitable rule was usually modified by provisions in the articles which provided for disclosure and abstention from voting at board meetings.

The statutory duty requires a director to disclose to the other directors the nature and extent of any interest, whether direct or indirect, that the director has in relation to a proposed transaction or arrangement with the company. There is no requirement for authorisation. The term "arrangement" is wider than the term "transaction" and includes agreements or understandings having no contractual effect (see *Duckwari Plc, Re*[65]). The reference to indirect interests means that the director himself does not need to be a party to the transaction for the duty to apply; another person's interest could amount to an interest on the part of the director. As stated in Section 3.10 above, the categories of persons "connected" with a director were broadened under CA 2006 s.252.

Disclosure is required before the company enters into the transaction or arrangement and can be made at a meeting of the directors, by notice in writing sent to the other directors, or by way of a general notice to the effect that the director has an interest in a specified body corporate or firm and is to be regarded as interested in any transaction or arrangement that may be made with that body or firm after the date of the notice, or that the director is connected with a specified person and is to be regarded as interested in any transaction or arrangement that may be made with that person.

The nature and extent of the interest must be declared and if, after disclosure, the declaration proves to be or becomes inaccurate or incomplete, a further declaration must be made correcting the earlier one, assuming that the company has not yet entered into the transaction or arrangement.

There are various circumstances specified where there is no requirement to make a declaration. No declaration is required where the director is not aware of having an interest or is not aware of the transaction or arrangement in question. However, it is expressly provided that the director is to be treated as being aware of matters of which they ought reasonably to

---

[65] *Duckwari Plc, Re* [1999] Ch. 253.

be aware. In the Parliamentary debate prior to enactment of CA 2006, the Attorney-General considered these words and stated that it should be judged objectively whether the director ought reasonably to be aware of a particular matter. From a practical point of view, this gives rise to directors having to undertake a certain amount of due diligence regarding their potential interests in order to avoid breaching the duty inadvertently.

Other situations where no declaration is required are: if the interest cannot reasonably be regarded as likely to give rise to a conflict of interest; if, or to the extent that, the other directors are already aware or ought reasonably to be aware of it; and if the interest concerns the terms of a director's service contract that are considered by a meeting of the directors or a committee appointed for the purpose.

CA 2006 s.180(4)(b) provides that the company's articles may contain provisions for dealing with conflicts of interest compliance which will prevent a breach of the general duty. The explanatory note to CA 2006 provides that conflicted directors may, subject to the company's articles, participate in decision taking relating to such transactions with the company although the articles may require that the directors must disregard the views of an interested director.

It should be noted that CA 2006 s.182 deals separately with declarations of interest in existing transactions or arrangements not already declared under s.177. This provision is dealt with in Chapter 7. While a breach of s.182 is a criminal offence, a breach of s.177 is not. The Attorney-General explained the distinction by referring to the fact that a breach of s.182 cannot affect the validity of the existing transaction or arrangement whereas a failure to declare an interest in a proposed transaction or arrangement could lead to other consequences such as voidability. This raises the issue (which is considered further below) that CA 2006 does not expressly set out the remedies applying to the general duties and therefore gives rise to some uncertainties, particularly where the statutory duty departs from the concepts developed by prior case law and in relation to common law and equitable duties.

In relation to the relevance of case law prior to CA 2006, the Solicitor-General confirmed that the general duty replaced the equitable principle that directors may not enter into contracts with their company or have an interest in any of the company's contracts. The authorities include *Aberdeen Railway Co v Blaikie Brothers*[66] and reflect the same principle that prevents an agent from contracting with his principal and a trustee from contracting with his trust (as determined in *Keech v Sandford*[67]).

---

[66] *Aberdeen Railway Co v Blaikie Brothers* (1854) 1 Macq. 461; [1843–60] All E.R. 249.
[67] *Keech v Sandford* 25 E.R. 223; (1726) Sel. Cas. Ch. 61.

If a company enters into a transaction with a conflicted director in circumstances where the director failed, before the transaction was entered into, to declare the nature and extent of his interest in the transaction, the company will by virtue of CA 2006 s.178 have the right to set aside the transaction (see *Transvaal Lands Co v New Belgium (Transvaal) Land and Development Co*[68]).

3.13 Consequences of breach of general duties

CA 2006 s.178 provides that the consequences of breach (or threatened breach) of the general duties are the same as would apply if the corresponding pre-CA 2006 common law rule or equitable principle applied. Each of the general duties (with the exception of the common law duty to exercise reasonable care, skill and diligence) are stated to be "enforceable in the same way as any other fiduciary duty owed to a company by its directors".

By way of elaboration, prior to the enactment of CA 2006, the Solicitor-General stated that:

"where those duties have been codified the courts will be able to identify the relevant rule or principle. Where they have been changed the courts will need to find the rule or principle that covers the same subject matter as the general duty contained in the statutory statement … the fact that the general duties might depart from common law rules and equitable principles in certain ways will not alter the circumstances flowing from their breach. The question will not be whether the rule or principle has been breached but what the consequences should be once it has been breached. The consequences of a breach of the fiduciary duty can include damages, compensation, restoration of a company's property, rescission of a transaction or a requirement of a director to account for any profits made as a result. They may also include injunctions or declarations, although those matters are primarily employed when a breach is threatened but has not yet occurred. The consequences of a breach of the duty of care and skill may include the court awarding compensation or damages."

3.14 Consent, approval or authorisation by members

CA 2006 s.180 contains various provisions relating to the general duties concerning board approval, shareholder authorisation and circumstances where approval or authorisation is not required if certain other approvals have been obtained or if certain matters are dealt with in the articles. This section should also be read with the provisions relating to ratification by a

---

[68] *Transvaal Lands Co v New Belgium (Transvaal) Land and Development Co* [1914] 2 Ch. 488.

company of conduct by a director amounting to negligence, default, breach of duty or breach of trust in relation to the company, which are set out in CA 2006 s.239.

First, s.180 makes it clear that, unless the company's constitution requires otherwise, the consent or approval of members of the company is not required in relation to:

(a)   the duty to avoid conflicts of interest where authorisation has been duly obtained by the directors in accordance with s.175; and

(b)   the duty to declare an interest in a proposed transaction or arrangement, where the declaration is duly made in accordance with s.177. This was a change from the common law rules and equitable principles which could have required a transaction or arrangement to be set aside if the consent or approval of the members of the company had not been obtained.

Secondly, there are circumstances where it is expressly stated that it is not necessary to comply with the provisions relating to the duty to avoid conflicts of interest (s.175) or the duty not to accept benefits from third parties (s.176). This is the case where the provisions of CA 2006 Pt 10 Ch.4 apply and, either approval is given under that chapter, or where it is provided that approval is not needed. CA 2006, Pt 10 Ch.4 (which is considered in Chapter 5 of this Guide) deals with the requirements for member approval in relation to four different types of transaction by a company with its directors:

(a)   long-term service contracts;
(b)   substantial property transactions;
(c)   loans, quasi-loans and credit transactions; and
(d)   payments for loss of office.

For each type of transaction, the basic requirement for member approval is set out followed by express exceptions to the basic rule and finally the consequences of breaching that rule.

Thirdly, s.180(4)(a) preserves "any rule of law" enabling the company to give authority, specifically or generally, for anything to be done (or omitted) by the directors, or any of them, that would otherwise be a breach of duty.

Under the common law rules, breaches of fiduciary duty could be authorised by ordinary resolution, although unlawful acts (such as unlawful dividends, unlawful returns of capital or acts otherwise in breach of statute or the general law) could not be authorised. Similarly, a shareholder authorisation may not be valid where it constitutes a "fraud on the minority". The common law rules in relation to shareholder authorisation reflect the principle that those to whom duties are owed may release fiduciaries from their legal obligations provided there is full disclosure in advance of the decision. Where breaches of fiduciary duties have been lawfully authorised (or ratified), the court will be obliged to refuse permission to a shareholder who has brought a derivative claim under CA 2006 Pt 11 to continue that claim.

Section 180(4)(b) provides that, where the articles contain provisions dealing with conflicts of interest, provided a director acts in accordance with those provisions, the director will not be held to be in breach of any of the general duties by acting in accordance with those provisions.

Save for these express exceptions, s.180(5) provides that the general duties will have effect (unless otherwise provided or the context otherwise requires) notwithstanding any enactment or rule of law. An example of a situation where CA 2006 does provide otherwise is s.247, which enables directors to make provision for the benefit of employees on the cessation or transfer of a company's business even if this would otherwise constitute a breach of the general duty to promote the success of the company.

As to ratification, the provisions in CA 2006 s.239 made significant changes to the pre-existing law. Previously, the common law allowed an interested shareholder to vote his or her shares on a matter in which he or she was interested. For this reason, the courts stopped short of accepting that *all* breaches of directors' duties could be ratified by ordinary resolution—as directors in breach could otherwise vote to forgive themselves in respect of the breach. The dividing line as to which breaches could be ratified and which could not was not easy to draw. For example, in *Daniels v Daniels*,[69] directors' negligence was not ratifiable, whereas in *Pavlides v Jensen*,[70] it was ratifiable. The distinction may lie in the fact that in the former case there was a misappropriation of corporate property while in the latter there was not. Under the statutory provision, any decision by a company to ratify conduct by a director amounting to negligence, default, breach of duty or breach of trust in relation to the company must be taken by the members without reliance on the votes of the director concerned (if a member of the company) and any member connected with him (although such person may attend and be counted in the quorum and otherwise take part in the proceedings of a shareholders' meeting). For these purposes a director includes a former director and "connected person" is given a very wide meaning. This concept of disqualification may have the benefit that breaches of all directors' duties are, in principle, ratifiable, compared with the common law position where the courts decided that not all breaches could be ratified, particularly where dishonesty or expropriation of corporate property was involved. However, whether the courts will in fact adopt such an approach remains to be seen.

---

[69] *Daniels v Daniels* [1978] Ch. 406; [1978] 2 W.L.R. 73; (1977) 121 S.J. 605.
[70] *Pavlides v Jensen* [1956] Ch. 565; [1956] 3 W.L.R. 224; (1956) 100 S.J. 452.

Section 239(6) makes it clear that the law on unanimous consent is expressly preserved. The explanatory notes to CA 2006 state that this has the effect that the restrictions imposed by this section as to who may vote on a ratification resolution will not apply when every member votes (informally or otherwise) in favour of the resolution. Also, the powers of the directors to agree not to sue, or to settle or release a claim made by them on behalf of the company are expressly preserved.

Finally, the section provides that any other enactment or rule of law imposing additional requirements for valid ratification or any rule of law as to acts that are incapable of being ratified by the company are not affected by this section. So, for example, unlawful acts or breaches of statute may not be ratified.

3.15 Direct duties to members

Earlier within this chapter, there have been references to areas where CA 2006 provisions on general duties of directors do not attempt to address all the legal principles existing at the time of its enactment. These include: the law relating to shadow directors; duties to creditors on impending insolvency; those fiduciary duties not covered by the general duties such as the duty to act fairly as between different members (this duty does not require equal treatment to all members, only that the treatment should be fair); the duty of confidentiality; and the remedies applying to breach of the general duties. This chapter concludes with a further category of duty which applies to directors, namely, the direct duty owed in certain circumstances to members of the company.

A director's duties are normally owed to the company. In certain exceptional circumstances, however, a director may be found to owe duties to the company's members (or potential investors in the company). Each case is likely to be very fact specific, however, case law suggests that for a direct duty to be owed there would need to be some special circumstances where the members or potential investors have conferred particular trust and confidence in the directors to protect their interests as shareholders (or potential investors) as opposed to solely protecting the interests of the company. The principal cases where such duties are likely to arise are considered below.

There will be occasions when directors, particularly of public companies, will be communicating with their shareholders. They owe a general duty to those shareholders to be honest and not to mislead (*Gething v Kilner*)[71] or (when seeking their approval of transactions or recommending particular courses of action) to make full (as well as honest) disclosure (*Normandy v*

---

[71] *Gething v Kilner* [1972] 1 W.L.R. 337; [1972] 1 All E.R. 1166; (1971) 116 S.J. 74.

Ind Coope & Co Ltd).[72] In addition, quite apart from the liability that can arise under Financial Services and Markets Act 2000 s.90 in respect of the general duty of disclosure in relation to prospectuses, directors could be personally liable for the tort of negligent misstatement: that is, if shareholders were to suffer loss by relying on negligent misstatements made by the directors (*Chez Nico (Restaurants) Ltd, Re).*[73] Such statements do not necessarily have to be made in writing (as in circulars); they can be made orally, as may be more likely in the case of dealings with shareholders in private companies with few shareholders.

The decision in *Percival v Wright*[74] is sometimes cited as authority for a general proposition that directors do not owe duties directly to the company's shareholders. The decision has been doubted in a number of cases both in the UK and elsewhere, where it has been held that, in certain special circumstances, directors can owe duties, including a duty of disclosure, vis-à-vis shareholders individually. In *Chez Nico (Restaurants) Ltd, Re,* Nico Ladenis (a high-profile restaurateur) had sought to exercise powers of compulsory acquisition of minority shares under CA 1985 s.429. A minority of shareholders objected and the court decided that, as a matter of law, the powers were not in fact exercisable in light of the particular events. However, the court noted with disapproval the failure of Mr Ladenis to give the minority shareholders sufficient or accurate information, but commented that, as the powers of compulsory acquisition were not exercisable, it was unnecessary to determine the issue of whether Mr Ladenis was under a fiduciary duty to disclose the true position to the minority shareholders. The court did, however, confirm its approval of the decision of the New Zealand Court in *Coleman v Myers,*[75] in which directors were held to be under such a duty to shareholders.

In *Platt v Platt,*[76] a director (who was also a shareholder) was held liable for negligent misrepresentation and breach of his fiduciary duties owed directly to his fellow shareholders. In that case, a director persuaded his brothers to transfer their shares to him for £1 to enable the business to be sold to the main supplier—the alternative, the director said, was to call in the receivers. When the sale to the supplier failed to materialise and no receivers were appointed, the brothers called for their shares to be returned to them. The director refused and subsequently sold all of the shares at a profit. The director had failed to give his brothers adequate or up-to-date financial or trading information about the company and had made it difficult for his brothers to check the facts with the supplier. It was held that, in the circumstances, the director was under a fiduciary duty to disclose matters which he knew or had reason to believe would be material to his

---

[72] *Normandy v Ind Coope & Co Ltd* [1908] 1 Ch. 84.
[73] *Chez Nico (Restaurants) Ltd, Re* [1991] B.C.C. 736; [1992] B.C.L.C. 192.
[74] *Percival v Wright* [1902] 2 Ch. 421.
[75] *Coleman v Myers* [1997] 2 N.Z.L.R. 225.
[76] *Platt v Platt* [1999] 2 B.C.L.C. 745.

brothers' decision to transfer their shares. The director was held liable for the loss of value of the brothers' shares.

In *Peskin v Anderson*,[77] former members of the RAC Club, who did not benefit from payments made on the disposal of a motoring services business, unsuccessfully alleged that the directors were in breach of fiduciary duty in not informing them of the proposed sale and thereby deprived them of the opportunity to be readmitted as members in order to be eligible for the windfall. The Court of Appeal examined the duties owed to shareholders. Mummery LJ stated:

> "The fiduciary duties owed to the company arise from the legal relationship between the directors and the company directed and controlled by them. The fiduciary duties owed to the shareholders do not arise from that legal relationship. They are dependent on establishing a special factual relationship between the directors and the shareholders in the particular case. Events may take place which bring the directors of the company into direct and close contact with the shareholders in a manner capable of generating fiduciary obligations, such as a duty of disclosure of material facts to the shareholders, or an obligation to use confidential information and valuable commercial and financial opportunities, which have been acquired by the directors in that office for the benefit of the shareholders, and not to prefer and promote their own interests at the expense of the shareholders ... There are, for example, instances of the directors of a company making direct approaches to, and dealing with, the shareholders in relation to a specific transaction and holding themselves out as agents for them in connection with the acquisition or disposal of shares; or making material representations to them; or failing to make material disclosure to them of insider information in the context of negotiations for a take-over of the company's business; or supplying to them specific information and advice on which they have relied. These events are capable of constituting special circumstances and of generating fiduciary obligations, especially in those cases in which the directors, for their own benefit, seek to use their position and special inside knowledge acquired by them to take improper or unfair advantage of the shareholders."

In *Sharp v Blank*,[78] a claim was brought against the directors of Lloyds TSB by certain shareholders of the bank alleging misrepresentations by the bank's directors concerning the acquisition of Halifax Bank of Scotland Plc and the recapitalisation of Lloyds TSB. The court struck out various claims that the directors had breached their fiduciary duties and held that although the directors had a duty to provide the shareholders with sufficient information to enable them to make an informed choice about the acquisition, they did not owe any wider fiduciary duties because no special relationship existed and they had not undertaken to act for the shareholders in any more extended sense. Nugee J reviewed the main authorities on the extent to which a director will owe duties to the company's members and summarised the position as follows:

---

[77] *Peskin v Anderson* [2001] B.C.C. 874; [2001] 1 B.C.L.C. 372.
[78] *Sharp v Blank* [2015] EWHC 3220 (Ch) at [9]–[13].

"I take it therefore to be established law, binding on me, that although a director of a company can owe fiduciary duties to the company's shareholders, he does not do so by the mere factor of being a director, but only where there is on the facts of the particular case a 'special relationship' between the director and the shareholders. It seems to me to follow that this special relationship must be something over and above the usual relationship that any director of a company has with its shareholders. It is not enough that the director, as a director, has more knowledge of the company's affairs than the shareholders have: since they direct and control the company's affairs this will almost inevitably be the case. Nor is it enough that the actions of the directors will have the potential to affect the shareholders—again this will always, or almost always, be the case. On the decided cases the sort of relationship that has given rise to a fiduciary duty has been where there has been some personal relationship or particular dealing or transaction between them."

Nugee J also observed that these special circumstances most commonly arise in small companies which are closely held and where the directors are dealing with the shareholders in respect of transactions where the directors stand to benefit personally.

Whilst these decisions show that English law recognises the duties of directors to shareholders in certain circumstances, it does not mean directors must at all times reveal all they know to shareholders or risk incurring liability. Frequently, directors will be under duties (e.g. regulatory duties or duties of confidentiality, whether owed to third parties or to the company itself) not to reveal information prematurely, nor to reveal it selectively. The courts will respect the bona fide views of directors as to the best interests of the company (as long as they are not unreasonably held) and will not seek to substitute their own views. But the courts have been increasingly reluctant to allow companies (and their shareholders or creditors) to suffer as a result of directors failing to conduct themselves in accordance with others' reasonable expectations of them or as a result of directors putting their own interests or other outside interests ahead of the company's interests.

At the time directors' duties were codified, there was a concern that CA 2006 might increase the exposure of directors to claims for breach of duty and that shareholders might seek to test and develop the law through the medium of the derivative claims procedure in CA 2006 Pt 11. The fears of some commentators that CA 2006 Pt 11 would open the floodgates to tactical shareholder litigation have not been realised.

3.16 Looking ahead

The events of the financial crisis of 2008 and more recent large scale corporate failures have all served to increase the public focus on directors' duties and the critical role that directors are expected to play in ensuring that companies are run responsibly, adopt high standards of corporate governance and remain appropriately accountable to their members and wider stakeholders, including employees, pensioners, customers, the environment and the wider community.

Whether it be in relation to the safeguarding of worker rights or pensions schemes, measures to clamp down on inappropriate or fraudulent activities or the protection of personal data, the responsibilities of companies from a legal and compliance perspective are on the increase, and the expectations placed upon companies and their directors are arguably greater than ever. The responsibilities and accountabilities of individual directors (alongside the collective responsibility of the board) is also an increasing area of focus and seen as an important means of embedding the right corporate culture within an organisation. An example of this is the emphasis placed on senior management oversight of financial crime compliance in the statutory guidance on adequate procedures under the Bribery Act 2010 and in regulatory initiatives such as the Senior Managers and Certification Regime (SMCR) in the context of regulated financial services firms. The principles behind SMCR in terms of their focus on improving the culture, governance and accountability of senior individuals and their awareness of conduct issues across the organisation are, arguably, of relevance to directors of all companies to some extent.

It is notable, however, that the codified general duties of directors and the proper performance by the directors of their duties remain a cornerstone of company law and good corporate governance.

The increased focus from a corporate governance perspective on the duty of directors under CA 2006 s.172, including the requirement for large companies to include in their strategic report a s.172(1) Statement (see Section 3.7 above), is likely to be a continuing area of development and focus. In this regard, there is a clear emphasis by the Government on the need for greater transparency from directors, in particular, on matters such as how, when setting and applying their dividend policy or making other capital allocation decisions, they have had regard to the long term implications and the interests of stakeholders generally.

In October 2018, the Government published the response to its consultation on "Insolvency and Corporate Governance" of March 2018. The consultation's focus was to explore ways to reduce the risk of major corporate failures occurring through poor governance or stewardship, and to improve the insolvency framework in such situations. It explored a number of wider issues that can be particularly relevant when companies get into financial difficulties, including the role and duties of directors. In its response, the Government acknowledges, amongst other things, the GC100 Guidance 2018 as a helpful new resource for directors and commits to bringing forward further proposals to strengthen access to training and guidance for directors, tailored to different sizes of company. The Government also indicates that it will consider whether some level of training should be mandatory for directors of all large companies.

Chapter 4

Potential Liabilities

Elliot Shear

Managing Director

W Legal Limited

4.1 Introduction

It is the very essence of English company law that a limited company is a separate legal entity from its shareholders—and yet it acts through persons appointed as directors. Directors are responsible for the day-to-day running of the company and for making decisions on the management of the company's business and control of its assets and yet their acts or omissions ordinarily expose the company to liability rather than the directors personally.

However, directors boast a complex and contrasting variety of characteristics—and these ensure that there are still circumstances in which directors may be personally liable to third parties for their acts or omissions as directors. These characteristics include the fact that a director is an agent of the company; however, unlike any other agent, a director determines how his principal (the company) acts. Also, a director is similar to a trustee in the sense that a director owes the company fiduciary duties in the same way a trustee owes duties to the beneficiaries of a trust (however, a director does not hold property like a trustee because, unlike a trust, the company can own and hold its own assets). A director is an officer, but not necessarily an employee, of the company. Finally, although generally directors are appointed as such, a person who acts as a director without ever being appointed as one (a shadow director or de facto director) can be subject to the same duties and liabilities as a validly appointed director.

Whether on a contractual, tortious or criminal basis; based on statute, various rules or miscellaneous codes; or in the potential minefield of a liquidation, directors must remain vigilant to protect their own personal position as directors, as well as fulfilling all of their duties to the company. While most of English company law is based on the obligations, responsibilities and potential liabilities faced by the company itself, this chapter makes clear that there are a host of specific areas where personal liability for directors is a real issue. These include very precise areas of contract law, as well as more general areas of tort and criminal law.

Directors of public companies are faced with an abundance of further potential personal liabilities—particularly where the company is listed.

Finally, directors need to note that not all of their conduct can be subsequently ratified by shareholders and that the circumstances in which their personal liability can be indemnified by the company are strictly limited. Consequently, the areas in which a director can be personally liable are likely to be far more extensive than many, even highly risk-averse, directors are aware.

4.2 Liability for exceeding authority

A director's authority is generally derived from both the company's articles of association and the express or implied terms of their service contract. They have authority to carry out expressly or impliedly authorised acts and their authority extends to any subordinate acts that are necessary, or reasonably incidental, to carrying out the authorised acts. The management of the company is generally entrusted to the directors through the articles. Although the articles are not automatically binding between a company and its officers, they may be expressly or impliedly incorporated into the contract between the company and a director.[1]

Other sources of a director's authority could include effective resolutions of the company or particular classes of shareholders and shareholders' agreements. A director's authority may also be implied by the particular office or job to which the director is appointed.[2] Finally, the director can derive authority from the subsequent ratification of their acts (discussed in Section 4.8 below).

Third parties who deal with directors acting in excess of their authority are protected by Companies Act 2006 (CA 2006) s.40(1) which provides that:

> "… [i]n favour of a person dealing with a company in good faith, the power of the directors to bind the company, or authorise others to do so, is deemed to be free of any limitation under the company's constitution."

These include limitations that derive from a resolution of the company, or class of shareholders, and from any agreement between the members of the company or of any class of shareholders.

In order to take advantage of CA 2006 s.40(1), third parties will not have to investigate whether the director was authorised to bind the company, or to

---

[1] *Globalink Telecommunications Ltd v Wilmbury Ltd* [2002] EWHC 1988 (QB); [2002] B.C.C. 958; [2003] 1 B.C.L.C. 145.
[2] *Hely-Hutchinson v Brayhead Ltd* [1968] 1 Q.B. 549; [1967] 3 W.L.R. 1408; (1967) 111 S.J. 830.

authorise others to bind it.[3] In addition, there is a presumption that the third party will be acting in good faith unless the contrary is proved. The presumption is further strengthened by a provision that an act will not be regarded as being in bad faith simply because the third party knows the act is beyond the powers of the director under the company's constitution. These provisions provide strong protection for third parties transacting with companies through their directors.

Directors who exceed their actual authority expose themselves to personal liability, as well as potentially being vulnerable to a derivative claim by a minority shareholder of the company.[4] They may be liable for breach of fiduciary duty and therefore liable to indemnify the company against any losses incurred by it in consequence of the transaction entered into. If the parties to the transaction include a director of the company or of its holding company, or a person connected with any such director, the transaction will be voidable at the instance of the company. The director, or any persons associated with him, may be liable to account to the company for any gain he has made directly or indirectly by the transaction and may be required to indemnify the company for any loss or damage resulting from the transaction.

4.3　Personal liability to shareholders

The relationship between shareholders and the company is generally regulated by the articles of association—and with the directors as the "thinking minds" of the company, this creates a duty for directors to protect the members' interests. The articles effectively act as a contract, and so shareholders can technically sue if their membership rights are infringed by the company, or in fact, the directors. Ultimately, the limited liability inherent to the company will make such a suit challenging to bring and a more likely route for a shareholder action against a director, personally, is the derivative action under CA 2006.

A derivative action is one where the shareholder's right of action is not personal to that shareholder but instead it is derived from the company's right of action, but the company has not exercised it.

Derivative actions against directors personally will require a cause of action arising from a director (or shadow director) acting in a manner involving negligence, default, breach of duty or committing a tort. This area of law is dealt with more fully in Section 10.3 of this book.

3　CA 2006 s.40(2)(b)(i).
4　CA 2006 s.40(4) and (5).

4.4 Potential contractual liability

A director is not generally personally liable for the company's contracts even where the director has signed on the company's behalf. However, there are certain very specific circumstances in which a director should be aware that he may be liable on company contracts.

4.4.1 Pre-incorporation contracts

As companies do not exist prior to their incorporation, pre-incorporation contracts are null and void. Pre-incorporation contracts are unenforceable either by or against the company because the company is not a party to the contract.[5] It is not possible to ratify pre-incorporation contracts because the company had no capacity to make them in the first place.[6]

A director will be personally liable at common law under the pre-incorporation contract if the counterparty can show that although the director ostensibly contracted as an agent of the company, he intended to be a party to the contract himself. The court will examine a range of factors such as how the (future) director signed the contract and the terms of the contract itself. As the only way in which a pre-incorporation contract can be given effect at common law is if the director contracted as a principal, the courts will fairly readily interpret the factual circumstances as having this legal result.[7]

The position, is, however, even stronger under legislation. CA 2006 s.51(1) provides that a director is personally liable if he enters into a pre-incorporation contract, purportedly on behalf of the company, prior to its incorporation. The terms of the section will apply even if all parties to the contract knew that the company had not been formed at the date of the contract.[8] The section applies "subject to any agreement to the contrary". This allows for the possibility of the pre-incorporation contract being novated to the company once it is formed.[9] If the director is personally liable, he can sue as well as be sued on the pre-incorporation contract.[10]

---

5   *Newborne v Sensolid (Great Britain) Ltd* [1954] 1 Q.B. 45; [1953] 2 W.L.R. 596; (1953) 97 S.J. 209.
6   *Kelner v Baxter* (1866–67) L.R. 2 C.P. 174; *Natal Land & Colonization Co Ltd v Pauline Colliery and Development Syndicate Ltd* [1904] A.C. 120.
7   *Newborne v Sensolid (Great Britain) Ltd* [1954] 1 Q.B. 45; [1953] 2 W.L.R. 596; (1953) 97 S.J. 209.
8   *Phonogram Ltd v Lane* [1982] Q.B. 938; [1981] 3 W.L.R. 736; [1981] Com. L.R. 228.
9   *Howard v Patent Ivory Manufacturing Co* (1888) 38 Ch. D. 156.
10 *Braymist Ltd v Wise Finance Co Ltd* [2002] EWCA Civ 127; [2002] Ch. 273; [2002] 1 B.C.L.C. 415.

4.4.2 Pre-trading certificate contracts

A private company may transact business as soon as it is incorporated, but a company that was registered as a public company when it was originally incorporated is not permitted to transact any business or exercise any borrowing powers until it has either been issued with a "trading certificate" by the registrar under CA 2006 s.761(1) or re-registered as a private company.

The consequence of transacting or borrowing without a trading certificate is that the company and the defaulting officer will be guilty of a criminal offence under CA 2006 s.767(2). The defaulting officer will either be liable to a fine on indictment or to a fine not exceeding the statutory maximum on summary conviction.

If the company enters into a transaction without a trading certificate, the transaction will remain valid.[11] However, if the company fails to comply with its obligations under the transaction within 21 days from being called upon to do so, the directors of the company are jointly and severally liable to indemnify the other party to the transaction in respect of any loss or damage suffered by him by reason of the company's failure to comply with those obligations. The directors who will be liable are those who were directors at the time the company entered into the transaction.

4.4.3 Contracts without proper disclosure of company details

Under CA 2006, provisions regarding the disclosure and display of a company's name are largely dealt with in the Company, Limited Liability Partnership and Business (Names and Trading Disclosures) Regulations 2015 (the 2015 Regulations)[12] which revoked and replaced the Companies (Trading Disclosures) (Amendment) Regulations 2009,[13] in force from October 2009 and, previously, the Companies (Trading Disclosures) Regulations 2008,[14] which came into force on 1 October 2008.

Where a company is seeking to enforce a contract that does not comply with the 2015 Regulations, those proceedings will be dismissed if the defendant can show that company has breached the 2015 Regulations or the defendant has otherwise suffered some loss as a result of the breach.

CA 2006 s.84 sets out the criminal consequences of any breach and provides that the company and any defaulting officer are guilty of an offence and are

---

[11] Companies Act 2006 s.767(3). At common law, a contract entered into in such a case where the trading certificate was never granted did not bind the company and was unenforceable against it (*Otto Electrical Manufacturing Co (1905) Ltd (Jenkins' Claim), Re* [1906] 2 Ch. 390).

[12] Company, Limited Liability Partnership and Business (Names and Trading Disclosures) Regulations 2015 (SI 2015/17).

[13] Companies (Trading Disclosures) (Amendment) Regulations 2009 (SI 2009/218).

[14] Companies (Trading Disclosures) Regulations 2008 (SI 2008/495).

liable to a fine on summary conviction not exceeding Level 3 on the standard scale and, in the event of a continued contravention, a daily fine not exceeding one-tenth of Level 3 on the standard scale.

The 2015 Regulations require a company to disclose its registered name in characters that can be read with the naked eye in or on all:

(a)   business letters, notices and other official publications of the company;
(b)   bills of exchange, promissory notes, endorsements and order forms;
(c)   cheques purporting to be signed by or on behalf of the company;
(d)   orders for money, goods or services purporting to be signed by or on behalf of the company;
(e)   bills of parcels, invoices and other demands for payment, receipts and letters of credit;
(f)   applications for licences to carry on a trade or activity;
(g)   all other forms of its business correspondence and documentation; and
(h)   its websites,

with additional specified particulars to appear on a company's business letters, order forms and web sites, including the company's registered number, registered office address and details of its paid up share capital (if any).[15]

Historically, the trading disclosures provision has been strictly enforced by the courts. Its object is to protect persons who deal with the company in ignorance of the fact that they are dealing with an entity with limited liability.[16] However, its scope has been extended by the courts to include not only those cases in which the words indicating the company's limited liability status are omitted but to cases where the word "limited" appeared but the company's name has been misstated by the omission of a word,[17] where the words in the company's name are transposed[18] and where

---

[15]   Company, Limited Liability Partnership and Business (Names and Trading Disclosures) Regulations 2015 (SI 2015/17) Pt 6 reg.25.
[16]   *Elizabeth Penrose v John Martyr* 120 E.R. 595; (1858) El. Bl. & El. 499; *Atkin v Wardle* (1889) 5 T.L.R. 734; *British Airways Board v Parish* [1979] 2 Lloyd's Rep. 361; (1979) 123 S.J. 319; *Blum v OCP Repartition SA* (1988) 4 B.C.C. 771; [1988] B.C.L.C. 170; [1988] P.C.C. 416.
[17]   *Hendon v Adelman* (1973) 117 S.J. 631, *LR Agencies Ltd rather than L & R Agencies Ltd*; *Barber & Nicholls Ltd v R & G Associates Ltd* (1981) 132 N.L.J. 1076, "(London)" omitted from the company name "R and G Associates (London) Limited". The abbreviations "Co" and "Ltd" are acceptable substitutes for "company" and "limited" respectively (*Banque de l'Indochine et de Suez SA v Euroseas Group Finance Co Ltd* [1981] 3 All E.R. 198; [1981] Com. L.R. 77 and *Stacey & Co Ltd v Wallis* (1912) 106 L.T. 544). Other abbreviations may be accepted where the abbreviation is one generally accepted and where no other word is similarly abbreviated— not, e.g. where "M" was substituted for "Michael" in the name "Michael Jackson (Fancy Goods) Limited" (*Durham Fancy Goods Ltd v Michael Jackson (Fancy Goods) Ltd* [1968] 2 Q.B. 839; [1968] 3 W.L.R. 225; [1968] 2 Lloyd's Rep. 98).
[18]   *Atkin v Wardle* (1889) 61 L.T. 23 (the company name, "South Shields Salt Water Baths Company Ltd", misstated as "Salt Water Baths Company Ltd, South Shields" and "South Shields Water Baths Company").

additional words have been added to the name.[19] By contrast, misspelling a company's name will not amount to a breach of the section provided that no danger of confusion arises from this.[20]

CA 2006 s.85 provides that minor variations in the company's name are not to be taken into account. Thus, no account is to be taken of whether: upper or lower case characters (or a combination of the two) are used; whether diacritical marks or punctuation are present or absent; or whether the name is in the same format or style as is specified under CA 2006 s.57(1)(b) for the purposes of registration, provided there is no real likelihood of names differing only in those respects being taken to be different names.

4.5 Potential tortious liability

4.5.1 Negligent acts and omissions of the company

In the majority of cases, a company's directors will not be responsible for the company's negligence, or other tortious acts or omissions, simply because they are officers of, and direct, the company.[21] This is the case even where the company is small and the director necessarily has a lot of power over its affairs; and also where the director is the sole director and shareholder of the company.[22] English law is mindful to preserve the principle that the company is separate and distinct in law from its directors, shareholders and officers and should therefore enjoy the benefit of limited liability.

> "Commercial enterprise and adventure is not to be discouraged by subjecting a director to such onerous potential liabilities."[23]

English law will, however, attach liability to the director where he has effectively made the tortious conduct his own, as opposed to the company's. Where it is sought to make a director liable for his company's tort, there will be a careful examination of the role personally played by the director in respect of the act complained of. A director will be liable with the company as a joint tortfeasor if:

---

[19] *Nassau Steam Press v Tyler* (1894) 70 L.T. 376, "Old Paris and Bastille Syndicate Ltd" rather than "Bastille Syndicate Ltd".

[20] e.g. "Primkeen" rather than "Primekeen" (*Jenice Ltd v Dan* [1994] B.C.C. 43; [1993] B.C.L.C. 1349).

[21] *Rainham Chemical Works Ltd (In Liquidation) v Belvedere Fish Guano Co Ltd* [1921] 2 A.C. 465 at 476.

[22] *British Thomson-Houston Co Ltd v Sterling Accessories Ltd* (1924) 41 R.P.C. 311, referred to in *C Evans & Son Ltd v Spritebrand Ltd* [1983] Q.B. 310; (1985) 1 B.C.C. 99316; [1985] 1 W.L.R. 317 at 325.

[23] *PLG Research Ltd v Ardon International Ltd* [1993] F.S.R. 197 at 238.

(a)   the director authorises, orders, directs or procures the commission of the tort; or

(b)   the director assumes responsibility for the negligent act or omission.

A director would not be treated as liable with the company as a joint tortfeasor if he did no more than carry out his constitutional role in the governance of the company.[24]

4.5.1.1   *Authorise, order, direct or procure*

If a director personally commits a tort, he will, of course, be liable for it and cannot escape liability merely because he has carried out the tort in the course of his duties as a director of a company.[25] Equally, if a director forms a company for the express purpose of doing a wrongful act, or expressly directs that the company do a wrongful act, the director will be individually responsible.[26]

However, for the director to be liable for his company's tort, express direction is not a necessity. A lesser form of control can attract liability. A director may be personally liable if he directs or procures the commission of a negligent act. The direction and procurement can be either express or implied.[27]

The question of what kind of participation in the act of the company will give rise to personal liability on the part of the director has been described as "an elusive question".[28] It will involve a careful examination of the personal involvement of the director and may raise difficult questions of degree about whether a director had ordered or procured the relevant acts to be done. Broad policy considerations may also be taken into account in deciding whether the conduct is of such a nature as to make the director personally liable.[29]

Although express and implied direction and procurement may attract personal liability, a director who merely "facilitates" a tort is not personally responsible for it. His conduct must at least amount to conduct that would render him liable as a joint tortfeasor if the company had not existed.[30] For

---

[24]   *Deakin v Card Rax Ltd (In Administration)* [2011] EWPCC 3 at [289].

[25]   *C Evans & Son Ltd v Spritebrand Ltd* [1985] 1 W.L.R. 317 at 323.

[26]   *Rainham Chemical Works Ltd (In Liquidation) v Belvedere Fish Guano Co Ltd* [1921] 2 A.C. 465.

[27]   *Performing Right Society Ltd v Ciryl Theatrical Syndicate Ltd* [1924] 1 K.B. 1 at 14–15, quoted in *C Evans & Son Ltd v Spritebrand Ltd* [1985] 1 W.L.R. 317 at 328.

[28]   *Mentmore Manufacturing Co Ltd v National Merchandising Manufacturing Co Inc* (1978) 89 D.L.R. (3d) 195 referred to in *C Evans & Son Ltd v Spritebrand Ltd* [1985] 1 W.L.R. 317 at 325–326.

[29]   *C Evans & Son Ltd v Spritebrand Ltd* [1985] 1 W.L.R. 317 at 330. See *Mancetter Developments v Garmanson and Givertz* [1986] Q.B. 1212; [1986] 2 W.L.R. 871; [1986] 1 All E.R. 449 and *AP Besson Ltd v Fulleon Ltd* [1986] F.S.R. 319 for examples of cases where directors have been found liable as joint tortfeasors.

[30]   *PLG Research Ltd v Ardon International Ltd* [1993] F.S.R. 197 at 238–239.

example, selling materials for the purpose of infringing a patent to the man who is going to infringe it, even knowing that the buyer is going to do so, may not amount to procuring a tort.

A director may be made jointly liable for a company's torts regardless of his state of mind. It may not be necessary for the director to know or have been reckless as to whether his acts were likely to be tortious.[31] The exception is where a particular mental state would be an element of the tort. If the claimant has to prove a particular state of mind or knowledge on the part of the defendant as a necessary element of the tort alleged, the state of mind of the director will be relevant. However, it is not a precondition of liability that there be a "knowing, deliberate, wilful quality" to the director's actions in order for liability to attach.[32]

4.5.1.2 *Assumption of responsibility for the negligent act or omission*

A director will be jointly liable with the company where he assumes responsibility to the victim, expressly or by implication, for the act or omission that constitutes the tort.[33] This will usually require the director to put himself into a special relationship with the victim, for example, writing letters or issuing invoices suggesting that the director, rather than the company, was personally answerable for the services owed in the particular circumstances.[34]

4.5.2 *Negligent misrepresentation*

A company may become liable in tort for negligent statements[35] for the economic loss suffered by a claimant on *Hedley Byrne* principles, namely where the company creates a special relationship with the claimant by assuming responsibility towards him, for example, by giving advice to the claimant in a professional capacity in the knowledge that that advice will be reasonably relied on.[36] The assumption of responsibility principle extends beyond the making of statements to the provision of services. In order to establish a cause of action the claimant will need to show that he relied on the assumption of responsibility by the company. In considering what amounts to an assumption of responsibility, the courts will apply an objective test. The primary focus is not on what the defendant thought or intended personally, but on whether what he said or did in his dealings

---

[31] *C Evans & Son Ltd v Spritebrand Ltd* [1985] 1 W.L.R. 317 at 329–330. This is at least the case in relation to infringements of Copyright Act 1956 s.1(2).

[32] *C Evans & Son Ltd v Spritebrand Ltd* [1985] 1 W.L.R. 317 at 330.

[33] *Fairline Shipping Corp v Adamson* [1975] Q.B. 180; [1974] 2 W.L.R. 824; [1974] 1 Lloyd's Rep. 133.

[34] See also *Yuille v B&B Fisheries (Leigh) Ltd, The Radiant* [1958] 2 Lloyd's Rep. 596 at 619–620.

[35] Even where there is a contractual duty in the same respect.

[36] *Hedley Byrne & Co Ltd v Heller and Partners Ltd* [1964] A.C. 465; [1963] 3 W.L.R. 101; [1963] 1 Lloyd's Rep. 485.

with the claimant as judged in the relevant context, means that the defendant assumed responsibility towards the claimant for the advice or services.

It is possible for a director to be personally liable in respect of a company's negligent misrepresentations or services. As with other forms of tortious conduct, a director will not be personally liable for negligent misrepresentations just because he is an officer of the company. In a small company, the director will almost inevitably have qualities and skills that are core to the advice or services offered by the company but that does not mean that the director will have assumed personal responsibility to the customers of the company. A director's personal liability will arise where the director, or someone on his behalf, conveyed, directly or indirectly, to the claimant that the director assumed personal responsibility towards him. In deciding whether a director has assumed responsibility to the claimant, the courts will investigate the oral and written exchanges between the director and the claimant to see whether they "cross the line". The claimant will also have to establish reliance as a matter of fact and it must have been reasonable for the claimant to have relied on an assumption of personal responsibility by the individual director. It is not sufficient for the company to have a special relationship with the claimant. There must have been an assumption of responsibility that creates a special relationship with the director himself.

4.5.3 Statutory liability

Misrepresentation Act 1967 s.2(2) provides that where a person has entered into a contract after a misrepresentation made to him otherwise than fraudulently, and he would be entitled to rescind that contract, then the court may award damages in lieu of rescission if it appears to the court that it would be equitable to do so. Subject to the exclusion and related exception inserted by the Consumer Protection (Amendment) Regulations 2014,[37] damages may be recovered under Misrepresentation Act 1967 s.2(3).

4.5.4 Fraudulent misrepresentation

The elements of the tort of deceit will be satisfied where a person makes a false representation to another person intending that they be induced to act on it and they do in fact rely on it, as a result of which they change their position to their detriment.[38] The representation may be oral, in writing or arise by implication from words or conduct. The representor must know or believe the representation to be untrue, or be careless, reckless, or indifferent as to its truth. Based on these principles, a director responsible for a prospectus (for example) will be liable in the tort of deceit if he signs or authorises the issue of a prospectus knowing or believing it to contain a

---

[37] Consumer Protection (Amendment) Regulations 2014 (SI 2014/870).
[38] See per *Derry v Peek* (1889) 14 App. Cas. 337.

false statement for the purpose of inducing the claimant to take up shares which the claimant does, and then subsequently suffers loss as a consequence.[39] The company will also be liable in respect of the director's act if it is within the scope of his authority but the director's liability remains. The claimant can combine the claim for deceit with a claim for statutory relief (e.g. under the Financial Services and Markets Act 2000 (FSMA) s.90) and a claim against the company for rescission,[40] although generally relief is either by way of damages or rescission.

The principles that apply to the assessment of damages payable where the claimant has been induced by a fraudulent misrepresentation to buy property are set out in the judgment of Lord Browne-Wilkinson in *Smith New Court Securities Ltd v Scrimgeour Vickers (Asset Management) Ltd*.[41] They are that the defendant is bound to make reparation for all the damage flowing directly from the transaction, even if not foreseeable, although it must have been directly caused by the transaction. The claimant is entitled to recover the full price paid by him but must give credit for any benefits received as a result of the transaction, which generally include the market value of the property at the date of acquisition, unless the application of this rule would prevent full compensation. The general rule will usually not apply where the misrepresentation has continued to operate after acquisition and has induced the claimant to retain the asset or if the claimant is by reason of the fraud locked into the property. The claimant is also entitled to recover consequential losses caused by the transaction. The usual principle of mitigation applies. Lord Browne-Wilkinson considered that it would be an over-elaboration to cross-check the computation by comparing what the value of the business would have been if the misrepresentation had not been true with the value of the contract price. This approach to the measure of damages can be contrasted with the law of negligence where the claimant's entitlement to recover losses will depend on what was foreseeable by reference to the scope of the duty owed by the defendant.

4.5.5 Misstatements in company reporting

Theoretically, a director can be liable for misstatements in the company's accounts. However, it would be unlikely to result in liability for investment decisions because the element of reliance in the tort of deceit would be difficult to establish. This is because (unlike with a selling document like a prospectus) there is no intention to induce reliance in respect of securities trading. A similar difficulty arises in relation to negligent misstatements in the company's accounts. Based on the principles in *Caparo Industries Plc v*

---

[39] *Andrews v Mockford* [1896] 1 Q.B. 372; cf. *Peek v Gurney* (1873) L.R. 6 HL 377; [1861–1873] All E.R. Rep. 116; also *Al Nakib Investments (Jersey) Ltd v Longcroft* [1990] 1 W.L.R. 1390; [1990] 3 All E.R. 321; [1990] B.C.C. 517.

[40] *Frankenburg v Great Horseless Carriage Co* [1900] 1 Q.B. 504.

[41] *Smith New Court Securities Ltd v Scrimgeour Vickers (Asset Management) Ltd* [1997] 4 A.C. 254.

Dickman,[42] there is no general duty of care owed to shareholders who rely on the company's statutory accounts to make investment decisions. This is because the purpose of the statutory accounts is to assist shareholders to exercise their corporate governance rights. Following the implementation of the Transparency Directive, concerns were raised that the distinction drawn in *Caparo* between corporate governance rights and investment decisions might be undermined in relation to company reporting required by the Transparency Directive because the Directive focuses on (and is indeed "animated by" the objective of) investor protection. Subsequently, the Government enacted FSMA s.90A to deal with these concerns.

FSMA s.90A creates a statutory liability scheme in relation to all disclosures made by a listed company through a recognised information service. FSMA s.90A creates a liability on listed issuers for fraudulent or reckless misstatements or from omissions amounting to a dishonest concealment of a material fact. From 1 October 2010, the liability under FSMA s.90A is extended to dishonest delays in publishing information, pursuant to amendments made by the Financial Services and Markets Act 2000 (Liability of Issuers) Regulations 2010.[43]

Holders, as well as acquirers and sellers, of securities may rely on s.90A. The section does not require issuers to intend acquirers to rely on the reported information and in that sense is broader in scope than the tort of deceit. It is a requirement that the investor must have reasonably relied on the information. Although the section does not extend liability to directors, directors may still be liable to the company in negligence. CA 2006 s.463 excludes directors from liability for negligence in relation to the directors' report and directors' remuneration report (and summary financial statements derived from them). However, it does not excuse directors where they know that the statement is untrue or misleading or are reckless as to those matters, or where directors know that an omission was a dishonest concealment of a material fact.

4.6 Potential criminal liability

Apart from crimes of strict liability, a person will only be convicted of a crime if he has committed the elements that constitute the crime, including the requisite state of mind, or mens rea. Accordingly, a director may be criminally liable in respect of any criminal acts of a company if the requisite mens rea can be proved against him individually. For example, a director may be guilty of conspiring with, or aiding and abetting, a company to commit a wrong.

---

[42] *Caparo Industries Plc v Dickman* [1990] 2 A.C. 605; [1990] 2 W.L.R. 358; [1990] 1 All E.R. 568.
[43] Financial Services and Markets Act 2000 (Liability of Issuers) Regulations 2010 (SI 2010/1192).

Legislation may make it an offence for a director of a company to enable the company to commit an offence in some way. Any number of formulations may be used. Common examples are formulations that make directors liable if they "cause or knowingly permit" the commission of an offence by a company, or if the offence occurred with the director's "consent or connivance" or as a result of his "neglect". In each case, the requisite conduct and mental element will need to be independently proven against the director.

Further, companies are obliged to comply with judgments and orders of the court and undertakings given by them to the court. RSC Order 45 r.5(1) Civil Procedure Rules relevantly provides that:

> "... [w]here a person required by a judgment or order to do an act within a time specified in the judgment or order refuses or neglects to do it ... or a person disobeys a judgment or order requiring him to abstain from doing an act, then, subject to the provisions of these rules, the judgment or order may be enforced by one or more of the following means, that is to say ... where that person is a body corporate, with the permission of the court, a writ of sequestration against the property of any director or other officer of the body; subject to the provisions of the Debtors Act 1869 and 1878, an order of committal against that person or, where that person is a body corporate, against any such officer."

In spite of the broad words of the rule, the courts will not make an order for committal for contempt against a director merely because he holds office and has knowledge of the order. An order for committal can only be made against an officer of a company where he can be shown to be in contempt[44] or where he is responsible for the company's breach of the order or judgment, whether by his actions or wilful failure to ensure the company's compliance with its obligations.[45] Directors cannot, however, be passive in the face of orders made, or undertakings given, restraining a company from doing certain acts. A director who is aware of the terms of such an order or undertaking is under a duty to take reasonable care to secure the company's compliance with it. Even if the director has not participated in the company's breach, he will be exposed to committal for contempt if the company breaches the order in circumstances where the director wilfully failed to take adequate and continuing steps to ensure that those to whom compliance had been delegated had not misunderstood or overlooked the obligations.[46]

---

[44] *Director General of Fair Trading v Buckland* [1990] 1 W.L.R. 920; [1990] 1 All E.R. 545; (1989) 5 B.C.C. 817.

[45] *British Concrete Pipe Association's Agreement, Re* [1982] I.C.R. 182 at 195.

[46] *Att-Gen of Tuvalu v Philatelic Distribution Corp Ltd* [1990] 1 W.L.R. 926; [1990] B.C.C. 30; [1990] B.C.L.C. 245.

4.7 Liability under the Bribery Act 2010

The Bribery Act 2010 came into force on 1 July 2011. The Act introduced a strict liability offence for companies that fail to prevent their employees giving bribes and further requires directors to ensure there are "adequate procedures" in place to prevent bribery in order to avoid personal criminal liability. Overseas companies will be caught by the Act if they carry on their business in the UK. The scope of this legislation was unprecedented in the UK making a director or an entire board far more likely to find themselves on the hook, personally, for a corrupt employee or third party. It is important to note that it is very difficult for directors to plead innocence where a company has committed a bribery offence—as the minds of the company, it is hard to separate directors from the corporate entity in order to avoid liability. Directors can also be found guilty even where the company is not.

Under s.14 of the Act the definition of who is a Senior Officer and can be personally liable for bribery is broad. It encompasses "… a director, manager, secretary or other similar officer …". Under the section, a senior officer can be personally liable if the organisation commits the offence of bribing, receiving a bribe or bribing a foreign public official if two conditions are met:

(a)   the senior officer must have a close connection with the UK. Broadly this means that he/she must be a UK citizen or ordinarily resident in the UK; and

(b)   the senior officer must have consented or connived in the bribery.

The Act created four principal offences, one of which is a corporate offence, which may be committed by a company and its directors. The two general offences relate to the paying and receiving of bribes, the latter is an offence which cannot be committed by a company but is purely a case of personal liability by the offender. In relation to paying bribes, it will be an offence to offer or give a financial or other advantage with the intention of inducing that person to perform a "relevant function or activity" "improperly" or to reward that person for doing so. With regards to receiving bribes, it will be a personal offence to receive a financial or other advantage intending that a "relevant function or activity" should be performed "improperly" as a result. A "relevant function or activity" includes any function that is of a public nature and any activity that is connected with a business. The individual who performs that activity must be expected to perform it in good faith or impartially or be in a position of trust.

An "improper performance" will be judged by whether it breaches the expectation of what a reasonable person in the UK would expect, in relation to the performance of the type of function or activity concerned. However, neither the function nor activity needs to have a connection to the UK.

The third offence is committed when an individual offers or gives a financial or other advantage to a foreign public official with the intention of influencing the foreign public official and obtaining or retaining business, where the foreign public official was neither permitted nor required by written law to be so influenced.

The fourth offence was new under the Act. This offence is committed by commercial organisations and liability can extend to its directors personally. It is committed where a person associated with a relevant commercial organisation (which includes not only employees, but agents, and external third parties) bribes another person (i.e. commits one of the above offences) intending to obtain or retain a business advantage; and the organisation cannot show that it had adequate procedures in place to prevent bribes being given.

All of the offences that were newly introduced by the Act have extra-territorial application. The corporate criminal offence will apply to commercial organisations that have a business presence in the UK (regardless of where the bribe is given or whether the procedures are controlled from the UK). With regards to directors, it will be a criminal offence to give, promise, or offer a bribe and to request, agree to receive or accept a bribe. The penalty for failing to comply with this is an unlimited fine for the company and the directors personally. Directors can also be punished with up to ten years' imprisonment.

However, there is a defence available if "adequate procedures" were in place. What constitutes an adequate procedure has not been clarified. However, the UK Government has produced guidance and suggested the following six principles will be sufficient:

(1) appropriate procedures;
(2) top-level commitment from the Board down;
(3) risk assessment;
(4) appropriate due diligence to ascertain which areas need to be looked at;
(5) communication (including training); and
(6) monitoring and review.

Under the Act (ss.1, 2 and 6), "Senior Officers", which includes directors, can be found personally liable for offences committed by their organisations if they are committed with their consent or connivance. A relatively recent example is *Director of the Serious Fraud Office v Mabey Engineering (Holdings) Ltd*,[47] a case which was initiated in the US and pre-dates the Act, in which the engineering group Mabey & Johnson pleaded guilty to breaching UN sanctions by the making of payments to Saddam Hussein's regime in return for contracts with Iraqi organisations and three senior executives were

---

[47] *Director of the Serious Fraud Office v Mabey Engineering (Holdings) Ltd* Unreported 2012.

subsequently convicted of the same offences on the basis of their consent or connivance. This case emphasises that there is in fact no requirement that the company itself be prosecuted, provided the offence can be proved against it. Any prosecution of the relevant senior person would have to establish, to the satisfaction of a jury, that the company had committed the offence in question.

4.8 Potential liabilities when issuing securities

Directors need to be aware of their responsibilities, obligations and potential liabilities as directors in connection with a proposed application for admission of a company's shares to the Official List of the Financial Conduct Authority and to trading on the London Stock Exchange's Main Market for listed securities. Attention should be drawn in particular to the personal liability to which a director may be exposed in relation to the contents of a prospectus prepared in accordance with FSMA, the prospectus rules made under FSMA Pt VI (the Prospectus Rules), the Financial Services Act 2012 (FSA), the Financial Services and Markets Act 2000 (Market Abuse) Regulations 2016[48] and the European Commission's Prospectus Regulation[49] (as amended by the Regulation 2017/1129 of 4 June 2017[50] (some parts of which do not take effect until 21 July 2019)) (the Prospectus Regulation).

It is important to note that some of the requirements in the context of preparing a prospectus have a continuing effect on a company's activities and those of the directors after admission. This applies particularly to the obligations imposed by the FSA Pt 7, which are discussed below.

Under the FSA, personal liability for a prospectus will not extend to an admission document for which a director of a company to be admitted to the AIM Market of the London Stock Exchange will be responsible. However, directors of AIM Market companies will still need to be conscious of their potential criminal liabilities under the financial services regime—and also the contractual and tortious liability they have expressly assumed by means of the responsibility statement they will have entered into.

4.8.1 Requirement for prospectus

FSMA s.85 requires that (unless one of a small number of exceptions apply) a prospectus approved by the FCA be made available to the public before:

---

[48] Financial Services and Markets Act 2000 (Market Abuse) Regulations 2016 (SI 2016/680).

[49] Regulation 809/2004 as regards information contained in prospectuses as well as the format, incorporation by reference and publication of such prospectuses and dissemination of advertisements [2004] OJ L149/3.

[50] Regulation 2017/1129 on the prospectus to be published when securities are offered to the public or admitted to trading on a regulated market [2017] OJ L168/12.

(a)   shares in a UK company are offered to the public in the UK; or
(b)   a request is made for the admission of such shares to trading on the
      London Stock Exchange's Main Market for listed securities.

The prospectus must be produced, approved and published in accordance
with the detailed requirements of FSMA, the Prospectus Rules and the
Prospectus Regulation. The Prospectus Regulation prescribes the detailed
information requirements of the prospectus. The CESR Recommendations
give guidance on the practical interpretation of the Prospectus Regulation.

In addition to those specific requirements, there is a general requirement
under FSMA s.87(2), (3) and (4) that the prospectus contain all information
which is necessary to enable investors to make an informed assessment of
the assets and liabilities, financial position, profits and losses and prospects
of the company and of the rights attaching to the shares to be listed. The
necessary information must be presented in a form which is comprehensible and easy to analyse and having regard to the particular nature of the
shares to be listed and the company.

If, after the date of approval of the prospectus by the FCA and before the
start of trading in the company's shares, there arises or is noted any
significant new factor, material mistake or inaccuracy relating to the
information included in the prospectus, the company must submit a
supplementary prospectus containing details of the new factor, mistake or
inaccuracy to the FCA for its approval. FSMA s.87(4) provides that an
investor who has already agreed to buy or subscribe for the relevant shares
may withdraw his acceptance within two working days after the date of
publication of any such supplementary prospectus.

4.8.2   *Responsibility for prospectus*

The Prospectus Rules set out the persons responsible for a prospectus.
These include the company, each director of the company and also each
person who has accepted (and is stated in the prospectus as having
accepted) responsibility for the whole or any part of it or who has
authorised any part of the prospectus.

Any liability may, therefore, be shared jointly among a number of persons.
The Prospectus Rules do not specify exactly how the liability will be shared
amongst those who are jointly responsible but if, for example, a director
were sued by a disgruntled investor, he could be liable for the full amount
of any loss, although he would be able to claim a right of contribution from
the other persons who are jointly responsible under the Civil Liability
(Contribution) Act 1978.

The Prospectus Regulation requires the prospectus to contain details of those who are responsible for the information contained in it and a responsibility statement to the following effect:

> "The Company and each of the Directors whose names appear on page [ ] of this document accept responsibility for the information contained in this document. The Company and the Directors declare that, having taken all reasonable care to ensure that such is the case, the information contained in this document is to the best of their knowledge in accordance with the facts and contains no omission likely to affect its import."

4.8.3 Civil liability under FSMA

Under FSMA s.90, the persons responsible for a prospectus are liable to pay compensation to any person who acquires shares in the company and who suffers loss in respect of them as a result of any untrue or misleading statement contained in the prospectus or the omission from it of any matter required to be included pursuant to the general duty of disclosure imposed by FSMA s.87.

Liability exists to initial subscribers or purchasers of shares in the context of fundraisings carried out in connection with a prospectus. In addition, although the position is not free from doubt, liability under FSMA probably also exists to persons who buy shares in the market who can demonstrate that their loss resulted from statements in omissions from a prospectus. There is no need to show reliance on the misstatement, provided the loss resulted from it. In broad terms, the measure of compensation will be calculated by comparing the value that the shares would have had if the prospectus had been correct with their actual value.

There are formal defences to this potential liability (and these are set out in FSMA Sch.10), which include the defence that a director will not be liable if, at the time the prospectus was submitted to the FCA, he had made such enquiries as were reasonable and reasonably believed that the particular statement was true and not misleading, or that the matter, the omission of which caused the loss, was properly omitted.

Another defence arises in respect of a statement made by or on the authority of an expert and included in the prospectus with the expert's consent, and where the director reasonably believed, at the time the prospectus was submitted to the FCA, that the expert was competent to make the statement and had consented to its inclusion in the form and context in which it was included, and in either case the director continued in this belief until the shares were acquired; or the shares were acquired before it was reasonably practical to bring a correction to the attention of those likely to acquire them; or before the shares were acquired the director took all reasonable steps to secure that a correction was brought to the attention of persons acquiring shares; or he continued in this belief until after commencement of dealings and the shares were acquired after such a lapse of time that he ought reasonably to be excused from liability.

A director shall also not be liable if the person suffering the loss acquired the shares in question knowing that the statement was false or misleading or knowing of the omitted matter or of the change or new matter.

Finally, even if a director cannot demonstrate reasonable belief in the accuracy of the prospectus at the time it was published, there is still a defence if he can show that:

(a)   before the shares were acquired a correction had been published in a manner calculated to bring it to the attention of potential investors; or

(b)   he took all reasonable steps to secure such publication and reasonably believed that it had taken place before the shares were acquired.

4.8.4   Criminal liability under FSMA and FSA

Financial Services Act 2012 (FSA) s.89 imposes potential criminal liability on a director. It provides that a person is guilty of an offence punishable by imprisonment and/or a fine if he:

(a)   makes a statement, promise or forecast which he knows to be misleading, false or deceptive in a material particular; or

(b)   dishonestly conceals any material facts; or

(c)   recklessly makes (dishonestly or otherwise) a statement, promise or forecast which is misleading, false or deceptive in a material particular.

A director would also be guilty of an offence if he does any of the above for the purposes of inducing, or is reckless as to whether it may induce, another person (whether or not the person to whom the statement, promise or forecast is made) to enter or offer to enter into, or to refrain from entering or offering to enter into, an investment agreement (which, broadly speaking, includes an agreement to buy, sell or underwrite shares). Recklessness in this context means either not caring whether a statement is true or closing one's eyes to the possibility that it may be false. The wording is sufficiently wide to include misstatements in or dishonest concealment of material facts from a prospectus.

FSA s.89 also provides that a person is guilty of an offence punishable by imprisonment and/or a fine if he does any act or engages in any course of conduct which creates a false or misleading impression as to the market in or the price or value of any investments, if he does so for the purpose of creating that impression and of thereby inducing another person to acquire, dispose of, subscribe for or underwrite those investments or to refrain from doing so or to exercise, or refrain from exercising, any rights conferred by those investments.

It is a defence for the person concerned to prove that he reasonably believed that his act or conduct would not create an impression that was false or misleading as to the matters mentioned above.

The maximum period of imprisonment for conviction of an offence under FSA s.89 is six months in the case of a summary conviction and seven years in the case of conviction on indictment. Fines on summary conviction are subject to the statutory maximum from time to time, but on indictment are not subject to any limit.

It is also an offence (under FSA s.89) for a person to provide information to the FSA which he knows to be, or to provide information recklessly which is, false or misleading in a material particular, in connection with an application for admission to the Official List or for approval of a prospectus or otherwise in purported compliance with any other requirement imposed by or under the FSA (which would include the Listing Rules, Prospectus Rules and Disclosure and Transparency Rules). Fines may be imposed for breach of this section.

FSA s.90 also creates an offence where a person gives a misleading impression as to the market in or the price or value of any relevant investments and has an intention to mislead the market.

Under the old Financial Services Market Act (FSMA) s.400, a director, member of the committee of management, chief executive, manager, secretary or similar officer of the company, or a person purporting to act in any such capacity, could also be guilty of an offence (punishable with imprisonment and/or a fine) committed by the company under FSMA if it is found to have been committed with his consent or connivance, or to be attributable to any neglect on his part. This has been extended to offences under the FSA (by virtue of an amendment in the same).

4.8.5   *Other criminal liability*

Under Theft Act 1968 s.19, a director is liable to imprisonment if he publishes or concurs in publishing a written statement or account (which includes a prospectus) which to his knowledge is or may be misleading, false or deceptive in a material particular, with the intent to deceive shareholders or creditors.

It is an offence under Fraud Act 2006 s.2 to make a false representation (by words or conduct as to any fact, law or state of mind of any person) whether express or implied either: knowing that the representation is false or misleading, or being aware that it might be. The victim of the representation need not actually rely upon it. A false representation in a prospectus could therefore lead to a criminal fraud charge if accompanied by the appropriate guilty intent.

It is an offence under Fraud Act 2006 s.3 to fail to disclose information where there is a legal duty to do so (e.g. statutory, contractual, custom from a trade or market, or a fiduciary relationship). Those who fail to make full disclosure pursuant to legal obligations will therefore be at risk from prosecution. This could include a deliberate failure to make disclosures in a prospectus in breach of the FSMA or Prospectus Rules requirements.

4.8.6 Other civil liability

4.8.6.1 Negligent misstatement

Where a director has been negligent in making a statement contained in the prospectus he may be liable under a claim for damages brought by a claimant who has suffered loss through acting in reliance on that statement.

This liability is reinforced by the inclusion of the responsibility statement in the prospectus. On the face of it this statement establishes a duty of care by the directors to persons who rely on statements in the prospectus and who suffer loss, where the loss was a reasonably foreseeable consequence of the negligent misstatement. Although the position is not free from doubt, case law has established that it is at least arguable that the duty of care extends to persons who buy shares in the market (i.e. it extends beyond persons who buy shares in a fundraising carried out on the admission of a company's shares to the Official List).[51]

4.8.6.2 Deceit

If a director has been fraudulent in misrepresenting facts stated (including a misleading omission) in the prospectus by making a statement either with knowledge of its falsity or being reckless as to whether it is true or false, he could be liable for damages to a shareholder or purchaser deceived by it. The measure of damages in an action for deceit is the actual damage suffered by the claimant.

A director will not be liable in an action for deceit if he can prove that he held an honest belief in the facts stated even though his belief was not based on reasonable grounds. He may not be liable if he can prove that the person suing him was not in fact misled by the statement. It is, however, no defence to the director that the claimant might easily have ascertained that the statement was untrue by independent enquiry.

---

[51] *Possfund Custodian Trustee Ltd v Diamond* [1996] 1 W.L.R. 1351; [1996] 2 B.C.L.C. 665.

4.8.6.3   *Contract and the Misrepresentation Act 1967*

If a prospectus contains an untrue or misleading statement or if there is an omission which renders any statement in the prospectus misleading, a person suffering loss from subscribing for or purchasing shares may have a remedy under the Misrepresentation Act 1967 which provides the remedies of rescission of the contract and/or damages.

In connection with an admission of a company's shares, the company will enter into an agreement with the financial adviser acting as its sponsor. Under that agreement the company will give to the sponsor certain warranties and indemnities. The warranties and indemnities from the company to the sponsor will relate to the accuracy and completeness of financial and other information concerning the group as contained in the prospectus and compliance by the company with other relevant legal requirements, including the Companies Act, FSMA, the Listing Rules, the Prospectus Rules, the Disclosure and Transparency Rules, the Admission and Disclosure Standards and the Prospectus Regulation.

If an action were to be brought against the sponsor by purchasers of the company's shares, the sponsor would rely on the warranties and indemnities given by the company and, in the event of a breach of warranty, would institute action against the company in relation to loss suffered by the sponsor as a result of any such claim. This is rare in practice but if such a claim was successful, the company may have a claim in turn against the directors.

4.8.6.4   *Duty of care*

The directors also owe to the company at common law a duty to exercise reasonable care and skill in the performance of their duties. If a breach of this duty results in a misstatement in the prospectus and the company is required whether under statute or at common law to compensate third parties who rely on the misstatement, the company may be able to recover its loss from the directors.

4.9   Potential Takeover Code liabilities

The City Code on Takeovers and Mergers (the Code) imposes another layer of responsibilities on all members of the board of directors of a public company involved in a takeover, in addition to their statutory and other responsibilities outlined in this Chapter. In the context of a takeover situation directors will need, in particular, to have regard to their duties under the CA 2006 to exercise independent judgment, to avoid conflicts of interest or duty, not to accept benefits from third parties, and to declare interests in proposed transactions or arrangements with the company.

Directors on the board of a target who are involved in a management buy-out, or who will remain involved with the business after completion of the takeover, will need to have particular regard to these statutory duties as well as their duties under the Code.

As the Code has a statutory footing, directors need to be even more aware of their responsibilities under the Code. The Panel on Takeovers and Mergers (the Panel) is the supervisory authority that polices the Code and the conduct of takeovers, and has certain statutory powers of enforcement under the CA 2006. For example, the Panel can ask the court to enforce compliance with its rulings (CA 2006 s.955) or require the payment of compensation to shareholders where there has been a breach of specific rules of the Code that deal with the offer price to be paid to target shareholders (CA 2006 s.954 and para.10(c) "Introduction to the Code").

It is a general principle of the Code that directors should act in the interests of the company as a whole and ensure, so far as they are reasonably able, that the Code is complied with in the conduct of an offer. The Code requires the target board to give its opinion on the offer to all target shareholders; however, the duties of the target directors in giving their views cannot always be easily reconciled with their general duty to promote the success of the company. In general, directors do not owe any duty to shareholders directly. However, in the context of a takeover some duties are owed directly to shareholders, particularly when it comes to deciding whether or not to recommend the offer to them. In summary, directors must not mislead shareholders and must form an honest opinion on the merits of the offer.

The Panel has accepted that the responsibility for supervising and monitoring an offer can rest with a committee of the board of a company. Nevertheless, every member of the board of directors will be required to accept responsibility for each document issued in connection with an offer and the individual responsibility of each director is not removed by delegation to a committee. This principle is emphasised in guidance notes on the responsibility of all the directors of a company during the course of an offer contained in Appendix 3 to the Code. Arrangements should, therefore, be made to ensure, among other things, that the entire board is provided promptly with copies of all documents and announcements issued by or on behalf of a company involved in a takeover which bear on the offer and that each director receives promptly details of other relevant matters.

Rule 19.1 of the Code creates a requirement for documents, advertisements or statements made in connection with a takeover to satisfy the highest standard of accuracy and to present information adequately and fairly. Rule 19.2 provides that each document (subject to certain exceptions found in r.19) issued to shareholders or advertisement published in connection with an offer must state that the directors of the bidder (and where appropriate the target) accept responsibility for the information contained in the document or advertisement for which they are responsible and that, to the best of their knowledge and belief (having taken all reasonable care to ensure that such is the case), the information contained in the document or advertisement is in accordance with the facts and, where appropriate, that it does not omit anything likely to affect the import of such information.

The notes to r.19.2 contain guidance on the application of the rule and expressly state that a responsibility statement extends to expressions of opinion as well as of fact. The inclusion of a responsibility statement in a takeover document (including a scheme document) or advertisement could expose the directors to a civil action in tort if he has failed to take reasonable care. For this reason alone no such document should be dispatched or issued unless each director has confirmed in writing that he or she accepts responsibility in terms of the responsibility statement contained in the document. The responsibilities which directors have as regards the standards of care and accuracy required in the preparation of documents and announcements under the Code are in addition to those responsibilities contained in statute and common law.

Directors will need to be particularly alive to CA 2006 s.953, which creates offences in relation to offer and response documents prepared in relation to takeover bids. If an offer document published in respect of the bid does not comply with the document offer rules then the person making the bid will commit an offence. Where the person making the bid is a body of persons (i.e. a board of directors) that body who caused the document to be published will be liable for committing the offence. Directors will only be liable if they knew that the offer document did not comply, or were reckless as to whether it complied, and failed to take all reasonable steps to ensure that it did comply. Directors may be liable on conviction on indictment to a fine or, on summary conviction, to a fine not exceeding the statutory maximum.

4.10 Ratification

The CA 2006 does not codify the common law on ratification of directors' breaches, and the common law restrictions on ratification are preserved by s.239(7).

Not all conduct by directors is capable of ratification by shareholders, but the law on which types of breach of duty are capable of ratification is unclear and the cases are difficult to reconcile. However, it is clear that shareholders cannot ratify (or authorise) breaches of duty which are fraudulent or are outside the powers of the company. On the other hand, it appears that an act which is merely negligent is ratifiable, even when it causes loss to the company. It also appears that if the directors exercised their powers in good faith but for improper purposes, that is also ratifiable.

Section 239 provides that ratification by a company of conduct by a director amounting to negligence, default, breach of duty or breach of trust in relation to the company must be by resolution of the members (s.239(1) and (2)).

Section 239(3) and (4) also sets out new requirements as to who can vote on a resolution to ratify a director's conduct. Section 239(3) provides that where the ratification resolution is proposed as a written resolution, the director himself (if a member) and any person connected with him are not eligible to vote on it. At a meeting where a resolution to ratify the conduct of a director is to be proposed, votes in favour of the resolution cast by the director concerned (if a member) and the votes of any member connected with him must be disregarded in determining whether the resolution is passed. The director and any member connected with him can still attend the meeting and be counted in the quorum (see CA 2006 s.239(4)). The definition of "connected person" for the purpose of s.239 is modified by s.239(5) and may also include other directors. However, nothing in s.239 affects the validity of a decision taken by unanimous consent of the members of the company, or any power of the directors to agree not to sue, or to settle or release, a claim made by them on behalf of the company (s.239(6)).

These new requirements mark a significant change from the position under the common law. The position is different when giving authorisation to directors before they take a particular action. In that case, the director concerned and any connected persons are not excluded and their votes will be counted.

4.11 Indemnity and insurance against liability

CA 2006 s.232 sets out the basic prohibition on provisions (in service agreements, letters of appointment, the articles of association or elsewhere) protecting directors from liability in connection with any negligence, default, breach of duty or breach of trust in relation to the company. Any provision that purports to exempt the director of a company (to any extent) from such liability is void (see s.232(1)) and any provision by which a company directly or indirectly provides an indemnity (to any extent) for a director of the company, or of an associated company, against such liability in relation to the company of which he is a director is void (see s.232(2)).

There are certain exceptions to the basic prohibition: the provision of insurance, qualifying third-party indemnity provisions (QTPIPs) and qualifying pension scheme indemnity provisions (QPSIPs).

Section 233 provides that the general prohibition does not prevent a company from purchasing and maintaining for a director of the company, or of an associated company, insurance against negligence, default, breach of duty or breach of trust in relation to the company.

Section 234 sets out what constitutes a QTPIP. A third-party indemnity provision is a provision for indemnity against liability incurred by the director to a person other than the company or an associated company. Such a provision will be a QTPIP if the requirements set out in s.234(3) are met:

(a)   the provision must not indemnify the director against any liability to pay a fine imposed in criminal proceedings or a sum payable to a regulatory authority by way of a penalty in respect of non-compliance with any requirement of a regulatory nature (however arising); and
(b)   the provision must not provide any indemnity against any liability incurred by the director:
  (i)   in defending criminal proceedings in which he is convicted;
  (ii)   in defending civil proceedings brought by the company, or an associated company, in which judgment is given against him; or
  (iii)   in connection with an application for relief in which the court refuses to grant him relief.

Section 234(4) sets out how "conviction", "judgment" and "refusal of relief" are to be interpreted and s.234(5) sets out when the conviction, judgment or refusal are to be interpreted as "final".

The applications for relief caught by s.234(3) are applications under CA 2006 s.661(3) or (4) (power of the court to grant relief in case of acquisition of shares by an innocent nominee) and CA 2006 s.1157 (the general power of the court to grant relief in the case of honest and reasonable conduct).

Section 235 provides that the general prohibition does not apply to QPSIPs. This exemption only applies to directors of a company where the company is a trustee of an occupational pension scheme (i.e. it does not cover directors who themselves are trustees of such schemes). In such circumstances provision may be made to indemnify the director against liability incurred in connection with the company's activity as a corporate trustee of the pension scheme. The permitted indemnity under a QPSIP can be wider than a QTPIP. The provision must not provide any indemnity against any liability of the director to pay a fine imposed in criminal proceedings or a sum payable to a regulatory authority by way of penalty in respect of non-compliance with any requirement of a regulatory nature (however arising). The provision must also not provide any indemnity against any liability incurred by the director in defending criminal proceedings in which he is convicted. Therefore unlike a QTPIP, a QPSIP can cover a director's liability to the pension trustee company itself, or to an associated company incurred in connection with the company's activities as a corporate trustee of the pension scheme.

CA 2006 ss.205 and 206 are also relevant. Generally, companies are prohibited from granting loans to their directors unless the transaction is first approved by a resolution of the members (see s.197). There are exceptions to this general rule. Subject to certain conditions, these exceptions include expenditure for defending proceedings (see s.205) and expenditure in connection with regulatory action or investigations (see s.206).

4.12   Statutory relief

In any proceedings against a director where negligence, default, breach of duty or breach of trust is established, the court may relieve the director of liability, either in whole or in part, if it is satisfied that the director acted honestly and reasonably, and that having regard to all the circumstances of the case, including those connected with his appointment, he ought fairly to be excused.[52] A company is entitled to elect whether to claim damages or an account of profits against a director for breach of his fiduciary duty and CA 2006 s.1157 applies whichever remedy is elected.[53] Section 1157 only applies to proceedings against a director by, on behalf of or for the benefit of his company for breach of his duty to the company as a director. It also applies to penal proceedings for the enforcement of specific duties imposed by the Companies Acts on the company's officers, but it cannot be used against strangers to the company.[54]

The section can be used to excuse a director from liability for negligence.[55] Conduct that is ultra vires the company may also be excused,[56] depending on the circumstances, because the provision is designed to protect honest directors and is "not to be construed in a narrow sense".

Where a director anticipates proceedings he may apply to the court for relief under CA 2006 s.1157(2). If proceedings are already pending, then only the court seised of those proceedings may grant the relief sought.[57]

When exercising its discretion under CA 2006 s.1157, all three requirements of CA 2006 s.1157(1) must be satisfied.[58] The director therefore has the onus of showing that he acted honestly, that he acted reasonably and that having

---

[52] CA 2006 s.1157.
[53] *Coleman Taymar Ltd v Oakes* [2001] 2 B.C.L.C. 749; (2001) 98(35) L.S.G. 32; (2001) 145 S.J.L.B. 209: liability to account being just as much a liability for this purpose as liability to pay damages, per Judge Robert Reid QC at 770.
[54] *Customs and Excise Commissioners v Hedon Alpha Ltd* [1981] Q.B. 818; [1981] 2 W.L.R. 791; [1981] 2 All E.R. 697.
[55] *D'Jan of London Ltd, Re* [1993] B.C.C. 646; [1994] 1 B.C.L.C. 561; *Barings Plc (In Liquidation) v Coopers & Lybrand (No.8)* [2003] EWHC 2371 (Ch); [2003] All E.R. (D) 294 (Oct).
[56] *Claridge's Patent Asphalte Co Ltd, Re* [1921] 1 Ch. 543.
[57] *Gilt Edge Safety Glass Ltd, Re* [1940] Ch. 495; [1940] 2 All E.R. 237.
[58] *Coleman Taymar Ltd v Oakes* [2001] 2 B.C.L.C. 749.

regard to all the circumstances of the case he ought fairly to be excused. The test imposed by CA 2006 s.1157 is an "essentially" subjective one, requiring an examination of all the circumstances of the case to ascertain whether the director concerned has acted honestly and reasonably and deciding whether on those grounds he ought to be excused. The subjective approach is limited to the "honesty" element of "honestly and reasonably", since reasonableness tests are by nature objective.[59] It follows that the court has no jurisdiction to grant relief from liability under CA 2006 s.1157 where the claim made against the officer involves the application of an objective standard to his behaviour.[60] The standard of reasonableness to be satisfied in the context of CA 2006 s.1157 is that of "a man of affairs dealing with his own affairs with reasonable care and circumspection" in such a case.[61] The question of what is reasonable may be assessed by reference to the company's past conduct.[62] Given the scope of the analysis that has to be undertaken, it is unlikely that an application for relief under CA 2006 s.1157would succeed on a summary judgment application.[63]

4.13 Insolvency

When a company is insolvent or verging on insolvent, the common law requires a shift in its directors' duties, away from shareholders towards creditors and what is in their best interests.[64] This duty is expressly preserved in CA 2006 s.172(3). Directors cannot, for example, cause an insolvent company to enter into an agreement to repay shareholders' debts or make distributions to shareholders out of the company's profits if this effectively amounts to a winding up of the company and an attempt to distribute the company's assets without proper provisions for all the creditors.[65] From the case law, it is not clear exactly when this shift in duty from shareholders to the creditors first occurs. In practice, it is both prudent and typical for directors to assume that the shift first occurs at around the time that the company first becomes unable to pay its debts by reference to the tests set out in Insolvency Act 1986 (IA 1986) s.123. Under IA 1986 s.123, a company is deemed to be unable to pay its debts if:

---

[59] *Coleman Taymar Ltd v Oakes* [2001] 2 B.C.L.C. 749.
[60] *Produce Marketing Consortium Ltd (In Liquidation) (No.1), Re* [1989] 1 W.L.R. 745; [1989] 3 All E.R. 1; (1989) 5 B.C.C. 399.
[61] *Duomatic Ltd, Re* [1969] 2 W.L.R. 114; (1968) 112 S.J. 922; [1969] 2 Ch. 365 at 377, per Buckley J.
[62] *Duomatic Ltd, Re* [1969] 2 Ch. 365 at 375 and 170, per Buckley J.
[63] *Equitable Life Assurance Society v Bowley* [2003] EWHC 2263 (Comm); [2003] B.C.C. 829; [2004] 1 B.C.L.C. 180.
[64] *Liquidator of West Mercia Safetywear Ltd v Dodd* (1988) 4 B.C.C. 30; [1988] B.C.L.C. 250; [1988] P.C.C. 212; *Kinsela v Russell Kinsela Pty Ltd* (1986) 4 N.S.W.L.R. 722; *MDA Investment Management Ltd (No.1), Re* [2003] EWHC 2277 (Ch); [2005] B.C.C. 783; [2004] 1 B.C.L.C. 217 at [70].
[65] *MacPherson v European Strategic Bureau Ltd* [2002] B.C.C. 39; [2000] 2 B.C.L.C. 683; (2000) 97(35) L.S.G. 36.

(a)   the company fails, within three weeks after its service on it, to pay or settle a statutory demand (a form of written demand for sums over £750);

(b)   execution or other process issued on a court judgment or order obtained against the company, is returned unsatisfied in whole or in part;

(c)   the company is unable to pay its debts as they fall due and this is proved to the court's satisfaction. This is commonly referred to as the cash-flow insolvency test; or

(d)   the value of the company's assets is less than the amount of its liabilities, taking into account its contingent and prospective liabilities, and this is proved to the court's satisfaction. This is commonly referred to as the balance sheet insolvency test.

The duty to act in the best interests of creditors is owed to the company, but in the event of a formal insolvency it is enforceable by the company's liquidator.[66] If the duty is not properly discharged and this causes creditors to suffer loss, a subsequently appointed liquidator can bring a claim against any culpable director to compensate the company's estate for the loss. IA 1986 s.212 provides a mechanism for bringing this kind of claim, as explained in more detail below.

A number of other potential causes of action against directors can arise where a company is insolvent and it enters into a formal insolvency process under IA 1986. These are summarised below as well.

4.13.1   *Personal Guarantees*

The directors of a company are generally not personally liable for the debts of a company. However, if a director has given a personal guarantee for the liabilities of the company, that director may be personally liable under the terms of the guarantee.

4.13.2   *Misfeasance*

In the course of winding up a company, the liquidator or any affected creditor, or with permission of the court, any contributory, may bring an action against a person who is or has been a director of the company who has "misapplied or retained, or become accountable for, any money or other property of the company, or been guilty of any misfeasance or breach of any fiduciary or other duty in relation to the company".[67]

This captures a wide range of conduct. By way of example, the breach of "fiduciary or other" duty could include a breach of the director's duty to

---

[66]   *Horsley & Weight, Re* [1982] Ch. 442; [1982] 3 W.L.R. 431; [1982] 3 All E.R. 1045.

[67]   IA 1986 s.212(1).

the company to act in the best interests of the company's creditors when the company was insolvent by reference to the tests set out above. The "other" duty may include negligence,[68] but it does not extend to all cases in which the company has a right of action against the officer of a company. It is limited to cases where there has been something in the nature of a breach of duty by an officer of the company and does not include a claim for repayment of an ordinary debt.[69] For example, a claim was brought against a director for the sum of the company's unpaid VAT in the months before liquidation.[70] In addition, the liquidator can only sue in respect of a cause of action vested in the company.[71]

The director may be examined and if found liable, the court may order the director personally to restore the company to its former position or otherwise compensate it for the consequences of his misconduct.[72] The remedy under IA 1986 s.212 is discretionary[73] such that the court may award a lower damages sum than that required to remedy the misfeasance in full.[74] The court also has a discretion where remedies sought go beyond those available at common law.[75] The court may relieve a director from liability under IA 1986 s.212 where the provisions of CA 2006 s.1157 apply, that is, where it appears to the court that the director acted honestly and reasonably and ought fairly to be excused.[76]

Although the shareholders can ratify breaches of duty by the directors where the company is solvent, if the breach occurs when the company is insolvent or becomes so as the result of the breach, the ratification will be ineffective.

It is well established that IA 1986 s.212 does not create new liabilities. It merely provides a simpler procedure for the recovery of property or compensation in a winding up. Sums or property recovered under IA 1986 s.212 are the product of a chose in action vested in the company prior to the liquidation and are accordingly considered to be assets of the company which are capable of being made the subject of a charge[77] or of being assigned by the company or the liquidator.[78] This contrasts with the proceeds of contribution orders against directors for fraudulent or wrongful

---

68 *Kyrris v Oldham* [2003] EWCA Civ 1506; [2004] B.C.C. 111; [2004] 1 B.C.L.C. 305.
69 *Etic Ltd, Re* [1928] Ch. 861.
70 *E D Games Ltd, Re* [2009] EWHC 223 (Ch).
71 *Ambrose Lake Tin & Copper Mining Co Ex p. Moss, Re* (1880) 14 Ch. D 390.
72 IA 1986 s.212(3).
73 *Westlowe Storage and Distribution Ltd (In Liquidation), Re* [2000] B.C.C. 851; [2000] 2 B.C.L.C. 590.
74 *Inland Revenue Commissioners v Richmond* [2003] EWHC 999 (Ch); [2003] S.T.C. 1394; [2003] 2 B.C.L.C. 442.
75 *Continental Assurance Co of London Plc (In Liquidation), Re* [2007] 2 B.C.L.C. 287; [2001] B.P.I.R. 733.
76 *Westlowe Storage and Distribution Ltd (In Liquidation), Re* [2000] B.C.C. 851; [2000] 2 B.C.L.C. 590.
77 *Anglo-Austrian Printing & Publishing Union (No.3), Re* [1895] 2 Ch. 891.
78 *International Championship Management Ltd, Re* [2006] EWHC 768 (Ch).

trading which are held for creditors but not as assets of the company. They are not, therefore, capable of being made the subject of a charge or of being assigned by the company.

4.13.3 Fraudulent trading

Directors are exposed to both civil and criminal liability for fraudulent trading.

Civil liability can arise under IA 1986 s.213, if in the course of the winding up of the company, it appears that any business of the company has been carried on to defraud its creditors, to defraud creditors of any other person, or for any fraudulent purpose.[79] This provision only applies if the company goes into liquidation.

On the application of the liquidator, the court may declare any person, including a director, knowingly party to the carrying on of business in this way liable to contribute to the company's assets as it thinks proper.[80]

The first element of IA 1986 s.213 requires the court to be satisfied that there was an intention to defraud creditors. This requires actual dishonesty on the part of the defendant.[81] The test for intention to defraud is subjective,[82] although the standard of dishonesty will be what reasonable and honest people consider to be dishonest, provided that the defendant realised that by those standards his conduct was in fact dishonest.[83]

The second element of 1986 s.213 IA requires the defendant to have participated in carrying on the business with intent to defraud. The defendant will not be liable for fraudulent acts of the company in which he did not participate; they are irrelevant to the claim against him.[84] However, the concept of participation is widely construed.[85] A defendant may be liable under the section even if a single creditor was defrauded by a single transaction, provided that the transaction could properly be described as a fraud on a creditor in the course of carrying on business.[86] Participation requires some form of positive act; passivity is not sufficient. There are circumstances in which a transaction that is dishonest will not amount to carrying on of the business for that purpose.[87] The phrase "carrying on business" does not require active trading and may include the collection of

---

[79] IA 1986 s.213(1).
[80] IA 1986 s.213(2).
[81] *Augustus Barnett & Son Ltd, Re* [1986] P.C.C. 167; [1986] 2 B.C.C. 98904 at 98907.
[82] *Bernasconi v Nicholas Bennett & Co* [2000] B.C.C. 921; [2000] B.P.I.R. 8; [2000] Lloyd's Rep. P.N. 285.
[83] *Twinsectra Ltd v Yardley* [2002] UKHL 12; [2002] 2 A.C. 164; [2002] 2 W.L.R. 802.
[84] *Bank of Credit and Commerce International SA (In Liquidation) (No.13), Re* [1999] B.C.C. 943.
[85] *Augustus Barnett & Son Ltd, Re* [1986] P.C.C. 167; [1986] 2 B.C.C. 98904.
[86] *Gerald Cooper Chemicals Ltd, Re* [1978] Ch. 262; [1978] 2 W.L.R. 866; [1978] 2 All E.R. 49.
[87] *Gerald Cooper Chemicals Ltd, Re* [1978] Ch. 262.

assets and distribution of their proceeds to discharge liabilities of the company.[88] A person who performs certain duties to the company, such as a secretary, may not be found to be "concerned in carrying on the business of the company" by performing the duties appropriate to their office and so may avoid liability.[89] The knowledge of a particular person in an organisation may be attributed to the board so rendering the company liable to a claim for fraudulent trading. This will happen where a company delegates sufficient authority to that person, such as giving them the ultimate decision-making power in respect of a transaction.[90]

The contribution that the defendant may be required to make should reflect and compensate for the loss which has been caused to creditors by the carrying on of the business in the fraudulent manner. Although under the predecessor law it was held appropriate to include a punitive as well as a compensatory element in the court's order, this is no longer the case.[91] To the extent that Parliament intended a punitive element, this is to be found in the criminal sanctions for fraudulent trading under CA 1986 s.993 (see below). Where two or more individuals are found liable under IA 1986 s.213, their respective liability is not automatically joint and several. Instead, a court can apportion liability on the basis of the degree of control each defendant had over the affairs of the company and the extent to which each defendant benefited from the fraud. This is similar to the approach taken in the context of wrongful trading—see below.[92] Any contribution payable by the director will be held for the benefit of its creditors generally rather than any particular creditor.

Criminal liability for fraudulent trading can arise under CA 2006 s.993 if a director knowingly carries on the business of a company with intent to defraud creditors of the company or for any other fraudulent purpose.[93] Unlike the civil sanctions under IA 1986 s.213, this applies whether or not the company is in the process of being wound up.[94]

The court will not construe the words "or any fraudulent purpose" as applying only to creditors. The section is wide and is intended to protect against "fraudulent trading and not fraudulent trading just in so far as it affects creditors".[95] Dishonesty is a necessary element of fraudulent trading and the same general standard of dishonesty applies as for criminal cases.[96]

---

[88] *Sarflax Ltd, Re* [1979] Ch. 592; [1979] 2 W.L.R. 202; [1979] 1 All E.R. 529.
[89] *Maidstone Building Provisions, Re* [1971] 1 W.L.R. 1085; [1971] 3 All E.R. 363; (1971) 115 S.J. 464.
[90] *Morris v Bank of India* [2005] EWCA Civ 693; [2005] B.C.C. 739; [2005] 2 B.C.L.C. 328.
[91] *Morphitis v Bernasconi* [2003] EWCA Civ 289; [2003] Ch. 552; [2003] 2 W.L.R. 1521.
[92] *Continental Assurance Co of London Plc (In Liquidation), Re* [2007] 2 B.C.L.C. 287; [2001] B.P.I.R. 733.
[93] CA 2006 s.993(1).
[94] CA 2006 s.993(2).
[95] *R. v Kemp (Peter David Glanville)* [1988] Q.B. 645; [1988] 2 W.L.R. 975; (1988) 4 B.C.C. 203.
[96] *R. v Lockwood* [1986] 2 B.C.C. 99333; [1986] Crim. L.R. 244.

The penalties for fraudulent trading are severe. CA 2006 s.993 provides that a person is liable to imprisonment or a fine, or both.[97] The punishment will depend on whether the conviction for fraudulent trading is summary or on indictment. A person who is guilty of fraudulent trading on conviction on indictment is liable to an imprisonment term not exceeding ten years or an unspecified fine (or both).[98] A person who is summarily convicted of fraudulent trading in England and Wales is liable to imprisonment for a maximum of 12 months or a fine (or both).[99] In Scotland and Northern Ireland, the period of imprisonment is slightly shorter, being six months.[100]

In addition to the civil and criminal sanctions above, a person who is declared to have traded fraudulently, or found guilty of fraudulent trading, may be made the subject of a disqualification order under Companies Directors Disqualification Act 1986 (CDDA 1986) ss.4 and 10. The maximum period of disqualification is 15 years.

4.13.4 *Wrongful trading*

Wrongful trading under IA 1986 s.214 was introduced as a mechanism for providing a civil remedy against directors whose mismanagement of the company had caused loss to creditors. An important difference between fraudulent and wrongful trading is that the basis of liability for wrongful trading is more akin to negligence than to dishonesty.[101]

Where a director knew or ought to have concluded that there was no reasonable prospect of the company avoiding an insolvent liquidation (the wrongful trading point) and he did not take every step available to him to minimise the potential loss to the company's creditors,[102] the court can require the director to contribute to the company's assets as it thinks proper.[103] These wrongful trading provisions only apply if the company goes into insolvent liquidation[104] and only the company's liquidator can bring the action.

Only persons who are or have been directors of the company are exposed to claims for wrongful trading. This can include shadow directors[105] and de facto directors.[106] This potentially brings a number of outsiders within the ambit of IA 1986 s.214: for example, turnaround specialists, lending banks,

---

[97] CA 2006 s.993(3).
[98] CA 2006 s.993(3)(a).
[99] CA 2006 s.993(3)(b)(i).
[100] CA 2006 s.993(3)(b)(ii).
[101] *Morris v Bank of India* [2005] EWCA Civ 693; [2005] B.C.C. 739; [2005] 2 B.C.L.C. 328.
[102] IA 1986 ss.214(2) and 214(3).
[103] IA 1986 s.214(1).
[104] IA 1986 s.214(2).
[105] IA 1986 s.214(7).
[106] *Hydrodan (Corby) Ltd (In Liquidation), Re* [1994] B.C.C. 161; [1994] 2 B.C.L.C. 180.

and parent companies, where they have exercised sufficient influence for them to be considered a shadow or de facto director.[107]

IA 1986 s.214(7) expressly states that shadow directors are treated as directors for the purpose of the wrongful trading provisions. A shadow director is someone in accordance with whose directions or instructions the directors of the company are accustomed to act.[108] A person is not to be regarded as a shadow director by reason only of providing advice in a professional capacity.[109]

A de facto director is a person who acts as a director without having been validly appointed. A de facto director can also be caught by the wrongful trading provisions.[110] In determining whether a person is caught, the crucial issue is whether that person has assumed the status and functions of a company director so as to make himself responsible as if he were a de jure director. Where there is a de jure corporate director of the insolvent company, a person who acts as de jure director of that corporate director would not automatically be considered a de facto director of the insolvent company simply by virtue of mere performance by him of his duties as a de jure director of the corporate director.[111] Something more will be required. The degree of control which the director of the corporate director exercised over that company would be relevant as would shareholder control of the corporate director.[112] It will not be sufficient to constitute someone as a director on the basis that he was in a position to control the actions of a company notwithstanding that he did not actually exercise the powers pertinent to his position.[113]

In addition, the section almost certainly extends to foreign directors, resident abroad, of a foreign company being wound up in England and Wales under the IA 1986.[114] A claim may also be made against the estate of a deceased director[115]

The director is judged on the basis of what he knew or ought to have known, the conclusions he should have reached and the steps he should have taken, as against a reasonably diligent person having both:

(a)   his general knowledge, skill and experience; and
(b)   the general knowledge, skill and experience that might be reasonably expected of someone carrying out the same functions as he did.

---

[107] *Tasbian Ltd (No.3), Re* [1992] B.C.C. 358.
[108] IA 1986 s.251 and CA 2006 s.251.
[109] CA 2006 s.251(2).
[110] *Tasbian Ltd (No.3), Re* [1992] B.C.C. 358.
[111] *Revenue and Customs Commissioners v Holland* [2009] EWCA Civ 625; [2010] Bus. L.R. 259; [2009] S.T.C. 1639.
[112] *Secretary of State for Trade and Industry v Hall* [2006] EWHC 1995 (Ch); [2009] B.C.C. 190.
[113] *Secretary of State for Trade and Industry v Hall* [2006] EWHC 1995 (Ch).
[114] *Howard Holdings Inc, Re* [1998] B.C.C. 549.
[115] *Sherborne Associates Ltd, Re* [1995] B.C.C. 40.

This is a combined objective and subjective test. It is objective in the sense that the director must exercise the general knowledge, skill and experience that a reasonable director would. Thus an inexperienced director cannot escape liability on the basis that he personally did not realise the company could not avoid insolvency in circumstances where a reasonable director would have done so.[116] The subjective part of the test takes into account the particular skills of the director in question. These particular skills are in addition to the skill set that the reasonable director is meant to have. So if a director has particular financial expertise that means he would have been aware of the unavoidable insolvency at an earlier point in time than a director who did not have that expertise, he will be held to the higher standard. A non-executive director is not expected to possess the same skill set as an executive director.[117]

In *D'Jan of London Ltd, Re*, the court held that the test set out in IA 1986 s.214(4) encapsulates the duty of directors at common law.[118] That position is also reflected in CA 2006 s.174, which codifies a director's duty to exercise reasonable care, skill and diligence in *D'Jan, Re* terms.

The knowledge to be imputed to a director in testing whether or not he knew or ought to have concluded that there was no reasonable prospect of the company avoiding insolvent liquidation is not limited to the documentary material actually available at the given time. The words "ought to know or ascertain", indicate that facts which, given reasonable diligence and an appropriate level of general knowledge, skill and experience, are capable of being ascertained, must be included.[119]

The steps that are required to minimise the potential loss to creditors so as to avoid liability in any particular case will depend on all the circumstances of that case at the relevant time. In deciding whether the steps taken were sufficient, the same objective and subjective standards discussed above will be applied. What is unlikely ever to be appropriate once the wrongful trading point has been reached, is for the director to simply ignore the situation and continue as normal, or to continue trading with some distant (unrealistic) hope that fortunes might change. If a director has in fact done all he can to minimise potential loss to creditors then he will not be liable for wrongful trading.

There is little guidance as to how any contribution order should be calculated. The cases decided so far indicate that it should be compensatory rather than penal, calculated with reference to the amount of the company's

---

[116] *Purpoint Ltd, Re* [1991] B.C.C. 121; [1991] B.C.L.C. 491.
[117] *Equitable Life Assurance Society v Bowley* [2003] EWHC 2263 (Comm); [2003] B.C.C. 829; [2004] 1 B.C.L.C. 180.
[118] *D'Jan of London Ltd, Re* [1993] B.C.C. 646.
[119] *Produce Marketing Consortium (In Liquidation) Ltd, Re (No.2)* [1989] 5 B.C.C. 569; [1989] B.C.L.C. 52.

assets that have been depleted by the director's conduct.[120] Loss which could not have been reasonably foreseen as a consequence of continued trading should not be taken into account, nor should loss attributable to other causes which would have been incurred in any event.[121] Where two or more individuals are found liable under IA 1986 s.214, their respective liability is not automatically joint and several—a court can apportion liability between them.[122] Any contribution payable by the director will be held for the benefit of its creditors generally rather than any particular creditor. Accordingly any receipt will not be caught by a charge over the company's assets and it is incapable of assignment.[123]

The defence under CA 2006 s.1157(1), that the director has acted honestly and reasonably and ought fairly to be excused does not apply to a wrongful trading claim as it is inconsistent with the objective standard imposed on the director.[124]

A person who is declared to have traded wrongfully may also be made the subject of a disqualification order under CDDA 1986 s.10. As with a declaration of fraudulent trading, the maximum period of disqualification is 15 years.

Of all the liabilities set out in this section, wrongful trading is likely to be the most difficult problem for directors of a company in financial difficulty, not least because of the imprecision in determining how far directors have to go to avoid liability. It is crucial that regular board meetings are called and that the commercial decisions of the directors are reported in full in the company's minutes.

4.13.5   Re-use of company name on "phoenix company"

IA 1986 s.216 restricts a director of a company that goes into insolvent liquidation from re-using the company's name or a similar name for a period of time following the insolvency of the first company in circumstances where he is a director or otherwise involved in the promotion, formation or management of the second or "new" company. The section is aimed at preventing directors of insolvent companies from simply rolling over the business into a new, undercapitalised company with the same or a similar name, without some protection for creditors who may (mistakenly)

---

[120] *Produce Marketing Consortium (In Liquidation) Ltd, Re (No.2)* [1989] 5 B.C.C. 569; [1989] B.C.L.C. 52 at 597 per Knox J.

[121] *Lexi Holdings Plc (In Administration) v Luqman* [2009] EWCA Civ 117; [2009] B.C.C. 716; [2009] 2 B.C.L.C. 1.

[122] *Continental Assurance Co of London Plc (In Liquidation), Re* [2007] 2 B.C.L.C. 287; [2001] B.P.I.R. 733.

[123] *Oasis Merchandising Services Ltd (In Liquidation), Re* [1998] Ch. 170; [1997] 2 W.L.R. 764; [1997] 1 All E.R. 1009.

[124] *Produce Marketing Consortium (In Liquidation) Ltd, Re (No.2)* [1989] 5 B.C.C. 569; [1989] B.C.L.C. 52.

believe that they are still dealing with the "old" insolvent company when in fact they are dealing with the "new" company.

The section applies to any person who was a director or shadow director of the insolvent company at any time in the period of 12 months before the day on which it went into liquidation. For a period of five years beginning with the day on which the company went into liquidation, any such director or shadow director cannot, except in exempted circumstances:

(a)   be a director of any other company that is known by a prohibited name; or
(b)   in any way, whether directly or indirectly, be concerned or take part in the promotion, formation or management of any company known by a prohibited name; or
(c)   be concerned or take part in the promotion, formation or management, whether directly or indirectly, in any business (not carried on by a company) known by a prohibited name.[125]

A prohibited name is one by which the company in liquidation was known (or by which any business carried on by that company was known) at any time in the period of 12 months before the day on which the company went into liquidation, or is a name so similar so as to suggest an association with that company.[126]

In considering whether the second name is sufficiently similar to the first to suggest an association between the two, the court will examine all the circumstances in which they were actually used or likely to be used, including such matters as the types of product dealt in, the location of the business, the types of customers dealing with the companies and those involved in the operation of the two companies.[127] The test is whether the similarity between the two names is such that it is probable that members of the public, comparing the names in the relevant context, would associate the two companies with each other.[128]

A director whose conduct contravenes IA 1986 s.216 is guilty of an offence and is liable to imprisonment or a fine, or both. In addition, he may be personally liable, jointly and severally with the company and any other person so liable, for the debts of the "new" company known by the prohibited name if he is involved in the "management" of that company, and those debts were incurred at a time when he was so involved.[129] A person does not have to be a director to be held personally liable for debts

---

[125] IA 1986 s.216(3).
[126] IA 1986 s.216(2).
[127] *Ricketts v Ad Valorem Factors Ltd* [2003] EWCA Civ 1706; [2004] B.C.C. 164; [2004] 1 B.C.L.C. 1.
[128] *Revenue and Customs Commissioners v Walsh* [2005] EWCA Civ 1291; [2006] B.C.C. 431.
[129] IA 1986 s.217(1)(a) and s.217(3)(a).

under this section. It is sufficient if he, whether directly or indirectly, takes part in the management of the company.[130]

A director can avoid liability under IA 1986 s.216 by obtaining leave of the court, or, where the new company is acquiring the whole or substantially the whole of the business of the company in liquidation under arrangements with an insolvency practitioner acting as its liquidator, administrator, administrative receiver or supervisor of a company voluntary arrangement, by giving a prescribed notice to creditors.[131]

4.13.6 Other actions

Other possible criminal causes of action against directors of insolvent companies under IA 1986, which are outside of the scope of this chapter, include:

(a) swearing a statutory declaration of solvency without having reasonable grounds for forming the requisite solvency opinion[132];

(b) fraud in anticipation of winding up[133];

(c) transaction(s) in fraud of creditors[134];

(d) misconduct in the course of the winding up[135];

(e) falsification of the company's books[136];

(f) making material omissions from the statement relating to the company's affairs[137]; and

(g) making false representations to creditors.[138]

---

[130] IA 1986 s.217(4).
[131] IA 1986 s.216(3) and Insolvency Rules 1986 (SI 1986/1925) r.4.228.
[132] IA 1986 s.89.
[133] IA 1986 s.206.
[134] IA 1986 s.207.
[135] IA 1986 s.208.
[136] IA 1986 s.209.
[137] IA 1986 s.210.
[138] IA 1986 s.211.

Chapter 5

Fair Dealing and Connected Persons

Stephen Hewes

5.1 Introduction

This Chapter looks at some of the provisions in Companies Act 2006 Pt 10 which deal with fair dealings between a director and their company (or another company in the same group) and between such companies and anyone connected with a director. It does not deal with the various obligations to disclose details of certain transactions or arrangements in the company's accounts. These provisions replaced the provisions of Companies Act 1985 Pt X following a lengthy process of review and consultation.[1] The Enterprise and Regulatory Reform Act 2013 Pt 6 made some further changes as from 1 October 2013, in particular introducing a new Ch.4A of Pt 10 dealing with payments to directors of quoted companies, and as from 10 June 2019 (subject to certain transitional arrangements) certain other changes will be made by the Companies (Directors' Remuneration Policy and Directors' Remuneration Report) Regulations 2019 (the 2019 Regulations).

5.1.1 Companies subject to the provisions

Before looking at various provisions in Pt 10, it is helpful to understand some of the defined terms which are used in those provisions. With the exception of Ch.4A, all of the provisions of Pt 10 apply to a "company". This means a company formed and registered under the Companies Act 2006, the Companies Act 1985, the Companies Acts 1948–1983, the Companies (Northern Ireland) Order 1986 or under certain earlier Acts (see s.1).[2] It includes unlimited companies. In contrast, "body corporate" includes bodies incorporated outside the UK, but not a corporation sole or a partnership that is not regarded as a body corporate under the law by which it is governed (see s.1173).

---

[1]   See Law Commission Consultation Paper No.153 and Law Commission Report No.261. For further background, see the *Consultation Document on Modern Company Law* published by the Company Law Review Steering Group in March 2000 and the *Final Report on Modern Company Law* published by the Company Law Review Steering Group in June 2001.

[2]   In this Chapter, all section references are to the Companies Act 2006 unless otherwise stated.

Chapter 4A currently applies to quoted companies. A quoted company is defined in s.385 and, broadly, is a company (as above) whose equity share capital is listed in the UK or EEA or is admitted to dealing on the New York Stock Exchange or Nasdaq. From 10 June 2019 (subject to transitional arrangements), Ch.4A will also apply to unquoted traded companies. An unquoted traded company is a traded company that is not a quoted company, and a traded company is defined in s.360C as a company any shares of which carry rights to vote at general meetings and are admitted to trading on a regulated market in an EEA State by or with the consent of the company.

5.1.2 Directors and their connected persons

The Pt 10 provisions apply to a "director". This is defined (see s.250) to include any person who occupies the position of director, "by whatever name called". This means that someone whom a company thinks it has appointed as a director is a director even if the appointment proves to be invalid. It also includes someone who acts as a director, even though the company has never appointed them as such. In some cases, it can also include an alternate director. A shadow director is treated as a director for the purposes of the relevant provisions (s.223), although if a person stops being treated as a shadow director this is not treated as a loss of office. A person is a shadow director if the directors of the company are accustomed to act in accordance with that person's directions or instructions. However, a person is not a shadow director just because the directors act on that person's advice given in a professional capacity. Also, a body corporate is not a shadow director of its subsidiaries just because the subsidiaries' directors are accustomed to act in accordance with the holding company's instructions or directions (s.251). Some of the provisions also apply to a person connected with a director. Those who come within this category are set out in s.252. As this is a fairly complicated provision, it is dealt with separately at the end of this Chapter in Section 5.10. For the purposes of the various provisions dealt with in this Chapter, it does not matter what law governs the transaction or arrangement in question (see s.259).

5.1.3 Subsidiaries, holding companies and wholly-owned subsidiaries

Some of the provisions in Pt 10 also relate to subsidiaries, holding companies and subsidiaries of holding companies. Section 1159 (and see s.1160 and Sch.6) sets out the definitions of "subsidiary", "holding company" and "wholly-owned subsidiary". In each case, the definition extends to bodies corporate as well as Companies Act companies and to sub-subsidiaries and holding companies of a holding company. A company is a subsidiary of another (which is therefore the holding company of that subsidiary) if one of three tests is satisfied. The first is if the holding company holds a majority of the voting rights in the subsidiary. The second is if the holding company is a member of the subsidiary and has the right to appoint or remove a majority of the directors. The third test is if the holding company is a member of the subsidiary and controls alone a majority of the voting rights, pursuant to an agreement with other shareholders or members.

5.1.4 Charities

There are particular rules for companies which are charities—see Charities Act 2011 ss.201 and 202. The Charity Commission must give its prior written consent where the members of the company give an approval under ss.190, 197, 198, 200, 201, 203, 217 or 218 and where the members give an affirmation under ss.196 or 214. Without the Commission's prior written consent, the approval or affirmation is ineffective (see Charities Act 2011 s.201). Prior written consent must also be obtained where the company does not need to obtain approval because it is a wholly-owned subsidiary (see Charities Act 2011 s.202). If the company does not obtain prior written approval, it is treated as if the exemption for wholly-owned subsidiaries did not apply.

5.1.5 Where approval is needed under more than one provision

In some cases, approval may be required under more than one section in Ch.4 of Pt 10 of the Act. For example, a director might buy a substantial asset but with the consideration left outstanding as a loan. In such cases, the requirements of each applicable section must be met, although a company can pass one resolution giving all the necessary approvals (see s.225).

5.2 Loss of office and retirement from office

Subject to the alternative regime for quoted companies contained in Ch.4A (see further below), the Companies Act 2006 requires companies to disclose payments to directors for loss of office or as consideration for retiring from office or in connection with their retirement from office. Such payments are unlawful unless they have been disclosed and approved by shareholders:

(a)   s.217 deals with payments by a company for loss of office to a director of the company or a holding company. Payments are prohibited unless they have been approved by the members of the company and, where payment is to a director of a holding company, by the members of the holding company;

(b)   s.218 deals with payments for loss of office made by any person to a director of a company in connection with the transfer of all or any part of the company's undertaking or property or of the undertaking or property of any subsidiary of the company. It prohibits any payments (i.e. not just those made by the company), unless details of the proposed payment (including its amount) are disclosed to members of the company (and each other company whose approval is needed) and the proposal is approved by the members of the company (or, where the transfer is the transfer of all or part of the undertaking or property of a subsidiary, by the members of each of the companies); and

(c) s.219 deals with any payments (again, not just those made by the company) made in connection with a transfer of shares in the company or in a subsidiary of the company, resulting from a takeover bid. A payment is prohibited unless it has been approved by a resolution of the holders of the shares to which the bid relates and any other holders of that class of shares. "Takeover bid" is not defined (the definitions in ss.943(7) and 953(9) only apply for the purposes of those respective sections). Section 219 applies to offers for all companies, whether or not the offer is subject to the City Code on Takeovers and Mergers. If the City Code does also apply, the company will also need to consider rr.21.1 (Restrictions on frustrating action—when share-holders' consent is required) and 25.5 (Offeree board circulars—directors' service contracts), as well as any Listing Rule requirements (see Section 5.6 below).

In each case, the requirement is for approval by way of an ordinary resolution, unless the company's articles of association require a higher majority. In the case of a private company, approval may be given by way of written resolution or a resolution passed at a general meeting, while public companies are not permitted to pass written resolutions and must therefore obtain approval in general meeting.

Companies Act 2006 Pt 10 Ch.4A, which was inserted by the Enterprise and Regulatory Reform Act 2013 (ERRA) as from 1 October 2013 (subject to transitional provisions which are no longer applicable), introduced alter-native requirements for payments to directors of quoted companies, including a requirement that a payment for loss of office to a director (or former director, or someone who is to be a director) of a quoted company cannot be made unless it is consistent with the approved directors' remuneration policy or is approved by resolution of the members passed in general meeting (s.226C). From 10 June 2019 (subject to transitional arrangements), Ch.4A will also be extended to apply to unquoted traded companies, and certain other amendments will be made to Ch.4A, by the 2019 Regulations. These provisions are dealt with in Section 5.2.8 below.

5.2.1 Payment for loss of office

Section 215 sets out a definition of "payment for loss of office" for the purposes of Ch.4 of Pt 10. It catches a payment to a director or past director of a company:

(a)   by way of compensation for loss of office as director of the company;
(b)   by way of compensation for loss of any office or employment in connection with the management of the affairs of the company or any subsidiary undertaking, either while the person is a director of the company or in connection with ceasing to be a director;
(c)   as consideration for, or in connection with, their retirement from office as director of the company; or
(d)   as consideration for, or in connection with, their retirement from any office or employment in connection with the management of the affairs of the company or any subsidiary undertaking, either while the person is a director of the company or in connection with ceasing to be a director.

In *Children's Investment Fund Foundation (UK) v Attorney General*,[3] it was stated that the words "in connection with" in s.215(1) are not to be narrowly construed.

The section makes it clear that compensation and consideration include non-cash benefits (confirming Lord Macfadyen's view in *Mercer v Heart of Midlothian Plc*).[4] It also makes clear that payments to a person connected with a director or to any other person on the direction of the director or a connected person or to another person for the benefit of a director or a connected person are all treated as payments to the director, and so are caught by the requirements. The section also provides that a person cannot avoid the relevant requirements by directing someone else to make a payment or getting someone else to make a payment for them.

Section 215(5), which was inserted by ERRA, makes it clear that nothing in ss.215–222 applies in relation to a payment for loss of office to a director of a quoted company (and, from 10 June 2019, of an unquoted traded company). These provisions therefore essentially now apply only to unquoted companies (and, from 10 June 2019, only to companies that are not traded companies). However, there are two exceptions. First, this is not the case (i.e. in this case ss.215–222 do apply) where s.226C does not apply to a payment by virtue of s.226D(6) (see Section 5.2.8 below). Secondly, this is not the case where Ch.4A does not apply because the payment for loss of office is required to be made under an agreement entered into before 27 June 2012 or in consequence of any other obligation arising before that date (ERRA s.82(5)).

---

[3]   *Children's Investment Fund Foundation (UK) v Attorney General* [2017] EWHC 1379 (Ch). Although the decision in the case was overruled by *Lehtimaki v Children's Investment Fund Foundation (UK)* [2018] EWCA Civ 1605, the relevant point referred to above was not affected by that judgment.
[4]   *Mercer v Heart of Midlothian Plc* 2001 S.L.T. 945; 2001 S.C.L.R. 701; 2001 G.W.D. 19–717.

5.2.2 Exception for payments in discharge of a legal obligation

A company does not need to obtain members' approval for payments which discharge a legal obligation. Section 220 makes it clear that a payment does not need to be approved if it is made in good faith:

(a)   in discharge of an existing legal obligation;
(b)   by way of damages for breach of an existing legal obligation;
(c)   by way of settlement or compromise of any claim arising in connection with the termination of a person's office or employment; or
(d)   by way of pension in respect of past services.

In order to be an "existing legal obligation", the obligation must be an obligation of the company or any body corporate associated with it. In addition, the obligation must not have been entered into in connection with, or in consequence of, the event giving rise to the payment for loss of office, where the company is making a payment for loss of office to a director or to a director of a holding company (i.e. within s.217). Where the company is making a payment for loss of office in connection with the transfer of the company's undertaking or property or in connection with a share transfer resulting from a takeover bid (i.e. within ss.218 or 219), an existing legal obligation means an obligation of the company or a body corporate associated with it that was not entered into for the purposes of, in connection with, or in consequence of, the transfer. If a payment falls within both ss.217 and 218 or within both ss.217 and 219, the test for payments within s.217 applies to determine whether there is an existing legal obligation. If there is a payment only part of which falls within the exception and part of which does not, the payment is treated as if each part is a separate payment.

Section 220 broadly follows the position which applied before the Companies Act 2006 (under which bona fide payment by way of damages for breach of contract or by way of pension for past service was excluded—see Companies Act 1985 s.316(3)). In practice, companies will often be able to rely on the exclusion in s.220 to avoid having to disclose payments and seek shareholder approval. Companies have sometimes been criticised for taking a generous view of what constitutes a bona fide payment by way of damages. In February 2008, the Association of British Insurers (ABI) and National Association of Pension Funds (NAPF) issued a joint statement on Executive Contracts and Severance and the ABI issued guidelines on policies and practices on executive remuneration in December 2009 which also include guidance on severance (the Investment Association Principles of Remuneration, issued in November 2018, still refer to this 2008 guidance). It can often be difficult to agree what reduction is appropriate to reflect the director's chance of finding another directorship. The Law Commission suggested (see Law Commission Consultation Paper

No.153) that directors would have the protection of Companies Act 1985 s.316(3) (which is similar to s.220) if they relied on proper legal advice, even if it were wrong.

Section 220 also reflects the Privy Council case of *Taupo Totara Timber Co v Rowe*,[5] which considered whether New Zealand Companies Act 1955 s.191 (which was identical to Companies Act 1985 s.312, which dealt with payments to a director for loss of office) applied to payments which a company has agreed to make to a director when he retires or loses office, before the retirement or loss of office occurs. The question in that case was whether a provision in the service contract of a managing director, which required the company to pay an amount of money to the director on resignation or dismissal, had to be approved by the company under s.191. The agreement did not fix the amount of the payment and the Privy Council held that s.191 only applied to payments which the company had not previously agreed to pay or which the company did not have a legal obligation to make. Accordingly, no disclosure to members or approval was needed.

The *Taupo Totara* case was followed in a case before the Outer House of the Court of Session, *Lander v Premier Pict Petroleum Ltd.*[6] In that case, Mr Lander, who was a company director, became entitled to a golden parachute payment under the terms of his service agreement if there was a change of control of the company and he gave notice to terminate his employment. He resigned in the circumstances envisaged by the contract, but the company refused to make the payment and argued that the payment was unlawful as it had not been disclosed and approved under Companies Act 1985 s.312. Lord Osborne rejected the company's argument. Following the Privy Council decision, he decided that the sections only apply to proposed payments: that is, that payments which the company was already legally obliged to pay were not covered by the sections. Section 220 reflects the decisions in the *Taupo Totara* case and *Lander v Premier Pict Petroleum Ltd.*

The position is, however, less clear where an obligation to make a payment is entered into shortly before a director loses office. In *Mercer v Heart of Midlothian Plc*, Lord Macfadyen's statements suggested that where a contractual payment was agreed just before resignation in order to ensure that Companies Act 1985 s.312 would not apply, it was not clear that the payment did not need approval. Lord Macfadyen thought it was likely that an agreement which is entered into on the basis that there will be a further period of continuing office would fall to be treated as a covenanted payment and so would fall outside the scope of the section. The position under s.220 is slightly different. The question to be asked is whether the legal obligation is entered into "in connection with, or in consequence of"

---

[5]   *Taupo Totara Timber Co v Rowe* [1978] A.C. 537; [1977] 3 W.L.R. 466; (1977) 121 S.J. 692.
[6]   *Lander v Premier Pict Petroleum Ltd* 1997 S.L.T. 1361; [1998] B.C.C. 248; 1997 G.W.D. 17–759.

the event giving rise to the payment or the transfer. These are wider tests, and so will make it harder for companies to argue that a legal obligation taken on about the time of the event or transfer is not connected and so is exempt from the need for approval.

5.2.3 *Memorandum setting out particulars and approval requirements*

Where a payment needs to be approved, a memorandum setting out particulars of the proposed payment, including its amount, must be made available to the members of the company whose approval is being sought (ss.217(3), 218(3) and 219(3)). If approval is being given by written resolution (in the case of a private company), the memorandum must be sent or submitted to every eligible member at or before the time when the proposed resolution is sent or submitted to them. An accidental failure to send or submit the memorandum to one or more members is disregarded unless the articles provide otherwise (s.224(1)). If approval is being given by passing a resolution at a meeting, the memorandum must be made available for inspection by members at the company's registered office for at least 15 days ending with the date of the meeting and at the meeting itself.

If the approval is for a payment in connection with a share transfer within s.219, if the person making the offer or any associate of that person (as defined in s.988) is a member, they are not entitled to vote on the resolution. If they would otherwise be entitled to do so, they are, however, entitled to receive a copy of any written resolution and to be given notice of the meeting at which the resolution is to be proposed and to attend that meeting, speak and, if present in person or by proxy, count towards the quorum (s.219(4)). Also for payments in connection with a share transfer within s.219, a payment will be deemed to be approved for the purposes of s.219 if a quorum is not present at the meeting and a quorum is again not present at an adjournment of the meeting at a later date (s.219(5)). There is no equivalent provision for payments which need approval under ss.217 or 218.

As explained above, in some cases approval may be required from the members of a holding company or a subsidiary as well as from the company itself. There are some helpful provisions (in ss.217(4), 218(4) and 219(6)) which provide an exception in two cases. The first is that no approval is required if the body corporate is a wholly-owned subsidiary of another body corporate. The second is that no approval is required for a body corporate that is not a UK-registered company: that is, a company registered under the Companies Act 2006 (see s.1158). The effect is broadly that companies incorporated outside the UK are exempt from the need for shareholder approval.

5.2.4   *Exception for small payments*

There is also an exception for small payments which applies to all three sections requiring approval (s.221(1)). A company does not need approval if the company or one of its subsidiaries makes the payment and the amount or value of the payment, together with the amount or value of any other relevant payments, does not exceed £200. What counts as an "other relevant payment" varies depending on whether the payment falls within ss.217, 218 or 219. Where s.217 applies, the "other relevant payments" are payments for loss of office by the company or any of its subsidiaries to the same director in connection with the same event. Where ss.218 or 219 applies, the "other relevant payments" are payments for loss of office paid in connection with the same transfer to the same director by the company or any of its subsidiaries.

5.2.5   *Civil consequences of breach*

The consequences of breaching ss.217–219 vary slightly (s.222). In all three cases, the recipient holds any payment received on trust:

(a)   payments made in contravention of s.217 are held on trust for the company making the payment. Any director who authorised the payment is jointly and severally liable to indemnify the company that made the payment for any loss resulting from it;

(b)   payments made in contravention of s.218 are held on trust for the company whose undertaking or property is being transferred (apparently, even if the payment was made by another person); and

(c)   payments made in contravention of s.219 are held on trust for the persons who have sold their shares as a result of the offer made (again, rather than for the person who made the payment). In addition, the person who receives the payment must bear any expenses they incur in distributing the payment to those shareholders, and cannot deduct them from the payment. There is no guidance as to how the payment is to be divided between the shareholders.

If a payment contravenes ss.217 and 218, only the civil consequences applying to payments which contravene s.218 apply. If a payment contravenes ss.217 and 219, only the civil consequences applying to payments which contravene s.219 apply, unless the court directs otherwise.

5.2.6   *Anti-avoidance provisions*

The sections contain some anti-avoidance provisions. These apply where a director is to cease to hold office or to hold any office or employment in connection with the management of the affairs of the company or any of its subsidiary undertakings in connection with a transfer falling within ss.218 or 219. In such a case, if a director is paid more per share than other

167

shareholders or is given any valuable consideration by someone other than the company in either case in connection with a transfer subject to ss.218 or 219, the excess price or the money value of the consideration is deemed to be a payment for loss of office (s.216).

5.2.7   Relationship with section 190

Section 190(6) makes it clear that a payment for loss of office is not also subject to the requirements in s.190 for substantial property transactions with directors or connected persons (see Section 5.5 below).

5.2.8   Loss of office payments to directors of quoted companies and unquoted traded companies

From 1 October 2013 (subject to transitional provisions which are no longer applicable), a payment for loss of office to a director of a quoted company can only be made if it is consistent with the approved directors' remuneration policy or if the payment is approved by resolution of the members of the company[7] (s.226C). The same is true for payments for loss of office to someone who is to be a director of a quoted company, or to someone who has been a director of a quoted company. The approved directors' remuneration policy is the most recent remuneration policy to have been approved by the members in general meeting. From 10 June 2019, this regime is also extended to unquoted traded companies by the 2019 Regulations, and will apply also to a chief executive officer (howsoever described) and any deputy chief executive officer of a company subject to Ch.4A if such person is not a director anyway.

The definition of a payment for loss of office is extended where a director of a quoted company is to cease to be a director or to hold any other office or employment in connection with the management of the company's affairs or any subsidiary undertakings' affairs. Where this is to happen in connection with the transfer of all or part of the company's undertaking or property or a subsidiary's undertaking or property or a transfer of shares in the company or a subsidiary resulting from a takeover bid, any price paid to the director for shares in the company which is higher than the price other shareholders could have obtained is taken to be a payment for loss of office, as is the money value of any valuable consideration given to the director by someone other than the company in connection with the transfer (s.226A(2),(3) and (4)). A payment by any person at the company's direction or a payment on behalf of the company is treated as a payment by the company (s.226A(6)). Payments to a person connected with a director or to

---

[7]   From when the 2019 Regulations apply to a company, if a payment is proposed to be made that is not consistent with the approved directors' remuneration policy then, rather than the payment itself needing to be approved, an amendment to the policy authorising the payment to be made must have been approved by resolution of the members of the company.

someone at the director's direction or for the director's benefit are caught as are payments to someone at the direction of a person connected with the director or for the benefit of a connected person. References to a director include references to a former director and to a person who is to become a director (s.226A(7)).

The requirements of Ch.4A of Pt 10 do not apply to payments for loss of office required to be made under an agreement entered into before 27 June 2012 or in consequence of any other obligation arising before that date (ERRA s.82(3)). However, if such an agreement or obligation is modified or renewed on or after that date, Ch.4A will apply (ERRA s.82(4)).

Where it is proposed to pass a members' resolution to approve a payment for loss of office, a memorandum setting out particulars of the proposed payment (including the amount) must be made available for inspection by members at the company's registered office for not less than 15 days ending with the date of the meeting. It must also be available at the meeting itself. The company must also make the memorandum available on its website from the first day the memorandum is made available for inspection until the company's next accounts meeting. The memorandum must explain how the proposed payment is inconsistent with the approved directors' remuneration policy. Failure to meet the requirement to make the memorandum available on the company's website does not affect the validity of a resolution approving a payment.

For companies that were quoted companies before 1 October 2013 (the day when ERRA s.79 came into force), s.226C did not apply to a payment for loss of office made before the earlier of: (i) the end of the first financial year of the company to begin on or after 1 October 2013; and (ii) the date from which the company's first directors' remuneration policy approved under s.439A takes effect (ERRA s.82(2)). For other companies, s.226C does not apply before the earlier of: (i) the end of the first financial year of the company to begin on or after it becomes a quoted company[8]; and (ii) the date from which the company's first directors' remuneration policy approved under s.439A takes effect[9] (s.226D(6)). Nothing in s.226C authorises a payment for loss of office that contravenes the company's articles of association (s.226D(5)).

An obligation to make a payment for loss of office which would contravene s.226C has no effect. If a contravening payment is made, the recipient holds the payment on trust for the company or other person making the payment. Any director who authorised the payment is jointly and severally liable to indemnify the company that made the payment for any loss resulting from it. The position is different if a contravening payment for loss of office is

---

[8] Or, from 10 June 2019, an unquoted traded company.
[9] Under the 2019 Regulations, only the second limb will be relevant for an unquoted traded company (unless the company already had a compliant directors' remuneration policy that had been approved by the members of the company before 10 June 2019).

made in connection with the transfer of all or part of the company's undertaking or property or those of a subsidiary. In this case the payment is instead held by the recipient on trust for the company whose undertaking or property is transferred (s.226E(3)). If a contravening payment for loss of office is made in connection with a transfer of shares in the company or a subsidiary resulting from a takeover bid, the recipient instead holds the payment on trust for shareholders who have sold their shares as a result of the bid and the recipient must bear any expenses of distributing that sum amongst the shareholders (s.226E(4)). The court can relieve a director from liability for authorising a payment, wholly or in part, if the director can show they acted honestly and reasonably and the court considers the director should be relieved of liability, having regard to all the circumstances of the case (s.226E(5)).

Where shareholder approval is required under Ch.4 (for example, because it involves a loan to the director), Ch.4A does not affect that requirement. However, where a payment to which s.226C applies also needs approval under Ch.4, approval obtained for the purposes of Ch.4 is treated as satisfying the requirements of s.226C(1)(b) (s.226F).

5.3   Disclosure of interests in transactions or arrangements

As explained in Chapter 3, s.177 sets out, as part of the statement of the general duties of directors, a director's duty to declare an interest in a proposed transaction or arrangement[10] with the company to the other directors. This duty is enforceable in the same way as any other fiduciary duty owed to the company and the consequences of breach are the same as would apply if the corresponding common law rule or equitable principle applied. In addition, s.182 requires a director to declare any interest in an existing transaction or arrangement the company has entered into. The section does not apply if, or to the extent that, the interest has been declared under s.177. In contrast to s.177, failure to comply with the requirements of s.182 is a criminal offence and a person guilty of an offence is liable to a fine (s.183).

A director who is in any way, whether directly or indirectly, interested in a transaction or arrangement that has been entered into by the company, or in a proposed transaction or arrangement with the company, must declare the nature and extent of that interest to the other directors of the company. Under s.182 the declaration must be made, and under s.177, the declaration can (but need not) be made, in one of three ways:

(a)   at a meeting of the directors;
(b)   by notice in writing in accordance with s.184; or

---

[10]   The term "arrangement" here includes understandings having no contractual effect: see *Duckwari Plc (No.2), Re* [1999] Ch. 253 at 260.

(c)   by a general notice in accordance with s.185.

In *Guinness Plc v Saunders*,[11] when considering the requirements of Companies Act 1985 s.317 which required a declaration of interest to be made at a meeting of the directors, it was held that declaration to a committee of the board was not enough. It seems likely the same will be true for the Companies Act 2006 provisions, except for declarations relating to a director's own service contract (see below).

If a declaration is made by notice in writing, the director must send the notice to the other directors. It can be sent in hard copy form by hand or by post. If the recipient has agreed to receive notices in electronic form and by electronic means, it can be sent by agreed electronic means in an agreed electronic form. Where a director declares an interest in accordance with s.184, the making of the declaration is deemed to form part of the proceedings at the next meeting of the directors after the notice is given. Section 248 requires companies to keep minutes of directors' meetings for at least ten years from the meeting and that section applies as if the declaration had been made at the next directors' meeting.

A director can also give a general notice in accordance with s.185. In that case, the notice must be given to the directors of the company to the effect that the director has an interest (as member, officer, employee or otherwise) in a specified body corporate or firm and is to be regarded as interested in any transaction or arrangement that may be made with that body corporate or firm after the date of the notice. A notice can also be given to the effect that the director is connected with a specified person (other than a body corporate or firm) and is to be regarded as interested in any transaction or arrangement that may be made with the specified person after the date of the notice. The notice must state the nature and extent of the director's interest in the body corporate or firm or the nature of their connection with the specified person. A general notice is not effective unless either it is given at a meeting of the directors or the director takes reasonable steps to secure that it is brought up and read at the first directors' meeting after the general notice is given.

The requirements of ss.177 and 182 also apply to shadow directors, but with some adaptations in the case of s.182 (s.187). "Shadow director" is defined in s.251 as any person in accordance with whose directions or instructions the directors of the company are accustomed to act. However, there is an exception for someone who gives advice in a professional capacity, such as a solicitor or accountant, provided the only reason that person would be treated as a shadow director is because of that advice. There is another exception for the purposes of some sections in the Companies Act 2006 (but not ss.182–187). Under this exception, a body corporate is not treated as a

---

[11]   *Guinness Plc v Saunders* [1988] 1 W.L.R. 863; [1988] 2 All E.R. 940; (1988) 4 B.C.C. 377.

shadow director of any of its subsidiaries only because the directors of the subsidiary are accustomed to act in accordance with the holding company's directions or instructions.

In the case of a declaration required by s.182, shadow directors can only declare their interests in a contract by a notice in writing to the directors in accordance with s.184 or by general notice in accordance with s.185 (a shadow director therefore cannot make a declaration of interest under s.182 at a meeting of the directors. A general notice given by a shadow director is not effective unless it is given by notice in writing in accordance with s.184, and the requirements of s.185(4) (which require a general notice to be given at a directors' meeting or require the director to take reasonable steps to secure the general notice is brought up and read at the next meeting of the directors after it is given) also do not apply.

The director's duty is not simply to disclose the fact that he or she has an interest, but also "the nature and extent of the interest". The declaration must make the director's colleagues "fully informed of the real state of things" (see *Imperial Mercantile Credit Assoc (In Liquidation) v Coleman*).[12] The fact that the interest is the same as other employees' or that it is an interest in another group company does not mean that it does not have to be disclosed.

The section does not require disclosure of interests which the director is not aware of or where the director is not aware of the transaction or arrangement in question. However, a director is treated as being aware of matters of which he ought reasonably to be aware. This will prevent directors burying their heads in the sand to avoid a disclosure obligation. A director also need not disclose an interest if it cannot reasonably be regarded as likely to give rise to a conflict of interest or if, or to the extent that, the other directors are already aware of the interest. The other directors are treated as being aware of anything of which they ought reasonably to be aware. A director also need not declare an interest if, or to the extent that, it concerns the terms of their service contract which have been, or are to be, considered at a directors' meeting or by a board committee appointed to consider those terms.

In the case of a declaration required by s.177, the declaration must be made before the company enters into the proposed transaction or arrangement and if it proves to be, or becomes, inaccurate or incomplete, a further declaration must be made (ss.177(3)–(4)). Any declaration required by s.182 must be made as soon as reasonably practicable. There is still a duty to make a declaration, even if this timing requirement has not been met

---

[12] *Imperial Mercantile Credit Assoc (In Liquidation) v Coleman* (1873) L.R. 6 (HL) 189 at 216 per Lord Chelmsford.

(s.182(4)). If a declaration under s.182 proves to be inaccurate or incomplete or becomes inaccurate or incomplete, a further declaration must be made (s.182(3)).

In the case of s.182, there are special requirements which apply if a company has a sole director, but is required to have more than one director (s.186). In this case, the declaration of interest must be recorded in writing and the making of the declaration is deemed to form part of the proceedings at the first meeting of the directors after the notice is given. The requirements of s.248 as to making and keeping of minutes apply as if the declaration had been made at that meeting. There are also separate requirements where a company enters into a contract with a director who is the sole member of the company (see s.231 and Section 5.4 below).

If a director fails properly to declare an interest when required to do so in accordance with s.177 in relation to a proposed transaction or arrangement, the consequences are the same as would apply if the corresponding common law rule or equitable principle applied (s.178(1)), meaning that the relevant transaction or arrangement may (subject to any applicable equitable defences) be liable to be set aside at the instance of the company and the director may be required to disgorge any gains or compensate the company for any loss.

Sections 182–187 do not contain any provisions setting out what the effect is on a contract if a director fails to declare an interest in an existing transaction or arrangement. This has, however, been considered by the courts in relation to Companies Act 1985 s.317, which contained an obligation on a director to declare an interest in a contract or a proposed contract. There does not seem to be any reason why the conclusions reached in relation to Companies Act 1985 s.317 should not be relevant to s.182.

If a director failed to comply with Companies Act 1985 s.317 this did not make the contract in which the director was interested unenforceable. In *Hely-Hutchinson v Brayhead Ltd*,[13] Lord Pearson said that s.317 merely created a statutory duty of disclosure and imposed a fine for non-compliance. This approach was approved, obiter, in *Guinness Plc v Saunders*.[14] Harman J also took this view in *Lee Panavision Ltd v Lee Lighting Ltd*,[15] concluding that remarks by Lord Templeman in the *Hely-Hutchinson* case that suggested a contract was voidable where there was a breach of contract were incorrect.

In *Craven Textile Engineers Ltd v Batley Football Club Ltd*,[16] the Court of Appeal held that the court did not have a general discretion to do what seemed "fair and just" if a director was in breach of s.317. In that case, a

---

[13] *Hely-Hutchinson v Brayhead Ltd* [1968] 1 Q.B. 549; [1967] 3 W.L.R. 1408; (1967) 111 S.J. 830.
[14] *Guinness Plc v Saunders* [1990] 2 A.C. 663; [1990] 2 W.L.R. 324; [1990] B.C.C. 205.
[15] *Lee Panavision Ltd v Lee Lighting Ltd* [1991] B.C.C. 620; [1992] B.C.L.C. 22.
[16] *Craven Textile Engineers Ltd v Batley Football Club Ltd* [2001] B.C.C. 679.

director claimed payment for work done and goods supplied to the company. He had failed to disclose his interest in the contract to the company. The Court of Appeal said it was impossible to restore the parties to their original positions and so rescission of the contract was not possible. The director was entitled to payment of his invoices notwithstanding the breach of s.317.

In *Runciman v Walter Runciman Plc*,[17] a question arose as to the position where a director failed to disclose an interest in a contract and a variation to that contract, but all the affected parties were aware of the director's interest in the contract. In that case, the director failed to disclose his interest in his own service contract in accordance with Companies Act 1948 s.199 (which was replaced by s.317). The director was wrongfully dismissed. The company conceded the claim but argued it was not bound by the contract because of the breach of s.199. Simon Brown J held that there was no suggestion that the director or his fellow directors had abused their position. Even if the section had not been complied with, the contract was not automatically invalid. The decision in this case was that the balance of justice did not require a "technical breach" of the section to render the variation unenforceable. This case shows that the courts have not necessarily been sympathetic to companies seeking to avoid obligations as a result of a technical breach of an obligation to declare an interest in a contract. Under s.182(6)(c) the position in relation to declarations of interest in a director's service contract is, in any case, now different. However, it is probably not safe to assume that the *Runciman* case means a company cannot ever avoid a contract where an interest has not been properly disclosed.

5.4 Contracts with directors who are sole members

If a limited company which has only one member enters into a contract with that member, there are particular requirements that the company must follow if the sole member is a director or shadow director of the company (see s.231). Section 231 applies to companies limited by shares or by guarantee, but not to unlimited companies. It does not apply to contracts entered into in the ordinary course of the company's business. There is no case law on what is the ordinary course of business in this context. However, in other contexts it has been held to mean "part of the undistinguished common flow of business done ... calling for no remark and arising out of no special or particular situation" (*Broome v Speak*).[18] The question will be one of fact which will depend on what the company does.

Unless the contract is in writing (in which case, the company need do nothing more), the company must ensure that the terms of the contract are

---

[17] *Runciman v Walter Runciman Plc* [1993] B.C.C. 223; [1992] B.C.L.C. 1084.
[18] *Broome v Speak* [1903] 1 Ch. 586.

either set out in a written memorandum or are recorded in the minutes of the first meeting of the directors of the company after the contract is made (see s.231(2)). If the company fails to meet this requirement, every officer who is in default is liable to a fine (see s.231(3)), but the validity of the contract is not affected (see s.231(6)). These requirements are in addition to any other statutory or other requirement which may apply to the contract (see s.231(7)).

5.5 Substantial property transactions involving directors

Companies are prohibited from entering into certain arrangements to transfer non-cash assets above a certain value to or from directors (or people connected with them), unless certain shareholder approvals have first been obtained or the arrangement is conditional on obtaining those approvals. Section 190 applies to transfers and proposed transfers[19] (both direct and indirect) to or from a director of the company or a director of any holding company of the company or to or from any person connected with such a director. Shadow directors are treated as directors for the purposes of the section (s.223(1)). For the prohibition to apply, there is no requirement that the director concerned (or any other person) acted dishonestly or that the transaction was to the disadvantage of the company.

"Non-cash asset" is defined in s.1163 as "any property or interest in property other than cash". For this purpose, cash includes foreign currency. Section 1163(2) extends the meaning of transfer or acquisition of a non-cash asset to include creating or extinguishing an estate or interest in any property or a right over property. It also includes the discharge of any person's liability other than a liability for a liquidated sum.[20] According to the Court of Appeal decision in *Granada Group Ltd v Law Debenture Pension Trust Corp Ltd*,[21] to fall within this definition an interest in or right over property will need to be one that is legally recognisable and enforceable. In *Duckwari Plc (No.1), Re*,[22] a company acquired either the benefit of a contract or a beneficial interest in the property which was the subject of the contract and the Court of Appeal held that the asset acquired was a non-cash asset for the purpose of Companies Act 1985 s.739(2) (now replaced by s.1163). Also, in *Ultraframe (UK) Ltd v Fielding*,[23] it was held that an exclusive licence of design right was a "non-cash asset". However, the grant of a purely personal right that is not derived from any existing property will not be

---

[19] See *Smithton Ltd v Naggar* [2014] EWCA Civ 939.

[20] In *Gooding v Cater* Unreported 13 March 1989 (Chancery Division), the court held that where a company discharged its own liability for damages for breach of a director's service contract, it did not have to obtain prior approval under Companies Act 1985 s.320 (which s.190 replaced).

[21] *Granada Group Ltd v Law Debenture Pension Trust Corp Ltd* [2016] EWCA Civ 1289.

[22] *Duckwari Plc (No.1), Re* [1995] B.C.C. 89; [1997] 2 B.C.L.C. 713; [1994] N.P.C. 109.

[23] *Ultraframe (UK) Ltd v Fielding* [2005] EWHC 1638 (Ch); [2006] F.S.R. 17; [2007] W.T.L.R. 835.

caught.[24] Although the better view is that a director (or connected person) subscribing for new shares in a company does not involve the acquisition of a non-cash asset, this point has not been judicially tested.

The section does not apply to a transaction so far as it relates to anything to which a director is entitled under their service contract or to payment for loss of office as defined in s.215 (s.190(6)).

Transfers of non-cash assets only need to be approved if the value of the asset exceeds £100,000 or (if less) it exceeds 10% of the company's asset value (although transfers of assets valued at £5,000 or less do not need to be approved) (s.191). Whether the value of the non-cash asset exceeds these thresholds must be determined when the arrangement in question is entered into. The company's asset value is its net asset value determined by reference to its most recent statutory accounts. Where no accounts have been prepared when the arrangement is entered into, the company's asset value is treated as being the amount of the company's called-up share capital. A company's statutory accounts are its annual accounts prepared in accordance with Pt 15 of the Act and its "most recent statutory accounts" are the accounts for which the time for sending them out to members (in accordance with s.424) is most recent. In *Micro Leisure Ltd v County Properties and Developments Ltd,*[25] the Scottish Court of Session held that the value of the asset can be the special value of the asset to the director and not the objective market value of the asset. The case related to Companies Act 1985 s.320, but there appears to be no reason why the same approach should not apply to s.191.

If there is an arrangement which involves more than one non-cash asset or if the arrangement is one of a series involving non-cash assets, the arrangement is treated as if it involved a non-cash asset of a value equal to the aggregate of all the non-cash assets involved in the arrangement or the series (s.190(5)). This prevents companies from splitting an arrangement into different parts to avoid the requirements applying to it.

There are various exceptions from the requirement to obtain approval. Section 190 only applies to companies as defined in s.1, but not to other bodies corporate. Therefore, an overseas body corporate entering into a transaction with one of its own directors or with a director of its UK-incorporated holding company will not (provided that the holding

---

[24] See *Terry v Watchstone Ltd* [2018] EWHC 3082 (Comm) where it was held that a right to an indemnity in respect of certain liabilities of a director was not property or an interest in property. See also *Mercer v Heart of Midlothian Plc* 2001 S.L.T. 945; 2001 S.C.L.R. 701; 2001 G.W.D. 19–717, where Lord Macfadyen thought it was "questionable" whether the benefits received by the former director (including seats in the director's box at Tynecastle Stadium on match days, access to the boardroom and a car park pass) amounted to a non-cash asset as they were a personal right against Heart of Midlothian rather than a right over property.

[25] *Micro Leisure Ltd v County Properties and Developments Ltd* 1999 S.L.T. 1428; [2000] B.C.C. 872; *Times* 12 January 2000.

company is not indirectly participating in the transaction) be caught. If the company is a wholly-owned subsidiary of another body corporate (as defined in s.1159(2)), no approval is needed wherever its holding company is incorporated (see s.190(4)(b)). Also, no approval is needed for transfers between members of the same wholly-owned group: that is, from a holding company to a wholly-owned subsidiary or vice versa, or from one wholly-owned subsidiary to another wholly-owned subsidiary in the same group (s.192(b)).

Approval is required if an arrangement is entered into when the company is in a members' voluntary winding up but not otherwise if the company is being wound up (s.193(1)(a)). It is also not required if the company is in administration within the meaning of the Insolvency Act 1986 Sch.B1 or the Insolvency (Northern Ireland) Order 1989.[26] Approval is not required if the transaction is with a person in their capacity as a member (s.192(a)): for example, where a director receives bonus shares in common with other members or shares under a scrip dividend arrangement, or where the company enters into an own share purchase with a director or connected person. Finally, no approval is needed if the director or a connected person effects a transaction on a recognised investment exchange (as defined in Financial Services and Markets Act 2000 Pt 18), such as the London Stock Exchange, through an independent broker as defined in s.194(2).

Section 190(1) provides that where approval is needed the arrangement must be approved "by a resolution of the members of the company", meaning an ordinary resolution unless the company's articles of association require a higher majority. If the arrangement is with a director of a holding company (or a connected person of such a director), it must also be approved "by a resolution of the members of the holding company" (s.190(2)), unless the holding company is not a UK-registered company (s.190(4)(a)). In the case of a private company, the requisite approval may be given by written resolution or a resolution in general meeting, whereas public companies are not permitted to pass written resolutions. In relation to Companies Act 1985 s.320 (which s.190 replaced), the requirement was held to be satisfied where all the shareholders of a company had unanimously agreed, at a meeting, to the transfer of company property to certain of those shareholders and directors, even though the meeting was described as a "board meeting" and no shareholders' resolution giving prior approval was passed.[27] In another case, approval of a transaction subject to s.320 without any formal resolution was held to be sufficient, applying *Duomatic Ltd, Re*.[28] There does not seem to be any reason why a court would come to a different conclusion in relation to s.190.

---

[26] The Insolvency (Northern Ireland) Order 1989 (SI 1989/2405 (NI 19)).
[27] See *Conegrade Ltd, Re* [2002] EWHC 2411 (Ch); [2003] B.P.I.R. 358; [2002] All E.R. (D) 19.
[28] *NBH Ltd v Hoare* [2006] EWHC 73 (Ch); also see *Duomatic Ltd, Re* [1969] 2 Ch. 365; [1969] 2 W.L.R. 114; [1969] 1 All E.R. 161.

The consequences of entering into an arrangement in breach of s.190 are set out in s.195. The company can avoid the arrangement and any transaction entered into in pursuance of the arrangement, unless one of a number of conditions has been satisfied. These are:

(a) that it is no longer possible to return the money or asset which was the subject of the arrangement or transaction;

(b) the company has been indemnified in pursuance of s.195 by some other person for the loss or damage it has suffered;

(c) a person who is not a party to the arrangement or transaction has acquired any rights in good faith, for value and without actual notice that s.190 had been breached, and those rights would be affected if the arrangement or transaction were avoided; or

(d) the members of the company affirm the arrangement by resolution within a reasonable period and, if the arrangement involves a transfer of an asset to or by a director of its holding company (or someone connected with that director), the arrangement is also affirmed by a resolution of the members of the holding company (s.196).

A transaction was not illegal just because Companies Act 1985 s.320 had been breached (see *Joint Receivers and Managers of Niltan Carson v Hawthorne*)[29] and the same would appear to be the case if s.190 is breached. Section 190(3) provides that a company is not subject to any liability by reason of a failure to obtain approval required by s.190. Also the transaction is not void ab initio. However, directors (both the director who enters into the arrangement or transaction and the directors who authorise it) and connected persons who enter into the transaction or arrangement are liable to account to the company for any gains made, directly or indirectly, as a result and to indemnify the company for any resulting loss or damage (s.195(3)). The liability to indemnify is a joint and several liability with anyone else who is liable under s.195. The liability arises whether or not the company avoids the arrangement or transaction and is in addition to any other liability. However, a director can avoid liability for an arrangement between the company and a person connected with them if they can show that they took "all reasonable steps" to secure the company's compliance with s.190 (s.195(6)). A person connected with a director and a director who authorised the arrangement or transaction can avoid liability if they can show that they did not know the relevant circumstances constituting the contravention when the relevant arrangement was entered into (s.195(7)). In *Duckwari Plc (No.2), Re*,[30] it was held that the liability to indemnify the company extends to a decline in the market value of an asset after it has been acquired. In *Duckwari Plc (No.3), Re*,[31] it was held that the director was not liable for the costs of borrowing that the company incurred to buy the

---

[29] *Joint Receivers and Managers of Niltan Carson v Hawthorne* (1987) 3 B.C.C. 454; [1988] B.C.L.C. 298 at 322.

[30] *Duckwari Plc (No.2), Re* [1999] Ch. 253; [1998] 3 W.L.R. 913; [1999] B.C.C. 11.

[31] *Duckwari Plc (No.3), Re* [1999] Ch. 268; [1999] 2 W.L.R. 1059; [1999] 1 B.C.L.C. 168.

asset in question. In *NBH Ltd v Hoare*,[32] it was held that the company that had acquired an asset from a company connected to a director could not recover any extra profit the company might have made when it sold the asset. In that case, the company had sold the asset for more than it had acquired it and so had not made a loss. The fact that the vendor had sold the asset to the company for more than the amount the vendor had paid to it was irrelevant. That was not the sort of "gain" with which the relevant sections were concerned. In *Murray v Leisureplay Plc*,[33] Arden LJ said that the costs of obtaining a due diligence report were a direct result of the arrangement for acquiring the relevant asset and could be recovered. However, the costs of hiring an additional director were not foreshadowed by the acquisition and could not be recovered under Companies Act 1985 s.322(3)(b) (reproduced in s.195(3)(b)).

5.6 Transactions with related parties

Companies that have a premium listing of equity securities by the Financial Conduct Authority (FCA) and are therefore subject to the Listing Rules are also subject to restrictions on transactions and arrangements between the listed company or any of its subsidiary undertakings and certain group directors or an associate of such a director. Under Ch.11 of the Listing Rules, if a listed company (or any of its subsidiary undertakings as defined in the FCA glossary) wishes to enter into a transaction or arrangement with a director or their associate or where the company or subsidiary undertaking and the director or associate are each investing in, or providing finance to, another undertaking or asset, broadly speaking it must meet certain disclosure requirements and obtain shareholder approval for the trans-action, unless an exception applies. The rules also apply to any other similar transaction or arrangement between a listed company or subsidiary undertaking and any other person if the purpose and effect is to benefit a director or associate. The requirements do not apply to transactions and arrangements in the ordinary course of business.

The company must ensure that the director does not vote on the resolution to approve the transaction and that the director takes all reasonable steps to ensure their associates do not vote. The Listing Rules contain guidance as to the approach to take where someone who is a party to a transaction or arrangement which is subject to shareholder approval becomes a related party after the notice of meeting has been sent out but before the meeting takes place. The company must send a further circular to shareholders containing additional information that would have been required if the person had been a related party when the transaction was entered into, which must be received at least one clear business day before the last time for lodging proxies for the meeting.

---

[32] *NBH Ltd v Hoare* [2006] EWHC 73 (Ch); [2006] 2 B.C.L.C. 649.
[33] *Murray v Leisureplay Plc* [2005] EWCA Civ 963; [2005] I.R.L.R. 946.

The directors who are subject to the Listing Rules requirements are the directors and shadow directors of the listed company, any of its subsidiary undertakings, any parent undertaking or any subsidiary undertaking of a parent undertaking. Anyone who was a director of such a company in the 12 months before the date of the transaction or arrangement is also caught by the requirements. "Associate" is widely defined to mean:

(a) that individual's spouse, civil partner or child (who together are referred to as "the individual's family");

(b) the trustees (acting as such) of any trust of which the individual or any of the individual's family is a beneficiary or discretionary object. There are exceptions for a trust which is an occupational pension scheme, as defined in the Financial Services and Markets Act 2000 (Regulated Activities) Order 2001 art.3(1),[34] or an employees' share scheme, as defined in s.1166 of the Act, provided, in each case, the trust does not have the effect of conferring benefits on persons all or most of whom are related parties;

(c) any company if the individual or any member or members (taken together) of the individual's family, or the individual and any such member or members (taken together), are directly or indirectly interested in the company's equity securities (or have a conditional or contingent entitlement to become interested) so that they are (or would be if the condition were met or the contingent interest became an interest) able:

    (i) to exercise or control the exercise of 30% or more of the votes able to be cast at general meetings on all, or substantially all, matters; or

    (ii) to appoint or remove directors holding a majority of voting rights at board meetings on all, or substantially all, matters; and

(d) any partnership in which the individual or any family member(s) (taken together) are directly or indirectly interested (or have a conditional or contingent entitlement to become interested) if they hold or control (or would hold or control) a voting interest of more than 30% or at least 30% of the partnership.

For the purpose of (c), where more than one director of the listed company, its parent undertaking or any of its subsidiary undertakings is interested in the equity securities of another company, then the interests of those directors and their associates will be aggregated when determining whether that company is an associate of the director.

If a listed company (or any of its subsidiary undertakings) proposes to enter into a transaction which might be a related-party transaction, the company must obtain guidance from a sponsor to assess the potential application of LR 11. If the company enters into a related-party transaction, the company must make a notification in accordance with LR 10.4.1R. Chapter 10 of the

---

[34] Financial Services and Markets Act 2000 (Regulated Activities) Order 2001 (SI 2001/544).

Listing Rules contains rules dealing with transactions by premium listed companies where the requirements depend upon the size of the transaction. LR 10.4.1R requires the company to notify certain details to a Regulatory Information Service as soon as possible after the terms of the transaction are agreed. The details are those that would be required for a Class 2 transaction, and also the name of the related party (i.e. the director or associate) and details of the nature and extent of the related party's interest in the transaction or arrangement.

The listed company must send a circular to shareholders containing certain prescribed information (see LR 11.1.7R(2)). This includes full particulars of the transaction together with the related party's name and the nature and extent of his or her interest in the transaction. Where an asset is being acquired or disposed of under a "related party" transaction where any percentage ratio (for the purpose of deciding what class the transaction is under Ch.10 of the Listing Rules) is 25% or more, there must be an independent valuation of the asset if "appropriate" financial information is not available. The directors of the listed company must state in the circular that the transaction is fair and reasonable as far as the security holders of the company are concerned, that the directors have been advised that this is the case by a sponsor and, if applicable, that the related party will not vote on the relevant resolution and has undertaken to take all reasonable steps to ensure their associates will not vote on the relevant resolution. The director who is a party to the related party transaction (or whose associate is a party to the related party transaction) must not take part in the board's consideration of the matter, and the circular must state this (see LR 13.6).

If there is a material change affecting anything the company is required to disclose in its circular to shareholders or there is a material new matter which the company would have had to disclose if it had arisen before the circular was published which the company becomes aware of before the meeting to approve the related-party transaction, the company must notify the FCA as soon as practicable and send a supplementary circular containing an explanation of the relevant matters (see LR 11.1.7CR and LR 10.5.4R). The company may have to adjourn the shareholder meeting if the supplementary circular cannot be sent at least seven days before the meeting (LR 10.5.5G). If there is a material change to the terms of a transaction after shareholder approval is obtained but before the transaction is completed, the company must comply again with the Listing Rule requirements (see LR 11.1.7AR). The FCA would (amongst other things) generally consider an increase of 10% or more in the consideration payable to be a material change to the terms of a transaction.

If a company (or any of its subsidiary undertakings) varies or novates an existing agreement with a director or associate, the variation or novation is caught, whether or not the original agreement was made when the director or associate was a related party.

There are various exceptions to the requirements (see LR 11.1.6R and LR11 Annex 1). These include:

(a) small transactions—these are defined by reference to various percentage ratios used for classifying transactions for Listing Rules purposes. Where all of these do not exceed 0.25%, the exception applies. If one or more ratio exceeds 0.25% but is less than 5%, the normal rules (including having to obtain shareholder approval) do not apply (LR 11.1.10R). In this case, before the company enters into the transaction or arrangement it must, instead, obtain a written confirmation from a sponsor that the proposed terms are fair and reasonable as far as the company's shareholders are concerned and as soon as possible after entering into the transaction or arrangement it must notify certain details to a Regulatory Information Service, including the identity of the related party, the value of the consideration for the transaction or arrangement and any other relevant circumstances.

If a company enters into more than one related party transaction or arrangement with the same director (or any of their associates) in a 12-month period, the transactions must be aggregated unless they have been approved by shareholders. If any percentage ratio is 5% or more for the aggregated transactions, the company must follow the usual requirements for the latest transaction and give details of all the transactions being aggregated in the circular to shareholders (LR 11.1.11R(2)). If one or more of the percentage ratios for the aggregated small transactions is more than 0.25% but all the percentage ratios for the aggregated small transactions are less than 5%, the company must obtain written confirmation from a sponsor that the terms of the latest small transaction are fair and reasonable as far as shareholders are concerned and notify the relevant details of all the aggregated small transactions to a Regulatory Information Service (LR 11.1.11R(3));

(b) certain issues of new securities or sales of treasury shares to a related party;

(c) exceptions for certain benefits in accordance with the terms of an employees' share scheme or a long-term incentive scheme;

(d) granting credit to a related party on normal commercial terms or of an amount and on terms no more favourable than those offered generally to group employees or a grant of credit by the related party on normal commercial terms on an unsecured basis;

(e) granting an indemnity to a director to the extent specifically permitted by the Act or maintaining an insurance contract for a director to the extent allowed by the Act or a loan or assistance to a director if specifically permitted by the Act;

(f) a related party underwriting an issue of securities provided certain conditions are met;

(g) a related party co-investing in, or providing finance to, another undertaking or asset with the listed company if, broadly, the related party's investment is no more than 25% of the company's and a sponsor has confirmed in writing to the FCA that the company's terms are no less favourable than those applying to the related party; and

(h) where the related party is (or was) a director (or shadow director) of an insignificant subsidiary or is (or was) a substantial shareholder in an insignificant subsidiary. This is a subsidiary undertaking which has contributed less than 10% of the profits of the listed company and has represented less than 10% of the assets of the listed company in each of the three financial years preceding the date of the transaction for which accounts have been published. (There are different rules if the subsidiary undertaking has been part of the group less than three years.)

For exceptions falling within paras (b)–(h) the transaction or arrangement must not have any unusual features.

If a director of a listed company is knowingly concerned in a breach of the Listing Rules requirements, the FCA can impose a fine on the director or publish a statement censuring the director (Financial Services and Markets Act 2000 s.91).

5.7 Loans to directors and related transactions

5.7.1 Loans

Subject to various exceptions, companies are prohibited from making loans to directors and persons connected with them and entering into similar transactions unless the transaction has been approved by shareholders' resolution, meaning an ordinary resolution unless the company's articles of association require a higher majority. The provisions are very detailed and quite complex; they contain various anti-avoidance provisions. Under the relevant sections of the Companies Act 1985 (ss.330–342) the requirements varied depending, broadly, on whether or not there was a public company in the company's group. When the Companies Act 2006 was originally introduced as a Bill, it was proposed that this distinction should be abolished, so all companies should be subject to the same requirements. However, at a late stage, the Bill was amended so that the provisions relating to quasi-loans, loans to persons connected with a director and credit transactions only apply to public companies or companies associated with a public company. A company is associated with a public company if either it is a subsidiary of a public company or it has a public company as its subsidiary or if both companies are subsidiaries of the same body corporate (s.256).

The basic prohibition applies to all companies. A company must not:

(a) make a loan to a director or to a director of its holding company; or

(b)   give a guarantee or provide any security in connection with a loan made by anyone to a director of the company or its holding company (see s.197(1)).

The prohibition does not apply if the transaction has been approved by a resolution of the members of the company. If the director is a director of the company's holding company, the transaction must also have been approved by a resolution of the members of the holding company (s.197(2)).

If the company is a public company or is associated with a public company, there is an additional restriction on loans to persons connected with a director of the company or a director of its holding company. In this case, the company also must not make a loan to such a connected person, or give a guarantee or provide any security in connection with a loan made by any person to such a connected person. As for loans to directors, the prohibition does not apply if the transaction has been approved by a resolution of the members of the company and, if the connected person is connected with a director of the company's holding company, also by a resolution of the members of the holding company (s.200).

For the purposes of ss.197–214 a director includes a shadow director (see s.223(1)) but, for these purposes, a body corporate is not treated as a shadow director of any of its subsidiaries only because the directors of the subsidiary are accustomed to act in accordance with the holding company's directions or instructions (see s.251(3)). It appears from the section that it does not matter whether the director is entering into the loan in another capacity, for example as a trustee of an employee share trust.

A "loan" is not defined. Generally, this involves an advance of money to or for someone on condition that it will be repaid in money or money's worth. It is not essential for interest to be paid on the money lent. In *Currencies Direct Ltd v Ellis*,[35] there was a dispute as to whether monies paid by the company to a director were a loan or remuneration for work and services. At first instance, Gage J found, on the facts, that most amounts were remuneration but that some amounts were loans. In the case of the amounts which were loans, there was an express written acceptance by the director of his liability to pay the sum on demand whereas there was no evidence that the other amounts were paid to the director as advances subject to an express or implied term that they be repaid. The Court of Appeal upheld this approach. In the case of *Ciro Citterio Menswear Plc v Thakrar*,[36] the court found that there was a loan of company funds where it was only evidenced by a debit entry in the company's computerised nominal ledger. The case considered an arrangement between the directors of the company to make unused credit balances on the directors' accounts available to other

---

[35]   *Currencies Direct Ltd v Ellis* [2002] EWCA Civ 779; [2002] B.C.C. 821; [2002] 2 B.C.L.C. 482.
[36]   *Ciro Citterio Menswear Plc v Thakrar* [2002] EWHC 662 (Ch); [2002] 1 W.L.R. 2217; [2002] 2 All E.R. 717.

directors. However, on the facts, the court held that the arrangements between the directors had not created a loan by the directors in favour of the director in question. It was the company which had partly funded the transfer of property. Agreeing to make money available probably does not, of itself, amount to making a loan until the money is actually advanced. In *Champagne Perrier-Jouet SA v HH Finch Ltd*,[37] the court held that a company which had paid a director's bills and supplied goods to a company he controlled, on credit, had not made a loan to him. However, such an arrangement would fall within the definition of a quasi-loan (see Section 5.7.2 below). Providing security is also not defined. However, it seems fairly clear that the section would catch a situation, for example, where a bank or other third party lends money to a director and the company enters into an agreement where, if the loan or interest is not repaid, the lender has rights against some or all of the company's assets or undertaking to recover the amount not paid.

Before a resolution is passed a memorandum must be made available to members setting out the nature of the transaction, the amount of the loan and the purpose for which it is required and the extent of the company's liability under any transaction connected with the loan. If the resolution is to be passed as a written resolution (in the case of a private company) the memorandum must be sent or submitted to every eligible member when the proposed resolution is sent or submitted to them (or beforehand). Accidental failure to send or submit the memorandum will be disregarded unless the articles provide otherwise (see s.224). If the resolution is to be passed at a meeting, the memorandum must be made available for inspection at the company's registered office for at least 15 days ending with the date of the meeting and at the meeting itself (s.197(3) and (4) and s.198(4) and (5)).

The requirement for approval under s.197 does not apply to wholly-owned subsidiaries (as defined in s.1159(2)) or to bodies corporate that are not UK-registered companies (as defined in s.1158) (s.197(5)).

5.7.2 *Quasi-loans*

A public company or a company associated with a public company must not:

(a) make a quasi-loan to a director of the company or a director of its holding company or to a person connected with such a director; or
(b) give a guarantee or provide any security in connection with a quasi-loan made by anyone to such a director or a person connected with them (see ss.198 and 200).

---

[37] *Champagne Perrier-Jouet SA v HH Finch Ltd* [1982] 1 W.L.R. 1359; (1983) 80 L.S.G. 93; (1982) 126 S.J. 689.

The prohibition does not apply if the transaction has been approved by a resolution of the members of the company. If the director is a director of the holding company or if the connected person is a person connected with a director of the company's holding company, it must also be approved by a resolution of the members of the holding company.

A quasi-loan is defined in s.199(1). It is a transaction under which one party (the creditor) agrees to pay a sum for another (the borrower) or in fact pays a sum for the borrower other than under an agreement. It also includes situations where the creditor agrees to reimburse expenditure incurred by a third party for the borrower or in fact reimburses such expenditure other than under an agreement. The terms of the transaction must include that the borrower (or a person on their behalf) will reimburse the creditor or that the borrower incurs a liability to reimburse the creditor. Examples of quasi-loans include a company paying for goods on behalf of a director, even if the director subsequently reimburses the company, and a company allowing a director to use a company credit card for private expenditure.

As for loans (see Section 5.7.1 above), there is a requirement to make a memorandum available to members giving prescribed details of the proposed quasi-loan before the written resolution or resolution at a meeting is passed (see s.198(4) and (5) and s.200(4) and (5)). The matters to be disclosed are the nature of the transaction, the amount of the quasi-loan and the purpose for which it is required and the extent of the company's liability under any transaction connected with the quasi-loan. The memorandum must be sent or submitted to every eligible member when the proposed written resolution (in the case of a private company only) is sent or submitted to them (unless it has already been sent or submitted). Accidental failure to send or submit the memorandum will be disregarded unless the articles provide otherwise (see s.224). If the resolution is to be passed at a meeting, the memorandum must be made available for inspection by members of the company at the company's registered office for at least 15 days ending with the date of the meeting and at the meeting itself. Also, as for loans, the requirement for approval does not apply to wholly-owned subsidiaries (as defined in s.1159(2)) or to bodies corporate that are not UK-registered companies (as defined in s.1158) (ss.198(6) and 200(6)).

5.7.3 Credit transactions

Unless the transaction has been approved by shareholders' resolution, a public company or a company associated with a public company is also prohibited from entering into a credit transaction as a creditor for the benefit of a director or a director of its holding company or a person connected with such a director (see s.201(2)(a)). Also, it cannot give a guarantee or provide any security in connection with a credit transaction made by anyone for the benefit of such a director or a person connected with them (see s.201(2)(b)). The prohibition does not apply if the transaction

186

(i.e. the credit transaction, the giving of the guarantee or the provision of the security) has been approved by a resolution of the members of the company and by a resolution of the members of the holding company if the director or connected person is a director of the holding company or a person connected with such a director.

Credit transaction is defined in s.202(1). It is a transaction under which one party (the creditor):

(a)   supplies any goods or sells any land under a hire-purchase agreement or a conditional sale agreement (defined in the Consumer Credit Act 1974—see s.202(3)); or
(b)   leases or hires any land or goods in return for periodical payments.

It also includes transactions where the creditor otherwise disposes of land or supplies goods or services on the understanding that payment is to be deferred. For this purpose, services means anything other than land or goods, and it does not matter whether payment is made in a lump sum, instalments, periodical payments, or in any other way.

Before a resolution approving a credit transaction is passed, a memorandum must be made available to members setting out the nature of the transaction, the value of the credit transaction and the purpose for which the land, goods or services sold or otherwise disposed of, leased, hired or supplied under the credit transaction are required and the extent of the company's liability under any transaction connected with the credit transaction. If the resolution is to be passed at a meeting, the memorandum must be made available for inspection by members at the company's registered office for at least 15 days ending with the date of the meeting and at the meeting itself. In the case of a written resolution (in the case of a private company), the memorandum must be sent or submitted to every eligible member when the written resolution is sent or submitted to them (or beforehand) (s.201(4) and (5)). Accidental failure to send or submit the memorandum will be disregarded unless the articles provide otherwise (see s.224).

As for loans and quasi-loans (see Sections 5.7.1 and 5.7.2 above), there is no need for shareholder approval if the company is a wholly-owned subsidiary or unless the company is a UK-registered company (as defined in s.1158) (s.201(6)).

5.7.4   Transactions or arrangements on behalf of another

Section 212 sets out when a transaction or arrangement is made "for" a person. In the case of a loan or a quasi-loan, it is made for them if it is made to them. In the case of a credit transaction, it is made for them if they are the person to whom goods, land or services are supplied, sold, hired, leased or otherwise disposed of under the transaction. A guarantee or security is made for a person if it is entered into in connection with a loan or quasi-loan made to them or a credit transaction made for them. In the case of a related arrangement falling within s.203 (see Section 5.7.5), it is made for them if they are the person for whom the transaction is made to which the arrangement relates.

5.7.5   Anti-avoidance provisions: related arrangements

Section 203 contains some anti-avoidance provisions which are relevant to the transactions which are prohibited under ss.197, 198, 200 or 201 unless the arrangement in question has been approved by a resolution of the members of the company and, if the director or connected person for whom the transaction is entered into is a director of its holding company or a person connected with such a director, also by a resolution of the members of the holding company. Section 203(1)(b) prohibits a company from assuming any rights, obligations or liabilities under a transaction or arranging for any rights, obligations or liabilities under a transaction to be assigned to it which it could not have entered into itself without shareholder approval under ss.197, 198, 200 or 201. So, for example, a company cannot take an assignment of a loan made by a third party to one of its directors and cannot assume obligations under a guarantee made in connection with a quasi-loan to a person connected with one of its directors or a director of one of its holding companies. In such cases, to decide whether the transaction would have required approval under ss.197, 198, 200 or 201 if it had been entered into by the company, the transaction is treated as being entered into on the date the arrangement is made for the company to assume the rights, liabilities or obligations (s.203(6)).

Section 203(1)(a) deals with more complicated avoidance techniques. A company cannot take part in any arrangement under which someone else (A) enters into a transaction which the company itself could not have entered into without obtaining approval under ss.197, 198, 200 or 201 and that person A obtains any benefit from the company or a body corporate associated with it pursuant to the arrangement. It does not matter whether it is the company, one of its subsidiaries or holding companies or a subsidiary of any of the company's holding companies which provides the benefit. The prohibition does not apply if the arrangement has been approved by a resolution of the members of the company and of the members of the holding company if the director or connected person for whom the transaction is entered into is a director of its holding company or a person connected with such a director. This section would stop a company entering into a "back-to-back" arrangement with a totally unconnected company to make loans to that company's directors in return for that company making loans to its directors or directors of its holding company. It would also stop an arrangement under which a third party provides a guarantee or security for a loan to a company's director under an arrangement for another group company to place business with that third party.

"Arrangement" is not defined, but will include understandings having no contractual effect.[38] In the Parliamentary debates when the section was first enacted, the Government stated that the section was intended to apply only where the benefit provided by the company or another group company was the quid pro quo for the transaction entered into by the third party. This makes it clear that if there is a usual course of dealing between the company and the third party, unconnected to the transaction between the third party and the director, this is not prohibited by the section. According to the parliamentary debates the burden of proof for proving there is an arrangement is on the person who alleges it exists.

Before a resolution approving an arrangement within s.203 is passed, a memorandum must be made available to members setting out the matters that would have to be disclosed if the company were seeking approval of the transaction to which the arrangement relates, the nature of the arrangement and the extent of the company's liability under the arrangement or any transaction connected with it. If the resolution is to be passed at a meeting, the memorandum must be made available at the company's registered office for at least 15 days ending with the date of the meeting and at the meeting itself. If the resolution is a written resolution (in the case of a private company only), the memorandum must be sent or submitted to every eligible member no later than the time the proposed resolution is sent or submitted to them.

An approval is not needed under s.203 if the company is a wholly-owned subsidiary, or if it is not a UK-registered company as defined in s.1158 (s.203(5)).

5.7.6 Exceptions

Given the breadth of the provisions in ss.197, 198, 200 and 201, it is not surprising that there are a large number of exceptions.

5.7.6.1 Exceptions for expenditure on defending proceedings, regulatory actions and investigations

A company does not need shareholder approval to provide funds to a director of the company or holding company or a person connected with them to meet expenditure incurred in defending certain proceedings if certain conditions are met (see s.205). The company can provide funds to meet expenditure incurred in defending any criminal or civil proceedings in

---

[38] See *Duckwari Plc (No.2), Re* [1999] Ch. 253 at 260.

connection with any alleged negligence, default, breach of duty or breach of trust by the director in relation to the company or an associated company or in connection with any application to the court by the director for relief under s.1157 (relief in a case of honest and reasonable conduct) or s.661(3) or (4) (relief in a case of an acquisition of shares by an innocent nominee). Funds can also be provided to meet expenditure to be incurred for those purposes or to enable a director to avoid incurring such expenditure. It must be a term of the loan that it is to be repaid, or (as the case may be) the company's liability is to be discharged, if the director is convicted in the proceedings, judgment is given against them in the proceedings or the court refuses to grant relief. It must also be a term that it is to be repaid or discharged not later than the date when the conviction, judgment or refusal of relief becomes final. This happens either when the period for bringing an appeal ends without the appeal being brought, or if an appeal or further appeal is brought and is disposed of. The section makes it clear that this happens when any appeal is abandoned or ceases to have effect or if the appeal is determined and the period for bringing any further appeal has ended without the appeal being brought.

Section 206 also makes it clear that a company does not need approval under s.197, 198, 200 or 201 for anything it does to provide one of its directors or a director of its holding company with funds to meet expenditure incurred in defending an investigation by a regulatory authority or against action proposed to be taken by a regulatory authority. This is also the case for anything done to provide funds for expenditure to be incurred for such purposes or to enable the director to avoid incurring such expenditure. Unlike under s.205, there is no requirement in s.206 for the funds to be advanced on particular terms or to be repaid if the regulatory authority finds against the director.

5.7.6.2   Intra-group loans

Because the provisions of ss.197, 198 and 200 are widely drawn, they could prevent one company in a group making a loan or quasi-loan to another company in the same group or entering into a guarantee or providing security in connection with a loan or quasi-loan by a third party to another group member without the relevant approvals. This could arise, for example, because a director of one group company is connected with another group company—for example, because the director holds 20% of its equity share capital (see Section 5.10 below). Approval under ss.197, 198 or 200 is not required to make a loan or quasi-loan to an associated body corporate or to give a guarantee or provide security in connection with a loan or quasi-loan made to an associated body corporate (s.208(1)). Similarly, approval is not required under s.201 to enter into a credit transaction as creditor for the benefit of an associated body corporate or to give a guarantee or provide security in connection with a credit transaction entered into by any person for the benefit of an associated body corporate (s.208(2)). Bodies corporate are associated if one is a subsidiary of the other or both are subsidiaries of the same body corporate (s.256).

5.7.6.3 *Minor/business transactions*

A company can make a loan or quasi-loan, give a guarantee or provide security in connection with a loan or quasi-loan without needing approval under ss.197, 198 or 200 if the aggregate of the value (calculated in accordance with s.211) of the transaction and of any other relevant transactions or arrangements does not exceed £10,000 (see s.207(1)). Section 210 sets out how "other relevant transactions or arrangements" are to be determined for the purposes of an exception to ss.197, 198, 200 or 201 (see Section 5.8 below). The requirement to aggregate certain transactions is intended to prevent the exception being used as a way of avoiding the basic prohibition—for example, by having a number of group companies making small loans to a director.

A company may enter into a credit transaction or enter into a guarantee or provide security in connection with a credit transaction without needing approval under s.201 if the aggregate of the value of the credit transaction, guarantee or security and of any other relevant transactions or arrangements does not exceed £15,000 (see s.207(2)). If the relevant amounts are more than £15,000, the exception can still apply if:

(a)   the company enters into the transaction in the ordinary course of its business; and
(b)   the value of the transaction is not greater than the value it is reasonable to expect the company would have offered to someone unconnected with the company and of the same financial standing, and the terms of the transaction are not more favourable than it is reasonable to expect the company to have offered to such a person (see s.207(3)).

5.7.6.4 *Exception for expenditure on company business*

Difficult questions can arise as to whether a company makes a loan to a director if it advances money to them to allows them to meet their business expenses. Although the better view is probably that normally there is not a loan to the director where money is provided in advance to meet expenses, it may be harder to reach this view if, for example, a director is advanced a large amount for a long period and can use this to meet personal expenditure, even if he or she subsequently repays the personal expenditure and any unused amounts. Section 204 provides an exception from the requirement for approval in ss.197, 198, 200 or 201 as long as certain requirements are met. Where the requirements are met, the company can do anything to provide a director, a director of its holding company or a person connected with such a director with funds to meet expenditure they have incurred or will incur or to enable the director or the connected person to avoid incurring such expenditure. This means, for example, that the company can arrange for goods or services to be available to the director so that he or she does not have to arrange and pay for these personally. The requirements are as follows:

(a) the expenditure must be incurred "for the purposes of the company" or "for the purpose of enabling him properly to perform his duties as an officer of the company". Following *Brady v Brady*,[39] there is a risk that the courts would adopt a narrow construction of what "for the purposes of the company" means; and

(b) the aggregate value of the transaction in question and any other relevant transactions or arrangements must not exceed £50,000.

5.7.6.5 Money-lending companies

Section 209 provides an exception from the prohibitions in ss.197, 198 and 200 for "money-lending companies". A money-lending company is a company whose ordinary business includes making loans or quasi-loans or giving guarantees or providing security in connection with loans or quasi-loans. Provided certain conditions are met, a money-lending company can make a loan or quasi-loan to anyone, or enter into a guarantee, or provide security in connection with a loan or quasi-loan without needing approval under ss.197, 198 or 200. The exception does not, however, extend to credit transactions. The conditions are as follows:

(a) the company must enter into the transaction (the loan, quasi-loan, guarantee or security) in the ordinary course of its business; and

(b) the terms of the transaction must not be more favourable than the company could reasonably be expected to have offered to a person of the same financial standing who was unconnected with the company and the value of the transaction must not be greater than could reasonably have been expected to be offered to such a person.

The section does not define what constitutes the "ordinary course of the company's business". It is generally thought that this means that the transaction must be consistent with the normal course of the company's business and of a kind and on a scale normal for the company. It does not matter that the company's normal practice differs from the normal practice of other similar companies.[40] A decision as to whether the conditions are met in any case will therefore involve some consideration of the company's usual approach.

---

[39] *Brady v Brady* [1989] A.C. 755; [1988] 2 W.L.R. 1308; (1988) 4 B.C.C. 390.
[40] See *Steen v Law* [1964] A.C. 287; [1963] 3 W.L.R. 802; [1963] 3 All E.R. 770 and, in contrast, *Countrywide Banking Corp Ltd v Dean (Liquidator of CB Sizzlers Ltd)* [1998] A.C. 338; [1998] 2 W.L.R. 441; [1998] B.C.C. 105.

There are special provisions which allow money-lending companies to give home loans to their directors or a director of one of their holding companies or to an employee on favourable terms or for a larger amount than would normally be the case (see s.209(3) and (4)). The conditions to be satisfied are:

(a) the loan must be made to facilitate the purchase or improvement of all or part of any dwelling house together with land occupied and enjoyed with that house or to replace a loan made by a third party which meets these requirements;

(b) the house must be the only or main residence of the person to whom the loan is made; and

(c) the company ordinarily makes loans to its employees and the terms of the loan in question are no more favourable than those on which such loans are ordinarily made.

The conditions mean that a company can lend a director a larger amount than it would lend to a comparable third party provided the terms of the loan are no better than are ordinarily made available to the company's employees. Note that the company must, in fact, ordinarily make loans to its employees for the exception to apply. However, the amount must not be so large as to fall outside the company's ordinary course of business.

5.8 Other relevant transactions or arrangements

Sections 210 and 211 set out how to determine what are "other relevant transactions or arrangements" for the purpose of the various exceptions from ss.197, 198, 200 or 201 and their value. The company must first identify all the relevant transactions and arrangements for the director or for one of their connected persons which the company or one of its subsidiaries has entered into relying on the particular exception it proposes to rely on for the proposed transaction or arrangement. So, for example, if the company proposes to rely on the exception in s.207 to make a loan to a director it must identify any other loans, quasi-loans, guarantees or security provided in connection with a loan or a quasi-loan under £10,000 that it or any of its subsidiaries has already made to the director or a connected person. The company must also identify any loan, quasi-loan, guarantee or security provided in connection with a loan or quasi-loan being entered into at the same time as the proposed transaction or arrangement. If the proposed transaction or arrangement is to be made for a director of a holding company or a connected person, the company must identify all the transactions for that director or a connected person entered into by the holding company or any of its subsidiaries (or being entered into at the same time as the proposed transaction or arrangement). If any of the earlier transactions were made by a company which was a subsidiary when the transaction was made but is no longer a subsidiary when the determination is being made, those transactions can be ignored.

Once all the relevant transactions or arrangements have been identified, the value of each must be determined in accordance with s.211 and aggregated with the value of the proposed transaction or arrangement to see if the limit for the proposed transaction is exceeded. For loans, the value is the amount of its principal. The value of a quasi-loan is the amount, or maximum amount, that the person to whom the quasi-loan is made is liable to reimburse the creditor. Where a guarantee or security is to be given (or has been given) it is the amount guaranteed or secured. Where there is a s.203 arrangement, the value is the value of the transaction to which the arrangement relates. The value of a credit transaction is the price that could reasonably be expected to be obtained for the goods, land or services to which the transaction relates if they had been supplied (at the time the transaction is entered into) in the ordinary course of business and on the same terms (other than price) as the terms on which they have been supplied, or are to be supplied. If it is impossible to express the value of a transaction or arrangement as a specific sum of money—whether because the amount of any liability is unascertainable or for any other reason and whether or not any liability has been reduced—the value is deemed to exceed £50,000 (s.211(7)), which means that the proposed transaction will not fall within any of the exemptions.

The value of any "other relevant transaction or arrangement" as determined is reduced by any amount by which the liabilities of the person for whom the transaction or arrangement was made have been reduced.

5.9 Civil consequences of contravening sections 197, 198, 200, 201 or 203

If a company enters into a transaction or arrangement in contravention of ss.197, 198, 200, 201 or 203, the transaction or arrangement is voidable at the company's instance except in four cases (s.213). The first is where the money or asset which is the subject of the transaction or arrangement can no longer be restored. The second is where the company has been indemnified for any loss or damage resulting from the transaction or arrangement. The third case is where a third party has acquired any rights in good faith, for value and without actual notice of the contravention and those rights would be affected if the transaction or arrangement were avoided. The fourth case is where the transaction or arrangement is affirmed by the members of the company and, where necessary, by the members of its holding company "within a reasonable period" (s.214).

Section 213 provides that a transaction made in contravention of ss.197, 198, 200, 201 or 203 is voidable at the instance of the company unless the provisions of ss.213(2) or 214 apply. It follows that neither s.213 nor public policy prevent a company from recovering a loan made to a director in contravention of s.197.[41]

If a transaction or arrangement is made with a director of the company or a director of a holding company, the director incurs liabilities. If the transaction or arrangement is made with a person connected with a director of the company or a holding company, both the person connected with the director and the director with whom that person is connected are liable under s.213, although the director can escape liability in this case if they show that they took all reasonable steps to make sure the company complied with the relevant section. In either case, any director of the company who authorised the transaction or arrangement is also liable. However, a director who authorised a transaction or arrangement will not be liable if they show that, at the time of the transaction or arrangement was entered into, they did not know the relevant circumstances constituting the contravention (s.213(7)). The same is true for a person connected with a director of the company or of its holding company if they can show they did not know the relevant circumstances constituting the contravention when the transaction or arrangement was entered into. In each case, the liability is incurred whether or not the transaction or arrangement is avoided (s.213(3)).

The liability in each case is twofold. First, it is to account to the company for any gain the director or connected person has made directly or indirectly by the transaction or arrangement. Secondly, it is to indemnify the company for any loss or damage which results from the transaction or arrangement. The liability to indemnify is a joint and several liability with anyone else liable under s.213. The liability does not prejudice any other liability a director or person connected with a director may incur. Also, nothing in s.213 excludes the operation of any other enactment or rule of law by virtue of which the transaction or arrangement may be called into question (s.213(8)). In *Neville (Administrator of Unigreg Ltd) v Krikorian*,[42] (which considered the position under Companies Act 1985 s.341) it was held that a director who knowingly allowed a practice to continue under which lending by the company to his co-director was treated as acceptable had authorised the individual payments which were made in accordance with that practice even though he did not have actual knowledge of each individual payment when it was made. The director was held jointly and severally liable for the indebtedness of his co-director. In *Queensway Systems Ltd v Walker*,[43] a co-director was found to be authorising an arrangement or transaction for the purposes of s.341(2), even though she did not know the relevant payments were being posted to a loan account. She knew

---

[41] See *Currencies Direct Ltd v Ellis* [2002] EWCA Civ 779; [2002] B.C.C. 821; [2002] 2 B.C.L.C. 482.

[42] *Neville (Administrator of Unigreg Ltd) v Krikorian* [2006] EWCA Civ 943; [2006] B.C.C. 937; [2007] 1 B.C.L.C. 1.

[43] *Queensway Systems Ltd v Walker* [2006] EWHC 2496 (Ch); [2007] 2 B.C.L.C. 577.

payments were being made and if she had applied her mind to the question of what payments were being made and whether there was any justification for them, she would have discovered there was no justification.

In the case of *Ciro Citterio Menswear Plc*,[44] the High Court held that in some cases breach of Companies Act 1985 s.330 could give rise to a constructive trust, even though neither s.330 nor s.341 Companies Act 1985 mentioned this. However, in that case the High Court held that a constructive trust had not arisen. The director was not in breach of his fiduciary duties and there was no straightforward misappropriation of the company's property.

5.10   Connected persons

Sections 252–255 set out when a person is connected with a director for the purposes of Companies Act 2006 Pt 10. A person (A) is connected with a director of a company if (but only if) A is:

(a)   a member of the director's family, i.e. (i) the director's spouse or civil partner; (ii) any other person (whether of the same or a different sex) with whom the director lives as partner in an enduring family relationship; (iii) the director's children or step-children (of any age); (iv) the children or step-children aged under 18 (and who live with the director, but who are not children or step-children of the director) of the director's partner; and (v) the director's parents (s.253). Note that the director's grandparents, grandchildren, sisters, brothers, aunts, uncles, nephews and nieces are not connected with the director even if they live with the director (s.253(3));

(b)   a body corporate with whom the director is connected (see below). As explained below, in two situations a body corporate connected with a director will not be treated as a connected person of that director;

(c)   a person acting as a trustee of a trust if the beneficiaries of the trust include the director, anyone in (a) above or a body corporate with which the director is connected (see below) or if the trustees have a power under the trust that can be exercised for the benefit of any of those people or bodies. However, trustees acting as trustees of an employees' share scheme (as defined in s.1166) or as trustees of a pension scheme will not be connected with a director merely because he is a beneficiary or potential object of the trust;

(d)   acting as the director's partner or acting as a partner of anyone in (a), (b) or (c);

(e)   a firm that is a legal person under the law by which it is governed in which the director is a partner;

(f)   a firm that is a legal person under the law by which it is governed, if one of the partners of that firm is connected with the director as set out in (a), (b) or (c) above; or

---

[44]   See *Ciro Citterio Menswear Plc v Thakrar* [2002] EWHC 662 (Ch).

(g)   a firm that is a legal person under the law by which it is governed (X), if the director is a partner in another firm which is a partner of X, or a person connected with the director as set out in (a), (b) or (c) is a partner in another firm which is a partner of X.

Put more simply, (e), (f) and (g) mean that if a director is a partner in a firm that is a legal person under the law by which it is governed, that firm and any other firm which the first firm is in partnership with are each connected with the director. Similarly, if a person connected with a director is a partner in a firm that is a legal person under the law by which it is governed, that firm and any other firm which the first firm is in partnership with are each connected with that director. The provisions in (e), (f) and (g) used only to apply to Scottish firms but now apply more broadly.

Section 254 sets out when a director is connected with a body corporate. There are two situations where this is the case. The first is if the director and persons connected with them are together interested in at least 20% of the nominal value of the equity share capital of the body corporate. Equity share capital means the issued share capital but not share capital which only has a limited right to participate in a distribution for both dividends and capital (see s.548). So, for example, preference shares with a fixed right to a dividend and a right only to the return of a fixed amount of capital, such as the amount paid on subscription of the shares, and no further right to participate in any surplus would not be equity shares. The second case where a director is connected with a body corporate is where they and the persons connected with them are together entitled to exercise more than 20% of the voting power at any general meeting of that body corporate or control the exercise of such voting power.

A director is taken to control a body corporate if (but only if) they or any person connected with them are interested in any part of that body's equity share capital (as defined in s.548—see above) or entitled to exercise (or control the exercise of) any part of the voting power at any general meeting of the body corporate and the director, their connected persons and any other directors of the relevant company together are interested in more than half of the equity share capital or can exercise (or control the exercise of) more than half the voting power at any general meeting of the body corporate (see s.255). If a director controls a body corporate (A) which can control the exercise of voting power at a general meeting of another body corporate (B), the director is treated as being able to exercise control over that voting power at B's general meetings (see ss.254(4) and 255(4)). If a company holds shares as treasury shares, those shares and the voting rights attached to them are disregarded for the purposes of working out if a director is connected with a body corporate or controls it (see ss.254(5) and 255(5)).

When working out whether a director is connected with a body corporate or is deemed to control it, there are special rules where a person connected with a director is:

(a)   a body corporate with which the director is connected; or
(b)   a trustee.

In the first case, the interests in shares or votes held by the body corporate are ignored unless the body corporate is also a connected person by virtue of being a trustee or a partner of the director or of someone else connected with them (see s.254(6)(a)). The interests of shares or votes held by a trustee of a trust are ignored provided the only reason the trustee would be treated as a connected person is because the beneficiaries of the trust include (or may include) a body corporate which is connected with the director (see s.254(6)(b)).

A person is not treated as being connected with a director if that person is himself or herself a director of the company (see s.252(3)).

As will be seen from the above, the definition of connected person is extremely wide and catches people, companies, trustees, firms and partners (including those incorporated overseas) which would not, ordinarily, be thought of as being connected with a director. The definition is further broadened by the rules set out in the Companies Act 2006 Sch.1 which apply when determining whether a director is connected with a body corporate or is taken to control a body corporate. Under this, any restrictions or restraints on the exercise of any right attached to an interest in shares are ignored, and a director will be treated as being interested in shares when he or she has agreed to buy them or has a right or obligation under which he or she can become entitled to exercise a right conferred by them (e.g. under a call option or a put option). A director is also treated as being interested in shares if they can exercise a right conferred by holding the shares (such as voting) or can control that right, even though they are not the registered holder. The provisions of Sch.1 should be considered carefully in each case to see whether the director has an interest.

Chapter 6

Service Contracts and Remuneration

Andrew Taggart, Partner and Jemima Coleman, Professional Support Lawyer

Herbert Smith Freehills LLP

6.1 Introduction

The legal issues relevant to directors' service contracts and remuneration are considered in this Chapter, together with the relevant best practice guidance.

This Chapter examines the following issues:

(a)   definition of a service contract;
(b)   authorisation by the board of the company's entry into service contracts with directors;
(c)   limits on the length of the term of a director's service contract;
(d)   disclosure of service contracts, both to shareholders and the wider public;
(e)   remuneration of directors;
(f)   other benefits provided to directors, for example pension arrangements and share option schemes; and
(g)   compensation payable to directors for loss of office.

6.2 Definition of a service contract and key provisions

The Companies Act 2006 (CA 2006) Pt 10 Ch.5 on "Directors' Service Contracts" sets out a definition of a director's "service contract" at s.227:

> "(1)   For the purposes of this Part [10], a director's 'service contract', in relation to a company, means a contract under which—
>
> (a)   a director of the company undertakes personally to perform services (as director or otherwise) for the company, or for a subsidiary of the company, or
>
> (b)   services (as director or otherwise) that a director of the company undertakes personally to perform are made available by a third party to the company, or to a subsidiary of the company."

The definition includes contracts of service (e.g. an executive service agreement), contracts for services and non-executive letters of appointment. The contract may relate to any services that a director undertakes personally to perform for the company or a subsidiary or where a director provides services through a third party (e.g. a personal services company) (CA 2006 s.227(1)(b)).

A shadow director (any person in accordance with whose directions or instructions the directors of the company are accustomed to act) (CA 2006 s.251) is covered by s.227, as are de facto directors (anyone who acts as if he is a director and is treated as such by the board but has not been validly appointed). For the purposes of the CA 2006, "director" is defined to include any person occupying the position of director, by whatever name called (CA 2006 s.250).

6.3 Authorisation of service contracts—compliance with the company's constitution

Any service contract with a director must be authorised in accordance with the company's articles of association. The articles identify the responsibilities and duties of individual directors and the board as a whole. The articles usually prescribe that vacancies may be filled or additional directors may be appointed by the board of directors (subject to the articles' maximum number of directors) and will state the quorum required in order for a board meeting to take place. Provisions relating to directors' powers, remuneration (e.g. limit on directors' fees), interests, voting rights, ability to count in the quorum as well as the procedure for removal of directors, and any references to board delegation of responsibility, may also be contained in the articles of association. The consequence of a failure to follow the articles is that any purported agreement will be void. These principles apply equally to any changes to the terms of directors' service contracts.

The directors must also comply with the codified directors' duties set out in CA 2006:

(a)   a duty to act within powers (s.171);
(b)   a duty to promote the success of the company (s.172);
(c)   a duty to exercise independent judgment (s.173);
(d)   a duty to exercise reasonable care, skill and diligence (s.174);
(e)   a duty to avoid conflicts of interest (s.175);
(f)   a duty not to accept benefits from third parties (s.176); and
(g)   a duty to declare interest in proposed transaction or arrangement (s.177).

These duties are discussed in more detail in Chapter 3 of this Guide.

In certain instances, the statutory duties provide for derogation where a director is acting in a way authorised by the company's constitution.

There is a general duty on directors to declare their interest in a *proposed* transaction or arrangement, breach of which is a civil offence. However, since October 2008, there has been no need for a director to declare an interest if it concerns terms of his service contract that have been or are to be considered (i) by a meeting of the directors; or (ii) by a committee of the directors appointed for the purpose under the company's constitution (CA 2006 s.177(6)(c)). However, the articles of association may prescribe that directors should declare their interest in such circumstances. There is a separate obligation to declare a direct or indirect interest in an *existing* transaction or arrangement that has been entered into by the company (CA 2006 ss.182–183), for which a failure to comply would be a criminal offence.

The board should approve service contracts and changes to their terms formally only after a proper consideration of the company's interests and after ensuring compliance with the articles and the codified directors' duties mentioned above. The minutes of the board meeting should confirm compliance with these formalities and a copy of the minutes, signed by the chairman of the meeting, should be kept as evidence that the proper procedure has been followed.

6.4   Limits on the length of the term of a service contract

6.4.1   *Statutory limits—CA 2006 section 188*

Executive and non-executive directors' service contracts where the guaranteed term of employment with the company or any subsidiary is, or may be, longer than two years, require shareholder approval (CA 2006 s.188). The terms of the contract must be made available for inspection for at least 15 days before the meeting to approve it, and at that meeting. Further, if more than six months before the end of the guaranteed term of a director's employment, the company enters into a further service contract (otherwise than in pursuance of a right conferred by or under the original contract on the other party to it), then CA 2006 s.188 will apply as if there were added to the guaranteed term of the new contract the unexpired period of the guaranteed term of the original contract (CA 2006 s.188(4)). If a service contract contains such a term and there has been no shareholder approval, the term will be void and the service contract will be deemed to be terminable on reasonable notice.

There are a couple of exceptions. Shareholder approval is not required for a long-term service contract between a wholly-owned subsidiary and one of its directors. Nor is shareholder approval required if the company is not a UK-registered company (CA 2006 s.188(6)).

The purpose of this section is to encourage the trend towards shorter length service contracts as contracts with a guaranteed term of over two years can be costly for the company to terminate early. These new provisions apply equally to non-executive directors' letters of appointment. It is expected that notice provisions will become much more common in non-executive directors' letters of appointment as a result. Previously, institutional shareholders have voiced concerns that the presence of notice provisions could make it easier for executive directors to remove non-executive directors, following a board-level disagreement. It may be that some organisations will prefer to obtain shareholder approval to obtain the safeguard of a long-term contract for their non-executive directors. A provision could even be inserted into such a contract in which the non-executive director agrees not to bring a claim for damages for any early termination of his appointment. A contractual waiver of such claims at the outset should be binding.

6.4.2   Corporate governance on service contract limits

The key source of corporate governance standards in the UK is the UK Corporate Governance Code (the Corporate Governance Code). The latest version, published by the Financial Reporting Council (FRC) in July 2018, applies to accounting periods beginning on or after 1 January 2019. The Code covers Board Leadership and Company Purpose; Division of Responsibilities; Composition, Succession and Evaluation; Audit, Risk and Internal Control; and Remuneration. The Code is applicable to all companies with a premium listing, whether incorporated in the UK or elsewhere. Rule 9.8.6 of the Listing Rules provides that the Corporate Governance Code applies on a "comply or explain" basis to all companies with premium listing of equity shares incorporated in the UK.[1]

The Corporate Governance Code states the following in relation to notice or contract periods:

> "Provision 39: Notice or contract periods should be one year or less. If it is necessary to offer longer periods to new directors recruited from outside the company, such periods should reduce to one year or less after the initial period. The remuneration committee should ensure compensation commitments in directors' terms of appointment do not reward poor performance. They should be robust in reducing compensation to reflect departing directors' obligations to mitigate loss."

A quoted company must set out its approach to exit payments in its remuneration policy which is subject to a binding vote. As discussed in more detail below (at Section 6.6.5), remuneration payments and payments

---

[1]   Copies of the Corporate Governance Code are available from the website of the FRC: *http://www.frc.org.uk* [Accessed 2 May 2019].

for loss of office must be consistent with the approved directors' remuneration policy or, if not, must be approved by shareholders.

The Investment Association (formerly the Association of British Insurers) republished its Principles of Remuneration in November 2018. This guidance states that:

> "Undeserved and excessive remuneration sends a negative message to all stakeholders, including the Company's workforce, and causes long term damage to the Company. Shareholders expect the Remuneration Committee to ensure that the remuneration structure is appropriate and to exercise relevant discretion to avoid these situations."

Shorter notice periods are one mechanism for avoiding an excessive severance payment on termination. When drawing up contracts, remuneration committees should calculate the likely cost of any severance and determine whether this is acceptable. The contract should make clear that if a director is dismissed following the use of a disciplinary procedure, a shorter notice period than that given in the contract would apply. In reality, this may be difficult to negotiate.

The Investment Association Principles of Remuneration also state that:

> "Remuneration structures should be set to promote long-term value creation through transparent alignment with the agreed corporate strategy. Remuneration policies should support performance, encourage the sustainable financial health of the business and promote sound risk management for the success of the company and to the benefit of all its stakeholders."

Further, the IA's Principles of Remuneration (para.8) state that company should follow the Principles and Guidance contained within the Investment Association and PLSA Statement on Executive Contracts and Severance. This provides that the one-year notice period should not be seen as a floor, and boards are strongly encouraged to consider contracts with shorter notice periods.[2] If it is necessary to offer longer notice periods, for example for incoming executives at companies in difficulties, the statement indicates that the termination and length of the contract need to be justified and need to reduce on a rolling basis.

The AIM Rules for Companies, published by the London Stock Exchange, require an AIM company to state on its website and in its admission document when admitting its shares to trading on AIM:

- The details of a recognised corporate governance code that the board of directors of the AIM company has decided to apply. For example, AIM companies may adopt the Quoted Companies Alliance (QCA)

---

[2]   See   *https://www.ivis.co.uk/media/5896/ABI_NAPF_Joint_Statement_14feb2008_2_v_5.pdf* [Accessed 2 May 2019].

Corporate Governance Code or the Financial Reporting Council's (FRC) UK Corporate Governance Code.
- How the AIM company complies with that code and where it departs from its chosen corporate governance code an explanation of the reasons for doing so.

In addition, all companies incorporated in England and Wales are bound by any corporate governance provisions contained in the Companies Act 2006.

6.5 Disclosure of service contracts

6.5.1 Statutory obligations

A company must keep copies of every director's service contract (or where there is no written contract, a memorandum of the terms) open to inspection by shareholders without charge (CA 2006 s.288).

This obligation applies regardless of the length of any service contract and whether or not it is terminable within 12 months. All the copies and memoranda must be kept available for inspection at the company's registered office or a place specified in regulations under s.1136 (CA 2006 s.228(2)). The copies and memoranda must be retained by the company for at least one year from the date of termination or expiry of the contract and must be kept available for inspection during that time (CA 2006 s.228(3)). As a result of the expanded definition of service contract in CA 2006 s.227, this section now applies to contracts for services and non-executive directors' letters of appointment. These provisions apply equally to variations of a director's service contract and accordingly any documents amending the terms of a service contract must also be open to inspection by shareholders (CA 2006 s.228(7)). The company must give notice in the prescribed form to the registrar as to the place of inspection and of any change to that place unless they have at all times been kept at the company's registered office (CA 2006 s.228(4)). The disclosure requirements apply even where the director's contract requires him to work wholly or mainly outside the UK. There are financial penalties for a failure to comply with these require-ments. It is a criminal offence for which every officer of the company who is in default may be held liable to pay a fine (currently up to £1,000) (CA 2006 s.228(6)). In a change from the previous position under CA 1985 s.318, the company is no longer liable under the criminal offence.

Where a shareholder is denied inspection the court can compel inspection or direct that the copy required be sent to the person requiring it (CA 2006 s.229(5)).

In addition to shareholders' right to inspect (without charge) the copies of service contracts held by the company mentioned above, shareholders' have the right, upon payment of the prescribed fee, to request copies of such directors' service contracts (or, if not in writing, a memorandum of its terms) (CA 2006 s.229). The copy must be provided within seven days of the company receiving the request. Where a shareholder is denied inspection the court can compel inspection or direct that a copy be sent to the person requiring it (CA 2006 s.229).

6.5.2 The Takeover Code guidance on disclosure

The Takeover Code aims to provide a framework within which takeovers of public companies are conducted and to ensure fair and equal treatment of all shareholders. The Takeover Code covers both takeovers by contractual offer from the bidder to purchase the target shareholders' shares and schemes of arrangement sanctioned by the court under CA 2006.

The Takeover Code r.25.5 requires particulars of service contracts of directors and proposed directors of the target or any of its subsidiaries to be disclosed in the first major circular from the target board advising shareholders of an offer (whether recommending acceptance or rejection of the offer). If any of the contracts have been entered into or amended within six months of the offer document, details of the previous arrangements must be provided (and, if there have been none, this should be stated).

The particulars to be disclosed include:

(a)   the name of the director under contract;
(b)   the date of the contract, the unexpired term and details of any notice periods;
(c)   full particulars of each director's remuneration including salary and other benefits;
(d)   any commission or profit-sharing arrangements;
(e)   any provision for compensation payable upon early termination of the contract; and
(f)   details of any other arrangements which are necessary to enable investors to estimate the possible liability of the company on early termination of the contract.

It is not acceptable to refer to the latest annual report, indicating that information regarding service contracts may be found there, or to state that the contracts are open for inspection at a specified place.

A criminal offence has been introduced where the offer document does not contain the required information (including certain employee information). This applies to bids covered by the directive (e.g. a bid for a company listed on the Official List); and to other bids (e.g. a bid for a company listed on AIM) or to schemes of arrangement from November 2006. It is therefore very important that the information disclosed in bid documents on employment matters is accurate and complete. Further discussion on these changes falls outside the scope of this Chapter.

However, the Takeover Code r.26 which requires various documents to be made available for inspection and published on a website for inspection by the other party, or by any competing offeror or potential offeror, from the time that the offer document or offeree board circular, as appropriate, is published until the end of the offer period (and any related competition reference period), no longer includes a requirement for all service contracts of offeree company directors to be disclosed.

6.5.3   Persons entitled to inspect

As can be seen from the above, different provisions apply to who is entitled to inspect under the Companies Act 2006, the Corporate Governance Code and the Takeover Code.

6.6   Remuneration of directors

6.6.1   Components of directors' remuneration

6.6.1.1   Salary

A significant part of a director's remuneration is likely to be his salary. In relation to listed companies, the salary level should be set by the remuneration committee in accordance with:

(a)   the principles contained in the Corporate Governance Code (see Section 6.6.2 below);
(b)   the Investment Association's Principles of Remuneration; and
(c)   other best practice guidance.

Where the organisation is regulated by the Financial Conduct Authority (FCA) or the Prudential Regulation Authority (PRA), remuneration should be set in accordance with the revised Remuneration Code of Practice applicable to FCA or PRA regulated firms, as appropriate. This sets out principles against which the regulator will assess the quality of firms' remuneration policies and any linkage between these policies and excessive risk-taking by staff. Key objectives of the code include making firms' boards focus more closely on ensuring that the total amount of remuneration paid by a firm is consistent with good risk management and that individual compensation practices provide the right incentives.

Remuneration arrangements for directors of quoted companies incorporated in the UK must be consistent with the company's remuneration policy (as discussed in more detail below). Further details of the factors influencing the level at which salaries should be set by the remuneration committee are set out below.

6.6.1.2 Bonus

In addition to his basic salary, a director may be eligible to receive a bonus under a scheme which is either discretionary or contractual. The nature of the scheme is crucial, particularly in assessing damages on an early termination of the service contract. If truly contractual, the director is entitled to the bonus calculated in accordance with the bonus formula and the company cannot refuse to pay it or withhold any part of it. If discretionary, the director will not be contractually entitled to the bonus even when any targets as to individual/company performance are met, though the company would be under the general duty not to act in breach of the duty of trust and confidence in the way it exercised the scheme—this means that it should not exercise its discretion in bad faith or capriciously.

When an employer exercises a discretion set out in a contract to determine a bonus, they must:

- act rationally—i.e. an employer must not determine a bonus that no reasonable employer would have determined in all of the circumstances; and
- not take into account irrelevant factors or fail to take into account relevant factors in determining the bonus. This reflects the UK Supreme Court's decision in *Braganza v BP Shipping*[3] which imported public law concepts into the law on employment contracts.

If an employer does not satisfy these requirements, there is a risk that an employee could successfully claim for a higher bonus from a court or tribunal, and even claim that the employer's conduct gave the employee grounds to claim they had been constructively dismissed.

In the case of *Patural v DB Services (UK) Ltd*,[4] a banker challenged an employer's decision to award him a smaller bonus than two colleagues who were entitled to a guaranteed bonus. On the facts the claim did not succeed, but the High Court accepted the relevance of public law concepts in light of *Braganza*. The court did express caution about this development, noting that private employers do not necessarily have the same duties as public authorities to act in the public interest, but it likely that we will see this type of public law argument run in future. Companies should consider carefully what factors are relevant to such decisions, in addition to ensuring that they act in good faith and that the decision itself is not capricious or irrational.

---

[3]   *Braganza v BP Shipping* [2014] UKSC 17.
[4]   *Patural v DB Services (UK) Ltd* [2015] EWHC 3659 (QB).

However, even prior to *Braganza*, the Court of Appeal decision in *Keen v Commerzbank AG*[5] suggests that an employee wishing to challenge the amount of a discretionary bonus has a high evidential hurdle to clear. In that case, the fact that the employer had paid less than the line manager's recommendation and less than reflected the success of the employee's team was insufficient, given the employer's wide discretion in fluctuating market and labour conditions. An employee will need strong evidence of irrationality or perversity, supported by independent evidence, to be able to proceed with his claim. An employer can rely on a condition of a bonus scheme that the employee must be in employment at the payment date to be eligible for a bonus.

Employers wishing to withhold a bonus from an employee who has left or is under notice on the bonus payment date should expressly provide this in the scheme rules. The decision in *Rutherford v Seymour Pierce Ltd*[6] indicates that it will be difficult to argue such a term could be implied without evidence of a clear unvarying practice, at the time of entering into the contract, of not paying bonuses in this situation.

Employers should be wary of pre-contractual statements or representations, for example by headhunters or recruitment consultants, which might be used as evidence of a contractual entitlement where the bonus is intended to be discretionary. Clearly, careful drafting of the scheme is essential where no contractual entitlement is intended.

Similarly, in the context of an existing employment relationship, there will be a strong presumption that promises concerning employment terms are intended to be legally binding. In *Attrill v Dresdner Kleinwort Ltd*,[7] the employer had made an oral promise in relation to the size of a bonus pool and, even though there was no certainty as to each individual employee's award, the Court of Appeal found that the employer had contractually committed to a minimum bonus pool from which it could not renege, despite deteriorating financial circumstances. The case involved assurances made to Dresdner Bank employees prior to the sale of Dresdner Bank from Allianz to Commerzbank. A senior employee announced a guaranteed minimum bonus pool for the relevant year in order to stem the tide of investment banker defections. Subsequently, Commerzbank's attitude to honouring the commitment changed; it sought to avoid paying out bonuses on the basis that payments were subject to a material adverse change clause and that the financial circumstances of the Bank justified non-payment. The Court of Appeal ruled that a promise concerning the size of a bonus pool was capable of being incorporated into individuals' contracts of employment. The promise was also sufficiently certain notwithstanding the lack of detail as to how much could be held back for contingencies. It was sufficient

---

[5]   *Keen v Commerzbank AG* [2006] EWCA Civ 1536; [2006] 2 C.L.C. 844; [2007] I.C.R. 623.
[6]   *Rutherford v Seymour Pierce Ltd* [2010] EWHC 375 (QB); [2010] I.R.L.R. 606.
[7]   *Attrill v Dresdner Kleinwort Ltd* [2013] EWCA Civ 394; [2013] I.R.L.R. 548.

that the employees had been told that the fund would be dealt with "in the usual way". Further, there was a clear intention to create a legally binding obligation, given the use of the word "guaranteed". It is important to ensure that any oral assurances given to staff are carefully considered and that contractual commitments are not inadvertently created. Any commitments on bonus pool should expressly refer to any circumstances in which the employer wishes to have the right to reduce the pool, such as significant financial deterioration or reduction in the number of eligible employees.

Entitlement under a bonus scheme will depend on the terms of the scheme, but common factors are the company's performance in the relevant financial year (or the performance of particular subsidiaries for which a director is responsible) by reference to profits and the individual director's performance. A High Court decision (*Fish v Dresdner Kleinwort Ltd*[8]) confirmed that there is no duty on employees to give up contractual bonuses due to the employer's financial losses. The employer's argument that a senior employee's duty of trust and confidence, good faith or fiduciary duty obliged him to waive his right to a contractual bonus when the employer suffered significant financial losses failed. Employees cannot be obliged to forego their contractually promised remuneration simply because the employer's financial situation changes after the promise is made.

Bonus awards commonly take the form of cash payments, but some companies have adopted deferred share bonus plans whereby a part of the bonus is payable in shares which must be held by the director for a minimum period.

6.6.1.3 Long-term incentive schemes

A long-term incentive scheme which offers a director the right to acquire shares in the parent company may be another component of a director's remuneration. Such arrangements will often take the form of a share option, where the director will benefit from any increase in share price, or the grant of a share award, where the director can acquire shares at nil or nominal cost. These awards will generally be dependent on the company's performance, assessed by reference to particular targets. Alternatively they may take the form of a deferred bonus award, whereby part of the director's annual cash bonus is taken in the form of shares and, if left with the trustees of the scheme for a certain period, may qualify the director for a matching allocation of additional free shares. Again, the level of any matching award will generally be dependent on the company's performance. Under the Listing Rules, long-term incentive schemes for directors (whether payable in cash, shares or any other security) have to be approved by the shareholders except in specified circumstances (LR 9.4).

---

[8]   *Fish v Dresdner Kleinwort Ltd* [2009] EWHC 2246 (QB); [2009] I.R.L.R. 1035.

The Corporate Governance Code 2018 states:

> "Provision 36: Remuneration schemes should promote long-term shareholding by executive directors that support alignment with long-term shareholder interests. Share awards granted for this purpose should be released for sale on a phased basis and be subject to a total vesting and holding period of five years or more. The remuneration committee should develop a formal policy for post-employment shareholding requirements encompassing both unvested and vested shares.
>
> Provision 37: Remuneration schemes and policies should enable the use of discretion to override formulaic outcomes. They should also include provisions that would enable the company to recover and/or withhold sums or share awards and specify the circumstances in which it would be appropriate to do so."

A recent example of the impact of media scrutiny of share awards and the rationale for reform involved the £100m pay package of Jeff Fairburn, Chief Executive of Persimmon, in 2018. The size of the award was largely due to share awards linked to the company's stock market value, which had doubled since he took over in 2013. Persimmon's success was partly due to the publicly-funded Help-to-Buy programme which stimulated the housing market. When the long-term incentive plan was set up in 2012, the shares were trading at £4. But by 2018, the shares were trading at £24. As there was no cap on the award of shares, it meant there was no limit to the pay-out. Mr Fairburn agreed to a reduction in his package to £75m following public outcry; but the company said it could not claw back any of the share awards. Mr Fairburn's departure was announced shortly thereafter by "mutual agreement and at the request of the company". The issue was said to be having a "negative impact" on the firm's reputation and on "Jeff's ability to continue in his role".

6.6.1.4   Golden hellos

Offer letters may provide for a cash bonus to be paid when the director commences employment. These are taxable as income in the normal way. They typically take the form of an immediate cash payment or a guaranteed bonus for the first year/part year of employment when a discretionary bonus scheme would otherwise operate. An immediate cash payment would normally become repayable if the director left within a specified period of commencing employment. Such payments can be justified where they are needed to attract the best recruits.

6.6.2 Requirements of the Corporate Governance Code in relation to directors' remuneration

Chapter 5 of the Corporate Governance Code 2018 contains provisions relating to remuneration.

The Code contains three key principles regarding remuneration:

> "P. Remuneration policies and practices should be designed to support strategy and promote long-term sustainable success. Executive remuneration should be aligned to company purpose and values, and be clearly linked to the successful delivery of the company's long-term strategy.
>
> Q. A formal and transparent procedure for developing policy on executive remuneration and determining director and senior management remuneration should be established. No director should be involved in deciding their own remuneration outcome.
>
> R. Directors should exercise independent judgement and discretion when authorising remuneration outcomes, taking account of company and individual performance, and wider circumstances."

Provision 34 provides that the remuneration of non-executive directors should be determined in accordance with the Articles of Association or, alternatively, by the board. Levels of remuneration for the chair and all non-executive directors should reflect the time commitment and responsibilities of the role. Remuneration for all non-executive directors should not include share options or other performance-related elements.

A remuneration committee should be established of non-executive directors, with a minimum membership of three. This committee should have delegated responsibility for determining the policy for executive director remuneration and setting remuneration for the chair, executive directors and senior management. It should review workforce remuneration and related policies and the alignment of incentives and rewards with culture, taking these into account when setting the policy for executive director remuneration.

The Corporate Governance Code 2018 states that only basic salary should be pensionable. The pension contribution rates for executive directors, or payments in lieu, should be aligned with those available to the workforce. The pension consequences and associated costs of basic salary increases and any other changes in pensionable remuneration, or contribution rates, particularly for directors close to retirement, should be carefully considered when compared with workforce arrangements (Provision 38).

6.6.3   The Investment Association's Principles of Remuneration

The Investment Association's (IA) Remuneration Principles and general Guidance was re-published in November 2018 in relation to the manner in which remuneration is determined and structured. The Remuneration Principles expound the importance of simplicity and clarity. They are not prescriptive but provide that remuneration structures should be set to promote long-term value creation: to support performance, encourage the sustainable financial health of the business and promote sound risk management for the success of the company and to the benefit of all its stakeholders. The IA highlight investor concern that shareholder consultation on remuneration is treated as a validation exercise by the Remuneration Committee, rather than as a process for obtaining the views of their major shareholders. Investors need to analyse a company's remuneration structure, taking account of the company, and provide clear feedback. It is predominantly for companies with a main market listing but is also relevant to companies on other public markets, such as AIM.

The Principles on Remuneration are divided into four: Remuneration Policies, Remuneration Committees, Remuneration Structures and Levels of Remuneration. There is also detailed guidance for Remuneration Committees to help apply the IA's Principles on Remuneration and ensure a proper level of shareholder protection. Relevant extracts from the Principles are set out below:

> "Remuneration Policies should be set to promote long-term value creation and should be clearly aligned with corporate strategy. Remuneration policies should support performance, encourage the sustainable financial health of the business and promote sound risk management for the success of the company and to the benefit of all its stakeholders. Non-executive directors, particularly those serving on the Remuneration Committee, should oversee executive remuneration; but the Chairman and whole Board should be appropriately engaged. Remuneration Committees need to exercise independent judgement and not be over-reliant on their remuneration consultants. Remuneration structures should be appropriate for the specific business, and efficient and cost-effective in delivering its longer-term strategy. Complexity is discouraged. Shareholders prefer simple and understandable remuneration structures. Remuneration structures should be designed to reward sustainable business performance and deliver long-term value to shareholders."

Forfeiture of all or part of a bonus or long-term incentive award before it has vested and been paid ("performance adjustment" or "malus"); and/or clawback of sums already paid should be permitted, according to the IA's Principles. Executives should build up a high level of personal shareholding to ensure alignment of interests with shareholders.

Shareholders would expect the Remuneration Committee to exercise relevant discretion in relation to levels of remuneration to avoid excessive remuneration pay-outs which adversely affect the company's reputation and sends a negative message to staff. The Board should explain why the chosen maximum remuneration level is appropriate for the company. The Board should be mindful of pay and conditions in the rest of the workforce. Further, the Board should consider the aggregate impact of employee remuneration (including executive director remuneration) on the finances of the company, its investment and capital needs, and dividends to shareholders.

Separately, the Pensions and Lifetime Savings Associations (PLSA) (formerly NAPF) published its Corporate Governance and Voting Guidelines 2018. This echoes some of the themes in the IA's Principles of Remuneration, including that remuneration committees should design rewards that drive long-term success and the importance of effective engagement with shareholders.

6.6.4 Role of the remuneration committee

It will be seen from the provisions of the Corporate Governance Code and the IA's Remuneration Principles set out above that the remuneration committee plays a vital role in setting the levels and structure of directors' remuneration.

The remuneration committee should ensure compensation commitments in directors' terms of appointment do not reward poor performance. They should be robust in reducing compensation to reflect departing directors' obligations to mitigate loss (Provision 39).

When determining executive director remuneration policy and practices, the remuneration committee should address the following:

- clarity—remuneration arrangements should be transparent and promote effective engagement with shareholders and the workforce;
- simplicity—remuneration structures should avoid complexity and their rationale and operation should be easy to understand;
- risk—remuneration arrangements should ensure reputational and other risks from excessive rewards, and behavioural risks that can arise from target-based incentive plans, are identified and mitigated;
- predictability—the range of possible values of rewards to individual directors and any other limits or discretions should be identified and explained at the time of approving the policy;
- proportionality—the link between individual awards, the delivery of strategy and the long-term performance of the company should be clear. Outcomes should not reward poor performance; and
- alignment to culture—incentive schemes should drive behaviours consistent with company purpose, values and strategy. (Provision 40)

6.6.5 Disclosure requirements

6.6.5.1 Directors' report and directors' remuneration report—Accounts and Reports Companies Act 2006 Pt 15

All UK companies are required to prepare and file annual accounts and a directors' report and to have those accounts audited (subject to certain exemptions on grounds of size). The company may choose which accounting regime to apply—either Companies Act accounts prepared in accordance with the Companies Act 2006 or IAS accounts prepared in accordance with the International Accounting Standards (IAS).

Every company must send a copy of its annual accounts and reports (which includes the remuneration report in the case of a quoted company) to every shareholder of the company, every holder of the company's debentures and every person who is entitled to receive notice of general meetings (CA 2006 s.423). Directors of a public company must lay before the company in general meeting, copies of its annual accounts and reports (CA 2006 s.437). A quoted company must, prior to its accounts meeting, give its members notice of an ordinary resolution, approving the directors' remuneration report, although entitlement of a person to remuneration is not made conditional on the resolution being passed (CA 2006 s.439). The directors of a quoted company must deliver a copy of the directors' remuneration report to Companies House (s.439).

Requirements for Companies Act accounts are set out in Regulations:

(a) the Large and Medium-sized Companies and Groups (Accounts and Reports) Regulations 2008[9] (as amended by the Large and Medium-sized Companies and Groups (Accounts and Reports) (Amendment) Regulations 2013[10] and the Companies (Miscellaneous Reporting) Regulations 2018 (the Accounts Regulations)[11]; and
(b) the Small Companies and Groups (Accounts and Directors' Report) Regulations 2008.[12]

These Regulations set out the detailed requirements in relation to disclosure of directors' remuneration. Listed companies also have to comply with the Disclosure and Transparency Rules in relation to obligations imposed on them regarding periodic financial reporting.

---

[9] Large and Medium-sized Companies and Groups (Accounts and Reports) Regulations 2008 (SI 2008/410).
[10] Large and Medium-sized Companies and Groups (Accounts and Reports) (Amendment) Regulations 2013 (SI 2013/1981).
[11] Companies (Miscellaneous Reporting) Regulations 2018 (SI 2018/860).
[12] Small Companies and Groups (Accounts and Directors' Report) Regulations 2008 (SI 2008/409).

It is the directors' duty to ensure that annual accounts are prepared in accordance with Companies Act 2006, although they may delegate the detailed preparation activity to others. Directors should ensure that annual accounts give a true and fair view and so they must be satisfied with the methods adopted. The board must approve the accounts; the accounts should be signed on behalf of the board by a director. A parent company of a group or large or medium-sized companies must prepare group accounts. There are penalties for non-compliance (CA 2006 s.419). Only small companies are not required to produce group accounts (CA 2006 s.399).

6.6.5.2   Directors' report

Directors must prepare a directors' report for each financial year of the company including the names of the directors and the principal activities of the company in the course of the relevant financial year (CA 2006 ss.415(1) and 416(1)). A parent company of a group which prepares group accounts must also prepare a group directors' report. The directors' report must be approved by the board of directors and signed on behalf of the board by a director or the company secretary. All companies (except small companies) must produce a business review as part of the directors' report.

The directors' report must include information about the company and its directors, a statement that all relevant information has been disclosed to auditors, and a business review.

For financial years ending on or after 1 October 2013, the enhanced business review under CA 2006 s.417 has been replaced by a new requirement for companies to produce a standalone Strategic Report, which is a separate part of the Annual Report.

The purpose of the Strategic Report is to inform shareholders of the company and help them to assess how the directors have performed their duty under s.172 (duty to promote the success of the company). The Strategic Report must contain a fair review of the company's business and a description of the principal risks and uncertainties facing the company. It should be a balanced and comprehensive analysis of the development and performance of the company's business during the financial year, and the position of the company's business at the end of the year, consistent with the size and complexity of the business. This report should set out key messages in relation to the company's strategy and its business model, performance, principal risks and remuneration. It must include disclosures on social and environmental matters and the gender make-up at various levels within the corporate structure (i.e. number of persons of each sex who are, respectively, directors, managers (excluding those who are also directors) and employees of the company). The purpose is to disclose information required by shareholders to understand the development, performance or position of the company's business (s.414C).

6.6.5.3   Directors' remuneration report

The directors of a quoted company have a duty to prepare a directors' remuneration report for each financial year (CA 2006 s.420(1)). This duty applies to every person who was a director of the quoted company immediately before the period for filing the accounts and failure to comply constitutes an offence punishable by a fine (CA 2006 s.420(2)). All other companies are required to provide details of directors' remuneration in the notes to the financial statements, but the disclosure is far simpler than for a directors' remuneration report. The remuneration report must be approved by the board of directors and signed on behalf of the board by a director or the company secretary (CA 2006 s.439).

The remuneration report forms part of the annual report and accounts. It must be sent to the quoted company's shareholders with notice of the AGM, laid before the meeting and a copy sent to Companies House.

The Companies Act 2006 and Sch.8 to the Accounts Regulations contain the requirements in relation to directors' remuneration reports for quoted companies. There are standardised methodologies for the disclosure and presentation of remuneration information that should be clear and prepared consistently from year to year. The measures apply to remuneration payments to directors of any UK incorporated quoted companies, whether they are executive or non-executive directors. A "quoted company" is defined in the Companies Act 2006 for this purpose as a company whose shares are listed on the Official List, officially listed in an EEA State or admitted to dealing on the New York Stock Exchange or Nasdaq. The directors' remuneration report must contain:

1)   Annual Statement—a statement by the chair of the remuneration committee: this must summarise the major decisions on directors' remuneration, any substantial changes relating to directors' remuneration made during the year and the context in which those changes and decisions occurred or were taken;

2)   Directors' Remuneration Policy—the company's policy on directors' remuneration (the "remuneration policy"); this will set out the company's forward-looking policy on remuneration and potential payments (including its approach to exit payments), and be subject to a binding shareholder vote at least every three years; and

3)   Annual Report on Remuneration—disclosures on how the remuneration policy was implemented in the financial year being reported on (the "annual report on remuneration"); this will set out the actual payments made to directors in the last financial year, including disclosure requirements such as the single total figure for remuneration and pay relative to company performance over the last 5–10 years, and be put to an annual advisory shareholder vote.

NB—For financial years beginning on or after 1 January 2019, the Annual Statement must also summarise any discretion which has been exercised in the award of directors' remuneration.

Once the remuneration policy comes into effect, it will apply in relation to all remuneration and loss of office payments to directors; such payments will need to be consistent with the company's approved remuneration policy, or else separately approved by a shareholder resolution, unless the payment is made as part of an agreement entered into before 27 June 2012, which has not been amended or renewed since. NB One can still come across pre-June 2012 contracts occasionally; usually a pay rise would constitute an "amendment" to a contract, but it is sometimes argued that the underlying contractual terms fall outside the scope of the remuneration policy on the basis that the contract was entered into before 27 June 2012. It is important to clarify this point as a payment made which is inconsistent with the remuneration policy will be void (and there are potential personal liabilities for any director approving a payment in contravention of an approved remuneration policy).

Remuneration payments to directors of all other types of UK incorporated companies (including other public companies) will continue to be subject to the existing regime in the Companies Act 2006, including, for example, the requirements in relation to payments for loss of office (which are discussed in more detail below at Section 6.8).

It is an offence for directors of quoted companies not to produce a directors' remuneration report or to produce a report which does not comply with the requirements of the Companies Act 2006.[13]

6.6.5.4 *Directors' remuneration report: annual report on remuneration*

The annual report on remuneration should include the information set out below.

(1) *A table in prescribed format containing the single total figure of remuneration for each director in the financial year.* It should reflect actual pay earned rather than potential pay awarded. The purpose of the table is to provide comprehensive disclosures on all types of remuneration, including fixed and variable elements as well as pension provision in a consistent format. Disclosure is required for

---

[13] Directors may be liable for fines for failure to: Prepare the directors' remuneration report (CA 2006 s.420(2)); Provide information to prepare the directors' remuneration report (CA 2006 s.421(4)); Ensure that any directors' remuneration report or revised directors' remuneration policy that is approved complies with the requirements of the CA 2006 (CA 2006 ss.422(2) and 422A(5)); Give notice of the resolution for the approval of the directors' remuneration report or directors' remuneration policy to shareholders (CA 2006 s.440(1) and (2)); Put the resolution on the directors' remuneration report or directors' remuneration policy to a vote (CA 2006 s.440(2)).

each director who has served as a director at any time during the relevant year. Each column must contain two sums: the sum for the relevant year and the corresponding sum for the preceding financial year. The FRC's Financial Reporting Lab has developed a methodology for how the inputs into the single figure should be calculated and stated: "It is important to note that investors' interest is not in the single figure itself; rather it is in understanding the components of the single figure, as well as how it develops over time. Accordingly, the disclosure that accompanies the table is just as important as the numbers. It is the related disclosure that is needed by investors to allow them to obtain a proper understanding of the components of remuneration". The table should include details of:

(a) salary and fees in respect of the relevant financial year;

(b) the gross value of all taxable benefits paid or payable in the year, e.g. medical insurance, car, club benefits and the value (where significant). Benefits received in advance of a director commencing qualifying service are to be treated as if received on the first day of the contract under which the person is employed, or under which the payment is made);

(c) the full bonus awarded related to the performance year and whether it was in cash or shares (including the full amount of any bonus that has been deferred save where deferral is subject to further performance measures or targets in a future financial year). Where an amount is deferred, the percentage deferred, whether it was deferred in cash or shares and, where relevant, whether the deferral was subject to any conditions other than performance measures should be disclosed. Do not include (i) vesting of deferred elements of previous years' bonus (i.e. any awards made in a *previous* period where final vesting is determined as a result of achievement of performance conditions relating to the year being reported on (or shortly after the end of that financial year)); nor (ii) sums deferred awards subject to the achievement of performance measures or targets in a future reporting period;

(d) LTIP awards where final vesting is determined as a result of the achievement of performance conditions that end in the year being reported on and any awards granted where the final value is not subject to future performance conditions. Here (i) the cash value of any monetary award should be disclosed; (ii) the value of any shares or share options vested (there is a formula for calculating the value by reference to the percentage of the LTIP award that vests in the financial year (or best estimate of the percentage that will vest in the financial year) multiplied by the market price of shares at the date on which the shares vest); and (iii) the value of any additional cash or shares receivable in respect of dividends accrued (actually or notionally). Where the market price of shares at the date on which the shares vest is not ascertainable at the date on which the remuneration report is

218

approved by directors, an estimate of the market price of the shares shall be calculated on the basis of an average market value over the last quarter of the relevant financial year. The cash amount the individual was or will be required to pay to acquire the shares must be deducted from the total in respect of an award of shares or share options. NB—For financial years beginning on or after 1 January 2019, there are additional reporting requirements including an estimate of the amount of the award attributable to share price appreciation and whether discretion has been exercised as a result of share price appreciation or depreciation.

If any cash or shares become receivable as a result of a bonus and/or LTIP award included above, the following information should be set out: details of the performance measure and relative weighting of each, within each performance measure, the targets set when the performance measure was agreed and the corresponding value of the award achievable, and for each performance measure, how the company performed against the targets set and measured. Where the company has a discretion in respect of an award, it should also disclose whether the discretion was exercised and, if so, at what stage in the performance cycle and how, that discretion was exercised; and

(e)   all pension-related benefits including, broadly speaking, (i) any payments (whether in cash or otherwise) in lieu of pension; (ii) the cash value of contributions paid or payable to a director's money purchase scheme; and (iii) the additional value achieved by the director during the financial year from participating in a defined benefit scheme calculated using the method set out in the Accounting Regulations 2008 Sch.8.

Information relating to non-executive directors may be set out in a separate table and there is also flexibility to add columns to the prescribed table where required. A single figure for the previous financial year should also be disclosed. Where any money or other assets in respect of any previous financial year are clawed back for any reason, in the financial year being reported on, then the claw-back can be shown as a negative figure in a separate column and deducted from the total, with a note explaining the reason for the reduction and how it was calculated. Where the prescribed calculations (other than in respect of recovery or withholding) result in a negative value, this must be expressed as a zero in the relevant column in the table.

(2)   *Total pension entitlements for each person who has served as a director of the company at any time during the relevant financial year.* Companies will need to set out details of pension schemes in operation and who is entitled to benefits under them within the policy report. As the value attributed to defined benefit pensions in the single figure table does not capture the total value of the benefit further information must be provided for each person who has served as a director of the company

at any time in the relevant financial year, and who has a prospective entitlement to defined benefits or cash balance benefits. The additional information includes details of accrued benefits under the scheme as at the end of the relevant year, the person's normal retirement date and the total value of any additional benefit that will be receivable on early retirement. Where the person has a right to more than one type of pension benefit separate details must be provided in respect of each type of benefit.

(3)　*Scheme interests awarded during the financial year.* This section covers disclosures of awards in respect of the financial year where the value will be determined according to the achievement of performance conditions in future periods. Companies are required to report details of scheme interests awarded to each person who has served as a director of the company at any time during the relevant financial year. Additional disclosure of the percentage of the award that would vest at different levels of performance will be required. The purpose of this is to ensure companies continue to provide information about the decisions the remuneration committee has taken about directors' potential future entitlement to remuneration and the potential liabilities of the company. A table will need to be inserted, setting out scheme interests awarded to the director during the relevant financial year which are subject to performance measures and targets in future periods. For each scheme interest, the type of interest awarded, the basis for the award, the face value of the award, the percentage that would vest at minimum performance, where the scheme interest is a share option, an explanation of any difference between the exercise price per share and the face value, and the relevant performance period. A summary of the performance measures and targets, if not set out elsewhere in the report, is also required. The regulations set out how "face value" should be calculated.

(4)　*Payments within the reporting year to past directors.* Details of any payments made in the relevant financial year to any person who was not a director of the company at the time the award was made but had previously been a director of the company, other than payments for loss of office (which are disclosed separately), those disclosed in the single total remuneration table or in previous directors' remuneration reports, payments which are below a de minimis threshold set by the company and stated in the report, regular pension benefits commenced in a previous year, dividend payments in respect of scheme interests retained after leaving office and payments in respect of employment (or any other contractual service performed for) the company other than as a director.

(5)　*Loss of office payments.* On termination of a director's appointment, the company will be required to issue a statement immediately setting out details of any exit payment and how it has been calculated. This information will need to be restated in the annual report on remuneration, as indicated below: for each person who was a director at any time during the relevant year, or previous years, the total amount of any payment for loss of office, an explanation of how each component was calculated, any other payment paid to or receivable in connection with termination, including outstanding incentive awards that vest on or following termination and, where a discretion was exercised, an explanation of how it was exercised. There is a carve-out for de minimis payments.

(6) *A statement of directors' shareholding and share interests.* The report must state any requirements on the director to own shares in the company and state whether or not those requirements have been met. Further, in tabular form: (i) the total number of shares and share options of which the director is the beneficial owner; (ii) details of scheme interests (not including interests included in the single remuneration figure or disclosed in the context of para.3 above) differentiating between shares and share options, and those with and without performance conditions; and (iii) share options which are (a) vested but unexercised; and (b) exercised in the relevant financial year should be set out.

(7) *A performance graph* should be included showing up to ten years' comparative total shareholder return, supplemented with a table setting out historic CEO total remuneration together with the CEO's annual bonus rates and long-term incentive vesting rates (both expressed as a percentage of the maximum opportunity in the relevant years).

(8) *The percentage change in remuneration of the chief executive officer.* A disclosure of the percentage change from the financial year preceding the relevant financial year in relation to salary, benefits and bonus included in the total remuneration of the CEO (as set out in the single figure table) and that of all of the employees of the company taken as a whole. Where the company is a parent company, the statement should relate to the group and not the company and the CEO reported on should be the CEO of the parent company.

(9) *CEO pay ratio.* This is the ratio of the CEO's total remuneration (single total figure of remuneration) to the median (50th), 25th and 75th percentile full-time equivalent remuneration of their UK employees. There is a prescribed format for the ratios table and the disclosure will need to build up in future years to eventually cover a ten year time span. Companies must also provide specific information and an explanation, including: the methodology chosen for calculating the ratios; any trend or changes to the median pay ratio compared to the previous year; and whether (and if so why) the company believes the ratio is consistent with the company's wider policies on UK employee pay, reward and progression.

(10) *The relative importance of spend on pay* in graph form comparing the reporting year spend to previous years. This should set out the expenditure of the company on: (i) remuneration paid to or receivable by all employees of the group; (ii) distributions to shareholders by way of dividend and share buyback; and (iii) any other significant

distributions and payments or other uses of profit or cash-flow deemed by the directors to assist in understanding the relative importance of spend on pay.

(11) *Statement of implementation of remuneration policy in the following financial year.* The report must contain a statement describing how the company intends to implement the approved directors' remuneration policy in the financial year following the relevant financial year which includes, where applicable: (i) the performance measures and relative weightings for each; and (ii) performance targets determined for the performance measures and how awards will be calculated. Other than in the first year, the statement should detail any significant changes in the way that the remuneration policy will be implemented in the next financial year compared to how it was implemented in the relevant financial year. Significant changes are likely to include changes in basic salary, maximum bonus, long-term incentive awards, target short-term and long-term incentive awards, any change in non-executive director fees etc.

(12) *Remuneration committee.* If a committee of the company's directors has considered matters relating to the directors' remuneration for the relevant financial year, the report must name each director, state whether any person provided the committee advice or services that materially assisted with the consideration on any matter, and name any person that has done so. In relation to any non-director who provided remuneration advice, the report must state the nature of any other services that that person has provided to the company during the relevant financial years, who appointed that person and how they were selected, and how the remuneration committee has satisfied itself that the advice was objective and independent.

(13) *A statement of shareholder voting.* Full details will need to be disclosed of the number of votes cast (and the number for, against and abstentions) in respect of the last AGM, both in relation to the policy report and the annual report on remuneration. If in relation to either the binding vote or the advisory vote there were substantial shareholder votes against the resolution, then the annual report on remuneration should include the reasons for that vote (where known to the company) and any actions taken by the directors in response.

Items (1)–(6) above (which correlate to paras 4–17 of Pt 3 of Sch.8 to the revised Accounts Regulations) will be subject to audit.

6.6.5.5 *Directors' remuneration policy*

The policy report should include disclosures in relation to the matters set out below.

(1) *Commencement.* The directors' remuneration policy must be prepared at least every three years.

(2) *Continuation of policies.* Where a directors' remuneration policy is to be put to a meeting of the company for approval and it is intended that provisions of the last approved directors' remuneration policy shall continue to apply after the approval of the policy, this must be specifically stated, along with which provisions shall continue to apply and for what period of time.

(3) *Non-executive directors.* A table should set out the fees to be paid to that director, any additional fees payable for any other duties to the company and such other items to be considered in the nature of remuneration under their letter of appointment.

(4) *Future pay policy.* A description of each component of the remuneration package for the company's directors in tabular form e.g. base salary, benefits, annual bonus, long term incentive plan and pension. The table should set out:

(a) how each component supports the short and long-term strategic objectives of the company (or group);

(b) an explanation of how that component of the remuneration package operates including whether there are any provisions for the recovery of sums paid or the withholding of the payment of any sum i.e. claw-back or malus provisions;

(c) the maximum potential value receivable;

(d) where applicable, a description of the framework used to assess performance including what performance measure(s), if any, are used, the relative weighting of each and the period of time over which they are measured. The amount that may be paid for minimum level of performance that triggers a payment under the policy and any further levels of performance set in accordance with the policy should be disclosed together with an explanation as to whether there are any provisions for the recovery of sums paid or the withholding of any sums. Accompanying notes should explain why any performance measures were chosen and how any performance targets are set, the reason for any component not being subject to performance measures (other than salary, fees, benefits or pension), any new components included which were not previously part of the remuneration package and an explanation of the differences, if any, from the company's policy on remuneration of directors to that of employees generally within the company (or group); and

(e) an explanation of any provisions to permit recovery of sums or withholding of payments.

The purpose of this element of the policy report is to give shareholders a better understanding of how the policy as a whole supports the success of the company over the long term. The Accounts Regulations state that the company should explain any new element of remuneration which did not form part of the remuneration package in the last directors' remuneration policy which was approved by members and set out the rationale for the change. There is a carve-out for information disclosure of which would, in the opinion of the directors, be commercially sensitive.

(5) *Approach to recruitment remuneration.* A statement of the principles underlying the approach to remuneration for new directors, i.e. the various components to be included in the package and the company's approach to each component. This includes the maximum level of variable remuneration which may be granted (which can be expressed in monetary terms or otherwise). The principles which the company would apply in relation to compensating new recruits for the forfeiture of any award under variable remuneration arrangements entered into with a previous employer should be stated.

(6) *Service contracts* including a description of obligations in service contracts (e.g. notice periods, remuneration, change of control provisions) plus any proposed obligation which could impact on remuneration or loss of office payments which is not disclosed elsewhere in the report. This requirement also applies to non-executive letters of appointment.

(7) *Illustrations of application of remuneration policy.* A chart which sets out what the company expects executive directors (not non-executive directors) to receive in different circumstances e.g. minimum, on-target and maximum total remuneration including fixed elements but not allowing for any share price appreciation, and all variable elements paid out in full. An explanation must be given of the assumptions underlying the scenario charts. The purpose of this disclosure is to improve transparency about the potential levels of payment to directors. The intention is for this disclosure to provide an indication of the expectations of the remuneration committee when setting pay rather than hard and fast estimates of future pay packages. The Companies (Miscellaneous Reporting) Regulations 2018 introduce new requirements in this regard for remuneration policies introduced on or after 1 January 2019, including a requirement where performance targets or measures relate to more than one financial year, to provide an indication of the remuneration receivable assuming share price appreciation of 50% during the relevant performance period, and a short description of the basis of the calculation.

(8) *Policy on payment for loss of office.* The policy must set out the company's policy on the setting of notice periods under directors' service contracts. The report must also state the principles on which loss of office payments will be determined, including an indication of how each component of pay will be dealt with when calculating the exit payment, any contractual provision agreed prior to the introduction of the revised Account Regulations that could impact on the termination payment, and what approach will be taken to consideration of the circumstances under which a director leaves and how his performance during his period of service is taken into account when exercising any discretion.

(9) *Statement of consideration of conditions elsewhere in the company.* How pay and employment conditions of employees of the company (or group) were taken into account when setting the policy for directors' remuneration. The statement must also set out whether, and if so, how, the company consulted with employees when drawing up this policy part. The purpose of this is to make reports more specific about what the pay policy is for the wider organisation and how that has impacted on the decisions taken by the remuneration committee.

(10) *Statement of consideration of shareholder views.* Whether, and if so, how, any views expressed by shareholders in respect of remuneration at the last AGM or during the financial year were taken into account in formulating the directors' remuneration policy. The purpose of this section is to disclose information about how the company has engaged with shareholders. NB—The 2018 Corporate Governance Code emphasises the board's responsibility for considering the needs of wider stakeholders (see, in particular, Principle D and Provisions 3, 5 and 41).

Investors often expect the future pay policy table to be disclosed annually, so they can easily locate the policy currently in force and consider how it has been implemented. If the policy report is being put to a binding vote, the remuneration committee should clearly outline any changes in the policy and explain why they are being made. The key aspect will be the level of detail provided by the companies in the policy table; and, in particular, the need to strike the right balance between providing enough flexibility for companies to attract and retain the right employees and for investors to have sufficient detail to ensure the policy has sufficient boundaries. Remuneration reports should provide context for a remuneration committee's decision; they should not be drafted using "boilerplate" precedents.

6.6.5.6 *Directors' remuneration report: consequences of breach*

Directors may be liable for fines for failure to:

(a) prepare the remuneration report;
(b) provide information to prepare the remuneration report;
(c) sign the remuneration report;
(d) give notice of the vote on the remuneration report to shareholders; or
(e) put the resolution on the remuneration report to a vote.

A director is only liable to compensate the company for any loss it suffers as a result of any untrue or misleading statement in, or omission from, the directors' report, directors' remuneration report or summary financial statements, if the director knew or was reckless as to whether the statement was untrue or misleading or knew the omission to be dishonest concealment of a material fact (CA 2006 s.463). The safe harbour also provides that liability of the director is only to the company and not to any third party.

6.7 Other benefits

6.7.1 Pension arrangements

Pension benefits may be a very significant element of a director's remuneration package. Benefits for directors may be provided through an existing company scheme set up for all employees (although often special sections may be appropriate offering a higher scale of benefits, a lower retirement age and special terms on early termination of employment), or through a separate pension scheme for executives, or via contributions to a director's personal pension arrangement.

Usually, benefits will be provided through registered pension schemes, in order to qualify for reliefs and exemptions from various taxes. However, since the Government has legislated to restrict tax relief on pension savings for high earners, there has been renewed interest in unregistered arrangements as a means of retirement benefit provision for senior executives and directors.

Tax relief on employer contributions to a registered pension scheme is given by allowing the contributions to be deducted as an expense in computing the profits of a trade, profession or investment business, and so reducing the amount of an employer's taxable profit. Employer contributions qualify for tax relief if they are made "wholly and exclusively for the purposes of the employer's trade".

Relevant UK individuals (broadly, those aged under 75, resident in the UK and with relevant UK earnings chargeable to income tax) who are active members of registered pension schemes will be entitled to tax relief on their contributions on an amount up to 100% of their earnings. Contributions over 100% of earnings are possible, although pension providers are not required to accept them and no tax relief would be available.

However, a tax charge (the "annual allowance charge") is payable where pension savings made by, or on behalf of, a member (therefore, including employer contributions) in a tax year are in excess of the annual allowance. Reducing the annual allowance has been a key feature of the restriction on tax relief for high earners since 2011. The annual allowance was reduced from £255,000 to £50,000 for 2011–2012, and has been £40,000 since 2014–2015. From 2016–2017, the annual allowance has also been "tapered" so that, broadly, it is reduced by £1 for every £2 by which the individual's taxable income (which includes employer pension contributions, rental income and dividends) exceeds £150,000, up to a maximum reduction of £30,000; meaning an individual earning £210,000 or more will have an annual allowance of £10,000. An individual's annual allowance will also be reduced if the member has accessed benefits in a money purchase arrangement.

Broadly, whether an individual will be liable for an annual allowance charge in any tax year will depend upon whether his pension savings (his "pension input amount") for his pension input period ending in that tax year exceed the annual allowance. For those individuals accruing benefits on a money purchase basis (excluding cash balance arrangements), the member's pension input amount will be the total of any tax relievable contributions made by or on behalf of the individual to his money purchase arrangement (including contributions made in respect of the individual by his employer). In relation to defined benefit accruals, in broad terms an increase in the value of the member's benefits will occur if the value of the individual's entitlements at the end of his pension input period is greater than the value at the start of the period.

The annual allowance charge operates by recouping relief on pension contributions and accruals from which the relevant individual has benefited. Any savings in excess of the annual allowance are added to the individual's net income and taxed at his marginal rate of 20%, 40% or 45%.

In addition, a single lifetime limit on retirement savings for tax purposes applies. Pension savings in excess of this "lifetime allowance" will be subject, on vesting, to a recovery charge of 55% if taken as a lump sum (and 25% if taken as pension). The occurrence of certain "benefit crystallisation events" (including becoming entitled to a scheme pension and death) triggers the test of an individual's pension savings against his or her available lifetime allowance. The lifetime allowance was reduced to £1 million from 2016–17 and increases by CPI each tax year from 2018–19 (meaning it will be £1,055,000 for 2019–20). Those whose retirement savings were close to, or in excess of, the lifetime allowance as at 6 April 2006 (the date when the pensions tax regime was overhauled and when the lifetime allowance was introduced), or when the lifetime allowance was reduced in 2012, 2014 and 2016, may have been able to take advantage of transitional protection. Depending upon the type of protection, individuals may be prevented from accruing any further pension benefits under registered pension scheme if their transitional protection is to be maintained.

The changes to the high earner tax regime led to interest from employers in unregistered pension schemes (known as employer-financed retirement benefit schemes (EFRBS)), which can be outside of the ambit of the tax restrictions described above. EFRBS are viewed as successor vehicles to pre-6 April 2006 "unapproved arrangements" (funded unapproved retirement benefit schemes (FURBS) and unfunded unapproved retirement benefit schemes (UURBS)). However, changes have been introduced to limit their usefulness in most cases.

EFRBS are subject to their own particular tax and National Insurance requirements (which are broadly more favourable to high earners when compared to the effects of the reduced annual and lifetime allowances). In essence, employer contributions to EFRBS are not subject to National Insurance charges/contributions or otherwise taxable at the time they are paid into the EFRBS; neither are they tax deductible until benefits start to be paid to the member (though, for contributions since 2017, they cease to be tax deductible at all five years after the accounting period in which the contributions are paid). National Insurance charges will not be payable when benefits are paid out of the EFRBS where the benefits are within the limits which apply to registered pension schemes and where the employment relationship has come to an end (including any consultancy arrangement). The employee pays tax on any benefit he or she receives from the EFRBS; and the normal inheritance tax rules apply. Monies held in EFRBS will not count towards the individual's lifetime allowance.

"Disguised remuneration" legislation has been introduced to limit the opportunity for using EFRBS to sidestep the reduced annual and lifetime allowances. Whilst unfunded arrangements continue to be feasible under the disguised remuneration regime (and HMRC has confirmed that these fall outside the new regime), more stringent restrictions apply in respect of funded arrangements. Broadly, contributions to funded EFRBS arrangements will be immediately taxable for the employee unless the contribution is made to a pooled arrangement, such that it cannot be attributed to a single employee. Whilst this means that multi-member defined benefit arrangements are likely to be feasible, the same will not apply to single-member or defined contribution arrangements, where contributions can be attributed to individual members.

The restrictions that have been put in place have greatly limited the usefulness of these arrangements, and HMRC has indicated that it will continue to monitor these arrangements and may legislate further if it finds evidence of abuse. There may be some circumstances where such arrangements may nevertheless offer an alternative structure for employers wishing to compensate employees for the loss of accrual in their registered pension schemes (or for the tax charge applying to such accrual).

6.7.2   Share schemes

6.7.2.1   Long-term incentive schemes

Another key component of a director's remuneration can be a long-term incentive scheme which typically offers the director the right to acquire shares in the company or its parent company. Such arrangements will often take the form of a market-value share option, where the director will benefit from any increase in share price, or the grant of a nil-cost or free share award, where the director can acquire shares at nil or nominal cost. These awards will generally be dependent on the company's performance, assessed by reference to pre-set targets.

Alternatively, they may take the form of a deferred and also, possibly, a matching bonus award, whereby part of the director's annual cash bonus is taken in the form of shares and, if left with the trustees of the scheme for a certain period, may qualify the director for a matching allocation of additional free shares. Again, the level of the matching award (if any) will generally be dependent on the company's performance.

Employee share schemes take different forms, but share schemes can broadly be divided into tax-advantaged share schemes and non-tax-advantaged shared schemes. Types of tax-advantaged share schemes include Company Share Option Plans (CSOPs); SAYE, save as you earn, sharesave or savings-related option schemes (SAYE); Enterprise Management Incentives (EMI) options and Share Incentive Plans (SIP). (NB—SAYE and SIPs are all-employee plans, not specifically for directors, although directors can participate.) Non tax-advantaged share schemes provide incentives but do not attract favourable tax treatment; these do not have statutory requirements regarding the company, the shares, the employee or the limits on participation so can be more flexible than a tax-advantaged scheme. Such schemes can be used by companies in addition to a tax-advantaged scheme, for example to grant options above the limits available in a tax-advantaged scheme.

6.7.2.1.1   Discretionary share option schemes

A discretionary share option scheme normally gives the director the right to acquire shares in the company at an exercise price equal to market value at the date of grant of the option. The option will normally be exercisable from the third anniversary of grant until the tenth anniversary of grant (provided the director is still in employment), although some companies will allow a proportion of the option to become exercisable where the director leaves in certain specified circumstances. These type of schemes are usually established in two parts; a tax-advantaged part (CSOP) (which normally attracts income tax and National Insurance Contributions reliefs on options over shares with an aggregated value of up to £30,000 per participant at the original grant price, provided the options are not exercised for at least three years from grant), and a non-tax-advantaged part (which provides for options in excess of this limit, which will usually be subject to income tax and National Insurance Contributions).

6.7.2.1.2 Enterprise management incentive (EMI) schemes

Tax-advantaged EMI options are a type of discretionary share option arrangement commonly used by smaller, often private trading companies. EMIs are designed to assist higher risk trading companies to attract key executives by offering them generous tax reliefs on share options over shares with a value of up to £250,000 at the date of grant.

On 18 June 2018, HMRC published a report which evaluates the impact of EMI on small and medium enterprises; the report found substantial evidence that EMI is fulfilling its core aims of improving recruitment and retention prospects for small and medium enterprises and supporting their future growth.

A company, whether quoted or unquoted, can qualify for an EMI provided its gross assets do not exceed £30 million, it has fewer than 250 full-time equivalent employees, it is not under the control of another company, it only has "qualifying subsidiaries" and has a "permanent establishment" in the UK. Certain trading activities will not qualify and there are detailed rules relating to the independence requirement, the trading requirement and the shares that can be used for EMI options.

Companies can seek advance clearance from HM Revenue & Customs that they meet the requirements.

There is an aggregate £3 million limit (calculated at the date of each relevant grant) on the total value of shares in the company over which unexercised options under an EMI scheme may exist at any time.

There is no requirement under an EMI scheme for a minimum period before exercise. Qualifying companies may consequently choose their own exercise periods provided the option is capable of being exercised within ten years of grant. There will normally be no income tax or National Insurance Contributions to pay when an EMI option is exercised provided the option was granted at no less than market value (options can be granted at a discount to market value, but any such discount is taxable on exercise). When the shares are sold, capital gains tax may be payable on any gain over the market value at grant (that is, the difference between the sale proceeds and the market value of the shares at grant).

An added advantage of incentivising employees by using EMI options is that, provided certain conditions are met, the one-year holding period in order to benefit from entrepreneurs' relief will commence from the date the EMI options are granted (rather than from the date the underlying shares are acquired) and the requirement that shareholders hold at least 5% of the capital and voting rights in the company will be dis-applied. The Finance Bill 2019 proposes extending the one-year period between grant and disposal to a two-year period. If enacted, this will have effect for disposals made on or after 6 April 2019.

6.7.2.1.3 Share award schemes

Share award schemes, unlike discretionary options, give the right to acquire shares at nil or nominal cost. The awards will generally be structured as a free share award, nil-cost option or as the award of restricted (forfeitable) shares. The extent, to which those shares may be received, usually at the end of a three-year period, will depend on the company's performance, assessed by reference to pre-set targets. The value of the shares received will generally be subject to income tax and National Insurance Contributions on vesting. Increasingly, companies are requiring their directors to defer part of their annual cash bonus which is then taken in the form of shares and, if not sold for a certain period, will qualify the director for a matching allocation of additional free shares. Again, the level of the matching award will generally be dependent on the company's performance.

6.7.2.1.4 "Phantom" share schemes

Phantom share schemes are cash bonus schemes made to look like a share option scheme, or other long-term incentive plan, with the amount of the cash bonus mirroring the gain which would have been made on a true share scheme. They are usually used where a share scheme is not possible, but where the company wishes to link part of the director's remuneration to the share price as an incentive.

Eligibility for participation in any such scheme will be determined by the particular scheme rules which may provide that the board or a board committee, namely the remuneration committee, shall determine whether an individual participates in a scheme in any given year, and the extent of that participation. It is therefore advisable not to refer to participation in incentive schemes in the director's service agreement, save to say that the director may be invited to participate in the company's relevant schemes, subject to their rules.

Under the Listing Rules, any scheme which may involve the issue of new shares requires shareholder approval (LR 9.4). A scheme which uses existing shares may also require shareholder approval if one or more of the directors is eligible to participate and the scheme involves conditions in respect of service and/or performance to be satisfied over more than one financial year.

The 2018 Corporate Governance Code states that remuneration schemes should promote long-term shareholdings by executive directors that support alignment with long-term shareholder interests. Share awards granted for this purpose should be released for sale on a phased basis and be subject to a total vesting and holding period of five years or more. The remuneration committee should develop a formal policy for post-employment shareholding requirements encompassing both unvested and vested shares (Provision 36).

The Investment Association's Principles of Remuneration (November 2018) states that long-term incentives exist to reward the successful implementation of strategy and the creation of shareholder value over a period appropriate to the strategic objectives of the company. The Principles states that the performance period for long-term incentives should be clearly linked to the timing of the implementation of the strategy of the business, which should be no less than three years. Further, "the use of additional holding periods is expected by investors, so that in total the performance and holding period should cover a period of at least five years". The Principles state that the Remuneration Committee should select a remuneration structure which is appropriate for the specific business, efficient and cost-effective in delivering the company's longer-term strategy. The Principles set out the views of investors on some common structures and highlight various issues to consider, for example in relation to performance conditions and the way the remuneration committees exercise discretion on vesting outcomes.

As a result of these provisions, long-term incentive plans for listed companies will generally either have a five year vesting period or a requirement that any shares acquired by a director under such a scheme may not be sold before the fifth anniversary of the grant.

6.8 Compensation for loss of office

6.8.1 Damages for early termination of a service contract

In the absence of a liquidated damages, or payment in lieu of notice (PILON), provision in the contract, or any misconduct or other contractual breach on the part of the director entitling the company to dismiss with immediate effect, the director will be entitled to damages for wrongful dismissal if he is dismissed summarily.

Before turning to the issue of how damages will be assessed, a brief word about the approach of HM Revenue and Customs to the tax treatment of termination payments. If there is a PILON provision expressly stated in the contract or implied by virtue of custom and practice, sums paid under this section or broadly equivalent to the monies due under it will be fully taxable unless the employer can show he has terminated in breach.

Damages for wrongful dismissal will be assessed by reference to the net loss the director has sustained as a result of the breach of contract for the balance of the term of the service contract or the notice period. The net loss is calculated by assessing the net salary that the director would have received during that period, plus a sum to represent the loss of any other contractual benefits (e.g. a car) for the period.

Historically termination payments which are not taxable under the Income Tax (Earnings and Pensions) Act 2003 (ITEPA) s.62 as general earnings or under any other provision may be exempt from tax up to the first £30,000 pursuant to ITEPA s.401. (Section 401 applies to payments made in relation to offices or employment, so will cover termination payments made to non-executive directors.)

A new regime in relation to tax treatment of termination payments came into effect in respect of terminations on or after 6 April 2018. Effectively, employers are now required to subject to tax and class 1 NICs an amount equivalent to the employee's basic pay for any periods of unserved notice. HMRC will tax fully (as earnings) such part of a termination payment as is deemed to be in respect of unworked notice; the balance can then benefit from the £30,000 tax exemption. This additional tax is calculated using "basic pay", which includes pay that would have been received had it not been salary sacrificed, but excludes overtime pay, bonuses, commission, allowances, benefits in kind etc. HMRC's updated Employment Income Manual states that the calculation must be done even where the employment is terminated without notice by making a contractual payment in lieu.

Any amount over £30,000 will be subject to income tax in the normal way, and a damages payment will need to be grossed up to take account of the tax that the director will have to pay on the excess over £30,000.

Payments under ITEPA s.401 are not generally liable to NICs, even if they exceed £30,000, as they are not "earnings". However, employer Class 1A NICs on termination payments over £30,000, will be introduced with effect from April 2020 (NB—At time of publication, this measure has been postponed twice already; but we understand that it is due to take effect from April 2020).

Further, in assessing appropriate damages the board would be entitled to make a deduction for accelerated receipt, that is, a deduction to reflect that the director will receive the sum immediately rather than in monthly instalments had he remained in employment. The percentage deduction should be set by reference to what the director might reasonably be expected to earn by way of interest on the total sum.

Entitlement to damages is subject to the director's duty to attempt to mitigate his loss by seeking suitable alternative employment, thereby reducing the damages payable by the company by the amount that the director might reasonably be expected to earn. The courts will expect the departing director to do everything he can to find another job. Initially, the director would be entitled to restrict his search to positions at a similar level, offering equivalent salary and other benefits, but after a period he might be expected to look at a lower level. Clearly, if the director already has another job this can be taken into account by the company in assessing what it should pay the departing director—provided that the company knows about it. This is why a director may be required to warrant in any settlement documentation that he has not already obtained another job or been offered one.

In light of this, it will be clear that the unexpired length of the contract is especially significant, as companies cannot assume that mitigation will significantly reduce their liability. In deciding the level of damages payable, the board will have to consider carefully the director's prospects of finding alternative employment and it would not be exercising its powers in the best interests of the company if it failed to do so. To take expert advice from, for example, a recruitment consultant experienced in board-level prospects would assist the board in discharging this responsibility. Board minutes should record the board's consideration of the mitigation issue and how and why it reaches its conclusions.

The remuneration committees should ensure that contracts protect the company from being exposed to the risk of payment in the event of failure. Annual bonuses should be contractually related to performance. In the event of early termination, there should be no automatic entitlement to bonuses or share-based payments. If the service contract is simply to include a notice period, damages for breach of which would then be subject to the director's duty to mitigate his loss, shareholders will expect reassurance that the board has taken steps to ensure that the director has mitigated his loss to the fullest extent possible.

The inclusion of a clause in the service contract providing for phased payments where the company continues to pay the departing executive on the usual basis for the outstanding term of the contract or, if earlier, until the executive finds new employment is a useful mechanism. Continued payment could be stated to be conditional on the executive making reasonable efforts to find other employment (and, possibly, providing the company with proof of this).

6.8.2   *Payments for loss of office—CA 2006 sections 215–222 and 226*

The CA 2006 ss.215–222 set out the general position with regard to payments for loss of office. NB—There is a separate regime for remuneration payments and payments for loss of office for directors of UK incorporated quoted companies, as discussed in more detail below.

Section 217(1) CA 2006 provides that:

> "A company may not make a payment for loss of office to a director of the company unless the payment has been approved by a resolution of the members of the company."

A payment for loss of office is defined in CA 2006 s.215 as a payment made to a director or past director of a company as:

(a)   compensation for loss of office as director of the company (s.215(1)(a));
(b)   compensation for loss of any other office or employment in connection with the management of the affairs of the company or of any subsidiary undertaking (s.215(1)(b));
(c)   consideration for or in connection with his retirement from office as a director (s.215(1)(c)); or
(d)   consideration for or in connection with retirement from any other "office or employment in connection with the affairs of the company" or any subsidiary undertaking while a director or in connection with ceasing to be a director (s.215(1)(d)).

The regime under the Companies Act 2006 for payments for loss of office is discussed in detail in Chapter 5, Section 5.2 "Loss of office and retirement from office".

Cash and non-cash benefits are expressly covered. Payments to a person connected with a director, or payments to any person at the direction of, or for the benefit of, a director or a person connected with him will be treated as payments to the director for the purposes of ss.217–221 and therefore require members' approval (s.215(3)). It is clear that a payment to a former director would be caught as there is an express reference to "past director" in CA 2006 s.215.

The requirement to obtain members' approval to a payment to a director or former director in respect of loss of employment is limited to where the employment relates to the management of the affairs of the company.

A company may not make a payment for loss of office to a director of its holding company unless the payment has been approved by a resolution of the members of the company making the payment (unless the subsidiary is wholly-owned) and the members of the holding company (CA 2006 s.217(2)). A memorandum setting out details of the proposed payment (including its amount) must have been made available to members of the company before approval is given.

Member approval is also required if the company wishes to make a payment for loss of office to a director of the company in connection with the transfer of the whole or any part of the undertaking or the property of the company or of the subsidiary of the company (CA 2006 s.218). In the case of payment for loss of office to a director in connection with the transfer of shares in the company (or in a subsidiary of the company) resulting from a takeover bid, approval is required of the holders of the shares to which the bid relates and of any holders of shares of the same class (CA 2006 s.219). Extending the requirement for members' approval to payments for loss of office in these circumstances is new. There is also a presumption that member approval will be required in respect of any payments made pursuant to an arrangement entered into as part of the agreement for the share transfer in question, or within one year before or two years after that agreement, and to which the company whose shares are the subject of the bid, or any person to whom the transfer is made, is privy (CA 2006 s.219(7)). Persons making the offer for shares in the company (and any associate of them) are excluded from voting on any resolution to approve a payment for loss of office in connection with a share transfer (CA 2006 s.219(4)).

Shareholder approval is not required for a payment made in good faith in one of the following situations:

(a)   in discharge of an existing legal obligation (defined as an obligation "that was not entered into in connection with, or in consequence of, the event giving rise to the payment for loss of office");
(b)   by way of damages for breach of such an obligation;
(c)   by way of settlement or compromise of any claim arising in connection with the termination of a person's office or employment; or
(d)   by way of pension in respect of past services (CA 2006 s.220(a)–(d)).

CA 2006 s.220 broadly follows the exception contained in the previous Companies Act, CA 1985 s.316(3), for bona fide payments made by way of damages for breach of contract, as discussed in Chapter 5, Section 5.2.2.

A payment made in accordance with a clearly drafted payment in lieu of notice, liquidated damages or change of control provision should not require shareholder approval under the Companies Act 2006 as it should fall within the exemption for payments made in discharge of an existing legal obligation.

It is likely that for a payment of damages to be made "in good faith" and to escape the need for shareholder approval, a deduction should be made to take account of mitigation and accelerated receipt. Similarly, in relation to the exception for compensation payable in respect of a settlement or compromise of claims arising from termination of employment, a sensible estimate of the amount of likely compensation for any statutory claims, together with an assessment of likely compensation for breach of contract and a careful consideration of the director's future prospects of employment will be needed if the proposed compensation is to fall within the exemption and avoid the need to obtain shareholder approval.

The final exemption which relates to "pension for past services" is intended to cover a payment made to a pension scheme on behalf of a director in connection with the loss of office or employment. However, the scope of the exemption is unclear and a cautious approach is advisable especially given the IA guidance on ensuring that executives do not depart on special or preferential pension terms (e.g. with limited or no actuarial reduction).

The civil consequences of breaching these sections are set out at CA 2006 s.222(1)–(3) and are discussed in Chapter 5, Section 5.2.5.

As mentioned above, there is a separate regime for remuneration payments and payments for loss of office for directors of UK incorporated quoted companies, which is set out in Ch.4A "Directors of Quoted Companies: Special Provision" CA 2006. Payments for loss of office for these purposes are defined in the same way as above (CA 2006 s.215). These provisions also cover "remuneration payments" which include any form or payment or other benefit made to a current, prospective or former director (other than a payment for loss of office).

As explained in Section 6.6.5.1 above, the remuneration policy report part of the directors' remuneration report must contain details of the amount of any compensation for loss of office paid to any person who was a director at any time during that year, broken down into what components of pay made up that compensation and the value of each component, an explanation of how the payment was calculated, any other payments paid to the person in connection with the termination of qualifying service and an explanation of how discretions allowed for within the policy on exit payments were exercised.

Once the remuneration policy comes into effect, it will apply in relation to all remuneration and loss of office payments to directors; such payments will need to be consistent with the company's approved remuneration policy, or else separately approved by a shareholder resolution.

NB—There is a carve-out for remuneration payments or payments for loss of office made to a director of a quoted company before the earlier of the end of the first financial year of the company to begin on or after the day on which it becomes a quoted company.

Companies cannot change their remuneration policy without putting it back to shareholders for approval. However, companies may put a revised remuneration policy back to shareholders for approval in between AGMs (i.e. at a general meeting which is not an accounts meeting); in practice this is unlikely to happen often given the expense of calling a general meeting.

The restrictions on loss of office payments apply when the company's first directors' remuneration policy approved by shareholders takes effect.

A payment made which is inconsistent with the remuneration policy will be void (and there are potential personal liabilities for any director approving a payment in contravention of an approved remuneration policy). An obligation, howsoever arising, to make a payment which would be in contravention of these new provisions has no effect (CA 2006 s.226E(1)). If a payment has already been made in contravention of these provisions, it is held by the recipient on trust for the company or other person making the payment, and in the case of a payment by a company, any director who authorised the payment is jointly and severally liable to indemnify the company that made the payment for any loss resulting from it (CA 2006 s.226E(2)). There are safe harbour provisions in relation to this liability; a court may relieve the director, either wholly or in part, from liability in any proceedings against the director, if the director shows he or she has acted honestly and reasonably, and the court considers, having regard to all the circumstances, that the director ought to be relieved of liability.

There are also specific provisions which apply where a payment for loss of office is made in the context of a takeover (CA 2006 s.226E(4)).

There are transitional provisions which cover payments required to be made as part of a legal obligation entered into before 27 June 2012, which has not been amended or renewed since; these fall outside the scope of the new regime.

To further improve transparency, in the event of a director leaving office, companies need to issue a statement setting out the name of the person concerned, particulars of any remuneration payment made or to be made to the person after ceasing to be a director and particulars of any payment for loss of office that the director has received or may receive in the future. The company should explain how the decision made relates to the policy on exit payments, how the circumstances under which a director leaves have been considered and how his performance during his period of service is to be taken into account. This statement must be published as soon as reasonably practicable and must be kept available until the next directors' remuneration report of the company is made available on the website.

6.8.3   *Golden parachutes and golden handshakes*

A director's service contract may provide for an enhanced severance payment to be paid on early termination of the contract. This may be a liquidated damages clause providing for a payment to be made on a breach of contract (usually known as a golden handshake). Or it may be a contingency payment providing for a payment to be made on the occurrence of a particular event, such as change of control, for example, where the employing company is taken over or its business is transferred outside the group (known as a golden parachute). Shareholders may challenge the use of a liquidated damages clause which involves agreement at the outset on the amount that will be paid in the event of severance. In order to be enforceable, the liquidated damages provision must be a genuine pre-estimate of the director's loss—if it is not, then it is likely to be unenforceable as a penalty. Best practice guidance encourages the drafting of liquidated damages clauses which provide for a reduction to take account of accelerated receipt and the duty to mitigate.

The clause will set out a formula as to how the director's entitlement is to be calculated. This is usually a multiplier of the number of years left to run under the service contract/the length of the notice period and the director's gross salary and, usually, a sum representing the other contractual benefits. A similar effect can be achieved by including a PILON clause in the contract.

The advantage of such provisions is that they avoid the uncertainties of quantifying the contractual damages for wrongful dismissal which would otherwise be payable. An advantage for the director is that no account is taken of the director's duty to mitigate his loss by seeking further employment. This, of course, can be a significant disadvantage to the employing company if it sees a former director walk straight into a new job following termination. The real advantage to the company of such a provision is the fact that, by paying out under the liquidated damages clause, the company will be acting in accordance with the service contract and will therefore be able to rely on any enforceable restrictive covenants in the service contract. By contrast, if it breaches the service contract in dismissing the director, it cannot rely on the restrictive covenants.

It is becoming less common to see liquidated damages clauses which do not provide for a reduction to take account of accelerated receipt and the duty to mitigate. The Court of Appeal upheld a liquidated damages provision in a chief executive's service contract; the clause provided for one year's gross salary, pension contributions and other benefits in kind, notwithstanding that no reduction was made for mitigation (*Murray v Leisureplay Plc*).[14] In considering whether the liquidated damages provision amounted to a penalty clause (i.e. representing more than a genuine pre-estimate of

---

[14]   *Murray v Leisureplay Plc* [2005] EWCA Civ 963; [2005] I.R.L.R. 946.

probable loss arising on termination), the majority of the Court of Appeal held that a clause will only be a penalty if the party seeking to avoid the terms can demonstrate that the sum payable on breach is "extravagant or unconscionable" compared with the greatest loss that could follow from the breach. Further, the commercial context could be taken into account. The fact that the executive, in this case, had agreed to significant post-termination restrictive covenants was relevant. Looking at the clause in its commercial context, it was considered appropriate for the employer to pay out the full liquidated damages payment without a reduction for mitigation in return for the executive's agreement to these important restrictions. Companies may now be more likely to be bound by liquidated damages provisions even where the provision permits a departing executive to receive more than they would have obtained in damages at common law.

Liquidated damages provisions are also unattractive from a tax perspective (fixed severance payments pursuant to a liquidated damages clause are subject to income tax and national insurance contributions which can lead to a significant uplift in the cost to the company). A liquidated damages payment will not attract the tax-free element of a termination payment referred to above (currently £30,000) as it is construed by the HM Revenue and Customs as a contractual payment and not a payment representing damages for wrongful dismissal.

6.8.4 Summary—key provisions in executive and non-executive contracts

The following key points should be considered in relation to an executive director's service contract (or contract for service):

(a) the board should approve service contracts and variations formally only after ensuring compliance with the articles and a proper consideration of the company's interests and the codified directors' duties;

(b) shareholder approval is required for contracts for a period of more than two years, otherwise the term will be void and the service contract deemed terminable on reasonable notice;

(c) the term or notice period should not normally be more than one year;

(d) shareholders may inspect directors' service contracts or memorandum of terms (where no written directors' service agreement) and request copies upon payment of a prescribed fee;

(e) remuneration should normally be partly linked to performance;

(f) no share option should be issued to directors at a discount (save as permitted by the Listing Rules);

(g) long-term incentive schemes are subject to restrictions; in normal circumstances, shares granted or deferred remuneration should not vest, and options should not be exercisable, in less than three years; and

(h) termination payments should be fair and not a "reward for failure".

The following key provisions should be considered in a non-executive director's letter of appointment:

(a) the time commitment expected to carry out the role should be disclosed;

(b) remuneration should reflect time commitment and responsibilities of the role; and

(c) no share options should be granted.

Chapter 7

Share Dealing by Directors and Connected Persons

Paul Lester, Partner

Cripps LLP

7.1   Introduction

Directors have a special relationship with the company of which they are officers, in part, because of their duties of good faith in their dealings with the company and, in part, because of the nature and amount of information they hold about the company and its business.

At common law, the duties of directors in relation to their dealings in shares were not particularly high. The case of *Percival v Wright*[1] is considered to be authority for the view that, in the absence of any misrepresentation on the part of the directors, since the duties of the directors were owed to the company, no action would lie in respect of a purchase of shares in a company by the directors even though the directors had information which, had it been known to the sellers, would have led them to put a higher value on their shares. This general approach is subject to there being no particular relationship between the directors and the shareholders in question which would lead to a fiduciary obligation existing (see comments made in *Chez Nico (Restaurants) Ltd, Re*[2] and *Peskin v Anderson*[3]).

The intuitive feeling that it is wrong for directors (and other persons) to deal in shares with the benefit of price-sensitive information has led to provisions, both statutory and non-statutory, with a view to restricting the freedom which directors would otherwise appear to have at common law. This has meant that, in relation to directors, English law has not had to become involved in developing theories of liability based on, for example, misuse of company property (confidential information), as has happened in the US. In the absence of such theories of liability which rely on interpretations of directors' duties to the company, this also means that the provisions of s.170 and following of the Companies Act 2006 (general duties of directors) are unlikely to apply to dealings in shares by directors. English

---

[1]   *Percival v Wright* [1902] 2 Ch. 421.
[2]   *Chez Nico (Restaurants) Ltd, Re* [1991] B.C.C. 736; [1992] B.C.L.C. 192.
[3]   *Peskin v Anderson* [2001] B.C.C. 874; [2001] 1 B.C.L.C. 372.

law in this area focuses, instead, on the principle of creating a level playing field to prevent someone gaining an unfair advantage over others from the possession of price-sensitive information. This is the "equality of information" rationale for prohibiting the use of inside information. The EU Market Abuse Regulation,[4] known as MAR, also adopts the equality of information approach, characterising insider dealing as consisting of "an unfair advantage being obtained from inside information to the detriment of third parties who are unaware of such information and, consequently the undermining of the integrity of financial markets and investor confidence".[5] Although insider dealing and market abuse offences are not specifically aimed at directors, they may well have greater implications for directors than for other shareholders of a company because of directors' privileged access to information about the company, its business, its financial position and prospects.

Directors are, of course, almost always in a privileged position compared to outsiders when it comes to information about a company of which they are officers. It is not considered necessary or desirable to prevent directors from dealing in shares completely. Indeed, share incentive plans of one sort or another are thought by many to be good since they are seen as a way of linking, at least in part, the fortunes of the directors to the fortunes of the company (although the UK Corporate Governance Code 2018 states that remuneration "for all non-executive directors should not include share options or other performance related elements"[6]). The relevant laws and regulations therefore operate so as only to prevent dealings when the information is material or significant. The disclosure obligations provide transparency, to ensure that dealings are subject to scrutiny by the public and by the regulators.

In the UK, insider dealing may constitute a criminal offence (governed by the Criminal Justice Act 1993, or CJA) and/or a civil offence under the market abuse regime (governed by MAR). Insider dealing under the CJA requires the more onerous criminal burden of proof ("beyond reasonable doubt"), whereas for market abuse under MAR the corresponding lower burden of proof ("balance of probabilities") applies. The perceived difficulty in successfully proving the necessary component parts of the criminal offence of insider dealing led to relatively few prosecutions under the criminal law in the 1980s and 1990s. This was part of the rationale behind the introduction of the civil market abuse regime.

Notwithstanding the differing standards of burden of proof, however, given the nature and gravity of an enforcement action brought under the market abuse regime, the Upper Tribunal (Tax and Chancery Chamber) and the courts will need to satisfy themselves fully that the individual in question is

---

4   Regulation 596/2014 on market abuse [2014] OJ L173/1.
5   MAR Recital 23.
6   UK Corporate Governance Code 2018 Provision 34.

guilty of the conduct alleged. Consequently, in practical terms the burden of proof in the civil regime is unlikely to be materially different from that under the criminal law.

When the civil market abuse regime came into force on 1 December 2001, responsibility for criminal prosecutions of insider dealing was also handed to the Financial Services Authority (FSA). In light of the perceived difficulties in bringing successful prosecutions for insider dealing, the FSA initially tended to focus its efforts on using its civil market abuse powers to safeguard the integrity of the markets. This gave the impression that the criminal insider dealing laws were unlikely to be used. This has changed significantly in recent years.

In its Business Plan for 2008–2009, the FSA stated its intention to take enforcement action in order to achieve "credible deterrence". With that came a willingness to use the full range of enforcement powers available to it, whether civil or criminal.

On 1 April 2013, the FSA's powers and responsibilities for enforcement of insider dealing and market abuse laws were transferred to the Financial Conduct Authority (FCA). In its Business Plan for 2013–2014, the FCA stated its commitment to continuing the FSA's previous strategy:

> "We will pursue a strategy of credible deterrence, taking tough and meaningful action against the firms and individuals who break our rules. We will continue to use the full range of our criminal, civil and regulatory powers to support our priority of securing better results for consumers and reinforcing our commitment to ensuring markets function well."

It is therefore clear that insider dealing and market abuse are both important weapons in the FCA's armoury in combating prohibited share dealings.

7.2. Insider dealing (under the Criminal Justice Act 1993)

The criminal offence of insider dealing is contained in CJA Pt V. The objective of the law is to prevent those with inside information from using this information to their advantage to make a profit when dealing with others. The relevant provisions depend on there being an individual (and not a body corporate) who is an "insider" who deals in securities of a company with the benefit of confidential information, or encourages somebody else to deal, or who improperly discloses that information to a third party. As will be seen below, a director who (as a director) has information about the company, will almost always be an insider. Therefore the key issues which need to be determined in relation to insider dealing by directors will tend to centre around the materiality or significance of the confidential information in question, or as to the availability of one of the exemptions, and not around whether the director is an "insider".

7.2.1 The Offences

The CJA creates three main offences:

(a) dealing in price-affected securities, that is dealing in securities on the basis of information which would, if made public, be likely to have a significant effect on the price of the securities;

(b) encouraging another to deal in price-affected securities; and

(c) improperly disclosing information which a person holds as an insider.

To establish liability, a number of elements have to be present. There must be "inside information", which is information which:

(a) relates to particular securities or to a particular issuer, or particular issuers, of securities (including information affecting its business prospects);

(b) is specific or precise;

(c) has not been made public; and

(d) if it were made public would be likely to have a significant effect on the price (or value) of any securities.

In contrast to the interpretative guidance provided under the market abuse regime, the CJA gives little or no guidance as to the meaning of key words and expressions. For example, no indication is given in the CJA as to the scope of the words "specific or precise" or what is a "significant" effect on the price of securities, which has resulted in a degree of uncertainty, particularly in relation to "significant". Although some counsel have expressed the view that significance should be calculated by reference to a (small) percentage of the market value of a share, there is no certainty as to what the percentage might be or even whether it is a percentage at all or an absolute amount. There is no judicial decision on the point and, until there is guidance from the courts, directors who have inside information which might have an effect on a share price should only deal with caution. If there is doubt about whether any particular piece of information might be price-sensitive and, if so, to what extent, a director might be well advised to seek professional advice from a broker (probably the company's broker or somebody else who follows the company closely). Although, as will be seen below, there is no defence of reasonable belief that information was not price-sensitive, a court is likely to look more favourably on a person who at least took reasonable steps to confirm that the information was not price-sensitive than one who did not.

Some guidance as to the meaning of "made public" is given in CJA s.58, which sets out four situations in which information will be treated as having been made public.

These are that:

(a) the information is published in accordance with the rules of a regulated market for the purpose of informing investors and their professional advisers (e.g. by making an announcement through a Regulatory Information Service);

(b) it is contained in records which are required by statute to be open to inspection by the public (e.g. at Companies House);

(c) it can be readily acquired by those likely to deal in any securities to which the information relates or of an issuer to which the information relates; or

(d) it is derived from information which has been made public.

If information is available otherwise than in the four circumstances listed above, it cannot be assumed that it has been made public for the purposes of the CJA. This is another area of uncertainty on which there is no judicial guidance.

However, s.58 does provide that information *may* be treated as having been made public even though the information:

(a) can be acquired only by persons exercising diligence or expertise;

(b) is communicated to a section of the public and not to the public at large;

(c) can be acquired only by observation;

(d) is communicated only on payment of a fee; or

(e) is published only outside the UK.

To establish liability for insider dealing, it must be proved that the individual concerned knew that the information was, in fact, inside information and that he/she had that information from an inside source. This also applies to "secondary" insiders who must know that the person from whom they have obtained information is an insider and that the information is inside information.

The information must be from an inside source. A person has information from an inside source if (and only if):

(a) he/she has the information through:
(i) being a director, employee or shareholder of an issuer of securities; or
(ii) having access to the information by virtue of his/her employment, office or profession; or

247

(b)   he/she receives the information directly or indirectly from a person who is a director, employee or shareholder of the issuer of securities.

Generally speaking, an individual who is a director of the company will fall squarely within (a) above, and will thereby satisfy the test as to requisite knowledge, so that if he/she holds inside information (as defined), his/her dealings will be caught by the CJA.

Once it has been established that an individual has satisfied the requirements described above (i.e. that he/she has inside information, with the requisite knowledge, from an inside source), it must then be established whether he/she has committed one of the three offences.

The meaning of the word "securities" in this context should be noted. The term "securities" can clearly cover a wide range of investments but the relevant securities for the purpose of the CJA are defined in s.54(1) and Sch.2. The securities may not just be shares, but include debentures, warrants, futures, options and contracts for differences. In general terms, the CJA is concerned with securities dealt in, or under the rules of, a "regulated market". These are markets specified for the purpose by order (s.60(1)), being London Stock Exchange markets (including AIM) and various other stock exchanges listed in the orders (including EEA stock exchanges, NASDAQ, LIFFE, NEX Exchange and CoredealMTS).

7.2.1.1   Dealing in price-affected securities (CJA section 52(1))

Price-affected securities are securities in relation to which there is information which would, if made public, be likely to have a significant effect on the price or value of those securities. A person deals in securities if he/she:

(a)   acquires or disposes of them;
(b)   agrees to acquire or dispose of them;
(c)   enters into a contract which creates the securities (relevant to derivatives); or
(d)   procures, directly or indirectly, an acquisition or disposal of the securities by any other person (which will often be his/her agent, nominee or a person acting under his/her instruction).

The dealing must take place on a regulated market or the individual must have relied upon (or have been himself/herself) a professional intermediary. "Professional intermediary" is a person who carries on a business of acquiring or disposing of securities (as principal or agent) or of acting as an intermediary between those taking part in any dealing in securities, or indeed any employees of such persons.

7.2.1.2   Encouraging another to deal (CJA section 52(2)(a))

It is also an offence for an individual who has information as an insider to encourage another person to deal in price-affected securities in relation to that information, knowing or having reasonable cause to believe that the dealing would take place on a regulated market or the individual was relying on (or was himself/herself) a professional intermediary.

The person receiving the information does not have to realise that the securities are in fact price-affected securities and the inside information does not actually have to be given to the recipient. It is the act of encouraging that is relevant (and, indeed, there need be no actual dealing).

7.2.1.3   Disclosing information (CJA section 52(2)(b))

An individual who has information as an insider will commit an offence if he/she discloses that information to another person otherwise than in the proper performance of his/her employment, office or profession.

7.2.2   Defences

The defences to the three offences outlined above are contained in CJA s.53. The defences vary depending on which of the three offences is alleged to have been committed and are as follows:

7.2.2.1   Defences to dealing and encouraging another to deal

An individual will not be guilty of an offence of dealing or encouraging another to deal if he/she can show that any one of the following applies:

(a)   that he/she did not at the time of the offence expect the dealing to result in a profit attributable to the fact that the information in question was price-sensitive information in relation to the securities (the "no profit/no loss" defence);

(b)   that at the time he/she believed on reasonable grounds that the information had been or would be disclosed widely enough to ensure that none of those taking part in the dealing would be prejudiced by not having the information (the "equality of information" defence); or

(c)   that he/she would have done what he/she did even if he/she had not had the information.

An individual will also not be guilty of an offence of dealing or encouraging another to deal by virtue of a special defence contained in CJA Sch.1, if:

(a) the information the individual has as an insider is "market information" and it was reasonable for a person in his/her position to have acted as he/she did despite having that information as an insider at the time; or

(b) he/she acted in connection with an acquisition or disposal which was under consideration or the subject of negotiation and with a view to facilitating the accomplishment of the relevant transaction, and the information he/she had was market information which arose directly out of his/her involvement in the particular transaction.

For the purpose of this defence, "market information" is information consisting of any of the following facts:

(a) the fact that securities of a particular kind have been or are to be acquired or disposed of, or that their acquisition or disposal is under consideration or the subject of negotiation;

(b) the number of those securities or the price (or range of prices) of those securities;

(c) the identity of the persons involved or likely to be involved in any capacity in an acquisition or disposal; or

(d) the fact that securities of a particular kind have not been or are not to be acquired or disposed of.

In deciding whether it is reasonable for an individual to have acted as he/she did whilst in possession of market information, three issues have to be taken into account:

(a) the content of the information;

(b) the circumstances in which he/she first had the information and in what capacity; and

(c) the capacity in which he/she now acts.

7.2.2.2 Defences to disclosing

An individual will not be guilty of an offence of disclosing inside information if he/she can show that:

(a) he/she did not at the time expect any person to deal in the securities on a regulated market or in reliance on a professional intermediary because of the disclosure of the information; or

(b) although he/she did expect the above, he/she did not expect the dealing to result in a profit attributable to the fact that the information was price-sensitive information relating to the securities.

It will be seen that dealings by a director, or encouraged by a director, for the benefit of himself/herself or another person in circumstances in which the securities are price-affected securities, will generally not fall within any of the defences described above. One circumstance in which there might be a defence, however, is when a director is in the exercise period for an option or for the conversion of a convertible security where the final date for the exercise of the option or for conversion falls during a period when the director would otherwise be prevented from dealing by reason of his/her holding inside information. In this case, it may well be possible to argue that the director would have done what he/she did even if the director had not had the information. In addition, depending on the nature of the information, the director may also be able to claim that he/she had market information and that it was reasonable for the director in his/her position to have acted as he/she did despite having that information as an insider at the time. The occasions on which these defences will be available, however, are likely to be rare.

7.2.3 Jurisdiction

There are rules governing the territorial scope of the offence of insider dealing, which vary according to the particular offence:

(a) the offence of dealing: in order to commit this offence, the transaction does not have to take place within the UK. However, the following requirements must be satisfied:
  (i)   the individual must have been within the UK at the time when he/she is alleged to have done any act which constitutes or forms a part of the dealing; or
  (ii) the market on which the dealing is alleged to have taken place is a market which is specified by order by HM Treasury as being regulated in the UK for the purposes of the CJA; or
  (iii) the professional intermediary was within the UK at the time when he/she is alleged to have done anything causing the alleged offence to have been committed.
(b) *the offences of disclosing and encouraging:* these offences can only be committed if:
  (i)   the defendant was within the UK at the time when he/she is alleged to have committed the offence; or
  (ii) the alleged recipient of the information or encouragement was within the UK at the time when he/she is alleged to have received the information or encouragement.

7.2.4 Penalties

An individual convicted of the offence under the CJA is liable to a fine and/or imprisonment (for a term not exceeding six months on summary conviction, or seven years on a conviction on indictment).

A transaction in securities, which is effected in breach of the insider dealing provisions of the CJA, will not be void or unenforceable. There is no provision in the CJA to compensate a "victim" of insider dealing and there are no other civil remedies, but there are provisions for compensation or penalties in other statutes. For example, if a person who has suffered loss as a result of insider dealing can be identified, the Powers of Criminal Courts (Sentencing) Act 2000 allows a court to make a compensation order requiring the person convicted by that court to pay compensation for any loss suffered as a result of the insider dealing. In addition, the Crown Courts have the power under the Proceeds of Crime Act 2002 to make an order confiscating the proceeds of crime.

7.3 Market abuse (under the Market Abuse Regulation 2014)

The civil market abuse regime was first introduced in the UK upon the coming into force of FSMA in 2001, and amended in 2005 by the Financial Services and Markets Act 2000 (Market Abuse) Regulations 2005 to implement the Market Abuse Directive, known as MAD.[7]

MAR repealed and replaced MAD and the UK civil market abuse regime (as set out in FSMA s.118) with effect from 3 July 2016. Although MAR has direct effect in the UK, primary and secondary legislation was amended through the Financial Services and Markets Act 2000 (Market Abuse) Regulations 2016[8] to ensure the compatibility of UK law with MAR. Changes to the FCA Handbook were also made.

According to MAR, market abuse "is a concept that encompasses unlawful behaviour in the financial markets and … should be understood to consist of insider dealing, unlawful disclosure of inside information and market manipulation" (Recital 7 of MAR). In the context of share dealing by directors and connected persons, this Chapter considers only the first two behaviours, that is insider dealing and unlawful disclosure of inside information.

7.3.1 The Offences

MAR art.14 states that a person shall not:

(a)   engage or attempt to engage in insider dealing;
(b)   recommend that another person engage in inside dealing or induce another person to engage in insider dealing; or
(c)   unlawfully disclose inside information.

---

[7]   Directive 2003/6 on insider dealing and market manipulation [2003] OJ L96/16.
[8]   Financial Services and Markets Act 2000 (Market Abuse) Regulations 2016 (SI 2016/680).

The prohibitions set out in MAR art.14 are based on the misuse of "inside information". Under MAR art.7(1), "inside information" includes the following types of information:

- information of a precise nature which has not been made public relating, directly or indirectly, to one or more issuers or to one or more financial instruments, and which, if made public, would be likely to have a significant effect on the prices of those financial instruments or on the price of derivative financial instruments (art.7(1)(a));
- for persons charged with the execution of orders concerning financial instruments, information conveyed by a client and relating to a client's pending orders in financial instruments which is of a precise nature relating, directly or indirectly, to one or more issuers or to one or more financial instruments and which, if made public, would be likely to have a significant effect on the prices of those financial instruments (art.7(1)(d)).

Information will be deemed to be of a precise nature if it indicates:

- a set of circumstances which exist or which may reasonably be expected to come into existence; or
- an event which has occurred or which may reasonably be expected to occur

where that information is specific enough to enable a conclusion to be drawn as to the possible effect of that set of circumstances or event on the prices of the financial instruments or the related derivative financial instrument.[9]

When considering the expression "may reasonably be expected", the European Court of Justice's decision in *Markus Geltl v Daimler AG*[10] in 2012 may be relevant. Although the case concerned MAD, the court decided that a reasonable expectation that an event will occur requires "a realistic prospect", rather than "a high probability", that it will occur.

Where inside information concerns a process which occurs in stages, each stage of the process as well as the overall process can constitute inside information. An intermediate step in a protracted process may in itself constitute a set of circumstances or an event which exists or where there is a realistic prospect that they will come into existence or occur, on the basis of an overall assessment of the factors existing at the time (MAR Recital 16). An intermediate step will be deemed to be inside information if, by itself, it satisfies the criteria of inside information as provided for in MAR art.7.[11]

---

[9] MAR art.7(2).
[10] *Markus Geltl v Daimler AG* (C-19/11) EU:C:2012:397.
[11] MAR art.7(3).

MAR Recital 18 expresses an aim to bring together the two component parts of the meaning of inside information:

"Legal certainty for market participants should be enhanced through a closer definition of two of the elements essential to the definition of inside information, namely the precise nature of that information and the significance of its potential effect on the prices of the financial instruments ..."

This is brought about in MAR art.7(4):

"For the purposes of [art.7(1)], information which, if it were made public, would be likely to have a significant effect on the prices of financial instruments ... shall mean information a reasonable investor would be likely to use as part of the basis of his or her investment decisions."

Article 7(4) therefore suggests a close connection between the "price sensitivity test" (information which, if made public, would have a significant effect on price) and the "reasonable investor test" (information that a reasonable investor would be likely to use as part of the basis for investment decisions).

The cases of *Massey v Financial Services Authority*[12] and *Hannam v Financial Conduct Authority*[13] may be relevant when considering the interplay between the "price sensitivity test" and the "reasonable investor test". Although those cases concerned the definition of "inside information" contained in the now repealed FSMA s.118C, the respective decisions of the Upper Tribunal (Tax and Chancery) are likely to be instructive in interpreting the provisions of MAR art.7(4). In *Massey*, the Tribunal decided that if a hypothetical reasonable investor would have been likely to use the relevant information as part of the basis of his decisions about purchasing the shares in question, that was enough to satisfy the test that the information was "inside information", even if Mr Massey had thought the price of the shares would probably be unaffected by the information. In *Hannam*, the Tribunal held that the two tests must be read in conjunction with each other, with the reasonable investor test providing a definition as to what would be likely to have a significant effect on price.

Assistance in interpreting the reasonable investor test is provided by MAR Recitals 14 and 15, which refer to "ex ante information" and "ex post information". Reasonable investors are considered to base their investment decisions on information which is already available to them (ex ante information). When deciding whether a particular piece of information would be likely to be taken into account by a reasonable investor, that information should be appraised on the basis of the ex ante information available, taking into consideration the totality of the issuer's activity, the

---

[12]   *David Massey v Financial Services Authority* [2011] UKUT 49 (TCC).
[13]   *Hannam v Financial Conduct Authority* [2014] UKUT 223 (TCC).

reliability of the source of the information and any other market variables likely to affect the financial instruments.[14]

Information available after the event (that is, ex post information) can be used to check the presumption that the ex ante information was price sensitive. However, ex post information is not to be used to take action against someone who drew reasonable conclusions from the ex ante information which was available to them.[15]

The FCA Handbook says that the following factors may be taken into account in determining whether information has been made public (and therefore whether or not it constitutes inside information):

- whether the information has been disclosed to a prescribed market or auction platform through a regulatory information service;
- whether the information is contained in records which are open to inspection by the public;
- whether the information is otherwise generally available including through the internet, or some other publication (including if it is available only upon payment of a fee) or is derived from information which has been made public; and
- whether the information can be obtained by observation by members of the public without infringing rights or obligations of privacy, property or confidentiality.[16]

"Financial instruments" for the purposes of MAR means the list of instruments specified in Section C of Annex 1 to Directive 2014/65 (the MiFID II Directive).[17] This includes:

- transferrable securities;
- money market instruments;
- units in collective investment undertakings;
- options, futures, swaps, forward rate agreements and other derivative contracts relating to securities, currencies, interest rates or yields; and
- financial contracts for differences.

7.3.1.1 *Engaging in insider dealing (MAR article 14(a))*

Insider dealing (for the purposes of MAR) arises where a person possesses inside information and uses that information by acquiring or disposing of, for its own account or for the account of a third party, directly or indirectly, financial instruments to which that information relates. The use of inside information by cancelling or amending an order concerning a financial

---

14   MAR Recital 14.
15   MAR Recital 15.
16   Market Conduct sourcebook para.1.2.12G.
17   Directive 2014/65 on markets in financial instruments [2014] OJ L173/349.

instrument where the order was placed before the person concerned possessed the information will also amount to insider dealing.[18]

There is a presumption under MAR that if a person in possession of inside information acquires or disposes of financial instruments to which the information relates, he has used that information.[19] That presumption is rebuttable. This effectively codifies the European Count of Justice's decision in *Spector Photo Group NV v Commissie voor het Bank-, Financie-en Assurantiewezen (CBFA)*[20] which held that the market abuse regime did not require the transactions to be carried out "with full knowledge of the facts" in order to be prohibited and that therefore it was not necessary to provide evidence of an intention to commit market abuse.

7.3.1.2 Recommending or inducing (MAR article 14(b))

Recommending or inducing another person to engage in insider dealing arises where the person possesses inside information and recommends, on the basis of that information, that the other person:

- acquires or disposes of financial instruments to which that information relates, or induces that person to do so (MAR art.8(2)(a)); or
- cancels or amends an order concerning a financial instrument to which the information relates, or induces that person to do so (MAR art.8(2)(b)).

The use of recommendations or inducements amounts to insider dealing where the person using the recommendation or inducement knows or ought to know that it is based on inside information.[21]

MAR art.8 applies to any person who possesses inside information as a result of:

(a) being a member of the administrative, management or supervisory bodies of the issuer;

(b) having a holding in the capital of the issuer;

(c) having access to the information through the exercise of an employment, profession or duties; or

(d) being involved in criminal activities.[22]

In addition to the four specific circumstances set out above, MAR art.8 will also apply to any person who possesses inside information and that person

---

[18] MAR art.8(1).

[19] MAR Recital 24.

[20] *Spector Photo Group NV v Commissie voor het Bank-, Financie-en Assurantiewezen (CBFA)* (C-45/08) EU:C:2009:806; [2010] Bus. L.R. 1416; [2011] B.C.C. 827.

[21] MAR art.8(3).

[22] MAR art.8(4).

knows, or ought to know, that it is inside information.[23] For these purposes, MAR Recital 26 states that the competent authorities should consider what a normal and reasonable person knows or should have known in the circumstances.

The FCA Handbook provides guidance on determining whether a person who possesses inside information ought to know that it is inside information for the purposes of MAR art.8(4), stating that the following factors may be taken into account:

- if a normal and reasonable person in the position of the person who has inside information would know or should have known that the person from whom he received it is an insider; and
- if a normal and reasonable person in the position of the person who has inside information would know or should have known that it is inside information.[24]

Further, for the purpose of being characterised as an insider for the purposes of MAR art.8(4), a person does not need to know that the information concerned is inside information.[25]

MAR makes clear that if the insider dealing is carried out by a legal person (such as a company), then the prohibitions in MAR art.8 also apply, in accordance with national law, to the individuals who participate in the decision to carry out the acquisition, disposal, cancellation or amendment of an order for the account of the legal person concerned.[26]

7.3.1.3   Unlawfully disclosing inside information (MAR article 14(c))

Unlawful disclosure of inside information arises where a person possesses inside information and discloses that information to any other person, except where the disclosure is made in the normal exercise of an employment, a profession or duties.[27]

The onward disclosure of recommendations or inducements referred to in MAR art.8(2) amounts to unlawful disclosure of inside information where the person disclosing the recommendation or inducement knows or ought to know that it was based on inside information.[28]

---

[23]   MAR art.8(4).
[24]   Market Conduct sourcebook 1.2.8G.
[25]   Market Conduct sourcebook 1.2.9G.
[26]   MAR art.8(5).
[27]   MAR art.10(1).
[28]   MAR art.10(2).

7.3.2   Defences

MAR contains defences in relation to market abuse in the form of recognising "legitimate behaviour" (for dealing and disclosing) as well as a safe harbour for taking "market soundings" (for disclosing).

7.3.2.1   Defences to dealing and disclosing (MAR article 9)

MAR Recital 29 states that "in order to avoid inadvertently prohibiting forms of financial activity which are legitimate, namely where there is no effect of market abuse, it is necessary to recognise certain legitimate behaviour".

MAR art.9 sets out certain types of legitimate behaviour which will not amount to engaging in insider dealing. For example, it will not be deemed from the mere fact that a legal person is in possession of inside information that that person has used that information and has thus engaged in insider dealing on the basis of an acquisition or disposal where that person:

(a)   has established, implemented and maintained adequate and effective internal arrangements and procedures (i.e. Chinese walls) that effectively ensure that the natural person who made, or influenced, the decision on its behalf to acquire or dispose of financial instruments was not in possession of the inside information; and

(b)   has not encouraged, made a recommendation to, induced or otherwise influenced the natural person who, on behalf of the legal person, acquired or disposed of financial instruments to which the information relates (MAR art.9(1)).

7.3.2.2   Defences to disclosing (MAR article 11)

MAR provides a "safe harbour" for the disclosure of inside information. Disclosure of inside information made in the course of a "market sounding" is deemed to be made in the normal exercise of a person's employment, profession or duties (and therefore does not infringe MAR art.10(1)) provided certain conditions are complied with.[29]

A market sounding (sometimes known as "pre-marketing") comprises the communication of information, prior to the commencement of a transaction, in order to gauge the interest of potential investors in a possible transaction and the conditions relating to it such as its potential size or pricing, to one or more investors by:

•   an issuer;

---

[29]   MAR art.11(4).

- a secondary offeror of a financial instrument in such quantity or value that the transaction is distinct from ordinary trading and involves a selling method based on the prior assessment of potential interest from potential investors; or
- a third party acting on behalf of or on account of a person referred to in either of the above circumstances.[30]

Disclosure of inside information by a person intending to make a takeover bid for the securities of a company or a merger with a company to parties entitled to the securities will also constitute a market sounding, provided that:

(a) the information is necessary to enable the parties entitled to the securities to form an opinion on their willingness to offer their securities; and

(b) the willingness of parties entitled to the securities to offer their securities is reasonably required for the decision to make the takeover bid or merger.[31]

Before conducting a market sounding, a disclosing market participant must consider whether the market sounding will involve the disclosure of inside information, make a written record of its conclusion and reasons therefor and provide such written records to the competent authority upon request.[32]

Before making a disclosure of inside information in the course of a market sounding, a disclosing market participant must:

- obtain the consent of the intended recipient to receive inside information;
- inform the intended recipient that he is prohibited from using that information by acquiring or disposing financial instruments relating to that information or cancelling or amending an order already placed concerning financial instruments to which the information relates; and
- inform the intended recipient that, by agreeing to receive the information, he is obliged to keep the information confidential.[33]

7.3.3 Jurisdiction

The prohibitions and requirements of MAR apply to actions and omissions, in the EU and in a third country, concerning financial instruments admitted to trading on a regulated market.[34] A "regulated market" is a market

---

[30] MAR art.11(1).
[31] MAR art.11(2).
[32] MAR art.11(3).
[33] MAR art.11(5).
[34] MAR art.2(4).

defined as such in Directive 2014/65 (the MiFID II Directive) art.4(1)(21) and regulated pursuant to Title III of that directive. As a result, behaviour undertaken outside the EU is capable of being caught by MAR.

MAR was accompanied by a Directive on Criminal Sanctions for Market Abuse,[35] known as CSMAD, which establishes that where market abuse has been committed by a person intentionally, that behaviour is to be treated as criminal conduct under the laws of the relevant EU Member State. However, the UK decided not to opt into CSMAD, on the basis that "the UK already covers all the offences in its criminal law and also goes further by capturing, for example, acts of market abuse that are committed recklessly, as well as those committed intentionally".[36] Accordingly, in the UK, breach of MAR will constitute a civil offence, not a criminal offence.

7.3.4 Penalties

There is an overlap between the criminal insider dealing regime (under CJA) and the civil market abuse regime (under MAR) because market abuse can cover conduct falling within the criminal insider dealing regime. Conduct which amounts to insider dealing will almost invariably also amount to market abuse. In addition, the civil market abuse regime has a wider territorial scope than the criminal insider dealing regime as it applies to any instrument admitted to trading on an EU-regulated market. This can have significant practical implications; for example, a director of a UK Plc who is in the US discloses inside information about his company (traded on the London Stock Exchange) to a US shareholder with the aim of encouraging that person to buy shares in the company. This would not amount to insider dealing under the CJA because of the CJA's limited territorial scope. However, it would be market abuse, as it would amount to recommending or inducing another to commit market abuse, as the behaviour is in relation to an investment traded on an EU-regulated market.

Owing to the overlap between the two regimes, there is a risk of multiple jeopardy. The FCA has the power to institute criminal proceedings in respect of insider dealing as well as to institute civil proceedings in respect of market abuse. However, the FCA has stated that it will bring either market abuse charges or insider dealing charges against any individual.

The FCA is prepared to bring different charges against different individuals in relation to the same case. In *R. v Calvert*[37] in 2010, Malcolm Calvert was convicted of five counts of insider dealing, sentenced to 21 months' imprisonment and ordered to pay a £473,955 confiscation order and £50,000 towards the FSA's costs. The insider dealing offences involved Mr Calvert instructing a friend, Mr Hatcher, to acquire shares and splitting the gains

---

[35] Directive 2014/57 on criminal sanctions for market abuse [2014] OJ L173/179.
[36] Statement by the Financial Secretary to the Treasury 20 February 2012.
[37] *R. v Calvert* Unreported 16 February 2010.

made between them. The FSA agreed to use its regulatory powers against Mr Hatcher, rather than bring a criminal prosecution, as Mr Hatcher had agreed to assist the FSA with its investigations and prosecution of Mr Calvert. Mr Hatcher was fined £56,098 for breaching the insider dealing behaviour provisions of the FSMA market abuse regime.[38] The FCA is a "specified prosecutor" for the purposes of the Serious Organised Crime and Police Act 2005, which in the case of serious criminal offences allows the FCA (with the consent of the Attorney General) to grant individuals immunity from prosecution and to enter into plea bargaining agreements.

7.4 Restrictions on PDMR transactions

As directors will inevitably possess more information about the company of which they are an officer compared with outsiders, it is considered desirable to regulate the manner in which directors deal in shares in their companies, even where such a dealing would not amount to insider dealing or market abuse.

MAR recognises this concept in respect of directors and other managers of companies:

> "Persons discharging managerial responsibilities should be prohibited from trading before the announcement of an interim financial report or a year-end report ... unless specific and restricted circumstances exist which would justify a permission by the issuer allowing a person discharging managerial responsibilities to trade."[39]

The relevant provisions are set out in MAR art.19(11):

> "Without prejudice to Articles 14 [*insider dealing*] and 15 [*market abuse*], a person discharging managerial responsibilities within an issuer shall not conduct any transactions on its own account or for the account of a third party, directly or indirectly, relating to shares or debt instruments of the issuer or to derivatives or other financial instruments linked to them during a closed period of 30 calendar days before the announcement of an interim report or a year-end report which the issuer is obliged to make public according to (a) the rules of the trading venue where the issuer's shares are admitted to trading, or (b) national law."

A "person discharging managerial responsibilities" (or a PDMR) means a person within an issuer who is a member of the administrative, management or supervisory body of that entity, or a senior executive who has regular access to inside information relating directly or indirectly to that entity and has power to take managerial decisions affecting the future

---

[38] Final Notice, Financial Services Authority (13 May 2009).
[39] MAR Recital 61.

developments and business prospects of that entity.[40] The FCA Handbook provides guidance that an individual may be a "senior executive" within the definition of PDMR irrespective of the nature of the contractual arrangements (if any) between the individual and the issuer.[41]

For these purposes an "issuer" is an entity which has:

- requested or approved admission of their financial instruments to trading on a regulated market; or
- in the case of an instrument traded on a multilateral trading facility (MFT) or an organised trading facility (OTF), approved trading of its financial instruments on an MTF or an OTF or has requested admission to trading of their financial instruments on an MTF.[42]

As AIM is an MTF, MAR art.19 applies to companies admitted to trading on AIM, as well as to companies admitted to the Main Market of the London Stock Exchange.

The restriction in art.19(11) is expressed to be separate from (and apply in addition to) the insider dealing offence in MAR art.14.

The dealing restriction applies only to PDMRs and does not apply to "persons closely associated" with them (or "PCAs") (see "Disclosure of interests" below). However, some issuers may extend the dealing restrictions to PCAs, as well as PDMRs, in their own share dealing codes.

A "closed period" under MAR is linked to the *mandatory* announcement of results. If an issuer makes a voluntary trading update (such as quarterly results or interim management statements) then there is no requirement under MAR to create a closed period. However, some issuers may decide to treat this as a closed period under the terms of their own share dealing codes. Further, under MAR a closed period lasts for 30 days, whereas some listed companies may adopt a longer period in the case of the period from the financial year end to the date on which the preliminary results are announced.

Issuers in the UK have previously treated a closed period as ending on the date of the preliminary announcement of results (rather than on the date the actual accounts are published) as this is how the FCA's Model Code used to operate. This approach might appear to be inconsistent with the provisions of MAR art.19(11). The European Securities and Markets Authority (ESMA) has provided clarification on this point. According to MAR, there should be only one closed period relating to the announcement of every interim financial report and another relating to the year-end report. If the

---

[40] MAR art.3(1)(25).
[41] DTR 3 G3.1.2A.
[42] MAR art.19(4).

preliminary announcement of results contains all the key information relating to the financial figures expected to be included in the year-end report, then the closed period will end on the date of the preliminary announcement. If the information which has been announced changes after it has been published, this will not trigger another closed period (although the issuer is likely to have a disclosure obligation under MAR art.17).[43]

There is scope for a PDMR to trade on his own account or for the account of a third party during a closed period provided that the issuer permits this. An issuer may allow such a trade:

(a)   on a case-by-case basis due to the existence of exceptional circumstances, such as severe financial difficulty, which require the immediate sale of shares (MAR art.19(12)(a));

(b)   due to the characteristics of the trading involved for transactions made under, or related to, an employee share or saving scheme, qualification or entitlement of shares, or transactions where the beneficial interest in the relevant security does not change (MAR art.19(12)(b)).

MAR art.19(14) empowers the Commission to adopt delegated acts in connection with the types of transactions covered by MAR art.19, which the Commission has done through Commission Delegated Regulation 2016/522 (the Delegated Regulation).[44]

In order for an issuer to allow a PDMR to trade during a closed period under one of the circumstances in MAR art.19(12), the Delegated Regulation art.7(1) requires the PDMR to be able to demonstrate that the particular transaction cannot be executed at another point in time, other than during the closed period.

"Exceptional circumstances" for the purposes of MAR art.19(12)(a) means circumstances with all of the following characteristics: extremely urgent, unforeseen, compelling, caused other than by the PDMR and the PDMR has no control over them.[45]

If exceptional circumstances do exist, the PDMR must first make a written request to the issuer in order to obtain prior permission to sell shares in the

---

[43]   ESMA Questions and Answers *On the Market Abuse Regulation* (version 14, 29 March 2019), Question 7.2.

[44]   Regulation 2016/522 supplementing Regulation 596/2014 as regards an exemption for certain third countries public bodies and central banks, the indicators of market manipulation, the disclosure thresholds, the competent authority for notifications of delays, the permission for trading during closed periods and types of notifiable managers' transactions [2016] OJ L88/1.

[45]   Delegated Regulation art.8(2).

issuer during a closed period. The request must set out why the sale of the shares is the only route reasonably available to obtain the necessary financing.[46]

Having received a request to trade from a PDMR, the issuer must decide whether the circumstances are "exceptional". The issuer must take into account the extent to which the PDMR:

- is facing a legally enforceable financial commitment or claim at the time of the request; and
- has to make a payment to a third party (including a tax payment) as a result of a situation entered into before the closed period began and the PDMR cannot reasonably make that payment otherwise than by an immediate sale of the shares.[47]

In relation to employee share schemes and employee savings schemes, an issuer may allow a PDMR to trade during a closed period if the PDMR:

- has been awarded financial instruments under an employee scheme (provided that certain conditions are fulfilled);
- has been awarded financial instruments under an employee scheme which takes place during the closed period provided that a pre-planned and organised approach is followed, taking into account certain matters;
- exercises options, warrants or convertible bonds under an employee scheme where the date for exercise expires within a closed period;
- acquires financial instruments in the issuer under an employee saving scheme, provided that certain conditions are fulfilled;
- transfers or receives financial instruments, provided that the instruments are transferred between two accounts of the PDMR in circumstances where the transfer does not result in a change in price of the instrument; and
- acquires qualification or entitlement to the issuer's shares (which is likely to include nil-paid rights allocated to a shareholder in connection with a rights issue or bonus issue) and the final date for acquisition under the issuer's statutes or by-laws falls during a closed period and the PDMR provides evidence of the reasons why the acquisition cannot take place at any other time.[48]

The insider dealing prohibition contained in MAR art.14 applies during closed periods referred to in MAR art.19(11) in the same way as it does at any other time. Accordingly, when an issuer allows a PDMR to trade under MAR art.19(2), the general insider dealing provisions still apply and the

---

[46] Delegated Regulation art.7(2).
[47] Delegated Regulation art.8(3).
[48] Delegated Regulation art.9.

PDMR must always give consideration as to whether or not the relevant transaction would constitute insider dealing.[49]

7.4.1 Dealing codes

Prior to the implementation of MAR on 3 July 2016, in relation to dealings by directors, Ch.9 of the Listing Rules of the FCA provided that a listed company must require its directors and appropriate employees, including persons discharging managerial responsibilities, to comply with a model dealing code and must take all proper and reasonable steps to secure such compliance. The FCA's Model Code restricted directors and senior employees from dealing in their company's securities at particular times and set out procedures for how permission for dealings by these categories of person must be obtained. The provisions of the Model Code applied in addition to the requirements of the rules against market abuse and the CJA in relation to insider dealing.

The introduction to the Model Code stated:

> "This code imposes restrictions on dealing in the securities of a listed company beyond those imposed by law. Its purpose is to ensure that persons discharging managerial responsibilities do not abuse, and do not place themselves under suspicion of abusing, inside information that they may be thought to have, especially in periods leading up to an announcement of the company's results."

With regard to AIM companies, prior to the implementation of MAR the AIM Rules contained provisions which prohibited PDMRs from dealing in securities during close periods and exemptions to those prohibitions.

In the period leading up to the implementation of MAR, the FCA recognised that the Model Code in its then current form would be incompatible with MAR (particularly with regard to the prohibitions to trading and the exceptions to those prohibitions, as well as with regard to the definitions of closed periods). Consequently the FCA decided that the FCA's Model Code would be withdrawn and deleted from the Listing Rules. The FCA initially proposed to replace the Model Code with a new set of rules and guidance on the systems and controls an issuer should adopt in relation to PDMR dealings. However, following feedback on its consultation paper, the FCA concluded that any replacement rules and guidance would be unduly onerous on issuers and PDMRs, potentially creating a confusing two-tier regime. As a result, the FCA removed the Model Code but did not introduce the proposed new rules and guidance, with listed companies expected to look to MAR art.19 alone.[50] In its Policy Statement

---

[49] ESMA Questions and Answers *On the Market Abuse Regulation* (version 14, 29 March 2019), Question 7.8.
[50] "A listed company ... should consider the obligations under the disclosure requirements" which include MAR art.19 (Listing Rules LR9.2.5).

16/13 issued on 28 April 2016, the FCA did, however, recognise the value which a common dealing code might provide: "We note the suggestion of an industry-led development of codes or best practice in this area and we would support such a development".

On 24 June 2016, the Institute of Chartered Secretaries and Administrators (ICSA), the GC100 and the Quoted Companies Alliance (QCA) jointly published a guidance note on MAR.[51] These bodies believed that:

> "it would be of great benefit for listed and quoted companies to be able to turn to an equivalent version of the FCA's Model Code with the introduction of a single, industry-led dealing code rather than a variety of, no doubt broadly similar, codes which would potentially create confusion in the market."

The guidance note issued jointly by ICSA, GC100 and the QCA contains three specimen documents:

- A specimen group-wide dealing policy. This is designed to be issued to all group employees as well as managers and directors, explaining the concept of market abuse. It sets out the times when an individual is not permitted to deal in shares in the company. It also explains that confidential information must not be disclosed except where disclosure is necessary as part of an individual's employment or duties.
- A specimen dealing code. The dealing code is divided into two parts. Part A sets out the clearance procedure which a PDMR and other employees must follow in order to be allowed to trade in the company's securities. Part B, which applies only to PDMRs, sets out the circumstances in which clearance to trade will be refused and the procedures to be followed by a PDMR once a transaction has been entered into in order to notify the company and the FCA of the dealing. The PDMR also has obligations in relation to dealings in the company's securities by persons who are closely associated with the PDMR. The code also contains templates for individuals to seek clearance to deal and to make notification of a dealing.
- A specimen dealing procedures manual. This manual is for use by the company secretary. The manual is divided into two parts. Part A contains the dealing requirements and clearance procedures for PDMRs and the other employees who are looking to deal in the company's securities. It also sets out when permission to deal will be refused. Part B sets out the circumstances when a PDMR may be permitted to deal during a closed period. The manual also includes guidance on the operation of employee share plans, awards and trusts in the context of share dealings and on the maintenance of insider lists.

Whilst there is no requirement for listed companies on the Main Market of the London Stock Exchange to operate a "model code", the AIM Rules do

---

[51] Guidance note, Market Abuse Regulation (MAR), Dealing code and policy document (June 2016).

require a company trading on AIM to have in place "a reasonable and effective policy setting out the requirements and procedures for directors' and applicable employees dealings in any of its AIM securities".[52] The AIM Rules do not prescribe the contents of the dealing policy beyond some high-level minimum requirements regarding matters such as the close periods during which directors cannot deal, when a director must obtain clearance to deal, procedures for obtaining clearance and how the AIM company will assess whether clearance to deal may be given.

It is an oddity that, in terms of regulating dealings of PDMRs, AIM companies are subject to a higher standard than companies admitted to the Main Market. The London Stock Exchange explains this anomaly: "Given the differences in nature, size and stage of development of AIM companies as compared to Main Market companies, the AIM rules may differ from the Listing Rules in certain respects".[53] The London Stock Exchange has made clear that compliance by an AIM company with MAR does not automatically mean that the company will have satisfied its obligations under the AIM Rules.[54] Likewise, compliance with the AIM Rules will not automatically mean that the company will have satisfied its obligations under MAR.[55]

The specimen dealing policy and code issued jointly by ICSA, GC100 and the QCA are stated to be intended for AIM companies as well as companies on the Main Market. As MAR art.19 applies to both Main Market companies and AIM companies, the dealing codes for Main Market companies and AIM companies are now likely to follow a similar format.

7.5 The Takeover Code

The City Code on Takeovers and Mergers (the Takeover Code) was established to ensure the fair and equal treatment of all shareholders in relation to takeovers and it contains a framework within which takeovers are conducted. The operation of the Takeover Code is overseen by the Panel on Takeovers and Mergers (the Panel), which draws its members from major financial and business institutions.

The Takeover Code will apply whenever a person makes an offer to the shareholders of certain types of company to acquire all or some of their shares, where the offeree company is:

---

[52] AIM r.21.
[53] London Stock Exchange's FAQs—The Market Abuse Regulation (Question 17).
[54] London Stock Exchange's FAQs—The Market Abuse Regulations (Question 8).
[55] AIM Guidance on AIM Rule 21; London Stock Exchange's FAQs—The Market Abuse Regulation (Question 9).

(a)   a listed public company having its registered office in the UK, the Channel Islands or the Isle of Man;

(b)   a non-listed public company having its registered office and its place of central management and control in the UK, Channel Islands or Isle of Man; or

(c)   a private company having its registered office and its place of central management and control in the UK, the Channel Islands or the Isle of Man but only if there has been some public market for its shares, or it has filed a prospectus, at any time during the ten years prior to the relevant date.

In determining where a company has its place of central management and control, the Panel will take into account (amongst other things) the country in which the majority of the directors (executive and non-executive) are ordinarily resident.

The Code also applies to:

(a)   a company having its registered office in the UK but admitted to trading on a regulated market in one or more Member States of the European Economic Area (EEA) but not on a regulated market in the UK;

(b)   a company having its registered office in another EEA Member State and admitted to trading only on a regulated market in the UK; and

(c)   a company having its registered office in another EEA Member State and admitted to trading on a UK regulated market and at least one other regulated market in the EEA (but not on a regulated market in the EEA Member State in which it has its registered office), provided that the securities of the company were first admitted to trading in the UK only, or were simultaneously admitted to trading on a UK-regulated market and at least one other regulated market of the EEA (and the company notifies the Panel and the other regulatory authorities that it has chosen the Panel to regulate it), or the Panel is the supervisory authority pursuant to the second paragraph of art.4(2)(c) of the Directive on Takeover Bids.[56]

The introduction to the Takeover Code makes it clear that the "spirit" of the Takeover Code is important and must be observed as well as the precise wording and the Panel has decided that if the "spirit" of the Takeover Code is not observed, this can be viewed as a breach, regardless of whether a particular rule has been broken. It can be seen, therefore, that the Takeover Code is not black and white, and is open to interpretation. If in doubt as to the meaning of any provision, it is advisable to seek clarification by consulting the Panel.

---

[56]   Directive 2004/25 on takeover bids [2004] OJ L142/12.

Directors are covered by the Takeover Code like other persons and will usually be regarded as "acting in concert" with their company. The general consequences of this are not described in this Chapter, but there are a number of rules in the Code which specifically deal with share dealings and their consequences:

(a) Rule 4.1: this rule prohibits dealings of any kind in securities of an offeree company by any person, other than the offeror, who is privy to confidential price-sensitive information about an offer or contemplated offer, prior to an announcement of the offer or contemplated offer or of the termination of discussions;

(b) Rule 4.2: this rule restricts dealings by the offeror and persons acting in concert with it (such as directors), by providing that such persons must not sell any securities in the offeree company during an offer period, unless consent from the Panel is obtained and following 24 hours' public notice that such sales might be made. If any such sales are made, neither the offeror nor persons acting in concert with it will generally be permitted to purchase securities in the offeree thereafter; and

(c) Rule 5: if a person (and persons acting in concert with him/her) is interested in shares carrying less than 30% of the voting rights in a company, he/she must not acquire an interest in other voting rights which, when aggregated with the existing holding, would carry 30% or more of the voting rights in the company. If a person (and his/her concert parties) already holds 30% or more, but not more than 50% of the shares carrying voting rights, then the person and his/her concert parties cannot acquire any further shares. The rule is subject to a number of limited exceptions (e.g. the rule does not apply if the shares are acquired from a single shareholder and no other acquisitions are made within a period of seven days of that acquisition).

7.6 Disclosure of interests

Prior to the implementation of MAR on 3 July 2016, for companies admitted to the Main Market of the London Stock Exchange, the disclosure of directors' dealings in shares was governed by the Disclosure and Transparency Rules of the FCA (DTR), and in particular DTR Ch.3. For companies admitted to AIM, the disclosure of directors' dealings in shares was governed by the AIM Rules.

Following the implementation of MAR, DTR Ch.3 has been largely deleted by the FCA and the AIM Rules have been amended. Accordingly, PDMRs and companies admitted to the Main Market and to AIM must comply with MAR art.19 with regard to the disclosure of dealings by PDMRs.

7.6.1 Disclosure under MAR

The rationale for a disclosure regime relating to managers' dealings is set out in MAR Recital 59:

"The notification of transactions conducted by [PDMRs] on their own account, or by a person closely associated with them, is not only valuable information for market participants, but also constitutes an additional means for competent authorities to supervise markets."

The requirement for a PDMR of an issuer to notify the issuer of a dealing in the shares of the issuer extends to "persons closely associated" with the PDMR (PCAs). A PCA in relation to a PDMR is:

(a) a spouse (or a partner considered to be equivalent to a spouse under national law);
(b) a dependent child;
(c) a relative who has shared the same household for at least one year; or
(d) a legal person, trust or partnership, the managerial responsibilities of which are discharged by the PDMR or by a spouse, child or relative referred to in (a), (b) or (c), or which is directly or indirectly controlled by such a person, or which is set up for the benefit of such a person, or the economic interests of which are substantially equivalent to those of such a person.[57]

PDMRs of an issuer, and PCAs of PDMRs, must notify the issuer of every transaction conducted on their own account relating to the shares or debt instruments of that issuer (or to derivatives or other financial instruments linked to such shares or debt instruments).[58]

In addition to notifying the issuer, the PDMR and PCA are required to notify the relevant competent authority (MAR art.19(1) and 19(2)). Although the obligation to notify the competent authority (in the case of the UK, the FCA) lies with the PDMR and PCA, it is likely that the issuer will wish to make the notification itself, having been informed of the transaction by the PDMR or PCA.

The notification to the issuer and to the FCA must be made promptly and in any event no later than three business days after the date of the transaction (MAR art.19(1)). In turn, the issuer must make public promptly any notification of a transaction it receives from a PDMR or PCA and in any event within three business days of the date of the transaction (MAR art.19(3)). There is a risk to the issuer that if a PDMR or PCA notifies an issuer of a transaction at the end of the third day after the transaction, the issuer may have insufficient time to be able to make a public announcement

---

[57] MAR art.3(1)(26).
[58] MAR art.19(1).

of the dealing within the required timeframe. As a result, an issuer may consider it appropriate to adopt a dealing code requiring PDMRs (and their PCAs) to notify the issuer of any dealing within two business days of that dealing.

A "transaction" under MAR art.19(1) includes a pledge or loan of financial instruments, persons professionally arranging or executing a transaction on behalf of a PDMR or PCA (including on a discretionary basis), and a transaction made under a life policy where the PDMR/PCA is the policy holder bearing the investment risk and the policy holder has power or discretion to make investment decisions, or to execute transactions, regarding specific instruments for that life policy.[59]

The types of transactions which must be notified under MAR art.19 are set out in the Delegated Regulation art.10. These include:

- acquisition, disposal, short sale, subscription or exchange;
- acceptance or exercise of a stock option;
- entry into an equity swap;
- transactions in derivatives;
- a contract for difference; and
- acquisition, disposal or exercise of rights, including put options, call options and warrants.

The obligation to make a notification under MAR art.19 applies once the total amount of transactions within a calendar year has reached a threshold of €5,000 (MAR arts 19(1) and 19(8)).

The threshold is calculated by adding all transactions (without netting). Transactions by PDMRs and PCAs should not be aggregated though.[60] A competent authority has power to increase the threshold to €20,000 provided that it informs the European Securities and Markets Authority (or ESMA) of its decision and the justification for that decision.[61] For the time being, the FCA has decided to adopt the threshold of €5,000.[62]

It is open to issuers to notify all transactions on a voluntary basis, irrespective of the €5,000 threshold. It is likely that many UK issuers will decide to require all transactions by PDMRs and PCAs to be notified to the issuer and, in turn, to the FCA.

When calculating whether the threshold has been reached where transactions have been carried out otherwise than in Euros, the exchange rate to be

---

[59] MAR art.19(7).
[60] ESMA Questions and Answers *On the Market Abuse Regulation* (version 14, 29 March 2019), Question 7.3.
[61] MAR art.19(9).
[62] DTR Ch.3 para.3.1.2B.

used should be the daily foreign exchange reference rate at the end of the day on which transaction was made as published on the website of the European Central Bank.[63]

A notification of a transaction must contain the following information:

(a) the name of the PDMR or PCA;
(b) the reason for the notification;
(c) the name of the issuer;
(d) a description of the financial instrument (and its identifier);
(e) the nature of the transaction (e.g. acquisition or disposal);
(f) the date and place of the transaction; and
(g) the price and volume of the transaction.[64]

The form of the notification (both for notifying the issuer and the competent authority) has been prescribed in the Annex to the Commission Implementing Regulation 2016/523.[65]

7.6.2 Disclosure under the Takeover Code

In the case of dealings covered by the Takeover Code, there are additional rules for disclosure of a director's dealings in the shares of the offeror and the offeree company.

Takeover Code r.8 provides for a disclosure regime whereby parties involved in a takeover are required to announce what holdings they have, and dealings they have made, in the shares of the other parties.

An "Opening Position Disclosure" is an announcement containing details of interests or short positions in, or rights to subscribe for, any relevant securities of a party to the offer (other than a cash offeror). A "Dealing Disclosure" is an announcement containing details of any dealing made in relevant securities of any party to the offer (other than a cash offeror). For the purpose of r.8, the expression "relevant securities" includes securities of the offeree company which are being offered for or which carry voting rights; equity share capital of the offeree company and an offeror; securities of an offeror which carry substantially the same rights as any to be issued as consideration for the offer; and securities of the offeree company and an offeror carrying conversion or subscription rights into any of the foregoing.

Takeover Code r.8.1 requires the offeror to make a public Opening Position Disclosure within ten business days of the announcement that first

---

[63] ESMA Questions and Answers *On the Market Abuse Regulation* (version 14, 29 March 2019), Question 7.1.
[64] MAR art.19(6).
[65] Regulation 2016/523 laying down implementing technical standards with regard to the format and template for notification and public disclosure of managers' transactions in accordance with Regulation 596/2014 [2016] OJ L88/19.

identifies it as an offeror (and of any announcement first identifying a competing offeror, other than a cash offeror). The offeror must also make a Dealing Disclosure if it deals in any relevant securities during an offer period, and such disclosure must be made by 12.00 noon on the business day following the day of dealing.

Rule 8.2 requires the offeree to make a public Opening Position Disclosure within ten business days of the commencement of an offer period (and of any announcement first identifying any offeror, other than a cash offeror). The offeree must also make a Dealing Disclosure if it deals in any relevant securities during an offer period, such disclosure to be made by 12.00 noon on the business day following the day of dealing.

Rule 8.3 requires any person who is interested in 1% or more of any class of any relevant securities of any party to the offer (other than a cash offeror) to make a public Opening Position Disclosure and, if he deals during the offer period, a Dealing Disclosure.

Rule 8.4 requires any person who is "acting in concert" with any party to an offer to make a public Dealing Disclosure if he deals in any relevant securities of any party to the offer (other than a cash offeror) during an offer period, either for his own account or for the account of discretionary investment clients. For the purposes of the Takeover Code, the directors of a company (together with their close relatives and related trusts) will be presumed to be acting in concert with the company. "Close relatives" is not defined, but would, at the least, include spouse and infant children (and may, depending on the circumstances, be wider).

A person who is acting in concert with a party to an offer does not need to make an Opening Position Disclosure itself. Instead, details of the person's position must be included in the Opening Position Disclosure made by the party to the offer with which he is acting in concert.

Therefore, directors will need to ensure that:

(a)   their holdings of relevant securities are included within any Opening Position Disclosure made by the company of which they are a director; and

(b)   they make a Dealing Disclosure if they deal in relevant securities during the offer period.

Rules 24 and 25 provide for the detailed information that has to be given in offer documents and defence documents respectively. As well as much detailed financial information and general information about the offer, r.24.4 (in the case of offer documents) and r.25.4 (in the case of defence documents) require that a detailed list of shareholdings and of dealings be disclosed. Thus, in the offer document, there must be disclosed (inter alia):

(a)   shareholdings in the offeror (in the case of a securities exchange offer only) and in the offeree company in which directors of the offeror are interested; and

(b)   if a director has dealt for value in the shares in question during the period beginning 12 months prior to the commencement of the offer period (and ending with the latest practicable date before the posting of the offer document), details of the dealings, including dates must be stated. If no such dealings have occurred this must be stated.

In the case of a defence document, r.25.4 requires that the first major circular from the offeree company board advising shareholders on an offer must disclose (inter alia):

(a)   the shareholdings in the offeree company and in the offeror in which directors of the offeree company are interested; and

(b)   if any director has dealt for value in the shares in question between the start of the offer period and the latest practicable date prior to the posting of the circular during the period beginning 12 months before the start of the offer period and ending with the latest practicable date before the posting of the circular, the details of any dealings, including dates. If no such dealings have occurred this must be stated.

7.7   Effect of Brexit

In recent years, the UK has been at the forefront among EU Member States in seeking to tackle market abuse. It is likely that this will continue to be the case notwithstanding the UK's withdrawal from the EU. As a result, the UK will maintain a civil market abuse regime at least equivalent to the European market abuse regime contained in MAR.

In June 2018, the Treasury published a paper setting out its intended approach to financial services legislation in the context of Brexit.[66]

The purpose of the European Union (Withdrawal) Act 2018 (EUWA) is to provide a functioning statute book on the day the UK leaves the EU. The EUWA achieves this by converting into UK domestic law the existing body of directly applicable EU law (including EU Regulations). It also preserves UK laws relating to EU membership, such as legislation implementing EU Directives. This body of law is referred to as "retained EU Law". The EUWA gives ministers power to prevent, remedy or mitigate any failure of EU law to operate effectively, or any other deficiency in retained EU law, through Statutory Instruments (SIs). The contingency planning through the use of the SIs is referred to as "on-shoring". The SIs are not intended to make policy changes other than to reflect the UK's new position outside the EU.

---

[66]   HM Treasury's approach to financial services legislation under the European Union (Withdrawal) Act (27 June 2018).

The Market Abuse (Amendment) (Exit) Regulations 2019 were enacted on 18 February 2019, the substantive provisions of which come into effect on "exit day" (scheduled to be 31 October 2019) in the event of a "no deal" Brexit. This SI addresses deficiencies in retained EU law related to market abuse, including the following:

7.7.1 Maintaining the scope of MAR

UK MAR will capture conduct related to instruments admitted to trading on both UK and EU exchanges. This ensures the FCA maintains the ability to pursue cases of market abuse related to financial instruments which affect UK markets.

7.7.2 Notification requirements

UK MAR will retain EU MAR's notification requirements for issuers to report to national competent authorities. This includes the obligations to report PDMR transactions.

7.7.3 Transfer of functions

Under UK MAR, the power and functions of ESMA will be transferred to the FCA to enable it to enforce MAR to the extent necessary for a properly functioning UK regime.

Chapter 8

Directors' Powers and Proceedings

Crowley Woodford, Employment Partner and Nick Williamson, Corporate Partner

Ashurst LLP

8.1 Directors' Powers

Company directors must exercise their powers on behalf of the company and such powers are not independent of the company. The power to act on behalf of the company comes from the company's constitution, which means the company's articles of association and resolutions passed pursuant to it. The articles usually give the directors a wide general power to manage the company subject to anything reserved to the shareholders. For example, the Model Articles for Private Companies[1] specify that "subject to the articles, the directors are responsible for the management of the company's business, for which purpose they may exercise all the powers of the company" but go on to confirm that the "shareholders may by special resolution, direct the directors to take, or refrain from taking, specified action".[2] As well as this power to direct the directors to take or refrain from taking specified action by special resolution, it is important to appreciate that the shareholders have a statutory power to remove any director by ordinary resolution.[3]

Unless the articles specifically restrict what the company is able to do, the directors have the freedom and flexibility to carry out their management powers to theoretically conduct an unlimited range of lawful activities. However, the Companies Act 2006 (the CA 2006)[4] also specifies certain transactions and procedures that must be approved by the shareholders (for example, in relation to substantial property transactions, long-term service contracts and loans or credit transactions with directors). The articles of most companies formed under older company legislation (prior to the CA 2006) included an extensive set of objects clauses specifying what the company was permitted to do. That is no longer the case for companies formed under CA 2006 but companies can still include restrictions in their

---

[1] In discussing the powers and proceedings of directors, this chapter refers to the default articles for private companies limited by shares incorporated under the Companies Act 2006 (Model Articles for Private Companies).

[2] Model Articles for Private Companies arts 3 and 4.

[3] CA 2006 s.168.

[4] CA 2006 Pt 10 Ch.4 (ss.188–225).

articles on what they are permitted to do. Therefore, it is always prudent for directors to check the articles to ensure there are no such restrictions on what the company, and consequently they, can do.

Any restriction in a company's constitution has no bearing on third parties who deal with the company in good faith. The validity of any act carried out by the directors cannot be called into question on the ground of any lack of capacity provided for in the company's constitution.[5] Thus, where the directors engage in transactions that are prohibited under the company's constitution, those transactions will still be valid and enforceable. Moreover, where a third party deals with a company in good faith, the power of the directors to bind the company is deemed to be free of any restriction in the company's constitution and the third party is not required to inspect the company's constitutional documents to determine whether there is any constitutional limitation on the directors' powers to authorise the transaction in question.[6] If the directors have entered a transaction that has exceeded their powers, they will be in breach of their statutory duty to act within their powers[7] and will be liable to the company accordingly.

In addition to the general power to manage the company set out in the articles, the directors also have the additional benefit of a number of specific statutory and common law powers (including, for example, the right to call general meetings of the members,[8] the right to inspect company records (see Section 8.4), the right to litigate on behalf of the company[9] and the power to make provision for employees on cessation of a company's business with the approval of the shareholders).[10]

8.2 Directors' Proceedings

8.2.1 Process at board meetings

8.2.1.1 Preliminaries

The articles will usually include the procedure for convening and conducting board meetings. There is no statutory prescribed notice period for board meetings but reasonable notice must be given to all the directors of board meetings. "Reasonable" is determined in the context of the company's usual practice and what is necessary to give the directors a realistic opportunity of attending the meeting.[11] The notice does not need to

---

[5]   CA 2006 s.39.
[6]   CA 2006 s.40.
[7]   CA 2006 s.171.
[8]   CA 2006 s.302.
[9]   *John Shaw & Sons (Salford) Ltd v Shaw* [1935] 2 K.B. 113 CA.
[10] CA 2006 s.247.
[11] *Browne v La Trinidad* [1887] 37 Ch D.1 CA.

be in writing[12] but must state the proposed time and place, and if not a physical meeting, how they will communicate. If a meeting is adjourned, no further notice is required if each director attending is made aware of the date when the meeting is being reconvened. In the absence of any restriction in the articles, the directors can also act informally and take decisions without a formal board meeting provided they act unanimously.[13]

8.2.1.2   Quorum and chairman

Every board meeting must be quorate before business can be validly transacted at the meeting. The quorum will be dictated by the company's articles. The Model Articles for Private Companies require a quorum of two[14] unless it is a sole director company.[15] The sole director of a company[16] may record his or her decisions using written resolutions or adapt a board minute template to record the fact that the "meeting" is of a sole director.

The Model Articles for Private Companies also give the directors the power to appoint a chairperson and specify that if the appointed chairperson is not participating in the board meeting within ten minutes of the start time, a new chairperson must be appointed.[17] Where a disagreement exists among board members, the chairperson's duty is to ensure that the views of each director are fairly heard and to attempt to find a consensus.

The chairperson does not automatically have a casting vote unless the articles of association specifically provide for it. The Model Articles for Private Companies include a casting vote for the chairperson[18] which may only be exercised in the event of an equality of votes (and so long as the chairperson is not barred from participating in the meeting). The casting vote is conferred upon the office of chairperson as opposed to the individual and therefore must be exercised as a fiduciary power in what the chairperson considers to be the best interests of the company as a whole.

8.2.1.3   *Participation and voting*

For companies with the Model Articles for Private Companies, the directors are deemed to participate in a board meeting (or part of a board meeting) when the meeting has been called in accordance with the company's articles and they can communicate with each other any information or opinions they have on any particular item of the business of the meeting.[19] It is not important how the directors communicate or whether they are in the same

---

[12]   Model Articles for Private Companies art.9(3).
[13]   *Charterhouse Investment Trust Ltd v Tempest Diesels Ltd* [1986] B.C.L.C. 1.
[14]   Model Articles for Private Companies art.11.
[15]   Model Articles for Private Companies art.7(2).
[16]   CA 2006 s.154.
[17]   Model Articles for Private Companies art.12(4).
[18]   Model Articles for Private Companies art.13.
[19]   Model Articles for Private Companies art.10.

location and therefore board meetings held, for example, by telephone, Skype or FaceTime are all acceptable so long as each director can communicate with the others sufficiently to participate. For companies with articles which predate the Model Articles for Private Companies (for example, Table A articles formed under CA 1985), it is advisable to ensure there is an article specifically permitting board meetings by such means. Whilst it is not hard to envisage a situation where the UK courts would support the approach in the Model Articles and allow the holding of telephone board meetings without express permission in the articles, at the present time, no such judicial authority exists. Companies that do hold telephone or remote meetings without express authority in their articles should either amend their articles in advance of such meeting(s) or hold the board meeting remotely and then seek shareholder ratification of that action.

In making decisions, directors must act in accordance with their statutory duties to the company.[20] The general rule about decision-making is that any decision of the directors must either be made by a majority of those directors attending and voting[21] or by a written resolution signed by all eligible directors[22] (an eligible director being a director who would have been entitled to vote on the matter had it been proposed as a resolution at a board meeting). It is important to check whether or not the articles give the chairperson a casting vote (as noted, the Model Articles for Private Companies[23] confer a casting vote on the chairperson). It is also good practice for the minutes to set out which directors voted for and against the resolutions proposed at the meeting. Every director is entitled to have the fact that he voted against a motion recorded in the minutes. This may be particularly important where the director is unhappy with the way the company is being steered.

8.2.1.4 Declaration of directors' interests

Every director is subject to a duty to declare the nature and extent of any direct or indirect interest that he or she has in a proposed transaction or arrangement with the company[24] (to be made before the company enters the transaction or arrangement). There is a similar obligation to declare an interest in an existing transaction or arrangement with the company (which the company has already entered into).[25] The most common way of making such declarations is at board meetings, in which case the board minutes must set out the nature and extent of the director's interest. The minutes should also record whether the director making the declaration is able or unable to vote and be counted in the quorum. This will depend on the

---

[20] CA 2006 ss.170–177.
[21] Model Articles for Private Companies art.7.
[22] Model Articles for Private Companies art.8.
[23] Model Articles for Private Companies art.13.
[24] CA 2006 s.177.
[25] CA 2006 s.182.

company's articles. Under the Model Articles for Private Companies,[26] a director making a declaration in relation to actual or proposed arrangements or transactions "is not to be counted as participating in the decision-making process for quorum or voting purposes" and so cannot participate in the board meeting (or the part of the meeting), except in certain limited circumstances.

Directors are also subject to a separate duty to avoid any situation in which they have an actual or potential interest that conflicts or may conflict with the interests of the company.[27] Provisions in a company's articles will often specify how such conflicts are to be managed. The independent non-conflicted directors will often authorise a particular director's conflict of interest in accordance with the provisions of the articles and company law.[28] In doing so, it will also often be necessary to impose particular restrictions on the conflicted director (including, for example, restrictions on receiving information, attending the meeting or part of the meeting, counting in the quorum or voting on any of the business to be considered at the meeting). The board minutes will need to reflect the conflict of interest and the processes adopted for managing it.

8.2.1.5 Decision-making

The directors should satisfy themselves that by entering into a particular document or transaction, they are acting in a manner that is likely to promote the success of the company[29] (which, in practice equates with promoting the long-term interests of the shareholders as a whole). In making their decisions, the directors are obliged to consider the interests of the company's employees, suppliers, customers and other relevant stakeholders. The directors must also have regard to the desirability of the company maintaining a reputation for high standards of business conduct and the impact of the company's operations on the community and the environment and any other relevant matters.

8.2.2 Board minutes

Directors' proceedings are largely regulated by the articles of association of the relevant company. However, the need for companies to take board minutes is a statutory requirement, every company being required to take "minutes of all proceedings at meetings of its directors".[30] The minutes do not need to be a verbatim record of the meeting. The Oxford English Dictionary defines "minutes" as "a summarized record of the proceedings at a meeting", and hence it is generally appropriate for minutes to record a

---

[26] Model Articles for Private Companies art.14.
[27] CA 2006 s.175.
[28] CA 2006 s.175.
[29] In accordance with CA 2006 s.172.
[30] CA 2006 s.248.

summary of the key points of the meeting including resolutions, decisions and the reasons for those decisions. Fines can be imposed on a company and its officers if they are in default of the statutory obligation to record minutes. The statutory position is reflected in the common law, which also provides a general duty on directors to "place on record, either in formal minutes or otherwise, the purport and effect of their deliberations and conclusions; and if they do this insufficiently or inaccurately, they cannot reasonably complain of inferences different from those which they allege to be right".[31] ICSA, the professional body for governance, has issued helpful guidance about minute taking at board meetings; this notes that "decisions as to format, style and content should be taken from a position of knowledge of the law and of regulatory and market practice as providing an accurate, impartial and balanced record of meetings".[32]

Companies sometimes find it convenient to pre-prepare draft board minutes. Case law has confirmed that

> "there is nothing improper in the use of such drafts, provided the meeting does deal with the business before it in the manner indicated in the draft, and that ... the directors present do have the discussions and make the decisions indicated in the draft".[33]

However, directors must have regard to the company's interests and their own judgment and not necessarily be guided solely by the contents of the pre-prepared board minutes.

If board minutes are drafted in advance, it is important to check that: the meeting actually takes place; the directors consider the issues at hand and agree to take the actions and pass the resolutions set out in the minutes; and the minutes reflect the proceedings of the meeting. Any amendments to the minutes can be made after the meeting and should be made before the minutes are filed in the company's books.

Minutes purporting to be authenticated by the chairman of the meeting (or the chairman of the next directors' meeting) are evidence of the proceedings at the meeting.[34] So, although there is no statutory requirement for the board minutes to be signed by the chairman, it is good practice do so. Until the contrary is proved, every such meeting is deemed to have been duly held and convened, all proceedings are deemed to have duly taken place, and all appointments at the meeting are deemed valid.

It is good practice to begin board minutes by setting out the names of those directors in attendance under the heading "Present" with the names and

---

[31] *Liverpool Household Stores Associataion, Re* (1890) 59 L.J. Ch. 616 at 619.
[32] ICSA guidance note: Minute taking, April 2017.
[33] *R. (on the Application of the Inland Revenue Commissioners) v Crown Court at Kingston* [2001] EWHC 581 (Admin).
[34] CA 2006 s.249.

capacities of anyone else present at the board meeting (including professional advisers) being recorded under a separate heading of "In attendance". Minutes should be dated so that it can be seen when any resolutions were passed or rejected, and it is common to record the place where the board meeting was held and at what time. The Model Articles for Private Companies state that if the directors are in different places, the location of one of them can be chosen.

CA 2006 s.248 requires that records of board minutes must be kept for at least ten years from the date of the meeting. The articles of the company should also be checked in relation to the length of time that board minutes need to be kept. The Model Articles for Private Companies provide that directors must ensure that the company keeps a record in writing for at least ten years from the date of the meeting. Board minutes can be held in hard copy or electronic form and they can be arranged as the directors see fit, so long as they are adequately recorded for future reference. If the minutes are stored in electronic format, they must be capable of being printed.

It is also best practice for the board minutes to set out the necessary filing requirements to implement or perfect resolutions passed at the meeting. There is no requirement for a private company to appoint a company secretary but a company without such an officer should specify in the board minutes the name of a person responsible for completing the filing and administrative functions. All officers of the company are required to maintain up-to-date records both at Companies House and in the company's statutory books, failing which those in default are liable to a fine.

Every company director has a common law right to inspect and copy the minutes of the company's board meetings. By contrast with shareholders' rights to inspect minutes of general meetings, generally shareholders have no rights under articles of association or the CA2006 to inspect and copy board minutes. The Model Articles for Private Companies include a provision stating that no person may inspect the company's accounting or other records unless authorised to do so by law, the directors or by ordinary resolution of the shareholders.[35]

---

[35] Model Articles for Private Companies art.50.

8.3 Delegation

8.3.1 Delegation to committees

8.3.1.1 General

A company must have express provision within its constitution before it may delegate any of its functions. There will usually be a provision to this effect in the company's articles. Private Company Model Articles art.5 provides that the directors of the company may delegate any of their powers conferred on them under the articles to any person or a committee consisting of one or more persons (although note that reg.72 of Table A, the predecessor to the Private Company Model Articles only permitted committees of the board to consist of directors). Such delegation may be subject to any terms and conditions as the directors think fit. Thus the powers of the directors may be delegated to one person or to a committee consisting of more than one person. The board, when resolving to make such delegation, must not only clearly define the ambit of the committee's authority, but also specify whether the powers granted to the committee are granted in exclusion or in addition to the board of directors' own powers. It should also be noted that if the directors so specify, any such delegation may authorise further delegation of the directors' powers by any person to whom they are delegated. Where the articles permit delegation of powers by the board of directors, this is a fiduciary power and therefore the directors should consider their duties as directors when considering delegation (including CA 2006 ss.171(b) and 172). The Model Articles (both for Private Companies and for Public Companies) do not contain any guidance on the types of powers that can be delegated by the board of directors. However, in the case of premium listed companies, the July 2018 version of the FRC's non-mandatory Guidance on Board Effectiveness (the Guidance on Board Effectiveness), which supplements the Corporate Governance Code, suggests that boards of directors should produce a schedule of matters reserved for the decision of the board.

Even if powers are granted exclusively to a committee, the board in all cases retains the ability to alter or revoke any authority given.[36] Such revocation can be effected by the board passing a resolution expressly revoking the authority of the committee. It can also occur implicitly where the board exercises a power that has been delegated to the committee where the original delegation gave authority solely to the committee.

The membership of a committee must be set out by the board, specifying if membership is to be for a fixed period or for such period until the member

---

[36] Any agreement that purports irrevocably to delegate the directors' powers would be viewed by the courts to be contrary to public policy and unenforceable.

resigns his position or is replaced. However, even if the appointment of a particular person to a committee was for a fixed period, it may be revoked immediately by the board.[37]

The ability to delegate some of the board's decision-making powers to committees is an invaluable way of facilitating company management. It allows directors to attend, overall, fewer management meetings each and thereby frees up more time to develop the commercial aspects of the company. Abuse of the committee structure as a means of excluding a particular director or minority of directors who are properly entitled and obliged to participate in the management, not just by voting but also by having general corporate financial and commercial information available to them, is not permitted.[38]

The aim of releasing some directors from the need to attend some meetings (as allowed by the committee structure) does not mean that it entitles a company to take matters discussed at committee meetings any less seriously. Good corporate governance recognises that some matters are better dealt with by committees, rather than by the whole board, particularly where directors are bound to be interested in the outcome, for example, producing general company policy on directors' pay.

It is advisable for the terms of reference establishing a committee or a company's articles of association to specify how that committee should record its proceedings and decisions. Model Articles for Private Companies art.6 provides that any such committee must follow procedures which are based so far as applicable on those provisions of the articles which govern the taking of decisions by directors, although the directors may make rules of procedure for all or any committees which prevail over rules derived from the articles if they are not consistent with them.

8.3.1.2   *Premium Listed Companies*

Under the 2018 version of the Corporate Governance Code applicable to financial years beginning on or after 1 January 2019, premium listed companies should establish three board committees as follows:

8.3.1.2.1   Audit committee[39]:

The audit committee's function is to establish formal and transparent policies and procedures to ensure the independence and effectiveness of internal and external audit functions and to satisfy itself on the integrity of financial and narrative statements.

---

[37] *Manton v Brighton Corp* [1951] 2 K.B. 393; [1951] 1 T.L.R. 1105; (1951) 115 J.P. 377.
[38] *Bray v Smith* (1908) 124 L.T. Jo. 293.
[39] Corporate Governance Code Provision 24.

8.3.1.2.2   Nomination committee[40]:

The nomination committee's role is to lead the process for appointments to the board and ensure an orderly succession plan. Its duties include the constant evaluation of the make-up of the board, in terms of skills, experience, independence and knowledge, to assess where and what type of new appointments need to be made.

8.3.1.2.3   Remuneration committee[41]:

The remuneration committee should ensure that remuneration policies and practices are designed to support the company's strategy and promote long-term sustainable success. In particular, executive remuneration should be aligned to the company's purpose and values and be clearly linked to the successful delivery of the company's long-term strategy. The remuneration committee should have delegated responsibility for determining executive directors' remuneration policy and setting remuneration for the chair, executive directors and senior management.

Independent non-executive directors should make up the entirety of the audit committee and the remuneration committee and the majority of the nomination committee. The Guidance on Board Effectiveness recommends[42] that, in the interests of transparency, the three committees should make available on the company's website their terms of reference, explaining their roles and the authority delegated to them by the board.

Regardless of the nature and number of matters delegated to committee level for listed companies, the Guidance on Board Effectiveness notes that regular meetings of the board are essential.[43]

8.3.2   *Where there has been no official delegation of authority*

While CA 2006 s.40 (as discussed above in Section 8.1) does not operate to extend directly the powers of anyone else other than the board of directors, such as a committee or any individual director, it is possible that, under the law of agency, the acts of an individual may still bind the company where there has been no official delegation of authority.

When can the third party rely on agreements it has made with this unauthorised person who acts beyond the bounds of his authority? The individual may bind the company to the agreement if it acts as the company's agent. The law of agency is complex but, essentially, the individual agent must have either actual authority (which clearly is not

---

[40]   Corporate Governance Code Provision 17.
[41]   Corporate Governance Code Provision 32.
[42]   Guidance on Board Effectiveness para.63.
[43]   Guidance on Board Effectiveness para.28.

applicable here) or ostensible authority to do the thing which he does on behalf of the company (his principal).

When will an individual have ostensible authority? What amounts to ostensible authority will vary with circumstances. If a company (or a person with actual authority for a particular matter) represents that an individual has authority delegated down to him for that matter, then the company will, if the third party relies on this representation, be bound by the acts of the individual and prevented from claiming that the individual did not have such authority. There is no such thing as a self-authorising agent. In some cases, ostensible authority arises not from a positive act, but from acquiescence by the company to an individual's assumed role, such as permitting a director or ex-director to continue to act as if he were still authorised to do so even though his authority had been terminated.

To determine what is usually or customarily within the scope of the authority of a particular agent, the relevant factors to consider include the principal's kind of business, the role of the office-holder in that business, current business practices and all other material circumstances.

8.4 Directors' access to company books

Directors have long had an acknowledged right (founded in the common law) to inspect the company's books and records, either at a board meeting or elsewhere, and to take copies of them. In the case of *Conway v Petronius Clothing Co*,[44] the court allowed inspection of "all books of account, management accounts, working papers, bank statements, cheque stubs, contracts and invoices" and in *Dilato Holding Pty Ltd v Learning Possibilities*,[45] the court permitted a director access to all company documents, subject to the proviso that sight of them should only be used for the purpose of performing his duties as a director (see below). In addition, CA 2006 s.388(1)(b) states that a company's accounting records must at all times be open to inspection by the company's officers.

The court has discretion as to whether or not to order an inspection. It is clear from the cases that the right will be enforced, not for the director's own advantage, but to enable him to carry out his duties as a director.

In *Oxford Legal Group Ltd v Sibbasbridge Services Plc*,[46] the Court of Appeal refused to enforce the right to inspect a company's accounts, not only where the purpose for which the inspection was sought was to injure the company,

---

[44] *Conway v Petronius Clothing Co* [1978] 1 All E.R. 185; (1978) 122 S.J. 15.
[45] *Dilato Holding Pty Ltd v Learning Possibilities* [2015] EWHC 592 (Ch); [2015] 2 B.C.L.C. 199.
[46] *Oxford Legal Group Ltd v Sibbasbridge Services Plc* [2008] EWCA Civ 387; [2008] Bus. L.R. 1244; [2008] B.C.C. 558.

but also where the purpose was improper. The court confirmed that the true nature of the right to inspect was in order to enable the director to carry out his role as such.

As the right to inspect is for the benefit of the company, it terminates on a director's removal from office. Almost invariably in cases where directors are refused access to the company books, the majority of directors will be seeking to get those denied access removed expediently as directors. Where an application by those refused access comes before the court and a general meeting of the company has already been convened for the purpose of removing the applicant(s) as director(s), the court will normally intervene only if it considers such intervention necessary for the protection of the company. Such were the allegations in the *Petronius* case, where misconduct was alleged against the applicant director and the court ruled that the balance of convenience was against making the order before a meeting had been held to consider the director's removal.

It will often be argued in such cases that the applicant plans to abuse the inspection, if granted by the court, to damage the interests of the company. Though a court will not allow a director to abuse his right by disregarding the confidence his office imposes, in the absence of clear proof from the respondent, it will be assumed that the applicant will inspect in the company's best interests and for its benefit.

There is no definitive English case law to confirm that a director is entitled to have an agent (for example a lawyer or accountant) examine and copy company documents on his behalf. However, in *Edman v Ross*,[47] the Court of New South Wales held that the right of a director to inspect the books and accounts of the company (and to take copies) may be exercised either by the director personally or by a proper agent on his behalf. In addition, in the *Dilato* case, the court order permitted the directors' professional advisers to inspect and copy the company's documents as well as the director, subject to provision of a confidentiality undertaking.

---

[47] *Edman v Ross* (1922) S.R. (NSW) 351.

Chapter 9

Corporate Governance

Jonathan Marks, Partner
Slaughter and May

> "Corporate governance is concerned with holding the balance between economic and social goals and between individual and communal goals. The governance framework is there to encourage the efficient use of resources and equally to require accountability for the stewardship of those resources. The aim is to align as nearly as possible the interests of individuals, corporations and society." (Adrian Cadbury)[1]

9.1 Introduction

Since the financial crisis of 2008, corporate governance has received an unprecedented amount of attention from politicians, regulators and the media. Rarely have issues relating to corporate governance attracted so much national interest. Controversies ranging from excessive executive remuneration to financial services scandals relating to LIBOR and PPI to the avoidance of pension fund liabilities have been regular news headlines. Shareholder rebellions, government inquiries into corporate ethics and executive resignations have become a common occurrence, while debates still continue about the best way to reconcile the competing interests of "individuals, corporations and society".

All this means there has been an ongoing focus on both regulatory oversight and the value of effective corporate governance. There have been calls for greater scrutiny of compliance functions by directors and allegations that senior executives have often exhibited a "wilful blindness" towards a toxic corporate culture within their organisations. Politicians have been quick to join the fray in recent years, using public forums such as Select Committee investigations to exert additional pressure on boards.

There continues to be considerable popular anger at what many perceive as clear examples of boardroom greed. In Britain, the pay gap between the executives of top companies and the "shop floor" has grown appreciably over the past two decades. The ratio of executive to average pay at FTSE 100 firms has jumped from 47 times to 120 times in the past 20 years. While the

---

[1] Adrian Cadbury, *Corporate Governance and Chairmanship: A Personal View* (Oxford University Press, 2002), p.354.

years following 2013 have produced some evidence of executive pay stabilising or even slightly declining amid a political climate harshly critical of excessive remuneration, there is plenty to suggest the issue will continue to be a salient source of criticism of corporate Britain. Between 2016 and 2017, the median pay of a FTSE 100 CEO rose by 11%, with the average FTSE 100 CEO taking home around 190 times the salary earned by the average UK employee. Some 44% of UK employees classed their CEO's pay as either "too high" or "far too high", and the Conservative Government has proved to be responsive to such sentiments, introducing various reporting requirements in respect of executive pay and executive engagement with the workforce.

Attitudes about the interrelationship between large companies and society are clearly changing. Until now, the theory of corporate governance in the UK has mainly been predicated on the belief that what is good for the shareholder is good for the company and good for the economy in general. In the wake of a financial crisis that saw the UK taxpayer pick up the tab to avoid the collapse of the UK banking system, the Walker Review raised the idea of an implicit social contract between shareholders, the company and the general public at large.[2] Political arguments calling for the promotion of "responsible capitalism" have increasingly gained ground. Amid growing concerns about the societal impact of widening income inequality, few politicians would now attest to being "intensely relaxed about people getting filthy rich", with a growing enthusiasm towards intervention against undesirable corporate behaviour demonstrated by Conservative Prime Minister Theresa May's statement that "big business needs to change … if big firms are abusing their roles … we should do something about it".

Increasingly, corporate governance has been seen as going to the very heart of the culture of an organisation. In April 2013, Barclays published the Salz Review, a wide-ranging (and in places highly critical) review of its corporate practices and governance procedures. The Salz Review acknowledged that:

> "A board has an important role to play in protecting the culture of its institution by overseeing how effectively management promotes and embeds its stated values. So the board must consider the tone it sets; and it should dedicate sufficient board and board committee time to discussing how values are being implemented internally and to assessing how the culture is developing and its impact on behaviours."[3]

This emphasis on corporate governance and the need to improve governance standards continues to grow, with Prime Minister Theresa May remarking in August 2017 that while

---

[2] Sir David Walker, *A Review of Corporate Governance in UK Banks and Other Financial Industry Entities: Final Recommendations*, 26 November 2009 (Walker Review), para.5.7, p.70.
[3] Salz Review, *An Independent Review of Barclays' Business Practices*, April 2013.

"... our system of corporate governance is rightly envied and emulated around the world.

We must continue to improve if we are retain our competitive edge. We have also seen worrying evidence that a small minority of our companies are falling short of the high standards we expect."[4]

9.1.1 Recent Developments in Corporate Governance

There have been several key developments in corporate governance in recent years:

(a)   remuneration: the Government has successfully introduced new legislation relating to executive remuneration, in effect from October 2013. This legislation gives shareholders a binding vote on the remuneration policy and increases the level of transparency required in relation to remuneration structures. Further legislation came into force in January 2019 requiring large listed companies to make additional disclosures in respect of executive pay. More generally, there has been a renewed focus on incentivising responsible behaviour and long-term performance. This is reflected in the updated codes of guidance issued by shareholder representative bodies such as the Investment Association (IA) and the Pensions and Lifetime Savings Association (PLSA);

(b)   diversity: the Hampton-Alexander Review, published in November 2016, called for FTSE 350 companies to set targets for female representation in the boardroom. As of June 2018, FTSE 100 firms were on track to meet the target of 33% female representation on boards by 2020 but the figures for the FTSE 250 gave less grounds for optimism. Since April 2017, companies with 250 or more employees have been subject to a statutory gender pay gap reporting requirement. Diversity continues to rise up the corporate governance reform agenda, with the Department for Business, Energy & Industrial Strategy (BEIS) consulting on a similar ethnicity pay reporting regime. The Financial Reporting Council (FRC) has revised the UK Corporate Governance Code (the Governance Code), the latest version of which applies to financial years beginning on or after 1 January 2019, to be more fulsome in its requirements in relation to diversity than any previous incarnation of the Governance Code;

(c)   stewardship: the role of investors in holding companies to account for corporate governance failings, and in engaging constructively with companies with regards to long-term strategy, has been emphasised repeatedly in recent years. The Kay Review looked in detail at the important role institutional investors must play in promoting high governance standards and the Stewardship Code has been amended

---

[4]   HM Government, *Corporate Governance Reform: The Government response to the Green Paper consultation*, August 2017, p.i.

to mirror several of Kay's proposals. There has been a continued focus on emphasising the importance of stewardship in ensuring effective governance, with a new Stewardship Code due to be published in the summer of 2019, following consultation; and

(d)   governance of large private companies: traditionally, corporate governance initiatives have focused on public listed companies on the basis that as ownership and control are generally more closely linked in private companies there is less need to regulate management's activities for the benefit of the shareholders. However, events such as the collapse of BHS and the issues relating to its pension scheme have highlighted the potentially severe impact the failure of large private companies can have, both economically and socially, while the impetus to improve the governance of large private companies has been strengthened by the increased extent to which large enterprises are now held by private equity investors, as opposed to being listed. Consequently, the Government has introduced secondary legislation requiring large companies of a significant size to report on their corporate governance arrangements. In concert with this development, the FRC published finalised principles for the corporate governance of large private companies in December 2018.

9.1.2   *Reforming Corporate Governance: The Walker Review and the UK Corporate Governance Code*

Sir David Walker was commissioned by the 1997–2010 Labour Government to investigate corporate governance failings at Britain's banks and similar financial institutions before the financial crisis. He produced his final recommendations in November 2009 (the Walker Review). The Walker Review placed a large portion of the blame for the crisis on boardroom behaviour and criticised boards for having failed to provide the necessary leadership to avert the crisis. It argued that boards too often lacked an effective challenge to dominant and over-ambitious executives. It also argued that boards too easily succumbed to arguments in favour of increased leverage and were complacent about low-frequency, high-impact risk factors.

The Walker Review comprised 39 different recommendations proposing changes in the key areas of board function and composition, risk management, remuneration and the role of institutional shareholders. An appeal for greater accountability unites these 39 recommendations. It is an appeal that operates on three key levels. First, within the boardroom, the Walker Review urged non-executive directors to do more to hold executives to account, particularly in managing risk and developing companies' overall strategy. It called for the creation of board-level risk committees, chaired by a non-executive director, which would have the power to scrutinise and block transactions where necessary. It recommended that non-executive directors be given personalised training under the regular review of the chairman. The Walker Review highlighted the need for non-executive directors to exercise a more rigorous "strength of character" in their dealings with executive directors. It proposed that "independence of mind" and an "atmosphere of challenge" should replace the current formal appearance of leadership, encouraging boards to contest undesirable executive decisions.

Secondly, the Walker Review called for the annual re-election of chairmen to improve accountability to companies' shareholders. To aid shareholders in bringing boards to account, the Walker Review also encouraged boards to undertake a "formal and rigorous" evaluation of its performance. It proposed that these reviews be facilitated every two to three years by an independent and qualified external reviewer.

Finally, beyond the boardroom, the Walker Review examined the role of shareholders in taking positive action to bring boards to account. The Walker Review made clear that responsibility for enforcing good governance rested as much with financial institutions' shareholders as with their boards, calling on institutional shareholders to take a more active role as "owners" of their companies. As a result of the Walker Review, the Combined Code was revised and republished as the "UK Corporate Governance Code" in May 2010.

The FRC stopped short of introducing the Walker Review recommendations that were suitable only for banks and financial institutions, such as the proposal that remuneration committees be responsible for setting firm-wide pay, but went further in other areas: specifically, all directors of FTSE 350 companies were recommended to put themselves up for annual re-election. This is a position that the Governance Code now applies to all directors, not merely directors of FTSE 350 companies. The FRC has stated that it hopes to encourage boards to be better balanced and avoid "group think", to promote proper debate in the boardroom, to improve risk management at board level, and to foster performance-related pay that is better aligned to the long-term interests of the company.[5] As such, the 2010 Governance Code closely mirrored the Walker Review, particularly in its desire for greater board accountability. This drive for accountability is perhaps best represented by the requirement for directors' annual re-election and the introduction of externally facilitated board reviews every three years for FTSE 350 companies.

9.1.3 The Kay Review: Focus on long-term success

On 22 June 2011, it was announced that the Government had appointed Professor John Kay to carry out an independent review into investment in UK equity markets and its impact on the long-term competitive performance and governance of UK quoted companies (the Kay Review). This

---

[5] FRC, *Revisions to the UK Corporate Governance Code (Formerly the Combined Code)*, May 2010.

followed a call for evidence from the then Department of Business, Innovation and Skills (BIS)[6] entitled *A Long-Term Focus for Corporate Britain*, published on 25 October 2010, which was the first stage of BIS' review into corporate governance and economic short-termism in capital markets.

Kay published his final report on the operation of UK equity markets in the UK in July 2012 (the Report). The Report is a wide-ranging narrative assessment of the state of the equity capital markets in the UK, and its impact on the long-term performance and governance of UK listed companies. Kay's principal concern is to examine how well equity markets enhance the performance of UK companies, and enable savers to benefit from the activity of businesses through returns to direct and indirect shareholders.

Throughout the Report, Kay highlights the damaging effect of decisions made with the aim of increasing shareholder value in the short term. The Report questions both the assumption of whether an increased share price is a measure of success at all, and whether the success of any management decision can truly be measured before its long-term effects on the company have been established. The Report makes clear that company directors have an explicit responsibility to promote the long-term success of their companies under the Companies Act 2006 (CA 2006) s.172(1)(a). Despite this being a matter of law, Kay states that in the process of carrying out his review he encountered many company directors who interpreted the provision to mean a duty to maximise the current share price of their company. With the decline of the individual shareholding and the rise in nominee holdings run by stock brokers and banks, and intermediation in other forms, the Report states that the relationship of trust between a long-term investor and the company with which it is familiar has broken down: "a by-product of the growth of intermediation has been a tendency to view the performance of the market through the eyes of intermediaries".[7] As the Report points out, intermediaries each have their own remuneration structure and business model and, as such:

> "the incentives that emerge from their reward systems may not correspond with the interests of savers, or the promotion of the better performance of the companies in which funds are invested ... The more extended is the chain of intermediaries, the more scope there is for such misalignment of incentives."[8]

Kay raises concerns that some investment intermediaries are interpreting their duties to their clients or to beneficiaries too narrowly to mean the duty to maximise short-term financial returns, and that this may lead them to set investment strategies with asset managers that focus on short-term performance metrics, create a disincentive to engagement, and do not take

---

6   BIS was succeeded by the Department of Business, Energy & Industrial Strategy (BEIS) in July 2016.
7   Report para.3.11.
8   Report para.4.12.

into account long-term factors including relevant environmental, social and governance factors which may be relevant to company performance. Kay suggests such an interpretation may be the product of advice—from lawyers and consultants—that seeks to protect the intermediary rather than to support them to act in the best interest of the client or beneficiary. As such, the Kay Review recommended that the Law Commission should be asked to review the legal concept of fiduciary duty as applied to investment intermediaries to address uncertainties and misunderstandings on the part of trustees and their advisers.[9] The Law Commission's response, published on 1 July 2014 and entitled "Fiduciary Duties and Investment Intermediaries", does not focus on recommendations for legislative reform but instead explains the nature of fiduciary (and other) duties and describes how these duties apply to investment intermediaries. The report concludes that the law permits trustees to make investment decisions that are based on non-financial (e.g. environmental, social or governance) factors, provided that: (i) there is good reason to think that scheme members share the concern; and (ii) there is no risk of significant financial detriment to the fund.

The most striking misalignment in relation to corporate behaviour, in the view of the Report, is the "bias towards action", which aligns individual intermediaries' rewards (and even those of company directors) with profits arising from current activities, rather than focusing on long-term returns. This may manifest itself as an incentive to promote reorganisations, acquisitions and disposals, alongside an increased volume of dealing activity in a company's shares.[10] Kay decries this "financialisation" of UK business, whereby growth takes place not organically but by aggressive programmes of acquisitions and disposals. The examples of ICI and GEC are cited as companies which "reacted to weaknesses in their operating activities by trading in businesses rather than by trading in chemicals or electrical goods". Kay notes that some companies appear to have given relatively too much attention to marketing and to the acquisition of businesses, and not enough to the fundamental research or development on which long-term success in their industry depends.[11]

The Review's general proposal to shift the market's emphasis towards long-term concerns revolves around establishing a closer bond of trust between company management and company stakeholders. Drawing strongly on the idea of stewardship, the Report advises company management to foster "trust and respect" between the company and its ultimate shareholders, and between all the intermediaries in between. The Report stresses the importance of stewardship: company management must

---

[9] *Ensuring Equity Markets Support Long-Term Growth: The Government Response to the Kay Review*, November 2012, p.26.
[10] See para.4.13, where the Report states that independent financial advisors recognise that clients are more willing to pay for advice to do something than to do nothing.
[11] Report para.1.26.

understand the needs and expectations of stakeholders, based on trust that the company will act in the best way for its shareholders.[12]

The Report therefore recommends that the UK Stewardship Code (discussed below) should be developed to incorporate a more expansive form of stewardship, focusing on strategic issues as well as questions of corporate governance. This idea is fundamental to the whole Report, as it points out that trust and engagement are the principal mechanisms through which information asymmetries and misalignment of incentives are removed, which is key to help savers and companies reach their long-term objectives. Anonymous relationships and high volumes of trades are unlikely to achieve this relationship.

While the Stewardship Code is not explicitly aimed at company directors, the Report makes it clear that the principles behind it are equally applicable, and that this is the approach which directors should take in the future. The most tangible recommendation is therefore that company directors (along with asset managers and asset holders) should adopt Good Practice Statements that promote effective stewardship and long-term decision making. Acting in line with these principles should prevent company directors from viewing the company "as a portfolio of businesses", or using the movement of the share price to measure performance, and in turn should move management approaches away from a "transaction based culture".[13] Additionally, the adoption of stewardship principles by all levels of the investment chain should be the first step to more productive and active engagement by the directors with asset managers and holders, and allow the company to disengage from the process of managing short-term earnings expectations and announcements.

The Kay Review provides the following "Good Practice Guidance for Company Directors." It suggests that directors should:

1.   understand their duties as directors under the CA 2006, and in particular acknowledge the relevance of considering long-term factors, including relevant environmental, social and governance issues, and the reputation of the company for high standards of business conduct, in fulfilling their duty to promote the success of the company;

2.   acknowledge that long-term value creation in the interests of shareholders is best served by strategies which focus on investing appropriately to deliver sustainable performance rather than treating the business as a portfolio of financial interests;

3.   act to ensure that the intermediation costs associated with a publicly traded company are kept to a minimum;

---

[12]   Report para.6.3.
[13]   Report para.6.26.

4. ensure that corporate reporting is focused on forward-looking strategy;
5. facilitate engagement with shareholders, and in particular institutional shareholders such as asset managers and asset holders, based on open and ongoing dialogue about their long-term concerns and investment objectives;
6. provide information, in the context of corporate reporting and ongoing shareholder engagement, which supports shareholders' understanding of company strategy and likely long-term creation of value, including by agreeing a range of performance metrics relevant to the company;
7. communicate information to shareholders which aids understanding of the future prospects of the company, even if this means going beyond (but not against) the strict requirements of accounting standards, for example on market valuations;
8. not allow expectations of market reaction to particular short-term performance metrics to significantly influence company strategy;
9. refrain from publishing or highlighting inappropriate metrics which may give a misleading impression of anticipated future company performance; and
10. be paid in a way which incentivises sustainable long-term business performance: long-term performance incentives should be provided in the form of company shares to be held until after the executive has retired from the business.

The Government response to the Kay Review (published in November 2012) was broadly supportive of the Report's recommendations. Embracing the guidelines above, it also suggested that other principles emerging from the Review should be included: that directors should consult major long-term investors over major board appointments, and that directors should seek to disengage from the process of managing short-term earnings expectations and announcements. Consistent with this approach, Kay's recommendation that mandatory quarterly reporting obligations should be removed was implemented in November 2014.

9.1.4 BEIS Green Paper on corporate governance reform

The genesis of the BEIS Green Paper on corporate governance reform, published in November 2016 (the BEIS Green Paper) was rooted in both an understanding that the UK's world-leading corporate governance framework owes its status to a longstanding tradition of periodic review and judicious subsequent amendment and a more context-specific concern from business that high-profile contemporary corporate scandals, such as the failure of BHS, threatened to allow the actions of a very small number of UK businesses to undermine the reputation of British business generally.[14]

---

[14] BEIS Green Paper, *Corporate Governance Reform* November 2016, p.4.

The BEIS Green Paper focused on three areas where it was felt the need to consider updates to the corporate governance framework was particularly acute, namely:

(a)   shareholder influence on executive pay;
(b)   measures to increase company engagement with non-shareholding stakeholders, in particular employees; and
(c)   the possibility of requiring the largest privately-held companies to comply with a specified corporate governance code.

Of particular note were the BEIS Green Paper's suggestions intended to "strengthen the wider stakeholder voice" in order to ensure that companies are run "not just with an eye to the interests of the board and the shareholders, but with a recognition of their responsibilities to employees, customers, suppliers and wider society".[15] This aim is consistent with the increasing impetus in recent years to require businesses to take a broader, more socially aware view of their activities and the impacts they create, first demonstrated by the inclusion of a requirement under CA 2006 s.172 for company directors to have regard to a range of stakeholder interests when acting to promote the success of the company. This trend is more recently demonstrated by the introduction of the Modern Slavery Act, which requires businesses exceeding a certain size to disclose how they have sought to remove slavery and human trafficking from both their own business and its supply chains.

The BEIS Green Paper's recommendations of most import in this sphere were those advocating stakeholder representatives on the board, and strengthened reporting requirements in relation to both stakeholder engagement and compliance with CA 2006 s.172. In relation to this first potential reform, the BEIS Green Paper particularly focused on the appointment of employee representatives to boards, noting that such appointments could "bring a new perspective to board discussions, particularly adding a longer-term perspective".[16] However, the BEIS Green Paper also acknowledges the many potential drawbacks of appointing employee representatives to company boards, in particular risks of tokenism (whereby a company could purport to be engaging with the workforce by appointing a workforce director but would continue in practice to fail to substantively engage with employees at every level in the business) and the risk of important decision-making being conducted in fora other than the board meeting. The BEIS Green Paper therefore makes clear that it does not propose mandating the appointment of employee representatives to boards. This hesitancy to be overly prescriptive endured in the ultimate implementation of this idea, with Provision 5 of the Governance Code (as applicable to financial years beginning on or after 1 January 2019) permitting boards to engage with the workforce by using

---

[15]   BEIS Green Paper, *Corporate Governance Reform* November 2016, p.34.
[16]   BEIS Green Paper, *Corporate Governance Reform* November 2016, p.40.

one, or a combination of, options which include (but do not require) the appointment of a director from the workforce. Companies can also put in place a workforce advisory panel, or designate a non-executive director as responsible for responding to employee concerns (both further means of board-workforce engagement suggested by the BEIS Green Paper). Alternatively, a company may put "alternative arrangements" in place so long as the company is able to provide a sufficient explanation as to why those alternative arrangements are considered effective.

Insofar as increased reporting is concerned the BEIS Green Paper recommended that stronger reporting requirements in relation to compliance with s.172 duties and engagement with non-shareholding stakeholders be put in place in order to provide greater confidence that boardroom decisions are being taken with regard to stakeholder interests.[17] This recommendation has been taken forward through secondary legislation introducing a range of additional reporting criteria that requires certain companies (generally larger concerns) to report on how they have had regard to employee and other stakeholder interests and the effect of that regard on the company's principal decisions during the financial year. Similarly, large companies must make a statement in their strategic report describing how their directors have had regard to the matters set out in the CA 2006 s.172(1)(a)–(f). More details on these new reporting requirements are set out at Section 9.4.9 of this Chapter.

The reporting requirements introduced by secondary legislation are equally applicable to private companies meeting the relevant thresholds. However, the BEIS Green Paper further considered requiring the UK's largest private companies to comply with a governance code. Again, this idea is symptomatic of the increasingly popular conception that good governance should not merely be concerned with regulating the relationship between the owners and the managers of a business (which is less of an issue in private companies where there is generally far more alignment in this respect than in listed entities), but should also regulate the relationship between the managers of a business and other stakeholders with a strong interest in that business, such as employees, customers and pension fund beneficiaries.[18] In order to achieve this, the BEIS Green Paper raises the possibility of developing a bespoke governance code for private companies which the largest privately-held companies would then be required to comply with (or explain why they do not feel that compliance is appropriate or possible). The Government response to the BEIS Green Paper supported this idea, leading to the development of the Wates Principles for large private companies and the introduction of a requirement (applicable to financial years beginning on or after 1 January 2019) for large private companies to "make a statement of corporate governance arrangements" in

---

[17]   BEIS Green Paper, *Corporate Governance Reform* November 2016, p.40.
[18]   BEIS Green Paper, *Corporate Governance Reform* November 2016, p.43.

their directors' reports. For more detail on the Wates Principles and the associated reporting regime, see Section 9.8 of this Chapter.

9.2 Background

The prominence of recent debates in corporate governance concerning boardroom diversity, remuneration, the promotion of investor stewardship, the introduction of an employee voice into company management, and the governance of large private companies all suggest that there is going to continue to be considerable interest in corporate governance reform in years to come.

But what is corporate governance? In 1992, the Cadbury Report[19] defined corporate governance as the system by which companies are directed and controlled. In introducing the report, it pointed out the effectiveness with which boards discharge their responsibilities as determining Britain's competitive position. It saw directors' freedom to drive their companies forward within the framework of effective accountability as being the essence of any system of good corporate governance. Boards of directors were regarded as responsible for the governance of their companies—with the shareholders' role in governance being to appoint the directors and the auditors and satisfy themselves that an appropriate governance structure was in place.

The separate roles of the board and the shareholders are long established. By the middle of the 19th century, it had become established practice for shareholders to elect the directors and for the directors to run the company. If the members were unhappy with the running of the company they could, in theory, change the board but not intervene in the management. Until their removal, the existing board continued to have control over the management of the company.

This has been an enduring theme in company law, reinforced by the Cadbury Report:

> "The formal relationship between the shareholders and the board of directors is that ... the directors report on their stewardship to the shareholders and ... the shareholders as owners of the company elect the directors to run the business on their behalf and hold them accountable for its progress."[20]

In the post-war years, some institutional investors took the view that it was cheaper to invest in successful companies and to avoid or divest from unsuccessful ones. If the company underperformed, shareholders just sold their shares. As the share price fell, it was at least possible that acquisitive

---

[19] *The Financial Aspects of Corporate Governance* 1 December 1992.
[20] *The Financial Aspects of Corporate Governance* 1 December 1992, para.6.1.

and more successful companies might move in with takeover proposals. Where institutional intervention did take place, it was often on an informal basis rather than through representations or other action at formal shareholder meetings. This environment provoked debate about the appropriate standards of corporate governance which it was desirable to promote.

The law currently provides a basic framework of corporate governance by specifying the minimum number of directors that companies may have, by regulating the conduct of directors in a limited way, by requiring disclosure of certain matters and by providing for certain decisions to be taken by the shareholders. Apart from these requirements, however, companies are generally free to establish their own systems of governance by means of provisions in their articles of association or by less formal internal rules. As a result, governance structures are not in the main prescribed by law but have developed out of business and commercial practice. The governance of listed companies is also influenced by the additional rules promulgated and administered by the UK Listing Authority of the Financial Conduct Authority (the FCA), which are mainly directed towards the protection of investors.

During the 1990s, the codes of practice developed by three committees (which were set up to examine corporate governance issues) introduced a new dimension. The approach adopted in those codes was to use self-regulation as a means of promoting and maintaining practices of good governance. The intention in each case was to establish a voluntary code, but with an emphasis on disclosure. The idea was to encourage transparency in corporate governance through disclosure obligations which would promote shareholder pressure to comply with best practice in appropriate cases.

The Cadbury Committee was set up in May 1990 as a result of public concern over high-profile corporate failures such as Polly Peck, BCCI and Maxwell. The objective of the Cadbury Committee was to help to raise the standards of corporate governance and the level of confidence in financial reporting and auditing by setting out clearly the responsibilities of directors and their relationship with auditors. The committee published its report, accompanied by its Code of Best Practice, in December 1992.[21]

Concern over what were considered to be excessive remuneration and compensation packages awarded to some directors resulted in the establishment of the Greenbury Committee in January 1995 to identify good

---

[21] *The Financial Aspects of Corporate Governance* 1 December 1992; *The Code of Best Practice* 1 December 1992.

practice in determining directors' remuneration. The committee published its report and Code of Best Practice in July 1995.[22]

Unlike the Cadbury and Greenbury Committees, the establishment of the Hampel Committee in November 1995 was not a reaction to public concern about the way in which companies regulated themselves, but rather to the two reports which had preceded it. The Hampel Committee was born out of the recommendation of Cadbury and Greenbury that a committee should follow up on the implementation of their findings. The aim was to draw up a set of principles and a code, based on Cadbury, Greenbury and its own conclusions.

Following the publication of the final report of the Hampel Committee, the London Stock Exchange (LSE) issued the Principles of Good Governance and the Code of Best Practice (the Combined Code) in June 1998, which was derived from the reports of the three committees on corporate governance. At the same time, the LSE published a new listing rule. This required listed companies to include in their annual reports and accounts specified details as to how they had complied with the Combined Code during the year under review, but it did not require listed companies to comply with the Combined Code. This was the basis of the "comply or explain" philosophy that still underpins UK corporate governance.

The Turnbull Committee was set up by the Institute of Chartered Accountants in England and Wales (ICAEW) to provide guidance for listed companies on how to implement the requirements in the Combined Code relating to internal control. Its report set guidelines for ensuring that companies have in place effective risk management and internal control systems.[23] It followed a principles-based approach and did not include detailed prescription as to how to implement the guidance. The same approach was adopted when the guidance was revised in October 2005.

Following the collapse of Enron in 2001, the Government appointed Derek Higgs in April 2002 to head a review of "the role and effectiveness of non-executive directors in the UK". This followed the Myners Review of institutional investment.[24] In addition, the FRC commissioned a report by Sir Robert Smith to clarify the responsibilities of audit committees and to develop the existing Combined Code guidance in this area.[25] The final reports from these exercises were published in January 2003 and included a revised version of the Combined Code which was due to take effect from 1 July 2003. However, following criticism of both the substance of certain

---

[22] *Directors' Remuneration—Report of a Study Group chaired by Sir Richard Greenbury* 17 July 1995.
[23] *Internal Control: Guidance for Directors on the Combined Code* September 1999.
[24] *Institutional Investment in the United Kingdom, a Review* March 2001.
[25] The Smith Report, *Audit Committees: Combined Code Guidance* January 2003. A modified version dated July 2003 forms part of the related guidance accompanying the Combined Code.

findings of the Higgs Review and the speed at which its findings were to be implemented through the revised Combined Code, the FRC did not publish the final version of the revised Combined Code until 23 July 2003. The revised version took effect from 1 November 2003. Following a review of the implementation of the Combined Code in 2005, the FRC consulted on a small number of changes to the Combined Code. These changes were incorporated in an updated version published in June 2006. Between April and July 2007 the FRC carried out a similar review of how the Combined Code was being implemented and proposed a small number of amendments in 2008. A revised Combined Code took effect in June 2008.

In response to the financial crisis in the last part of the previous decade, the Labour Government appointed Sir David Walker to head an inquiry into banks' corporate governance. The Walker Review published its final report in November 2009. The report included a list of recommendations for how the Combined Code should be reformed. The FRC brought forward its review of the Combined Code scheduled for 2010 to accommodate the Walker Review's recommendations. While the Walker Review focused specifically on corporate governance in financial services firms, the FRC's remit was wider as the Combined Code applied to all listed companies regardless of industry sector. For this reason, some recommendations were adopted while some were deemed inappropriate.

As a consequence of the Walker Review, the name of the Combined Code was changed from "The Combined Code on Corporate Governance" to "The UK Corporate Governance Code". It was hoped that this title would make its status as the UK's recognised corporate governance standard for companies clearer to foreign investors and to foreign companies listed in the UK, which, as a result of changes to the Financial Services Authority (FSA) Listing Regime in April 2010, are required to report against the Governance Code if they have a premium listing.[26] The first version of the Governance Code was published in May 2010, although several subsequent versions have incorporated further amendments since this time. The most recent version of the Governance Code was published in July 2018 and will have to first be reported against in respect of financial years beginning on or after 1 January 2019. The main changes to the Governance Code included provisions meaning that boards should foster greater engagement with stakeholders, particularly members of the workforce, and that where there is a significant vote against a resolution recommended by the board, the board should consult with shareholders in order to understand the reasons for their dissatisfaction.

Historic developments have shown that additions to the Governance Code can bring about change in process and practice relatively quickly: for example, just two years after the Governance Code first recommended that

---

[26] See LR 9.8.7 R. From 1 April 2013, the Listing Rules formed part of the Financial Conduct Authority Handbook.

FTSE 350 companies put all directors up for re-election annually, nearly all of those companies and a good many smaller ones were doing so.[27]

There is currently a high level of compliance with the provisions of the Governance Code. The FRC noted in October 2018 that 72% of FTSE 350 companies declare full compliance with the Governance Code, while 95% comply with all but a handful of Governance Code provisions.[28]

Following the publication of Sir John Kingman's independent review of the FRC in December 2018, which recommended the abolition of the FRC and its replacement by an independent statutory regulator with stronger powers, the Business Secretary Greg Clark confirmed that the Government would replace the FRC with a new regulator. Kingman's review proposes that the new regulator have responsibility for maintaining and promoting the Governance Code.[29] Given the fact Kingman commends the outgoing FRC's effective custody of the "world-leading" Governance Code as one of the organisation's few "clear strengths",[30] it seems unlikely the new regulator's approach to the Governance Code will drastically depart from that of the FRC.

Corporate Governance: A Short History

1992	Cadbury Report	Responded to controversial UK governance failures such as Polly Peck and BCCI and the Robert Maxwell scandal: roles of chairman and chief executive separated; requirement introduced for two independent NEDs; and requirement introduced for audit committee of NEDs.
1995	Greenbury Report	Responded to public outcry over executive pay levels (such as at British Gas): introduced requirement for a remuneration committee of NEDs; and long-term performance related pay introduced.
1998	Hampel Report	Reviewed the implementation of the Cadbury and Greenbury Reports: introduced the Combined Code on corporate governance; and the approach was principles-based, as opposed to consisting of detailed guidelines.

---

[27] FRC, *Developments in Corporate Governance 2012: The impact and implementation of the UK Corporate Governance and Stewardship Code* December 2012, p.1.
[28] FRC, *Annual Review of Corporate Governance and Reporting 2017/2018* October 2018, p.32.
[29] Sir John Kingman, *Independent Review of the Financial Reporting Council* December 2018, p.21.
[30] Sir John Kingman, *Independent Review of the Financial Reporting Council* December 2018, p.6.

1999	Turnbull Report	Introduced a requirement for the board to review its systems of internal control and risk management.
2003	Higgs Report	Responded to corporate failings in the US, such as Enron, Worldcom and Tyco; followed the "comply or explain" principle (in contrast to US authorities, who favoured mandatory regulation in the Sarbanes-Oxley Act); introduced a requirement for at least half of board to be independent NEDs; and introduced annual board and director evaluation.
2003	Smith Report	Responded to concerns regarding auditor independence: sets out guidance on the role and responsibilities of audit committees; and focuses on independence of external auditors and level of non-audit services provided.
2009	Walker Review	A review of governance of the UK banking industry in response to the global financial crisis. Many of Walker's recommendations were incorporated into the renamed "UK Corporate Governance Code" in 2010.
2010	Stewardship Code	Aimed to improve the level of engagement between institutional investors and companies. A revised version was published in September 2012.
2011	Guidance on Board Effectiveness	Published by the FRC as a replacement for the 2003 Higgs guidance. Provides guidance on ss.A and B of the then Governance Code regarding leadership and board effectiveness.
2012	Kay Review	A review of long-term decision making practices in the UK equity markets. Made several recommendations relevant to corporate governance and stewardship.
2012	Guidance on Explanations	FRC report on the form discussions should take between companies and investors, providing guidance on the quality of explanations companies should provide.
2013	Legislation on directors' remuneration report	Amendments to the CA 2006 are brought into force, giving shareholders a binding vote on companies' future remuneration policies.
2016	Hampton-Alexander Review	Government commissioned review on the promotion of women in FTSE companies. Recommended that FTSE 350 companies aim for a minimum of 33% female representation on their boards by 2020. Subsequent reports published in November 2017 and November 2018.

2017	BEIS Green Paper	The Government's response to the BEIS Green Paper invited the FRC to revise the Governance Code to allow for a strengthened non-shareholder stakeholder voice at board level.
2018	New Governance Code	The FRC published a new version of the Governance Code, revised in light of the BEIS Green Paper and the related BEIS Select Committee Inquiry. The new Governance Code will apply to accounting periods beginning on or after 1 January 2019.

In terms of legislation, the provisions introduced by the CA 2006 remain the key developments of recent years. The Companies Bill (formerly called the Company Law Reform Bill) received Royal Assent on 8 November 2006, and followed on from a review of company law begun as far back as 1998. The CA 2006 contains about 1,300 sections and is said to be one of the longest ever UK statutes. The Act replaced virtually all of the Companies Acts 1985 and 1989, much of the Companies (Audit, Investigations and Community Enterprise) Act 2004, and the Directors' Remuneration Report Regulations 2002.

The changes introduced by the CA 2006 included:

- the codification of directors' duties with an obligation to have regard to specific matters;
- various additional rights for shareholders, including the right for a registered member of a listed company to nominate a third party to receive information from the company and, in the case of all companies if their articles so provide, to exercise voting rights;
- a statutory process for bringing derivative claims in the name of the company with additional rights for shareholders to those previously provided under the common law; and
- certain additional requirements for a company's business review (building on the provisions introduced previously in controversial circumstances).

Before considering the changes most directly relevant to corporate governance in more detail, further consideration is given to certain of the provisions of the FCA's Listing Rules and Disclosure Guidance and Transparency Rules, the Governance Code and the Stewardship Code.

9.3   The Listing Rules and Disclosure Guidance and Transparency Rules

The Listing Rules, the Prospectus Rules and the Disclosure Guidance and Transparency Rules provide important protection to the holders of shares listed on the Main Market of the London Stock Exchange. Revised Listing Rules came into force in July 2005 but have been regularly updated since then to take account of changes in legislation and the introduction of new legislation. At the time of writing, the rules had most recently been amended in July 2018.

Consistent with the move towards "principles-based" regulation undertaken by the FSA, the Listing Rules contain two listing principles and six premium listing principles applicable to companies with a premium listing (as well as more detailed rules and guidance).[31] The listing principles are that:

(a)   a listed company must take reasonable steps to establish and maintain adequate procedures, systems and controls to enable it to comply with its obligations (Listing Principle 1); and

(b)   a listed company must deal with the FCA in an open and co-operative manner (Listing Principle 2).

The premium listing principles are that:

(a)   a listed company must take reasonable steps to enable its directors to understand their responsibilities and obligations as directors (Premium Listing Principle 1);

(b)   a listed company must act with integrity towards the holders and potential holders of its premium listed securities (Premium Listing Principle 2);

(c)   all equity shares in a class that has been admitted to premium listing must carry an equal number of votes on any shareholder vote. In respect of certificates representing shares that have been admitted to premium listing, all the equity shares of the class which the certificates represent must carry an equal number of votes on any shareholder vote (Premium Listing Principle 3);

(d)   where a listed company has more than one class of securities admitted to premium listing, the aggregate voting rights of the securities in each class should be broadly proportionate to the relative interests of those classes in the equity of the listed company (Premium Listing Principle 4);

(e)   a listed company must ensure that it treats all holders of the same class of its premium listed securities and its listed equity shares that

---

[31]   The listing principles are set out in LR7.2.1 R, and the premium listing principles are set out at LR7.2.1 AR, with the related guidance included at LR7.2.2 G, LR7.2.3 G, and LR7.2.4 G.

are in the same position equally in respect of the rights attaching to those premium listed securities and listed equity shares (Premium Listing Principle 5); and

(f) a listed company must communicate information to holders and potential holders of its premium listed securities and its listed equity shares in such a way as to avoid the creation or continuation of a false market in those premium listed securities and listed equity shares (Premium Listing Principle 6).

The Listing Rules include guidance in relation to Listing Principle 1. The guidance states that Listing Principle 1 is intended to ensure that the relevant listed companies have adequate procedures, systems and controls to enable them to comply with their obligations under the Listing Rules, Disclosure Guidance and Transparency Rules, and corporate governance rules. The guidance goes on to note that, in particular, the FCA considers that listed companies should place an emphasis on ensuring that they have adequate procedures, systems and controls in relation to identifying whether any obligations arise under LR 10 (Significant transactions) and LR 11 (Related party transactions), and the timely and accurate disclosure of information to the market. Further guidance is provided in relation to the latter. The FCA notes that timely and accurate disclosure of information to the market is a key obligation of listed companies. The guidance then provides that, for the purposes of Listing Principle 1, a listed company should have adequate systems and controls to be able to ensure that it can properly identify information which requires disclosure under the Listing Rules, Disclosure Guidance and Transparency Rules, or corporate governance rules in a timely manner. The company must also ensure that any such information identified is properly considered by the directors and that such a consideration encompasses whether the information should be disclosed.

The detail of the Listing Rules is outside the scope of this Chapter. Nonetheless, there are certain provisions of significance in this context. LR 9.8 contains various provisions relating to the publication of a listed company's annual report and accounts. A company incorporated in the UK with a premium listing is required (amongst other things) to include the following in its annual report and accounts (note that LR 9.8.6 R(3) will be updated in due course to refer to equivalent provisions of the Governance Code published in July 2018, and to take account of the fact that this latest version of the Governance Code does not contain specifically identified "Main Principles"):

"9.8.6 R(3)   statements by the directors on:

(a)   the appropriateness of adopting the going concern basis of accounting (containing the information set out in provision C.1.3 of the UK Corporate Governance Code); and

(b) their assessment of the prospects of the company (containing the information set out in provision C.2.2 of the UK Corporate Governance Code);

prepared in accordance with the 'Guidance on Risk Management, Internal Control and Related Financial and Business Reporting' published by the Financial Reporting Council in September 2014;

(5) a statement of how the listed company has applied the Main Principles set out in the UK Corporate Governance Code, in a manner that would enable shareholders to evaluate how the principles have been applied;

(6) a statement as to whether the listed company has:
    (a) complied throughout the accounting period with all relevant provisions set out in the UK Corporate Governance Code; or
    (b) not complied throughout the accounting period with all relevant provisions set out in the UK Corporate Governance Code and if so, setting out:
        (i) those provisions, if any, it has not complied with;
        (ii) in the case of provisions whose requirements are of a continuing nature, the period within which, if any, it did not comply with some or all of those provisions; and
        (iii) the company's reasons for non-compliance ..."

An overseas company with a premium listing must include in its annual report and accounts a statement of how it has complied with the Governance Code in the same way as for UK-incorporated companies with a premium listing.[32] It must also disclose the unexpired term of the service contract of any director proposed for election or re-election at its forthcoming annual general meeting. If any director standing for election or re-election does not have a service contract, a statement to that effect must be included.[33]

A company with a standard listing (either incorporated in the UK or overseas) is not required by the Listing Rules to state how it has complied with the Governance Code. However, it must publish a corporate governance statement detailing its approach to corporate governance.[34]

DTR Chapter 7 ("Corporate Governance") was introduced in the Eighth (and amendments to the Fourth and Seventh) Company Law Directives in June 2008.[35] DTR 7.2 requires all companies listed in the UK, whether with a premium or standard listing, incorporated in the UK or overseas, to make

---

[32] LR 9.8.7 R.
[33] LR 9.8.8 R.
[34] See LR 14.3.24, LR 18.4.3 (2) and DTR 7.2.
[35] The Statutory Audit Directive (Directive 2006/43 on statutory audits of annual accounts and consolidated accounts [2006] OJ L157/87) and the Company Reporting Directive (Directive 2006/46 amending Council Directives 78/660 on the annual accounts of certain types of companies, 83/349 on consolidated accounts, 86/635 on the annual accounts and consolidated accounts of banks and other financial institutions and 91/674 on the annual accounts and consolidated accounts of insurance undertakings [2006] OJ L224/1).

corporate governance statements in their directors' reports.[36] Alternatively, the corporate governance statement can be included in a separate report published together with the annual report, or on the issuer's website, in which case there must be a cross-reference to this in the directors' report.[37] Companies with a premium listing must refer to the fact that they are subject to the Governance Code.[38] As under the Listing Rules, a company must explain which parts of the Governance Code it departs from and its reasons for doing so.[39] Guidance states that compliance with the LR 9.8.6 R(6) (above) will satisfy this requirement.[40]

The Disclosure Guidance and Transparency Rules also set out the content requirements for this corporate governance statement. The corporate governance statement must contain a description of the main features of the company's internal control and risk management systems in relation to the financial reporting process.[41] The Disclosure Guidance and Transparency Rules provide that the corporate governance statement must also contain the information required by the Large and Medium-sized Companies and Groups (Accounts and Reports) Regulations 2008[42] Sch.7 para.13(2)(c), (d), (f), (h) and (i), where the issuer is subject to the requirements of that paragraph.[43]

In addition, the corporate governance statement must contain a description of the composition and operation of the issuer's administrative, management and supervisory bodies and their committees.[44] Guidance provides that where a company with a premium listing follows the recommendations on disclosure relating to particular provisions in the Governance Code,[45] this last requirement will be met.[46]

Under the Listing Rules, a company with a premium listing must ensure that the auditors review each of the following before its annual report is published[47]:

---

[36] DTR 7.2.1 R.
[37] DTR 7.2.9 R.
[38] DTR 7.2.2 R.
[39] DTR 7.2.3 R(1)(b).
[40] DTR 7.2.4 G.
[41] DTR 7.2.5 R. DTR 7.2.10 R states that an issuer which is required to prepare a group directors' report within the meaning of s.415(2) of the CA 2006 must include in that report a description of the main features of the group's internal control and risk management systems in relation to the process for preparing consolidated accounts.
[42] Large and Medium-sized Companies and Groups (Accounts and Reports) Regulations 2008 (SI 2008/410).
[43] DTR 7.2.6 R.
[44] DTR 7.2.7 R.
[45] For example, Governance Code A.1.1, A.1.2, B.2.4, C.3.3, C.3.8, D.2.1. (note that references are to the version of the Governance Code published in April 2016—DTR 7.2.8 G will be updated in due course to refer to equivalent provisions of the Governance Code published in July 2018).
[46] DTR 7.2.8 R.
[47] LR 9.8.10 R.

- LR 9.8.6 R(3) (statement by the directors on the appropriateness of adopting the going concern basis of accounting); and
- the parts of the statement required by LR 9.8.6 R(6) (corporate governance) that relate to the following provisions of the Governance Code (note that references are to the version of the Governance Code published in April 2016 – LR 9.8.10 R will be updated in due course to refer to equivalent provisions of the Governance Code published in July 2018):
  (a)   C.1.1;
  (b)   C.2.1;
  (c)   C.2.3; and
  (d)   C.3.1–C.3.8.

The Auditing Practices Board provides guidance for auditors when reviewing a company's statement in relation to Governance Code compliance in accordance with LR 9.8.10 R.[48]

In addition, the annual report and accounts of a UK-incorporated company with a premium listing must include a report to shareholders by the board which contains all of the matters set out in LR 9.8.8 R. This rule requires that the report must contain details of the unexpired term of any service contract of any director proposed for election or re-election at the forthcoming annual general meeting, and, if any such director does not have a service contract, a statement to that effect.

9.3.1   Comply or explain

The Governance Code and the related disclosure provisions under the Listing Rules and Disclosure Guidance and Transparency Rules seek to encourage both companies' boards and their shareholders to consider whether their companies are being governed in shareholders' best interests. LR 9.8.6 R(5) requires companies with a premium listing to state how they have applied the "Main Principles" of the Governance Code, which represent certain broad concepts believed to underpin effective board governance. Beyond this, however, LR 9.8.6 R(6)(b) permits a degree of flexibility in respect of how companies adhere to both these "Main Principles" and all other relevant provisions of the Governance Code. This is known as "comply or explain": where a company with a premium listing does not apply the "Code Provisions", it must disclose how and why it has done things differently. Shareholders are then able to decide whether it is necessary to put pressure on the board to make changes to the way that the company is governed. Flexibility in the application of the Governance Code Provisions is seen as being achievable by fostering an informed dialogue between the company and its shareholders. Companies are to review and explain their governance policies, including any special circumstances

---

[48] *Developments in Corporate Governance Affecting the Responsibilities of Auditors of UK Companies* Bulletin 2009/4 December 2009.

311

which in their view justify departure from generally accepted best practice, and shareholders and others should show flexibility in the interpretation of the Governance Code, taking into account the explanations they receive and judging them on their merits. The Listing Rules will be updated in due course to take account of the fact that the latest version of the Governance Code does not contain specifically identified "Main Principles."

Notwithstanding that the Governance Code encourages such an approach, this has not always been how shareholders have responded in practice. In 2009, the FRC canvassed the views of a number of chairmen at FTSE 100 and 250 companies as to the effectiveness of the old Combined Code.[49] While many chairmen saw the lack of prescription of the Combined Code as a key strength, concern was expressed at the use of a box-ticking approach to governance evaluation. The new version of the Governance Code published in July 2018 sets out a number of features of what the FRC considers to be a meaningful explanation, in order to provide a benchmark for companies when providing explanations and shareholders when assessing them. These features are:

- the explanation should set out the background, provide a clear rationale for the action it is taking, and explain the impact that the action has had; and
- where departure from a particular provision is intended to be limited in time, the explanation should indicate when the company expects to conform to the provision.[50]

The FRC notes that although the quality of explanations continues to vary, generally companies remain reluctant to explain non-compliance with Governance Code provisions and are still not providing sufficient detail to allow shareholders to understand a company's decision to depart from a provision. While better explanations include company specific context and information on mitigating actions taken to avoid any additional governance risk arising from non-compliance, other companies limit their explanations to "boiler-plate reporting" and give no information as to why alternative governance arrangements were considered acceptable. In terms of improving explanations going forward, the FRC emphasises the importance of the company explaining how its alternative approach is consistent with the spirit of the provision it is departing from.[51]

A report by the Association of British Insurers (the ABI) made similar observations, and suggested that companies should follow the guidance listed below, in order that explanations offered by the company are sufficiently detailed. Explanations should reflect the following:

---

[49] FRC, *Review of the Effectiveness of the Combined Code. Summary of the Main Points Raised at Meetings with the Chairman of FTSE Companies* July 2009.
[50] Governance Code, p.2.
[51] FRC, *Annual Review of Corporate Governance and Reporting 2017/2018* October 2018, pp.33–34.

(1)   *company-specific context and historical background*: a company should consider the context in which it is making its governance decisions, providing details of the business specific reasons (such as any unique characteristics of the business model, strategy or ownership structure);

(2)   *convincing and understandable rationale*: a company should justify why the governance decision taken is proportionate in the light of the context already provided. It should aim to provide a cogent description of the link between the business-specific context and the governance model employed;

(3)   *mitigating action to address any additional risk*: a company should specify what action it intends to take. It should contemplate whether mitigation measures are appropriate to safeguard the interests of shareholders and, if not considered necessary, explain why;

(4)   *time-bound*: companies should consider whether certain Governance Code departures should only be in place for a limited period of time (for example, a NED may serve more than nine years where there is a desire to maintain continuity while new NEDs gain appropriate experience);

(5)   *specify deviations from the provisions as well as from main principles*: companies should link their explanation specifically to the relevant Governance Code provision, demonstrating that they have considered how the Governance Code provisions support the main principles; and

(6)   *explain how the alternative is consistent with the Governance Code principles and contributes to the objective of good governance*: companies should consider this criteria as an underlying principle for all governance reporting. Essentially, the focus should be on assessing whether the alternative arrangements are aligned with the main principles of the Governance Code and fulfil the underlying objective of good governance.

There were some calls in response to the European Commission's Green Paper on an EU Corporate Governance Framework for regulatory oversight of the quality of explanations provided by companies in the case of non-compliance. However, the Commission concluded that such prescriptive regulation would undermine the flexibility which lies at the heart of the "comply or explain" system. The European Commission stated in its December 2012 Action Plan that it intends to undertake an initiative to improve corporate governance reports, in particular the explanations where companies have sought to explain non-compliance with national corporate governance codes. To this end, the Commission published a recommendation on the quality of corporate governance reporting in April 2014. The Commission advises that for each departure from a specific recommendation of the appropriate corporate governance code a company should:

(a)   explain in what manner the company has departed from a recommendation;

(b)   describe the reasons for the departure;

(c) describe how the decision to depart from the recommendation was taken within the company;

(d) where the departure is limited in time, explain when the company envisages complying with a particular recommendation; and

(e) where applicable, describe the measure taken instead of compliance and explain how that measure achieves the underlying objective of the specific recommendation or of the code as a whole, or clarify how it contributes to the good corporate governance of the company.

9.4 The UK Corporate Governance Code: Key Themes

The Governance Code was previously known as the "Combined Code on Corporate Governance". When first established by the Hampel Committee, the Combined Code was designed as a statement of "broad principles" that should be applied "flexibly and with common sense to the varying circumstances of individual companies".[52] The philosophy behind the Combined Code was always to serve as a general guide to good practice rather than as a checklist of "hard and fast" rules.[53]

The Walker Review in the wake of the financial crisis heralded potentially the biggest shake-up of corporate governance since the Combined Code was first introduced. Many argued that the crisis exposed identifiable weaknesses in companies' systems of corporate governance, such as a failure to give proper risk oversight at board level, and a failure to appropriately hold executives to account or to rein in the remuneration incentives that helped allow a culture of short-termism to develop.

Nevertheless, in spite of these failings, the Walker Review endorsed the UK's unitary board system and affirmed that the Combined Code remained broadly fit for purpose. Its opinion was that the financial crisis was more the result of a failure of behaviour than a failure of process and that the "comply or explain" approach of the Combined Code was well-suited to the task of bringing into effect the necessary behavioural change for reform of corporate governance. Indeed, a prescriptive, "box-ticking" approach to governance was firmly rejected, and the flexibility offered by a code of practice was held up as having distinct advantages over other regulatory or legislative solutions. Eschewing a radical restatement of principles, the Walker Review focused instead on trying to reform board culture through key changes in the Combined Code's emphasis.

The FRC conducted a review of the Combined Code in parallel with the Walker Review in 2009 to see how best to incorporate its recommendations. The FRC review's main conclusion echoed the Walker Review's call for behavioural change by stating that more attention needed to be paid to

---

[52] Hampel Report, para.1.11.
[53] Phrase comes from the Hampel Report, para.1.11.

"following the spirit of the [Governance] Code as well as its letter". The changes it introduced focused on altering the "tone" of the Combined Code by making limited but significant changes to its principles and provisions in order to guide board behaviours. Chairmen are now encouraged to report personally in their annual statements on how the principles have been applied in order to try to challenge what the FRC calls the "fungus" of "boiler-plate reporting." By doing so, the FRC sought to encourage genuine engagement with the "spirit" of the Governance Code.

The most significant Walker Review recommendations were incorporated through changes to the provisions of the then Governance Code. These introduced the requirements that chairmen must oversee personal training for each director, an external evaluation of the board of every FTSE 350 company should be facilitated every three years, and directors of FTSE 350 companies should stand for re-election every year. These changes were introduced with a view to improving board accountability to shareholders, to emphasise the importance of having non-executive directors who can provide an effective "challenge" to executive leadership, and to elevate the board's role in risk management.

Governance principles came under closer scrutiny following the Parliamentary Commission on Banking Standards' report on the failure of HBOS.[54] This report highlighted that one of the failings of the bank that contributed to its catastrophic downfall was a lack of an appropriate balance of skills on the board across all divisions that the bank operated in. While board members had a thorough understanding of the bank's retail operations (with several directors having had direct expertise in this area), the board lacked expertise in corporate, international and treasury operations. As a result, there was much less rigorous oversight of these operations and management decisions were often left unscrutinised and unchallenged. The report ultimately found that "[t]hese weaknesses in senior management were instrumental in the pursuit by these three divisions of the policies and practices that led to devastating losses".[55]

Similarly, the Salz Review recommended that the Barclays board should include an appropriate diversity of experience, noting that the benefit of this is that it helps the board "to challenge effectively the performance of management, to satisfy itself that risk management systems are robust, and to test business practices".[56]

The version of the Governance Code published in September 2014, in the aftermath of these reports, sought to respond to such concerns, noting the problems arising from "groupthink" which had been exposed as a result of

---

[54] *"An Accident Waiting to Happen": The Failure of HBOS*, Parliamentary Commission on Banking Standards, Fourth Report of Session 2012–13 HL Paper 144, HC 705, 4 April 2013.
[55] *"An Accident Waiting to Happen": The Failure of HBOS*, Parliamentary Commission on Banking Standards, Fourth Report of Session 2012–13 HL Paper 144, HC 705, para.53.
[56] Salz Review, *An Independent Review of Barclays' Business Practices* April 2013, para.9.24.

the financial crisis. This version of the Governance Code introduced a requirement on directors to report on how they have assessed the future prospects of the company, taking into account the principal risks it faces. The period over which the assessment is required to be made is not prescribed, but contemporary guidance suggests it should typically be "significantly longer than 12 months", thus requiring broad, holistic consideration of the company's viability going forward.[57]

Even as the financial crisis recedes into the past, continued recognition of "a widespread perception that executive pay has become increasingly disconnected from both the pay of ordinary working people and the underlying long-term performance of companies", and that companies "need to do more to reassure the public they are being run, not just with an eye to the interests of the board and the shareholders, but with a recognition of their responsibilities to employees, customers, suppliers and wider society" prompted the BEIS Green Paper, published in November 2016.[58]

The Government published its response to that Green Paper in August 2017, inviting the FRC to consult on revising the Governance Code to include a principle "strengthening the voice of employees and other non-shareholder interests at board level", and to "give remuneration committees greater responsibility for demonstrating how pay and incentives align across a company".[59] The FRC duly consulted and amended the Governance Code as appropriate, publishing the new Governance Code in July 2018. This iteration of the Governance Code also includes important changes in relation to workforce engagement, significant votes against resolutions and diversity, which are explored under the relevant headings below.

9.4.1 Leadership

"Leadership", part of the heading of the first section of the Governance Code, brings into focus the most important role that boards are expected to provide: it emphasises the point that it is the board, as opposed to simply the management, that is required to govern a company and dictate its strategy. A fundamental statement of the role of the board is provided in Principles A and C:

> "A successful company is led by an effective and entrepreneurial board, whose role is to promote the long-term sustainable success of the company ... The board should ensure that the necessary resources are in place for the company to meet its objectives and measure performance against them. The board should also establish a framework of prudent and effective controls, which enable risk to be assessed and managed."

---

[57] FRC, *Guidance on Risk Management, Internal Control and Related Financial and Business Reporting* September 2014, p.19.
[58] BEIS Green Paper, *Corporate Governance Reform* November 2016, p.16, p.34.
[59] HM Government, *Corporate Governance Reform* August 2017, p.4, p.19.

Effective leadership by the board requires leadership from within it, and this is a role expressly provided to the chairman by the Governance Code.[60] The chairman is key to setting the board's agenda. He should ensure enough time and appropriate information is available for strategic discussion. The chairman should also ensure that the right culture is fostered and that the board is marshalled such that all directors contribute effectively and that appropriate checks and balances are in place to executive power.

In effect, the chairman's role is to be responsible for the working of the board, for the balance of its membership and for ensuring that all directors, executive and non-executive alike, are able to play their full part in its activities. By contrast, the role of the chief executive is to run the business and to implement the policies and strategies adopted by the board. Effective division between chairman and chief executive was always central to the Combined Code[61] and goes back to the Cadbury Report, which recommended separating the two roles to "ensure a balance of power and authority, such that no one individual has unfettered powers of decision".[62]

The importance of having a strong chairman, who is independent of the chief executive, has been highlighted by the governance failings brought to light by the financial crisis, where chief executives were insufficiently held to account at some financial institutions. The Walker Review called the role of the chairman "paramount" and changes to the Combined Code were designed to encourage chairmen to play a more positive role in board-rooms.[63] The ability of the chairman to head up a strong non-executive presence on the board is considered equally important. The FRC's Guidance on Board Effectiveness suggests that the chairman should "foster relationships based on trust, mutual respect and open communication ... between non-executive directors and the executive team".[64]

The Walker Review was very critical of the failure of non-executive directors to provide an effective "challenge" to executive power. As a consequence, a new Principle was introduced to the version of the Governance Code published in June 2010, setting out the role of non-executive directors.[65] Non-executives are considered vital to the proper operation of a unitary board system. They are there to provide an effective challenge to the potential short-termism and self-interest of executive directors and to promote the long-term success of the company.[66] By way of example, the Salz Review for Barclays suggested that it is important for

---

[60] Governance Code, Principle F.
[61] Now Governance Code, Provision 9.
[62] The Cadbury Report, para.4.9.
[63] ICSA Guidance Note, *The Roles of Chairman, Chief Executive and Senior Independent Director under the Combined Code* September 2004.
[64] FRC, *Guidance on Board Effectiveness* July 2018, p.18.
[65] Now Governance Code, Principle H.
[66] ICSA, *Improving Board Effectiveness* July 2010.

non-executive directors to acquaint themselves more closely with the values and management of a company.[67] The review noted that a key factor in achieving this was for boards to consider regularly the time commitments realistically expected for non-executive directors. In order for non-executives to hold adequately executive decisions to account, boards should put into action a plan for non-executive directors to engage actively with the major business of the bank.[68]

The Governance Code also recommends that, even where the roles of chairman and chief executive are held by different people, there should be a recognised senior independent non-executive director other than the chairman who must meet the test of independence and to whom concerns can be conveyed.[69] The Higgs Review concluded that the senior independent non-executive director should be available to shareholders if they have reason for concern that contact through the normal channels (i.e. the chairman or chief executive) has failed, although this conclusion was criticised as undermining the role of the chairman.[70] The Governance Code currently requires that the senior independent non-executive director serve as an intermediary between the chairman and the shareholders.[71]

The Governance Code emphasises the importance of the role of the senior independent non-executive director. The Walker Review called for the position not only to be an alternative channel of communication for the expression of dissatisfaction from outside the board but also to perform a similar role within it. Senior independent non-executive directors should act as an intermediary and arbitrator, if need be, between the chairman and chief-executive, or the chairman and the non-executive directors, ensuring that the non-executive directors are able to contribute effectively. Senior independent non-executive directors should be the "lightning conductor" for non-executives to express their concerns, when necessary, and, given the "inevitable tendency towards collegiality in boards" which can lead to "excessive deference in colleagues" that "stifles critical enquiry and challenge", the senior independent non-executive director "should be the potentially negative charge on the board".[72] In order to facilitate frank contributions from the other non-executives, the senior independent non-executive director should lead meetings without the chair present in order to appraise the chair's performance. The senior independent non-executive director should also provide critical support as a "sounding board" to the chairman.[73]

---

[67] Salz Review, *An Independent Review of Barclays' Business Practices* April 2013, paras 9.25–9.32.
[68] Salz Review, *An Independent Review of Barclays' Business Practices* April 2013, para.9.37.
[69] Governance Code, Provision 12.
[70] The *Higgs Report*, paras 7.4 and 7.5.
[71] Governance Code, Provision 12.
[72] Walker Review, paras 4.27 and 4.28.
[73] Governance Code, Provision 12.

9.4.2   *Effectiveness*

The importance of having appropriate input from non-executives on the board to protect the company's interests was brought into sharper focus by the financial crisis. One of the ways in which the Hampel Committee recommended that the board of a company can achieve its role effectively was to ensure that the board was not dominated by one individual or a group of individuals. To promote this end, the Combined Code provided that the board should include non-executive directors of sufficient calibre and number for their views to carry significant weight in the board's decisions. The Hampel Committee recommended that non-executive directors should comprise not less than one-third of the board. The Higgs Review went further, putting particular emphasis on greater non-executive presence. The Higgs Review version of the Combined Code stated that at least half of the board, excluding the chairman, should be non-executive directors, and that the board should identify in its annual report the non-executive directors that it determines to be independent.[74] The Governance Code currently requires an "appropriate combination" of executive and non-executive directors on the board.[75] It also requires of all companies subject to the Governance Code that at least half the board, excluding the chairman, should be comprised of independent non-executive directors.[76] Prior to the introduction of the latest version of the Governance Code this provision only applied to companies within the FTSE 350. The exemption for "smaller companies" was removed from the Governance Code on the grounds that "even smaller companies should strive for the highest standards of corporate governance".[77]

The independence of non-executives has long been viewed as a key issue in assessing their ability to perform their role. However, in the wake of the financial crisis, concerns at the lack of banking qualifications and industry experience of non-executives at Northern Rock, the Royal Bank of Scotland and elsewhere has resulted in refinement to this approach. The Walker Review questioned whether independence should be the overriding concern when recruiting non-executive directors: boards should sometimes give greater weight to experience over independence and should be ready to depart from independence criteria where required.[78]

The Governance Code places the independence of non-executives in a broader context. In addition to its stipulations about the proportion of independent directors, it also requires that a board should contain a

---

[74]   Combined Code (June 2008), A.3.1.
[75]   Governance Code, Principle G.
[76]   Governance Code, Provision 11.
[77]   FRC, *Proposed Revisions to the UK Corporate Governance Code* December 2017, p.11.
[78]   Walker Review, para.3.8, p 44. See also Grant Thornton, *Are They Experienced? A Review of FTSE 350 Non-Executive Director Experience* 2009.

combination of skills, experience and knowledge.[79] Nevertheless, independence still remains very important and a non-executive should ideally be expected to show an "independence of mind and spirit, of character and judgement".[80] The board should still identify in the annual report each non-executive it considers to be independent.[81]

The criteria for independence are based largely on a joint statement issued by the ABI and the National Association of Pension Funds (NAPF) in 1999.[82] Whilst the Governance Code leaves the final judgement as to whether a director can be considered independent in the hands of the board, it lists a number of circumstances that may lead the board to conclude that a director should not be considered independent. In essence, a director is considered independent when the board determines that the director is independent in character and judgement, and there are no relationships or circumstances which could affect, or appear to affect, the director's judgement. Relationships or circumstances which are likely to impair, or could appear to impair, a non-executive director's independence include, but are not limited to, whether a director:

(a) is or has been an employee of the company or group within the last five years;
(b) has, or has had within the last three years, a material business relationship with the company either directly or as a partner, shareholder, director or senior employee of a body that has such a relationship with the company;
(c) has received or receives additional remuneration from the company apart from a director's fee, participates in the company's share option or a performance-related pay scheme, or is a member of the company's pension scheme;
(d) has close family ties with any of the company's advisers, directors or senior employees;
(e) holds cross-directorships or has significant links with other directors through involvement in other companies or bodies;
(f) represents a significant shareholder; or
(g) has served on the board for more than nine years from the date of their first appointment.[83]

In its initial draft of the revised Governance Code to apply to accounting periods beginning on or after 1 January 2019, the FRC proposed turning the indicators set out above into strict criteria, meaning that if any of the factors applied to a particular director, the company should not consider that director independent. However, responses to the FRC's consultation

---

[79] Governance Code, Principle K.
[80] Walker Review, p.44.
[81] Governance Code, Provision 10.
[82] A joint ABI/NAPF Statement, *Responsible Voting* July 1999, Appendix 1, 19.
[83] Governance Code, Provision 10.

yielded overwhelmingly negative feedback, with the effect that determinations of independence remain at the board's discretion. Therefore, the board remains free to disregard the presence of any of the above relationships or circumstances, though it must explain in the annual report why it considers a director to be independent notwithstanding their existence. Indeed, additional disclosures in relation to why the board considers particular directors to be independent are likely to be required as a result of revisions to the Governance Code. The Governance Code now makes clear that the factors it lists as possibly compromising independence are not exhaustive, thus inviting comment on any other circumstances that could possibly compromise a director's independence. Furthermore, for the first time the Governance Code explicitly requires a "clear explanation" of why a particular director is considered independent by the board where circumstances exist to suggest he or she may not be.

The FRC also proposed that additional measures be added to the Governance Code to ensure the chair's independence. A proposal that the chair not only be independent on appointment, but remain so throughout his or her tenure was ultimately not implemented, with the FRC conceding that it was sufficient for the chair to demonstrate objective judgement throughout his or her tenure, thereby retaining the ability to become closely involved with the company and its executive personnel.[84] However, the Governance Code does now require that the chair does not remain in post beyond nine years from the date of their first appointment to the board.[85] The FRC intends that this change will encourage board refreshment and diversity, and therefore permits the nine-year period to be extended by a limited time in order to facilitate effective succession planning and the development of a diverse board.[86] Extensions will be particularly permissible in circumstances where the chair was an existing non-executive director on appointment, though a clear explanation should be provided in relation to any extension.[87]

Following the financial crisis, there has been renewed focus on the calibre of non-executive director appointments in the financial sector. In particular, the FSA sought to improve oversight of the effectiveness of non-executive directors of regulated firms. The FSA emphasised the important role played by non-executive directors in challenging firms substantive policy decisions.

In his speech of May 2009, Hector Sants (then-CEO of the FSA) suggested that non-executive directors must be expected to demonstrate higher levels of competence in the future. As such, the FCA has recently focused on the need for relevant and broad sector expertise, independence of thought and

---

[84] FRC, *Feedback Statement, Consulting on a revised UK Corporate Governance Code* July 2018, p.12.
[85] Governance Code, Provision 19.
[86] Governance Code, Provision 19; FRC, *Feedback Statement, Consulting on a revised UK Corporate Governance Code* July 2018, p.12.
[87] Governance Code, Provision 19.

the ability to avoid the "herd mentality". While historically many non-executive director positions were seen as part-time, there is now a growing trend towards greater time commitment in fulfilling the duties of a non-executive director. Firms are expected to build upon the technical expertise of their non-executive directors by providing ongoing training and the FSA has called upon non-executive directors to make greater use of independently employed advisers. In larger, more complex or risky firms, it has become more common for the regulator to interview non-executive director candidates applying for roles such as chair of the audit, risk or remuneration committees.

The FSA was replaced by the FCA and the Prudential Regulation Authority (the PRA) in April 2013. The FCA has taken a similar approach to the supervision of non-executive directors of FCA regulated firms. Any person wishing to take on the position of a non-executive director in a regulated firm must first be approved by the FCA to perform Controlled Function 2 (CF2) (which is a Significant Influence Function (SIF)). In order to be approved, such non-executive directors must satisfy certain criteria in relation to their integrity and honesty, and also their competence. Once approved, non-executive directors have to comply with the FCA's Statements of Principle for Approved Persons (APER) and are accountable to the FCA when their conduct falls below these standards.

The FCA expects non-executive directors to ask the challenging questions and to understand the business models and sources of profit of the firm, together with the risks that those entail. Non-executive directors should, therefore, expect the FCA to assess their competence and, if they fail to meet the standards the FCA requires of them, to be held to account by the FCA.

Also relevant to non-executive directors of FCA regulated firms is the Senior Managers and Certification Regime (SMCR). Banks have been subject to SMCR since March 2016, with the regime to be extended to financial services firms solely regulated by the FCA in December 2019. Under the SMCR persons who perform designated Senior Management Functions (SMFs) must be approved to do so, meet certain standards of fitness and propriety on an ongoing basis, and comply with two tiers of conduct rules. Non-executive directors will perform SMFs where they hold positions such as company chair, board committee chair, or senior independent director. Non-executive directors not performing SMFs must comply with only one tier of conduct rules.

From a broader perspective, beyond that of regulated financial services firms, various corporate governance reports suggest that one way of promoting an effective and balanced board is for there to be a transparent policy and system for recruiting new directors. This is advocated in the Governance Code which provides that the board should establish a nomination committee to lead the process for appointments.[88] The process by which nominations are made should be identified in the annual report, and a majority of the members of the nomination committee should be independent non-executives.[89] The aim of the nomination committee is to promote objectivity in the appointment of directors, which is crucial in guaranteeing a balanced board not dominated by a particular individual or group of individuals. If a chairman chairs the nomination committee they should stand down when the recruitment of a new chairman is under discussion.[90]

The Walker Review raised a number of concerns relating to the recruitment of appropriately qualified directors. Whilst emphasising the fact that industry and professional experience should be an important factor when assessing the suitability of new directors, the Walker Review still implicitly supported the idea of recruiting from as wide a pool as possible. Indeed, the Walker Review was concerned that increasing demands placed on directors and an increase in their legal liabilities might have the effect of reducing the pool from which directors can be chosen. Another of the Walker Review's concerns was that greater demands placed on non-executive directors' time might deter talented candidates and curb the enthusiasm or ability of companies to allow executives to take up non-executive positions elsewhere.[91] It has become increasingly common for boards to recruit new directors via external recruitment consultancies. As a result, the Governance Code was amended in September 2012 to state that, where such an external search consultancy has been used, it should be identified in the annual report and a statement should be made as to whether it has any connection with the company. The Governance Code also notes that open advertising and/or an external search consultancy should generally be used for the appointment of the chair and non-executive directors.[92]

The Walker Review called for a substantial increase of time commitment from non-executives at banks and financial institutions, from 25 to around 35 days a year.[93] This recommendation was not adopted by the Governance Code as it was felt that it was too prescriptive outside the financial services sector. Nevertheless, the Governance Code explicitly states that "non-executive directors should have sufficient time to meet their board responsibilities".[94]

Chairmen are responsible for ensuring that directors receive accurate, timely and clear information.[95] It is especially important in the light of the

---

[88] Governance Code, Provision 17.
[89] Governance Code, Provision 23 and Provision 17.
[90] Governance Code, Provision 17.
[91] Walker Review, paras 2.20–2.22, 3.9 and 3.20.
[92] Governance Code, Provision 20.
[93] Walker Review, Recommendation 3, pp.48–49.
[94] Governance Code, Principle H.
[95] Governance Code, Principle F.

Walker Review to ensure that non-executives are properly informed of the company's operations and business concerns going into meetings in order to effectively engage with the executives. To this end, all directors should have access to the advice of the company secretary, who is responsible for advising the board on all governance matters.[96]

A major Walker Review proposal that the FRC included in the Governance Code was the provision that an external evaluation should be conducted on boards of FTSE 350 companies at least every three years.[97] This Governance Code Provision was designed to introduce more objectivity in the board review process.[98] The Governance Code provides that where board evaluations have been externally facilitated, the external evaluator must now be identified in the annual report.[99] When consulting on prospective amendments to the Governance Code in 2018 the FRC initially proposed requiring all companies to undertake an externally facilitated evaluation every three years. However, concerns about the burden in terms of cost and management time this would impose on smaller companies, as well as the lack of an adequate pool of organisations providing board evaluation services meant this proposal was dropped.[100]

The Walker Review suggested that an evaluation statement should underline the independence of the process by indicating any other business relationships between the external reviewer and the company and, where a relationship does exist, that the board is satisfied that any potential conflict has been appropriately managed. The Walker Review also said that it would be desirable for the statement to provide some indication of the outcomes of the evaluation process, but at the same time appreciated that the sensitivity of information might make publication of the results undesirable. Current Pension Investment Research Consultants (PIRC) guidelines state that companies should describe the appraisal process (for both executives and non-executives), along with the criteria used and minimum requirements. The company should also disclose the general outcomes of appraisals of individual directors, committees and the board as a whole, and identify the director or committee responsible for the process.[101]

On 12 December 2012, the ABI published its *2012 Report on Board Effectiveness* following a review of the annual reports of all FTSE 350 companies.[102] One of the key topics it focused on was the promotion of effective board evaluation. The ABI emphasised that board evaluations

---

[96] Governance Code, Provision 16.
[97] Walker Review, Recommendation 12, Now Governance Code, Provision 21.
[98] FRC, *Final Report*, para.3.41.
[99] Governance Code, Provision 21.
[100] FRC, *Feedback Statement, Consulting on a revised UK Corporate Governance Code* July 2018, p.9.
[101] Pension Investment Research Consultants UK Shareholder Voting Guidelines (March 2018), p.8.
[102] Excluding 56 investment trusts.

should be carried out by an independent party not subject to a conflict of interest. As such, this should preclude those who provide other services to the company (such as search agents) who assist in the recruitment of directors, auditors and remuneration consultants. If the company does decide to appoint an evaluator with a past business relationship, the directors should take steps to explain in their annual report the previous relationship and how any potential conflict of interest has been managed. The ABI recommended that companies should explain the performance evaluation process and disclose any significant recommendations and the changes or improvements that the board has committed to following the review. The board evaluation should not simply be a "box-ticking" exercise, where directors effectively go through the motions of being evaluated: the outcomes of these evaluations should be different year-on-year as they constructively reflect upon the performance of the individual board members. The Salz Review concurred with this, recommending that the Barclays' board should be "actively engaged in the process of improving its own effectiveness, including through regular and rigorous evaluations" and that the board "should report openly on the evaluation process, set forward-looking objectives for improvement and explain progress against these objectives".[103]

The Governance Code now requires that all directors should be subject to annual re-election.[104] Previously, this provision only applied to companies in the FTSE 350. Despite being controversial upon its introduction, with concerns raised that it might encourage short-termism among directors, FTSE 350 companies quickly adopted a high level of compliance, with 96% of FTSE 350 companies proposing the full board for annual re-election by 2012.[105]

9.4.3 Diversity

The promotion of diversity on boards has been a particular concern for some years now. In February 2011, as advised by the Davies Report on women on boards, the FRC consulted on the issue of gender diversity at boardroom level. Lord Davies recommended that FTSE 100 boards should aim for a minimum of 25% female representation by 2015. In May 2011, the FRC published a consultation document, concerned with whether further steps were required to reach the goal of more diverse boards, what (if any) these changes should be and when they should be introduced.

In a response published by the GC100 in July 2011, several changes were suggested to Principles B.1 and B.2 of the then Governance Code, to include the promotion of "diversity on the board, including gender". The GC100

---

[103] Salz Review, *An Independent Review of Barclays' Business Practices* April 2013, para.9.75.
[104] Governance Code, Provision 18.
[105] Grant Thornton, "Corporate Governance Review 2012: The Chemistry of Governance" December 2012.

suggested that companies were better placed themselves to evolve and advance a diverse managerial culture, whilst accommodating existing sex discrimination legislation. In response to the consultation process, in October 2011, the FRC published changes to Provision B.2 of the then Governance Code, adding a new supporting principle so as to require listed companies to report annually on their diversity policy, including gender, and any measurable objectives that the board has set for implementing the policy along with progress made in achieving these objectives. These changes were incorporated into the edition of the Governance Code published in September 2012.

The publication of the Davies Report resulted in some momentum towards improved gender diversity on boards. From 1 March 2012 to 1 March 2013, women secured 34% of FTSE 100 and 36% of FTSE 250 board appointments. This compares with 18.5% and 11.9% respectively in the year to 1 March 2012. As at 1 March 2013, women accounted for 17.3% of FTSE 100 and 13.2% of FTSE 250 directors, up from 12.5% and 7.8% respectively (an increase of nearly 40%).[106] The 25% female representation target set by the *Davies Report* was achieved by the FTSE 100 in 2015.[107]

Despite such progress, it was still evident that there were significant further improvements to be made. In particular, increased female representation was almost entirely accounted for by an increased number of female non-executive directors, with the percentage of female executive directors remaining broadly static. As at November 2012 there were 6.7% female executive directors in the FTSE 100, in contrast to 21.6% non-executive directors, and only between 5 and 6% of executive directors in the FTSE 250 and below were female.[108] While by November 2016, there had been some improvement in the amount of women reaching executive positions, with women holding just under 19% of executive committee positions in the FTSE 100, it was widely recognised that a "bottleneck" at this level and below was impeding more women progressing into executive roles.[109]

This prompted the Hampton-Alexander Review (published in November 2016), which recommended that the entire FTSE 350 should aim for a minimum of 33% female representation on their boards by 2020, with the FTSE 100 being set an additional target of ensuring 33% female representation across their executive committees and direct reports to their executive committees, also by 2020. This latter target was extended to FTSE 250 companies in October 2017, albeit accompanied by a recognition that it may take such companies longer to meet the target given their later starting date. In November 2018, the Hampton-Alexander Review published an update on progress so far. While female representation on FTSE 100 boards now

---

[106] Lord Davies, *Women on Boards: Progress Review*, April 2013, p.2.

[107] *Hampton-Alexander Review*, November 2016, p.9.

[108] FRC, *Developments in Corporate Governance 2012: The Impact and Implementation of the UK Corporate Governance and Stewardship Codes*, December 2012, p.13.

[109] *Hampton-Alexander Review*, November 2016, p.6.

stands at just over 30%, meaning that the target of 33% representation by 2020 is well within reach, the representation of women on FTSE 100 executive committees and in roles directly reporting to the executive committee has only reached 27%.[110] There is therefore some work to do if the latter target is to be reached by 2020, particularly in light of the fact that between 1 July 2017 and 30 June 2018, 65% of relevant appointments went to men.[111] The FTSE 250 has made more modest progress in placing women on boards, with female representation at just under 25%. The Hampton-Alexander Review concludes this means unless progress picks up considerably in the next two years, the FTSE 250 is unlikely to meet its 2020 target.[112]

The increased focus on diversity as a vital element of good corporate governance extends much deeper than achieving a more equitable gender balance on boards. Since April 2017, companies with 250 or more employees have been subject to a statutory gender pay gap reporting regime requiring them to report on the size of the pay gap between their male and female employees. The Governance Code now requires nomination committees to "oversee the development of a diverse pipeline for succession", expanding the remit of nomination committees to nurture diverse talent downstream of board level.[113] Indeed, the new Governance Code published in June 2018 has a considerably greater focus on diversity than its predecessors. In particular, reporting requirements on diversity are more fulsome, with the annual report having to describe the work of the nomination committee with particular reference to:

(a)   the process used in relation to appointments, its approach to succession planning and how both support developing a diverse pipeline;

(b)   the policy on diversity and inclusion, its objectives and linkages to company strategy, how it has been implemented and progress on achieving the objectives; and

(c)   the gender balance of those in senior management and their direct reports.[114]

The new Governance Code also broadens how diversity is defined, stating that boards should seek to promote not only diversity of gender, but also diversity of social and ethnic backgrounds and cognitive and personal strengths.[115] The FRC stopped short of adding a reporting requirement in relation to ethnic diversity to the Governance Code, recognising the significant challenges and practical difficulties of collecting data on ethnicity. However, it does encourage companies to think about providing more information about different aspects of diversity in their workforce,

---

[110] *Hampton-Alexander Review* November 2018, p.24, p.10.
[111] *Hampton-Alexander Review* November 2018, p.11.
[112] *Hampton-Alexander Review* November 2018, p.26.
[113] Governance Code, Provision 17.
[114] Governance Code, Provision 23.
[115] Governance Code, Principle J.

other than gender.[116] BEIS concluded a consultation on potentially introducing an ethnicity pay reporting regime to apply to employers in January 2019. Responses received in the course of the consultation (which focused on seeking companies' views on precisely what information should be disclosed to gauge the extent of ethnic pay disparities) will be used to inform how the Government takes forward its stated policy aim to introduce mandatory ethnicity pay reporting.

9.4.4 Financial and Business Reporting

> "The board should present a fair, balanced and understandable assessment of the company's position and prospects."[117]

The Governance Code emphasises the need for directors to report that the business is a going concern in the company's annual or half-yearly financial statements, with supporting assumptions or qualifications as necessary.[118] The FRC provides guidance in relation to assessing whether the company is a going concern and any related disclosures that may be required.[119] The Governance Code requirement is reinforced by LR 9.8.6 R(3), which requires a UK-incorporated company with a premium listing to include in its report and accounts a statement made by the directors on the appropriateness of adopting the going concern basis of accounting and their assessment of the prospects of the company.

The presumption that a company is a going concern—namely that the company will continue in operational existence for the foreseeable future—is one of the fundamental accounting concepts[120] upon which the preparation of a company's accounts is based. It is presumed that a company is a going concern unless the published accounts contain a clear statement to the contrary. In any case, the directors are under a duty to ensure that the accounts present a true and fair view of the financial affairs of the company, and so the application of this basic principle would require disclosure in the accounts if there are factors which cast doubt on the going concern presumption.

The board's responsibility to present a balanced and understandable assessment of the company's position and prospects also extends to interim and other price sensitive public reports and reports to regulators.

---

[116] FRC, *Feedback Statement, Consulting on a revised UK Corporate Governance Code* July 2018, pp.15–16.
[117] Governance Code, Principle N.
[118] Governance Code, Provision 30.
[119] See FRC, *Guidance on Risk Management, Internal Control and Related Financial and Business Reporting* September 2014.
[120] International Standard on Auditing (UK and Ireland) (ISA) 570 "Going Concern" (June 2016). See also, APB's guidance to auditors in assessing companies' Corporate Governance and Going Concern Statements, Bulletin December 2009. In June 2012, the FRC published the Sharman Inquiry's final report into going concern and liquidity risk.

The Governance Code provides that directors should include in the annual report an explanation of the company's position, performance, business model and strategy.[121] This requirement was added in response to a House of Commons Treasury Committee recommendation for companies to set out "in a short business review, in clear and jargon-free English, how the firm has made (or lost) its money and what the main future risks are judged to be".[122] The aim is both to help shareholders and potential investors understand the company's business risks and also to serve as another prompt to the board to consider their long-term business model.[123]

In line with concerns raised in the Green Paper on European Corporate Governance, the European Commission amended the Accounting Directive to increase disclosure of non-financial risks. In its Action Plan, the Commission had stated that it believes that boards should give broader consideration to the entire range of risks faced by their companies. Therefore, it has extended the reporting requirements with regards to non-financial parameters in order to help in establishing a more comprehensive risk profile of the company, enabling more effective design of strategies to address those risks. The chief means of transposition of these requirements into UK law has been the insertion of s.414CA and s.414CB into the CA 2006, which requires certain types of large companies (including traded companies) which have more than 500 employees, to include a non-financial information statement as part of their strategic report. It is hoped that this additional focus on non-financial aspects will encourage companies to adopt a sustainable and long-term strategic approach to the development of their businesses. More detail on the non-financial information statement can be found in Section 9.6.6 of this Chapter.

While the Kay Report does not make specific recommendations in relation to information reporting, it discusses the principles behind information provision in line with those of effective stewardship. It suggests that the reporting of performance, and the metrics and models used, should be clear, relevant and timely. Disclosure of information should be related closely to the needs of users and directed to the creation of long-term value. It should promote good risk-adjusted long-term returns from the companies in which savers' funds are invested. When determining reporting obligations, the relevance to investors should be the principal criterion, and the reporting of data irrelevant to long-term value creation should be reduced. Furthermore, risks reported on should be related to this value-creation, rather than to only short-term volatility.

The report questions the philosophy that markets inevitably operate better when provided with large quantities of data. Kay observes that the

---

[121] Governance Code, Provision 27.
[122] House of Commons Treasury Committee, *Banking Crisis: Reforming Corporate Governance and Pay in the City*, May 2009.
[123] FRC, *Final Report*, p.26.

so-called "efficient market" hypothesis has placed undue reliance on information disclosure as a response to divergences in knowledge and incentives across the equity investment chain. The effect of this has seen large quantities of data provided to market participants (much of which is of little value to its users):

> "Such copious data provision may drive damaging short-term decisions by investors, aggravated by well-documented cognitive biases such as excessive optimism, loss aversion and anchoring."[124]

To a large extent companies' reporting is determined by regulation, and the report laments the increase of measures to increase comparability between reports (which it sees as an encouragement towards anonymous markets). Reports should rather include information that is of specific relevance to the industry in which the company operates. For example, the report argues that, for industries with long-term investment horizons (such as oil, mining or pharmaceuticals) profitability can only be assessed over a period of many years, and frequent reporting prematurely is simply "noise" in the financial system. For this reason, financial information for such businesses should, if appropriate, give discursive rather than statistical information where possible to both asset holders and asset managers. In the same way, mark-to-market accounting practices should be avoided when they give no useful information about the long-term value creation of an asset.

The report stresses the importance of non-financial, narrative reporting for complete transparency. Narrative reporting should put the financial results in context, highlight important factors and communicate strategy and risks to investors in an understandable, engaging and concise format, without obscuring the key information in a morass of superfluous detail and marketing speak, needlessly lengthening reports or confusing investors.

Seven years on from the publication of the Kay Report the quality of corporate reporting remains under scrutiny. In October 2018, the FRC announced that it would launch a major project to challenge existing thinking about corporate reporting and to consider how company reporting could be improved to better meet the needs of both shareholders and other stakeholders. The FRC anticipates that the project will re-evaluate the ongoing fitness for purpose of the current mainstays of corporate reporting, including critiquing the usefulness of the annual report as currently constituted. In particular, the project is likely to focus on how reporting regimes should be adapted in order that businesses are held accountable not merely by shareholders but also by wider stakeholders. The FRC plans to publish a paper consolidating the outcomes of the project in the second half of 2019, which it believes will ultimately result in calls for a number of changes to regulation and practice in respect of company reporting.

---

[124] *The Kay Review of UK Equity Markets and Long-Term Decision Making* July 2012, p.10.

9.4.5   *Risk management and internal control*

> "The board should establish procedures to manage risk, oversee the internal control framework, and determine the nature and extent of the principal risks the company is willing to take in order to achieve its long-term strategic objectives."[125]

A major theme of the Walker Review was the need for boards to take more responsibility for a company's risks. Following the Walker Review, the FRC expanded the Main Principle relating to risk management in the then Governance Code to make explicit the board's role in managing risk.

Under the Governance Code, the role of boards in managing risk is essentially twofold. The board must make decisions as to the strategic risk that a company is prepared to take and must also involve itself in monitoring a company's risk management and internal control systems. In fulfilling the latter, the Governance Code recommends that directors conduct a review, at least annually, of the effectiveness of the system of internal controls, and that the directors report to shareholders that they have done so in the annual report. The review should cover all material controls, including financial, operational and compliance controls and risk management systems.[126] This contrasts with the Sarbanes-Oxley Act s.404 which is concerned only with internal controls over financial reporting.[127] The version of the Governance Code published in July 2018 has been commended by the Institute of Risk Management for placing a greater emphasis on risk management than previous incarnations of the Governance Code, notably through stating in Principle D that "the board should ... establish a framework of prudent and effective controls, which enable risk to be assessed and managed".

The Turnbull Committee first issued guidance for directors on how to comply with this aspect of the Combined Code in 1999. After the FRC established the Turnbull Review Group in 2004, the Turnbull guidance was re-published in October 2005 to incorporate a small number of changes. Among other things, the re-published guidance encouraged boards to use the internal control statement as an opportunity to help shareholders understand the risk and control issues facing a company.

On 12 October 2009, the ICAEW Foundation published a report by Independent Audit Ltd on risk governance in non-financial services companies. The report concluded that the principles of the Turnbull guidance remain relevant but their usefulness depends on the manner in which they are implemented.

---

[125] Governance Code, Principle O.

[126] Governance Code, Provision 29.

[127] This was a factor in the Turnbull Review Group deciding not to follow the model of requiring a company's management to make a statement on the effectiveness of internal controls over financial reporting and the external auditor to issue an attestation report.

In September 2014, the FRC issued new guidance replacing the Turnbull guidance, entitled *Guidance on Risk Management, Internal Control and Related Financial and Business Reporting.*

The guidance is based on the adoption by a company's board of a risk-based approach to establishing a sound system of internal control and to reviewing its effectiveness. The guidance notes that this should be incorporated by a company into its normal management and governance processes and should not be treated as a separate exercise to meet regulatory requirements.

The guidance puts responsibility for a company's risk management and internal control onto the directors. In order to achieve this, they must ensure the design and implementation of appropriate risk management and internal control systems that identify the risks facing the company and enable the board to make a robust assessment of the principal risks. The board is also responsible for determining the level of risk the company is willing to expose itself to in order to achieve its strategic objectives.[128] The guidance states that the board should take various factors into account when determining what would constitute a sound system of risk management for their particular company:

(a) the nature and extent of the risks facing the company which the board regard as desirable or acceptable for the company to bear;

(b) the likelihood of the risks concerned materialising;

(c) the company's ability to reduce the likelihood of the risks materialising and the impact on the business of risks that do materialise;

(d) the exposure to risks before and after risks are managed or mitigated, as appropriate;

(e) the operation of the relevant controls and control processes;

(f) the effectiveness and relative costs and benefits of particular controls; and

(g) the impact of the values and the culture of the company on the effectiveness of the systems.[129]

The guidance outlines certain matters which should be encompassed within an internal control system. The guidance also states the characteristics which an effective system of internal control should have. The system should:

(a) be embedded in the operations of the company; and

---

[128] FRC, *Guidance on Risk Management, Internal Control and Related Financial and Business Reporting* September 2014, p.5.

[129] FRC, *Guidance on Risk Management, Internal Control and Related Financial and Business Reporting* September 2014, p.9.

(b)   be capable of responding quickly to evolving risks to the business arising from factors within the company and to changes in the business environment.[130]

Although the board formulates the company's policies on internal control, it is the role of management to implement and take day-to-day responsibility for board policies on risk management and internal control. Management should also ensure internal responsibilities and accountabilities are clearly established, understood and embedded at all levels of the organisation. All employees have some responsibility for internal control, and should understand their responsibility for behaving according to the culture.[131]

The guidance indicates the responsibilities within companies for reviewing the effectiveness of internal controls:

(a)   it sees this as an essential part of the board's responsibilities stating that the board needs to exercise reasonable care, skill and diligence in forming its own view based on the evidence provided to it;

(b)   on-going monitoring and review is stated to be an essential component of a sound system of control. The board should regularly receive and review reports on risk management and internal control, and should also make an annual assessment for the purpose of making its statement on the effectiveness of the company's risk management and internal control systems in the annual report; and

(c)   management is accountable to the board for monitoring the system of internal control and for providing assurance to the board that it has done so.[132]

An example of poor risk control was identified by the Parliamentary Commission on Banking Standards in their report on the downfall of HBOS.[133] The report noted that the main reporting line of the divisions of the bank was to divisional management rather than to the group-level risk team. The report found that this caused a disparity between divisional risk functions and group risk functions.[134] It was apparent that "[t]he status of the Group risk functions was low relative to the operating divisions".[135]

---

[130] FRC, *Guidance on Risk Management, Internal Control and Related Financial and Business Reporting* September 2014, p.8.

[131] FRC, *Guidance on Risk Management, Internal Control and Related Financial and Business Reporting* September 2014, p.5.

[132] FRC, *Guidance on Risk Management, Internal Control and Related Financial and Business Reporting* September 2014, p.10.

[133] *"An Accident Waiting to Happen": The Failure of HBOS*, Parliamentary Commission on Banking Standards, Fourth Report of Session 2012–13 HL Paper 144, HC 705, 4 April 2013.

[134] *"An Accident Waiting to Happen": The Failure of HBOS*, Parliamentary Commission on Banking Standards, Fourth Report of Session 2012–13 HL Paper 144, HC 705, 4 April 2013, paras 54, 64.

[135] *"An Accident Waiting to Happen": The Failure of HBOS*, Parliamentary Commission on Banking Standards, Fourth Report of Session 2012–13 HL Paper 144, HC 705, 4 April 2013, para.64.

These factors led the Parliamentary Commission to conclude that the bank's poor risk control was an important factor in explaining why the high-risk activities of certain divisions of the bank were not properly analysed or checked at the highest levels within the bank.[136]

The Salz Review also noted its concern that the responsibility for oversight of operational risk had not been explicitly based to an established, suitable body by Barclays and reputational risk was not prioritised in the framework of board decision-making.[137] The review recommended that the Barclays board should make clear which committees have primary oversight of conduct, reputational and operational risks across the Barclays group. Furthermore, its terms of reference should make clear where the primary responsibilities lie for different aspects of operational risk, and where oversight of all financial and non-financial risks comes together.[138]

The guidance suggests further issues that the board may wish to consider and discuss with management in relation to monitoring and review of risk management systems and related public reporting requirements. The guidance also provides for what the board should consider in making public statements on internal control and the content of such statements.[139]

9.4.6 Audit Committee and auditors

"The board should establish formal and transparent policies and procedures to ensure the independence and effectiveness of internal and external audit functions and satisfy itself on the integrity of financial and narrative statements."[140]

The Governance Code recommends that this objective should be achieved by establishing an audit committee of at least three members (or, in the case of companies below FTSE 350 level, at least two members), who should all be independent non-executive directors. The Chair of the board should not be a member, while at least one member should have recent and relevant financial experience.[141] A company that applies these recommendations will also satisfy the requirements of the Disclosure Guidance and Transparency Rules Ch.7.[142]

---

[136] *"An Accident Waiting to Happen": The Failure of HBOS*, Parliamentary Commission on Banking Standards, Fourth Report of Session 2012–13 HL Paper 144, HC 705, 4 April 2013, para.64.

[137] Salz Review, *An Independent Review of Barclays' Business Practices* April 2013, para.9.65.

[138] Salz Review, *An Independent Review of Barclays' Business Practices* April 2013, para.9.70.

[139] See FRC, *Guidance on Risk Management, Internal Control and Related Financial and Business Reporting* September 2014, Appendix C.

[140] Governance Code, Principle M.

[141] Governance Code, Provision 24.

[142] DTR 7.1.1 AR provides that at a majority of members of the audit committee must be independent and at least one member must have competence in accounting and/or auditing.

The role of the audit committee includes monitoring of financial statements, reviewing significant financial reporting judgments and reviewing the company's internal audit function and financial controls. The audit committee is responsible for making recommendations to the board concerning the appointment of the external auditor and for monitoring the external auditor's independence, objectivity and effectiveness. The audit committee should also develop and implement policy on the engagement of the external auditor to supply non-audit services.[143]

The FCA has stated that a company that applies the Governance Code's recommendations will meet the minimum requirements set out by the Disclosure Guidance and Transparency Rules.[144] The Disclosure Guidance and Transparency Rules also require an issuer to make a statement available to the public disclosing which body carries out the audit committee functions, but provide that this can be included in the corporate governance statement in the annual report under DTR 7.2 (see Listing Rules above).[145]

The audit committee is responsible for preparing a report, which should discuss (amongst other things) the significant issues that it has considered in relation to the financial statements, and how these issues were addressed. It should also provide an explanation of how it has assessed the effectiveness of the external audit process and the approach taken to the appointment or reappointment of the external auditor. The report should also provide information on the length of tenure of the current audit firm and when a tender was last conducted.[146]

There have been concerns that long-term relationships with auditors were damaging the impartiality of the audit process. In particular, it was felt that the consulting and advisory services provided by the Big Four accountancy firms (PricewaterhouseCoopers (PwC), KPMG, Ernst & Young and Deloitte) as an increasingly significant part of their overall business may come into conflict with their duties as auditors (where audit firms should, of course, take a wary, outside view of a company's accounts, in the service of investors not management). As a result, legislation implementing relevant European law now requires certain companies (including all those with securities listed on a regulated market) to put their external audit contract out to tender at least every ten years and limits an external auditor's tenure to 20 years.[147]

The recent collapse of Carillion has prompted additional scrutiny of the relationship between auditors and the companies which engage them. The

---

[143] Governance Code, Provision 25.
[144] DTR 7.1.3 R. DTR 7.1.7 G states that in the FCA's view compliance with relevant provisions of the version of the Governance Code published in April 2016 will result in compliance with the DTRs.
[145] DTR 7.1.5 R and 7.1.6 G.
[146] Governance Code, Provision 26.
[147] CA 2006 s.494ZA.

joint report of the BEIS and Work and Pensions Committees into Carillion's collapse was scathing about the UK corporate governance environment generally, calling on the Government to "reset our systems of corporate accountability in the long-term public interest".[148] The report was particularly critical of the failings of KPMG (in its capacity as Carillion's long-time external auditor) to "challenge management … and voice professional scepticism towards Carillion's aggressive accounting judgments".[149] Such behaviour is presented as indicative of the current state of the statutory audit market as a "cosy club" comprised of the various members of the Big Four which is ultimately "incapable of providing the degree of independent challenge needed".[150] Given the propensity for this "lack of meaningful competition" in the statutory audit market to "create conflicts of interest at every turn",[151] the report successfully recommended that the Government refer the statutory audit market to the Competition and Markets Authority (CMA), with the CMA to consider both breaking up the Big Four into more audit firms and detaching audit arms from those providing other professional services.[152] The CMA has until October 2019 to complete its review. However, an update paper published in December 2018 suggests that the CMA is favourably disposed to requiring firms to structurally separate audit and non-audit services, and to introducing a mandatory joint audit concept where company accounts would have to be signed off by two audit firms. The mandatory joint audit concept could potentially require that each auditor pair contains one challenger to the Big Four.

The joint report into Carillion was also highly critical of the FRC, describing it as "timid in challenging Carillion on the inadequate and questionable nature of the financial information it provided and wholly ineffective in taking to task the auditors who had responsibility for ensuring their veracity".[153] Dismay at the obvious failings of the various audit firms involved with Carillion also led to the commission of an independent review of the FRC, which is responsible for the regulation of auditors in the UK. In his review of the FRC, Sir John Kingman recommended that the FRC be abolished and replaced by a new organisation, the Audit, Reporting and Governance Authority (ARGA). Kingman proposes that ARGA should be a stronger, more independent regulator than the FRC with greater statutory powers. In particular, Kingman argues that ARGA should jettison the

---

[148] Joint Report from the Business, Energy and Industrial Strategy and Work and Pensions Committees, *Carillion* 16 May 2018, p.86.
[149] Joint Report from the Business, Energy and Industrial Strategy and Work and Pensions Committees, *Carillion* 16 May 2018, p.53.
[150] Joint Report from the Business, Energy and Industrial Strategy and Work and Pensions Committees, *Carillion* 16 May 2018, p.85.
[151] Joint Report from the Business, Energy and Industrial Strategy and Work and Pensions Committees, *Carillion* 16 May 2018, p.84.
[152] Joint Report from the Business, Energy and Industrial Strategy and Work and Pensions Committees, *Carillion* 16 May 2018, p.85.
[153] Joint Report from the Business, Energy and Industrial Strategy and Work and Pensions Committees, *Carillion* 16 May 2018, p.61.

"excessively consensual"[154] approach to regulation of auditors adopted by the FRC and instead exert greater "purchase"[155] over audit firms—something Kingman recommends is achieved through the adoption of registry powers by ARGA.[156] The Government has stated that it intends to take forward the recommendations set out in the Kingman review and replace the FRC with a new independent regulator with stronger powers. To this end, the Government is currently consulting on Sir John Kingman's recommendations, with a further consultation on detailed proposals for the new regulator to be scheduled once such proposals have been developed. The deadline for responses to the current consultation is 11 June 2019.

9.4.7 Remuneration

Executive pay has come under increasing scrutiny in recent years, and successive governments have made clear their desire to push for greater oversight and value-for-money for shareholders. Following a slight attenuation in shareholder pre-occupation with the issue in 2017, dissatisfaction with perceived excesses in executive remuneration is again very much to the fore. A study published by the Chartered Institute of Personnel and Development (CIPD) in August 2018 found that between 2016 and 2017 the median pay of FTSE 100 chief executives rose by 11%. A PwC analysis of the first 24 AGMs held by FTSE 100 companies in 2018 evidenced an appreciable increase in shareholder discontent with perceived pay inflation, with 20% of FTSE 100 companies facing votes of greater than 20% against a pay resolution, compared with a corresponding figure of 7% for 2017.

The current impetus to arrest the perceived spiralling growth in executive pay dates back to the publication of a consultation paper on executive remuneration in September 2011 by BIS, outlining reform proposals to improve the transparency of board remuneration, the role of shareholders and the remuneration committee, and the promotion of good practice. This was followed by the "shareholder spring" of April and May 2012, where shareholders refused to back pay plans for a number of boards, including UBS, Citigroup, Barclays, AstraZeneca and Inmarsat. The chief executives of Trinity Mirror and Aviva both faced a revolt on their pay packages, and had to step down in the face of shareholder rebellion. While the much publicised events of the "shareholder spring" did for some time encourage greater pay restraint—a 2013 report by consultant Towers Watson suggested that of the 35 FTSE 100 chief executives who had already disclosed their salaries for that year, 11 had their pay frozen and the median increase was 2.5% (below the rate of inflation), while in 2017, the CIPD reported that mean pay for FTSE 100 chief executives in fact declined by 17% between 2015 and 2016—the issue remains firmly on the agenda of shareholders, legislators and corporate governance bodies. Historically, remuneration has

---

[154] Sir John Kingman, *Independent Review of the Financial Reporting Council* December 2018, p.8.
[155] Sir John Kingman, *Independent Review of the Financial Reporting Council* December 2018, p.28.
[156] Sir John Kingman, *Independent Review of the Financial Reporting Council* December 2018, p.29.

been the subject of two major reviews. In 1995, the Greenbury Review was set up to produce guidelines to combat what were perceived to be excessive remuneration practices. It established the idea of having a remuneration committee staffed by non-executive directors. The Walker Review produced proposals to curb excessive pay in the financial sector and attempt to tie it more closely to risk and discourage short-termism, introducing concepts like bonus "claw-back". The FRC preferred not to be too prescriptive for remuneration at non-financial firms. It rejected some Walker recommendations, such as the suggestion that remuneration committees should set the parameters of firm-wide pay, saying that such recommendations were not appropriate beyond the financial sector. To an extent, it argued, financial sector remuneration, with its large number of high earners below board level whose activities could have a material impact on the company's risk exposure, is unique to the issues and concerns facing the financial sector.

Nevertheless, the Governance Code continues to include a clear statement of the need for executive remuneration to be "clearly linked to the successful delivery of the company's long-term strategy.[157] Remuneration schemes should "promote long-term shareholdings by executive directors that support alignment with long-term shareholder interests"[158] and in determining remuneration policy the remuneration committee should ensure that "reputational and other risks from excessive rewards, and behavioural risks that can arise from target-based incentive plans, are identified and mitigated".[159] The Governance Code also advises that remuneration schemes and policies should include provisions that would enable the company to recover and/or withhold sums or share awards in specified circumstances.[160]

Principle P makes it clear that only "executive remuneration" should be performance-related and Provision 34 is explicit that non-executive directors' pay should not include share options "or other performance-related elements". In this way, non-executive pay should not risk compromising non-executive independence and objectivity. The Governance Code provides that where remuneration consultants have been appointed, the consultants must be identified in the annual report.[161]

The Salz Review identified several issues concerning the functioning of Barclays' Remuneration Committee: it found that the information given to the Remuneration Committee regarding employees' pay was too complex and should have been delivered in "an easily digestible form", detailing each component of the total amount to be paid to individual senior executives. Furthermore, it found that the Remuneration Committee may have concluded that its role was to focus more on regulatory requirements

---

[157] Governance Code, Principle P.
[158] Governance Code, Provision 36.
[159] Governance Code, Provision 40.
[160] Governance Code, Provision 37.
[161] Governance Code, Provision 35.

and the size of the overall bonus pool, than the detailed oversight of individual compensation, with the salaries of key senior individuals being the exception. To remedy these issues, it recommended that small control function committees review pay at the business unit level, before being passed to the Remuneration Committee.[162]

The Kay Report observes that the modal tenure of a corporate chief executive is between three and five years, whereas the consequences from important decisions will have repercussions for many years after that period has ended. Therefore, incentive schemes which pay out during the term of office of the director encourage them to adopt strategies with positive effects in the short term, irrespective of the long-term implications. In such circumstances, directors will favour strategies which create immediately apparent effects over less obvious long-term benefits. The Report therefore notes that any bonuses should be paid in shares and that the required holding period of these shares should extend well beyond the director's tenure with the company. The Governance Code now requires that share awards granted for the purpose of aligning the interests of executive directors with those of long-term shareholders should be released for sale on a phased basis and be subject to a total vesting and holding period of five years or more.[163]

The European Commission December 2012 Action Plan on corporate governance reflects similar concerns. The Commission believes that companies could benefit from remuneration policies which stimulate longer-term value creation and genuinely link pay to performance. Poor remuneration policies and/or incentive structures lead to unjustified transfers of value from companies, their shareholders and other stakeholders to executives. Therefore, and taking into account existing oversight possibilities, shareholders should be enabled to exercise better oversight of remuneration policies applying to directors of listed companies and the implementation of those policies. Reflecting the absence of a right for shareholders to vote on remuneration in many Member States, the Shareholder Rights Directive has been amended to require that shareholders are given the right to vote on remuneration policy.

Among the most radical concrete measures achieved in relation to excessive remuneration in recent years is the cap on bankers' bonuses introduced in the Fourth Capital Requirement Directive (CRD IV). Under the terms of this cap, key risk-takers at banks operating within Europe must be remunerated in accordance with a basic ratio of 1:1 fixed-to-variable pay, a ratio which may rise to 1:2 with the explicit approval of a supermajority of shareholders. It has been suggested by Mark Carney, Governor of the Bank of England, that the UK may jettison the cap following its exit from the EU.

---

[162] Salz Review, *An Independent Review of Barclays' Business Practices* April 2013, para.11.58–11.71.
[163] Governance Code, Provision 36.

Prior to the introduction of the cap, commentators suggested that the natural economic response to a bonus cap expressed as a percentage of fixed pay would be an increase in the fixed pay base, sparking fears that the resulting increased fixed cost would reduce the bank's ability to retain, or claw back, capital in the event of underperformance against expectations. Supporters and detractors of the cap have reached differing conclusions regarding the extent to which this has occurred in practice. Following implementation of the cap, concerns were raised that institutions were circumventing restrictions on the permitted proportion of variable pay through the use of "allowances"—payments that institutions purported to be fixed pay, but which could in fact be reduced or withdrawn. In response, European Banking Authority Guidelines published in December 2015 made clear that in order for "allowances" to be properly classified as fixed remuneration they must be, inter alia, non-discretionary and non-revocable.

More recently, criticisms of excessive remuneration have tended to focus not only on levels of executive pay per se, but on the considerable disparities between directors' remuneration and that of the wider workforce. Such disparities are highlighted by the findings of a report published by the Equality Trust in March 2017 that the average annual pay of a chief executive of a FTSE 100 company is 386 times that of the average annual pay of a worker earning the statutory UK "National Living Wage". The extent of inequality in remuneration has attracted denunciation from across the political spectrum, with Prime Minister Theresa May criticising an "irrational, unhealthy and growing gap between what … companies pay their workers and what they pay their bosses".

Such sensitivities are clearly reflected in the updated Governance Code. Provision 33 gives the remuneration committee an expanded remit to "review workforce remuneration and related policies and the alignment of incentives and rewards with culture, taking these into account when setting the policy for executive director remuneration". The purpose of requiring the remuneration committee to "review" the pay of the wider workforce alongside performing its traditional function of determining executive remuneration is to ensure that the remuneration committee takes into account the level of benefits available to the workforce when deciding executive pay.[164] This is bolstered by the reporting requirement to describe what engagement with the workforce has taken place to explain how executive remuneration aligns with wider company pay policy.[165] The new Governance Code is also for the first time explicit that pension contribution rates for executive directors should be aligned with those available to the workforce,[166] challenging the past trend for executive directors to enjoy more generous pension arrangements than rank-and-file employees. The intention of these changes to the Governance Code is that by requiring

---

[164] FRC, *Guidance on Board Effectiveness* July 2018, p.34.
[165] Governance Code, Provision 41.
[166] Governance Code, Provision 38.

remuneration committees to link their consideration of executive benefits with workforce benefits, a sense that directors' remuneration is increasing at a rate far beyond that enjoyed by the workforce can be tempered. In this context, "workforce" refers only to persons engaged by the company under an employment contract or a contract, or other arrangement to do work or provide services personally.[167]

The effect of these Governance Code provisions is supplemented by additional reporting requirements that have been introduced through secondary legislation.[168] In respect of financial years beginning on or after 1 January 2019, quoted companies with more than 250 employees will be required to include in their remuneration reports the ratio of the total pay of their chief executive to the median, 25th and 75th percentile remuneration of their UK employees. This will be accompanied by an ongoing requirement to explain year-on-year changes to the ratio. Quoted companies will also be obliged to set out in their remuneration reports what amount (or estimate thereof) of a director's pay awarded as a result of the achievement of certain performance measures and targets is attributable to an increase in share price, and, where discretion has been exercised in respect of such a pay award, how the resulting level of award was determined and whether that discretion was exercised as a result of share price appreciation or depreciation.[169] In the same vein, the remuneration reports of quoted companies will be required to contain a statement in respect of each executive director indicating the maximum remuneration such a director might receive in the event of a 50% appreciation in the company's share price over the performance period of any target that director is subject to which relates to more than one financial year.[170] BEIS have indicated this last provision must be complied with in any new remuneration policies put to shareholders from 1 January 2019.[171] This approach is intended to focus the attention of remuneration committees on the question of whether executive pay awards can be justified with reference to a company's performance. These reporting requirements build upon those in force since October 2013 requiring quoted companies to include a table in their remuneration reports showing the single total figure of remuneration received by each director in both the financial year subject

---

[167] FRC, *Guidance on Board Effectiveness* July 2018, p.34.
[168] See the Large and Medium-sized Companies and Groups (Accounts and Reports) Regulations 2008 (SI 2008/410) Sch.8 Pt 3 paras 19A–19G, as amended by the Companies (Miscellaneous Reporting) Regulations 2018 (SI 2018/860).
[169] See the Large and Medium-sized Companies and Groups (Accounts and Reports) Regulations 2008 (SI 2008/410) Sch.8 Pt 3 para.7 and para.12, as amended by the Companies (Miscellaneous Reporting) Regulations 2018 (SI 2018/860).
[170] Large and Medium-sized Companies and Groups (Accounts and Reports) Regulations 2008 (SI 2008/410) Sch.8 Pt 4 para.35A, as amended by the Companies (Miscellaneous Reporting) Regulations 2018 (SI 2018/860).
[171] BEIS, *The Companies Miscellaneous Reporting Regulations 2018 Q&A* November 2018, p.6.

to the report and the financial year before that. The table must also break down the different types of remuneration that make up the single total figure of remuneration.[172]

9.4.7.1 Statutory remuneration regime

On 27 June 2012, BIS announced a package of measures to address failings in the corporate governance framework for directors' remuneration. The Enterprise and Regulatory Reform Act 2013 (ERRA) amended the CA 2006 to introduce new requirements regarding the disclosure and governance of directors' remuneration. Its amendments came into force on 1 October 2013.

The ERRA reforms consist of three principal elements:

- a binding shareholder vote on remuneration policy, including the policy on termination payments;
- an advisory shareholder vote on implementation of the remuneration policy; and
- new rules on disclosure, both of the policy to be adopted for the future and of the remuneration of the directors in the last financial year.

The new rules, which are set out in Ch.4A of Pt 10 and Ch.9 of Pt 15 of the CA 2006, apply to quoted companies, which are those which are officially listed in the UK (whether Premium or Standard) or the EEA or on the NYSE or Nasdaq.

The CA 2006 was amended by ERRA to introduce the following restrictions on the payment of remuneration to directors:

- a quoted company must not make a remuneration payment to a director (or a proposed/former director) unless:
  - the payment is consistent with a remuneration policy that has been approved by shareholders; or
  - the payment is specifically approved by shareholders;
- no person may make a payment for loss of office to a director or former director of a quoted company unless:
  - the payment is consistent with a remuneration policy that has been approved by shareholders; or
  - the payment is specifically approved by shareholders.

Shareholders' approval of a remuneration policy will be by ordinary resolution and must be renewed at least every three years. If a company fails the binding vote, it will have to continue using the existing policy until a revised policy is approved by shareholders. Once the policy has been approved, companies will not be able to make payments outside its scope. If

---

[172] See the Large and Medium-sized Companies and Groups (Accounts and Reports) Regulations 2008 (SI 2008/410) Sch.8 Pt 3 paras 4–12.

a payment is made in breach of these requirements it will be held on trust for the company or other person who paid it (or in the case of a takeover, the shareholders whose shares were acquired in the takeover); and the directors who approved the payment must indemnify the company for any loss. The requirement for the remuneration report (other than the part containing the remuneration policy) to be subject to a resolution of shareholders at the meeting at which accounts (for the financial year to which the remuneration report relates) are laid remains in place.

The rules on disclosure in the directors' remuneration report are detailed and complex.[173] While the precise requirements are outside the scope of this chapter, further information can be found in Section 6.6.5 of Chapter 6 on Service Contracts and Remuneration.

9.4.8 Communication

> "In order for the company to meet its responsibilities to shareholders and stakeholders, the board should ensure effective engagement with, and encourage participation from, these parties."[174]

There has been no shortage of commentary on the role of shareholder meetings in the governance of companies. In 1995, with the encouragement of the Department of Trade and Industry (DTI), as it then was,[175] a joint City/industry working group was established "to suggest practical ways in which the relationship between UK industry and institutional shareholders can be improved as a stimulus for long-term investment and development".[176]

Virtually all participants in the working group's consultation exercise viewed the AGM, as then constituted, as an "expensive waste of time and money". Criticisms referred to poor attendance by institutional shareholders and to the hijacking of proceedings by special-interest groups or by individuals with questions irrelevant to most people attending the meeting.

The solution recommended by the working party was to change the format of the AGM to make it a more interesting and rewarding event so that major investors saw value in attending. Thus:

(a)   an updated trading statement would be provided at the meeting and operational managers would make presentations;

---

[173] See the Large and Medium-sized Companies and Groups (Accounts and Reports) Regulations 2008 (SI 2008/410) Sch.8, as amended.

[174] Governance Code, Principle D.

[175] The DTI became known as the Department for Business, Innovation and Skills (BIS) in June 2009. BIS was succeeded by the Department of Business, Energy & Industrial Strategy (BEIS) in July 2016.

[176] *Developing a Winning Partnership—How Companies and Institutional Investors are Working Together* (The Myners Report), February 1995.

(b)   shareholders would be encouraged to submit their questions in advance;

(c)   questions which were not of general interest would be referred to the relevant director or manager after the meeting; and

(d)   institutions should accept their responsibilities to take an active and involved interest in constitutional governance.

In 1996, the DTI issued a consultative document[177] raising a number of specific questions in this context:

(a)   Should the Companies Act be amended to render it easier for shareholders to requisition resolutions?

(b)   Should there be additional provisions to allow and regulate questions asked by members, both private and corporate, at AGMs?

(c)   Should the law make it easier for the beneficial owners of shares (particularly with the introduction of CREST) to attend shareholder meetings when their shares were held by nominees?

The Institute of Chartered Secretaries and Administrators (ICSA), with support from the DTI, established a working party to deal with the issues raised by the responses to the DTI's consultative document. The working party issued a guide to what was considered best practice in the conduct of AGMs.[178] The guide sets out 24 principles as to best practice at AGMs.

The guide emphasises the importance of good communication with shareholders, including in relation to questions at the AGM (which should be encouraged) about past performance, results and intended future performance. The guide also advocates the provision of an updated trading statement at the AGM, together with a report from at least one executive director. Given the length of time which can elapse between the release of the preliminary announcement and the holding of the annual meeting, this may be a useful way in which to encourage attendance.

The Hampel Committee had two main recommendations in this area:

(a)   the practice of some companies in mounting a full business presentation with a question and answer session should be examined and perhaps followed by other companies; and

(b)   without a poll being demanded, companies should announce the total proxy votes for and against each resolution, once it has been dealt with by the meeting on a show of hands. The Committee was of the view that this would be likely to encourage an increase in shareholder voting.

---

[177] DTI, *Shareholder Communications at the General Meeting* April 1996.
[178] *A Guide to Best Practice for AGMs* September 1996.

The Guidance on Board Effectiveness issued in conjunction with the latest Governance Code contains the following advice on AGMs:

(a)   non-executive directors should use the AGM (or any other general meeting) as an opportunity to understand the concerns of shareholders;

(b)   at least 20 working days' notice of the AGM should be given, to ensure shareholders have sufficient time to consider the issues and discharge their stewardship duties effectively; and

(c)   the chairs of the audit, remuneration and nomination committees should be available to answer questions at the AGM, and should be encouraged to make a statement on the activities and achievements of their committee over the past year.[179]

In March 2010, the LSE published a practical guide to investor relations which emphasised the importance of shareholder meetings for good communication, saying that shareholder meetings should be used as a discussion forum where management is as transparent as possible about the running of the business.[180] The continuing attention paid to shareholder communication highlights the importance for the good governance of a company of maintaining a sound relationship with its shareholders.

In September 2012, the main Governance Code principle relating to the presentation of the annual report was amended to require that the board presents a *fair* assessment of the company's position and prospects (in addition to the previous requirement that the assessment be balanced and understandable), a requirement that remains present in the version of the Governance Code published in 2018.[181] The board is also required to establish arrangements to enable it to ensure that the information is presented in compliance with this requirement. Additionally, the board will also be required to confirm that the report and accounts, taken as a whole, are fair, balanced and understandable and provide the information needed for shareholders to assess the company's performance, business model and strategy.[182]

The updated Governance Code also requires companies to pay greater heed to shareholder dissension communicated to the company through voting at general meetings. Provision 4 states that where 20% or more of votes have been cast against a resolution recommended by the board, the company should explain, when announcing voting results, what actions it intends to take to consult shareholders in order to understand the reasons behind the result. The company must then publish an update on the views received from shareholders and the actions it has taken no more than six months after the general meeting at which the shareholder dissent was expressed.

---

[179] FRC, *Guidance on Board Effectiveness* July 2018, p.11.
[180] LSE, *Investor Relations: A Practical Guide* 15 March 2010, p.49.
[181] Governance Code, Principle N.
[182] Governance Code, Provision 27.

The board should then provide a final summary in the annual report (and in the explanatory notes to the resolutions at the next shareholder meeting if appropriate) on what impact the feedback from shareholders has had on its decisions, and any further actions or resolutions proposed. This change to the Governance Code gives significant protest votes that nevertheless fall short of defeating a proposed resolution major new import. Companies will have to bring the original protest vote back to the attention of its shareholders both six months after such a vote and then again in the annual report. This places a substantial onus on a company which has suffered a significant protest vote to be able to demonstrate that dialogue with shareholders has occurred and that substantive measures have been taken to assuage shareholder concerns. Moreover, suffering a protest vote will impact any company's reputation in the governance sphere, given that the IA maintains an easily searchable public register of companies that have faced significant protest votes from shareholders, including a "Repeat Offenders" list that details all those companies that have appeared on the IA's register for two consecutive years on account of shareholder dissent towards the same resolution.

9.4.9 Wider engagement

A key new concern of the revised Governance Code is to foster greater engagement between companies and their non-shareholding stakeholders. In particular, the promotion of workforce engagement has been high on the agenda of the current Conservative Government, with the Prime Minister initially championing the long-standing trade union aspiration that company boards be required to include worker representatives. The eventual Governance Code position, though far more flexible from a company's perspective, still introduces an important new obligation for company boards to "engage with the workforce" in order better to "understand ... [its] views".[183] The broad scope of this requirement is emphasised by the FRC's decision to extend the definition of "workforce" applicable in this context to capture "the complexity and diversity of modern contractual relationships between companies and individuals undertaking work for them".[184] The Guidance on Board Effectiveness therefore notes that references to "workforce" include both staff with formal contracts of employment and other members of the workforce affected by the decisions of the board. Such other members of the workforce may include individuals engaged under contracts of service, agency workers, and remote workers, regardless of their geographical location.

Provision 5 of the Governance Code requires that boards engage with the workforce using one or a combination of the following methods:

---

[183] Governance Code, Provision 5.
[184] FRC, *Guidance on Board Effectiveness* July 2018, p.15; FRC, *Proposed Revisions to the UK Corporate Governance Code* December 2017, p.8.

(a)   a director appointed from the workforce;
(b)   a formal workforce advisory panel; and
(c)   a designated non-executive director.

The Governance Code also permits boards to put in place "alternative arrangements" to those set out above, so long as they explain what alternative arrangements are in place and why they consider those arrangements to be effective. At this early stage, it seems likely that companies will avail themselves of the full extent of the flexibility afforded to them by Provision 5. ICSA have commented that "it is likely that the optimum solution for any company will be a combination of some, all or none of these methods and probably something else". In particular, companies seem averse to satisfying the requirement by simply appointing a director from the workforce. An ICSA poll published in October 2018 found that 71% of companies surveyed felt that including workforce representatives on boards was a bad idea, while only 9% stated that they were currently considering it.

A survey of FTSE 100 companies published by the Practical Law Company, also in October 2018, found that the two single most popular expected means of compliance with Provision 5 were the designation of a non-executive director as responsible for workforce engagement and adoption of alternative arrangements. Adoption of alternative arrangements will likely prove popular at least initially as this method of compliance will enable companies to build on the existing mechanisms they have developed to take soundings from their workforce, such as opinion surveys, employee forums, and internal reporting from senior human resources managers to the board. The Governance Code requirement that the board should keep engagement mechanisms under review so that they remain effective[185] should result in workforce engagement methods continuing to evolve and improve as companies become more experienced in compliance year-on-year.

The Governance Code requirements in relation to workforce engagement are supplemented by new reporting requirements introduced by secondary legislation.[186] Pursuant to these requirements, for financial years beginning on or after 1 January 2019 companies with more than 250 employees must contain a statement in their directors' report summarising how the directors have engaged with employees and how the directors have had regard to employee interests, and the effect of that regard, including on the principal decisions taken by the company during the financial year. The disclosure of information concerning impending developments or matters in the course of negotiation which would, in the opinion of the directors, be seriously prejudicial to the interests of the company if disclosed is not required. This

---

[185] Governance Code, Provision 5.
[186] See the Large and Medium-sized Companies and Groups (Accounts and Reports) Regulations 2008 (SI 2008/410) Sch.7 Pt 4 paras 11 and 11A, as amended by the Companies (Miscellaneous Reporting) Regulations 2018 (SI 2018/860).

new obligation is in addition to the existing need to describe the actions that have been taken during the financial year to:

(a) provide employees systematically with information on matters of concern to them as employees;
(b) consult employees or their representatives on a regular basis so that the views of employees can be taken into account in making decisions which are likely to affect their interests;
(c) encourage the involvement of employees in the company's performance through an employees' share scheme or by some other means; and
(d) achieve a common awareness on the part of all employees of the financial and economic factors affecting the performance of the company.

Additionally, large companies must make a statement in their strategic report describing how the directors have had regard to the matters set out in the CA 2006 s.172(1)(a)-(f), one such matter being the interests of the company's employees.[187]

The updated Governance Code also requires boards to actively consider the needs and views of all their stakeholders. Principle D states that "in order for the company to meet its responsibilities to shareholders and stakeholders, the board should ensure effective engagement with, and encourage participation from, these parties". This Principle is buttressed by the associated reporting requirement of Provision 5, which obliges the board to "understand the views of the company's other key stakeholders and describe in the annual report how their interests and the matters set out in s.172 of the CA 2006 have been considered in board discussions and decision-making". The Guidance on Board Effectiveness notes that a business' stakeholders are likely to include its workforce, customers, and suppliers and may also include other stakeholders specific to a given company's circumstances such as regulators, government, bondholders, banks and other creditors, trade unions, and community groups. It is for the board to identify and prioritise key stakeholders, recognising that it may be faced with complex decisions whose impacts will benefit some stakeholders but disadvantage others. Such decisions should be made in the long-term interests of the company, and therefore in the interests of the company's most important stakeholders—those with a vested interest in the long term future of the company.[188]

In the consultation over the revised Governance Code, concerns were expressed that Principle D and Provision 5 could be viewed as extending the existing duty owed by directors to "have regard" to certain stakeholder matters while acting so as to promote the success of the company for the

---

[187] See CA 2006 s.414CZA.
[188] FRC, *Guidance on Board Effectiveness* July 2018, p.12.

benefit of its members as a whole.[189] However, the introduction to the Governance Code is clear that "nothing in this [Governance] Code overrides or is intended as an interpretation of the statutory statement of directors' duties in the CA 2006". The paramount responsibility of directors to consider the interests of shareholders therefore remains unchanged, though in order to comply with Principle D and Provision 5 the board will have to ensure effective engagement with stakeholders and be able to demonstrate how stakeholder views have been considered in reaching decisions. The GC100 has published guidance on how directors may discharge their s.172 duties with regards to stakeholders in which it recommends directors take steps to embed in their company a culture which is consistent with the company's goals in relation to stakeholders.[190] The Governance Code itself now stresses the importance of a company's culture, noting that all directors must promote the desired culture,[191] while the board should assess and monitor culture, and, where it is dissatisfied, seek assurance that management has taken corrective action.[192]

As with employee matters, reporting requirements in relation to other stakeholder matters have recently been introduced by secondary legislation applying to financial years beginning on or after 1 January 2019. As described above, large companies must make a statement in their strategic report describing how the directors, when performing their duty to act in the way most likely to promote the success of the company for the benefit of its members as whole, have had regard to the matters set out in the CA 2006 s.172(1)(a)–(f). This statement should include, amongst other things, details of how directors have had regard to the need to foster the company's business relationships with suppliers, customers and others, and the impact of the company's operations on the community and the environment.[193] Additionally, large companies will be required to include a statement in their directors' report summarising how the directors have had regard to the need to foster the company's business relationships with suppliers, customers and others, and the effect of that regard, including on the principal decisions taken by the company during the financial year. The disclosure of information concerning impending developments or matters in the course of negotiation which would be seriously prejudicial to the interests of the company if disclosed is not required.[194]

---

[189] CA 2006 s.172(1).
[190] See GC100, *Guidance on Directors' Duties: Section 172 and Stakeholder Considerations* 22 October 2018.
[191] Governance Code, Principle B.
[192] Governance Code, Provision 2.
[193] See CA 2006 s.414CZA.
[194] See the Large and Medium-sized Companies and Groups (Accounts and Reports) Regulations 2008 (SI 2008/410) Sch.7 Pt 4 paras 11B and 11C, as amended by the Companies (Miscellaneous Reporting) Regulations 2018 (SI 2018/860).

9.5 The Stewardship Code

While the Governance Code provides guidelines for ideal board governance, it can do little to regulate the extent to which shareholders enforce
good governance in practice. Shareholders have received increasing
criticism for their failure to monitor properly the companies they owned
before and during the financial crisis. In particular, the Kay Review
emphasised the important role that effective stewardship has to play in
promoting the long-term growth of listed companies.

The Walker Review expressed the belief that a situation in which feedback
is given to a company solely through movements in its share price "cannot
be regarded as a satisfactory ownership model".[195] The Walker Review
called for a fundamental change in investor behaviour. It argued that before
the crisis investors were at best uninterested in burdening themselves with
the task of engaging with banks' boards and at worst exacerbated
management errors by taking short-term views and encouraging banks to
accumulate ever more leverage in a bid to improve balance sheet
efficiency.[196] The Walker Review proposed a Stewardship Code to operate
in parallel to the Governance Code and to be monitored by the FRC. To this
end, the Walker Review recommended that the FRC adopt as the
Stewardship Code the "Code on the Responsibilities of Institutional
Shareholders", prepared by the Institutional Shareholders' Committee
(ISC). The FRC published a consultation paper in January 2010 inviting
respondents to comment on the ISC text, the disclosure requirements of the
Stewardship Code, and exactly which institutional shareholders should be
encouraged to subscribe to it.[197] Subsequently, the ISC code was adopted
with only a few minor amendments and published by the FRC as "The UK
Stewardship Code" (the Stewardship Code) in July 2010.

Following limited updates to the Stewardship Code in 2012, the FRC
included an overview consultation on the Stewardship Code in its larger
consultation on the Governance Code in 2017. A full consultation and draft
revised Stewardship Code was published on 30 January 2019, with the final
version to be published in the summer of 2019. However, Sir John
Kingman's review of the FRC has called the ongoing existence of the
Stewardship Code into question, noting that it "requires a fundamental
shift in approach ... to focus on outcomes and effectiveness, not on policy
statements", and "that if the [Stewardship] Code remains simply a driver of
boilerplate reporting, serious consideration should be given to its abolition".[198] It remains to be seen whether the final version of the revised

---

[195] Sir David Walker, *A Review of Corporate Governance in UK Banks and other Financial Industry
Entities: Final Recommendations* (Walker Review), para.5.7, p.70; see also "Sir David Walker:
Conformity not compliance" *The Financial Times* 12 April 2010.
[196] Walker Review, Ch.5, "The role of institutional shareholders: communication and
engagement", pp.68–89.
[197] FRC, *Consultation on a Stewardship Code for Institutional Investors* January 2010.
[198] Sir John Kingman, *Independent Review of the Financial Reporting Council* December 2018, p.46.

Stewardship Code will satisfy the criteria put forward in the Kingman review, but given Sir John Kingman is not the sole critic of the current incarnation of the Stewardship Code—the IA has stated that while the Stewardship Code has "met its objectives and helped attract companies and capital to the UK" now is an "opportune time for it to be fully refreshed and focused on best practice and the activity that goes on between companies and investors day to day"[199]—it seems extensive changes are likely. The Stewardship Code applies to institutional investors and is designed to set out a model of responsible long-term investor engagement.[200]

Concerns about stewardship are not new but date back to when a code on corporate governance was first suggested. The principle of "comply or explain" hinges on shareholders taking sufficient interest in the disclosures that companies make. When the Cadbury Committee proposed the idea of a corporate governance code in 1992, it acknowledged that such a code could only succeed if sufficient interest was shown by investors in how boards chose to apply it.[201] A key aspiration of the Stewardship Code is to encourage investors to take a long-term perspective on their investments and by doing so commit time and resources to considering corporate governance issues and developing relationships with investee companies.

As well as bettering corporate governance, the Stewardship Code also aims to improve the investment process for end investors. Originally, the Combined Code was designed to fix what might be described in economics as the "agency problem", where the alignment of interests of principal (the shareholders) and agent (the board) is sometimes obscured because of the information gap and the self-interest of directors.[202] The Stewardship Code is an attempt to fix another agency problem: that between end investors (be they pension funds, insurance companies or the general public) and investment managers.[203] By encouraging greater transparency in requiring managers to state openly their policies on engagement, as well as publishing how they have voted and the activities they have conducted, the Stewardship Code aims to help investors differentiate managers and scrutinise their commitment to corporate governance and long-term value creation.[204] The need to encourage investment managers to take an active interest in stewardship is arguably becoming all the more acute as the UK

---

[199] See Financial Times, *UK Stewardship Code in line for significant overhaul* 5 January 2019.

[200] Note the Stewardship Code states that it is directed at "institutional investors, by which is meant asset owners and asset managers with equity holdings in UK listed companies". The introduction to the Stewardship Code states that "broadly speaking, asset owners include pension funds, insurance companies, investment trusts and other collective investment vehicles".

[201] *Report of the Committee on the Financial Aspects of Corporate Governance* 1 December 1992, para.2.5.

[202] Walker Review, para.1.12, p.26.

[203] Walker Review, para.5.2, p.68.

[204] See the section "Clear mandates" to ISC paper *Improving Institutional Investors' Role in Governance* June 2009. The Stewardship Code requires disclosure of the information listed under Principles 1, 5, 6 and 7.

equity investor profile increasingly shifts away from UK long-only institutions to overseas investors, tracker funds and hedge funds—market participants traditionally less concerned about the long-term promotion of good governance in their investees.

9.5.1 The stewardship principles

The Stewardship Code is a collection of principles that have been developed over the course of the last thirty years. In 1991, at the time of the Cadbury Review, the ISC published a statement on "The Responsibilities of Institutional Shareholders in the UK". When the Combined Code was established in 1998 it contained a section (Section E) that comprised a number of non-binding recommendations addressed to institutional share-holders. The March 2001 Myners Review of shareholder activism recommended that those responsible for pension scheme investments should have a duty actively to monitor and communicate with the management of investee companies and to exercise shareholder votes where those would enhance the value of the investment. The Department of Work and Pensions jointly with the Treasury then issued a consultation paper in February 2002, "Encouraging Shareholder Activism".[205] In response to this, the ISC issued a Statement of Principles on 21 October 2002, which was a voluntary code of practice setting out the responsibilities of institutional investors in relation to the companies in which they invest.[206] The Higgs Review recommended that institutional investors apply the ISC Statement of Principles, and, as a consequence, it was explicitly referred to in Principle E.1 of the Combined Code.

The ISC Statement of Principles was updated in September 2005 and June 2007, when it was released alongside a framework for voting disclosure. In response to recommendations of the Walker Review, the ISC converted its Statement of Principles into a code in November 2009, which was adopted by the FRC's January 2010 consultation paper as the draft Stewardship Code. The ISC Principles form the seven principles of the Stewardship Code. These principles provide that institutional investors should:

(a)   publicly disclose their policy on how they will discharge their stewardship responsibilities;

(b)   have a robust policy on managing conflicts of interest in relation to stewardship and this policy should be disclosed;

(c)   monitor their investee companies;

(d)   establish clear guidelines on when and how they will escalate their stewardship activities;

(e)   be willing to act collectively with other investors where appropriate;

(f)   have a clear policy on voting and disclosure of voting activity; and

(g)   report periodically on their stewardship and voting activities.

---

[205] *Encouraging Shareholder Activism—A Consultation Document* 4 February 2002.
[206] ISC, *The Responsibilities of Institutional Shareholders and Agents in the UK.*

The Stewardship Code operates like the Governance Code on a "comply or explain" basis. Unlike the Governance Code, however, there is no absolute obligation to have regard to the Stewardship Code's recommendations as a matter of course. The Walker Review recognised that the willingness of institutional investors to involve themselves in active engagement is dependent on the investment mandates under which they operate.[207] To accommodate this, the Walker Review recommended that institutional investors have a responsibility to disclose the business model they are using and, where they do adhere to an active-engagement business model, state this on their website along with the extent to which they commit to the Stewardship Code. Foreign investors are also encouraged to commit to the Stewardship Code on a voluntary basis.

Regulators had to deal with several regulatory issues when considering the introduction of the Stewardship Code. The Stewardship Code encourages investors to engage in collective action with other investors to secure more influence over boards. Concerns were raised in the July 2009 consultation paper to the Walker Review that such action might breach concert party provisions of the Takeover Code r.9 and the "acting in concert" rules of the FCA's controllers regime which derives from the EU Acquisitions Directive (and which requires persons "acting in concert" to notify the FCA of an intention to acquire an aggregate holding exceeding 10% of the shares in a financial institution).[208] In response, the Walker Review called for the creation of "safe harbours", saying there was a need to recognise the distinction between collective action that is designed to achieve a degree of control on a continuing basis and that which sets out to achieve "a limited, specific and relatively immediate objective". As a result, the Takeover Panel issued a statement which made clear the circumstances in which collective action would not be deemed "control seeking".[209]

The Walker Review also acknowledged concerns that an activist approach to governance might lead to penalties for market abuse in instances where managers acquire inside information through their communications with the board. The Walker Review asserted that where advance notice is received by fund managers of an intended change in the board or in some aspect of the company's strategy, the fund manager should be rigorous in ensuring its compliance arrangements prevent the information being leaked to the relevant trading desk.[210]

The FSA published a letter in 2009 to the ISC explaining how its rules on market abuse apply to activist shareholders who wish to work with other

---

[207] Walker Review, para.5.2, p.68. The ISC's "Improving institutional investors' role in governance" (June 2009) recommended that mandates clearly express the type of commitment to corporate governance.
[208] Walker Review, Annex 7, pp.151–152.
[209] Takeover Panel, Practice Statement No.26 on 9 September 2009.
[210] Walker Review, para.5.14, p.73.

shareholders to promote effective corporate governance in companies.[211] The FSA also discussed how shareholders engaging in collective action would not necessarily be deemed to be acting in concert in relation to its rules on the disclosure of major shareholdings and change in control. Nevertheless, some major institutional shareholders were not satisfied that the FSA had provided enough clarity on these concerns.[212]

9.5.2 Adoption of the Stewardship Code

The Walker Review recognised that languishing shareholder engagement was partly a result of the structure of the stock market and modern investment management practices. While institutional investors manage more money than ever before, portfolio theory has encouraged portfolio diversification and low conviction investment strategies among managers.[213] That this trend has been accompanied by an increasing tendency for a higher proportion of the monies intended for stock market investment to be allocated to passive funds has only compounded investor reticence to engage.

There are several barriers to meaningful shareholder engagement. One obvious issue is whether end investors are likely to forego real returns in order to support the promotion of less tangible gains in corporate governance. The needs and demands of investors differ enormously— clearly the provisions of the Stewardship Code are not appropriate for all investors. Typically the Stewardship Code is most applicable to long-only institutions such as life assurance and pension funds, where investors are looking for long-term returns.

In the case of pension funds, managers' mandates will be decided by pension fund trustees. One might expect ensuring effective corporate governance to be relatively low down on trustees' list of priorities. Trustees' primary responsibility is to pay pensions for current and future fund members and this is the reason for their preoccupation with raising dividends and asset values, especially at a time when many pension funds are in actuarial deficit. Active engagement in corporate governance is likely to be an expensive exercise for managers, and trustees may not want these costs passed on to pension scheme investors.

A major challenge to the efficacy of the Stewardship Code (and shareholder engagement more generally) is the declining interest of traditional long-term UK equity-holders. Data published by the Pensions Regulator and Pension Protection Fund in November 2012 showed a reduced

---

[211] FSA, Letter to Keith Skeoch, ISC Chairman, *Shareholder Engagement and the Current Regulatory Regime* 19 August 2009; FSA, Press Release, "FSA provides clarity for activist shareholders" 19 August 2009; see also, FSA Market Watch Issue No.20 May 2007.

[212] e.g. *Response from BlackRock to the Financial Reporting Council's Consultation on a Stewardship Code for Institutional Investors* 16 April 2010, p.3.

[213] Walker Review, paras 5.3 and 5.7.

allocation to equities amongst Defined Benefit pension schemes and, within equities, a falling UK share. Encompassing both Defined Benefit and Defined Contribution pension schemes, the asset allocation of the average pension fund to UK equities stood at 18% in 2011, down from 46% a decade earlier.[214] Pension funds and insurance companies may long have held great sway over the UK stock market, but there can be no doubt that the influence of UK-based institutional shareholders has been in decline over the course of the last 20–25 years. It is now questionable how powerful UK long-only institutions overall really are, particularly given the growing influence of overseas investors, hedge funds and sovereign wealth funds. The proportion of UK-listed companies owned by overseas shareholders reached 53.9% by the end of 2016. This is in contrast to 1990 when equivalent overseas holdings were just 11.8%. Equally, UK pension funds and insurance companies' collective ownership of 52.1% of the stock market has declined to just 7.9% in the same period.[215]

A survey by the Chartered Financial Analysts Institute (CFAI) suggested that foreign investors' interest in the stewardship of UK companies was particularly low in comparison to engagement among UK pension and insurance funds.[216] There has also been a rise in the number of index-tracker funds which account for a significant proportion of the investment in the FTSE 100 share index. These tracker funds are less incentivised than active fund managers to be concerned about the way in which their investee companies are governed.

The FRC sought responses from institutional investors about the Stewardship Code in its January 2010 consultation paper.[217] Most respondents identified the size of funds under management to be the biggest factor determining whether or not the Stewardship Code would be adopted. Funds of £1 billion or more were identified by the CFAI as most likely to adopt the Stewardship Code because of the size of their resources and influence and the fact that economies of scale would share out the burden of the costs of engagement among individual investors.[218] Several respondents recognised that smaller funds would only be able to commit themselves to corporate governance by outsourcing voting and other engagement activities to third parties.

Other major issues raised by respondents were that public disclosure of voting and engagement activities would cause concerns about confidentiality, and that there would be a danger of engagement becoming too

---

[214] Pensions Regulator and Pension Protection Fund, *The Purple Book: DB Pensions Universe Risk Profile 2012* November 2012.

[215] Institute of Chartered Accountants in England and Wales, Letter to Susannah Haan at the FRC, 13 April 2010, p.3; Office for National Statistics, *Ownership of UK quoted shares 2016* November 2017, p.8.

[216] CFAI, Letter to Susannah Haan at the FRC, 30 April 2010, pp.6–7.

[217] FRC, *Consultation on a Stewardship Code for Institutional Investors* January 2010.

[218] CFAI, Letter to Susannah Haan at the FRC, 30 April 2010, p.7.

compliance-orientated. Concerns were raised that companies might actually prefer to engage with non-signatories to avoid having to disclose confidential information, and that the excessive use of tick-box compliance might lead to a deterioration in the quality of engagement, as in the case of the ERISA legislation in the US where "a rise in voting has not led to a rise in responsible ownership".[219]

In spite of these concerns, there are now a considerable number of signatories to the Stewardship Code. In January 2019, the FRC reported that there were 280 signatories, including most of the largest investors in UK equities (though the most notable exceptions were sovereign wealth funds, who have been slow to embrace the stewardship principles). Signatories are designated as either Tier 1, in which case they provide a "good quality and transparent description of their approach to stewardship and explanations of an alternative approach where necessary" or Tier 2, in which case they "meet many of the reporting expectations but report less transparently on their approach to stewardship or do not provide explanations where they depart from provisions of the [Stewardship] Code".[220] In February 2019, approximately 75% of signatories were designated as Tier 1.

The FRC published a new version of the Stewardship Code in September 2012. While the seven key principles remained unchanged, there were some minor adjustments to address some perceived shortcomings in the original version. The main changes to the Stewardship Code included:

- clarification of the respective responsibilities of asset managers and asset owners for stewardship, and for stewardship activities that they have chosen to outsource;
- clearer reporting requirements, including on the policy on stock lending; and
- inclusion of provisions to encourage asset managers to have the processes that support their stewardship activities independently verified, to provide greater assurance to their clients.

The FRC warns that a distinction should be drawn between constructive shareholder engagement and a more confrontational approach. Clearly, remuneration has been an area of heated debate in recent years—but, while (as the FRC suggests) a greater willingness on the part of shareholders to challenge board decisions is welcome, more effort will be required to embed the culture and practice envisaged by the Stewardship Code:

> "There needs to be a level of engagement that looks more like ownership than confrontation. A 'no' vote is not necessarily evidence of success if it means a failure to engage constructively on the part of the company or its shareholders."

---

[219] ABI, *Response to the FRC's Consultation on a Stewardship Code for Institutional Investors*, p.4.
[220] FRC, *Proposed Revision to the UK Stewardship Code* January 2019, pp.4–5.

In March 2013, ICSA published guidance on the relationship between companies and their investors and how to facilitate good engagement practices. The guidance emphasises four key messages: the need to develop an engagement strategy, the importance of getting housekeeping issues right, strengthening the conversation on strategy and long-term performance and providing feedback in a way that adds value for all participants.[221] In the same month, the European Commission published a Green Paper on the long-term financing of the European economy, which considered the role that financial institutions and financial markets can play in enhancing long-term financing and the importance of the ease with which SMEs can access bank and non-bank funding. One factor that this consultation raises is the incentives that may encourage greater long-term shareholder engagement and refers to ideas such as granting increased voting rights, or dividends, to long-term investors.

As noted above, the Kay Report identified some major challenges for regulators and standard-setters in the promotion of greater investor engagement. The report's recommendations generally reflected the aims of the Stewardship Code in promoting long-termism in a healthy equity market—though it urged the FRC to develop a more holistic approach in relation to the Stewardship Code by going beyond narrowly based discussion on remuneration.

The draft version of the revised Stewardship Code (the final version of which is scheduled to be published in the summer of 2019) attempts to answer Sir John Kingman's criticism that the current Stewardship Code is insufficiently focused on outcomes and effectiveness.[222] The FRC propose introducing a much more robust reporting regime than that contained in the current Stewardship Code, which simply asks that institutional investors report periodically on their stewardship and voting activities.[223] Under the prospective new regime, in order to become a signatory to the Stewardship Code entities would be required to submit a policy and practice statement. This statement would set out what category of signatory status the entity is applying for (from a choice of: asset owner, asset manager, or service provider), and confirm how the entity's policies and practices enable them to apply the applicable principles and comply with the applicable provisions of the Stewardship Code.[224] Where the entity is not compliant with a provision, a meaningful explanation of an alternative approach would be required.[225] Subsequent to becoming a signatory, entities would be further required to produce an annual activities and outcomes report. This report would require signatories to:

---

[221] *Enhancing Stewardship Dialogue*, Guidance prepared by the Institute of Chartered Secretaries and Administrators 14 March 2013.

[222] Sir John Kingman, *Independent Review of the Financial Reporting Council* December 2018, p.10.

[223] Stewardship Code, Principle 7.

[224] FRC, *Proposed Revision to the UK Stewardship Code—Revised UK Stewardship Code* January 2019, p.4.

[225] FRC, *Proposed Revision to the UK Stewardship Code* January 2019, p.13.

(a)   detail their compliance with their policy and practice statement and any departures from that statement;

(b)   describe the activities they have undertaken to implement the provisions of the Stewardship Code in the preceding 12 months; and

(c)   provide an evaluation of how well stewardship objectives have been met, and/or have enabled clients to meet theirs, and the outcomes achieved.[226]

The FRC also proposes a new definition of stewardship to be used in the revised Stewardship Code. Stewardship would be defined as the:

> "responsible allocation and management of capital across the institutional investment community to create sustainable value for beneficiaries, the economy and society. Stewardship activities include monitoring assets and service providers, engaging issuers and holding them to account on material issues, and publicly reporting on the outcomes of these activities."[227]

In demonstrating this broader concern for the wider society and economy, the draft Stewardship Code is looking to move beyond being "simply a driver of boilerplate reporting", a characteristic for which it was criticised by Sir John Kingman.[228] In keeping with this new approach, the draft Stewardship Code makes explicit reference to environmental, social, and governmental concerns. For instance, it obliges signatories to demonstrate how they take into account material environmental, social, and governmental factors in their investment approach.[229]

The European Commission Action Plan on corporate governance identifies several key areas for development in relation to the promotion of stewardship. The issue of shareholder identification has been discussed in some detail: only when companies can easily identify their shareholders can an effective dialogue between company and investor take place. With regard to suitable reforms, responses to the Commission's Green Paper on corporate governance were varied. Some respondents felt that requiring issuers to offer a forum to shareholders on their corporate websites was sufficient. Others spoke out in favour of a fully-fledged EU shareholder identification mechanism. Many respondents suggested lowering the thresholds for notification of major holdings in the Transparency Directive instead. Ultimately, the Commission amended the Shareholder Rights Directive, introducing changes designed to make it easier for companies to identify their shareholders, thus facilitating better engagement between companies and their investors. The amended Directive came into force in June 2017, with Member States having until 10 June 2019 to transpose its

---

[226] FRC, *Proposed Revision to the UK Stewardship Code—Revised UK Stewardship Code* January 2019, p.4.

[227] FRC, *Proposed Revision to the UK Stewardship Code—Revised UK Stewardship Code* January 2019, p.1.

[228] Sir John Kingman, *Independent Review of the Financial Reporting Council* December 2018, p.10.

[229] FRC, *Proposed Revision to the UK Stewardship Code—Revised UK Stewardship Code* January 2019, p.7.

provisions into national law. The main thrust of the amended Directive is to require Member States to give companies the right to identify their shareholders. Given the CA 2006 Pt 22 already permits public companies to investigate the identity of their shareholders, specific UK transposition measures would be limited to proposed amendments to the FCA handbook in respect of institutional investor and asset manager engagement policies, institutional investors' investment strategies and arrangements with asset managers, and transparency of asset managers. Such amendments will only be made in the event that the UK leaves the EU with an implementation period during which EU law continues to apply to the UK for a pre-determined period. In the event the UK leaves the EU with no such implementation period agreed, the FCA will not proceed with the proposed amendments.[230]

The Commission requested that the European Securities and Markets Authority (ESMA) develop guidance to increase legal certainty on the relationship between investor co-operation on corporate governance issues and the rules on acting in concert in the Takeover Bids Directive and the Transparency Directive in order to make shareholder co-operation easier. In response ESMA published a public statement entitled "Information on shareholder co-operation and acting in concert under the Takeover Bids Directive" that contains a "white list" of activities that will not, in and of themselves, lead to a conclusion that shareholders co-operating to engage in such activities are acting in concert. It is hoped that this will promote greater collaboration (particularly between powerful institutional shareholders) in providing constructive oversight of companies' corporate governance standards. In the UK, major shareholders have for some years proved able to engage in co-ordinated activism to promote higher corporate governance standards in their investee companies by forming investor groups such as the IA (which represents investment managers) and PLSA (which represents pension schemes). These investor groups are able to represent their members by putting the case for improved governance standards to investee companies without their members having to be concerned about being accused of acting in concert with fellow members.

9.6 The corporate governance implications of the CA 2006

Aside from the developments of the Governance Code and the Stewardship Code, the 1997–2010 Labour Government's reforms in the field of corporate governance had also looked to promote wider participation of shareholders in the affairs of the companies in which they invest. Before the Stewardship Code, a number of legislative changes were introduced on the basis of "enhancing shareholder engagement and a long-term investment culture". Many of the changes under the CA 2006 were introduced with this objective in mind.

---

[230] FCA, *Consultation on proposals to improve shareholder engagement* January 2019, p.5.

In its White Paper in March 2005, the Government commented that:

> "Shareholders have a key role to play in driving long-term company performance and economic prosperity. Informed, engaged shareholders—or those acting on their behalf—are the means by which the directors are held to account for business strategy and business performance and by which investment decisions are taken which reflect the best use of capital. However, the investment chain has become increasingly complex, with the result that communication up and down the chain, and the exercise of ownership rights and responsibilities have become more difficult."[231]

Improving shareholder participation has long been a goal of the European Commission: the principal aims of the Shareholder Rights Directive were to facilitate shareholder communication and increase rights to information.

9.6.1 Shareholder communications

Various changes have been introduced to improve the timeliness and transparency of company information and proceedings with a view to increasing shareholder dialogue and engagement.

They include the following provisions of particular relevance to public companies:

(a)   a reduction in the time allowed for companies to file their annual accounts. This is intended to reflect improvements in technology and the increased rate at which information becomes out of date. For public companies it has been reduced from seven months to six months (s.442(2)(b));

(b)   the requirement for AGMs to be held within six months of the end of the financial year for public companies (s.336). This is intended to provide a more timely opportunity to hold the directors of a public company to account.[232] Conversely, the default provision is that private companies will no longer be required to hold an AGM;

(c)   the publication of the full reports and accounts on the websites of quoted companies (s.430);

(d)   a public company is required to meet the cost of circulating resolutions received from members who hold not less than 5% of the voting rights or at least 100 members holding an average of £100 or more in nominal amount of its paid-up share capital if received before the financial year end (s.338);

(e)   enhanced rights for proxies to vote on a show of hands as well as a poll and to speak (ss.284, 285, 324 and 329);

(f)   the disclosure of the results of polls taken at general meetings by quoted companies on their websites (s.341)[233];

---

[231] BIS, *Company Law Reform* March 2005, p.15.
[232] CA 2006 Explanatory Notes, para.538.
[233] Section 341 was amended by the Companies (Shareholders' Rights) Regulations 2009 (SI

(g)   the independent scrutiny of a polled vote where requested by a minority of members of a quoted company (members who hold not less than 5% of the voting rights, or 100 or more members each holding an average of £100 or more in nominal amount of its paid-up share capital (s.342)). There is a period of a week to exercise the right, for example on a controversial resolution or where there appears to be a problem relating to voting procedures[234]; and

(h)   the grant of rights to indirect investors allowing them a greater role in company proceedings (CA 2006 Pt 9).

The Salz Review was of the opinion that the Barclays board should "design, adopt and publish from time to time a communications policy for promoting effective and open communication with shareholders and encouraging their participation in general meetings".[235] The review further added that in its shareholder reports, Barclays should provide:

> "complete, relevant, balanced, accessible and understandable information about the Group, its performance, risks and prospects, with an emphasis on the quality and candour of information rather than its quantity. In particular, its annual report should include not only information as to its financial performance but also a prominent report on the successes and challenges in fulfilling its stated purpose."[236]

The improvement of company communications with shareholders continues to remain high on the agenda of investor groups. In its corporate governance policy and voting guidelines published in January 2019, PLSA remarked that ensuring their messages are clearly understood by investors is a "crucial" means by which companies can achieve effective engagement with shareholders. In particular, the PLSA guidelines call for increased disclosure of relevant details relating to:

(a)   corporate culture and working practises;
(b)   succession planning, insofar as is feasible; and
(c)   the external board evaluation process, including, as far as is possible, the conclusions drawn from the evaluation and any subsequent actions taken.

2009/1632) to give more detailed disclosure requirements for "traded companies", where traded companies are companies traded on regulated markets in the EEA, including the UK.

[234] CA 2006 Explanatory Notes, para.342.

[235] Salz Review, *An Independent Review of Barclays' Business Practices* April 2012, p.119 Recommendation 15.

[236] Salz Review, *An Independent Review of Barclays' Business Practices* April 2012, p.119 Recommendation 15.

9.6.2 Exercise of members' rights by non-members

Investors increasingly hold their shares through an intermediary or a chain of intermediaries. The UK Government has accepted that there are advantages in this and that it is, in any event, sometimes a regulatory requirement. However, it is undoubtedly the case that such an approach does not facilitate shareholder engagement.

The CA 2006 contains a number of provisions which attempt to overcome the problems which this can cause. The Explanatory Notes to the CA 2006 (the Explanatory Notes) explain that these provisions have been designed to make it easier for investors to exercise their governance rights fully and responsibly.

The CA 2006 contains provisions which allow all companies whose articles enable them to do so to extend certain rights to persons nominated by the registered member, including rights in respect of resolutions and meetings and to appoint a proxy.[237] Typically, any such nomination is expected to be in favour of a beneficial holder of the shares, but the relevant section permits anyone to be nominated. However, only the member can enforce these rights and they do not affect the requirements for the transfer of a member's interest.

The CA 2006 also contains special provisions for nominations in respect of information rights in listed companies.[238] A registered member of such a company will have the right to nominate a person on whose behalf he holds shares to receive communications sent to members and to require copies of accounts and reports. The enjoyment of such information rights by the nominated person may be enforced against the company by the member as if they were rights conferred by the company's articles.

A company will have an opportunity to check annually whether nominated persons wish to retain their information rights. A company will have the right to terminate a nominated person's information rights, if the company asks the nominated person if he wishes to retain such rights and does not receive a response within 28 days. However, only one such enquiry can be made in any 12-month period.

The Secretary of State may, by regulation, amend the provisions in relation to information rights to extend or restrict the classes of companies to which such provisions apply, make other provision as to the circumstances in which a nomination may be made or extend or restrict the rights conferred by a nomination.[239]

---

[237] CA 2006 s.145.
[238] CA 2006 ss.146–150.
[239] CA 2006 s.151.

9.6.3 *Powers in relation to institutional investors*

Even before the Walker Review, the then Labour Government had long been concerned with ensuring greater engagement by institutional shareholders. Under the CA 2006 s.1277, the Secretary of State and the Treasury have the power to make regulations requiring institutional investors to disclose information about the way in which shares held by them in quoted companies have been voted.[240] Section 1280 provides that the regulations made by the Secretary of State or the Treasury may require the institutions to which the section applies to disclose detailed information on, for example, the exercise or non-exercise of voting rights and any instructions given or delegations made relating to their exercise or non-exercise.

So far, this power has not been exercised. There is already a voluntary framework on voting disclosure published by the ISC in June 2007 and designed to operate in conjunction with the ISC Statement of Principles which currently forms the Stewardship Code.[241] The voting framework works on a "comply or explain" basis, where institutions can decide against making their voting record publicly available so long as they explain why they have done so. At the time of introduction, the ISC noted that much had already been achieved in recent years in terms of the improvement in voting disclosure.

The provisions supply the Government with an alternative line of attack if the voluntary framework is seen to be failing. Therefore, in the event that the Stewardship Code is eventually abolished, use of the provisions would seem to become more likely. Nevertheless, these provisions proved very controversial when debated in the House of Lords, where issues were raised similar to those discussed in the FRC consultation on the Stewardship Code. One such point was that compulsory disclosure might lead to a compliance-orientated approach to voting, which might perversely result in a decline in the quality of engagement.

9.6.4 *Electronic communications*

For some companies—particularly those with large shareholder bases—the ability to communicate electronically with members and nominated persons can result in significant cost savings. The then-Labour Government also saw electronic communications as providing the opportunity to enhance the "immediacy and transparency of dialogue between companies and shareholders".[242]

---

[240] CA 2006 ss.1277–1280.
[241] ISC, *Institutional Shareholders' Committee Framework on Voting Disclosure* June 2007.
[242] BIS's Company Law Reform White Paper, March 2005, p.18.

Under the CA 2006,[243] a company may communicate by email with persons who have agreed to receive documents via email (or, in the case of communications with a company, if the company is deemed to have agreed to receive email communications by a provision in the companies legislation).

The CA 2006 provides that a company may communicate by means of a website with persons who have agreed, or are deemed to have agreed, to receive such communications. A member or nominated person will be deemed to have agreed to receive communications by means of a website if:

(a)   members of a company have resolved to approve the use of website communications or the articles of the company permit such communications; and

(b)   the company requests the member or nominated person to agree to receive website communications and does not receive an answer within 28 days.

A member or nominated person will not, however, be deemed to have agreed to accept such communications if the company's request does not explain clearly the consequences of failing to respond or the company seeks his or her agreement more than once in any 12-month period.

Where a member of a company has received information from the company otherwise than in hard-copy form, he is entitled to require the company to send him a version of the information in hard-copy form.

Electronic communications by quoted companies are also the subject of rules issued by the then FSA for the purpose of implementing the Transparency Directive—now the Disclosure Guidance and Transparency Rules. The rules provide that a decision to use electronic means to convey information (through either email or website) must be taken in a general meeting of the company.[244] The use of electronic means must not depend on the residence of the recipient.[245] It had been thought that this will restrict the use of such means to cases where local securities laws do not make it necessary to restrict distribution. However, the FSA indicated that it would not regard the principle of equality of treatment of shareholders as being breached merely because an issuer does not offer to communicate electronically with shareholders where legal restrictions in certain jurisdictions mean that this is not possible.[246] Furthermore, DTR 6.1.8 R(4) states that the written consent of direct shareholders or, in certain cases, indirect shareholders entitled to acquire, dispose of or otherwise exercise voting rights must be obtained to the use of electronic communications. Consent is deemed to have been obtained if no objection is received within a

---

[243] CA 2006 ss.1143–1148 and Schs 4 and 5.
[244] DTR 6.1.8 R(1).
[245] DTR 6.1.8 R(2).
[246] UKLA Publications, Disclosure and Transparency Note, 7 October 2010, p.34.

reasonable period of time.[247] However, DTR 6.1.8 R(4) does not apply where the issuer in question is a company within the meaning of the CA 2006, in which case the provisions of the CA 2006 Sch.5 in relation to electronic communications apply instead.[248] Issuers have been advised that the requirements of DTR 6 (insofar as they apply) should be interpreted in a manner consistent with the relevant provisions of the CA 2006.

9.6.5 *Auditors and accounts*

Reforms were introduced in the CA 2006 which were intended to allow limitation of auditors' liability, improve the quality of the audit process and simplify auditing and accounting procedures.

An auditor will be able to limit its liability in respect of the audit by agreement with the company. Agreements of this kind will be valid in respect of one financial year only and are subject to shareholder approval.[249]

The agreement may not limit the auditor's liability to less than the amount which is fair and reasonable in the circumstances, having regard to the auditor's responsibilities, its contractual obligations to the company and required professional standards. An agreement that purports to limit the auditor's liability to less than this amount takes effect as if it limited the auditor's liability to that amount. This provision allows the court to impose its view of what is fair and reasonable and thus involves a material element of uncertainty for auditors. The CA 2006 states that it is immaterial how a liability limitation agreement is framed; in particular, the limit on the amount of the auditor's liability need not be a sum of money, or a formula, specified in the agreement.

The debate over limitation of auditors' liability was one of the most highly publicised aspects of the CA 2006. The decision to allow auditors to limit their liability by contract was seen as balanced by the creation of a new criminal offence in relation to auditors' reports. This is committed where an auditor knowingly or recklessly causes its report on the company's annual accounts to include any matter that is materially misleading, false or deceptive.[250]

The provisions on the limitation of auditors' liability are broadly consistent with the European Commission recommendation published in 2008 on measures to limit the civil liability of auditors and audit firms carrying out statutory audits of companies registered and listed in European Member

---

[247] DTR 6.1.8 R(4)(a).
[248] In particular, see CA 2006 Sch.5 para.6 and paras 8–10.
[249] CA 2006 Pt 16 Ch.6.
[250] CA 2006 s.507.

States.[251] The position is less compatible with that of the SEC in the US, however, where the rules oppose firms entering into auditor liability limitation agreements. It is generally thought that companies which are dual-listed in the UK and US may not be able to enter into liability limitation agreements without breaching US regulations on auditor independence. The FRC guidance on auditor liability limitation agreements suggested that the FRC has had discussions with the SEC on the impact of its rules on UK SEC registrants, but the FRC has not yet provided further advice on this issue. The GC100 published an updated version of its guidance on the SEC rules in July 2009.[252]

CA 2006 provisions designed to improve the value and quality of the audit include:

(a)   a power to make rules to require companies to disclose the content of audit engagement letters (s.493);

(b)   a right for a specified proportion of shareholders in a quoted company to require website publication of matters relating to the audit, or about the auditors ceasing to hold office, which the shareholders propose to raise at the next meeting of shareholders (s.527);

(c)   a requirement that the auditor of a public interest company (a definition which includes issuers with transferable securities admitted to trading on a regulated market) must, on ceasing to hold office, send to the company a statement of its reasons for ceasing to hold office (s.519); and

(d)   a requirement that the "senior statutory auditor", who will be the individual identified by the audit firm (in accordance with EU guidelines or, in the absence of such guidelines, guidance issued by the Secretary of State), signs the auditor's report for and on behalf of the firm (ss.503 and 504).

As described more fully in Section 9.4.6, the audit market is likely to be subject to further significant change in the near future, as it faces both the introduction of a new, more empowered regulator in place of the FRC and potential attempts by the CMA to challenge the Big Four's dominance of the market for statutory audit services.

9.6.6   Strategic report

In October 2013, the requirement for companies to produce a business review as part of the directors' report pursuant to the CA 2006 s.417 was repealed and replaced with a duty to prepare a strategic report, set out at s.414A. The requirements in respect of the strategic report are set out at

---

[251] Commission of the European Communities, *Commission Recommendation concerning the limitation of the civil liability of statutory auditors and audit firms* 5 June 2008.
[252] GC100 Update Note: Auditors' Limitation of Liability Agreements: Draft Revised June 2009.

s.414B to s.414D. The CA 2006 states that the purpose of the strategic report is to inform members of the company and help them assess how the directors have performed their duty under s.172.[253] FRC guidance recommends that this aim is fulfilled by meeting five main content-related objectives, namely:

(a)   to provide insight into the entity's business model and its main strategy and objectives;
(b)   to describe the principal risks the entity faces and how they might affect its future prospects;
(c)   to provide relevant non-financial information;
(d)   to provide an analysis of the entity's past performance; and
(e)   to provide information to enable shareholders to assess how directors have had regard to stakeholders and other matters when performing their duty under the CA 2006 s.172.[254]

In terms of the requirements prescribed by the CA 2006 itself, s.414C states that the strategic report must contain a fair review of the company's business, a description of the principal risks and uncertainties facing the company, and, if applicable, the information required by s.414CZA, s.414CA, and s.414CB (which concern, respectively, the statements about s.172(1) and non-financial information to be given by the directors). According to FRC guidance, the requirement to describe the principal risks and uncertainties facing the company obliges disclosure of only those facts and circumstances that are (or should be) considered material to an understanding of the development, performance, position or future prospects of the business. As a result, the number of items disclosed will generally be relatively small, with no need to disclose all risks and uncertainties that may affect the company.[255] The principal risks and uncertainties that are disclosed in the strategic report should be sufficiently specifically described that shareholders are able to understand why exactly they are material to the company.[256]

The character of the review is further prescribed by s.414C(3), which states that the review should comprise a balanced and comprehensive analysis of the development and performance of the company's business during the financial year and the position of the company's business at the end of that financial year. The FRC has advised that in order to achieve the required balance, the report should address the positive and negative aspects of the entity's development, performance, position and prospects, ensuring shareholders are not misled as a result of information contained in or omitted from the strategic report.[257] The FRC also interprets the requirement of comprehensiveness as reflecting the breadth of information that

---

[253] CA 2006 s.414C(1).
[254] FRC, *Guidance on the Strategic Report* July 2018, p.16.
[255] FRC, *Guidance on the Strategic Report* July 2018, p.19.
[256] FRC, *Guidance on the Strategic Report* July 2018, p.30.
[257] FRC, *Guidance on the Strategic Report* July 2018, p.21.

should be included in the strategic report rather than the depth of information, meaning that it is not necessary for the strategic report to cover all possible matters in detail to be considered comprehensive.[258]

Where necessary to aid understanding of the company's development, performance or position, the strategic report should also include analysis with reference to financial key performance indicators, and, where appropriate, other key performance indicators, including those in respect of environmental and employee matters.[259] The FRC recommends that the key performance indicators used should be those the directors judge to be most effective in assessing progress against objectives or strategy, monitoring principal risks, or measuring the development, performance or position of the company.[260] Key performance indicators (both financial and non-financial) should be presented consistently over time to allow for year-on-year comparisons to be made.[261] Companies producing a non-financial information statement compliant with s.414CB(1)–(6) shall be treated as complying with the requirements in respect of other key performance indicators.[262] There is more detail on non-financial information statements below.

Additional requirements applicable only to quoted companies are set out at s.414C(7)–(8). Companies producing a non-financial information statement compliant with s.414CB(1)–(6) shall be treated as complying with the requirements of s.414C(7), other than insofar as that section requires the provision of information about community issues.[263] Where fully applicable, s.414C(7) requires the inclusion of:

(a)   the main trends and factors likely to affect the future development, performance and position of the company's business; and
(b)   information about environmental matters (including the impact of the company's business on the environment), the company's employees, and social, community and human rights issues,

including information about the policies the company has in place in relation to those matters, and the effectiveness of those policies. Such information must be provided to the extent necessary to give an understanding of the future development, performance or position of the company's business. Where any such information is not contained in the strategic report, the strategic report must state which kinds of information have been omitted. FRC guidance advises companies take a broad view when considering trends and factors germane to a businesses' performance, examining both internal and external trends. In respect of external trends,

---

[258] FRC, *Guidance on the Strategic Report* July 2018, p.21.
[259] CA 2006 s.414C(4).
[260] FRC, *Guidance on the Strategic Report* July 2018, p.35.
[261] FRC, *Guidance on the Strategic Report* July 2018, p.36.
[262] CA 2006 s.414CB(7)(a).
[263] CA 2006 s.414CB(7)(b).

the strategic report should analyse relevant developments taking place in society more generally, as well as those occurring in the company's chosen sector.[264] The FRC also provides guidance on how companies should consider information in relation to environmental matters, the company's employees and social, community and human rights issues.[265] Generally speaking, such information should not be considered in isolation, but should be integrated throughout the report. In particular, such information should be considered alongside discussion of the company's strategy and business model, principal risks and uncertainties, and key performance indicators. Furthermore, disclosures should not be limited to the matters and issues explicitly set out by the CA 2006. Rather, an entity should consider which other resources and relationships are necessary for an understanding of the development, performance or position of its business. This could potentially include relationships with suppliers and pension schemes.[266]

Quoted companies are also required by s.414C(8) to include the following information in their strategic reports (though companies producing a non-financial information statement compliant with s.414CB(1)–(6) shall be treated as complying with the requirement to produce a description of their business model)[267]:

(a)   a description of the company's strategy;
(b)   a description of the company's business model; and
(c)   a breakdown showing at the end of the financial year, the number of persons of each sex who were directors, senior managers, and employees of the company.

When describing their strategies and business models as required, companies should have regard to Provision 1 of the Governance Code, which states that companies "should describe in the annual report how opportunities and risks to the future success of the business have been considered and addressed, the sustainability of the company's business model and how its governance contributes to the delivery of its strategy" in order to satisfy the requirements of both the Governance Code and the CA 2006 with as few as possible disclosures. The FRC advises that the description of the entity's business model should also "explain how it generates and preserves value over the longer term" and demonstrate how the business model described is "consistent with the entity's purpose".[268] To that end, the description of the company's strategy should disclose the objectives the company seeks to use that strategy to meet.[269]

---

[264] FRC, *Guidance on the Strategic Report* July 2018, p.28.
[265] See FRC, *Guidance on the Strategic Report*, July 2018 para.7A.42.
[266] FRC, *Guidance on the Strategic Report* July 2018, p.32.
[267] CA 2006 s.414CB(7)(c).
[268] FRC, *Guidance on the Strategic Report* July 2018, p.27.
[269] FRC, *Guidance on the Strategic Report* July 2018, p.26.

In satisfying the requirements of s.414C there is no requirement to disclose any information about impending developments or matters in the course of negotiation if such a disclosure would, in the opinion of the directors, be seriously prejudicial to the interests of the company.[270]

The requirement to include a non-financial information statement in the strategic report is applicable to (amongst other types of company) large traded companies with more than 500 employees (or, if the traded company is a parent company, where the group which that traded company heads has more than 500 employees).[271]

The content requirements for the non-financial information statement are contained in s.414CB. This provision requires the non-financial information statement to contain, at minimum, information relating to:

(a) environmental matters (including the impact of the company's business on the environment);
(b) the company's employees;
(c) social matters;
(d) respect for human rights; and
(e) anti-corruption and anti-bribery matters.

Such information must be provided to the extent necessary for an understanding of the company's development, performance and position and the impact of its activity. The FRC has provided guidance on the questions companies should consider in relation to each of the disclosures required here.[272] Broadly speaking, the FRC encourages companies to consider both how their activities impact stakeholders and society and how they themselves are impacted by stakeholders and society, in particular where such impacts could affect the long-term success of the company.[273]

Companies subject to the requirement to produce a non-financial information statement must also include the following information in that statement:

(a) a brief description of the company's business model;
(b) a description of the policies pursued by the company in relation to the matters mentioned at (a)–(e) above and any due diligence processes implemented by the company in pursuance of those policies;
(c) a description of the outcome of those policies;
(d) a description of the principal risks relating to the matters mentioned at (a)–(e) above arising in connection with the company's operations and, where relevant and proportionate, a description of its business

---

[270] CA 2006 s.414C(14).
[271] CA 2006 s.414CA.
[272] See FRC, *Guidance on the Strategic Report* July 2018, p.48.
[273] See FRC, *Guidance on the Strategic Report* July 2018, p.48.

relationships, products and services which are likely to cause adverse impacts in those areas of risk, and a description of how it manages the principal risks; and

(e)   a description of the non-financial key performance indicators relevant to the company's business.

The FRC advises that the description of each policy should be clear, concise and proportionate to the risks posed and be accompanied by a description of any due diligence processes that a company has in place to ensure that the policies described are adhered to throughout the group.[274] In the event the company does not pursue a policy in relation to any of the matters in relation to which it is obliged to describe its policies, it must provide a clear and reasoned explanation for not doing so.[275] The FRC counsels that the board should undertake a broad consideration of potential risks in order to fulfil its obligation here, having regard to risks that are both financial and non-financial in nature, and risks resulting from factors both within and beyond the board's control. It is necessary to consider both risks posed to the company and risks that the company's activities pose to wider society. Disclosure is only necessary where risks are identified as material to the development, performance, position or future prospects of the company or where the company's activity poses a significant risk externally.[276]

By way of example of potentially relevant non-financial key performance indicators, the FRC cites measures related to product quality, customer complaints, environmental matters or employee metrics. Companies should also consider disclosing key performance indicators that measure the external impact of a businesses' activities.[277]

It is important to note that the content requirements of the non-financial information statement do not require the disclosure of information concerning impending developments or matters in the course of negotiation which, in the opinion of the directors, would be seriously prejudicial to the commercial interests of the company if disclosed. This is provided that such non-disclosure would not prevent a fair and balanced understanding of the company's development, performance or position, or the impact of the company's activity.[278]

Both s.414C(12) (in relation to the strategic report generally) and s.414CB(5) (in relation to the non-financial information statement, where such statement must be provided) require the inclusion, where appropriate, of references to and additional explanations of amounts included in the company's annual accounts. Where a company produces a non-financial information statement compliant with s.414CB(1)–(6) it shall be treated as

---

[274] See FRC, *Guidance on the Strategic Report* July 2018, p.49.
[275] CA 2006 s.414CB(4).
[276] See FRC, *Guidance on the Strategic Report* July 2018, p.44.
[277] FRC, *Guidance on the Strategic Report* July 2018, p.52.
[278] CA 2006 s.414CB(9).

complying with s.414C(12) insofar as s.414C(12) relates to those other provisions of s.414C that a company producing such a non-financial information statement shall be treated as complying with.[279]

As explained elsewhere, large companies must include a statement in their strategic report describing how the directors have had regard to the matters set out in s.172(1)(a)–(f) when performing their duty under s.172.[280]

9.6.7 Codification of directors' duties

The CA 2006 codified directors' duties with a view to reflecting in statute the current common law position, but with some significant changes.

The CA 2006 provides that directors owe the following duties[281]:

(a) to act in accordance with the company's constitution and for proper purposes;
(b) to promote the success of the company;
(c) to exercise independent judgment;
(d) to use reasonable care, skill and diligence;
(e) to avoid conflicts of interest;
(f) not to accept benefits from third parties; and
(g) to declare interests in proposed transactions or arrangements.

Whilst the detail of these duties is outside the scope of this Chapter, certain of the changes are relevant in this context.

9.6.8 Duty to promote the success of the company

This duty requires a director to act in the way he "considers, in good faith, would be most likely to promote the success of the company for the benefit of its members as a whole".[282] In fulfilling this duty, a director is required to have regard (amongst other matters) to:

(a) the likely long term consequences of any decision;
(b) the interests of the company's employees;
(c) the need to foster the company's business relationships with suppliers, customers and others;
(d) the impact of the company's operations on the community and the environment;

---

[279] Namely CA 2006 s.414C(4)(b), s.414C(7) (except as it relates to community issues), and s.414C(8)(b).
[280] CA 2006 s.414CZA.
[281] CA 2006 ss.171–177 (both inclusive).
[282] This is subject to the directors' duty to consider or act in the interests of creditors in certain circumstances. See CA 2006 s.172(3).

(e)   the desirability of the company maintaining a reputation for high standards of business conduct; and

(f)   the need to act fairly as between members of the company.

The list is not exhaustive but it is intended that it:

> "highlights areas of particular importance which reflect wider expectations of responsible behaviour, such as the interests of the company's employees and the impact of the company's operations on the community and the environment."[283]

9.6.9   The meaning of "success"

The Government stated that, for most companies, "success" is defined in commercial terms. In a debate in the House of Lords, the Attorney-General said the following:

> "... What is success? The starting point is that it is essentially for the members of the company to define the objectives that they wish to achieve. Success means what the members collectively want the company to achieve. For a commercial company, success will usually mean long-term increase in value. For certain companies, such as charities and community interest companies, it will mean the attainment of the objectives for which the company has been established.[284] But one can be more refined than that. A company's constitution and the decisions that a company makes can also go on to be more specific about what is the appropriate success model for the company. I have indicated that usually for a company it will be a long-term increase in value, but I can imagine commercial companies that would have a different objective as to their success."

9.6.10   "Enlightened shareholder value"

One of the main questions raised at the beginning of the Company Law Review process was whether directors' duties should continue to be owed solely to the company, except in limited cases, or whether directors should be required as a matter of law to account directly to third parties, e.g. employees, suppliers and local communities. The conclusion was that the existing position should remain: the CA 2006 provides that a director's duties are owed to the company rather than third parties.

However, the 1997–2010 Labour Government favoured an approach known as "enlightened shareholder value". This requires a director to have regard to the interests of third parties in fulfilling his or her duties to the company. This approach is reflected in the statutory duty to promote the success of

---

[283] CA 2006 Explanatory Notes para.326.
[284] See CA 2006 s.172(2).

the company in CA 2006 s.172. When fulfilling this duty, a director must have regard, among other things, to the interests of employees and the various other factors set out above.

The 1997–2010 Labour Government's desire to introduce this list of factors as matters to which directors must have regard caused considerable debate. The Government maintained consistently that directors will need to do more than pay "lip-service" to each of these factors when making decisions: directors will be required to give due and proper consideration to them. Indeed the Explanatory Notes state that the duty to exercise reasonable care, skill and diligence in CA 2006 s.174 will apply. The Explanatory Notes emphasise that:

> "It will not be sufficient to pay lip service to the factors and in many cases the directors will need to take action to comply with this as part of the duty [in s.172]."[285]

Critics expressed particular concern that this would make decision-making more onerous. Further, critics claimed that these factors would increase the likelihood of directors' actions being challenged in the courts and would lead to greater judicial interference in business decisions particularly given the new statutory provisions relating to derivative claims. There was, therefore, concern that the increased risk of litigation will make directors more risk-averse.

Those in favour of the introduction of these factors, however, claimed that the risks which they pose to directors were exaggerated. They argued, first, that the director's basic duty remains a subjective one: the director must act in the way he considers, in good faith, would promote the success of the company. Further, a director is only obliged to have regard to the factors listed above; a director is not required actively to promote the interests of the environment, the community and so forth.

The Explanatory Notes provide some support for this view, stating that:

> "The decision as to what will promote the success of the company, and what constitutes such success, is one for the directors' good faith judgment. This ensures that business decisions on, for example, strategy and tactics are for the directors, and not subject to decision by the courts, subject to good faith,"

and (having noted the duty to exercise reasonable care, skill and diligence in this context) go on to state that:

> "At the same time the duty does not require a director to do more than good faith and the duty to exercise reasonable care, skill and diligence would require, nor would it be possible for a director acting in good faith to be held

---

[285] CA 2006 Explanatory Notes para.328.

liable for a process failure which would not have affected his decision as to which course of action would best promote the success of the Company."[286]

Southern Counties Fresh Foods Ltd, Re[287] confirmed that the test under (at least the first limb of) s.172(1) remains subjective in nature (that is, one looks at whether the director honestly believed that he acted in a way most likely to promote the company's success). This mirrors the pre-2006 Act position as set out in *Smith & Fawcett, Re.*[288] It should not be taken to mean that directors' decisions are immune from challenge.

There were fears that there would be an increase in the amount of litigation faced by directors from activist shareholders seeking to test the courts' approach to these factors. One particular source of concern was that shareholders would be able to commence derivative actions using the new statutory provisions.[289] The CA 2006 put the old common law right to bring a derivative action on a statutory footing while removing some of the barriers that had previously made bringing a derivative action difficult for shareholders, such as the necessity to show that directors had personally benefited from the alleged wrongdoing. Derivative actions are brought by shareholders on behalf of the company for wrongs committed by directors in breach of their duties. As directors' duties are now codified, it was thought that this would also make derivative actions easier, while the obligation to have regard to third parties such as employees and the community might increase the range of potential causes of action. At the same time, the Government hoped that the drafting of the CA 2006 on derivative action would encourage greater shareholder activism.

Fears that the floodgates of litigation would be opened to activist shareholders have so far proved ill-founded and there have been relatively few cases to date. This is partly to do with the procedure by which a shareholder must bring a derivative action. Shareholders must first get the permission of the court to bring a claim. Courts have so far been very restrictive in the way they have applied their own tests for allowing a derivative action.[290] One factor courts consider is whether a person acting in accordance with the director's duty to promote the success of the company would not seek to continue the claim. It is often hard to prove the action in question is in the interests of the company. Further, members may be dissuaded by the costs of losing an action to a company able to run up far greater legal expenses, especially since the benefit gained from a successful claim will go to the company rather than directly to shareholders. Success

---

[286] CA 2006 Explanatory Notes paras 327 and 328.
[287] *Southern Counties Fresh Foods Ltd, Re* [2008] EWHC 2810 (Ch).
[288] *Smith & Fawcett, Re* [1942] Ch. 304; [1942] 1 All E.R. 542.
[289] See CA 2006 Pt 11.
[290] Cases where permission has been refused include: *Mission Capital Plc v Sinclair* [2008] EWHC 1339 (Ch); [2008] B.C.C. 866; *Franbar Holdings Ltd v Patel* [2008] EWHC 1534 (Ch); [2009] 1 B.C.L.C. 1; *Stimpson v Southern Landlords Assoc* [2009] EWHC 2072 (Ch); [2010] B.C.C. 387; and *Kleanthos v Paphitis* [2011] EWHC 2287 (Ch); [2012] B.C.C. 676; (2011) 108(36) L.S.G. 19.

may be more likely under a contractual claim for a breach of the terms of any shareholder's agreement. Shareholders may also prefer to pursue their interests directly through an unfair prejudice petition.

When the CA 2006 first came into force, there were also concerns that directors' greater exposure to liability would increase bureaucracy and discourage risk-taking. There is no evidence to suggest that the CA 2006 has had this effect. The CA 2006 may have encouraged directors to record the reasons for their decisions and consider their duties more fully than before, but compliance with the legislation is unlikely materially to have increased bureaucracy in a well-managed company. Further, the directors' duties are largely a codification of what already existed in common law, and as such have not made directors any more risk-averse than they were before the introduction of the CA 2006.[291]

9.6.11 Changes to the CA 2006 introduced by the Shareholder Rights Directive

The Shareholder Rights Directive (the Directive) was implemented in the UK on 3 August 2009 by the Companies (Shareholders' Rights) Regulations 2009 (the Regulations).[292] The Directive hoped to improve shareholder participation by enabling shareholders to exercise their voting rights and rights to information more easily. It was also anticipated that its implementation across Europe would solve some of the problems associated with cross-border voting. The CA 2006 was already relatively advanced in terms of the rights given to shareholders. Rather than bring in new legislation, it was felt that the best response would be to introduce the parts of the Regulations that added weight to the CA 2006 in certain respects. ICSA has published guidance on the implications of the changes made to the CA 2006 in practice.[293]

Some changes to the CA 2006 apply to all companies, others to those traded on regulated markets in the EEA, including the UK (traded companies).[294] Draft legislation in relation to the UK leaving the EU proposes altering the definition of "traded company" to encompass companies who are admitted to trading on either UK or EU regulated markets. The LSE Main Market is a regulated market, but AIM is not.

The Shareholder Rights Directive was amended in 2017, with the primary intention of making it easier for companies to identify their shareholders.

---

[291] Directors may wish to refer for guidance to GC100, *Companies Act (2006)—Directors' Duties* 7 February 2007, GC100, *Companies Act 2006—Directors' Conflicts of Interest* 18 January 2008, and GC100, *Guidance on Directors' Duties: Section 172 and Stakeholder Considerations* 22 October 2018.

[292] Companies (Shareholders' Rights) Regulations 2009 (SI 2009/1632).

[293] ICSA Guidance on the Implementation of the Shareholder Rights Directive 29 July 2009.

[294] CA 2006 s.360C.

Section 9.5.2 contains further details about these amendments, including information concerning the proposed implementation of such amendments in the UK.

9.6.11.1 *Voting*

Under the CA 2006 as amended, a proxy has the powers to vote twice in the same meeting if representing more than one member.[295] This enables a proxy to implement conflicting voting instructions from two or more shareholders. If a proxy is appointed by several members with instructions to vote the same way, the proxy is entitled to vote only once, "for" or "against" as applicable. Where, however, one or more of the members instructs him to vote "for" and one or more member instructs him to vote "against", the proxy is then entitled to vote twice, both "for" and "against." This is the only stated exception to the general rule that a proxy only has one vote on a show of hands.

The Directive clarifies the position where a member appoints more than one proxy in respect of different shares within the same shareholding. In this case, each appointed proxy has one vote on a show of hands. This enables nominee shareholders to appoint the underlying beneficial owners as proxies in respect of those shares in which they have an interest. The Directive also puts on a statutory footing the common law position that a proxy is required to vote in accordance with any voting directions provided by the appointing shareholder.[296] This introduces an extra statutory duty for the proxy in addition to his common law duty as agent. If it is found that a proxy has not voted in accordance with instructions, this will not invalidate the results of the meeting.

The Directive also permits companies to offer advance voting on a poll.[297] This is to enable members to cast a vote in advance of a meeting, separate to their rights to appoint a proxy. The provision was primarily designed for European Member States with no proxy systems or more restrictive proxy practices. It should be noted that this is a permissive provision, so companies are not required to offer advance voting, but may do so through amending their articles if they wish.

9.6.11.2 *Notice of meetings*

The old CA 2006 distinction between the minimum requirements of 14 days' notice for a general meeting and 21 days' for an AGM was modified slightly by the Directive. Under the Directive, there is a general requirement that the notice period for all meetings of traded companies should be at least 21

---

[295] CA 2006 s.285(2).
[296] CA 2006 s.324A.
[297] Incorporated into the CA 2006 in s.322A.

days.[298] This is subject to an exception, however. A general meeting of a traded company (as opposed to an AGM) may be called on 14 days' notice so long as a special resolution has been passed at a previous meeting to that effect, and so long as the company offers the facility to allow shareholders to vote by electronic means. This will be met if the company offers the facility to shareholders to appoint a proxy by means of a website.

While the wording of this provision in the CA 2006 affords flexibility to a company to call a meeting at 14 days' notice, voting guidelines issued by Institutional Shareholder Services (ISS) provide that the authority to hold a general meeting on 14 days' notice (which is now typically sought by companies at their AGMs) should only be used in limited and time-sensitive circumstances where its use would clearly be to the advantage of shareholders as a whole. To that end, companies should provide assurance that the shorter notice period will only be used when merited. Should companies call short-notice general meetings inappropriately, ISS warns that it may recommend against renewing the authority at subsequent meetings.[299]

There is also a requirement that the matters set out in the notice for a meeting must be made available on a traded company's website.[300] There are also additional content requirements for notices of meetings. Traded companies must include the voting record date, the procedure on how to attend and vote and a statement of the member's right to ask questions (for more on which, see below), amongst other things.[301]

9.6.11.3 Shareholders' rights to call meetings, have questions answered and add agenda items

While the original provisions of the CA 2006 allowed members of public companies to require directors to call a general meeting so long as they had the support of 10% of the voting share capital of the company, the Directive has reduced this threshold to 5%.[302]

The Directive also introduced a general right that shareholders must have their questions answered at general meetings. This was possibly the Directive's biggest statement of intent in relation to shareholder empowerment. Consequently the CA 2006, as amended, states that at a general meeting of a traded company, the company must cause to be answered any question relating to the business being dealt with at the meeting put by a member attending the meeting.[303]

---

[298] CA 2006 s.307A.
[299] ISS, *United Kingdom and Ireland Proxy Voting Guidelines: Benchmark Policy Recommendations* 6 December 2018, p.26.
[300] CA 2006 s.311A(1)(a).
[301] CA 2006 s.311.
[302] CA 2006 s.303.
[303] CA 2006 s.319A.

This general principle that all questions should be answered is not without its drawbacks, however. If every question were to be answered it would add extra time and cost to meetings which could jeopardise the company's interests or simply result in meetings becoming side-tracked. For this reason, exceptions to this general principle have been introduced and the CA 2006 provides that no answer needs to be given if it is undesirable in the interests of the company or the good order of the meeting.[304] Further no answer need be given if to do so interferes unduly with the preparation of the meeting, involves the disclosure of confidential information, or if the answer has already been given on a website in the form of an answer to a question.[305]

Shareholders also have a right to require traded companies to add items to their AGM agendas.[306] This is in addition to rights under the CA 2006 to require the circulation of statements and resolutions.[307] The rules are the same as for requisitioned resolutions. Shareholders must have 5% of total voting rights or 100 members entitled to vote, with an average of at least £100 paid-up share capital per member. The request must be received no later than six weeks before the meeting or, if later, the time notice is given. The company must bear the cost of circulating the details of such agenda items if the request is received before the end of the financial year preceding the AGM.[308] As in the case of requisitioned resolutions, a company can refuse to include a matter in the AGM business if it is defamatory of any person, or frivolous or vexatious.[309]

Finally, amendments to the CA 2006 have removed the chairman's casting vote. The chairman will no longer be able to make the ultimate decision if there are equal votes on an ordinary resolution at a general meeting. Any provision giving the chairman a casting vote in a general meeting in a company's articles will be void.

9.7 Further power to legislate

The UK Government took various powers to introduce further changes to companies legislation using subordinate legislation. Of particular relevance to corporate governance, the Government provided the FSA with the power for the UK Listing Authority (UKLA) to make corporate governance rules relating to issuers whose securities have been admitted to a regulated market in order to take account of the UK's Community obligations.[310] Draft legislation (in connection with the UK's planned exit from the EU)

---

[304] CA 2006 s.319A(2)(c).
[305] CA 2006 s.319A(2)(a) and (b).
[306] CA 2006 ss.338A and 340A.
[307] CA 2006 ss.338, 339 and 340.
[308] CA 2006 s.340B.
[309] CA 2006 s.338A(2).
[310] FSMA s.89O.

currently proposes amending this power so that it simply allows the FCA to make corporate governance rules in respect of issuers whose securities have been admitted to trading on a regulated market. In addition, the Government took a similar power to make regulations for such issuers, for the purposes of implementing or dealing with corporate governance matters arising out of or related to EU obligations. These regulations may be made by reference to any specified code on corporate governance—which might include the Governance Code—and create new criminal offences punishable by a fine.[311] Draft legislation (also in connection with the UK's planned exit from the EU) proposes repealing this power.

9.8 Governance of large private companies

Traditionally, efforts to improve corporate governance have focused on listed companies, with large privately-held companies given much freer rein to determine their own governance arrangements. BEIS' Green Paper on corporate governance reform reflects that the reason for this divergent treatment historically has been the perception that since "the owners of privately-held businesses do not need the same levels of reassurance and information as owners of public companies because ownership and control are usually closely intertwined", the mandatory application of stringent governance regimes to large private companies is inappropriate.[312]

Nevertheless, high profile instances of failure by large private companies, along with an increasingly widely-held conviction that good governance should not simply be pre-occupied by regulating the relationship between a company's shareholders and the board, but should also focus on how the board serves other stakeholders with a "strong interest in whether a business is well run"[313] has created a momentum in favour of greater prescription of governance requirements for large private companies.

Additionally, there has been recognition that the conduct of certain large private companies risks undermining the public's trust in business generally. Recent years have seen the much publicised collapse of BHS, with its attendant adverse implications for members of the BHS pension scheme, and a parliamentary inquiry criticising Sports Direct for the working practices to which its employees were subject. Given that private companies constitute a substantial and expanding part of the British economy as "increasing numbers of large businesses"[314] choose to operate as private businesses, the imperative to ensure high governance standards among large privately-held companies has become all the more acute.

---

[311] CA 2006 s.1273.
[312] BEIS Green Paper, *Corporate Governance Reform* November 2016, p.43.
[313] BEIS Green Paper, *Corporate Governance Reform* November 2016, p.43.
[314] BEIS Green Paper, *Corporate Governance Reform* November 2016, p.44.

In its November 2016 Green Paper on corporate governance reform, BEIS included a section exploring whether and to what extent the UK's largest privately-held businesses should meet higher minimum corporate governance and reporting standards. The paper considers the adoption of a bespoke governance code for unlisted companies by the largest privately held businesses on a voluntary basis, as well as the possibility of applying certain reporting requirements to all companies above a certain size irrespective of whether the company is listed or not. The Government's August 2017 response to that Green Paper encouraged the development of a set of corporate governance principles suitable for large private companies, to which large private companies could voluntarily adhere.

Consequently, a coalition established by the FRC and chaired by Sir James Wates developed the Wates Corporate Governance Principles for Large Private Companies, the final version of which was published in December 2018. The Wates Principles are consciously flexible and high-level, in order that they will be of use to both private companies large enough to be statutorily obliged to report on their corporate governance arrangements and smaller private companies.[315] Companies voluntarily adhering to the Wates Principles should do so on an "apply and explain basis", where they explain how each Wates Principle is specifically applicable to their own organisation and then detail how their own governance arrangements address the Wates Principle in question. Unlike the Governance Code, the Wates Principles are not supplemented by additional provisions which an entity must either comply with or explain its non-compliance. Instead, each Wates Principle is accompanied by supporting guidance to assist companies in explaining their approach to applying each Wates Principle.[316] It is hoped that this approach will lead to good governance practices in large private companies being substantively developed, as opposed to simply encouraging box-ticking.[317]

The six Wates Principles are as follows:

(a)   Purpose and Leadership: An effective board develops and promotes the purpose of a company, and ensures that its values, strategy and culture align with that purpose.

(b)   Board and Composition: Effective board composition requires an effective chair and a balance of skills, backgrounds, experience and knowledge, with individual directors having sufficient capacity to make a valuable contribution. The size of a board should be guided by the scale and complexity of the company.

---

[315] FRC, *The Wates Corporate Governance Principles for Large Private Companies* December 2018, p.1.
[316] FRC, *The Wates Corporate Governance Principles for Large Private Companies* December 2018, p.8.
[317] FRC, *The Wates Corporate Governance Principles for Large Private Companies* December 2018, p.1.

(c) Director Responsibilities: The board and individual directors should have a clear understanding of their accountability and responsibilities. The board's policies and procedures should support effective decision-making and independent challenge.

(d) Opportunity and Risk: A board should promote the long-term sustainable success of the company by identifying opportunities to create and preserve value, and establishing oversight for the identification and mitigation of risks.

(e) Remuneration: A board should promote executive remuneration structures aligned to the long-term sustainable success of a company, taking into account pay and conditions elsewhere in the company.

(f) Stakeholder Relationships and Engagement: Directors should foster effective stakeholder relationships aligned to the company's purpose. The board is responsible for overseeing meaningful engagement with stakeholders, including the workforce, and having regard to their views when taking decisions.

The introduction of the Wates Principles deliberately coincides with the introduction by secondary legislation of a requirement for large private companies to make a "statement of corporate governance arrangements" in their directors' reports. In relation to financial years beginning on or after 1 January 2019 companies subject to the requirement must state:

(a) which corporate governance code, if any, the company applied in the financial year;

(b) how the company applied any corporate governance code it reports applying; and

(c) if the company departed from the corporate governance code it reports applying, the respects in which it did so, and its reasons for so departing.

If the company has not applied any corporate governance code for the financial year, the statement of corporate governance arrangements must explain the reasons for that decision, and explain what arrangements for corporate governance were applied for that year.[318] The Wates Principles may be used as the corporate governance code large private companies report in respect of in their statements of corporate governance arrangements. The extent to which the Wates Principles are adopted by large private companies as a framework for their corporate governance arrangements will become apparent in 2020, when reporting on financial years beginning on or after 1 January 2019 will commence.

The requirement to make a statement of corporate governance arrangements is applicable to companies that satisfy either or both of the following

---

[318] Large and Medium-sized Companies and Groups (Accounts and Reports) Regulations 2008 (SI 2008/410) Sch.7 Pt 8 para.26, as amended by the Companies (Miscellaneous Reporting) Regulations 2018 (SI 2018/860).

conditions (though companies already subject to the requirement to make a corporate governance statement under DTR 7.2 are exempted from this particular requirement)[319]:

(a)   it has more than 2000 employees; or
(b)   it has a turnover of more than £200 million and a balance sheet total of more than £2 billion.[320]

The ICAEW has been critical of both the content of the Wates Principles and the lack of an enforcement body to ensure that large private companies are abiding by their chosen governance code to the extent they claim to be in their statements of corporate governance. In the absence of organisations like the IA actively providing oversight of the governance practices adopted by large private companies this would seem to be problematic. Such a role could be performed indirectly by ratings agencies or potentially by any successor organisation to the FRC.

---

[319] Large and Medium-sized Companies and Groups (Accounts and Reports) Regulations 2008 (SI 2008/410) Sch.7 Pt 8 para.22, as amended by the Companies (Miscellaneous Reporting) Regulations 2018 (SI 2018/860).
[320] Large and Medium-sized Companies and Groups (Accounts and Reports) Regulations 2008 (SI 2008/410) Sch.7 Pt 8 para.23, as amended by the Companies (Miscellaneous Reporting) Regulations 2018 (SI 2018/860).

Chapter 10

Directors Facing Disputes

Michael Hatchard, Retired Partner

Skadden, Arps, Slate, Meagher & Flom (UK) LLP

Michael Todd QC

Erskine Chambers

This Chapter is divided into two parts. Section 10.1 covers disputes within the board of a company. Sections 10.2–10.4 cover disputes between the board and members of the company. Chapters 12 and 13 address regulatory investigation and disqualification of directors. The notion that a non-executive directorship is a comfortable retirement berth may readily be dispelled. Whilst it may have been thought that the problem was the introduction into statute law of codified directors' duties, there have been more fundamental causes for any discomfort that exists.

There can be no doubt that the introduction of the "new" statutory duties in the Companies Act 2006 had the potential for disquiet. The value of the introduction of those duties has been viewed by legislators and directors from opposite ends of the telescope.

So far as the legislature was concerned, and however inelegantly they may have done so, they were seeking to inform, and to clarify for directors the scope of their responsibilities, so as to enable them to better fulfil their duties.

But from the directors' perspective, to replace reasonably well understood common law and fiduciary duties with newly articulated statutory "general duties", and then to legislate that "the general duties shall be interpreted and applied in the same way as the common law rules or equitable principles, and regard shall be had to the corresponding common law rules and equitable principles in interpreting and applying the general duties", if not an exercise in obfuscation, had the potential for confusion and, potentially, disaster.

However, it is not the introduction of these statutory duties which has given rise to the increased volume of disputes; it is accountability and shareholder activism. The two go hand in hand. A perceived lack of accountability leads inexorably to increased activism. And the activist now has a range of tools at its disposal, to redress the perceived wrongs; wrongs, that is, to the company of which it is a shareholder and to the shareholder itself or as a member of a class.

10.1 Disputes within the board

The performance of a board of directors reflects the sum of its parts. Individuals differ in their backgrounds, opinions and objectives. Diversity is a strength, but members of a board can sometimes find themselves at odds with others.

In practice, a board may continue running a company for years without rigid formality. However, the absence of a good record will weaken the ability of the board to defend its conduct. Differences may be resolved through compromise. This Section addresses situations where compromise fails and irreconcilable positions are taken, first from the standpoint of the majority and then the minority. It also addresses the position where the board is deadlocked.

10.1.1 Majority standpoint

Disagreement leading to a split majority board decision is not generally fatal in the absence of special constitutional voting provision. However, where relations have become contentious, the controlling majority might seek to exclude an objectionable director from day to day management or restrict the flow of company information. However, any attempt to do so, particularly in circumstances in which that director is an appointee of an activist shareholder, or even in a joint venture company in which there is, at least, an expectation of management participation, may result in litigation.

10.1.1.1 Exclusion from proceedings and information

While the day to day operations of a company happen outside the board room, the strategy of the board for the promotion of the success of the company, and thus the framework within which the directors will conduct that day to day business, will usually be determined by the board. Should any further decision of the board be required, each director has the right:

(a) to be notified of a proposed board meeting in sufficient time to attend (or the meeting may be invalid); and
(b) to attend board meetings.

This right of attendance is fundamental, given the responsibilities associated with the office of director, and has proved to be enforceable by injunction.[1]

The procedures for notification of board meetings are commonly provided in the articles of association and may be supplemented by practices generally observed by the company. Where relations are strained, reliance on formality with the aim of side-lining a particular director, for example not using readily available means of communication,[2] would be open to attack if it can be shown that a reasonable effort to give notice was not made with material consequences for the excluded director. Similarly, failing to supply information necessary to allow the directors to perform their functions breaches an entitlement that lasts while the director is in office. A court is likely to order inspection rights, if there is no reason to suppose the director is likely to be removed from office, unless it is satisfied that the director's intention is to abuse confidence and materially injure the company[3] or the purpose of inspection is improper.[4]

Delegation of particular functions to committees or officers may operate in practice to limit participation. Such a power of delegation may legitimately be used, for example, to exclude a director against whom the company has a claim from participation in any consideration of the merits of such a claim. However, the power to delegate is a fiduciary power that may not be improperly used to exclude, for no good reason, a director from decision making and information flows. An over-riding consideration in the case of a director shareholder is the potential to invoke s.994[5] (see Section 10.4.1.7(a) below).

10.1.1.2 Removal of directors

The articles can include procedures to remove a director, for example by conferring a power of removal on a specified majority of the directors. In

---

[1] *Hayes v Bristol Plant Hire Ltd* [1957] 1 W.L.R. 499; [1957] 1 All E.R. 685. A director has a sufficient proprietary interest to maintain an action for the injunction. The underlying conclusion is founded on a judgment of Sir George Jessel MR that itself relied on an assumption that the relevant articles gave a right to attend meetings that must be upheld. See also *Pulbrook v Richmond Consolidated Mining Co* (1878) 9 Ch. D. 610.

[2] *Mitropoulos v Greek Orthodox Church and Community of Marrickville & District Ltd* (1993) 10 A.C.S.R. 134.

[3] *Official Receiver v Watson* [2008] EWHC 64 (Ch); [2008] B.C.C. 497; [2008] All E.R. (D) 188 at 181. *Conway v Petronius* [1978] 2 W.L.R. 72: refusal of an immediate order for inspection in circumstances where the relevant director might be removed from office by resolution in general meeting, absent evidence that intervention was necessary for the protection of the company or the protection of the director. The risk of improper use of materials is also a factor to weigh in the balance of convenience assessment of the court when considering relief. Section 388 refers to the right of inspection of accounting records by the company's officers in similar terms to Companies Act 1948 s.147 considered in *Conway v Petronius*.

[4] *Oxford Legal Group Ltd v Sibbasbridge Services Plc* [2008] EWCA 387; B.C.C. 558.

[5] In this Chapter, all section references are to the Companies Act 2006 unless otherwise stated.

the absence of such a power, the board has no inherent right to remove a director from office (as distinct from termination of employment or curtailment of delegated authority). Without special provision in the articles, the directors are removable only by some action on the part of the members. This can be achieved either:

(a)   by exercise of a power conferred by or introduced into the articles; or
(b)   through use of the absolute right to remove a director pursuant to s.168.

Before starting the process to remove a director, an assessment should be undertaken to confirm whether he is already disqualified from holding office or whether there was any procedural defect in his appointment. The various bases of disqualification are reviewed in Chapter 2, Section 2.6.

It is also of prime importance to consider whether there were any special terms of office conferred at the time of appointment and any implications of removal that need to be managed. Assess, for example, whether the board can function effectively without the relevant director, for instance as a result of quorum requirements or contractual commitments dictating board procedure. Review whether the relevant director exercises any delegated authority that must be cancelled. Determine whether removal of the director will trigger any breach of commitment and, if so, whether the rights of appointment are contractual or class rights.[6] The financial implications, especially in the case of executive directors or where breach of a contractual commitment will result from removal, will also need to be anticipated.

The s.168 procedure is reviewed and summarised in Chapter 2. The statutory procedure for removal of a director under s.168 is inalienable and by its terms operates notwithstanding any agreement between the company and the director.[7] However, it does rely upon shareholders voting by the necessary majority and the shareholders (which may include the relevant

---

6   *Cumbrian Newspapers Group Ltd v Cumberland & Westmorland Herald Newspaper & Printing Co Ltd* [1987] Ch. 1; [1986] 3 W.L.R. 26; (1986) 2 B.C.C. 99227.
7   CA 2006 s.168. See also *Link Agricultural Property Ltd v Shanahan* (1998) 28 A.C.S.R. 498 CA (Vic). The corresponding CA 1985 s.303 also provided that the power to remove directors would operate notwithstanding anything in the company's articles, but that reference has been omitted in CA 2006 s.168 on grounds of redundancy on the premise that anything contained in the articles that is contrary to the provisions of the Companies Acts, or against general law, will have no effect. See *Bushell v Faith* [1970] A.C. 1099; [1970] 2 W.L.R. 272; (1970) 114 S.J. 54, which demonstrates the ability to introduce provisions in a company's articles conferring weighted voting rights on shares held by a director to counteract a resolution to remove him as a director. The provisions were held to be effective with the result that the statutory power to remove the director was effectively circumvented. In *Criterion Properties Plc v Stratford UK Properties LLC* [2002] EWCA Civ 1883; [2003] 1 W.L.R. 2108; [2003] B.C.C. 50, and [2004] UKHL 28; [2004] 1 W.L.R. 1846; [2004] B.C.C. 570, where provisions in an agreement with the company would give rise to significant, negative commercial consequences for the company in the event of removal of identified directors from office and thereby act as a fetter on the freedom of shareholders to remove directors

director) are free to fetter their voting rights contractually as they choose.[8] Even the exercise of this inalienable statutory right may be subject to equitable constraints, where, for example, the relationship between the shareholders contemplates that it will only be exercised in particular circumstances and not capriciously.[9]

Special notice is required of a resolution to remove a director under s.168.[10] Section 312 contains the relevant provisions governing the giving of special notice, which can be given by the board. The board is otherwise able to ensure that the requirements in s.312 are observed. While the s.312 procedure would apparently require a meeting to remove a director under s.168 to be held on a minimum of 28 days' notice, the effect of the relief in s.312(4) is to allow the meeting to be convened within a shorter period, provided notice of the intention to move the resolution has first been given to the company.

Section 169 imposes certain procedures for notification of a removal proposal under s.168 to the relevant director and confers rights on the director to publish a response of a reasonable length, at the expense of the company, save where the right to make representations is being abused. The board will be concerned to manage the surrounding publicity and will have the resources of the company at its disposal for that purpose. It will also have the initiative and in particular will control the timing and procedure of the meeting.

There is no particular form that the removal resolution must take, although it is often expressed to the following effect:

> "THAT, special notice having been received by the Company, Mr X be removed as a director of the Company pursuant to Section 168 of the Companies Act 2006."

The director concerned, even if not a member of the company, is entitled to speak at the meeting, in addition to requiring his written representations to be read out (if not previously sent to members).[11]

In addition to the statutory right of removal, articles sometimes provide for the removal of a director by shareholder resolution. Such an article may be useful in bypassing the detailed statutory procedures that apply where reliance is placed on s.168. Section 168(5) provides that the statutory power does not derogate from any power to remove a director that may exist apart from s.168. Hence, the practice has grown up that the articles permit

---

under CA 1985 s.303 (now substantially in s.168), it was acknowledged that the approval of such an agreement might demonstrate an improper exercise of board power.

8   *Holmes v Life Funds of Australia Ltd* [1971] 1 NSWLR 860.
9   *Ebrahimi v Westbourne Galleries* [1973] A.C. 360.
10 CA 2006 168(2).
11 CA 2006 s.169(2) and (4).

shareholders by special resolution to remove a director as an effective alternative to the power and procedures in s.168. While s.168 does not carry over from CA 1985 s.303 the confirmation that the statutory right to remove a director applies notwithstanding anything in the articles, according to CA 2006 Explanatory Note 68, the omission was made on grounds of redundancy on the premise that anything contained in the articles that is contrary to the provisions of the Companies Acts, or against general law, will have no effect.

If a company's articles do not contain a provision for removal of a director, in the absence of any class rights to appoint and remove directors,[12] there is no reason why a general meeting should not pass two resolutions, the first a special resolution altering the articles to insert such a power, and the second implementing the removal.

Unless the vacancy created by the removal is filled at the shareholders' meeting, the board can fill it if so permitted by the articles (see, for example, Model Articles for Private Companies Limited by Shares (the Model Articles) art.17).[13] A director appointed by shareholder resolution in place of a person removed under the statutory power in s.168 will be treated for the purposes of any retirement provisions in the articles as if appointed on the date of appointment of the replaced director.[14] The retirement requirements applicable in the case of an appointment by the board under a power to fill casual vacancies will depend on the terms of the articles.

Removal of a director under s.168 or under a power in the articles does not, unless otherwise agreed, deprive him of any compensation or damages (see the discussion at Section 6.8 above) payable on termination either as a director or in respect of any appointment that terminates with his directorship.[15] It may also, in certain circumstances, be the foundation of a claim by a director shareholder under s.994 (see Section 10.4.1.7 below).

---

[12] *Cumbrian Newspapers Group Ltd v Cumberland & Westmorland Herald Newspaper & Printing Co Ltd* [1987] Ch. 1; [1986] 3 W.L.R. 26; (1986) 2 B.C.C. 99227.

[13] Companies (Model Articles) Regulations 2008 (SI 2008/3229).

[14] CA 2006 s.168(4).

[15] CA 2006 s.168(5)(a). While the entitlement to directors' fees may be qualified under the articles in the event of termination, entitlements under a contract of employment are unaffected save by their terms, certainly for early termination of a fixed-term contract. *Southern Foundries (1926) Ltd v Shirlaw* [1940] A.C. 701; [1940] 2 All E.R. 445 (note the dissenting judgments in relation to the particular operation of the principle in circumstances where a controlling shareholder exercised rights conferred post-contract to remove a director rather than the company acting itself and the pragmatic if somewhat strained analysis supporting the majority conclusion that the actions of the shareholder and the company were either merged or interdependent); *Shindler v Northern Raincoat Co* [1960] 1 W.L.R. 1038; [1960] 2 All E.R. 239; (1960) 104 S.J. 806. See *Read v Astoria Garage (Streatham) Ltd* [1952] Ch. 637; [1952] 2 All E.R. 292; [1952] 2 T.L.R. 130, which supports the theory that, where there is no specified contractual duration, termination by removal from office may not found a claim in damages for contractual breach if the terms of the contract provide for automatic termination of appointment on loss of directorship. Much depends on the terms of the contract in any particular case.

The statutory written resolution procedure for private companies laid down in s.288 is not available to pass a resolution to remove a director under s.168.[16] In relation to articles permitting members' resolutions to be in writing, it is clearly not possible to rely on an article such as reg.5 of Pt II of the 1948 Table A, which is expressly "[s]ubject to the provisions of the Act". It is questionable whether reliance can be placed on an article such as reg.53 of the 1985 Table A, even though not so qualified, because it is inconsistent with the statutory special notice provisions and the provisions of the Act conferring on the director concerned the right to speak in his own defence at the meeting in response to proposed removal under s.168.

10.1.2 Individual Director standpoint

A director who is in dispute with the other members of the board has the benefit of a number of rights:

(a)   to be informed about the company's affairs and have access to information necessary to allow the director to perform his functions as discussed in Section 10.1.1.1 above[17];

(b)   to have the assistance of an expert when making an inspection of company information[18];

(c)   to call a meeting of the board in compliance with the applicable notice provisions adopted by the board or set out in the company's articles;

(d)   not to be excluded from board meetings.[19] Any director under threat of ejection should take care to give instructions for notification of board meetings that are both efficient and consistent with any notification provisions in the articles; and

(e)   in the case of a company that is required to observe the UK Corporate Governance Code (the Code) under applicable listing rules, to demand adequate and timely information consistent with the Code requirements, ensure unresolved boardroom differences are suitably recorded and otherwise require observance of Code requirements.

As described above, the director also has the right to make representations to the members in the event that a resolution for his removal from office is proposed under s.168,[20] and to speak at the meeting at which the resolution is proposed.[21]

---

[16]   CA 2006 s.288(2)(a).

[17]   *Conway v Petronius Clothing Co Ltd* [1978] 1 W.L.R. 72; [1978] 1 All E.R. 185; (1978) 122 S.J. 15 and *Burn v London and New South Wales Coal Co* [1890] 7 T.L.R. 118, 9 Digest (Reissue) 197, 1190 which confirm a general right of access to any information of the company necessary for the director to perform his functions, in contrast to the statutory reference to accounting records being open for inspection by the company's officers, now in s.388.

[18]   *West-Transvaalse Boeresake (Edms) Bpk v Pierterse* 1955 (2) SA 464 PD (Tvaal); *Conway v Petronius Clothing Co Ltd* [1978] 1 W.L.R. 72; [1978] 1 All E.R. 185; (1978) 122 S.J. 15.

[19]   *Hayes v Bristol Plant Hire Ltd* [1957] 1 W.L.R. 499; [1957] 1 All E.R. 685.

[20]   CA 2006 s.169(3) and (4).

[21]   CA 2006 s.169(2).

10.1.3 Boardroom deadlock

The board of a company may be deadlocked because one or more directors refuses to attend board meetings (so as to prevent there being a quorum) or because the directors are equally divided on a question and the chairman either does not have or is not prepared to use a casting vote.

As an alternative or perhaps an adjunct to removal of a director, the members in a general meeting have an inherent default power to fill vacancies in the board.[22] In addition, an article in the form of the Model Articles art.17[23] empowers the general meeting to appoint additional directors, subject to any limit on the total number of directors imposed by the articles that cannot by its terms be adjusted by ordinary resolution.

While the powers of the board are usually delegated by the company's articles, the members may pass a special resolution to take the conduct of the business of the company away from the directors, but an ordinary resolution is insufficient except and to the extent that the articles require the directors to comply with directions given by the members in general meeting.[24]

Under articles that adopt or replicate the Model Articles art.4(1),[25] the general meeting can give directions to the board by special resolution. Article 4(2) provides that no such resolution invalidates anything which the directors have done before the passing of the resolution.[26]

If the directors are unable by reason of dysfunction (e.g. because they cannot secure a quorum whether by reason of overall lack of numbers or dispute) to exercise the powers given to them under the articles, the company in general meeting can perform the functions delegated to the board, certainly to appoint additional directors and perhaps to exercise other powers.[27]

---

[22] *Munster v Cammell Co* (1882) 21 Ch. D 183; *Barron v Potter* [1914] 1 Ch. 895, which distinguished *Blair Open Hearth Furnace Co v Reigart* (1913) 108 L.T. 665, in which it was held that if the directors have delegated power to fill vacancies, that excludes any implied concurrent right of members; see also *Integrated Medical Technologies Ltd v Macel Nominees Pty Ltd* (1988) 13 A.C.L.R. 110, SC (NSW) in which it was held that any attempt in the articles to confer an exclusive power of appointment on the board must be clearly expressed. The principle in *Blair* was doubted by Lord Hanworth M.R. in *Worcester Corsetry Ltd v Witting* [1936] Ch. 640, although the ratio of the decision turned on the construction of the particular articles.

[23] See also reg.78 of the 1985 Table A.

[24] *Automatic Self-Cleansing Filter Syndicate Co Ltd v Cuninghame* [1906] 2 Ch. 34; *Gramophone & Typewriter Ltd v Stanley* [1908] 2 K.B. 89 at 105, dicta of Fletcher Moulton and Buckley LJJ; *Quin & Axtens Ltd v Salmon* [1909] A.C. 442.

[25] See also reg.70 of the 1985 Table A.

[26] See also reg.70 of the 1985 Table A.

[27] *Barron v Potter* [1914] 1 Ch. 895.

The procedure by which to convene a general meeting in the absence of an effective board is addressed at Chapter 8.

As a last resort, a member may apply to the court to act either under its inherent power or under Supreme Court Act 1981 s.37(1) for the appointment of a receiver to manage the affairs of the company. Alternatively, if the deadlock reflects a stalemate at the shareholder level, the remedy discussed in Section 10.4 below or a winding up on the just and equitable ground may provide the solution.

In the unreported case concerning a dispute as to control of the affairs of Westward Television, on an application for injunctive relief to prevent purported appointees to the board holding themselves out as the legitimate board of the company, Dillon J stated that if no agreement could be reached pending resolution of the dispute at trial, he would be prepared to appoint a receiver to manage the affairs of the company during that interim period.

Such an appointment is sometimes made over property as a preservation measure pending determination of competing entitlements to that property. In *BAT Industries Plc v Windward Prospects Ltd*,[28] the court was concerned with an application by BAT for the appointment of a receiver over claims which it contended were vested in Windward for in excess of $800 million against its former sole shareholder, Sequana SA, and former directors. The basis of the application was that BAT contended there was a real risk that at least some of those claims may have imminently become time-barred, that Windward had taken no effective steps to preserve the claims, and that the appointment of a receiver was necessary to ensure that all Windward's claims were protected and preserved, and not lost to Windward and its creditors, including BAT. The court found that justice and convenience did require the appointment of a receiver.

However, such an appointment is invasive and will interfere with the management of the company's affairs unless the scope of the receivership is limited to particular assets. Receivers being officers of the court, any interference with them or the carrying out of their functions may amount to a contempt of court.

10.2 Disputes between directors and members

As a generality, directors owe their fiduciary duties to the company, not its members and the company alone is entitled to enforce those obligations. However, a director may face a claim for breach of a shareholder's personal rights; that is, rights vested in the shareholder and other potential liabilities addressed in Section 4 above. In this Section 10.2 we address the rights that

---

[28] *BAT Industries Plc v Windward Prospects Ltd* [2013] EWHC 3612 (Comm).

a shareholder has under the company's constitution, and the extent to which those rights can be enforced by the shareholder.

Section 10.3 below considers the circumstances in which a shareholder can bring an action in the name of the company to obtain redress for a wrong done to the company (a "derivative" action). Section 10.4 below addresses the right of a shareholder to bring an action under s.994 to obtain a remedy for unfairly prejudicial conduct.

As an alternative, an aggrieved minority might instead draw the matters complained of to the attention of relevant authorities to provoke investigation and remedy. The alternatives are considered in Chapter 12.

Which route to follow in mounting a dispute will be a function of resource and the remedy sought. A personal action may be brought to address a wrong done to a shareholder personally, for example refusal to register a transfer of shares. It may also be brought to ensure compliance with the articles, or to ensure that powers conferred by the articles are exercised for the purposes for which they were conferred. A derivative suit is designed to remedy a wrong done to and the loss suffered by the company. An unfair prejudice claim under s.994 is the route most likely to result in separation. In all instances, the implications of privilege, proper use and access to corporate information must be weighed.

Where the true nature of the claim is a dispute between shareholders, the company will be a nominal defendant. Any advice given to the company will not be privileged from disclosure to the shareholders during the course of the proceedings. Where the proceedings concern the propriety of an exercise of fiduciary powers by the directors, for example as to the allotment of shares, where there is a case to be answered, the directors will be required to justify their actions, and disclosure of relevant correspondence and any advice given to the board is likely to be sought. Where the claim is brought for the benefit of the company itself, a claim for an account by the directors may be sought, requiring them to account for their actions and for any funds of the company expended or dissipated.

10.2.1 Personal actions

This Section identifies a range of contractual and statutory rights and protections that form a key element of the minority shareholder protections. In exercising their powers, the directors need to be sensitive to the inherent limits on their authority and the potential for shareholders to intervene.

There is a complex interaction between a member's right to bring proceedings in an individual capacity and the derivative action discussed in Section 10.3 below where the acts complained of cause damage to the company. If the claimant can establish that the conduct has constituted a breach of some legal duty owed to him personally and the court is satisfied that such breach has caused him personal loss, separate and distinct from any loss occasioned to the company, a personal action can be mounted.[29] A member is also entitled to ensure that powers conferred on directors, being powers delegated by the company's articles, are exercised for the proper purposes, that is to say, for the purposes for which they were conferred, notwithstanding that the duty to do so is owed to the company. Such an entitlement exists irrespective of any loss being suffered by the member by reason of that breach of duty.

10.2.1.1 *Shareholders' personal rights*

Section 33 provides that the provisions of the company's constitution bind the company and its members to the same extent as if there were covenants on the part of the company and of each member to observe those provisions. This contract is generally recognised as the basis of the legal relationship between the company and its members in addition to its operation as between the members themselves.

However, this does not mean that every shareholder necessarily has the right to enforce all of the rights that the contract appears on its face to confer. The decided cases are not entirely consistent and to some extent turn on their facts. Nonetheless, the general view is that s.33 gives contractual effect to a provision in the constitution only insofar as it gives rights to or imposes obligations on a member in his capacity as a member,[30] most certainly when in common with other members or a class of members (insider rights) and not, for example, as a director[31] or as a professional adviser to the company[32] (outsider rights) whether or not the director or adviser is also a shareholder. It is certainly the case that a member seeking to enforce a provision vested in him as a member should expect to succeed under established principle more readily than in an action to uphold a provision that does not touch on the member qua member. The difficulty in any attempt to uphold outsider rights by enforcing provisions in a company's articles has not been affected by the Contracts (Rights of Third Parties) Act 1999, which excludes s.33 from its scope.[33] So for example, the common provision in articles permitting the grant of indemnities to directors does not confer on the director an enforceable right to indemnity.

---

[29] *Walker v Stones* [2001] Q.B. 902; [2001] 2 W.L.R. 623; [2001] B.C.C. 757.

[30] *Hickman v Kent or Romney Marsh Sheepbreeders Assoc* [1915] 1 Ch. 881. For further analysis, see Section A Part 2 Law Commission Consultation Paper 142. See cases referred to in fn.70 for discussion of the distinction between rights enjoyed by the company and those of individual shareholders.

[31] *Browne v La Trinidad* (1887) 37 Ch. D 1; but see *John v PricewaterhouseCoopers (formerly Price Waterhouse) (Costs)* [2002] 1 W.L.R. 953—an appointment made "on the footing of the Articles" may have the effect of incorporating provisions of the articles into a director's terms of appointment.

[32] *Eley v Positive Government Security Life Assurance Co Ltd* (1876) 1 Ex. D. 88.

[33] Contracts (Rights of Third Parties) Act 1999 s.6(2).

A contractual indemnity must be entered into between the company and the director to confer a right of indemnity on the director.

Even if the provision of the company's constitution that has been breached is one that creates "insider rights", the member may not be able to bring a personal action to enforce it. If for example the breach involves only an internal corporate irregularity, such as an irregularity in the conduct of a meeting that is trivial or can readily be remedied by reconvening a meeting at which it is expected that a majority will prevail in a manner that renders the breach nugatory, it may not be possible to mount a personal claim.

10.2.1.2   Impact of the rule in Foss v Harbottle[34]

The refusal by the courts to uphold personal actions by shareholders in respect of breaches of internal corporate irregularities stems from the "majority rule"[35] and "proper claimant"[36] principles generally attributed to the decision in *Foss v Harbottle*, set out in the case of *Edwards v Halliwell*[37] and restated in *Prudential Assurance Co Ltd v Newman Industries Ltd (No.2)*.[38] The "rule in *Foss v Harbottle*" is discussed in more detail in Section 10.3.1 below.

The courts have not been consistent in relation to the ability of a shareholder to challenge internal corporate irregularities; in certain instances the line adopted has been to restrain individual action in reliance on an extension of the *Foss v Harbottle* principle, while in other cases, the courts have permitted a shareholder to enforce his contractual right under the articles. Shareholders have, for example, been allowed to bring personal actions involving defective or inadequate notice of meeting,[39] improper adjournment of meetings[40] or the right to have their votes counted,[41] but have been refused any remedy when a valid demand for a poll was wrongfully rejected by the chairman of the meeting even though, so it appears, the outcome of the particular poll would have reversed the result on a show of hands.[42]

---

[34]   *Foss v Harbottle* 67 E.R. 189; (1843) 2 Hare 461.

[35]   The will of the majority of members of the company should in general prevail.

[36]   A breach of duty owed to the company is a wrong for which the company and not its investors should seek a remedy. In determining whether to seek redress, the company may legitimately take into account balancing factors such as the relative return on investment of time and other resources in litigation.

[37]   *Edwards v Halliwell* [1950] 2 All E.R. 1064; [1950] W.N. 537; (1950) 94 S.J. 803.

[38]   *Prudential Assurance Co Ltd v Newman Industries Ltd (No.2)* [1982] Ch. 204.

[39]   *Musselwhite v CH Musselwhite & Son Ltd* [1962] Ch. 964; [1962] 2 W.L.R. 374; (1962) 106 S.J. 37.

[40]   *Byng v London Life Assoc Ltd* [1990] Ch. 170; [1989] 2 W.L.R. 738; (1989) 5 B.C.C. 227.

[41]   *Pender v Lushington* (1877) 6 Ch. D. 70; *Oliver v Dalgleish* [1963] 1 W.L.R. 1274; [1963] 3 All E.R. 330; (1963) 107 S.J. 1039.

[42]   *MacDougall v Gardiner* (1874–75) L.R. 10 Ch. App. 606.

If a general principle can be extracted from the authorities, it may be that where a breach of internal procedure damages the company first and foremost and incidentally affects all members, it should be resolved by corporate action, save where an exception to the rule in *Foss v Harbottle* applies (see Section 10.3.1 below).[43] Contrastingly, where the principal wrong is done to an individual member, that individual may seek redress unless the matter complained of is open to ratification by ordinary resolution. In cases of substantial wrongdoing, it is in any event likely to be appropriate to seek a remedy under s.994.

10.2.1.3 Transactions outside the company's powers

The rule in *Foss v Harbottle* does not prevent a shareholder from bringing a personal action to restrain the directors from acting beyond their powers save in respect of acts done in fulfilment of a legal obligation that results from a prior act of the company.[44] While the principle was acknowledged in *Smith v Croft (No.2)*[45] that a shareholder can have locus to bring an action to recover on behalf of a company property or money transferred or paid in an ultra vires transaction, and that an ultra vires act cannot be ratified by any majority of the members, it was held that if a majority of independent shareholders, acting in good faith, do not wish such an action to be continued, the will of that majority should prevail. This assumes that the shareholder promoting the action is not able to demonstrate a loss beyond that which is merely reflective of the loss suffered by the company as a result of the ultra vires transaction.

10.2.1.4 Amendments to the company's articles

A shareholder may be able to challenge a special resolution altering the company's articles on the grounds that the resolution was not passed bona fide (i.e. without fraud or malice) for the benefit of the company as a whole (i.e. the shareholders as a general body), or breached a class or special right or discriminated between majority and minority shareholders,[46] or (as discussed below) that the alteration was unfairly prejudicial to his interests for the purposes of s.994.

---

[43] See also *Burland v Earle* [1902] A.C. 83 at 93: "It is an elementary principle of the law relating to joint stock companies that the court will not interfere with the internal management of companies acting within their powers and in fact has no jurisdiction to do so." This rule is attributed by Lord Davey at 93 to the decision in *Foss v Harbottle* 67 E.R. 189; (1843) 2 Hare 461.

[44] CA 2006 s.40(4).

[45] *Smith v Croft (No.2)* [1988] Ch. 114; [1987] 3 W.L.R. 405; (1987) 3 B.C.C. 207.

[46] *Allen v Gold Reefs of West Africa Ltd* [1900] 1 Ch. 656; *Greenhalgh v Arderne Cinemas Ltd* [1951] Ch. 286; (1950) 94 S.J. 855; cf. *Sidebottom v Kershaw Leese & Co Ltd* [1920] 1 Ch. 154 and *Shuttleworth v Cox Bros & Co (Maidenhead) Ltd* [1927] 2 K.B. 9. In determining whether an amendment of the articles is bona fide for the benefit of the company, the test is by reference to the opinion of the shareholders; their bona fides will only be called into question if the

The High Court of Australia decision in *Gambotto v WCP Ltd*[47] adopted an interesting approach in relation to the assessment of validity of amendments made to the constitution of a company although not followed to date in the English courts.[48] The Australian court stressed the proprietary nature of a share and rejected a test based simply on the amendments being bona fide in the interests of the company as a whole. Instead, the court distinguished between amendments allowing expropriation by the majority of the shares of the minority or of valuable proprietary rights attaching to the shares and other amendments to the constitution giving rise to a conflict of interest. The court determined that the test applicable to the first category would be whether the power to alter the constitution had been exercised for a proper purpose and if so, whether the exercise of that power would not operate oppressively in relation to minority shareholders. For amendments falling into the second category, the court decided that, if regularly approved, such amendments would prima facie be fair, unless shown to be beyond a purpose contemplated by the constitution or oppressive.

10.2.1.5   Shareholders' agreements

Accepting that the law relating to enforcement of rights and obligations provided for in the articles is complex and, depending on what is intended, may not provide comprehensive protection for an individual shareholder, those wishing to regulate their relationship as shareholders should consider whether a shareholders' agreement is appropriate to supplement the constitution. A shareholders' agreement gives rise to specific contractual rights as between the parties that are enforceable in the normal course.[49]

If the company is a party to the agreement, then any restriction on its statutory powers contained in the agreement (such as a restriction preventing it from increasing its authorised share capital except by special resolution) will be void as far as the company is concerned, but assuming the severability or disapplication of the provision in as far as it would otherwise bind the company, so as to avoid fettering the inalienable statutory powers of the company, parallel restrictions assumed by shareholders who are parties to the agreement will be enforceable amongst them.[50]

---

circumstances are so oppressive or extravagant as to cast suspicion on their honesty. Benefit of the company will be assumed unless no reasonable man could consider it so (at 11, 17d onwards).

[47]   *Gambotto v WCP Ltd* (1995) 182 C.L.R. 432.
[48]   *Constable v Executive Connections Ltd* [2005] EWHC 3 (Ch); [2005] 2 B.C.L.C. 638; *Citco Banking Corp NV v Pusser's Ltd* [2007] UKPC 13; [2007] Bus. L.R. 960; [2007] B.C.C. 205. See *Arbuthnott v Bonnyman* [2015] EWCA Civ 536.
[49]   Provisions in a shareholders' agreement may also attach as class rights to shares; see *Harman v BML Group Ltd* [1994] 1 W.L.R. 893; [1994] B.C.C. 502; [1994] 2 B.C.L.C. 674.
[50]   *Russell v Northern Bank Development Corp Ltd* [1992] 1 W.L.R. 588; [1992] B.C.C. 578; [1992] B.C.L.C. 1016; applying the principle established in *Southern Foundries (1926) Ltd v Shirlaw* [1940] A.C. 701; [1940] 2 All E.R. 445 at 739 and *Allen v Gold Reefs of West Africa Ltd* [1900] 1 Ch. 656 at 671.

10.2.1.6   *Statutory rights*

The Companies Acts and the Insolvency Act 1986 provide shareholders with a disparate collection of other direct or indirect rights. The principal rights of shareholders in the Companies Acts,[51] which may in relevant circumstances be considered in parallel with the minority protection regime, are:

(a)   to challenge a special resolution passed by a private company approving a payment out of capital for the redemption or purchase of its shares (s.721);

(b)   to apply to the court in the event that it proves impracticable to call or conduct a meeting by conventional means (s.306);

(c)   if representing not less than 5% of the issued shares or any class thereof,[52] to challenge a special resolution of a public company to re-register as a private company (s.98);

(d)   if representing not less than 5% of the total voting rights[53] of a public company, to require distribution of notice of a resolution to be proposed at the next annual general meeting (s.338);

(e)   if representing not less than 5% of the total voting rights, to requisition an extraordinary general meeting (s.303);

(f)   if representing not less than 10% of the shares,[54] to apply for the appointment of inspectors under CA 1985 s.431, which may lead to the Secretary of State bringing a petition under s.995 for an unfair prejudice remedy under CA 2006 Pt 30 (see Section 10.4 below); and

(g)   if representing not less than 15% of the relevant class, to challenge a resolution varying the rights attaching to a class of shares passed in accordance with s.630 (s.633).

Principal rights available to shareholders under the Insolvency Act 1986 are:

(a)   to object to a business or property transaction approved under Insolvency Act 1986 s.110 (Insolvency Act 1986 s.111); and

(b)   to petition the court for the company to be wound up on the ground that it is just and equitable to do so (Insolvency Act 1986 s.122(1)) and a related restraining remedy under Insolvency Act 1986 s.126.[55]

---

[51]   Others can be found in CA 2006 ss.125, 168, 229, 563, 803 and 981.

[52]   Or being not less than 50 members.

[53]   Or being not less than 100 members holding shares in the company on which there has been paid up an average sum, per member, of not less than £100.

[54]   Or being not less than 200 members.

[55]   Other rights that may be available to a contributory during a winding up can be found in Insolvency Act 1986 ss.133, 147, 155, 167, 168, 188 and 212, and operate in addition to powers exercisable by the liquidator.

10.3 Derivative actions

A "derivative action" is a proceeding which a shareholder may bring to enforce a cause of action vested in the company. It has to be distinguished from a personal action of the type described in Section 10.2.1 above, which shareholders may bring in their own right to enforce a right vested in them personally.

CA 2006 Pt 11 Ch.1 (Derivative claims in England and Wales or Northern Ireland) sets out the legislative provisions relating to derivative claims that came into force with effect from 1 October 2007. The provisions largely reflect the recommendations of the Law Commission for a "new derivative procedure with more modern, flexible and accessible criteria for determining whether a shareholder can pursue an action".[56]

The premise for a derivative action is based on the notion that an individual shareholder should only be able to bring such an action in exceptional and limited circumstances. The common law derivative action continues to apply in respect of events prior to 1 October 2007 and informs the application of the statutory derivative action. It also survives as the derivative procedure where a member of an ultimate holding company brings a complaint about conduct of affairs of a subsidiary[57] and in respect of overseas companies.[58]

Under the common law, as a generality, a member cannot bring an action on behalf of the company for an injury done to the company; the company is the injured party and the action vests in it. The common law derivative action relies on an exception to this rule where the matter complained of constitutes a fraud on the minority, including fraud proper as well as breach by a director of fiduciary duty to the company in circumstances in which the wrongdoers are in control of the company.

Following the introduction in 1948[59] of the prejudice remedy (now in s.994) the significance of the common law derivative action diminished. The Law Commission, in its *"Shareholder Remedies" Report 246*, nonetheless identified in the derivative action a remedy that serves a useful purpose in providing a mechanism for shareholders to intervene in the face of corporate wrongs. However, the common law remedy is complicated and unwieldy, employing uncertain concepts such as "wrongdoer control". Further, the common law action is available only to a minority shareholder if able to prove that

---

[56] Law Commission Report No.246 para.6.15.
[57] The High Court has held that the common law continues to apply in relation to "multiple" derivative actions, where the claimant is not a member of the relevant company but is a member of its holding company. *Fort Gilkicker Ltd, Re* [2013] EWHC 348 (Ch); [2013] 3 W.L.R. 164; [2013] B.C.C. 365. *Bhullar v Bhullar* [2015] EWHC 1943 (Ch).
[58] *Konamaneni v Rolls-Royce Industrial Power (India) Ltd* [2002] 1 W.L.R. 1269. *Abouraya v Sigmund* [2014] EWHC 277 (Ch).
[59] Companies Act 1948 s.210, now in s.994.

the matter complained of conferred a benefit on the controlling sharehold-ers, or that the failure of the directors to bring an action constitutes fraud on the minority. This narrows the already limited circumstances in which a minority shareholder can bring a derivative action to circumstances of serious mismanagement where the majority have profited in some way from the negligence.

As a result, CA 2006 introduced a new derivative procedure that replaced the common law action (save for its transitional application to matters arising prior to 1 October 2007,[60] "multiple" derivative actions brought by persons other than members of the abused company and in respect of overseas companies) and operates subject to tight judicial control with the objective of allowing justified actions to develop in stages. This offers the potential to mitigate the substantial costs typically associated with derivative actions while guarding against nuisance litigation.

Despite its limitations, the derivative action retains a number of potential advantages when compared to a s.994 prejudice action. First, a claimant in a derivative action does not need to prove unfairly prejudicial conduct by the defendants.[61] Secondly, while a "multiple" or "double" derivative action (where the derivative action is brought by a non-member, for example by minority shareholders in a holding company wishing to take action on behalf of a subsidiary) would not be possible under s.994, such an action is possible under the common law derivative action regime under CA 2006 Pt 11 Ch.1 (Derivative claims in England and Wales or Northern Ireland).[62] Furthermore, whereas s.994 has to a substantial extent evolved as an exit remedy, the derivative action is designed to provide a solution for shareholders that wish to retain their investment.[63] The s.994 procedure by contrast provides a personal remedy, it is not dependent on court approval to commence the action, the scope of the claim is broader, it cannot be derailed by authorisation or ratification of the conduct complained of and, should the suitable remedy be through a derivative process, Section 996(2)(c) empowers the court to authorise civil proceedings to be brought in the name and on behalf of the company by such person or persons and on such terms as the court may direct, providing a route back to a corporate remedy through the prejudice action.

The right to bring the statutory derivative action is subject to obtaining the court's approval to allow the action to proceed, satisfying a two-stage test. First, the court must dismiss the application if the applicant cannot establish

---

[60] Companies Act 2006 (Commencement No.3, Consequential Amendments, Transitional Provisions and Savings) Order 2007 (SI 2007/2194) Sch.3 para.20.

[61] The remedy under s.995 is only available where the court is satisfied that an unfair prejudice has occurred.

[62] *Fort Gilkicker Ltd, Re* [2013] EWHC 348 (Ch); [2013] 3 W.L.R. 164; [2013] B.C.C. 365. Note, however, that this was a first instance decision and a diversity of views have been expressed about this decision.

[63] Law Commission Report 246 para.6.11.

a prima facie case and secondly, the court may use its discretion to refuse or grant leave to continue a derivative claim taking into account specified matters. Historically, the common law action did not require court permission but the application of CPR 19.9 is such that an assessment of the existence of a prima facie claim and entitlement to pursue a derivative action under the exception to the rule in *Foss v Harbottle* must be established at a preliminary stage. Rights have been reserved to alter or add by regulation to the circumstances that should be taken into account by the court in refusing or giving permission to bring or continue derivative claims.[64]

The incidence of derivative claims remains low, the unfair prejudice remedy being the preferred mechanism by which minority shareholders can obtain relief and a personal remedy.

Civil Procedure Rules r.19.9 applies to all derivative claims other than a claim made pursuant to CA 2006 s.996, establishing the procedures to be observed for the conduct of claims.

This Chapter contains a review, in Sections 10.3.1–10.3.6, of the common law position, because the common law criteria continue to be relevant in respect of causes of action that arise before 1 October 2007, multiple derivative actions and in respect of overseas companies and influence the statutory derivative action described in Sections 10.3.7 and 10.3.8 below.

10.3.1 The position under the common law—the rule in Foss v Harbottle

The derivative action has its origins in the principle of majority rule and the principle that the company that suffers the wrongdoing is the proper plaintiff, principles referred to as the rule in *Foss v Harbottle*.[65] This rule, substantially restated in *Prudential Assurance Co Ltd v Newman Industries Ltd (No.2)*,[66] has operated according to the following principles:

(a)   the proper claimant in an action in respect of a wrong alleged to be done to a corporation is prima facie the corporation;

(b)   where the alleged wrong is a transaction that might be made binding on the corporation by a simple majority of the members, no individual member of the corporation is allowed to maintain an action in respect of that matter because, if the majority confirms the transaction, *cadit quaestio* (the question is at an end); or, if the majority challenges the transaction, there is no valid reason why the company should not sue;

---

[64]   CA 2006 s.263(5). The section has been disapplied specifically in relation to entities taken into ownership by the Treasury.

[65]   *Foss v Harbottle* 67 E.R. 189; [1843] 2 Hare 461.

[66]   *Prudential Assurance Co Ltd v Newman Industries Ltd (No.2)* [1982] Ch. 204; [1982] 2 W.L.R. 31; [1982] 1 All E.R. 354.

(c)   the rule has no application if the alleged wrong is ultra vires the corporation, because the majority of members cannot confirm the transaction;

(d)   the rule has no application if the transaction complained of could validly be undertaken or sanctioned only by a special resolution, because a simple majority cannot confirm a transaction which requires a greater majority; and

(e)   the rule has operated subject to a true exception where what has been done amounts to fraud or possibly oppression or unfairness[67] and the wrongdoers are themselves in control of the company.

At first instance in *Prudential Assurance Co Ltd v Newman Industries Ltd (No.2)*,[68] Vinelott J promulgated a broader exception to the rule in *Foss v Harbottle*, so as to allow individual shareholder action whenever the justice of the case so required. This broad exception was rejected on appeal.[69] The decision at first instance that, as a result of a finding of fraud, individual shareholders were entitled to damages for the loss of value in their shares as a personal claim was also held to be misconceived in that the damage complained of was damage suffered by the company. To recover under a personal claim, the case would need to be made of a loss to personal assets caused by the fraudulent act, separate and distinct from the loss suffered by the company. No claim can be founded for personal loss that is merely a reflection of the loss suffered by the company unless the company has no cause of action to sue and recover the loss.[70] The foundation of the rule is

---

[67]   *MacDougall v Gardiner* (1874-75) L.R. 10 Ch. App. 606; *Edwards v Halliwell* [1950] 2 All E.R. 1064; [1950] W.N. 537; (1950) 94 S.J. 803.

[68]   *Prudential Assurance Co Ltd v Newman Industries Ltd (No.2)* [1981] Ch. 257; [1980] 3 W.L.R. 543; [1980] 2 All E.R. 841.

[69]   *Prudential Assurance Co Ltd v Newman Industries Ltd (No.2)* [1982] Ch. 204 at 221. See also *Harris v Microfusion 2003-2 LLP* [2016] EWCA Civ 1212. Compare Australia's *Biala Pty Ltd v Mallina Holding Ltd (No.2)* (1993) 11 A.C.S.R. 785.

[70]   *Prudential Assurance Co Ltd v Newman Industries Ltd (No.2)* [1982] Ch. 204 at 223; see also *Johnson v Gore Wood* [2002] 2 A.C. 1; [2001] 2 W.L.R. 72; [2001] 1 All E.R. 481 in which the House of Lords identified two circumstances in which an individual shareholder might sue, namely: (i) where the company had no cause for action, the shareholder claim being measured by a reduction in the value of his shareholding and thus a reflective loss; and (ii) where the shareholder had a separate cause of action distinct from that of the company in respect of a breach of duty owed independently to the shareholder, representing a personal loss that was separate and distinct from loss suffered by the company; see also *Giles v Rhind* [2002] EWCA Civ 1428; [2003] Ch. 618; [2003] 2 W.L.R. 237, which represents an attempt to introduce a wider exception where the wrong-doing had disabled the company, doubted in *Gardner v Parker* [2004] EWCA Civ 781; [2005] B.C.C. 46; [2004] 2 B.C.L.C. 554 and criticised in *Waddington Ltd v Chan* [2008] HKCU 1381 but further considered in *Stevenson v Southwark LBC* [2011] EWHC 108 (QB), also *Day v Cook* [2001] EWCA Civ 592; [2003] B.C.C. 256; [2002] 1 B.C.L.C. 1, *Ellis v Property Leeds (UK) Ltd* [2002] EWCA Civ 32; [2002] 2 B.C.L.C. 175 and *Shaker v Al-Bedrawi* [2002] EWCA Civ 1452; [2003] Ch. 350; [2003] 2 W.L.R. 922; the burden is on the defendant to establish that the whole claim is reflective and recoverable by the company.
In the US, where courts have held that directors and controlling shareholders of closely held corporations owe other investors a higher level of fiduciary duty than needs to be observed in the case of publicly held corporations, there is also precedent permitting a personal action as a means of providing direct compensation to a shareholder for loss

the need to avoid double recovery and double jeopardy arising from the same facts, regardless of the capacity in which claims might be brought, and to protect the company's creditors.[71]

This emphasises the scope and essential character of derivative action; it seeks relief to the extent, and no larger than, that which the company itself would have if it were the claimant. For this reason, a shareholder is able to assert a cause of action which arose before he became a shareholder because it is the company's and not his substantive right that is being enforced.[72] This contrasts with claims under s.994 when the conduct complained of is an unfair prejudice to some part of the members, not the company.

There may be circumstances where the conduct giving rise to the claim might most suitably be addressed through a derivative suit that technically cannot be commenced where the more flexible prejudice claim might be open. Section 996 allows the court to sanction a derivative claim as a remedy in prejudice proceedings, so allowing a corporate remedy where a derivative suit could not have been initiated but is appropriate.

10.3.2 Fraud on the minority

The common law exception described in Section 10.3.1(e) above was recognised because, without it, the minority's grievance could never have reached the court since the wrongdoers themselves, being in control, would not allow the company to sue.[73] To come within the exception, the claimant must show:

(a) that what had been done amounts to fraud; and
(b) that the wrongdoers are in control. While this was at one time considered to be simply a majority control requirement, the exception is available where control of the company is split 50:50[74] and it is sufficient to establish whether or not an independent organ of the company is or would prevent proceedings for proper purpose, for the benefit of the company.[75]

---

sustained by a close corporation where all shareholders are joined in the action. However, this tendency to permit personal actions is more evident in states that do not make statutory provision for oppression actions. US courts have also been prepared to provide an individual remedy where the corporation is no longer a going concern or where there has been a change of control of the corporation and derivative action would not provide an adequate remedy.

[71] *Gardner v Parker* [2004] EWCA Civ 781; [2005] B.C.C. 46; [2004] 2 B.C.L.C. 554.
[72] See CA 2006 s.260(4). See also *Seaton v Grant* (1866–67) L.R. 2 Ch. App. 459.
[73] *Prudential Assurance Co Ltd v Newman Industries Ltd (No.2)* [1982] Ch. 204 at 211. See Lord Denning MR at 390A-D in *Wallersteiner v Moir (No.2)* [1975] Q.B. 373.
[74] *Abouraya v Sigmund* [2014] EWHC 277 (Ch) at [17].
[75] Described by Lord Davey at 93 in *Burland v Earle* [1902] A.C. 83 suggesting majority voting control, in *Smith v Croft (No.2)* [1988] Ch. 114 at 183–185, the independent organ test was recognised and it was confirmed that regard should be had to the views of the independent shareholders.

In this context, "fraud" means "fraud in the wider equitable sense of that term, as in the equitable concept of a fraud on a power" and does not require proof of deliberate or dishonest breach of duty.[76] Examples include:

(a)   attempts by the majority to sell worthless assets to the company, while concealing a commission paid to a director who procured the arrangement[77];

(b)   the majority diverting business from the company to themselves in breach of their fiduciary duties[78]; and

(c)   the majority compromising, on terms which were disadvantageous to the company, litigation against bodies in which the majority was interested.[79]

In the absence of actual fraud (in the sense of deliberate or dishonest breach of duty) the exception has no application where the wrongdoers did not themselves benefit. It certainly does not extend to mere negligence or breach of duty on the part of the directors,[80] unless the negligence resulted not only in harm to the company but personal benefit for the directors.[81] Even in such a case, if an independent majority vote that proceedings not be taken, the action would fail provided the majority do not use their voting powers to confer benefit on themselves that in effect expropriates from the minority. In *Smith v Croft (No.2)*,[82] a case in which the purported wrongdoers had voting control, it was held that a minority shareholder's derivative action should not be allowed to continue if an "independent organ" of the company did not wish it to be pursued. The nature of an independent organ might vary from one company to another, but it could consist of a majority of the independent shareholders or directors (i.e. those not associated with the wrongdoers). The test of independence is whether the relevant parties are capable of reaching a determination as to a course of action that in their view is bona fide for the benefit of the company as a whole.[83]

Wrongdoer control could arise through a direct or indirect holding of a majority of the shares in the company, and could also extend to a situation

---

[76]   *Estmanco (Kilner House) Ltd v Greater London Council* [1982] 1 W.L.R. 2; [1982] 1 All E.R. 437; 80 L.G.R. 464 at 12. Further held on the facts that the sum total of the facts represented such an abuse of power as to have the same effect as a fraud on the minority although there was no financial gain to the majority.

[77]   *Atwool v Merryweather* (1867–68) L.R. 5 Eq. 464 (Note).

[78]   *Cook v Deeks* [1916] 1 A.C. 554.

[79]   *Menier v Hooper's Telegraph Works* (1873–74) L.R. 9 Ch. App. 350. Consultation Paper on *Shareholder Remedies* CPNo 142 1996, para.4.11.

[80]   *Pavlides v Jensen* [1956] Ch. 565; [1956] 3 W.L.R. 224; (1956) 100 S.J. 452.

[81]   In *Daniels v Daniels* [1978] Ch. 406; [1978] 2 W.L.R. 73; (1977) 121 S.J. 605, the court held that if directors benefit personally from the negligence at the company's expense, this might constitute fraud on the minority. See also *Abouraya v Sigmund* [2014] EWHC 277 (Ch) at [19] and *Harris v Microfusion 2003-2 LLP* [2016] EWCA Civ 1212.

[82]   *Smith v Croft (No.2)* [1988] Ch. 114.

[83]   *Smith v Croft (No.2)* [1988] Ch. 114 at 186.

where control lies with the wrongdoers together with those likely to vote with them as a result of influence or apathy.[84]

A major problem for the claimant is the need to show that there is a prima facie case of fraud, and sufficient control by the wrongdoers, at a preliminary hearing, as the court should not proceed upon the hypothesis that all the allegations of fraud and control in the statement of claim are facts.[85] The court should also assess whether a hypothetical, reasonable independent board could reach a conclusion that it was appropriate to bring proceedings.[86] This could have the effect of turning the preliminary application into a mini trial, while upholding the purpose, to avoid multiple claims where the company itself is competent to bring proceedings but might for its own reasons determine not to do so. It was suggested in the *Prudential* appeal proceedings[87] that it might be right for a judge trying the preliminary issue to grant a sufficient adjournment to enable a meeting of shareholders to be convened, so that a conclusion could be reached in the light of the conduct of the members. In the decision *Airey v Cordell*,[88] Warren J stayed the action for a period to allow time for the parties to see if they could agree a proposal to address the unfairness.

The fraud exception has been materially repackaged in the s.260 statutory derivative action that has replaced the common law derivative action other than in respect of claims relating to matters arising prior to 1 October 2007, multiple derivative actions and overseas companies.

10.3.3 Ultra vires or illegal transactions

Alleged wrongs that are ultra vires the company (through restrictions in the constitution) or illegal (such as the unlawful reduction of capital) or criminal provide a prima facie basis for the shareholder's common law action. They simply fall outside the majority rule principle and there is no need to show fraud on the minority.[89]

---

[84] *Prudential Assurance Co Ltd v Newman Industries Ltd (No.2)* [1982] Ch. 204 at 219E.
[85] *Prudential Assurance* [1982] Ch. 204 at 221G–222A. This was described in *Smith v Croft (No.2)* [1988] Ch. 114 at 139 as giving rise to a halfway house in this very special type of case. See also David Richards at [53] in *Abouraya v Sigmund* [2014] EWHC 277 (Ch): "the claimant must demonstrate a prima facie case that the company...is entitled to the relief claimed. A prima facie case is a higher test than a seriously arguable case and I take it to mean a case that, in the absence of an answer by the defendant, would entitle the claimant to judgment. In considering whether the claimant has shown a prima facie case the court will have regard to the totality of the evidence placed before it on the application".
[86] *Airey v Cordell* [2006] EWHC 2728 (Ch) at [75].
[87] *Prudential Assurance* [1982] Ch. 204 at 222A.
[88] *Airey v Cordell* [2006] EWHC 2728 (Ch).
[89] *Smith v Croft (No.2)* [1988] Ch. 114.

10.3.4 Where a special resolution is required

A shareholder may bring an action to prevent reliance on an ordinary resolution to sanction a matter that the Act or the articles requires to be approved by special resolution.[90] Although traditionally presented as an exception to the rule in *Foss v Harbottle* (as set out in Section 10.3.1(d) above), such a claim is legitimate to allow a requirement of the law or constitution to be enforced in response to an irregularity.

10.3.5 Further obstacles

Assuming that a complaint constitutes an exception to the rule in *Foss v Harbottle*, a number of further tests would need to be satisfied to persuade the court to allow the common law action to proceed. The court exercises a discretion whether to grant permission and will have regard to all relevant factors. In particular:

(a) whether the wrong complained of could, as a matter of law, properly be ratified or approved. If the act complained of amounts to a breach of duty by the directors, only disinterested members might ratify the actions of the directors and thus wrongdoer controllers could not achieve ratification.[91] Where the conduct is of a kind that discriminates between the minority and the majority, purported ratification would be no bar to the minority shareholder's common law action.[92]

(b) whether the claimant comes "with clean hands". The common law derivative action is an equitable remedy. As a result, the minority shareholder is barred from bringing it if he knowingly benefited from the relevant act or event; acquiesced or delayed.[93]

(c) whether the claimant has a legitimate interest in the company. A nominee shareholder seeking to proceed against the wishes of the beneficial owner would not have a legitimate interest.[94]

---

[90] *Pavlides v Jensen* [1956] Ch. 565; [1956] 3 W.L.R. 224; (1956) 100 S.J. 452.

[91] CA 2006 s.239.

[92] *Cook v Deeks* [1916] 1 A.C. 554. Had a relevant majority previously determined to dissolve the company or that it should close its business or could not pursue an opportunity, there would have been no breach of duty in subsequently taking the benefit of a contract personally; cf. *Regal (Hastings) Ltd v Gulliver* [1967] 2 A.C. 134; [1942] 1 All E.R. 378 if a breach of fiduciary duty in the guise of a director making a profit from his position is not validly approved or ratified, the director will be liable to account; see also *Hogg v Cramphorn* [1967] Ch. 254; [1966] 3 W.L.R. 995; (1966) 110 S.J. 887 and *Bamford v Bamford* [1970] Ch. 212; [1969] 2 W.L.R. 1107; (1969) 113 S.J. 123.

[93] *Nurcombe v Nurcombe* [1985] 1 W.L.R. 370; (1984) 1 B.C.C. 99269; (1984) 81 L.S.G. 2929 at 378; *Barrett v Duckett* [1995] B.C.C. 362; [1995] 1 B.C.L.C. 243.

[94] *Abouraya v Sigmund* [2014] EWHC 277 (Ch). See also *Estmanco (Kilner House) Ltd v Greater London Council* [1982] 1 W.L.R. 2 where there was no financial loss to the company and the minority members but other injury to them.

(d) whether a reasonable board of directors would consider it to be in the best interests of the company to pursue the proceedings.[95]

(e) whether some other adequate remedy is available to the minority shareholder.[96]

(f) whether the company is in liquidation. If the company is in liquidation, there is normally no need for a minority shareholder to bring a derivative action to obtain redress against the wrongdoers, as the liquidator can bring an action in the name of the company if there is a reasonable cause of action; and if he refuses, the shareholder may be able to obtain an order requiring the liquidator to bring the action[97] or an order permitting the shareholder to bring an action in the name of the company.[98]

10.3.6 Costs

A further, substantial, obstacle has been the burden of the costs of the action. It was held by the Court of Appeal in *Wallersteiner v Moir (No.2)*[99] that legal aid was not available to a shareholder bringing a derivative action, and legal aid is now largely unavailable anyway for money claims.[100] However, following *Wallersteiner v Moir (No.2)*, the claimant may apply for an indemnity out of the assets of the company for the costs incurred by him in bringing the action on the company's behalf (commonly called a *Wallersteiner* order).

The ability to apply for such an indemnity is now set out in the Civil Procedure Rules, r.19.9E.[101] Under this rule, the court may order the company "to indemnify the claimant against any liability for costs incurred in the permission application or in the derivative claim or both".[102]

According to the judgment in *Wallersteiner v Moir (No.2)*, providing it is reasonable and prudent in the company's interest for a claimant to bring a derivative action, and it is brought by him in good faith, the court may

---

[95] *Abouraya v Sigmund* [2014] EWHC 277 (Ch) at [26]. See also *Kleanthous v Paphitis* [2011] EWHC 2287 at [75].

[96] *Barrett v Duckett* [1995] 1 B.C.L.C. 243 at 250. See also CA 2006 263(3)(f).

[97] Insolvency Act 1986 ss.112(1) and 168(5).

[98] *Barrett v Duckett* [1995] 1 B.C.L.C. 243 at 255.

[99] *Wallersteiner v Moir (No.2)* [1975] Q.B. 373; [1975] 2 W.L.R. 389; (1975) 119 S.J. 97.

[100] The Access to Justice Act 1999 set up alternative systems of funding for civil cases in England and Wales, including funding under the Community Legal Service, conditional fee agreements and litigation funding agreements.

[101] The new procedure was introduced by Civil Procedure (Amendment) Rules 2007 (SI 2007/2204) r.7.

[102] CPR r.19.9E applies to derivative actions under CA 2006 Pt 11 Ch.1, whether issued or taken over by a member, and to claims by members of a trade union or by members of an incorporated body, to which CA 2006 Pt 11 Ch.1 does not apply. The rule applies where the claim form for the derivative action was issued on or after 1 October 2007. See Civil Procedure (Amendment) Rules 2007 (SI 2007/2204) r.21. Where a claim was begun before 1 October 2007 the rules of court in force immediately before that date apply. Those rules are set out at Practice Direction 19C para.8(2).

order an indemnity in favour of the claimant (whether the action ultimately succeeds or not).[103] The court may have regard to the ability of the claimant to finance the claim himself[104] and may order that part of the costs be borne by the claimant regardless of his means.[105] Where the company is a quasi-partnership, then the court may consider the granting of an indemnity by the company to be unjust since the successful claimant will be entitled to recover a proportion of his costs from the defendant and be entitled to a lien and an indemnity over the assets recovered for the remainder and, where the claimant is unsuccessful, it would be unfair for the company (in effect the successful defendant) to bear any of the costs.[106] In practice the courts have been cautious, assessing the suitability of indemnities according to the circumstances, staging or limiting indemnities in appropriate circumstances or refusing them where the burden on the company would be unfair.[107]

The majority of the Court of Appeal in *Wallersteiner v Moir (No.2)*[108] considered that contingency fees (where the advisers to the petitioner are entitled to a share in the proceeds if the action is successful) could not be used as a mechanism to fund derivative actions. However, the introduction of rules permitting conditional fee arrangements[109] (allowing recovery from losing opponents of uplifted success fees, in addition to normal fees, and premiums for after-the-event legal expenses insurance) provides an alternative for the claimant to protect himself from full exposure to costs unless and until he obtains an indemnity out of the assets of the company.

10.3.7 Derivative action under CA 2006

Section 260 introduced the statutory derivative action that largely replaced the common law derivative action in respect of matters occurring from 1 October 2007.[110]

The provisions of CA 2006 generally prescribe a wider range of circumstances in which a derivative action may be brought by a shareholder

---

[103] *Wallersteiner v Moir (No.2)* [1975] Q.B. 373 at 392 and 403.

[104] *Smith v Croft (No.1)* [1986] 1 W.L.R. 580; (1986) 2 B.C.C. 99010; [1986] B.C.L.C. 207. In this case, Walton J suggested that it was for the claimant to show that he did not have sufficient resources to finance the action and that he genuinely needed an indemnity from the company. However, this more restrictive approach was not followed in *Jaybird Group Ltd v Greenwood* [1986] B.C.L.C. 319 at 327. See also *Iesini v Westrip Holdings Ltd* [2009] EWHC 2526 (Ch); [2010] B.C.C. 420; [2011] 1 B.C.L.C. 498 at [125].

[105] *Smith v Croft (No.1)* [1986] 1 W.L.R. 580; (1986) 2 B.C.C. 99010; [1986] B.C.L.C. 207 at 597–598.

[106] *Halle v Trax BW Ltd* [2000] B.C.C. 1020 as applied in *Mumbray v Lapper* [2005] EWHC 1152 (Ch); [2005] B.C.C. 990.

[107] *Wishart v Castlecroft Securities Ltd* [2009] CSIH 65; *Hughes v Weiss* [2012] EWHC 2363 (Ch); *Bhullar v Bhullar* [2015] EWHC 1943 (Ch).

[108] *Wallersteiner v Moir (No.2)* [1975] Q.B. 373 at 403.

[109] Under the Access to Justice Act 1999.

[110] See above. Transitional provisions address the basis on which claims related to events preceding that date may be brought.

against a director[111] when compared with the common law derivative action, most particularly where a director's negligence is actionable. Also, the statutory derivative claim can be brought even if a director has not benefited personally from the breach. Further, it is not necessary for the shareholder to show that those who have allegedly breached their duty control the majority of the shares in the company.[112] However, the statutory remedy is restrictive in comparison to the common law claim in that a derivative claim under CA 2006 Pt 11 Ch.1 may be brought "only in respect of a cause of action arising from an actual or proposed act or omission involving negligence, default, breach of duty or breach of trust by a director of the company",[113] or pursuant to an order in proceedings under s.994. As such, a derivative claim will be available in the event of breach by a director or directors of the general duties as codified in CA 2006 Pt 10 Ch.2, including the duty to exercise reasonable care, skill and diligence.[114]

Section 260 defines a "derivative claim" as comprising three parts. First, a derivative claim brought under s.260 must be brought by a member of the company.[115] It is immaterial whether the cause of action arose before or after the person seeking to bring or continue the derivative claim became a member of the company[116] and a "member of the company" includes a person who is not a member but to whom shares in the company have been transferred or transmitted by operation of law, for example where a trustee in bankruptcy or personal representative of a deceased member's estate acquires an interest in a share as a result of the bankruptcy or death of a member.[117] Secondly, a cause of action must vest in the company and arise from an act or omission involving negligence, breach of duty or trust by a director or shadow director.[118] Finally, the relief must be sought on behalf of the company (as opposed to the member).

Derivative claims may be brought against the directors (which includes shadow directors and former directors) themselves or against third parties.[119] The statutory explanatory notes anticipate that derivative claims against third parties "would be permitted only in very narrow circumstances, where the damage suffered by the company arose from an act

---

[111] *Iesini v Westrip Holdings Ltd* [2009] EWHC 2526 (Ch) at [75].

[112] This nonetheless is a factor the court may take into account; see *Wishart, Petitioner* [2009] CSIH 65; 2010 S.C. 16; 2009 S.L.T. 812 at [38]. Also *Bamford v Harvey* [2012] EWHC 2858 (Ch). If the company is in liquidation, it is likely the court will be disinclined to permit a derivative suit while the liquidator is able to determine whether or not to pursue a claim on the merits.

[113] CA 2006 s.260(3).

[114] CA 2006 s.174.

[115] In contrast, see above for "multiple" derivative claims brought by a non-member outside the statutory regime; see *Fort Gilkicker Ltd, Re* [2013] EWHC 348 (Ch); [2013] 3 W.L.R. 164; [2013] B.C.C. 365.

[116] CA 2006 s.260(4).

[117] CA 2006 s.260(5)(c).

[118] CA 2006 s.260(3), (5)(a) and (b).

[119] *Iesini v Westrip Holdings Ltd* [2009] EWHC 2526 (Ch) at [75].

involving a breach of a duty etc. on the part of the director (e.g. for knowing receipt of money or property transferred in breach of trust or for knowing assistance in a breach of trust)".[120]

10.3.8 *Procedure to bring a derivative claim under CA 2006*

10.3.8.1 *Application for permission to continue a derivative claim or continue a claim made by the company as a derivative claim*

Pursuant to ss.261 and 262, the court's permission (or leave, in Northern Ireland) must be obtained in order to continue a derivative claim or to continue a claim made by the company as a derivative claim. The court has a broad discretion to give directions as to the evidence that is required to be provided by the company in advance of the full hearing and as to the conduct of the proceedings generally, including powers to adjourn and give such directions as it thinks fit. The court is also given the power to exercise a broad discretion in determining the outcome of such an application and there is scope for significant judicial involvement throughout the process including controls over any settlement.[121]

The claim is initiated by issuing a claim form and application notice.[122] There is no requirement to obtain the leave of the court prior to issuing the claim form. However, the member must apply for leave to continue the claim, thereby providing the court with the ability to assess whether a prima facie case exists and to develop a process for the conduct of the proceedings that is appropriate in the circumstances.[123]

If a prima facie case,[124] is not established, the court must dismiss the application and it may make any consequential orders it considers appropriate (e.g. a costs order against the member). The onus of proof is on the member to establish that a prima facie case exists on the evidence filed with the claim. If the court is satisfied on the strength of evidence filed by the member, it may give directions as to the evidence to be provided by the company or adjourn the proceedings to enable evidence to be obtained. On further hearing of the application, the court may give permission to continue the claim on such terms as it thinks fit, refuse permission and dismiss the application or adjourn the proceedings and give directions as it thinks fit.

---

[120] Companies Act 2006 Explanatory Notes prepared by the Department of Business, Innovation and Skills.

[121] CPR 19.9 and CPR Practice Direction 19C: Derivative Claims para.7.

[122] CPR 19.9–19.9F and CPR Practice Direction 19C: Derivative Claims.

[123] For a review of this standard, see A. Keay and J. Loughrey, "Derivative Proceedings in a Brave New World for Company Management and Shareholders" [2010] J.B.L. 3. See also comments of David Donaldson QC in *Langley Ward Ltd v Trevor* [2011] EWHC 1893 (Ch) on the importance of the two-stage process introduced by CA 2006.

[124] *Abouraya v Sigmund* [2014] EWHC 277 (Ch) at [53]—see above.

Where a member wishes to apply for the permission (or leave) of the court to continue as a derivative claim a claim that has been brought by a company, the member must also convince the court that:

"(a)   the manner in which the company commenced or continued the claim amounts to an abuse of the process of the court;

(b)   the company has failed to prosecute the claim diligently; and

(c)   it is appropriate for the member to continue the claim as a derivative claim."[125]

These requirements reflect the Law Reform Commission's concern to prevent undue interference by members with existing litigation. It was explained during the debates on the Companies Bill 2006 in Committee Stage in the House of Commons that an objective was to provide the member with a right to claim where a company has brought proceedings to prevent a derivative claim and the company has not prosecuted the claim diligently in the sense that it has not pursued the claim in a reasonable way without undue delay so as to have the effect of frustrating someone else's ability to bring a claim.

10.3.8.2   *Application for permission to continue a derivative claim brought or continued by another member*

Where a member wishes to apply for permission (or leave) of the court to continue a derivative claim brought or continued by another member, equivalent standards to those described above when convincing the court to permit a member to continue as a derivative claim a claim brought by the company will apply pursuant to s.264. Similarly, if a prima facie case for giving permission (or leave) is not established, the court must dismiss the application and may make any consequential order it considers appropriate but, if the application is not dismissed, the court may give directions as to the evidence to be provided by the company or adjourn the proceedings to enable evidence to be obtained. On further hearing of the application, the court may give permission to continue the claim on such terms as it thinks fit, dismiss the application or adjourn the proceedings and give such directions as it thinks fit.

10.3.8.3   *Court's discretion in determining whether to grant permission to continue a derivative claim*

The court is granted a wide discretion to consider all relevant factors when determining whether a derivative claim should continue. CA 2006 specifies circumstances in which permission must be refused and the factors that the court must take into account in making its determination. Unless the parties otherwise agree, these further requirements should be addressed after permission (or leave) to continue a derivative claim has initially been

---

[125] CA 2006 s.262(2).

granted, at a second stage when considering evidence developed by the company as directed after a prima facie case has been established. In practice, in assessing the prima facie case, there is likely to be a tendency to merge the assessment with some consideration of these further requirements.

In determining whether a prima facie case has been established, the existence of a good cause of action on the part of the company and negligence, default, breach of duty or trust by a director of the company must be established. At the second stage, the court must form a provisional view on the strength of the claim, considering the requirements in s.263(2).[126]

Pursuant to s.263(2), the court *must* refuse permission to continue a derivative claim under ss.261 or 262 if it is satisfied:

"(a) that a person acting in accordance with Section 172 (duty to promote the success of the company) would not seek to continue the claim, or

(b) where the cause of action arises from an act or omission that is yet to occur, the act or omission has been authorised by the company, or

(c) where the cause of action arises from an act or omission that has already occurred, the act or omission—
(i) was authorised by the company before it occurred, or
(ii) has been ratified by the company since it occurred."

By its terms, the court should only refuse permission if satisfied that no director would seek to continue the claim for s.263(2) purposes.[127] However, pursuant to s.263(3), the court must also take account of the importance a person acting in accordance with s.172 (duty to promote the success of the company) would attach to continuing the claim and will consider the prospects of success, the ability of the company to recover damages, the disruption to the company's business, the costs and potential damage to the company, in effect some level of assessment as to reasonable business judgement.[128]

As noted by Lewison J in the case of *Iesini v Westrip Holdings Ltd*, weighing these considerations is essentially a commercial decision that the court is ill-equipped to undertake, except in a clear case. Evidence of the commercial view of independent directors is therefore likely to prove significant, and should be taken into account under s.263(3)(b). As is the case for the common law derivative action, authorisation or ratification will operate as a bar to continuation of a derivative claim. If not already

---

[126] *Iesini v Westrip Holdings Ltd* [2009] EWHC 2526 (Ch).
[127] *Iesini v Westrip Holdings Ltd* [2009] EWHC 2526 (Ch) at [86].
[128] *Franbar Holdings Ltd v Patel* [2008] EWHC 1534 (Ch); [2008] B.C.C. 885; [2009] 1 B.C.L.C. 1 at [36]. See also at [30] and [36] for commentary that the lack of a fully developed case is not fatal to the ability of a director to determine that a claim should be continued. Also *Iesini v Westrip Holdings Ltd* [2009] EWHC 2526 (Ch) at [85]. *Wishart, Petitioner* [2009] CSIH 65; 2010 S.C. 16; 2009 S.L.T. 812 at [37].

authorised or ratified, the likelihood (but not merely the possibility)[129] that the company will authorise or ratify the matter complained of, if invited to do so, is to be considered by the court under s.263(3)(c).

Provision for ratification of conduct by a director amounting to negligence, default, breach of duty or breach of trust in relation to the company is made in s.239 and applies to conduct on or after 1 October 2007. Conduct prior to that date is subject to the law relating to ratification applicable immediately before that date. The section does not affect any enactment or rule of law imposing additional requirements for valid ratification including rules that certain acts are incapable of ratification.[130]

Section 239 imposes an additional restriction not applicable at common law, that a decision by a company to ratify conduct by a director must be made by the members without reliance on votes in favour of the ratification cast by the director or any member connected with him.[131] Ratification at common law does not exclude related party voting.[132] Moreover, s.263(4) requires the court to take account of any evidence before it as to the views of members of the company who have no personal, direct or indirect, interest in the matter.[133] The court might be expected to require evidence from the company in that regard, in addition to the other factors it must take into account as described above and the discretionary considerations summarised below.

Having navigated the requirements in s.263(2), the court must *take into account* the following considerations listed in s.263(3) in making its determination:

(a)   whether the member is acting in good faith in seeking a remedy for the company[134];

---

[129] *Franbar Holdings* [2008] EWHC 1534 (Ch) at [47].

[130] CA 2006 s.239(7) and *Franbar Holdings* [2008] EWHC 1534 (Ch) at [44] and [45], although the basis for determination of what is incapable of ratification is confused. The full scope of what is incapable of ratification remains unclear although clearly including expropriation of company property and diversion of company opportunity: *Cook v Deeks* [1916] 1 A.C. 554.

[131] See CA 2006 ss.252 and 254 defining connectedness for this purpose.

[132] *Regal (Hastings) Ltd v Gulliver* [1967] 2 A.C. 134; [1942] 1 All E.R. 378 at 150.

[133] For an interpretation of the nature of interest for this purpose, see *Iesini v Westrip Holdings Ltd* [2009] EWHC 2526 (Ch) at [129].

[134] See *Nurcombe v Nurcombe* [1985] 1 W.L.R. 370; (1984) 1 B.C.C. 99269; (1984) 81 L.S.G. 2929 at 376; *Goldsmith v Sperrings Ltd* [1977] 1 W.L.R. 478; [1977] 2 All E.R. 566; (1977) 121 S.J. 304; a dominant purpose to benefit the company is sufficient despite the existence of some collateral purpose unrelated to the benefit of the company—*Iesini v Westrip Holdings Ltd* [2009] EWHC 2526 (Ch) at [121]. See also *Franbar Holdings* [2008] EWHC 1534 (Ch) at [32]–[34]—an objective to enhance the buy-out value of a minority holding is not evidence of bad faith, nor is a poorly developed case. Note also that the claimant will be disqualified if he participated in the wrong to which the complaint relates: *Iesini* [2009] EWHC 2526 (Ch); [2010] B.C.C. 420; [2011] 1 B.C.L.C. 498 at [122].

(b) the importance a person acting in accordance with s.172 (duty to promote the success of the company) would attach to continuing the claim;

(c) whether the company is likely to authorise or ratify the matter;

(d) whether the company has decided not to pursue the claim; and

(e) whether the act or omission in respect of which the claim is being brought gives rise to a cause of action that the member could pursue in his own right.

The considerations in s.263(3) are discretionary, not mandatory, unlike the factors to be considered under s.263(2). There is no guidance or restriction as to the sequence in which the factors in ss.263(2) and (3) should be considered but they are complementary and provide the court with the opportunity to explore the context and take into account views of any independent directors and shareholders. As experience develops, the Secretary of State has authority to amend both s.263(2) and (3), after consulting such persons as he considers appropriate.

Assembling the evidence required to demonstrate the likelihood of authorisation or ratification by the company in order to satisfy the consideration referred to in para.(c) above might impose an evidentiary burden on the company depending on the circumstances.[135] As a practical matter, the adjournment procedures envisaged in s.261 allow time to demonstrate whether authorisation or ratification will be forthcoming. The fact that weight is attached to the prospect of authorisation or ratification echoes the suggestion made in *Prudential Assurance Co Ltd v Newman Industries Ltd (No.2).*[136]

The attention required to be given to any decision of the company not to pursue a claim and the associated requirement in s.263(4) to have particular regard to the views of members of the company who have no personal interest in the matter[137] allows the court to bar a derivative claim for a breach of a director's duty even though incapable of ratification or where for their own reasons other disinterested members do not support the claim.[138]

As to the last identified factor to be taken into account, the prospect of an alternative remedy available to the member arising out of the act or omission would include an unfair prejudice petition in the alternative to derivative action[139] and rights to bring a claim conferred under a

---

[135] See *Stimpson v Southern Landlords Assoc* [2009] EWHC 2072 (Ch) for use of a questionnaire to elicit shareholder views.

[136] *Prudential Assurance Co Ltd v Newman Industries Ltd (No.2)* [1982] Ch. 204.

[137] Those who are not implicated in the alleged wrongdoing, and who do not stand to benefit otherwise than in their capacity as members of the company. *Iesini v Westrip Holdings Ltd* [2009] EWHC 2526 (Ch) at [129] and [130].

[138] See *Smith v Croft (No.2)* [1988] Ch. 114.

[139] Where a s.994 petition has been initiated, the prospect of success in seeking permission to

shareholders agreement.[140] The common law required all remedies to be taken into account including those available to the company.[141]

Concern has been voiced that the statutory derivative claim inappropriately enhances the ability of minority members to bring derivative claims and exposes directors to more claims and liability. However, deterrent features in the statutory process include the requirement to establish a prima facie case at the outset and the broad discretion vested in the court to reject applications in the preliminary hearings or exploit the power to adjourn and give directions as circumstances dictate.[142]

The capacity to assemble evidence in response to a prima facie case that is relevant to the court's consideration of the identified discretionary factors and any other factor to which the court should have regard allows a geared approach to assessment of the merits at a preliminary stage without embarking on a mini trial.[143]

The financial exposure of the petitioner to a costs order should circumstances merit remains unchanged and serves as a deterrent. Obversely, the scope for sequenced preliminary procedures while evidence is assembled offers the potential to allow for a more phased process than had emerged under the common law action. It remains the case that, should the shareholder be successful in a derivative action, any damages awarded are payable to the company and not to the shareholder.

All told, billed as "a weapon of last resort",[144] the procedure in relation to derivative claims maintains many strong deterrent elements. The multiplicity of considerations to be addressed by the court and the uncertain depth of consideration to be applied at the preliminary stages leaves plenty of scope for the courts to reject applications. The introduction of the statutory derivative claim has not and is unlikely to result in a dramatic increase in litigation in this area.

10.3.8.4   Costs

While the principle was established in *Wallesteiner v Moir (No.2)*[145] that an indemnity for costs from the company should be available for derivative

---

bring a derivative action even on a consolidated basis is likely to be reduced (see *Franbar Holdings* [2008] EWHC 1534 (Ch) at [53]) unless the remedy likely to be available under s.994 is less suitable.

[140] See *Bamford v Harvey* [2012] EWHC 2858 (Ch); [2013] Bus. L.R. 589; [2013] B.C.C. 311, where a director's application for permission to commence derivative proceedings was refused where the director had express authority to litigate the claim under a shareholders agreement.

[141] *Barrett v Duckett* [1995] 1 B.C.L.C. 243 at 372.

[142] See *Iesini v Westrip Holdings Ltd* [2009] EWHC 2526 (Ch) at [108].

[143] See *Fanmailuk.com Ltd v Cooper* [2008] EWHC 2198 (Ch).

[144] *Hansard*, HL, Vol.679 (Official Report) cols GC4-5 (Lord Goldsmith) 27 February 2006.

[145] *Wallesteiner v Moir (No.2)* [1975] Q.B. 373.

actions, and that once a prima facie case has been established the court ought normally to order the company to indemnify the claimant against his costs,[146] the courts have been cautious not to unfairly burden the company or its shareholders and will take account of the circumstances. Indemnity may be refused where it would otherwise prejudice the defendants or where the outcome of the claim is quite uncertain despite the relatively low hurdle to obtain permission to proceed having been negotiated. Indemnity might be ordered on a staged or partial basis or might be open to modification in the event of material change of circumstance.[147]

10.3.8.5 Company Participation

In any derivative claim, the company must be made a party; it is the person on whose behalf and for whose benefit the claim is being brought. It needs and wants to be a party so that it may enforce any judgment given in its favour.

The company, although a necessary party, being unable properly to bring the proceedings in its own right and in its own name, will be a nominal party. It will be required to give disclosure of documents, and may be required to disclose privileged materials.[148] It may also be required to provide an indemnity to the member pursuing the claim on its behalf and for its benefit. Where however, an independent majority of the board consider that it is not in the interests of the company that the claim be pursued, the company may choose to adduce evidence to that effect on any application to continue the claim as a derivative claim. The court will have due regard to any such evidence.[149]

A derivative claim may be thought by activist shareholders to be a more attractive form of proceeding than a claim under s.994. Whilst a s.994 claim has the merits of (1) the breadth of the claims that may be brought; and (2) the breadth of the relief that may be granted, it has the downside that the usual relief that is granted, or is offered, is an order that the claimant's shares be purchased at a fair value. A refusal to accept any such "reasonable" offer is often followed by a strike out application, on the ground that the claimant cannot reasonably expect to do any better if the claim was fought and was successful. The potential for any negotiation, therefore, is limited. On the other hand, in a derivative action, the remedy of a "buy out" is not available to the court. The action, if well founded, will be fought to a conclusion unless a negotiated settlement is reached before then. Until such a settlement is reached, or the action is fought, substantial costs, both financial and in terms of management time will be expended,

---

[146] *Iesini v Westrip Holdings Ltd* [2009] EWHC 2526. Civil Procedure Rules r.19.9E.
[147] See Section 10.3.6 above. Also *Wishart v Castlecroft Securities Ltd* [2009] CSIH 65; *Bhullar v Bhullar* [2015] EWHC 1943 (Ch).
[148] *Hydrosan, Re* [1991] B.C.L.C. 418.
[149] *Kleanthous v Paphitis* [2011] EWHC 2287 (Ch).

distracting the directors from their management of the company's business and the pursuit of its success. Those costs should not be underestimated. To the activist shareholder, this may well be seen to create a suitable, or even ideal, environment within which to pursue its claims by negotiation, rather than at trial.

10.4 Statutory unfair prejudice remedy (section 994)

The statutory remedy for unfairly prejudicial conduct is notable for two reasons; the breadth of both the jurisdiction and of the remedies that may be granted. In *Saul D Harrison*,[150] Hoffmann LJ explained the concept of unfairness. He said that it involved conduct which amounted to a breach of conduct, a breach of duty, or was inconsistent with a legitimate expectation which the complainant had as to the manner in which the affairs of the company would be conducted.

It was that last element which extended the jurisdiction of the court, the other two elements being otherwise recognised by the law in the more traditional forms of action. Where the court is satisfied of the unfair prejudice, it has a wide discretion to grant the forms of relief set out in s.996 for the purpose of remedying the unfairness, many of which would not be available in a traditional form of action for breach of contract or breach of duty.

That said, the courts have been astute to recognise that these complaints arise out of a business or commercial relationship, the terms of which are often set out in some detail in written agreements between the parties, and have, thus, been slow to recognise the existence or legitimacy of expectations outside of those agreements.

Further, whilst s.996 affords a menu of different reliefs which may be granted or fashioned to meet the unfair prejudice, it must be recognised that the usual remedy is a "buy out" order, reflecting the desire, as stated by Hoffmann LJ in *Saul D Harrison*, that what the complainant really wants in such a situation is to have his shares purchased at a fair price.

10.4.1 The requirements of section 994[151]

Section 994(1) provides:

> "A member of a company may apply to the court by petition for an order under [Pt 30 CA 2006] on the ground (a) that the company's affairs are being or have been conducted in a manner that is unfairly prejudicial to the interests of members generally or of some part of its members (including at least himself),

---

[150] *Saul D Harrison & Sons Plc, Re* [1995] 1 B.C.L.C. 14.
[151] Replacing CA 1985 s.495, substantially without alteration, with effect from 1 October 2007.

or (b) that an actual or proposed act or omission of the company (including an act or omission on its behalf) is or would be so prejudicial."

The remedy was first introduced in Companies Act 1948 s.210 and related to conduct that was oppressive to some part of the members. The narrower concept of oppression was replaced by the requirement now reflected in s.994[152] that the relevant conduct be unfairly prejudicial. The opportunity was also taken when replacing the remedy in the Companies Act 1980 to address other defects in s.210.

Under s.210 it was necessary to demonstrate that the facts would have justified a winding up on the just and equitable ground. Section 994 imposes no such requirement.[153] It also makes clear that a single act or omission, and threatened conduct of a kind that would otherwise support a petition, can justify relief. Further, to supplement the fraud on the minority exception to the rule in *Foss v Harbottle*, the power of the court was extended to authorise proceedings to be brought against a third party in the name of the company and on such terms as the court should direct. Finally the right of persons entitled to shares by transmission to petition was specifically confirmed.[154] It was anticipated that the amendments now reflected in s.994 should enable a petitioner to obtain relief where he could demonstrate sufficient prejudice to his interests as a result of conduct that damaged the value of the company, for example, through negligence or abuse of corporate assets, where the conduct complained of might fall short of fraud on the minority. Nonetheless there was a concern to achieve an appropriate balance such that the court should not interfere with bona fide commercial decisions taken on behalf of the company.

An amendment introduced in the Companies Act 1989 removed a defect that impeded reliance upon the remedy where the interests of some but not all of the members were unfairly prejudiced.

While successful petitions under s.210 were rare, the remedy introduced in 1980 and now reflected in s.994 has spawned a very high level of activity and has generally proved far more successful although a strong case for further reform has been made as reflected in the Law Commission *Shareholder Remedies* Report 246.[155]

The remedy was introduced as an alternative to a winding up on the just and equitable ground and is substantially relied upon as an exit mechanism

---

[152] Originally Companies Act 1980 s.75 and then consolidated in CA 1985 s.49.

[153] *O'Neill v Phillips* [1999] 1 W.L.R. 1092; [1999] B.C.C. 600; [1999] 2 B.C.L.C. 1 at 1098–1100; *Hawkes v Cuddy* [2009] EWCA Civ 291; [2010] B.C.C. 597; [2009] 2 B.C.L.C. 427 at [104].

[154] These changes were all recommended by the Jenkins Committee: Cmnd.1749 of 1962, see paras 199–212.

[155] In the event, no material reform was introduced in CA 2006. In particular, the opportunity was not taken to adopt proposals for reform made by the Law Commission and summarised in Section 10.4.5 below.

for the damaged shareholder while not destroying the company. In distinguishing circumstances in which a claim under s.994 is more appropriate than a derivative claim, if the substance of the claim relates to breach of duty or other conduct that is actionable by the company, a derivative claim is more suitable whereas a complaint relating to mismanagement of the company should be pursued on the grounds of unfair prejudice. However, reliance on s.994 to address breaches of duty which have caused loss to the company has been successful even though the circumstances would warrant a derivative claim.[156] Evidently, should this trend develop, it opens the way to circumvent the need to pursue a derivative claim. Nonetheless, provided the remedy is corporate, the outcome can be rationalised with the core reflective loss presumption, that a shareholder cannot sue to make good a loss which would be made good should the company's assets be replenished, through action against the party responsible for the loss.[157]

While the unfair prejudice claim applies to all Companies Act companies,[158] it has proved particularly relevant to private companies, in circumstances where shareholders may also be directors and the distinction between the interests of an individual as an investor and his responsibilities as a director is blurred. Despite the remedy, shareholders in private companies where disputes of the kind to which s.994 applies are more likely to arise will generally be well served to make appropriate provision in shareholders' agreements or the articles to establish controls over the conduct of the company's affairs, manage disputes and provide an exit solution in the event that issues in dispute cannot otherwise be resolved satisfactorily.

The jurisdiction under s.994 comprises a number of elements addressed in the following sections.

10.4.1.1   The complainant must be a member

In general, the petitioner under s.994 must be a member[159] at the time of bringing the petition. The petitioner need not have been a member at the time of the conduct to which the complaint relates.[160] Any person to whom shares have been transferred or transmitted by operation of law is, although not a registered member, permitted to petition.[161] A former member is unable to petition under s.994, even if he discovers that unfairly prejudicial conduct occurred while he was a member.

---

[156] *Company (No.005287 of 1985), Re* [1986] 1 W.L.R. 281; (1985) 1 B.C.C. 99586; (1986) 83 L.S.G. 1058 at 284.
[157] *Johnson v Gore Wood & Co (No.1)* [2002] 2 A.C. 1; [2001] 2 W.L.R. 72; [2001] 1 B.C.L.C. 313 at 337.
[158] CA 2006 s.994(3).
[159] CA 2006 s.112 defines member.
[160] *Lloyd v Casey* [2002] 1 B.C.L.C. 454.
[161] CA 2006 s.994(2). *McCarthy Surfacing Ltd, Re* [2006] EWHC 832 (Ch).

A separate, but similar, right is given by s.995 to the Secretary of State to petition if he has received an inspector's report or obtained information by exercising his powers to do so, and it appears to him that the affairs of the company are being, or have been, conducted in a manner that is unfairly prejudicial to the interests of the members generally or of some part of the members, or that any actual or proposed act or omission of the company (including an act or omission on its behalf) is or would be so prejudicial.

10.4.1.2 *The complaint must be made in the petitioner's capacity as a member*

Section 994 refers to members' interests including at least the petitioner. It has been held that, while the expression "interests" is wider than "strict legal rights",[162] the interests must be those of the petitioner qua member, and not in some other capacity; that is, the conduct complained of must adversely affect or jeopardise the value or quality of the shareholder's interest.[163] There may be circumstances where conduct affecting a member in some other capacity may nonetheless also affect the member as a member because it breaches a term on which he agreed to participate as a member. For example, where the value of membership is inextricably connected with a management role, removal from management may prejudice the member's interests as a member.[164]

10.4.1.3 *Effect on other members*

The matter complained of need not affect the petitioner alone: it can affect all members (e.g. a fall in share value), even though the others do not complain.

10.4.1.4 *Conduct of the company's affairs*

It is not necessary for the conduct to be continuing at the time of presentation of the petition.[165] While the act complained of need not be continuing and a failure to act may prove sufficient,[166] if the offending conduct has been put right and cannot recur, or can be remedied by the petitioner, no court-imposed remedy will be required or available.[167] If the

---

[162] See *Company (No.00477 of 1986), Re* [1986] P.C.C. 372; [1986] B.C.L.C. 376 at 378; *JE Cade & Son Ltd, Re* [1991] B.C.C. 360; [1992] B.C.L.C. 213.

[163] *Company (No.004475 of 1982), Re* [1983] Ch. 178; [1983] 2 W.L.R. 381; [1983] B.C.L.C. 126 at 189; *JE Cade & Son Ltd, Re* [1991] B.C.C. 360; [1992] B.C.L.C. 213; but see the remarks of Vinelott J in *Company (No.002567 of 1982), Re* [1983] 1 W.L.R. 927. See also *O'Neill v Phillips* [1999] 1 W.L.R. 1092 which, while confirming that the prejudice must be suffered as a member, noted that the requirement should not be too narrowly or technically construed. See also commentary of Ralph Gibson LJ in *Nicholas v Soundcraft Electronics Ltd* [1993] B.C.L.C. 360.

[164] *O'Neill v Phillips* [1999] 1 W.L.R. 1092.

[165] *Company (No.001761 of 1986), Re* [1987] B.C.L.C. 141 at 143.

[166] *Company (No.001761 of 1986), Re* [1987] B.C.L.C. 141.

[167] *Legal Costs Negotiators Ltd, Re* (also known as *Morris v Hateley*) [1999] B.C.C. 547; [1999] 2

conduct is liable to recur, the court will assert jurisdiction.[168] It follows that it is not, in general, apt for persons in control of a company as directors and shareholders to bring a petition, even where relations with a minority shareholder have totally broken down, for example in an effort to squeeze out the minority in reliance on s.994, notwithstanding some prior or even current improper conduct of the minority shareholder in any management role.[169] Although there is no express restriction in s.994, where the petitioner can himself readily put an end to the alleged unfair prejudice, the court would usually strike out a s.994 petition brought by majority shareholders unless they do not have control so as to be able to remedy the offending conduct.[170]

There is no limitation period applicable to a petition under s.994, and so historic conduct can be relied upon, but inexcusable delay may bar relief.[171]

Although s.994 makes reference to a proposed act or omission of the company, proposed conduct of the company that is merely speculative may be insufficient.[172]

10.4.1.5 Meaning of "the company's affairs"

The conduct complained of must be conduct by the defendant of the company's affairs, rather than conduct by shareholders of their own affairs or the exercise of their individual rights, and will be construed liberally.[173] The offending conduct must be concerned with acts done by the company or those authorised to act on its behalf[174] for example, a decision by the board or under delegated authority from the board or within the scope of

---

B.C.L.C. 171 at 198c; (1999) 96(13) L.S.G. 31; and see *Grandactual Ltd, Re* [2005] EWHC 1415 (Ch); [2006] B.C.C. 73; [2005] All E.R. (D) 313.

[168] *Kenyon Swansea Ltd, Re* [1987] B.C.L.C. 514 at 521, referred to with approval by Peter Gibson LJ in *Legal Costs Negotiators Ltd, Re* (1999) 2 B.C.L.C. 171 at 198b.

[169] *Legal Costs Negotiators Ltd, Re* (1999) 2 B.C.L.C. 171 at 198 and 201.

[170] *Parkinson v Eurofinance Group Ltd* (2001) 1 B.C.L.C. 720. Also *Cool Seas (Seafoods) Ltd v Interfish Ltd* [2018] EWHC 2038 (Ch) in which minority shareholder consent was contractually required for various matters including commencement of a breach of duty claim by the company against directors appointed by the minority. Taking account of the totality of restraint represented by the reserved matters requiring minority consent, Rose J allowed the petition. The decision is also an example of shareholder responsibility for the conduct of its nominee directors.

[171] *Company (No.005134 of 1986) Ex p. Harries, Re* [1989] B.C.L.C. 383 at 397–398.

[172] *Aske (BSR) Plc, Re* (1998) 2 B.C.L.C. 556 at 578.

[173] *Hawkes v Cuddy* [2009] EWCA Civ 291 at [48] and [50]. See also commentary in *Sikorski v Sikorski* [2012] EWHC 1613 (Ch) at [56] that s.994 was not normally to be used for the resolution of disputes between shareholders, although those arrangements could be relevant to the extent they impact on the conduct of the affairs of the company.

[174] *Legal Costs Negotiators Ltd, Re* (1999) 2 B.C.L.C. 171; *Arrow Nominees Inc v Blackledge* [2000] C.P. Rep. 59; [2001] B.C.C. 591; [2000] 2 B.C.L.C. 167.

authority of the board.[175] Conduct wholly in another capacity (even if that conduct affects the company) will not support a complaint.[176]

A refusal by a minority shareholder to sell shares, or disagreements between shareholders relating to their disposal of or dealings with their shares, or breach of a shareholders agreement will not constitute conduct of the company's affairs even where the company may have an incidental involvement such as registration of a transfer made in breach of a pre-emption provision.[177] Similarly, disagreements as to the operation of a shareholders' agreement typically will not constitute conduct of the company's affairs.[178]

Actions or omissions in compliance or contravention of the articles of a company may or may not constitute conduct of the company's affairs depending on the precise facts.[179] Should controlling shareholders procure that a company takes no action to preserve its interests in the face of competing objectives of the controlling shareholders, or associated breach of directors duties, maintaining that policy of passive neglect of the company's interests will qualify as conduct of the company's affairs. Whether doing so is conduct that is unfairly prejudicial will turn on the facts.[180] The success of any petition under s.994 based on a breach of duty is likely to depend upon evidence that the controlling shareholders have failed to act and that derivative action is not appropriate.

Particularly in a group context, where a subsidiary has an independent minority, the parent company must accept that, insofar as it competes with the interests of its subsidiary, there will be an obligation to conduct affairs so as to deal fairly with the subsidiary.[181] Representative directors of the majority shareholder may find themselves in a delicate position where competing demands arise, but in those circumstances the burden will fall on the controlling shareholder to behave with evident fairness towards the minority shareholders and allow its representative directors to act in the best interests of the subsidiary. Exploiting control to guide the subsidiary to

---

[175] *Hawkes v Cuddy* [2009] EWCA Civ 291 at [50].
[176] *Charterhouse Capital Ltd, Re* [2014] EWCA Civ 536 at [45]. *Company (No.001761 of 1986), Re* [1987] B.C.L.C. 141; *O'Neill v Phillips* [1999] 1 W.L.R. 1092; *Sikorski v Sikorski* [2012] EWHC 1613 (Ch).
[177] *Leeds United Holdings Plc, Re* [1997] B.C.C. 131; [1996] 2 B.C.L.C. 545. *Coroin Ltd (No.2), Re* [2012] EWHC (Ch): breach of obligations under a shareholders agreement. See *Graham v Every* [2014] EWCA Civ 191 at [38]: where breach of pre-emption provisions result in a purely administrative role such as registration of a new member, that is not sufficient conduct of the companies' affairs for this purpose.
[178] *Unisoft Group Ltd (No.3), Re* [1994] B.C.C. 766; [1994] 1 B.C.L.C. 609; *Leeds United Holdings Plc, Re* [1997] B.C.C. 131; [1996] 2 B.C.L.C. 545, but see *Scottish Co-operative Wholesale Society Ltd v Meyer* [1959] A.C. 324; [1958] 3 W.L.R. 404; 1958 S.C. (H.L.) 40.
[179] *Charterhouse Capital Ltd, Re* [2015] EWCA Civ 536 at [45].
[180] *Wilkinson v West Coast Capital* [2005] EWHC 3009 (Ch); [2007] B.C.C. 717.
[181] *Scottish Co-operative Wholesale Society Ltd v Meyer* [1959] A.C. 324 at 341.

a policy of inaction, restraint or omission is sufficient connection between the conduct of the controlling shareholders and the company's affairs for these purposes.

Where the affairs of members of a group of companies are, to a significant extent, treated as if they were a single enterprise, actions taken by the parent company in its own interests may be regarded as acts done in the conduct of the affairs of the subsidiary, even if the two companies are engaged in different types of business and despite general principles of separate corporate personality.[182] Obversely, conduct of the affairs of a wholly-owned subsidiary may give rise to allegations of unfair prejudice to the interests of members of the parent company.[183] This conclusion is justified by reference to the risk of diminution in value of the members' interests in the parent company that is reflective of the loss of value of the parent company's investment in the subsidiary as a result of the matters giving rise to the allegations. While this runs counter to the principle that a member should have no personal remedy and logically not enjoy any other personal cause of action when the loss is reflective, perhaps central to any determination whether a claim under s.994 is appropriate in the alternative to a derivative action in such circumstances will be whether, following a derivative action, the relationship between the shareholders is such that an exit remedy under s.994 would be more appropriate.

While the commercial realities will be an influential factor in determining the appropriate remedy, the mere capacity of one enterprise to exercise direct or indirect control over the affairs of another should not be expected to prove sufficient of itself to establish an adequate connection for this purpose.[184]

10.4.1.6 Meaning of "interests"

Although the expression "interests of members" in s.994 limits the interests in question to those of the members qua members, it is not limited to strict legal rights under the company's constitution, and the court may have regard to wider equitable considerations.[185] However, the petitioner must usually show some breach of the terms on which the members have agreed, or have an understanding, that the affairs of the company should be conducted.[186]

---

[182] *Nicholas v Soundcraft Electronics Ltd* [1993] B.C.L.C. 360.

[183] *Gross v Rackind* [2004] EWCA Civ 815; [2005] 1 W.L.R. 3505; [2005] B.C.C. 11.

[184] *Grandactual Ltd, Re* [2005] EWHC 1415 (Ch); [2006] B.C.C. 73; [2005] All E.R. (D) 313.

[185] See *Macro (Ipswich) Ltd, Re* [1994] 2 B.C.L.C. 354 at 404—examples of interests included damage to the value of the company and the absence of independent directors; *Rotadata Ltd, Re* [2000] B.C.C. 686; [2000] 1 B.C.L.C. 122; *Gamlestaden Fastigheter AB v Baltic Partners Ltd* [2007] UKPC 26; [2007] Bus. L.R. 1521; [2007] B.C.C. 272 where account was taken of the member's loan capital in the company.

[186] *O'Neill v Phillips* [1999] 1 W.L.R. 1092 at 1098–1100.

This agreement need not necessarily be a formal agreement, but in appropriate circumstances can be a "legitimate expectation"[187] of the petitioner, breach of which might have formed the basis of a petition to wind up the company on the "just and equitable" ground set out in Insolvency Act 1986 s.122(1)(g). In the case of *Ebrahimi v Westbourne Galleries Ltd*[188] (where the majority had exercised their legal right to remove the petitioner from his directorship), the House of Lords determined that it was both impossible and undesirable to give an exhaustive statement of the circumstances in which equitable considerations should be taken into account in determining whether a person's rights had been interfered with, but indicated that the circumstances might include one or probably more of the following elements:

(a)   an association formed or continued on the basis of a personal relationship, involving mutual confidence—this element will often be found where a pre-existing partnership has been converted into a limited company;

(b)   an agreement, or understanding, that all or (if there are sleeping shareholders) some of the shareholders shall participate in the conduct of the business; and

(c)   a restriction upon the transfer of the members' interest in the company—so that, if confidence is lost or one member is removed from management, he cannot take out his stake and go elsewhere.

This parallel between circumstances in which an exercise of strict legal rights will nonetheless justify a remedy under s.994 and the "just and equitable" ground for winding up is not intended to mean that the conduct complained of will not be unfair unless it would justify a winding up order on that ground. It is quite clear that whereas there was such a requirement in the former Companies Act 1948 s.210, that standard is not replicated in

---

[187] *Saul D Harrison & Sons Plc, Re* [1994] B.C.C. 475; [1995] 1 B.C.L.C. 14, although this expression was qualified in *O'Neill v Phillips* [1999] 1 W.L.R. 1092 such that only to the extent equitable principles dictate should a remedy be available. Most US states provide a remedy in response to misconduct by those that control a corporation. A common theme in the development of such remedies is to relate them closely to breach of good faith and fair-dealing obligations by majority shareholders or, at its broadest, the frustration of "reasonable expectations" of shareholders. The reasonable expectations standard has enabled US courts to adapt the remedy to address the greater intimacy of business relationships that tend to exist in close corporations, permitting the court to assess the understanding of the parties and then determine whether the conduct of controlling shareholders is contrary to that understanding. In determining the particular characteristics that bind participants in a close corporation, US courts have tended to distinguish subjective aspirations, frustration of which would not justify relief, and expectations that were known to and concurred with by other shareholders. In assessing expectations, the US courts have been prepared to look beyond rights and benefits anticipated by a shareholder in that capacity, to take account of an individual's collateral expectations as an officer or employee.

[188] *Ebrahimi v Westbourne Galleries Ltd* [1973] A.C. 360; [1972] 2 W.L.R. 1289; (1972) 116 S.J. 412.

425

s.994. The parallel is not in the conduct that the court will treat as justifying the remedy but in the principles upon which it determines that the conduct is unjust, inequitable or unfair.[189]

The expression "quasi-partnership" is not prescribed but identifies an enterprise where the participants should not be expected to rely solely on their constitutional and contractual rights and liabilities, where equitable considerations qualify those rights and liabilities.[190] It has been used to describe companies in which some or all of the elements in paras (a)–(c) above exist although they are not exhaustive or essential characteristics.[191] Qualification as a quasi-partnership is a function of mutual understanding and legitimate expectation.[192] The distinction between companies which are quasi-partnerships and those that are not is important in understanding what attitude a court will take on a petition under s.994. Where it is established that the company has the characteristics of a quasi-partnership, minority participants will in effect have an additional string upon which to rely, namely the breach of legitimate expectations that may go beyond the articles or agreements between shareholders, statutory obligations or directors' duties. However, it is not sufficient for the petitioner merely to establish that the company is a quasi-partnership in order to obtain a remedy under s.994. He must also show either a breach of the legal terms on which the business of the company is to be conducted or, in the context of a quasi-partnership, use by the majority of their strict legal entitlements in a manner that equity would regard as contrary to good faith.[193]

In identifying these hurdles, the House of Lords decision in *O'Neill v Phillips* represents a landmark limitation on excessive reliance upon s.994 by shareholders petitioning on the strength of broad based disappointments. Section 994 does not provide a right to exit at will, even if it is possible to establish that the company is a quasi-partnership, simply because there has been a loss of trust, confidence or good relations.[194] Deadlock and the inability of the company to conduct its business as initially contemplated is not in itself sufficient.

Nonetheless, where an event occurs that puts an end to the basis upon which parties have entered into a quasi-partnership, making it unfair that some shareholders should insist upon the continuance of the association,

---

[189] *O'Neill v Phillips* [1999] 1 W.L.R. 1092; also *Hawkes v Cuddy* [2009] EWCA Civ 291 at [104].
[190] *Re a Company (No.002015 of 1996)* [1997] 2 B.C.L.C. 1 at 18e.
[191] *Re a Company (No.002015 of 1996)* [1997] 2 B.C.L.C. 1 at 19a.
[192] *Re a Company (No.005685 of 1988) Ex p. Schwarcz (No.2)* [1989] B.C.L.C. 424 at 440c.
[193] *O'Neill v Phillips* [1999] 1 W.L.R. 1092 at 1098–1100. The Law Commission *Shareholder Remedies* Report 246 at para.4.11 references its suggestion that conduct could be unfairly prejudicial merely based on breaches of legitimate expectations, a concept adopted in *Saul D Harrison & Sons Plc, Re* [1994] B.C.C. 475; [1995] 1 B.C.L.C. 14. In *O'Neill*, Lord Hoffmann qualified this broad interpretation on the basis that a balance must be struck between the breadth of discretion given to the court and the principle of legal certainty.
[194] See also *Hawkes v Cuddy* [2009] EWCA Civ 291 at [108], rejecting *Guidezone Ltd, Re* [2001] B.C.C. 692; [2000] 2 B.C.L.C. 321.

the conduct of the majority to maintain that continuation in changed circumstances may be sufficient to support a petition.[195]

It will in general be difficult to demonstrate a quasi-partnership other than in small, possibly very small, companies. It is highly unlikely that a petitioner would be able to demonstrate that all members of a public company with a substantial number of shareholders were parties to some informal arrangement sufficient to qualify the contractual obligations and rights conferred by the constitution save perhaps in circumstances where there are two or more major shareholdings and there is a background of special co-operation or participation, for example, among founding shareholders.[196] As a general presumption those holding shares in a traded company should expect to rely on the strict constitutional arrangements and legal rights although conduct designed to undermine the position of minorities will fall within the scope of a s.994 petition. Nevertheless, a minority may hold the directors to account for any misuse or abuse of fiduciary power. Thus in *Howard Smith Ltd v Ampol Petroleum*,[197] a minority shareholder successfully challenged an allotment of shares by the directors the principal purpose of which was to dilute a particular existing shareholding, so as to facilitate a bid for the company which the board favoured. Such an abuse of power could now be brought within a s.994 proceeding. A sale or transfer of assets to a new company in which a minority may not be interested may also be susceptible to challenge even if the price paid was a fair price, if the purpose of the transaction was to exclude the minority from participating in that business.

10.4.1.7 *Meaning of "unfairly prejudicial"*

This leads to consideration of the meaning of the expression "unfairly prejudicial". There is a vast body of case law in the context of the s.994 remedy, reflecting the courts acknowledgement that, while the conduct must be prejudicial and unfairly so, the protection afforded by the section has to be worked out on a case-by-case basis and the words "unfairly prejudicial" should be applied flexibly to meet the circumstances.[198] The relevant conduct must be prejudicial, causing harm of a commercial nature, adverse to the company or shareholder value. It may encompass disregard of a member's rights without financial consequences although this is more challenging to establish.[199] To be unfair, account must be taken of legal

---

[195] *Hawkes v Cuddy* [2009] EWCA Civ 291 at [108] referring to *O'Neill v Phillips* [1999] 1 W.L.R. 1092 at 1101.

[196] *Blue Arrow Plc, Re* (1987) 3 B.C.C. 618; [1987] B.C.L.C. 585; [1988] P.C.C. 306; *Tottenham Hotspur Plc, Re* [1994] 1 B.C.L.C. 655; *Astec (BSR) Plc, Re* [1999] B.C.C. 59; [1998] 2 B.C.L.C. 556 at 590; *CAS (Nominees) Ltd v Nottingham Forest FC Plc* [2002] B.C.C. 145; [2002] 1 B.C.L.C. 613 at 627.

[197] *Howard Smith Ltd v Ampol Petroleum* [1974] A.C. 821.

[198] per Neill LJ in *Saul D Harrison & Sons Plc, Re* [1994] B.C.C. 475.

[199] *Coroin Ltd, Re* [2012] EWHC 2343 (Ch) at [630] and [631]. Also, *Elgindata (No.1), Re* [1991] B.C.L.C. 959.

rights and any equitable considerations driven by the petitioner's legitimate expectations which may be limited to the constitutional legal rights unless there are other relevant agreements or understandings, for example but not necessarily based on a quasi-partnership relationship. Management decisions that prejudice the petitioner's interests are insufficient; it is an assumed risk of investment that wider interests of the company may provoke decisions that prejudice individual interests and courts will be reluctant to characterise management decisions as unfair unless directors have exceeded their powers or exercised them for illegitimate or ulterior purpose.[200] A claim for alleged unfairly prejudicial conduct based upon a misuse of powers may be difficult to substantiate where it impacts equally on all shareholders, be they directors or otherwise, as such an effect may serve to undermine any allegation of impropriety.[201]

In the case of *O'Neill v Phillips*,[202] Lord Hoffmann identified two aspects of unfairness: some breach of the agreed terms for the conduct of the affairs of the company; and use of the agreed terms in a manner that equity would regard as contrary to good faith.

In its 1996 Consultation Paper,[203] the Law Commission analysed the petitions under the section presented to the Companies Court at the Royal Courts of Justice between January 1994 and December 1995, and identified the following principal allegations pleaded (listed in order of frequency):

(a)   exclusion from management: by far the most common allegation was that the petitioner had been excluded from the management of the company,[204] and this exclusion would be likely to entitle the petitioner to relief if the court finds that he has a legitimate expectation to participate and that exclusion was unfairly prejudicial to his interests qua member.[205] The conduct of the petitioner, and the way in which he was excluded, would be relevant.[206] The Law Commission has recommended that in the case of a private company limited by shares, in which substantially all the members are directors, there should be a statutory presumption that the removal of a shareholder as a director or from substantially all his functions as a director is unfairly prejudicial conduct. While this recommendation is not reflected in terms in the CA 2006, as noted in *O'Neill v Phillips*, this would not seem very different in practice from the way in which the provision is interpreted. The key point, however, is that the unfairness is not so much in the exclusion alone as in the exclusion without a reasonable offer to buy out the relevant shareholder (see Section 10.4.2 below);

---

[200] See Neill LJ in *Saul D Harrison & Sons Plc, Re* [1994] B.C.C. 475 under "Unfair prejudice".
[201] *OS3 Distribution Ltd; Watchstone Group Plc v Quob Park Estate Ltd* [2017] EWHC 2621 (Ch).
[202] *O'Neill v Phillips* [1999] W.L.R. 1092 at 1098.
[203] The Law Commission Consultation Paper No.142, Appendix E Table 1.
[204] *Richards v Lundy* [1999] B.C.C. 786; [2000] 1 B.C.L.C. 376.
[205] *Quinlan v Essex Hinge Co Ltd* [1997] B.C.C. 53; [1996] 2 B.C.L.C. 417.
[206] *RA Noble & Sons (Clothing) Ltd, Re* [1983] B.C.L.C. 273.

(b)   failure to provide information: although the failure to comply with the various requirements of the Companies Acts to provide members with information may be grounds for a petition under s.994 (unless the failure is trivial), it is more commonly linked to an allegation of exclusion from management. However, a deliberate policy not to consult the petitioner on major issues on which he has a legitimate expectation to be consulted could amount to unfair prejudice[207];

(c)   misappropriation of assets: there have been a number of successful petitions under the s.994 remedy where the majority have been shown to have misappropriated the company's assets (often by selling them at an undervalue to a company controlled by them) or diverted business, which should have gone to the company, to another business owned by them or otherwise acted to run down the value of the company while transferring value to themselves.[208] These cases show that a petition under s.994 is not barred even though the facts would have warranted the bringing of a derivative action or a personal action based on the directors' breach of duty;

(d)   failure to remunerate/pay a dividend: the fact that a company's failure to pay a dividend affects all shareholders equally is no longer relevant following the amendments introduced by the Companies Act 1989 and reflected in s.994. The petitioner will, however, have to show a legitimate expectation that dividends would be paid in order to overcome the objection that it is for the directors to decide what the company's policy should be on the retention or distribution of the company's profits. Failure to pay dividends is often linked to a complaint about excessive remuneration of the directors (see (f) below)[209];

(e)   mismanagement: the courts have been reluctant to interfere in the management of a company's business by the directors. Mere disagreement over the manner in which the business of a company is being operated or the policies of the board will not support action under s.994. Section 994 will not provide an exit mechanism or financial top-up for a shareholder who is simply disappointed with the company's performance or disagrees with decisions of the board over the direction the company should take or who has fallen out with the majority. Generally, the courts have been alive to the potential to exploit the threat of litigation under the s.994 remedy as leverage and as an instrument of oppression of a company and the controlling majority.[210] However, it has been acknowledged[211] that serious or

---

[207] per Nourse J in *RA Noble & Sons (Clothing) Ltd, Re* [1983] B.C.L.C. 273 at 289.
[208] e.g. *London School of Electronics Ltd, Re* [1986] Ch. 211; [1985] 3 W.L.R. 474; (1985) 1 B.C.C. 99394; *Company (No.005287 of 1985), Re* [1986] 1 W.L.R. 281; (1985) 1 B.C.C. 99586; (1986) 83 L.S.G. 1058; *Antoniades v Wong* [1998] B.C.C. 58; [1997] 2 B.C.L.C. 419.
[209] *Shamsallah Holdings Pty Ltd v CBD Refrigeration and Airconditioning Services Pty Ltd* (2001) 19 A.C.L.C. 517.
[210] *Howard Smith Ltd v Ampol Petroleum Ltd* [1974] A.C. 821; [1974] 2 W.L.R. 689; 118 S.J.L.B. 330 at 832; *Rock (Nominees) Ltd v RCO (Holdings) Plc (In Members Voluntary Liquidation)* [2004] EWCA Civ 118; [2004] B.C.C. 466; [2004] 1 B.C.L.C. 439; see also *Fisher v Cadman* [2005] EWHC 377 (Ch); [2006] 1 B.C.L.C. 499.

persistent mismanagement which the majority has done nothing to correct or which reflects a course of conduct previously accepted but nonetheless inconsistent with constitutional requirements that a shareholder is seeking to revive could amount to unfair prejudice; and

(f) excessive remuneration: if the remuneration paid to the defendant has clearly been in excess of what he deserved by comparison to his contribution to the company's business, that has been held to be unfairly prejudicial to the interests of the petitioner.[212]

Other commonplace allegations include oppressive conduct of board meetings[213]; breach of agreement; breach of statute[214]; improper allotment of shares[215]; breach of articles; decisions made for the benefit of related companies rather than shareholders in the company[216]; use of company funds to defend oppressive proceedings[217]; and other breaches of fiduciary duty.

The test of unfair prejudice is an objective one, to be applied flexibly according to the circumstances in the context of the commercial relationship.[218] It is not necessary for the petitioner to show bad faith or a conscious intention to prejudice the petitioner. Rather, the test is one of unfairness, not unlawful or even underhand conduct.[219] Indeed, as noted above, in the context of quasi-partnerships, the unfairness may consist of reliance on legal rights in circumstances where ethical considerations make it unfair to do so because the proposed exercise is outside either that which can fairly be regarded as having been in the contemplation of the parties when they became members or some later established understanding.[220] Thus, what may be fair between competing business people may not be fair in a quasi-partnership company context.

10.4.2 Obstacles

Even if the petitioner is able to demonstrate unfairly prejudicial conduct within the ambit of s.994, there are further obstacles that he must overcome to obtain relief under s.994. These are:

---

[211] *Elgindata (No.1), Re* [1991] B.C.L.C. 959 at 993; *Macro (Ipswich) Ltd, Re* [1994] 2 B.C.L.C. 354.

[212] *Cumana Ltd, Re* [1986] B.C.L.C. 430, see also *Dalkeith Investments Pty Ltd, Re* (1984) 9 A.C.L.R. 247.

[213] Young J in *John J Star (Real Estate) Pty Ltd v Robert R Andrew (Australasia) Pty Ltd* (1991) 6 A.C.S.R. 63 at 66.

[214] *DR Chemicals Ltd* (1989) 5 B.C.C. 39.

[215] *DR Chemicals Ltd* (1989) 5 B.C.C. 39 but see for contrast *CAS (Nominees) Ltd v Nottingham Forest FC Plc (Application for Disclosure)* [2001] 1 All E.R. 954; [2002] B.C.C. 145; (2000) 97(40) L.S.G. 42. See also *Dalby v Bodilly* [2004] EWHC 3078 (Ch); [2005] B.C.C. 627.

[216] *Brenfield Squash Racquets Club Ltd, Re* [1996] 2 B.C.L.C. 184.

[217] *DG Brims & Sons Pty Ltd, Re* (1995) 16 A.C.S.R. 559.

[218] *Guidestone Ltd, Re* [2000] B.C.L.C. 321.

[219] *DR Chemicals Ltd* (1989) 5 B.C.C. 39.

[220] *O'Neill v Phillips* [1999] 1 W.L.R. 1092.

(a) Conduct of the petitioner: in contrast to the situation where the shareholder wishes to bring a derivative action (see Section 10.3 above), in the case of a petition under s.994 it is not necessary for him to come "with clean hands". However, his conduct will be taken into account by the court in deciding whether conduct which was clearly prejudicial was also unfair.[221] Acceding to habitual breach of the constitutional procedures required to be observed in the conduct of a company's affairs may restrict the availability of a remedy in respect of those breaches.[222]

(b) Availability of an alternative remedy: this divides itself into three, namely: (i) the existence of pre-emption rights in the company's articles of association; (ii) in the absence of pre-emption rights, the existence of a fair offer by the other shareholder(s) to buy the petitioner's shares; and (iii) the availability of a ready market for the shares:

   (i) Pre-emption rights: if the company's articles contain (as the articles of many private companies do) provisions requiring (or entitling) a shareholder to offer his shares for purchase by the other shareholders (or, in some cases, by the company itself) before he can transfer them elsewhere, and he does not take advantage of those provisions, it might be argued that he has failed to exploit a remedy that is available in the alternative to an order under s.994. However, such provisions often require the shares to be valued on an "open market value" basis, and the value of a minority shareholding will often be valued on a discounted basis (i.e. at less than the pro rata value of the shares), and so to the disadvantage of the shareholder in contrast to the basis of valuation usually applied in the buy-out remedy available under s.994.[223] There may be other factors (such as the valuation procedures or the commercial impact of the conduct complained of) that render the provisions inappropriate as a fair alternative to a remedy under s.994. It is now accepted that the existence of such provisions does not represent a bar to proceedings under the s.994 remedy,[224] but an open offer to purchase the minority shareholder's shares at a fair price, which is calculated on a pro rata basis and otherwise fairly, will make it an abuse of process for the petitioner to continue an action.[225]

---

[221] *London School of Electronics Ltd, Re* [1986] Ch. 211; [1985] 3 W.L.R. 474; (1985) 1 B.C.C. 99394; and see *DR Chemicals Ltd, Re* (1989) 5 B.C.C. 39. See also *Richardson v Blackmore* [2005] EWCA Civ 1356; [2006] B.C.C. 276. In *Interactive Technology Corp Ltd v Ferster* [2016] EWHC 2896 (Ch) at [325], the petitioners conduct resulted in refusal of relief even in circumstances of unfair prejudice.

[222] *Fisher v Cadman* [2005] EWHC 377 (Ch); [2006] 1 B.C.L.C. 499.

[223] See Section 10.4.3 for further commentary on valuation.

[224] See *Isaacs v Belfield Furnishings Ltd* [2006] EWHC 183 (Ch); [2006] 2 B.C.L.C. 705.

[225] *Virdi v Abbey Leisure Ltd* [1990] B.C.C. 60; [1990] B.C.L.C. 342; *Company (No.000836 of 1995), Re* [1996] B.C.C. 432; [1996] 2 B.C.L.C. 192; but see *Rotadata Ltd, Re* [2000] B.C.C. 686; [2000] 1 B.C.L.C. 122 at 132.

(ii) Offer to buy the petitioner's shares: a reasonable offer to buy the petitioner's shares at a fair price (to be determined by competent expert valuation if not agreed, with each party having the right to make submissions), with equality of access to relevant company information and a fair mechanism to deal with the petitioner's shares may be enough to prevent the petition under s.994 from being successful. If the company is a quasi-partnership, the basis of valuation may need to be on a pro rata, rather than discounted, basis to be sure of success, although the court has a discretion in all cases.[226] There may be difficulties in deciding the date as at which the valuation is to be made, as this will need to be fair in context[227] and so will vary with the circumstances of the case but typically should be as close as possible to the actual date of sale and appropriately reflect an assessment of the impact of future events, whether positive or negative.[228] Failure to include in the offer terms a contribution to the costs incurred in response to the claim may not be fatal but any assessment of the adequacy of the offer will have regard to what is reasonable in the circumstances. The respondent might expect a reasonable grace period following a breakdown in relations to frame and finance an offer before he must necessarily also take into account the costs incurred by the petitioner in seeking relief. If a respondent has made a reasonable offer, the prejudice complained of will not be unfairly prejudicial and he will be entitled to have the petition struck out.[229]

(iii) Ready market: an obstacle to proceedings under s.994 that is particularly acute for a shareholder in a public company is the availability of a ready market for the shares.

(c) Triviality or resolution: where an investment turns out to be worse that it was, that does not entitle a shareholder to cash in the investment where the facts do not demonstrate a degree of unfairness that justifies the intervention of the court, despite the circumstances leading to a degree of distrust. Trivial and technical infringements will not justify a remedy.[230]

(d) Costs: as with derivative actions (see Section 10.3.6 above) the issue of costs is pervasive. The old legal aid regime was replaced by a system of public funding that expressly excludes funding for matters relating

---

[226] *Bird Precision Bellows Ltd, Re* [1986] Ch. 658; [1986] 2 W.L.R. 158; (1985) 1 B.C.C. 99467 at 669; and see *O'Neill v Phillips* [1999] 1 W.L.R. 1092 also *North Holdings Ltd v Southern Tropics Ltd* [1999] B.C.C. 746; [1999] 2 B.C.L.C. 625 at 639.

[227] See *London School of Electronics Ltd, Re* [1986] Ch. 211; [1985] 3 W.L.R. 474; (1985) 1 B.C.C. 99394. See also *Bee Tee Alarms Ltd, Re* [2006] All E.R. (D) 157 (Mar).

[228] *Bilkus v King* (also known as *Clearsprings (Management) Ltd, Re*) [2003] EWHC 2516 (Ch); [2003] All E.R. (D) 470 (Oct). See also *Wilkinson v West Coast Capital* [2005] EWHC 3009 (Ch); [2007] B.C.C. 717; [2005] All E.R. (D) 346 (Dec).

[229] *O'Neill v Phillips* [1999] 1 W.L.R. 1092 at 10.

[230] *Parkinson v Eurofinance Group Ltd* [2001] 1 B.C.L.C. 720 at 748e. *Metropolis Motorcycles Ltd, Re* [2007] 1 B.C.L.C. 520 at 561–2.

to company law.[231] Moreover, as the petition is by the shareholder in his own right, the court has no discretion to grant the petitioner an indemnity out of the company's assets for his costs, a material point of distinction when compared with the derivative action. The Law Commission, in its 1996 Consultation Paper,[232] cites examples of the cost and length of proceedings seeking the s.994 remedy, including the case of *Elgindata (No.1), Re*,[233] in which the hearing of the petition lasted 43 days, costs totaled £320,000 and the shares, originally purchased for £40,000, were finally valued at only £24,600. In the case of *O'Neill v Phillips*,[234] the original petition was issued in January 1992 and the House of Lords decision was handed down in May 1999. The rules permitting conditional fee and litigation funding arrangements have now provided an alternative method of funding these petitions.[235]

(e)   No removal or diminution by contract: members may be restricted from presenting a petition under s.994 where they have agreed to remove or restrict their rights pursuant to contract.[236]

10.4.3   Remedies available

Section 996 provides:

"(1)   —If the court is satisfied that a petition under [CA 2006 Pt 30] is well founded, it may make such order as it thinks fit for giving relief in respect of the matters complained of.

(2)   —Without prejudice to the generality of subsection (1), the court's order may—

(a)   —regulate the conduct of the company's affairs in the future;

(b)   —require the company—(i) to refrain from doing or continuing an act complained of, or (ii) to do an act that the petitioner has complained it has omitted to do;

(c)   —authorise civil proceedings to be brought in the name and on behalf of the company by such person or persons and on such terms as the court may direct;

(d)   —require the company not to make any, or any specified, alterations in its articles without the leave of the court;

---

[231] The system was brought in under the Access to Justice Act 1999 (see above). Access to Justice Act 1999 Sch.2 sets out services that are excluded from funding under the Community Legal Service regime.
[232] The Law Commission Consultation Paper "Shareholder Remedies" No.142, p.104 onwards.
[233] *Elgindata (No.1), Re* [1991] B.C.L.C. 959.
[234] *O'Neill v Phillips* [1999] 1 W.L.R. 1092.
[235] These alternative means of funding are referred to in Access to Justice Act 1999 Pt II.
[236] *Fulham Football Club (1987) Ltd v Richards* [2010] EWHC 3111 (Ch); [2011] Ch. 208; [2011] 2 W.L.R. 1055, in which it was held that the statutory rights under s.994 were not inalienable but could be removed or diminished by contract. In that case the members had agreed that disputes could be referred to arbitration and the petition under s.994 was accordingly stayed.

(e) —provide for the purchase of the shares of any members of the company by other members or by the company itself and, in the case of a purchase by the company itself, the reduction of the company's capital accordingly."

The court must establish unfair prejudice before the power to grant relief under s.996 arises. Accordingly, it has no power under s.996 to grant interim relief although it may exercise other powers in appropriate circumstances.[237] Section 996 confers no power to order a winding up and limited power to award damages in view of the implication for creditors.[238]

The decision as to the appropriate remedy is a matter of judgment, in the discretion of the court.[239] The court will take into account all relevant interests. The remedy is not limited to any remedies sought by the petitioner. The unacceptability to the petitioner of the relief that the court considers appropriate will be a major consideration but the court may make such order as it thinks fit.[240]

By far the most common form of relief sought is the purchase of the petitioner's shares.[241] In its 1996 Consultation Paper,[242] the Law Commission noted that, in petitions presented to the Companies Court at the Royal Courts of Justice between January 1994 and December 1995 seeking relief under the s.994 remedy, 69.9%[243] sought this form of relief. As noted in Section 10.4.2(b)(ii) above, issues arise in relation to the basis of valuation of the shares (whether on a discounted basis, which is more likely where the shareholding is an investment,[244] or pro rata basis, traditionally where the relationship is a quasi-partnership although where fairness dictates in other circumstances too; whether on a going concern basis or a "break-up" basis; and whether selling costs in connection with any value realisation should be taken into account[245]),[246] the date as at which the valuation is to be made[247] and whether allowance should be made for the impact of the unfair

---

[237] Senior Courts Act 1981 s.37(1).

[238] However, see *Sikorski v Sikorski* [2012] EWHC 1613 (Ch).

[239] See *Hawkes v Cuddy* [2009] EWCA Civ 291 for a discussion at [80]–[92].

[240] *Hawkes v Cuddy* [2009] EWCA Civ 291 at [85]–[91], clarifying the Law Commission Consultation Paper No.142 "Shareholder Remedies" para.10.2 as supporting only the proposition that the petition must specify the relief sought by the petitioner but that that is not to the exclusion of the court's discretion on remedies.

[241] But see *Brenfield Squash Racquets Club Ltd, Re* [1996] 2 B.C.L.C. 184; also *Elliott v Planet Organic Ltd* [2000] B.C.C. 610; [2000] 1 B.C.L.C. 366.

[242] The Law Commission Consultation Paper "Shareholder Remedies" No.142 Appendix E.

[243] Taking into account that any given petition may include reference to more than one form of relief.

[244] See *Elgindata (No.1), Re* [1991] B.C.L.C. 959. See also *Irvine v Irvine* [2006] EWHC 583 (Ch); [2006] 4 All E.R. 102; [2007] 1 B.C.L.C. 445 and *Annacott Holdings Ltd, Re* [2013] EWCA Civ 119; [2013] 2 B.C.L.C. 46 in which it was held, reversing a prior decision, that no discount should be applied for lack of marketability of the shares.

[245] *Annacott Holdings Ltd, Re* [2013] EWCA Civ 119.

[246] *Strahan v Wilcock* [2006] EWCA Civ 13; [2006] B.C.C. 320; [2006] 2 B.C.L.C. 555.

[247] See *Bilkus v King* [2003] EWHC 2516 (Ch); [2003] All E.R. (D) 470 (Oct), for a review of relevant considerations in selecting a valuation date; also *Profinance Trust SA v Gladstone*

prejudice.[248] All these factors are circumstance specific and matters of discretion for the court. The capacity of the purchaser should not be a consideration unless it goes to the substance of the remedy. The suitability of the purchaser will be a consideration including whether it is appropriate for the company to be the purchaser, when the interests of creditors and financial impact on the company should be taken into account.[249] While more probable by far that any buy-out would be by a majority or in appropriate circumstances the company, the court has authority to order that the minority acquire the shares of the majority.[250]

The persons against whom remedies may be sought are unlimited. There must, however, be some nexus between the unfairly prejudicial conduct and the relief granted. Section 996 confers on the court power "to make such order as it thinks fit for giving relief in respect of the matters complained of". Thus a director may be ordered to compensate the company for any misappropriation of assets, or for any damage he has caused to the company. He may be required to cause any creature company to disgorge any profits which it has made illegitimately at the expense of the company. A director may be ordered to perform, or be restrained from doing, some act which is, or would be unfairly prejudicial.

The courts have been prepared to grant relief to the company under a s.994 petition on the basis that the broad discretion allowed to the court under s.996 permits it to grant the same relief that it would have granted in a derivative claim.[251]

Generally the courts will apply equitable considerations so as to arrive at a result that is, in all the circumstances, fair as between the parties and provides appropriate relief.[252]

[2001] EWCA Civ 1031; [2002] 1 W.L.R. 1024; [2002] B.C.C. 356 and *Cumana Ltd, Re* [1986] B.C.L.C. 430 and *Annacott Holdings Ltd, Re* [2013] EWCA Civ 119, in which "quasi-interest" was awarded for the period from the valuation date.

[248] *Scottish Co-operative Wholesale Society v Meyer* [1959] A.C. 324 at 364 (starting point to value on the assumption the unfair prejudice has not occurred).

[249] *Hawkes v Cuddy* [2009] EWCA Civ 291 at [84]. *Phoenix Office Supplies Ltd, Re* [2002] EWCA Civ 1740 at [30].

[250] *Re a Company (No.00836 of 1995)* [1996] B.C.C. 432.

[251] *Clark v Cutland* [2003] EWCA Civ 810; [2004] 1 W.L.R. 783; [2004] B.C.C. 27 at [2].

[252] See *Bird Precision Bellows Ltd, Re* [1986] Ch. 658; [1986] 2 W.L.R. 158; (1985) 1 B.C.C. 99467 at 672; *Scottish Co-operative Wholesale Society Ltd v Meyer* [1959] A.C. 324; [1958] 3 W.L.R. 404; 1958 S.C. (H.L.) 40 at 369; *Jermyn Street Turkish Baths Ltd, Re* [1970] 1 W.L.R. 1194; [1970] 3 All E.R. 57; (1970) 114 S.J. 583 at 1208; *Guinness Peat Group Plc v British Land Co Plc* [1999] B.C.C. 536; [1999] 2 B.C.L.C. 243; [1998] N.P.C. 168; *O'Neill v Phillips* [1999] 1 W.L.R. 1092; *Elgindata (No.1), Re* [1991] B.C.L.C. 959; *Profinance Trust SA v Gladstone* [2001] EWCA Civ 1031. In terms of fashioning remedies, the US courts have provided a rich seam of alternatives for consideration. In addition to dissolution or buy-out, in many US states a court can appoint a provisional director to resolve deadlock and to enable the corporation to function. The appointment of a custodian represents an alternative that is more intrusive in the sense that a custodian need not operate with the approval or acquiescence of board members. Other remedies recognised in many US states include: (a) alteration of the corporation's constitution; (b) intervention in actions of the corporation; (c) prohibition of planned

10.4.4 *Procedure*

In *North Holdings Ltd v Southern Tropics Ltd*,[253] the judges emphasised the need for active case management at an early stage in order to reduce the time and expense involved in ascertaining a fair price for the petitioner's shares, and for use of the power to require a joint expert or the appointment of an assessor, which would lead to a reduction in the number of striking out applications. This was an appeal concerning the former s.459 action under earlier court procedure rules, but such cases shall continue to be of importance in light of the unchanged ethos behind the CPR.

Applications under s.994 are now governed by the Companies (Unfair Prejudice Applications) Proceedings Rules 2009[254] (the 2009 Rules) and (as far as not inconsistent with those Rules) the CPR, in particular Pt 49 CPR (Specialist Proceedings) and the Practice Directions made under it.[255] The 2009 Rules replaced the Companies (Unfair Prejudice Applications) Proceedings Rules 1986 (the 1986 Rules)[256] that applied to any petition to the court before 1 October 2009.[257]

An application under s.994 is made by petition in the form set out in the Schedule to the 2009 Rules ("with such variations, if any, as the circumstances may require").[258] The court will then fix a hearing for a day, i.e. "the return day", on which the petitioner and any respondent (including the company) shall attend before the registrar or district judge for directions, unless the court otherwise directs.[259] At least 14 days before the return day the petitioner must serve a sealed copy of the petition on the company and every respondent named in the petition.[260]

On the return day, or any time after it, the court shall give such directions as it thinks appropriate with respect to various matters.[261]

---

actions; (d) sale of assets; (e) alterations to the board of directors; (f) ordering an account of corporate assets or an investigation; (g) requiring declaration of a dividend; (h) identifying constructive dividends paid through controlling shareholder remuneration and directing a corresponding dividend to non-participating shareholders; (i) ordering a rebalancing in the shareholding structure; (j) treating related corporations as grouped for the purposes of determining appropriate relief; (k) imposing damages payments; (l) installation of effective accounting systems or management controls; and (m) directing dissolution at a future date if differences have not in the meantime been resolved.

[253] *North Holdings Ltd v Southern Tropics Ltd* [1999] B.C.C. 746; [1999] 2 B.C.L.C. 625; and see also *Rotadata Ltd, Re* [2000] B.C.C. 686; [2000] 1 B.C.L.C. 122.

[254] Companies (Unfair Prejudice Applications) Proceedings Rules 2009 (SI 2469/2009), made under Insolvency Act 1986 s.411.

[255] See the Chancery Guide 2013 issued by the Chancery Division, paras 20.2 and 20.3.

[256] Companies (Unfair Prejudice Applications) Proceedings Rules 1986 (SI 1986/2000).

[257] Companies (Unfair Prejudice Applications) Proceedings Rules 2009 (SI 2469/2009) r.7.

[258] Companies (Unfair Prejudice Applications) Proceedings Rules 2009 (SI 2469/2009) r.3(1).

[259] Companies (Unfair Prejudice Applications) Proceedings Rules 2009 (SI 2469/2009) r.3(3).

[260] Companies (Unfair Prejudice Applications) Proceedings Rules 2009 (SI 2469/2009) r.4.

[261] Companies (Unfair Prejudice Applications) Proceedings Rules 2009 (SI 2469/2009) r.5.

The petitioner may additionally seek a winding-up order on "just and equitable" grounds under Insolvency Act 1986 s.122(1)(g) in the alternative, relief which is not available under s.994.[262] However, Insolvency Act 1986 s.125(2) provides that the court is not to make a winding-up order on these grounds:

> "if the court is … of the opinion both that some other remedy is available to the petitioners and that they are acting unreasonably in seeking to have the company wound up instead of pursuing that other remedy."

The Practice Direction supplementing CPR Pt 49[263] states:

> "(1)   —Attention is drawn to the undesirability of asking as a matter of course for a winding up order as an alternative to an order under section 994 of the Companies Act 2006. The petition should not ask for a winding up order unless that is the remedy which the petitioner prefers or it is thought that it may be the only remedy to which the petitioner is entitled."

A petition to wind up a company can lead to devastating consequences for the company, not least under its contractual commitments and the restriction on disposal of property pending the court order.[264]

10.4.5 Reform

In the past, the Law Commission[265] has made a number of proposals with the aim of simplifying the unfair prejudice remedy and, in particular, ensuring active case management by the court.

Many of the Law Commission's proposals on procedure have been addressed by previous revisions of the CPR. For example, the court now has the power to strike out a claim or a defence which, in the court's view, discloses no reasonable grounds for bringing or defending the claim.[266] Another important innovation is that the CPR have given the court greater flexibility to make costs orders that take account of the way a party has conducted the proceedings and, in making an order for costs, the court must now consider whether it is reasonable for a party to raise, pursue or

---

[262] The Law Commission had proposed that the law should be altered to make a winding-up order available as a remedy in its *Shareholder Remedies* Report 246, para.4.35. In the period between January 1994 and December 1995, 37.3% of petitions under CA 1985 s.459 sought relief under Insolvency Act 1986 s.122(1)(g) in addition (see Appendix J).

[263] PD 49B para.1 to CPR Pt 49.

[264] Insolvency Act 1986 s.127.

[265] The Law Commission Report "Shareholder Remedies" 246.

[266] CPR r.3.4. This rule refers to the ability of the court to strike out a "statement of case". Though this term is defined to cover formal pleadings such as a particulars of claim and a defence, a similar application of the rule can likely be achieved by the court in the case of petitions under s.994, using its inherent power to make any order of its own initiative as part of the exercise of its case management powers (CPR r.3.3).

contest a particular allegation or issue.[267] Such increased powers should act as a deterrent to a party contemplating pressing ahead with weak or insubstantial allegations in a s.994 case.

In addition to the above, the recommendation that Alternative Dispute Resolution (ADR) should be encouraged in shareholder disputes wherever appropriate and that an amendment be made to the 1986 Rules so as to include an express reference to its use is reflected in the possible directions which a court may give on or any time after the return day under the 2009 Rules.[268]

Other proposals for reform made by the Commission include:

(a) the addition of winding up to the list of s.996 remedies available in proceedings under s.994;

(b) amendment to raise the following presumptions:
  (i) that in certain circumstances,[269] exclusion from participation in the management of a company will be presumed to be unfairly prejudicial (unless the respondent shows otherwise); and
  (ii) where the first presumption is not rebutted, and the court is satisfied that it ought to order a buy-out of the petitioner's shares, a presumption that the shares will be valued on a pro rata (rather than a discounted) basis;

(c) the introduction of a time limit for bringing a s.994 claim, although it was recommended that the time limit would apply only to the conduct which forms the basis of the unfair prejudice claim and that there should be no time limit imposed on other "background" matters to which the parties may refer in order to support or refute the claim[270]; and

(d) the amendment of Table A, now the Model Articles, by the insertion of a new regulation providing a "no-fault" exit route for disgruntled shareholders so that they do not have to resort to bringing costly proceedings under s.994 in order to have their shares bought out.[271] The inclusion of this new regulation would be optional and would allow the company to decide on the circumstances giving rise to the exit rights and the method of valuation of the shares in question.

---

[267] CPR r.44.3.

[268] Companies (Unfair Prejudice Applications) Proceedings Rules 1986 (SI 1986/2000) r.5(f).

[269] The circumstances in which a presumption of unfair prejudice on exclusion from management will arise are set out in the draft Bill in Appendix A to the 1997 Report. The type of companies envisaged are private companies limited by shares where substantially all the members of the company are directors and where prior to his removal as a director or his exclusion from management, the petitioner held, in his own name, at least 10% of the voting rights in the company (Law Commission Report "Shareholder Remedies" 246, paras 3.26–3.70).

[270] The Law Commission Report 246 paras 4.22 and 4.23.

[271] The exit article is set out in draft reg.119 in Appendix C to the Law Commission Report "Shareholder Remedies" 246.

None of these proposals is reflected in the CA 2006 restatement and marginal revision of the s.994 remedy. In relation to the recommendation referenced in (d) above, a structure to address disagreement that is suitable in context should be developed between shareholders and their representatives at the outset of a relationship or at least while harmonious relations prevail, whether in the constitution or the broader commercial framework regulating affairs between the members.

Chapter 11

Duties of Directors Facing Insolvency

Hamish Anderson

Consultant

Norton Rose Fulbright LLP

11.1 Introduction

Company directors who are facing the actual or prospective insolvency of their companies retain all of the duties they would have even if the company was fully solvent. Certain general duties formerly based on common law rules and equitable principles were brought within the ambit of statutory law by the Companies Act 2006 (CA 2006) which nonetheless specifies that the codified rules shall be interpreted and applied according to the rules and principles on which they are based. However, the onset of insolvency imposes a further set of duties, mostly under the Insolvency Act 1986 (IA 1986), and adds a new dimension to the fiduciary duties of directors which reflects the significant position of the company's creditors as opposed to its shareholders when insolvency is in prospect. CA 2006 is silent on this matter except that the statutory duty for a director to "act in the way he considers, in good faith, would be most likely to promote the success of the company for the benefit of its members as a whole" (CA 2006 s.172(1)) is expressed to be subject to any rule of law requiring directors in certain circumstances to consider or act in the interests of a company's creditors.

This Chapter deals with a number of statutory duties under the Insolvency Act 1986 which were enacted specifically to protect the creditors of insolvent companies, the cases surrounding the issue of directors' fiduciary duties when the company is insolvent or prospectively insolvent, and certain other duties under the CA 2006, the EU Market Abuse Regulation and the Financial Conduct Authority's rules which frequently become an issue on the prospective insolvency of the company. However, reference should also be made to Chapter 13 for commentary on those sections of the Company Directors' Disqualification Act 1986 which deal with insolvency.

In considering their duties, directors should always keep it in the forefront of their minds that each company in a group is a separate legal entity and that they must discharge their duties to each company rather than the

441

group as a whole. It may therefore be necessary to recognise and address conflicts of interest which arise between companies within a group.

11.2 Statutory duties under IA 1986

All of the provisions which are discussed in this part of this Chapter apply where a company has become subject to a formal insolvency procedure, either liquidation or administration. The liquidator or administrator then has the power to look back to the period shortly before a formal insolvency and bring proceedings, either for compensation against the directors personally or to undo certain transactions entered into by the directors during that period.

11.2.1 Wrongful trading (IA 1986 sections 214 and 246ZB)

A liquidator or administrator (or their assignee) is entitled to apply to the court for an order making a person liable to contribute to the company's assets if the following conditions apply (IA 1986 ss.214(2) (liquidation) and 246ZB(2) (administration)):

(a)   the company has gone into insolvent liquidation/administration;
(b)   at some time before the commencement of the process, that person knew or ought to have concluded that there was no reasonable prospect that the company would avoid going into insolvent liquidation or administration; and
(c)   that person was a director of the company at the time.

IA 1986 ss.214(3) (liquidation) and 246ZB(3) (administration) afford a defence to proceedings for wrongful trading by providing that the court shall not make an order to contribute with respect to any person if it is satisfied that, after they first knew or ought to have concluded that there was no reasonable prospect that the company would avoid going into insolvent liquidation or administration, they took every step with a view to minimising the potential loss to the company's creditors that they ought to have taken.

The Act also provides guidance on the knowledge, skill and experience which is expected of directors in the following terms (IA 1986 ss.214(4) and (5) (liquidation) and 246ZB(4) and (5) (administration)):

> "(4)   … the facts which a director of a company ought to know or ascertain, the conclusions which [the director] ought to reach and the steps which [the director] ought to take are those which would be known or ascertained, or reached or taken, by a reasonably diligent person having both—

(a) the general knowledge, skill and experience that may reasonably be expected of a person carrying out the same functions as are carried out by that director in relation to the company, and

(b) the general knowledge, skill and experience that that director has.

(5) The reference in subsection (4) to the functions carried out in relation to the company by a director of the company includes any functions which he does not carry out but which have been entrusted to him."

For these purposes the sections define entering into insolvent liquidation/administration as entering into the process when the assets of the company are insufficient for the payment of its debts and other liabilities and the expenses of the process (ss.214(6) (liquidation) and 246ZB(6) (administration)), i.e. balance sheet insolvency.

11.2.1.1 Comments

There are relatively few reported cases in which the wrongful trading legislation has been considered and, as yet, the case law concerns liquidation because the extension of wrongful trading powers to administrators only happened in 2015. In an early but still important decision (*Produce Marketing Consortium (In Liquidation) Ltd, Re (No.2)*),[1] Knox J characterised the method of establishing the quantum of the relevant director's liability as follows (at 553):

"In my judgment the jurisdiction under s 214 is primarily compensatory rather than penal. Prima facie the appropriate amount that a director is declared to be liable to contribute is the amount by which the company's assets can be discerned to have been depleted by the director's conduct which caused the discretion under sub-s (I) to arise. But Parliament has indeed chosen very wide words of discretion... the fact that there was no fraudulent intent is not of itself a reason for fixing the amount at a nominal or low figure, for that would amount to frustrating what I discern as Parliament's intention in adding s 214 to s 213 in the 1986 Act, but I am not persuaded that it is right to ignore that fact totally."

Morris v Bank of India[2] established that interest could be added to the award.

In the subsequent case of *DKG Contractors Ltd, Re*,[3] the court simply ascertained the date on which the directors ought to have concluded that there was no reasonable prospect of avoiding insolvent liquidation and made an order rendering the directors liable to pay a contribution equal to the amount of trade debts incurred by the company after that date. Although a precise method of calculating the liability has not been established, the principle that it is compensatory and not penal is not in

---

[1] *Produce Marketing Consortium (In Liquidation) Ltd, Re (No.2)* (1989) 5 B.C.C. 569; [1989] B.C.L.C. 520.

[2] *Morris v Bank of India* [2004] EWHC 528 (Ch); [2005] 1 All E.R. (Comm) 209; [2004] B.C.C. 404.

[3] *DKG Contractors Ltd, Re* [1990] B.C.C. 903.

doubt. In *Continental Assurance Co of London Plc, Re*,[4] it was held that it was not enough merely to say that, if the company had not still been trading, a particular loss would not have been suffered by the company. In order to impose liability on directors there must be sufficient connection between the wrongfulness of the directors' conduct and the company's losses.

More recently the principles were re-examined in *Ralls Builders Ltd, Re*[5] where the court treated establishing the increase (or reduction) in the net deficiency during the relevant period as the starting point and declined to make an order in the absence of any loss caused by delay in the commencement of insolvency proceedings.

In practice, if the directors of a company cease trading as soon as they reach the conclusion that there is no reasonable prospect of avoiding insolvency proceedings, then, assuming that their opinion was a reasonable one and they were not dilatory in reaching it, there should be little risk of a successful claim for wrongful trading being brought. This is because there will be no time for losses to accumulate between the directors reaching the relevant decision and the commencement of the liquidation or administration of the company. In *Continental Assurance Co of London Plc, Re* (above), Park J considered the difficult position of directors balancing their wish to avoid liability for wrongful trading with making proper efforts to avoid liquidation if possible. He said (at [817]):

> "An overall point which needs to be kept in mind throughout is that, whenever a company is in financial trouble and the directors have a difficult decision to make whether to close down and go into liquidation, or whether instead to trade on and hope to turn the corner, they can be in a real and unenviable dilemma. On the one hand, if they decide to trade on but things do not work out and the company, later rather than sooner, goes into liquidation, they may find themselves in the situation of the respondents in this case – being sued for wrongful trading. On the other hand, if the directors decide to close down immediately and cause the company to go into an early liquidation, although they are not at risk of being sued for wrongful trading, they are at risk of being criticised on other grounds. A decision to close down will almost certainly mean that the ensuing liquidation will be an insolvent one. Apart from anything else liquidations are expensive operations, and in addition debtors are commonly obstructive about paying their debts to a company which is in liquidation. Many creditors of the company from a time before the liquidation are likely to find that their debts do not get paid in full. They will complain bitterly that the directors shut down too soon; they will say that the directors ought to have had more courage and kept going. If they had done so, the complaining creditors will say, the company probably would have survived and all of its debts would have been paid. Ceasing to trade and liquidating too soon can be stigmatised as the cowards' way out."

---

4   *Continental Assurance Co of London Plc, Re* [2007] 2 B.C.L.C. 287; [2001] B.P.I.R. 733.
5   *Ralls Builders Ltd, Re* [2016] EWHC 243 (Ch); [2016] B.C.C. 293. See also *Brooks v Armstrong* [2016] EWHC 2893 (Ch); [2017] B.C.C. 99.

Directors whose companies are facing financial difficulties should always have regular board meetings and at each meeting consider the prospects for the company and minute their reasons for the view they take and their reasons for any decision to continue trading. Up-to-date financial information must be available. Directors should also consider taking professional advice because the courts, in deciding what conclusions a director should have reached, have been prepared to place some weight upon whether advice was taken and, if so, what that advice was (*Ralls Builders* above). In the context of disqualification proceedings, it has been held that a director must keep himself informed about the financial affairs of the company and play an appropriate role in its management (*Galeforce Pleating Co Ltd, Re*).[6] This is directly relevant to the "functions" of the directors when applying the wrongful trading test. Ignorance of the financial position will not be a valid defence to any claim for wrongful trading. Directors are expected to apply the general knowledge, skill and experience that may reasonably be expected of a person carrying out the same functions as are carried out (or entrusted to) the relevant director in relation to the company. This point was also emphasised in *Produce Marketing Consortium Ltd (No.2), Re* above. The standard of conduct required is not lower because the commercial activity in question is inherently risky (*Singla v Hedman*—a case concerning the film industry).[7]

In *Hawkes Hill Publishing Co Ltd (In Liquidation), Re*,[8] it was held that whether a company has a reasonable prospect of avoiding an insolvent liquidation cannot be determined on the basis of a snapshot of its financial position at any particular time but must be based on rational expectations of what the future might hold. Helpfully, the judge added that directors are not clairvoyant and the fact that they fail to see what eventually comes to pass did not necessarily mean that they are guilty of wrongful trading. To similar effect, the court commented in *Idessa (UK) Ltd (In Liquidation), Re*[9] that care should be taken not to invoke hindsight and that proper regard should be paid to the difficult choices which can confront directors in deciding whether to allow trading to continue. In *Ralls Builders* (above), Snowden J said (at [173]):

> "... the court does not approach the question of whether a director ought to have concluded that his company had no reasonable prospect of avoiding an insolvent liquidation with the benefit of 20:20 hindsight."

Wrongful trading was found to have occurred in *Roberts v Frohlich*[10] where directors, who had started a speculative development project in good faith,

---

6   *Galeforce Pleating Co Ltd, Re* [1999] 2 B.C.L.C. 704.
7   *Singla v Hedman* [2010] B.C.C. 684.
8   *Hawkes Hill Publishing Co Ltd (In Liquidation), Re* [2007] B.C.C. 937; [2007] B.P.I.R. 1305; (2007) 151 S.J.L.B. 743.
9   *Idessa (UK) Ltd (In Liquidation), Re* [2011] EWHC 804 (Ch); [2012] B.C.C. 315; [2012] 1 B.C.L.C. 80.
10 *Roberts v Frohlich* [2011] EWHC 257 (Ch); [2012] B.C.C. 407; [2011] 2 B.C.L.C. 625.

displayed "blind optimism" when allowing it to continue some two months later by when they knew that funding conditions could not be met. Wrongful trading was also found in *Kudos Business Solutions Ltd (In Liquidation), Re*[11] where services were marketed on behalf of the company which its director had nothing more than a speculative hope would ever be provided. The court commented that this was not a case of a director properly taking the view that it was in the interests of the company and its creditors that it be allowed to trade out of its difficulties. However, in the later case of *Langreen Ltd, Re*,[12] a wrongful trading claim was dismissed because the liquidator, in a case based on hindsight, failed to show on a balance of probabilities that the continued trading of another undercapitalised company was without a prospect of success.

Once the directors of a company have reached the conclusion that there is no reasonable prospect of avoiding insolvency proceedings, they have a choice. Either the company must cease trading immediately and go into liquidation or administration, or they may attempt to rely on the defence, that they took every step with a view to minimising the potential loss to the company's creditors that they ought to have taken.

This second option is a high-risk option for the following reasons:

(a)   although it is a defence to wrongful trading for the director to prove that he has taken these steps, the burden of proof shifts from the liquidator to the director himself (*Idessa (UK) Ltd, Re* above)[13]; and

(b)   the meaning of "every step he ought to have taken" will depend on the facts of the case.[14]

The scope of the minimising loss defence was considered in *Ralls Builders* (above). In that case the continued trading, whilst not resulting any increase in the overall net deficiency, had benefitted some existing creditors at the expense of new creditors. Snowden J said (at [245]):

"Given the express wording of s.214(3) ('every step'), I think that it is plain that s.214(3) is intended to be a high hurdle for directors to surmount. I therefore think that it is right to construe s.214(3) strictly and to require a director who wishes to take advantage of the defence offered by that subsection to demonstrate not only that continued trading was intended to reduce the net deficiency of the company, but also that it was designed appropriately so as to minimise the risk of loss to individual creditors. Otherwise a director could make out the defence under s.214(3) by claiming that he traded with a view to

---

[11]   *Kudos Business Solutions Ltd (In Liquidation), Re* [2011] EWHC 1436 (Ch); [2012] 2 B.C.L.C. 65.

[12]   *Langreen Ltd, Re* Unreported, 21 October 2011.

[13]   See also *Brooks v Armstrong* [2015] EWHC 2289 (Ch).

[14]   *Brooks v Armstrong* [2015] EWHC 2289 (Ch).

reducing the overall deficiency for creditors as a general body, irrespective of how he achieved that result as between creditors."[15]

Any director who considers that he will have to rely on this defence should take detailed legal advice at the time.

Practical problems often arise in relation to wrongful trading in circumstances where a period of continued trading may enhance the value of an asset which the company wishes to sell. It is sometimes suggested that, in such circumstances, the directors of a company have a positive duty to continue trading after reaching the point where they consider there is no reasonable prospect of avoiding insolvent liquidation. Such continued trading will, so the argument goes, have the effect of minimising the potential loss to creditors by a better value being achieved for the asset in question than would be achieved on a liquidation or other insolvency procedure. The author's view is that this interpretation is incorrect. The provisions which refer to the concept of minimising potential loss to creditors concern a *defence* to proceedings for wrongful trading. A director who manages to avoid any proceedings for wrongful trading being brought against him in the first place will not be relying on this subsection. The usual and clearest way to avoid the possibility of proceedings for wrongful trading being brought is to cease trading as soon as it becomes clear that insolvency proceedings are inevitable.

Continuing to trade in order to enhance the sale proceeds of an asset may increase the actual proceeds of sale of the company's assets, but may not necessarily benefit the creditors of the company as a whole. It is often the case that secured creditors put pressure on company directors to maximise the proceeds of a particular asset by continued trading. However, if that continued trading involves incurring further credit from unsecured creditors, those unsecured creditors will in fact have suffered increased losses as a result of the continued trading. The directors will, effectively, have benefited one set of creditors at the expense of another set (as happened in *Ralls Builders*). Under such circumstances, the directors of the company could be found liable for wrongful trading and may also have exposed themselves to liability for fraudulent trading—see below).

An issue which has been discussed in the case law surrounding wrongful trading is whether a director can plead CA 2006 s.1157(1) in his defence to wrongful trading proceedings. CA 2006 s.1157(1) (which replicates the former CA 1985 s.727) provides as follows:

> "If in proceedings for negligence, default, breach of duty or breach of trust against—

---

[15] Although the defence was not available to the directors in *Ralls Builders Ltd, Re* [2016] EWHC 243 (Ch), the case failed because of the absence of an increased net deficiency (see above).

(a)   an officer of the company, or
(b)   a person employed by a company as auditor (whether he is or is not an officer of the company),

it appears to the court hearing the case that the officer or person is or may be liable but that he acted honestly and reasonably, and that having regard to all the circumstances of the case (including those connected with his appointment) he ought fairly to be excused, the court may relieve him, either wholly or in part, from his liability on such terms as it thinks fit."

In an earlier judgment in the *Produce Marketing* case, Knox J held that in CA 1985 s.727 a subjective test applied, whereas in IA 1986 s.214, particularly in subss.(3) and (4), an objective test applied. It was difficult to see how the two sections could be used in conjunction. Knox J therefore held that CA 1985 s.727 was not available to the directors in wrongful trading proceedings.[16] However, in the later case of *DKG Contracts Ltd, Re* (above), CA 1985 s.727 was pleaded. The judge held that the directors had acted honestly but not reasonably and declined to grant the relief sought. It is notable in this case that there were other breaches of duty in addition to wrongful trading and that the earlier decision of Knox J appears not to have been drawn to the attention of the court. In *Brian D Pierson (Contractors) Ltd, Re*,[17] the court followed *Produce Marketing* in holding that s.727 does not apply to wrongful trading claims. This was consistent with the court having a discretion as to the amount of any award under s.214 and, in the author's view, the point should be regarded as settled.

11.2.2   Fraudulent trading (IA 1986 sections 213 and 246ZA)

Fraudulent trading is set out in IA 1986 s.213. It is as follows:

"(1)   If in the course of the winding up of a company it appears that any business of the company has been carried on with intent to defraud creditors of the company or creditors of any other person, or for any fraudulent purpose, the following has effect.

(2)   The court, on the application of the liquidator may declare that any persons who were knowingly parties to the carrying on of the business in the manner above-mentioned are to be liable to make such contributions (if any) to the company's assets as the court thinks proper."

IA 1986 s.246ZA, which was introduced in 2015, extends the jurisdiction to administration and is otherwise in substantially the same terms. Case law on the longer-established liquidation jurisdiction can therefore be treated as equally applicable to cases brought by administrators. Like wrongful trading claims, fraudulent trading claims are assignable (IA 1986 s.246ZD).

---

[16] *Produce Marketing Consortium Ltd (No.1) Ltd, Re* [1989] 1 W.L.R. 745; (1989) 5 B.C.C. 399; [1989] B.C.L.C. 513.
[17] *Brian D Pierson (Contractors) Ltd, Re* [1999] B.C.C. 26; [2001] 1 B.C.L.C. 275; [1999] B.P.I.R. 18.

The essential difference between fraudulent trading and wrongful trading is that fraudulent trading involves dishonest intent, described in this section as "intent to defraud".[18] Fraudulent trading is also a criminal offence under CA 2006 s.993. In *R. v Hollier*,[19] the court treated carrying on business "for any fraudulent purpose" as being a distinct ground for conviction which was separate from carrying on the business with intent to defraud creditors.

Given the connotations of dishonesty in fraudulent trading, a strong measure of proof is required, and this jurisdiction is consequently rarely invoked. But under ss.213 and 246ZA, which cover the civil liability to pay compensation, it is also possible for the fraudulent acts of an employee to be vicariously attributed to the person of a company.[20]

The Court of Appeal has held that a business can be carried on with intent to defraud creditors even though only one creditor is actually defrauded by a single transaction.[21] However, *Morphitis v Bernasconi*[22] shows that the section does not apply in every case where an individual creditor is defrauded but only where the business has been carried on with intent to defraud.

Earlier, *Sarflax Ltd, Re*[23] established that, even where the company is insolvent, preferring one creditor over another does not, per se, constitute fraud within the meaning of the provisions (although it could constitute a breach of fiduciary duty and expose the director to a disqualification risk as well as giving rise to an action under s.239, as to which see below).

It might be thought, in view of the lower standard of proof required in respect of wrongful trading, that the fraudulent trading jurisdiction has become redundant. This, however, is wrong for several reasons. Fraudulent trading is available as a civil claim against any person who is "knowingly a party to" the carrying on of the company business with intent to defraud (even persons outside the jurisdiction—*Bilta (UK) Ltd (In Liquidation) v Nazir*[24]). Thus on this aspect, liability under ss.213 and 246ZA is wider than liability for wrongful trading, because mere participants are potentially liable—for their involvement in the fraudulent act, while the only people being made liable under ss.214 and 246ZB are directors, albeit including shadow directors[25] (*Morris v Banque Arabe Internationale d'Investissement SA*

---

[18] As to the meaning of dishonesty for these purposes, see *Pantiles Investments Ltd, Re* [2019] EWHC 1298 (Ch) applying the test as stated in *Ivey v Genting Casinos (UK) Ltd* [2017] UKSC 67; [2018] A.C. 391.

[19] *R. v Hollier* [2013] EWCA Crim 2041.

[20] *Morris v Bank of India* [2005] EWCA Civ 693; [2005] B.C.C. 739; [2005] 2 B.C.L.C. 328.

[21] *Gerald Cooper Chemicals, Re* [1978] Ch. 262; [1978] 2 W.L.R. 866; [1978] 2 All E.R. 49.

[22] *Morphitis v Bernasconi* [2003] EWCA Civ 289; [2003] Ch. 552; [2003] 2 W.L.R. 1521.

[23] *Sarflax Ltd, Re* [1979] Ch. 592; [1979] 2 W.L.R. 202; (1979) 123 S.J. 97.

[24] *Bilta (UK) Ltd (In Liquidation) v Nazir* [2015] UKSC 23; [2016] A.C. 1.

[25] IA 1986 ss.214(7) and 246ZB(7).

(No.2)[26] in which the alleged participant was a bank). The court has jurisdiction to make respondents jointly and severally liable for the resultant loss.[27]

The second circumstance in which fraudulent trading liability is more widely available than wrongful trading arises because the fraud does not have to be directed at the company itself or even the company's own creditors. If the business of the company is being conducted: (a) with intent to defraud the creditors of another person; or (b) for any fraudulent purpose, the knowing participant is exposed to potential liability.[28] This means that, unlike ss.214 and 246ZB, the focus of the liability is not necessarily on the imminence of the company's liquidation and the putative defendant's awareness of that fact but rather it is on the propriety of undertaking liabilities.

Although it will normally be proper to infer intent to defraud where a company continues to carry on incurring credit when the directors know that there is no reasonable prospect of the creditors receiving payment,[29] that is not the only circumstance in which fraud may be established. Thus it may be fraudulent to promise creditors that a parent company will stand behind its subsidiaries when the promisor knows that this is not true, even though he might genuinely, properly and reasonably consider that the subsidiary is sound. In that kind of case, wrongful trading would not be established, but fraudulent trading might be if the promisor was a party to carrying on the business.[30] Considerations of fraudulent trading could also arise where directors cause a company to incur new liabilities to suppliers which they know will not be paid in accordance with the terms of supply despite having a genuine belief that the company will be able to avoid insolvent liquidation, for example through some form of rescue or restructuring.

11.2.3 Misfeasance

IA 1986 s.212 enables "misfeasance" proceedings to be brought against directors (and others) during the course of a company liquidation. This sometimes causes confusion. Although "misfeasance" is a convenient generic term for misconduct, s.212 is purely procedural in that it enables action to be taken more efficiently but it does not create any additional obligations on the part of directors (or others). The subject-matter of misfeasance proceedings brought under s.212 will always be breach of a

---

[26] *Morris v Banque Arabe Internationale d'Investissement SA (No.2)* [2002] B.C.C. 407; [2001] 1 B.C.L.C. 263; (2000) 97(42) L.S.G. 43.

[27] *Overnight Ltd (In Liquidation), Re* [2010] EWHC 613 (Ch); [2010] B.C.C. 796; [2010] 2 B.C.L.C. 186.

[28] *Pantiles Investments Ltd, Re* [2019] EWHC 1298 (Ch).

[29] *William C Leitch Bros Ltd, Re (No.1)* [1932] 2 Ch. 71 at 77.

[30] *Augustus Barnett & Son Ltd, Re* [1986] B.C.L.C. 170; (1986) 2 B.C.C. 98904; [1986] P.C.C. 167.

duty identifiable elsewhere in the applicable legislation or under general law. Any limitation period will be that applicable to the underlying claim.[31]

11.2.4 Transactions which can be overturned by liquidators or administrators

By way of preliminary comment on the various provisions considered in this Section 11.2.4, the jurisdiction is restitutionary. It has been held that the powers of the court do not extend to making orders against directors whose only role has been to direct the company to enter into the impugned transaction but who received no personal benefit from it.[32] Such a director may nonetheless face misfeasance proceedings if he or she acted in breach of duty.

11.2.4.1 Transactions at an undervalue (IA 1986 section 238)

IA 1986 s.238 deals with transactions at an undervalue. The section applies where a company goes into administration or into liquidation. For the purposes of this section and for s.239 (see Section 11.2.4.3 below) the administrator or liquidator is referred to as the "office holder".

A company enters into a transaction with a person at an undervalue if (IA 1986 s.238(4)):

"(a) the company makes a gift to that person or otherwise enters into a transaction with that person on terms that provide for the company to receive no consideration, or
(b) the company enters into a transaction with that person for a consideration the value of which, in money or money's worth, is significantly less than the value, in money or money's worth, of the consideration provided by the company."

The Act further provides, in subs.(5), as follows (IA 1986 s.238(5)):

"The court shall not make an order under this section in respect of a transaction at an undervalue if it is satisfied—

(a) that the company which entered into the transaction did so in good faith and for the purpose of carrying on its business, and
(b) that at the time it did so there were reasonable grounds for believing that the transaction would benefit the company."

Difficulties can arise in respect of what amounts to a "transaction" for the purposes of s.238. (A number of the relevant cases have been decided in relation to transactions defrauding creditors which offend IA 1986 s.423, see Section 11.2.4.6 below, which incorporates the same test and are therefore

---

[31] *Brown v Button* [2011] EWHC 1034 (Ch); [2011] 2 B.C.L.C. 597.
[32] *Johnson v Arden* [2018] EWHC 1624 (Ch).

equally applicable in this context). It has been held that that the payment of a dividend is a transaction for these purposes[33] as is a purchase by a company of its own shares.[34] There are open questions as to whether a payment can, without more, amount to a "transaction".[35]

On the question of undervalue, s.238 requires a comparison to be made between the outgoing and incoming values of the transaction, the court is not required to have reference to expert evidence but is entitled to take a common sense approach.[36]

The question sometimes arises as to whether security given by a borrower for indebtedness which has been outstanding for a period before the giving of security could be characterised as a transaction at an undervalue. This point was considered in *MC Bacon Ltd (No.1), Re*[37] which has been the leading case on transactions at an undervalue and preferences. The case concerned a company which was in financial difficulties and had given security in respect of its existing overdraft at the time when it was insolvent. When the company subsequently went into liquidation, the liquidator commenced proceedings under ss.238 and 239 to have the security set aside. Millett J held that a transaction of this type could not be a transaction at an undervalue, and stated:

> "In my judgment, the applicant's claim to characterise the granting of the bank's debenture as a transaction at an undervalue is misconceived. The mere creation of a security over a company's assets does not deplete them and does not come within the paragraph. By charging its assets the company appropriates them to meet the liabilities due to the secured creditor and adversely affects the rights of other creditors in the event of insolvency. But it does not deplete its assets or diminish their value. It retains the right to redeem and the right to sell or remortgage the charged assets. All it loses is the ability to apply the proceeds otherwise than in satisfaction of the secured debt. That is not something capable of valuation in monetary terms and is not customarily disposed of for value ... in my judgment, the transaction does not fall within sub-s (4), and it is unnecessary to consider the application of sub-s (5) which provides a defence to the claim in certain circumstances."

In *Hill v Spread Trustee Co Ltd*,[38] however, doubt was cast on this part of the judgment in *MC Bacon* in the Court of Appeal and the point should now be regarded as open pending further consideration by the Court of Appeal. In principle, it seems that the grant of security will more easily withstand challenge as a transaction at an undervalue (and also as a preference, as to

---

[33] *BTI 2014 LLC v Sequana SA* [2019] EWCA Civ 112; [2019] 1 B.C.L.C. 347.

[34] *Dickinson v NAL Realisations (Staffordshire) Ltd* [2017] EWHC 28 (Ch); [2018] B.C.C. 506.

[35] *Hampton Capital Ltd, Re* [2015] EWHC 1905 (Ch); [2016] B.C.L.C. 374; *Kiss Cards Ltd, Re* [2016] EWHC 2176 (Ch); [2017] B.C.C. 489; *Payroller Ltd v Panda Consultants Ltd* [2018] EWHC 3161 (QB).

[36] *Hollier, Re* [2010] EWHC 3155 (Ch); [2014] B.P.I.R. 927.

[37] *MC Bacon Ltd (No.1), Re* [1990] B.C.C. 78; [1990] B.C.L.C. 324.

[38] *Hill v Spread Trustee Co Ltd* [2006] EWCA Civ 542; [2007] 1 W.L.R. 2404; [2007] Bus. L.R. 1213.

which see below) where it is given in return for forbearance (as was the case in *MC Bacon*). *Hill v Spread Trustee Co Ltd* concerned the more egregious situation of the grant of security being a transaction defrauding creditors (as to which also see below).

In *Mistral Finance (In Liquidation), Re*,[39] it was held that a re-grant of security where the previously granted security was void for want of registration did not amount to a transaction at an undervalue, but was a preference (see Section 11.2.4.3 below).

The giving of a guarantee is a more obvious example of a transaction which may be a transaction at an undervalue but the court will have regard to the circumstances in which a guarantee is given. In *Tailby v HSBC Bank Plc*,[40] the court dismissed an application by a trustee as bankruptcy under IA 1986 s.339 (the analogous provision which applies to bankruptcies) where a guarantee had been given as part of ordinary commercial lending to companies which were, at the time, profitable. The relevant "transaction" was the whole package including the facility as well as the guarantee.

11.2.4.2 Relevant time

The court will not make an order in respect of a transaction at an undervalue unless the company entered into the transaction at a "relevant time" (IA 1986 s.240). In order to have occurred at a relevant time:

(a)   the transaction must take place at a time in the period of two years ending with the "onset of insolvency" (see Section 11.2.4.4 below) (or while an administration is pending); and
(b)   at the time of the transaction the company must be unable to pay its debts within the meaning of s.123 IA 1986 or become unable to pay its debts within the meaning of that section in consequence of the transaction.

The burden of proof is on the applicant office-holder[41] but, if the office holder shows that a transaction has occurred for which no sufficient consideration is apparent from the company's books and records, it is for the recipients to satisfy the court that sufficient consideration has been given (*Kiss Cards Ltd, Re* above). Unless the contrary is shown by the respondent, the second requirement (contemporaneous insolvency) is presumed where the person with whom the company enters into the transaction is connected with the company. This may be a difficult burden of proof to discharge where the issue turns on whether the company will be able to meet liabilities which are due to be paid at some future date because,

---

[39]   *Mistral Finance (In Liquidation), Re* [2001] B.C.C. 27.
[40]   *Tailby v HSBC Bank Plc* [2015] B.P.I.R. 143.
[41]   *Stanley & Wood v TMK Finance Ltd* [2010] EWHC 3349 (Ch); [2011] B.P.I.R. 876; [2011] Bus. L.R. D93.

the further forward the projection is made, the more difficult it is to establish (on a balance of probabilities) that the company can reasonably be expected to meet those liabilities upon maturity.[42] A company may be cash-flow solvent but balance sheet insolvent, or vice versa, at any particular time but a company with some assets (however illiquid) and no debts cannot be insolvent on either ground.[43]

11.2.4.3 Preferences (IA 1986 section 239)

This provision applies in similar circumstances to those relating to IA 1986 s.238: that is, if a company goes into administration or liquidation. Section 239(4) describes the nature of a preference:

> "For the purposes of this section ... a company gives a preference to a person if—
>
> (a) that person is one of the company's creditors or a surety or guarantor for any of the company's debts or other liabilities, and
> (b) the company does anything or suffers anything to be done which (in either case) has the effect of putting that person into a position which, in the event of the company going into insolvent liquidation, will be better than the position he would have been in if that thing had not been done."

For a company to "suffer" something to be done for these purposes, it must permit something to happen which it has the power to stop or obstruct: *Klempka v Miller*.[44] Under subs.(5), the court shall not make an order unless the company which gave the preference was "influenced in deciding to give it by a desire to produce in relation to that person the effect mentioned in subsection (4)(b)".

The concept of a "desire to prefer" was introduced in the IA 1986 when the previous law of "fraudulent preference" was radically recast. The leading case on both transactions at an undervalue and preferences, *MC Bacon Ltd (No.1), Re* (above), gives some guidance as to the interpretation of this subsection. As mentioned in Section 11.2.4.1 above, the case concerned a company which had encountered financial difficulties. It gave security to its bank to secure its overdraft facilities, which were advanced to it before the security was given. This situation is clearly extremely common in the negotiations that companies have with their bankers when the company is in financial difficulties and facing insolvency. Millett J held that the giving of security in these circumstances was not a preference because the

---

[42] *Casa Estates (UK) Ltd, Re* [2013] EWHC 2371 (Ch), on appeal, [2014] EWCA Civ 383; [2014] B.C.C. 269.
[43] *Salter v Wetton* [2011] EWHC 3192 (Ch); [2012] B.P.I.R. 63.
[44] *Klempka v Miller* [2008] EWHC 3554 (Ch); [2010] B.C.C. 309; [2009] B.P.I.R. 549.

company was not "influenced by a desire to prefer" the bank. Millett J interpreted the concept of being "influenced by a desire to prefer" as follows (at 335–336):

"It is no longer necessary to establish a *dominant* intention to prefer. It is sufficient that the decision was *influenced* by the requisite desire. That is the first change … The second change is made necessary by the first, for without it, it would be virtually impossible to uphold the validity of a security taken in exchange for the injection of fresh funds into a company in financial difficulties. A man is taken to intend the necessary consequences of his actions, so that an intention to grant a security to a creditor necessarily involves an intention to prefer that creditor in the event of insolvency. The need to establish that such intention was dominant was essential under the old law to prevent perfectly proper transactions from being struck down. With the abolition of that requirement intention could not remain the relevant test. Desire has been substituted. That is a very different matter. Intention is objective, desire is subjective. A man can choose the lesser of two evils without desiring either. It is not, however, sufficient to establish a desire to make the payment or grant the security which it is sought to avoid. There must have been a desire to produce the effect mentioned in the sub-section, that is to say, to improve the creditor's position in the event of an insolvent liquidation. A man is not to be taken as *desiring* all the necessary consequences of his actions. Some consequences may be of advantage to him and be desired by him; others may not affect him and be matters of indifference to him; while still others may be positively disadvantageous to him and not be desired by him, but be regarded by him as the unavoidable price of obtaining the desired advantages. It will still be possible to provide assistance to a company in financial difficulties provided that the company is actuated only by proper commercial considerations. Under the new regime a transaction will not be set aside as a voidable preference unless the company positively wished to improve the creditor's position in the event of its own insolvent liquidation. There is, of course, no need for there to be direct evidence of the requisite desire. Its existence may be inferred from the circumstances of the case, just as the dominant intention could be inferred under the old law. But the mere presence of the requisite desire will not be sufficient by itself. It must have influenced the decision to enter into the transaction. It was submitted on behalf of the bank that it must have been the factor which 'tipped the scales'. I disagree. That is not what sub-s (5) says; it requires only that the desire should have influenced the decision. That requirement is satisfied if it was one of the factors which operated on the minds of those who made the decision. It need not have been the only factor or even the decisive one. In my judgment, it is not necessary to prove that, if the requisite desire had not been present, the company would not have entered into the transaction. That would be too high a test."

This approach was supported in *Fairway Magazines Ltd, Re*,[45] where a company issued security for advances utilised to reduce an overdraft liability guaranteed by a director. It was held that the debenture was not a preference because the company was solely influenced by commercial considerations, namely the need to raise money from another source in

---

[45] *Fairway Magazines Ltd, Re* [1992] B.C.C. 924; [1993] B.C.L.C. 643.

order to continue trading. Mummery J made the point, however, that the desire to influence the creditor does not have to be the sole or decisive influence in making the decision. Later, in *Stealth Construction Ltd, Re*,[46] the court emphasised that it is the decision to prefer, rather than the giving of the preference pursuant to that decision (which could be later for administrative reasons), which has to be influenced by the desire.

Where the beneficiary of the preference is connected with the company otherwise than by reason only of being its employee at the time the preference was given, the desire to prefer is presumed (s.239(6)) unless the contrary is shown. Once the office holder has proved that the relevant disposition has occurred within the relevant period (see below), the evidential burden therefore shifts to the respondent to explain the transaction.[47] The presumption can apply even where one director is imposing terms on his co-director if there is a joint decision to give a preference.[48] However, in *Reynolds DIY Stores Ltd, Re (No.2)*,[49] where the presumption also applied, the liquidators' case was nonetheless dismissed because they failed to establish that the company was unable to pay its debts.

This section also provides that the fact that something was done in pursuance of the order of a court is not enough to prevent the doing or suffering of that thing from constituting the giving of a preference (s.239(7)).

As in the case of a transaction at an undervalue, IA 1986 provides that a transaction of this type will only be a preference if the company enters into it at a "relevant time". The "relevant time" is described as follows in IA 1986 s.240:

(a)   where the beneficiary of the preference is a person who is connected with the company (otherwise than by reason only of being its employee), at a time in the period of two years ending with the onset of insolvency;

(b)   where the preference is not given in favour of a connected person, a time in the period of six months ending with the onset of insolvency (s.240(1)); and

(c)   in either case, when an administration is pending.

As for transactions at an undervalue, the company must be unable to pay its debts within the meaning of IA 1986 s.123 at the time of, or as a consequence of, the preference. (In contrast to s.238, this is not presumed in the case of a connected person; see *Reynolds DIY Stores Ltd (No.2), Re* above

---

[46]   *Stealth Construction Ltd, Re* [2011] EWHC 1305 (Ch); [2012] 1 B.C.L.C. 297; [2011] B.P.I.R. 1173.
[47]   *MSD Cash & Carry Plc, Re* [2018] EWHC 1325 (Ch); [2018] B.C.C. 686.
[48]   *Taylor v Ziya* [2012] B.P.I.R. 1283.
[49]   *Reynolds DIY Stores Ltd, Re (No.2)* [2012] EWHC 4370 (Ch).

but, at the time of writing, the Government is proposing to introduce amending legislation extending the presumption to s.239 cases).

11.2.4.4   *The onset of insolvency*

The "onset of insolvency" is relevant to both transactions at an undervalue and preferences and is defined in s.240(3) which refers to the onset of proceedings rather than the financial condition of the company. The definition has become more complicated since its original enactment because of the expansion of the ways in which administration and liquidation can be commenced but, that aside, the rules are clear and the detail should be consulted in any case where the precise timing of a transaction is a critical factor. In summary, the overall effect is that the onset of insolvency will be no later than the formal commencement of the insolvency proceedings but may be slightly earlier, for example where liquidation or administration results from a court order in which case the relevant date is the date on which the application for the order was made.

11.2.4.5   *Effect of an order*

The court has a wide discretion as to the terms of the order it makes under ss.238 or 239, but the essential principle is that these are "claw-back" provisions designed to restore the position to what it would have been if the impugned transaction had not occurred. The relevant office-holder will be seeking to undo a transaction which has either depleted the assets of the insolvent estate (in the case of a transaction at an undervalue) or given one creditor a privileged position in relation to the general body of creditors (in the case of a preference). As such, the beneficiaries of the transaction are the target of the proceedings (subject to the provisions of IA 1986 s.241(2)–(3C) which provides protection for beneficiaries who did not have full knowledge of the circumstances of the transactions from which they benefited, as to which see further *Whitestar Management Ltd, Re*[50]), rather than the director of the company responsible for entering into the transaction (*Johnson v Arden* above). However, the potential sanctions against directors who are responsible for procuring companies to carry out such transactions are equally significant and are set out in CDDA 1986, which is described in Chapter 13 below and, depending on the circumstances, there is also a risk of misfeasance proceedings for breach of duty.

11.2.4.6   *Transactions defrauding creditors*

Directors should also be aware of IA 1986 s.423, which concerns transactions defrauding creditors. This provision applies to all companies,

---

[50]   *Whitestar Management Ltd, Re* [2018] EWHC 743 (Ch); [2018] B.P.I.R. 1524.

whether or not insolvent, and can apply to transactions taking place outside the jurisdiction.[51] The essential ingredients of a transaction defrauding creditors are as follows:

(a) a person must enter into a transaction at an undervalue. The definition of "transaction at an undervalue" is exactly the same as in relation to IA 1986 s.238 except that it contains a further provision which is only relevant to individuals and not to companies (IA 1986 s.423(1));

(b) the court may make an order under s.423 if it is satisfied that the person entered into such a transaction for the purpose of:

(i)   "putting assets beyond the reach of a person who is making, or may at some time make, a claim against him"; or

(ii) "otherwise prejudicing the interests of such a person in relation to the claim which he is making or may make" (IA 1986 s.423(3)).

The court may in such circumstances make such order as it thinks fit (s.423(2) IA 1986) for:

"(a) restoring the position to what it would have been if the transaction had not been entered into, and

(b) protecting the interests of persons who are victims of the transaction."

Proceedings may be brought by the liquidator or administrator of the company, or by a victim of the transaction. A "victim", for these purposes, includes anyone who is prejudiced by the transaction, not just those creditors that the debtor may have had in mind when entering the transaction.[52] However, whilst the concept of a "victim" is relevant to who may bring an application, the concept of the persons who may be prejudiced (see (b)(i) and (ii) above), thus triggering the potential application of s.423, is even wider. All that has to be shown is that the transaction was entered into for the purpose of defrauding any person who had made or might at some time make a claim (*Fortress Value Recovery Fund I LLC v Blue Skye Special Opportunities Fund LP* above). It does not matter if the prejudice would have happened anyway; it is the prejudicial purpose that triggers the jurisdiction.[53] Conversely, it is not enough to show the effect of the impugned transaction without the proscribed purpose.[54]

There is no requirement for a s.423 application that the company be insolvent or go into liquidation or administration within a particular time limit from the date on which the company entered into the transaction. Although actual or pending insolvency need not be proved, it will, in

---

[51] *Fortress Value Recovery Fund I LLC v Blue Skye Special Opportunities Fund LP* [2013] EWHC 14 (Comm); [2013] 1 All E.R. (Comm) 973; [2013] B.P.I.R. 276.

[52] *Sands v Clitheroe* [2006] B.P.I.R. 1000; *Ali v Bashir* [2014] EWHC 3853 (Ch); [2015] B.P.I.R. 211.

[53] *Hill v Spread Trustee Co Ltd* [2006] EWCA Civ 542; [2007] 1 W.L.R. 2404; [2007] Bus. L.R. 1213 and *Pathania v Tashie-Lewis* [2018] EWHC 362 (Ch).

[54] *Bibby ACF Ltd v Agate* [2013] B.P.I.R. 685; *JSC BTA Bank v Ablyzov* [2018] EWCA Civ 1176; [2018] B.P.I.R. 898; *Farrell, Re* [2019] EWHC 119.

practice, be much easier for any person invoking s.423 to prove the requisite purpose where a company was in financial difficulty when the transaction occurred.

The Court of Appeal held in *Inland Revenue Commissioners v Hashmi*[55] that prejudice to the creditor does not need to be the sole or even dominant purpose. The same case was generally regarded as authority for the proposition that the test was whether prejudice was a real and substantial purpose of the transaction and not merely a consequence or by-product.[56] However, in the more recent case of *JSC BTA Bank v Ablyazov*,[57] the Court of Appeal held that the word "substantial" was an unnecessary gloss on the language of s.423 and that the correct test was simply whether the transaction was entered into for the prohibited purpose even if there were one or more other purposes. Establishing purpose requires the court to have regard to the subjective state of mind of the transferor.[58] There is no presumption that a debtor has the proscribed purpose because of the existence of adverse claims; the court must decide on the evidence as a whole and the inferences which it can properly draw from that evidence (*JSC BTA Bank*, above).

In *Concept Oil Services Ltd v En-Gin Group LLP*,[59] a corporate reorganisation which left a debtor company as an empty shell was held to have been a transaction at an undervalue contrary to s.423 but every case turns on its own facts.

Any transaction which could be attacked under s.423 is likely, in the case of a company, also to be actionable by virtue of a breach of fiduciary duties by the directors, as is set out in more detail below. Although most of the reported cases on this section in fact relate to individuals, company directors need to be aware of it since the types of transaction it refers to, those which involve taking assets "out of the reach" of creditors, of course will almost inevitably end in the insolvency of the relevant company. Any deliberate attempt to try to make a company "judgment proof" can not only be attacked under s.423 but can also easily lead to sanctions being taken against the directors under the CDDA 1986 (see again Chapter 13 below).

---

[55] *Inland Revenue Commissioners v Hashmi* [2002] EWCA Civ 981; [2002] B.C.C. 943; [2002] 2 B.C.L.C. 489.
[56] *Williams v Taylor* [2012] EWCA Civ 1443; [2013] B.P.I.R. 133.
[57] *JSC BTA Bank v Ablyazov* [2018] EWCA Civ 1176.
[58] *Pagemanor Ltd v Ryan (No.2)* [2002] B.P.I.R. 593; *BTI 2014 LLC v Sequana SA* [2019] EWCA Civ 112, [2019] 1 B.C.L.C. 347; *Farrell, Re* [2019] EWHC 119.
[59] *Concept Oil Services Ltd v En-Gin Group LLP* [2013] EWHC 1897 (Comm).

11.3 Fiduciary and statutory duties of directors

The fiduciary duties of directors are of crucial importance for all company directors, not just those whose companies are facing insolvency. However, where a company is insolvent, or prospectively insolvent, cases have established the role of directors' fiduciary duties in protecting creditors as a class, not just shareholders, where it is the creditors as well as the shareholders of the company who stand to lose if the directors breach their duties.

11.3.1 Nature of fiduciary and statutory duties

In exercising their powers, directors have a duty to act bona fide in the interests of the company.[60] If they do so, the courts will not interfere in their actions unless there are no reasonable grounds for that belief.

The CA 2006 introduced a statutory statement of seven general duties which are set out in ss.170–177. Those duties are:

*   to act within powers;
*   to promote the success of the company;
*   to exercise independent judgment;
*   to exercise reasonable care, skill and diligence;
*   to avoid conflicts of interest;
*   not to accept benefits from third parties; and
*   to declare an interest in a proposed transaction or arrangement.

These duties are owed to the company, not to individual shareholders or creditors. Where the company is solvent, the company means its shareholders as a class.[61] The shareholders as a class can therefore choose to approve the directors' acts. Shareholder approval of the transaction will be sufficient in the case of a solvent company to absolve the directors from liability for the breach.[62] However, if the company is insolvent its shareholders are not the only people concerned. Creditors also stand to lose if, for example, the directors procure that the company makes a gift to a third party.

11.3.2 Insolvent companies

This situation had to be considered in the decision of the High Court of Australia in *Walker v Wimborne*.[63] The company went into liquidation and the liquidator challenged certain transactions which had taken place while the company was insolvent. These transactions included the payment of salaries to employees of other group companies and the making of an

---

[60] *Smith and Fawcett, Re* [1942] Ch. 304; [1942] 1 All E.R. 542.
[61] *Regal (Hastings) v Gulliver* (1967) 2 A.C. 134; [1942] 1 All E.R. 378.
[62] *Parke v Daily News (No.2)* [1962] Ch. 927; [1962] 3 W.L.R. 566; (1962) 106 S.J. 704.
[63] *Walker v Wimborne* (1976) 137 C.L.R. 1.

unsecured loan to another insolvent group member. It was held by the court that these acts amounted to misfeasance by the directors. Mason J made the following comments:

> "In this respect it should be emphasized that the directors of a company in discharging their duty to the company must take account of the interests of its shareholders and its creditors. Any failure by the directors to take into account the interests of creditors will have adverse consequences for the company as well as for them ...
>
> The transaction offered no prospect of advantage to [the company], it exposed [the company] to the probable prospect of substantial loss, and thereby seriously prejudiced the unsecured creditors of [the company]."

One mistake sometimes made by the directors of companies facing insolvency is that they attempt to protect their position by obtaining a resolution of shareholders approving the transaction made in breach of their duties. Logically, if the breach of fiduciary duties has implications for creditors as well as shareholders, the shareholders' consent will be insufficient to absolve the directors of liability for breach of fiduciary duty. This point was considered in the Australian case of *Kinsela v Russell Kinsela Pty Ltd*.[64] In that case, the company leased its premises to its shareholders, at a time when it was insolvent, for a very low rent. The court held that the transaction was effected in breach of duty to the company and Street CJ made the following observation in relation to the ineffectiveness of authorisation by the shareholders:

> "It is, to my mind, legally and logically acceptable to recognise that, where directors are involved in a breach of their duty to the company affecting the interests of shareholders, then shareholders can either authorize that breach in prospect or ratify it in retrospect. Where, however, the interests at risk are those of creditors I see no reason in law or in logic to recognize that the shareholders can authorize the breach. Once it is accepted, as in my view it must be, that the directors' duty to the company as a whole extends in an insolvency context to not prejudicing the interests of creditors ... the shareholders do not have the power or authority to absolve the directors from that breach."

A similar point was considered in *Liquidator of West Mercia Safetywear Ltd v Dodd*.[65] In this case, the company, West Mercia, was a wholly-owned subsidiary of AJ Dodd & C Ltd. Both companies were insolvent. Mr Dodd, a director of both companies, caused sums to be transferred by West Mercia to Dodd. This had the effect of reducing Mr Dodd's liability under a personal guarantee he had given in support of Dodd's overdraft. Clearly, the payment was made for the benefit of its shareholder. The Court of Appeal held that once a company was insolvent the interests of the

---

[64] *Kinsela v Russell Kinsela Pty Ltd* (1986) 4 NSWLR 722.
[65] *Liquidator of West Mercia Safetywear Ltd v Dodd* (1988) 4 B.C.C. 30; [1988] B.C.L.C. 250; [1988] P.C.C. 212.

creditors overrode those of the shareholders. Since West Mercia was known by Mr Dodd to be insolvent when the transfer took place and the transfer was a preference made to relieve Mr Dodd of his personal liability, Mr Dodd had breached his duty. The approval of the shareholders was in this case ineffective because creditors become prospectively entitled, through the mechanism of liquidation, to displace the power of the shareholders and directors to deal with the company's assets. (*West Mercia* has been cited in numerous subsequent cases and is generally treated as the leading English authority on the changed nature of directors' duties when insolvency supervenes.)

In *Colin Gwyer & Associates Ltd v London Wharf (Limehouse) Ltd*,[66] the point was reinforced. Where a company is solvent the court has to ask itself "could an honest and intelligent man, in the position of the directors, in all the circumstances, reasonably have believed that the decision in question was for the benefit of the company". Where the company is insolvent, the question is asked with the substitution of "creditors" for "company". However, this does not restrict directors from acting inconsistently with the interests of a particular creditor where it is in the interests of the general body of creditors.[67] CA 2006 provides that the statutory duties are to be interpreted and applied in the same way as the common law or equitable principles on which they are based, and regard is to be had to those principles in applying them (CA 2006 s.170(4)). In *GHLM Trading Ltd v Maroo*,[68] the court held that the statutory duty (under CA 2006 s.172; see Section 11.1 above), to promote the success of the company for the benefit of its members became, in the event of insolvency, a duty to have regard to the interests of the company's creditors as a class (as opposed to the interests of any particular creditor). It followed that a director who acted to advance the interests of one creditor without believing it to be in the interests of the creditors generally will commit a breach of duty (and the fact that the conditions for a preference claim under s.239 might not be met was not determinative).

The underlying principle is that directors are not free to take action which risks creditors going unpaid, without first considering their' interests rather than those of the shareholders. The duty, when it arises, is a subjective duty to have regard to the interests of creditors but, if there has been no actual consideration of those interests (without overlooking matters which would objectively be considered to be material), the court will apply an objective test to determine whether an honest and reasonable man in the position of

---

[66] *Colin Gwyer & Associates Ltd v London Wharf (Limehouse) Ltd* [2002] EWHC 2748 (Ch); [2003] B.C.C. 885; [2003] 2 B.C.L.C. 153.
[67] *Miller v Bain (Director's Breach of Duty)* [2002] 1 B.C.L.C. 266.
[68] *GHLM Trading Ltd v Maroo* [2012] EWHC 61 (Ch); [2012] 2 B.C.L.C. 369. For another example, see *Pantiles Investments Ltd, Re* [2019] EWHC 1298 (Ch).

the director could reasonably have believed that the matter under consideration was for the benefit of the company.[69]

In *Pro4Sport Ltd, Re*,[70] a claim of breach of duty failed because the respondent director had considered the interests of creditors and had honestly concluded that a sale of assets to a connected company was in their best interests. Recent examples of cases where a breach of the duty to have regard to the interest of creditors was established include *PV Solar Solutions Ltd, Re*[71] (remuneration drawn in breach of the company's articles) and *LRH Services Ltd v Trew*[72] (carrying out a corporate reorganisation which made an insolvent liquidation inevitable).

11.3.3 Prospectively insolvent companies

A problem for directors emerges when considering at what point the creditors begin to become significant for the directors in considering their duties? Although it may be difficult to identity the relevant point in time when the duty arises on the facts of a case, it was accepted in *BTI 2014 LLC v Sequana SA* at first instance (above) that there is a single threshold and that the duty does not arise in respect of some decisions and not others depending upon the gravity of the company's financial position.[73]

Identifying the trigger point is not a question which can simply be answered by reference to the statutory test (under the Insolvency Act 1986 s.123) of whether the company is "unable to pay its debts", even as elucidated by the Supreme Court in *BNY Corporate Trustee Services Ltd v Eurosail-UK 2007-3BL Plc*.[74]

Previous cases on when the duty arises were recently, and comprehensively, reviewed by the Court of Appeal in *Sequana* (above). The court held that the duty arises the directors know or should know that the company is or is likely to become insolvent. "Likely", in this context, means probable. Having noted the potential tension between the duty of directors to promote the success of the company for the benefit of members (CA 1985 s.172(1)) and the duty to have regard to the interests of creditors unless the latter duty (once engaged) was to be treated as paramount, the court expressly declined to rule on whether creditors' interests were paramount (that not being an issue which arose on the facts of *Sequana*).

---

[69] *HLC Environmental Projects Ltd, Re* [2013] EWHC 2876 (Ch); [2014] 2 B.C.L.C. 337; *Wessely & another v White* [2018] EWHC 1499 (Ch).
[70] *Pro4Sport Ltd, Re* [2015] EWHC 2540 (Ch); [2016] B.C.C. 390.
[71] *PV Solar Solutions Ltd, Re* [2017] EWHC 3228 (Ch); [2018] B.C.C. 196.
[72] *LRH Services Ltd v Trew* [2018] EWHC 600 (Ch).
[73] [2016] EWHC 686 (Ch); [2017] 1 B.C.L.C. 453, on appeal [2019] EWCA Civ 112; [2019] 1 B.C.L.C. 347 where the acceptance of these points was recorded without further comment.
[74] *BNY Corporate Trustee Services Ltd v Eurosail-UK 2007-3BL Plc* [2013] UKSC 28; [2013] 1 W.L.R. 1408; [2013] Bus. L.R. 715.

Where the matter under consideration is a distribution or other uncommercial transaction for the benefit of themselves or shareholders, other rules may be make the interests of creditors relevant before insolvency. An interesting case on this point is *Aveling Barford Ltd v Perion Ltd*[75] where a motion to set aside a judgment in default of defence was taken to the High Court. Aveling Barford was in liquidation. Perion was controlled by the same person as Aveling Barford. A property owned by Aveling Barford had been sold to Perion; and this fact was known to the directors of both Aveling Barford and Perion. The shareholders of Aveling Barford had consented to the transaction. Aveling Barford was solvent at the time but did not have any distributable reserves: it had an accumulated deficit on the profit and loss account. It would not have been able to make distributions to its shareholders. Hoffmann J took the view that the directors of Aveling Barford had acted in breach of their fiduciary duty to the company by selling the property at an undervalue and that Perion had the necessary notice of the breach of fiduciary duty to be held a constructive trustee of the benefit. Hoffmann J also held that the consent of the shareholders was ineffective to waive the breach even though Aveling Barford was solvent at the time. His reasoning was based on the fact that the company did not have distributable reserves and the transaction was effectively a dressed up distribution to shareholders because of the close connection between Perion and Dr Lee, the company's ultimate shareholder. Although the judgment is not grounded in an analysis of when it is the duty of directors to have regard to the interests of creditors, the court treated the rule that capital cannot be returned to shareholders (other than by following the correct statutory procedures) as being a rule for the protection of creditors such that its breach was a "fraud on creditors" which was incapable of ratification by shareholders. In light of this decision, company directors should always consider the position of creditors if there is any prospect of entering into a transaction which benefits a party associated with a shareholder, even though the company may be technically solvent at the time.

Despite the uncertainties as to the scope of the duty to have regard to the interests of creditors (as and when it arises), the duty is a duty owed to the company and not to the creditors themselves. It will therefore only be actionable by or on behalf of the company (e.g. by an office holder), but a creditor could use the misfeasance procedure (see Section 11.2.3 above) to ensure that the company's claim was brought.

---

[75] *Aveling Barford Ltd v Perion Ltd* (1989) 5 B.C.C. 677; [1989] B.C.L.C. 626; [1989] P.C.C. 370.

11.4 Public companies and listed companies: duties to shareholders

The duties of the directors of public companies and listed companies to their shareholders are complex and are covered elsewhere in this Guide. However, there are one or two legal provisions which, although relevant to all directors of such companies, tend to pose particular problems on insolvency and are therefore areas which the directors of such companies should always consider if there is any danger of insolvency approaching. These provisions include the maintenance of capital provisions under CA 2006 and (in relation to listed companies) the disclosure of information requirements under the EU Market Abuse Regulation (MAR).[76]

11.4.1 *Serious loss of capital (CA 2006 section 656)*

CA 2006 s.656 provides as follows:

> "(1) Where the net assets of a public company are half or less of its called-up share capital, the directors must call a general meeting of the company to consider whether any, and if so what, steps should be taken to deal with the situation.
>
> (2) They must do so not later than 28 days from the earliest day on which that fact is known to a director of the company.
>
> (3) The meeting must be convened for a date not later than 56 days from that day.
>
> (4) If there is a failure to convene a meeting as required by this section, each of the directors of the company who—
>   (a) knowingly authorises or permits the failure, or
>   (b) after the period during which the meeting should have been convened, knowingly authorises or permits the failure to continue, commits an offence.
>
> (5) A person guilty of an offence under this section is liable—
>   (a) on conviction on indictment, to a fine;
>   (b) on summary conviction, to a fine not exceeding the statutory maximum.
>
> (6) Nothing in this section authorises the consideration at a meeting convened in pursuance of subsection (1) of any matter that could not have been considered at that meeting apart from this section."

This provision is an important one for directors of public companies coming close to insolvency. The requirement to convene a meeting is, of course, a problem for directors who are in emergency negotiations for some scheme to save the company, since the publicity involved in convening a general meeting at this time may be inconvenient for the company. However, it is essential that directors are aware of their duty and convene the necessary meeting to avoid incurring penalties. The directors should also be aware that the section does not impose upon them a duty to remedy the situation

---

[76] Regulation 596/2014 on market abuse [2014] OJ L173/1.

in any way, but simply to call a meeting to consider what steps, if any, should be taken to deal with the situation.

11.4.2 The Listing Rules and MAR

Where a company is listed on the London Stock Exchange, the directors must ensure that it continues to comply with its obligations under both the Listing Rules and the disclosure requirements under MAR arts 17, 18 and 19. MAR art.17, the purpose of which is to promote prompt and fair disclosure of relevant information to the market, needs careful consideration in this context. Article 17 requires an issuer to notify a Regulatory Information Service as soon as possible of any inside information (as defined) which directly concerns it. However, an issuer may be able to delay the disclosure of inside information in circumstances where immediate disclosure is likely to prejudice legitimate interests, where the omission to disclose will not be likely to mislead the public and the information can be kept confidential.

Clearly, the obligation to disclose inside information can become a serious issue for the directors of listed companies where insolvency is in prospect. It is highly likely that the company's financial condition will be or become such as to warrant a notification under MAR art.17. Equally, the directors may well be reluctant to notify if they are involved in negotiations for a rescue of the company, since the announcement may prejudice the negotiations and worsen the company's problems. ESMA Guidance on when an issuer may have "legitimate interests" in delaying disclosure includes when:

> "the financial viability of the issuer is in grave and imminent danger, although not within the scope of the applicable insolvency law, and immediate public disclosure of the inside information would seriously prejudice the interests of existing and potential shareholders by jeopardising the conclusion of the negotiations designed to ensure the financial recovery of the issuer."[77]

In the Disclosure Guidance published by the FCA,[78] the FCA states that in its view, a company may (subject to certain requirements) be able to delay public disclosure of the fact that it is in rescue negotiations (or the substance of those negotiations) but the exception does not extend to permitting the company to delay public disclosure of the fact that it is in financial difficulty. Further, in the FCA's view, it does not permit a company to delay disclosure of inside information on the basis that its subsequent negotiations to deal with the situation will be jeopardised by the disclosure of its financial condition.

---

[77] European Securities and Markets Authority MAR Guidelines on the Delay of Disclosure of Inside Information published on 21 October 2016.
[78] FCA Disclosure Guidance and Transparency Rules sourcebook.

It should be noted that the disclosure of inside information, including information relating to financial performance, cannot be delayed merely so that it can coincide with a scheduled announcement of a periodic financial report.

Directors should be aware that the penalties for breach of the MAR disclosure requirements can be significant.

When a company to which the Listing Rules and the MAR disclosure requirements apply is under financial pressure, those requirements need to be carefully and continuously monitored if the directors are to comply with their obligations.

11.4.3   MAR articles 14 and 15 and Financial Services Act 2012 (FSA)

There are other provisions which, although of general application, may involve particularly difficult judgments when a company is experiencing any sort of solvency crisis—particularly where there the crisis is a short-term liquidity crisis and there are grounds for supposing that it is capable of resolution.

MAR arts 14 and 15 deal with market abuse. Examples of when market abuse will occur include the unlawful disclosure of inside information and market manipulation. Where a director has engaged in market abuse or has permitted others to do so, the Financial Conduct Authority can impose civil penalties.

In addition, FSA ss.89 and 90 provide criminal penalties for directors who (in summary) knowingly or recklessly make false or misleading statements or who dishonestly conceal any material facts in order to induce dealings in relevant investments or agreements in relation to them, or who otherwise create a false or misleading impression as to the market in, price or value of relevant investments.

These matters are covered in more detail in Chapter 4.

11.5   Practical matters

The combined effect of the statutory provisions set out in this Chapter, together with the cases in the areas of fiduciary duties and the powers of the court to make disqualification orders against directors, require the directors of companies facing insolvency to take into account a wide range of responsibilities when carrying out their functions. Clearly, no two companies are the same and detailed legal advice should always be taken in relation to the circumstances of any particular company where an insolvency issue has arisen. However, directors of a company facing insolvency should always consider the following practical guidelines:

(a)   take professional advice from insolvency specialists;
(b)   convene regular meetings to consider the company's financial position and keep under constant review the issue of whether the company has a reasonable prospect of avoiding insolvency proceedings;
(c)   every member of the board should ensure that he is adequately informed of the position of the company and should perform (and be seen to perform) his functions actively. Directors who leave other directors to cover for them can be penalised;
(d)   ensure that all information about the company, in particular its financial details, is adequate and up to date and available to all directors;
(e)   give careful consideration to deciding whether all actions taken by the board are in the commercial interests of the company (having regard also to the matters specified in CA 2006 s.172, as to which see Section 11.1 above);
(f)   consider the effect of any proposed transaction on the interests of creditors. Even where the company is of doubtful solvency rather than clearly insolvent, the interests of creditors may become the determining factor in relation to any allegations of breach of fiduciary duty. The board must never attempt to rely on shareholder approval to absolve it from a breach of fiduciary duty where the solvency of the company is in doubt;
(g)   consider the interests of all its creditors and not just a particular class (e.g. its bankers). Boards of directors are often pressed by certain powerful creditors to take action which is detrimental to other creditors. Directors can be penalised for acting in this way;
(h)   where the company is a listed company, the board should consider carefully its duties in relation to disclosure of information which could cause movements in the price of its shares;
(i)   each member of the board should consider his conduct carefully in relation to all relevant duties, not just those relating to insolvency. The insolvency of a company may be the trigger for scrutiny of the conduct of a director in relation to any aspect of his conduct;
(j)   where there is conflict amongst members of the board, each member must be seen to act positively to comply with his duties, since the sanctions relate to members individually not collectively. Where a member of the board disagrees with his co-directors, he should take active steps to make his views known (and recorded) and to obtain the information he needs to make the necessary decisions;
(k)   all proceedings of the board should be carefully minuted and checked by each member of the board. In particular, the reasons for entering into any transaction and the reasons for the board's belief that the company can continue to trade should be recorded fully. Clearly the members of the board will need evidence that they behaved properly; and

(l)   if taking legal advice, the directors should consider also taking that advice from advisers independent to those advising the company.

In a group situation, all the foregoing must be done in respect of each affected company and directors must be astute to consider the interests of the creditors of each company as separate constituencies. In the event of insolvency proceedings, their conduct will be considered on a company-by-company basis and even if several companies within a group, or the entire group, become subject to insolvency proceedings, it cannot be assumed that the same office-holders will be responsible for all the companies and thus be able to understand any group-wide perspective.

Chapter 12

Regulatory Investigations

Rob Dedman, Gareth Rees QC, Aaron Stephens

Partners, King & Spalding

12.1   Introduction

Since the financial crisis, investigations into misconduct by companies, and their directors and senior management, have not only become much more frequent and commonplace but have also grown in scale and complexity. The level of financial and other penalties applied as a result of such investigations has increased markedly.

In the financial services sector, the advent of changes to the regulation of senior managers (which includes Directors), and the calls for an increase in personal accountability that followed the financial crisis, have led to greater numbers of investigations being opened into senior executives (up to and including board members) on a personal basis.

Increasingly, investigations are becoming multi-authority in scope. Business issues are now leading more regularly to civil and criminal investigations into the conduct of directors and staff, and where there is overlap between agencies (as there is, for example, between the financial services and accounting sectors) it is common to see two, or more, agencies investigating the same or similar misconduct. This can mean that multiple penalties are applied, within the same jurisdiction, for the same misconduct.[1]

Finally, for those companies who operate in multiple jurisdictions around the globe, the level of co-operation, and indeed co-ordination, between regulators and prosecutors in different countries has significantly increased in the post-crisis period. Multi-agency international investigations can be extremely complex, with overlapping regulatory requirements, differential approaches to enforcement from agencies in different jurisdictions, different legal privilege regimes and the challenges of handling multiple requests for documents and testimony. As such, they require careful handling, and

---

[1]   This is not just a US phenomenon (though it is most prevalent in that jurisdiction). The UK financial services regulators have in the past investigated, and penalised under their own regimes, misconduct arising out of the same factual circumstances. e.g. both UK financial services regulators levied financial penalties on RBS Plc totalling £56m for an IT failure that affected a large number of UK consumers (see: *https://www.bankofengland.co.uk/news/2014/november/pra-fines-rbs-natwest-and-ulster-bank* [Accessed 10 May 2019]).

nearly always involve instructing counsel in all relevant jurisdictions, married with careful co-ordination by the lawyers representing the firm in the various jurisdictions in which investigations are launched.

12.2 Investigations under the Companies Acts and by the Financial Services Regulators

12.2.1 Content of this section

This section will, by way of example, concentrate on the regulatory schemes that have most interaction with company directors, namely:

(a) the Financial Conduct Authority (FCA) and Prudential Regulation Authority (PRA) in the financial services sector; and

(b) companies investigations under the Companies Act 1985 (the CA 1985).

A separate section below will deal with investigations by the Financial Reporting Council into company directors who are also accountants.

12.2.2 Regulators act under statutory powers

The key point to note about regulators' powers to investigate is that they derive from legislation, and are exercised in the context of broader regulatory functions that are also conferred on the agency concerned by Parliament. This means that the power of regulators to investigate is constrained by the statutory framework within which the particular regulator operates. The FCA and PRA, for example, have statutory objectives set out in the Financial Services and Markets Act 2000 (FSMA) which give each regulator a clear steer as to the objectives they are to seek to advance when exercising their regulatory functions.

In practice, this means that regulators often determine the approach to investigations by reference to the extent to which the investigation, and the potential regulatory outcome arising from it, has an impact on their statutory objectives.

12.2.3 Powers to commence investigations

12.2.3.1 Low barriers to entry

A common feature of nearly all regulatory schemes is that the statutory threshold for commencing an investigation is generally very low indeed. The governing statute will set the parameters within which an investigation may be opened. Some statutes confine the nature of the investigation; while others allow a broad investigation into almost any aspect of the affairs of a company, and the actions of its directors.

In the financial services sector, under FSMA s.168, the FCA or PRA may open an investigation if it appears to the regulator that there are circumstances suggesting that a person (which may include an individual director) may have contravened a rule made by that regulator, may be guilty of misconduct, or may be guilty of one or more of a variety of offences under FSMA and other legislation. The power may also be exercised if it appears to the regulator that there are circumstances suggesting a person may not be a fit and proper person to perform functions in a financial services firm.

The powers of the FCA and PRA to investigate are among the widest possessed by UK regulators, in that they are not confined to questions of misconduct. Under FSMA s.167, either regulator can open a general investigation into the nature, conduct or state of the business of a regulated firm if in its view "there is good reason for doing so". As noted, s.168 allows an investigation to be opened if the regulator considers that there are "circumstances suggesting" misconduct. And FSMA s.169 entitles the regulators to open an investigation in support of overseas regulators who exercise similar functions, if requested by the overseas regulator to do so. There is no requirement under s.169 for the FCA or PRA to suspect misconduct within the UK in order to open an investigation.

Companies Act investigations offer an example of the type of investigation whose nature is confined by statute. CA 1985 s.432(2) permits the Insolvency Service[2] (on behalf of the Secretary of State) to appoint inspectors to investigate the affairs of a company if it appears to him that there are circumstances suggesting (among other things) that a company is being operated with intent to defraud creditors or for a fraudulent or unlawful purpose, or that the management of the company has been guilty of fraud misfeasance, or other misconduct towards the company or its members. Section 442 contains a power to investigate the ownership of a company.[3]

Where the Insolvency Service uncovers other misconduct in the course of a company investigation, its guidance suggests it would normally seek to refer that to a regulator or agency with responsibility for those issues.

---

[2] The Insolvency Service deals with civil and criminal investigations. Prior to January 2017, criminal investigations and enforcement were handled by the Department for Business, Innovation and Skills (BIS) Criminal Enforcement Team (CET). The CET is now housed within the Insolvency Service.

[3] Investigations of this type may also be concerned with potential offences under the Companies Act 2006, Insolvency Act 1986 and/or Company Directors Disqualification Act 1986.

12.2.3.2   *Approach to opening investigations*

Many regulators will set out their approach to opening investigations in a published policy, or guidance note. These policies will often give an indication not only of the internal process for opening investigations (for example, who makes the decision) but also the criteria on which the regulator will determine whether it will do so. Further information may also be gleaned from any published document (including public speeches) that sets out the authority's regulatory priorities.

For example, the FCA sets out in its Enforcement Guide (EG), which can be found in the FCA handbook, the process by which it will determine whether to launch an enforcement investigation. EG also explains how the FCA selects its cases; how it will assist overseas regulators, and how it will deal with cases where other authorities have an interest. And the FCA publishes its enforcement referral criteria on its website.[4] In April 2019, the PRA published its referral criteria for the first time.[5]

In line with the new executive accountability arrangements under the Senior Managers and Certification Regime, both financial services regulators will consider, at the outset (and at various points during the investigation) whether they should also open investigations into the conduct of any senior managers or other staff.

Guidance issued by the Insolvency Service, which carries out investigations under the CA 1985, states that it will open an investigation if there is sufficient "good reason" to do so, and opening the investigation is in the public interest.

12.2.3.3   *Legal challenges to the launch of an investigation rarely succeed*

The corollary of the low statutory bar for opening investigations, and the breadth of matters that may be subject to an investigation, is that legal challenges to a decision by a regulator to open an investigation very rarely succeed in all but the most extreme cases. This means that, in practice, case law as to the process for opening investigations is relatively rare.

Discussions with regulators considering launching investigations therefore tend to be aimed at seeking to convince the regulator that some other form of action (informal, or non-disciplinary, in nature) would take less time, and be a better use of the regulator's scarce resources.

---

4   See *http://www.fca.org.uk/about/enforcement/referral-criteria* [Accessed 10 May 2019]. At time of writing, that page made clear that the key question the FCA will ask is whether an enforcement investigation is likely to further the FCA's aims and statutory objectives.

5   See *https://www.bankofengland.co.uk/-/media/boe/files/prudential-regulation/pra-statutory-powers/pra-investigation-referral-criteria* [Accessed June 12 2019].

12.2.4   Scoping investigations

12.2.4.1   Discussions as to scope

Even though it can be difficult to challenge a decision to open an investigation through the courts, it will be crucial for the directors of the company under investigation to understand not only the statutory basis for the investigation, but also the extent to which this drives, or limits, the scope of the investigation itself. This is important not only because it goes to the heart of whether the regulator has the power to investigate the misconduct alleged, but also because the scope of an investigation has a direct (and significant) impact on the company, both in terms of direct cost and the management time that will need to be spent on it.

An early conversation with the investigating authority—and a timely challenge to any proposal that goes beyond the scope of the case—can therefore be very helpful in terms of determining the parameters of the investigation at an early stage. In practical terms, it can also result in the regulator having a better understanding of the impact of requesting documents and information from the company concerned, and may lead to requests being cut back.

As such, it is important for Directors to remain vigilant, to ensure that the requests made by the regulator are reasonably and properly made.

12.2.4.2   The notice of appointment

It follows from the points made above that the document in which the regulator records the scope of its investigation and (if appropriate) the reasons for launching an investigation in the first place, is a vital document for the company and its directors, in that it not only allows the company to judge the likely direction of the investigation, but is also the trigger for a variety of actions on the part of the company (for which see later) which will be needed in order to determine its approach to the investigation itself, its potential exposure in terms of liability, and any employment law issues that may arise. For the directors, it is also the primary trigger to discharge their duties under the Companies Act.

In almost all cases,[6] the statute requires the regulator concerned to issue a notice of appointment. In practice, these normally set out, at a minimum:

---

[6]   The limited circumstances in which a regulator may not be under an obligation to provide a notice of appointment to the subject of an investigation are generally set out in the relevant statute. e.g. for the FCA and PRA, FSMA s.170(3) lists the circumstances in which the regulator is not required to give a notice of appointment. Circumstances include if giving notice of the investigation would be likely to end in the investigation being frustrated.

(a)   which regulator is making the appointment;
(b)   the statutory provisions under which an appointment is made;
(c)   the reasons for making the appointment (often these will do little more than recite the statutory provisions underlying the appointment, although in recent years the financial services regulators have come under pressure to include more detail in their notices of appointment)[7];
(d)   who has been appointed to investigate (very often this will be named individuals). This is important because it sets out who has been authorised to exercise the powers of the regulator concerned; and
(e)   the date of appointment.

The key with any notice of appointment is that both the company and the directors need to be as clear as possible not only on the scope of the investigation itself, but whether the company is the subject of the investigation or is being asked for assistance. The distinction is important and if the regulator is not clear, then the company should seek clarification as a matter of urgency.

In some cases the subject might be an individual director or employee currently working at the company, and when this is the case, the company will also need to take employment law advice as to what steps ought to be taken as regards that individual's employment (for which see below).

12.2.4.3   Scoping meetings

Most regulators will, on opening an investigation, arrange a scoping meeting with the subject of the notice of appointment to discuss the investigation, its scope, the regulator's expectations on matters such as document preservation and how the regulator intends the investigation to proceed.

If lawyers have been instructed, they should represent the company at the scoping meeting, though it is usual for at least one representative of the company (often a senior, in-house lawyer or compliance officer) to attend alongside the firm's external counsel.

The scoping meeting is important, because it provides an opportunity to have a face to face discussion (often with a sizable part of the investigation team, and its most senior members) not only on what the investigation is aiming to consider, but also how the regulator proposes to go about investigating. It also provides an opportunity to discuss more prosaic matters such as how document requirements should be handled, in what format the regulator would like to receive data, and how the regulator should approach witnesses at the firm.

---

[7]   The Insolvency Service guidance expressly states that it does not tell company directors the specific reasons why the Service is investigating their company.

12.2.4.4   Confidentiality of the investigation

The regulators

For most regulators, the starting point is that most investigations remain confidential until such time as the investigation has concluded and regulatory action is published.

In the financial services sector, both the FCA and PRA generally start from the position that they do not disclose the existence of an investigation, save in exceptional circumstances. Reasons why they might make an investigation public are set out in their published policies, and include:

(a)   assisting the investigation by encouraging witnesses to come forward; and
(b)   preventing or deterring more widespread misconduct.

Even when the PRA and FCA decide to do so, it is generally only the *fact* of the investigation that is made public; the regulators do not generally publish a detailed description of the investigation, or the identity of any individuals under investigation. That said, recent public pressure to be more open and transparent has led the financial services regulators to publish information about ongoing investigations more regularly than had been the case in the pre-financial crisis period, though the amount of information they put in the public domain about ongoing investigations is still relatively minimal.

For Companies Act investigations, the Insolvency Service guidance makes clear that these are confidential, but that the Service may issue a press release at the conclusion of the investigation if there is follow-up action.

The company

Some regulators will specify that the company must keep the investigation confidential,[8] and there may be the possibility of additional regulatory penalties for failing to do so.

However, a company that is under investigation must also consider other legal and regulatory requirements to which it is subject when determining whether it must disclose the existence of an investigation, for example notifying other regulators and, if the firm is listed, the financial markets. This is considered in more detail below.

---

[8]   This may include a requirement that a specified individual or individuals within the company not be informed of the investigation.

12.2.5 Powers to compel information

12.2.5.1   Wide powers

The powers afforded to regulators to compel the production of information and documents are broadly consistent across the regulatory spectrum. In the course of an investigation, the regulators can require the production of information from:

(a)   the subject of the investigation (it is worth noting that the power to compel the production of information and documents often extends to other group companies and connected persons)[9]; and

(b)   in certain circumstances, any person who has information relevant to the investigation (this can include individuals).[10] The circumstances in which a regulator can require information from a person entirely unconnected with the investigation will depend on the nature of the matter under investigation. In some cases, for example the financial services context, such information may only be sought if the regulator considers it to be "necessary or expedient" for the purposes of the investigation; in others the statutory test may be different.

In Companies Act investigations, past and present "officers and agents" of the company have a duty to produce documents, meet the inspectors and give the inspectors all assistance in connection with the investigation that they are reasonably able to give (see CA 1985 s.434(2)). Officers of the company include the board of directors and senior managers, whereas agents of the company include its bankers, solicitors, auditors and accountants (s.434(4)). In addition, inspectors can require the same level of co-operation from officers and agents of other bodies corporate, or any other person, if the inspectors consider that such a person may be in possession of information relating to a matter which they believe to be relevant to the investigation (s.434(2). Finally, an individual may be required to give evidence under oath, and the inspectors may administer an oath accordingly (s.434(3)).

12.2.5.2   Limits

There are limits on the exercise of information gathering powers. These are considered in more detail below.

---

[9]   See, in the financial services context, FSMA s.171. For Companies Act investigations, see CA 1985 s.434.

[10]   See, in the financial services context, FSMA s.172. For Companies Act investigations, see CA 1985 s.434.

12.2.5.3   *Approach to exercise of powers*

Most regulators set out in a public document their approach to the exercise of powers. In many cases, rather than serving a finalised requirement to provide information, the regulator will provide a draft version of the requirement, and seek a discussion with the subject of the requirement as to:

(a)   scope (i.e. is it asking for the right information, or too much?);
(b)   methodology for obtaining the information (this may include a discussion as to systems to be searched, date ranges, and search terms); and
(c)   timeline for compliance.

In the financial services sector, this discussion offers an opportunity for the subject to engage constructively with the regulator concerned to ensure the regulator has not cast the net too widely, and to discuss the impact of a particular proposal on the firm's ability to respond to the requirement in a timely manner. While in most cases the regulator will not be dissuaded from issuing a requirement in substantially similar form to the draft, the ability to manage regulatory expectations as to what may be able to be provided, and when, offers a valuable opportunity to have an open discussion with the regulator as to what is readily achievable, in what time period, and the impact of the regulator adopting one approach or another.

It is also worth noting that, almost universally, the statutes confer on the regulators an ability to enter premises under warrant to obtain information.[11] However, a regulator may only do so if it first secures a warrant from a justice of the peace. The requirements that must be met for a warrant to be issued vary from case to case, but usually comprise reasonable grounds for believing that:

(a)   documents which a person has failed to provide pursuant to a previous requirement are to be found on the premises; or
(b)   documents are on the premises of a person, and that a requirement (if issued) would not be complied with, or the documents would be likely to be removed, tampered with or destroyed.

There are various offences that may be committed where any person intentionally obstructs the exercise of any rights conferred by a warrant or fails (without reasonable excuse) to comply with any requirement imposed by a warrant.

Company inspectors have the power, in certain circumstances, to enter premises without a warrant (see CA 1985 s.453A or s.453B).

---

[11]   See, e.g. CA 1985 s.448 and, in the financial services sector, FSMA s.176.

12.2.5.4 Consequences of failure to provide information, or providing false or misleading information

Regulatory statutes normally provide for a range of criminal offences in relation to:

(a)   failure to comply with a requirement to provide information;
(b)   falsification, concealment, destruction or disposal of a document, or causing or permitting any of them; and/or
(c)   provision of false or misleading information.

For example, in the financial services context, FSMA s.177(4) provides that a person who provides information which he knows to be false or misleading in a material particular, or recklessly provides such information, is guilty of a criminal offence, which carries the penalty of a fine or imprisonment for a period of up to two years, or both.

In addition to dealing with issues of false or misleading information, in the financial services context, FSMA s.177(2) provides for a power for the regulators to refer to the court a failure to co-operate. If the court is satisfied that there was no reasonable excuse for the failure to co-operate, it may deal with the person as if they were contempt of court, which is punishable by imprisonment or a fine. In practice, such referrals happen very rarely indeed, and the court's initial response is usually to give the individual a further chance to co-operate with the investigation before exercising its power to treat them as if they were in contempt.

For Companies Act investigations, a person who gives false or misleading information to an inspector under oath will commit an offence under the Perjury Act 1911. In addition, it is an offence if any officer of a company destroys, mutilates or falsifies (or is privy to the destruction, mutilation or falsification of) a document affecting, or relating to the company's property or affairs, or makes (or is privy to the making of) a false entry in such a document (CA 1985 s.450(1)). There is also an offence of providing false information in the CA 1985 s.451.[12] Further, under s.436 of the 1985 Act, if a person fails to comply with a requirement to provide information, or refuses to answer a question, the inspector has similar powers to the FCA and PRA to refer the matter to the court.

---

[12]   Whether the person provides information which he knows to be false in a material particular, or recklessly provides information which is false in a material particular.

12.2.6 Powers to compel testimony

12.2.6.1 Interviews

Almost all regulators have the power to require the specified subjects to attend before them and answer questions in the context of a regulatory investigation. In the financial services context, for example, FSMA ss.171 and 172 permit the regulators to compel:

(a)   the person under investigation;
(b)   any person connected with that person[13]; and
(c)   (in certain circumstances) any other person.

Company inspectors have the right to do so under the CA 1985 s.434.

This means that, in the regulatory context, there is effectively no right to silence in enforcement investigations.

Often, regulators will provide a bundle of relevant documents prior to an interview to allow the subject of the interview, and their lawyers, to prepare in advance.

Interviews are generally recorded, and regulators will normally begin interviews with a warning about the consequences of a refusal to answer questions or providing false or inaccurate information in response to questioning.

12.2.6.2 Consequences of providing false or inaccurate information or refusing to answer questions

As set out above, providing false or inaccurate information will generally result in the commission of a criminal offence by the person being interviewed. A failure to co-operate may, as set out above, be referred to the court for further action.

12.2.6.3 Limits to powers

There are limits on the exercise of powers to compel testimony. These are considered in more detail below.

12.2.6.4 Legal advice and assistance during interviews

In regulatory interviews, the subject of the interview is generally permitted to have a lawyer with them for the interview, and may seek and obtain legal advice during the interview. Where the company is under investigation, the

---

[13]   What constitutes a "connected person" is defined in that section.

regulators are generally reluctant to allow the company's lawyers to be in the room for the interview, due to the potential for conflicts of interest to arise. In such cases, the subject of the interview is generally provided with an independent legal adviser.

12.2.7 Decision-making at the regulator during an investigation

12.2.7.1 Who is responsible for decision-making

It will be important for the company to ascertain who at the regulator has responsibility for decision-making throughout the course of the investigation, and in particular whether any decisions to expand the scope of the investigation are taken by the investigation team or by a more senior committee. The reason for this is not because the regulator will invite representations on that question—it will not—but because understanding who is responsible for the decision-making process will assist in dealing with the regulator as the investigation progresses. The key is to maintain, as far as possible, an open dialogue with the regulator as the investigation progresses, so that issues can be raised in a constructive manner without—unless absolutely necessary—resorting to long chains of correspondence.

12.2.7.2 Keeping up to date with the investigation

Linked with the previous point, the experience of regulators feeding back regularly to the company, or its directors (or indeed any other subject of the investigation) is patchy. While the financial services regulators, in particular, have said publicly that they recognise the need to be transparent, and will look to give more regular feedback as to progress during the investigation, this does not always occur in practice.

As such, companies should consider speaking to the investigation team early to diarise regular feedback meetings at which the regulator is invited to give feedback on progress, and next steps. Although there are some potential downsides to this (in that some may feel that being uppermost in the regulator's mind means that the investigation might proceed more quickly than they would like), ensuring that the directors are informed of the regulator's timelines is important in terms of allowing them to manage the risks to the company posed by the investigation.

12.2.8 Outcomes of investigations

12.2.8.1 Range of potential outcomes

There are a range of potential sanctions available to investigating authorities to deal with misconduct. Most regulators have a public policy setting out how they will apply those sanctions in practice, including a method for calculating financial penalties. While those policies generally allow for a wide margin of discretion for the regulators, they do allow for a structured discussion as to how the regulator has arrived at the level of sanction that it intends to impose (albeit that regulators are rarely disposed to move during discussions on the level of sanction).

In the financial services sector, the FCA and PRA both have a range of powers over firms and individuals, including public censure and fining. In relation to individuals, they also have the power to suspend and prohibit them from holding certain functions (or indeed any function) in the financial services industry. In addition to imposing sanctions on firms and individuals, the financial services regulators will often consider the extent to which the company concerned has recompensed consumers, or remediated the failings identified through the enforcement investigation. While proactively taking such actions up front rarely results in an enforcement investigation concluding with no findings against the firm, it can count as a mitigating factor when the regulators are considering the level of penalty to impose at the end of the process. It can also lead to a public acknowledgement by the regulator that the firm has remedied the issues which led to the investigation in the first place.

In CA 1985 investigations, Inspectors are required by s.437 to produce a report to the Secretary of State, who may provide it to persons set out in that section, or indeed publish it. Such reports may also go through a so-called "Maxwellisation" process, where individuals subject to criticism may be given the opportunity to comment on the criticism of them before the report is finalised.

12.2.8.2   Settlement process

Most regulators offer a process to subjects of investigation where, in return for accepting an early settlement of the investigation, they provide a discount in the level of penalty to be applied at the end of the case. For companies, this reduction in the amount of the penalty—which can be significant, as much as 30% in financial services cases—means that firms are generally incentivised to settle as a means of reducing the eventual fine that will need to be paid. Individuals, by contrast, contest matters more regularly—in part because the impact on an individual's reputation from an enforcement outcome (and consequently their ability to continue to work in the relevant sector) is generally quite significant.

Regulators will generally allow for a time period (normally around 28 days) within which a settlement must be concluded, or the matter will proceed to a formal, and normally independent, decision making process. Extensions can be granted to that 28-day period in exceptional circumstances, but in practice extensions are relatively rare.

In the financial services sector, the PRA offers a staggered discount, which reduces at each stage.[14] A subject that settles at Stage 1 (before the independent decision-making process in front of the Enforcement Decision Making Committee (EDMC) commences, for which see below) will receive a 30% discount on penalty. The discount then drops to 20%, 10% and finally 0% as the independent decision-making process gathers pace. The FCA's system is rather more complex. It, too, offers a 30% discount for the earliest possible settlement, and then a sliding scale of discount for a subject who wishes to take the matter before the Regulatory Decisions Committee (RDC), depending on whether the subject wishes to challenge the facts, the law, the penalty or any combination of them.

12.2.8.3   *Contesting cases before regulators*

Although regulatory decisions are generally cast as administrative (rather than judicial) in nature, almost all regulators have an independent committee, separate to the enforcement investigation, that hears contested cases and determines what action the regulator should take.

In the financial services context, the FCA's RDC and the Bank of England's EDMC (which takes contested decisions on behalf of the PRA) both follow similar procedures. The enforcement case is presented, with a recommendation, in a report. On the strength of that report, the committee then decides whether to issue a Warning Notice. The Warning Notice (which is not published[15]) is provided to the subject of the proposed action. The subject of the action then has a certain period within which to make representations to the committee. The representations can be in writing, or in person. Having heard those representations, and considered any response from the investigation team, the committee then decides what action the regulator should take, and—if it decides to take action—issues the subject with a Decision Notice. The Decision Notice is generally published if the party exercises their right (see below) to take the matter to the Tribunal. If the subject does not go to the Tribunal, or once the Tribunal hands down a judgment, the regulators will issue a Final Notice. It is with the Final Notice that the decision becomes operative (and at that point, for example, that any fine becomes due).

12.2.8.4   *Independent Tribunals*

Finally, although the detail is beyond the scope of this chapter, in almost all cases if the company or a person subject to action is aggrieved with the outcome of the investigation, they have the right (subject to time limits) to

---

14   At the time of writing, the PRA was consulting on the removal of the staggered discount. If the PRA makes this change, the effect would be that the discount offered will become a flat 30% during the settlement period, reducing to zero after that period concludes.

15   Although the fact it has been issued may be publicised in certain cases.

take a decision of a regulator to a specialist tribunal.[16] In most cases, the tribunal will hear the issue afresh (and consider evidence of fact, as well as submissions on the law). Following hearing evidence and legal submissions from both parties, it will issue a judgment in which it will make its findings, and direct the regulator to take particular action in accordance with them. There are onward appeals from the decision of the tribunal, but these are generally on a point of law only.

12.3 Investigations by the Accountancy Regulator

12.3.1 Content of this section

The Financial Reporting Council (FRC) is the UK's independent regulator responsible for promoting transparency and integrity in business. Its primary role as a regulator is as the Competent Authority for audit in the UK. The Enforcement Division of the FRC investigates and prosecutes audit breaches although a Recognised Supervisory Body (RSB)[17] also undertakes enforcement action for some statutory audits.

In December 2018, the "Independent Review of the FRC" produced by Sir John Kingman recommended—among other things—that the FRC ought to be replaced with an Audit, Reporting and Governance Authority (ARGA), a new regulator which he recommended ought to be given clear statutory powers and objectives. In March 2019, the Department for Business, Enterprise and Industrial Strategy issued a consultation document in which it accepted the Kingman Review's main recommendations. Further reform to the system of regulation for accountants, including the establishment of ARGA, is therefore likely to follow.

As a result, while this section will concentrate on the FRC's Accounting Scheme in force at time of writing, significant changes are expected to be made to the system of regulation for accountants over the coming years.

12.3.2 The Accountancy Scheme (the Scheme)

Until 2016, the FRC used long established procedures under the Account-ancy Scheme and the Actuarial Scheme, which are contractual arrange-ments between the FRC and various professional bodies. These arrangements require the FRC to undertake investigations into the conduct of members of the professional bodies whose conduct, in the course of their professional activities, amongst other things including as a director, falls

---

[16] In the case of the PRA and FCA, the review is carried out by the Tax and Chancery Chamber of the Upper Tribunal, with specialist financial services panel members.

[17] These are: Association of Chartered Certified Accountants (ACCA); Chartered Accountants Ireland (CAI); Institute of Chartered Accountants in England and Wales (ICAEW) and Institute of Chartered Accountants of Scotland.

significantly short of the standards reasonably to be expected or is likely to bring discredit to the member or to his profession. This is misconduct under the Scheme.

The Scheme is not a statutory arrangement and the director must be a member of an accountancy or actuarial professional body[18] which participates in the Scheme for it to engage. It is the individual's membership of the Scheme that provides for the FRC to have the power to investigate and if appropriate to bring a case against an accountant or actuary who is a director (the "member director").

It is common for accountants to hold senior executive and non-executive positions in public companies, whereas actuaries are rarely appointed to such roles. It follows that the recent FRC cases involving disciplinary proceedings against member directors under the scheme have all been accountants (with only one actuary being subject to enforcement by the FRC).

12.3.3 Opening investigations

The Conduct Committee of the FRC decides if a member director is liable to investigation and it will do so where:

(a) the matter raises or appears to raise important issues affecting the public interest in the UK; and
(b) there are reasonable grounds to suspect that there may have been misconduct.

Prior to 2016, the Companies Act 2006 required an RSB, as regulator of statutory auditors, to have an independent body to deal with potential misconduct affecting the UK public interest. Hence the wording in (a) above. In 2016, the introduction of new legislation removed the regulation of Statutory Audit[19] from the auspices of the Scheme. However, the Scheme continued to operate for all other accountants including member directors.

The UK public interest test has the effect of limiting, in effect, the member directors who are liable to be investigated under the Scheme to those who hold senior positions in public companies.

---

[18] For accountants the professional bodies are the Association of Chartered Certified Accountants (ACCA); Chartered Accountants Ireland (CAI); Institute of Chartered Accountants in England and Wales (ICAEW) and Institute of Chartered Accountants of Scotland as well as Chartered Institute of Management Accountants and Chartered Institute of Public Finance Accountants.
[19] See Statutory Auditors and Third Country Auditors Regulations 2016 (SI 2016/649).

12.3.4 Powers of investigators

The Scheme provides many of the powers that are available to those with responsibility to investigate directors under a statutory regime. Member directors are required to attend for interview and to provide material relevant to the investigation. The member director is required to answer all questions and the answers are admissible in any proceedings before a tribunal.[20]

A member director is required to provide information and explanation relevant to any matter under investigation and to permit the inspection and taking of copies of documents which are under the control of the member director. This includes, to the extent reasonable, the requirement "to supply copies of documents and other information (in whatever form it may be held, including any associated software necessary to facilitate a review by the FRC) at his or her own expense".[21]

The Scheme is supported by the Accountancy Regulations 2014 which provide further procedural rules on the process to be followed in an investigation.

12.3.5 Regulatory Outcomes

Much like other regulators, the FRC will usually afford the subject of an enforcement action the possibility of early settlement involving a reduction in penalty. The terms of the settlement are negotiated with the FRC's Executive Counsel, and are then sent to an independent Tribunal, which will determine whether it would be appropriate for the proposed settlement to be entered into, having regard to the purposes for which the Scheme was established.

If settlement cannot be reached (or if the FRC considers settlement would not be appropriate), then the FRC will issue the subject of the investigation with a formal complaint, which will proceed via the FRC's Conduct Committee to the Tribunal for hearing.

In the period since 2012, these powers of investigation and prosecution have been used in respect of member directors on a number of occasions. The FRC website provides details of the outcomes of cases settled before the Tribunal but, more frequently, settled by agreement between the FRC and the parties.

For conduct which involves a breach of integrity there have been long periods of exclusion from acting as an accountant. Sometimes the same

---

[20] See *R. v Institute of Chartered Accountants of England and Wales Ex p. Nawaz* [1997] EWCA Civ 1530.
[21] See Accountancy Scheme, 8 December 2014 para.14.

conduct is investigated by other regulators or prosecuting agencies including the FCA and the SFO. It is also possible that the Insolvency Service will seek to enforce director disqualification proceedings under the Company Directors Disqualification Act 1986 for misconduct based on the same facts.

12.4 Criminal Investigations

12.4.1 Content of this section

There are a number of agencies which have powers to investigate and prosecute criminal offences against companies and their directors, including: the Serious Fraud Office (SFO), the FCA, the PRA, the National Crime Agency (NCA) and the Police supported by the Crown Prosecution Service (CPS). In addition, the Insolvency Service carries out criminal investigations under the Companies Acts.

This part of this Chapter will concentrate on the powers available to criminal investigators, with particular reference to investigations carried out by the SFO.

The Director of the SFO is the decision-maker named in the Criminal Justice Act 1987 (the CJA 1987), the legislation from which the SFO derives its powers and functions. The Director may delegate certain of those functions to others in the SFO. Many of those delegations are set out in the policies and guidance that appear on the SFO's website. As such, the remainder of this Chapter will refer to the SFO, rather than talking about the "Director".

12.4.2 Powers to commence investigations

The SFO is one of a relatively small number of institutions in which the investigative and prosecutorial functions for criminal offences are both carried out in-house.[22] As such, the SFO brings prosecutions of cases it has itself investigated; it does not make use of the Crown Prosecution Service.

The SFO's role is to prosecute offences of serious and complex fraud, bribery and corruption and, under the Criminal Finances Act 2017, the offence of failure to prevent facilitation of overseas tax evasion.

Its Statement of Principle sets out that in doing so, the SFO will take into account the actual or intended harm that may be caused to:

(a)   the public;

---

[22]   The FCA also carries out criminal prosecutions in-house.

(b)   the reputation or integrity of the UK as an international financial centre; or

(c)   the economy or prosperity of the UK,

and whether the complexity and nature of the suspected offence warrants the application of the SFO's specialist skills, powers and capabilities to investigate and prosecute.

The decision to launch an investigation is taken by the Director of the SFO under the CJA 1987 s.1(5).

12.4.3   Powers to compel information

The SFO has broad powers to compel information once it has commenced a formal investigation:

(a)   CJA 1987 s.2(3) permits the SFO to compel the production of information at a specific time and place,[23] and to require the person producing them to provide an explanation of any of them. The SFO may also require a person to state where the documents may be found; and

(b)   the SFO may also apply under s.2(4) to a justice of the peace for a warrant to search premises. A warrant will only be granted if there are reasonable grounds for believing that, in relation to any documents:

- a person has failed to comply with an obligation under s.2, it is not practicable to serve them with a notice under s.2(3) or the service of a notice might seriously prejudice the investigation; and

- the documents are on the premises specified by the SFO.

Note that, in a 2018 case arising out of the Unaoil investigation, the Administrative Court held that the SFO's s.2 powers were intended to have extraterritorial effect, provided that the recipient of the notice has a sufficient connection with the UK (which will be a fact-specific assessment).[24] As such, there is the potential for a UK resident company to be served with a s.2 notice requiring production of information held overseas. In addition, the Crime (Overseas Production Orders) Act 2019[25] (COPA Act) will enable a UK investigating agency (like the SFO) to obtain a UK court order that will compel a company in a foreign country (like an internet service provider in the US) to produce specified electronic data to it for the

---

[23]   Under s.2A(1) of the 1987 Act, the SFO may also use the powers in s.2(2) and 2(3) prior to the commencement of an investigation to support a determination as to whether to open an investigation into bribery which has an international element. The SFO Operational Handbook notes that any notices served under that power must seek information that is necessary, reasonable and proportionate for that purpose only.

[24]   *R. (on the Application of KBR Inc) v Director of the Serious Fraud Office* [2018] EWHC 2368 (Admin).

[25]   Which received Royal Assent on 12 February 2019.

purposes of an investigation. The UK court order may be served directly on—and will be effective against—the US company without the involvement or supervision of any US authority or court, thus sidestepping the inefficiencies of the traditional mutual legal assistance (MLA) process.

Finally, it is worth noting that the SFO's s.2 powers can be exercised in an international context:

(a) to assist the Attorney Generals of the Isle of Man, Jersey and Guernsey in equivalent investigations in those jurisdictions; and

(b) to assist overseas investigators under various international agreements establishing processes for MLA between investigators investigating various types of crime.

Section 2 notices generally give a time for compliance in the future, although in some circumstances will be issued in order to seek to compel production on a "here and now" basis.

Where the SFO serves a s.2 notice on a company, it will normally name, and be served on, an individual at the company who will be responsible for compliance with the requirements of the notice. The SFO will also provide instructions as to how it wishes the information to be delivered to it. Those instructions may contain technical information about the format of any electronic media, and as a result—in addition to obtaining the relevant information—there should be early engagement with IT professionals inside the company to assist with any formatting issues.

12.4.4 *Interviews and witness testimony*

CJA 1987 s.2(2) permits the SFO to compel the following to answer questions or provide information:

(a) the person under investigation; or

(b) any other person who it has reason to believe has relevant information.

There is, therefore, no right to silence in a s.2 interview. The SFO Operational Handbook notes that, while obtaining documents from a suspect is permitted by s.2(3), caution should be used in exercising s.2 powers in respect of a suspect, particularly given the fact that under s.2(8) of the 1987 Act, compelled testimony from an individual cannot be used in a criminal prosecution of that individual save in limited circumstances (for which, see below).

There is no absolute right to have a legal adviser present in a s.2 interview.[26] The SFO's guidance on s.2 interviews makes clear that:

(a)   the person being interviewed may *request* a named lawyer be present, but generally no more than one lawyer will be permitted to be in the room;

(b)   the lawyer will be permitted to attend the interview if the SFO believes it likely that they will assist the purpose of the interview, or that they will provide essential assistance to the interviewee (i.e. legal advice or pastoral support); and

(c)   the firm must notify the SFO of their request seven days prior to the interview (or three days after receiving the s.2 notice, whichever is the later), including the name of the lawyer, the reasons why they meet the SFO's policy, and a number of written undertakings from the firm concerned. If a lawyer cannot give the required undertakings then the SFO guidance makes clear that they are unlikely to be allowed to attend the interview.

The guidance further makes clear that the lawyer's role in the interview is limited. They may advise the interviewee in the event that a matter of legal professional privilege arises in the interview. But otherwise, they must not do anything which undermines the free flow of information. In case of any infraction or obstruction, the SFO will reserve the right to exclude a lawyer who does not comply with its guidance.

While notes can be taken by the lawyer, they cannot make their own recording on behalf of the interviewee.

Interviews of suspects will generally be carried out under caution, with the relevant provisions of the Police and Criminal Evidence Act 1984 applying. In such interviews, an individual cannot be compelled to answer questions and has a right to be accompanied by a lawyer.

SFO interviews are tape recorded. In the context of a s.2 interview, and depending on the circumstances, the witness may, in due course, be provided with a copy of the recording and/or a transcript. In the context of an interview under caution, the legal representative of the suspect should request a copy of the recording immediately at the end of the interview. Where a transcript is prepared—and if there are transcription errors—there will generally be an opportunity to provide corrections to the transcript.

---

[26]   This was confirmed by the Administrative Court in *R. (on the application of Lord) v Director of the Serious Fraud Office* [2015] EWHC 865 (Admin).

12.4.5 Failure to provide information, or providing false or misleading information

As with the regulatory system, there are specific criminal offences relating to failure to provide information, or providing false or misleading information, set out in the CJA 1987 s.2 namely:

(a) failing to comply without reasonable excuse with a requirement imposed under s.2 (up to six months' imprisonment, or a fine, or both)[27];

(b) making, knowingly or recklessly, statements which are false or misleading in a material particular (up to two years' imprisonment, or a fine, or both)[28]; and

(c) falsifying, concealing destroying or disposing of documents (or causing any of those to occur) in circumstances where a person knows or suspects that an investigation by the police or the SFO into serious or complex fraud is being or is likely to be carried out (up to seven years' imprisonment, a fine, or both).[29]

As to what constitutes a "reasonable excuse" the SFO Operational Handbook suggests adopting a common sense approach and that it will generally wish to help recipients of notices overcome any practical obstacles to compliance. It goes on to state that if, following discussion a s.2 notice cannot (for a reasonable excuse) be complied with and new terms are agreed, then the SFO will issue a new notice, cancelling the old one. This regularly occurs in practice.

The SFO may also issue a s.2 notice in draft for comment and discussion, before issuing the formal notice.

12.4.6 Decision making during investigations

12.4.6.1 Pre-charge decisions

As set out above, the Director of the SFO is given the power in the CJA 1987 to take decisions relating to the investigation, although in practice those functions (particularly over the issue of s.2 notices) are delegated to others in the organisation.

The legal representative of a suspect may wish to engage with the relevant Case Controller and/or Head of Division during the period prior to any charging decision being made, and will generally make written representations as to why their client should not be charged. It may be necessary to

---

[27] CJA 1987 s.2(13).
[28] CJA 1987 s.2(14).
[29] CJA 1987 s.2(16).

escalate such matters to the level of the Director, but generally only after appropriate engagement with the Case Controller and/or Head of Division.

12.4.6.2   *The decision to bring a criminal charge*

Any decision to bring a criminal charge will be made by the Director of the SFO in accordance with the provisions of the *Code for Crown Prosecutors* (the Code). The Code contains a two-stage test (known as the "Full Code Test") which the SFO will need to meet before launching a prosecution (or indeed continuing a prosecution that has commenced):

(a) *The Evidential Test*—The SFO must first be satisfied that there is sufficient evidence to provide a realistic prospect of conviction (defined in the Code as being objectively more likely than not). As part of this they will consider what the defence may be to a charge, and how likely the defence is to affect the prospects of a conviction. Matters the prosecutor will consider include: the admissibility of evidence, how reliable and credible the evidence is, and the extent to which there is any other material that might affect the sufficiency of that evidence. If the case does not pass the evidential test, it should not proceed, regardless of the public interests at stake.

(b) *The Public Interest Test*—Provided the evidential test is met, the SFO will then go on to consider whether the prosecution is required in the public interest. The Code notes that a prosecution will normally take place unless the prosecutor is satisfied that the public interest factors against prosecution outweigh those in favour. Matters the Code suggests should be considered include: the seriousness of the offence, the level of the suspect's culpability, the circumstances of and harm caused to the victim, the suspect's age and maturity when the offence was committed, the impact on the community, the proportionality of prosecution as a response, and whether sources of information require protecting.

When considering a criminal charge against a corporate institution, the SFO will also consider the *Joint Prosecution Guidance on Corporate Prosecutions*. Where potential bribery is at issue, the SFO will also consider the *Prosecution Guidance of the Director of the SFO and the Director of Public Prosecutions on the Bribery Act 2010*.

12.4.7   *Deferred Prosecution Agreements (DPAs)*

Under the Crime and Courts Act 2013, the SFO has the power to enter into DPAs with companies in respect of which it has carried out investigations. The SFO and Crown Prosecution Service have produced detailed guidance as to the approach to DPAs in the *Deferred Prosecution Agreements Code of Practice*.

A DPA is an agreement by which the company concerned and the SFO agree:

(a)   the facts of the matter giving rise to the DPA (an admission of guilt is not necessary on the part of the company);

(b)   the company will pay a penalty; and, as a result

(c)   the SFO will not prosecute the company for the offence charged by the indictment (the indictment is effectively suspended).

In the UK, DPAs apply to organisations alone; they cannot be concluded with individuals. As a result, while Directors may sign a DPA on behalf of the company, they will not themselves be subject to a DPA directly.

Various other terms may be attached to a DPA, including: compensation for victims, payment of prosecution costs, disgorgement of profits, requiring improvements in compliance programmes and the appointment of an independent corporate Monitor.

A UK DPA must be approved by the court, which will scrutinise whether the DPA is likely to be in the interests of justice and that its proposed terms are fair, reasonable and proportionate.

If a company breaches a DPA, the SFO will first seek agreement from the company as to actions to rectify the breach. If these cannot be agreed, the SFO may apply to the court seeking a finding of a breach of the DPA and a hearing on remedies. For more serious breaches, the court may order that the DPA is terminated, which would leave the SFO free to pursue a prosecution of the matter on the indictment which was suspended as a result of the DPA.

It is also important to note that the existence of a DPA with a company does not prevent the SFO from bringing a prosecution against its directors or other individuals for their own actions in relation to the matters the subject of the DPA.

12.5   Limits on investigative powers

12.5.1   Investigators enjoy a wide discretion

The key point to note is that, in general terms, investigators enjoy a wide discretion in the way that they carry out their investigations, and the courts tend to be reluctant to interfere in the investigative process unless there is a clear indication that the investigator is acting beyond their powers.

That having been said, there are a number of potential limits on investigators that may arise in the course of an investigation. As a legal challenge is very much a "nuclear" option, formal challenges to investigative steps are relatively rare. However, these limits may also be used to frame a discussion with the investigating authority as to its approach to specific parts of the investigation.

12.5.2 Potential limits on investigators

12.5.2.1 The scope of the investigation

It goes without saying that limitations on the scope of the investigation, whether imposed directly by statute or as a result of the way the investigation has been scoped when launched, will limit the investigator's freedom to manoeuvre during the investigation. In particular, the scope of the investigation—as set out in the notice of appointment (or other terms of reference)—will constrain the investigator to require only information that could conceivably be relevant to the scope as defined.

In practice, however, it is often difficult for the recipient of a requirement to provide information to test whether or not the terms of the requirement fall within the scope of the investigation, and hence to mount a challenge to it. In any event, most investigating authorities have the power to extend the scope of an existing investigation, subject to their own internal decision-making processes, so even where the company can make a compelling case for the requirement being out of scope the authority may just choose to widen the scope of the investigation to include it.

12.5.2.2 Duty to act fairly

Investigating authorities are under the normal public law duty to act fairly in carrying out their investigative functions. While in practice, it is rare for challenges on fairness grounds to succeed in dissuading an investigating authority from embarking on a particular course of action, they can be useful in framing a discussion as to the impact of the investigation on individuals, and how those impacts may be mitigated.

For example, fairness would generally dictate that:

(a) witnesses be given reasonable notice that they are required to attend an interview with the investigating authority;

(b) they should also be given advance notice of the matters in respect of which they are to be interviewed, and often (particularly in regulatory proceedings) the authorities provide written material in advance to aid the witness' preparation;

(c)   during the interview, the witness may be permitted to have a legal adviser with them,[30] though the adviser's role will be limited (for example the adviser may not answer questions on the witness' behalf);

(d)   witnesses should not be led to believe that their evidence will be kept confidential, particularly because investigators may wish to put that evidence to others, or include it in a report or as the basis for further action; and

(e)   witnesses will normally be supplied with a transcript of their evidence (and interviews are often recorded and a copy of the recording supplied), and given the opportunity to review for transcription errors in the information provided, or any further comments.[31]

12.5.2.3   Legal Professional Privilege

Information, whether stored in documentary form or otherwise, which falls within the scope of legal professional privilege ("LPP") is almost always exempt from requirements to disclose:

(a)   in documentary form; or
(b)   verbally during the course of an interview.

In many cases, this limitation on investigative power arises out of the common law, however some statutes also specifically carve out legally privileged information from the types of material of which an investigating authority can compel production. For example:

- FSMA s.413 contains a list of "protected items" which a person is not obliged to disclose to the financial services regulators. The s.413 list broadly mirrors the ambit of LPP;
- CJA 1987 s.2(9) provides that a person cannot be required by the SFO to disclose information that they would be entitled to refuse to disclose on the grounds of LPP in the High Court; and
- CA 1985 s.452(1) has a similar restriction for company investigations.

In the UK, LPP broadly splits into two categories:

(a)   *Legal Advice Privilege*—the privilege that applies to confidential communications that pass between a client and a lawyer (acting in his/her professional capacity) in connection with the provision of legal services. This privilege means that all communications that form part of the continuum of the client/lawyer relationship will be

---

[30] Recently the authorities have been more strict in noting that the presence of a lawyer is not an automatic right, and in circumstances where the company is also under investigation, individuals ought to be provided with legal advisers independent of the company. In those circumstances the company's lawyers are generally not permitted to attend, even in an observer capacity.

[31] Though note that this may not happen in cases, for example, where to do so might compromise an ongoing investigation.

privileged from disclosure/discovery, even those communications that do not specifically seek, or convey, legal advice. In that context, however, it is worth noting that the position under English law is nuanced, in that the decision of the Court of Appeal in *Three Rivers No.5*[32] means that privilege can be lost if legal advice is widely circulated within an organisation beyond those who were responsible for the original instruction; and

(b) *Litigation Privilege*—the privilege that attaches to confidential communications passing between a party or its lawyers and any third parties, for the purpose of obtaining information or advice in connection with adversarial litigation. However, for this privilege to apply the litigation must either be in progress or in "reasonable contemplation", and the communication must be for the sole or dominant purpose of conducting that litigation.

Communications in either category will not be protected if they occurred for the purpose of committing a fraud or crime. It is also worth noting that lawyers may be required to furnish the name and address of their client.

In the internal investigations context in particular (for which see below) the ambit of legal privilege is highly fact specific, and will require significant input from legal counsel. The ambit of litigation privilege in particular has been subject to significant discussion in the courts. The Court of Appeal in *SFO v ENRC*[33] helpfully clarified the law on litigation privilege insofar as it relates to internal investigations, holding that—in both the civil and criminal context—it covers legal advice and work aimed at heading off, avoiding or settling proceedings in the same way as it covers advice or work aimed at resisting or defending those proceedings.

Even though investigating authorities recognise that they cannot compel production of legally privileged material, they have in recent years become more aggressive at challenging claims to privilege. As a result they will often adopt the position that:

(a) material is not privileged at all. The SFO, for example, sometimes adopts this position in respect of interview notes produced during internal investigations, arguing that these are factual, rather than containing legal advice. When carrying out internal investigations, care should be taken to produce documents in such a way that they are not vulnerable to such a challenge. Moreover, if faced with such a challenge, the company should take advice on privilege from its legal advisers. Some authorities, including the SFO, carry out a so-called "privilege review" within a team at the agency which is ringfenced

---

[32] *Three Rivers DC v Governor and Company of the Bank of England (No.5)* [2003] Q.B. 1556.
[33] *Director of the Serious Fraud Office v Eurasian Natural Resources Corp Ltd* [2018] EWCA Civ 2006.

from the investigation team.[34] Other models involve instructing Counsel independent of both parties to carry out the review, or litigating the matter before the courts[35]; and

(b) even if it is, the company should waive privilege and provide the material to receive full credit for co-operating with the authority concerned. Before agreeing to do so, the company should consider carefully the ramifications that might flow from such a decision. Such ramifications might include losing privilege over the material in other fora (including other criminal, regulatory or civil proceedings in the UK or elsewhere).

12.5.2.4 Other obligations that may limit disclosure

Normal rules of confidentiality, and data protection legislation, would not normally prevent disclosure of information pursuant to a binding requirement to provide it issued by an investigating authority. However, some statutory regimes do recognise the special status of certain types of material.

Banking confidentiality

Information subject to banking confidentiality is one example of a type of information which is afforded special status. For example, FSMA s.175(5)[36] provides that no-one can be required to disclose information in respect of which he owes a duty of banking confidence unless:

(a) they are the person under investigation, or a member of that person's corporate group;

(b) the person to whom the duty of confidence is owed is under investigation, or a member of that person's corporate group is;

(c) the person to whom the duty is owed consents to disclosure; or

(d) the imposition of the requirement to disclose has been expressly authorised by the regulator.

A similar provision appears in the CJA 1987 s.2(10) in respect of the SFO, where the gateways are limited to (a) consent from the person to whom the duty is owed, and (b) an authorisation by the Director of the SFO or a person designated by him.

---

[34] The SFO has in recent years started to use a machine learning algorithm to assist that process.

[35] See, e.g. *R. (on the application of Ford) v Financial Services Authority (FSA)* [2011] EWHC 2583 (Admin), in which the High Court considered a claim to privilege asserted by Mr Ford—who was subject to FSA enforcement proceedings—over certain documents sought to be relied upon by the FSA in the context of those proceedings.

[36] A similar provision appears at CA 1985 s.452(1A) for company investigations.

Communications data

In view of the sensitive nature of communications data held by telecommunications providers, the Investigatory Powers Act 2016[37] imposes certain specific requirements on investigating authorities seeking such data directly from telecommunications providers. Those requirements are beyond the scope of this chapter, however it is worth noting that this does not prevent the investigating authority seeking records of phone calls (for example call logs) directly from the company under investigation.

12.6 Products of the investigation

12.6.1 Outputs of the investigation

The outputs of an investigation will depend to a very great extent on what the statute requires. While every investigation will have working papers (for example governance and management documents, decision logs, internal memoranda recommending one course of action or another), these are very likely to be kept confidential within the investigating authority concerned.

Some statutes require a report to be produced by the investigator, for example under FSMA s.167 or CA 1985 s.437. These may, or may not, be published depending on what the statute requires. In the financial services context, for example, s.167 reports are not published. Companies Act reports may be provided by the Secretary of State to a range of recipients, or published.

In addition, some authorities will produce a report at the conclusion of an investigation for internal consumption to support any recommendations by the investigation team for a particular course of action. For example, both the FCA and PRA will, in many cases (particularly when they feel the matter is likely to be contested) produce what is known as a "Preliminary Investigation Report", setting out the findings of the investigation and any regulatory breaches they consider to have occurred as a result. These findings will normally be referenced to particular pieces of evidence on which the team intends to rely. Disclosure of these reports is normally provided in advance of any contested hearing before the FCA's RDC or the Bank of England's EDMC.

---

[37] Which replaced relevant provisions of the Regulation of Investigatory Powers Act 2000.

12.6.2 Use of compelled testimony in criminal proceedings

Due to the additional protections afforded to defendants in criminal proceedings and the right to a fair trial enshrined in the ECHR art.6, compelled testimony from investigations can only be used in very limited circumstances in UK criminal proceedings.[38]

The question concerning the use of compelled testimony in criminal proceedings is particularly fraught in the US context, due to the privilege against self-incrimination as enshrined in the 5th Amendment of the US Constitution and as interpreted by the courts. In the US criminal context, the use of testimony obtained by compulsion, or evidence derived from that testimony, would not generally be permissible in a criminal trial against the person from whom it was compelled.[39] As such, and following high profile acquittals in cases concerning manipulation of LIBOR,[40] regulators and prosecutors seek to co-ordinate in order to ensure that evidence obtained by compulsion in UK regulatory interviews does not taint US criminal proceedings.

12.6.3 Use in civil proceedings

The civil courts have a wide discretion in the exercise of their case management powers to allow evidence to be introduced in civil proceedings, and as a result there is no blanket prohibition on evidence that has been obtained by compulsion being used in civil proceedings.

While in certain circumstances public authorities may (i) be under duties to seek the views of individuals who have given evidence as to the disclosure of their evidence; (ii) consider redacting portions of documents that criticise individuals; or (iii) consider applying public interest immunity, directors or companies who provide information under compelled powers should not assume that information could never be used in civil litigation.

For example, in *Omers Administration v Tesco Plc*[41] the High Court required Tesco to disclose a number of documents that had been provided to it by the SFO in the course of negotiations relating to a Deferred Prosecution Agreement. Those documents had been obtained by the SFO from third parties using its powers of compulsion under the CJA 1987 s.2. The High Court considered the interests of the various parties to the case, and the individuals named in the documents, and came to the view that in the

---

[38] See, in financial services investigations, FSMA s.174 and, in the SFO context, the CJA 1987 s.2(8) and 2(8AA).

[39] An unwilling witness who invokes the 5th Amendment may be compelled to testify in US federal proceedings, but only if the Government grants the witness full "use and derivative use" immunity from prosecution. See *Kastigar v United States* 406 U.S. 441 (1972).

[40] See *United States v Allen* No.16-898 (2d Cir. 2017).

[41] *Omers Administration v Tesco Plc* [2019] EWHC 109 (Ch).

circumstances the balance favoured disclosure, potentially subject to redaction and specific steps to maintain confidentiality as between the parties to the litigation.

12.6.4 Disclosure of information gathered in the course of investigations

12.6.4.1 General prohibitions on disclosure

Almost all statutes under which investigating authorities exercise powers of compulsion contain provisions restricting the authority from disclosing information received in the course of carrying out their functions. For example, FSMA s.348 prevents the FCA or PRA from disclosing non-public information relating to the business or other affairs of any person that they receive in the course of carrying out their functions.[42] It is a criminal offence for the regulators to disclose information in breach of s.348, or for another party to disclose such information if the party received it from the FCA and/or PRA.

Similar duties arise under the CA 1985 s.449 in respect of information obtained during company investigations. The SFO, for its part, is under a duty of confidence in relation to information it obtains in the course of its functions.

The FRC is also subject to confidentiality requirements set out in the Accountancy Regulations reg.48(a).

12.6.4.2 Gateways permitting disclosure

In each case, the statute then sets up a series of so-called "gateways" through which information subject to confidentiality may be disclosed:

(a)   for the SFO, these are contained in the CJA 1987 s.3(5)[43];
(b)   for the CA 1985 they are in s.451A and Schs 15C and 15D to that Act;
(c)   for the FCA and PRA, these are contained in regulations made under FSMA s.349[44]; and
(d)   for the FRC these are in the Accountancy Regulations reg.48(c).[45]

---

[42]   Note under s.348, the FCA and PRA can disclose information if it is effectively anonymised.
[43]   There may also be gateways in other legislation, e.g. the Proceeds of Crime Act 2002 s.348.
[44]   Financial Services and Markets Act (Disclosure of Confidential Information) Regulations 2001 (SI 2001/2188) as amended.
[45]   This allows the FRC to disclose to those involved in the matter, and for the information to be used in any public hearing. The same information may be disclosed, "to any regulatory body, any investigation or prosecution authority, or to any person, body or authority carrying out a similar role similar to that of regulation, investigation or prosecution in any part of the world, subject to any statutory prohibition on disclosure."

Gateways can be complicated (particularly in the financial services context, where they implement various international obligations to share information between national supervisory bodies), but broadly they tend to permit disclosure to other bodies having similar functions to the authority making the disclosure, for certain specified purposes. Those purposes can include:

(a)　criminal investigations;
(b)　civil regulatory investigations;
(c)　certain civil proceedings (for example under the Company Directors Disqualification Act 1986); or
(d)　the performance of other statutory functions.

Gateways are specific to each authority, and are discretionary in nature. The existence of a gateway does not, therefore, give rise to a legal requirement on an investigating authority to disclose information; rather it provides a legal conduit through which such disclosures may be made if the authority is so minded. In practice, there are often significant amounts of information exchanged between authorities on almost a daily basis (particularly as between the FCA and PRA) where authorities are co-operating on supervision, or investigation, of companies and individuals. This can occur domestically within the UK, but often also occurs internationally between authorities in different jurisdictions, where appropriate gateways exist.

Many authorities have concluded Memoranda of Understanding with their counterparts (both in the UK and abroad) which seek to put a framework for understanding in place as to how they will exchange information. While these are not legally binding agreements, they nevertheless give an insight into the level of co-operation that may be occurring between authorities in different jurisdictions.

12.6.5　Freedom of Information

All UK public authorities are subject to the Freedom of Information Act 2000 (FOIA).[46] As such, any person may request, under FOIA, information held by those public authorities. Public authorities have 20 working days to respond to a request for disclosure made under FOIA.[47]

Unless the public authority concerned can rely on an exemption from disclosure contained in FOIA, it must disclose the requested information. The detail of FOIA is beyond the scope of this Chapter, however there are a number of exemptions commonly used by authorities seeking to resist disclosure of material relating to investigations:

---

[46]　FCA, PRA and SFO are all subject to FOIA. The FRC is also subject to FOIA in respect of some of its functions.
[47]　This can be extended in certain circumstances, e.g. to consider the public interest in maintaining confidentiality under certain exemptions to disclosure in FOIA.

(a) *Statutory confidentiality*—Information subject to a statutory prohibition on disclosure (see above) is exempt from disclosure under FOIA s.44.

(b) *Data Protection*—Information that is the personal data of individuals protected under data protection legislation will be exempt from disclosure under FOIA s.40.[48]

(c) *Criminal Investigation*—Information held for the purposes of criminal investigations will be exempt from disclosure under FOIA s.30, subject to the public interest in maintaining the exemption outweighing the public interest in disclosure.

(d) *Civil Investigation*—Information held for the purposes of civil (i.e. regulatory) investigations will be exempt from disclosure under FOIA s.31, subject to the public interest test above.

(e) *Commercial interests*—A public authority may refuse to disclose on the grounds that disclosure would or would be likely to be prejudicial to the commercial interests of any person, subject again to the public interest test above.

The requester has the right to complain to the Information Commissioner if they consider that the public authority concerned has failed to apply FOIA correctly, with an onward right of appeal for both parties to the First Tier Tribunal.

In practice, the application of exemptions means that information concerning investigations and proceedings (whether criminal or regulatory) rarely comes into the public domain via FOIA. There is, however, no requirement on the part of the authority concerned to inform any person that a request has been made under FOIA for information that relates to them, or to know in advance should information about the investigation fall to be disclosed.[49]

12.7 Other types of inquiry

12.7.1 *Other potential types of inquiry*

Where there has been a significant failure or misconduct in a company that has had widespread effects, in addition to formal investigations, the company may come under pressure as a result of the instigation of a number of other types of inquiry.

---

[48] Though the authority may have to carry out a balancing exercise under data protection legislation to consider the harm that could be caused to the person concerned by disclosure.

[49] Authorities do on occasion inform affected parties in advance, and will occasionally seek their assistance in making arguments to the Information Commissioner or the Tribunal concerning the impact of disclosure. Public sector contracts may also contain express provisions to this effect.

12.7.1.1   Parliamentary Select Committees

A growing feature of the UK political landscape is the advent of more regular inquiries into misconduct at significant companies by UK Parliamentary Select Committees. The inquiries can be commenced either as a result of a significant event at a company, including a criminal or regulatory investigation.

Select Committees, which are made up of Backbench MPs from across the political spectrum, will come together to take evidence from the investigating authority concerned and the company (usually by calling its senior executives to give oral evidence at a committee session), and will produce a report.

In the financial services sector, the Treasury Committee of the UK Parliament has been active in carrying out inquiries into a variety of issues, including the failure of HBOS Plc, and the financial issues in the crisis and post-crisis period at the Co-operative Bank Plc. It has also called senior bank executives to account for their approach to a variety of consumer-related issues, including debt collection practices.

In the non-financial services sector, inquiries have been carried out into a variety of issues arising in large companies, including data protection and privacy, offshore tax planning, and advertising during election campaigns.

Select Committee inquiries can have significant pitfalls for the unwary. There are no rules of evidence, and Select Committees have the ability—in addition to calling oral evidence—to seek disclosure of papers from organisations and individuals appearing before them. The ambit of that ability, and how the Committee exercises it (and might potentially enforce it), is beyond the scope of this chapter; however, any company or director subject to a demand from a Parliamentary Select Committee to appear before it, or to provide information to it, should seek legal advice at the earliest opportunity.

Questioning of senior executives in select committee sessions can be adversarial, and requires careful preparation. Ensuring that those appearing before the committee have appropriate advice during the preparation phase (from lawyers and communications advisers), as well as a sound knowledge of the facts, is vital.

12.7.1.2   Public Inquiry

Where issues of significant public interest arise, the relevant Secretary of State may decide to order a public inquiry. These inquiries, normally chaired by senior members of the judiciary, are inquisitorial proceedings designed to find facts, and make recommendations for the future. Public inquiries have powers to compel the production of information, and can call witnesses (who will normally give evidence under oath). Questioning is generally carried out by a counsel to the inquiry, although lawyers representing other interested groups may also have the opportunity to question witnesses.

Again, involvement in public inquiries requires significant preparation on the part of the company and its directors, particularly if the directors are to be called to give evidence. As such, legal advice should be sought at the earliest opportunity.

12.7.1.3 *Regulatory Reviews*

In the post-crisis world, regulators are coming under increased pressure to carry out independent reviews when there has been a serious regulatory failure.[50] The regulator concerned will appoint an independent person, and a supporting secretariat, to carry out the review.[51] It will allow full access to its records, and members of its staff, for the purposes of the review.

Generally, reviews are carried out in order to learn lessons from previous failures, and make recommendations for the future. However, at least one past review[52] has made recommendations concerning future enforcement investigations arising out of the issues which were the subject of the review.

Often, during the course of such reviews, the company and its directors will be invited to provide documents and observations to assist the independent person in coming to their conclusions. In addition, officers and senior employees of the company may be interviewed by the independent person to gather their recollections and views of what happened in the time period under review.

Past reviews have criticised the actions of senior executives at companies whose failure forms part of the subject matter of the review. For example, the *PRA/FCA Review of the Failure of HBOS Plc* found that ultimate responsibility for the failure of that Bank lay with its Board of Directors. Companies invited to participate in regulatory reviews should therefore understand that the review will not necessarily confine itself to commenting on the actions of the regulator.

---

[50] In the financial services sector, this requirement is enshrined in statute: see the Financial Services Act 2012 Pt 5.

[51] In the financial services sector, see, e.g. the *FCA/PRA Review into the Failure of HBOS Plc* (and the accompanying review of Enforcement decision making by Andrew Green QC), and the *PRA review of the prudential regulation of the Co-operative Bank Plc during the period 2008–2013*.

[52] Carried out by Andrew Green QC into the FSA's enforcement decision making related to HBOS Plc.

Where a regulatory review proposes to criticise individuals, it will generally give them the opportunity—through the process known as "Maxwellisation"[53]—to see the potential criticisms and make representations on them.

As such, it is vital that individuals who are asked to provide input to regulatory reviews are appropriately prepared for any interview process, and that the company concerned remains relatively close to the review process as it proceeds, so that it is (and any affected individuals are) in a position to engage appropriately with any Maxwellisation process as the review reaches its concluding stages.

12.7.1.4 *Independent Inquiry carried out by the company*

In cases where significant wrongdoing has been uncovered, whether by investigation or otherwise, the company itself may come under pressure—from Parliamentarians or the public where significant consumer detriment has occurred—to carry out an independent inquiry into its own actions, or those of its senior executives.

Such an inquiry is normally conducted by a senior member of the judiciary, a senior lawyer or City figure, with support from a secretariat.

Aside from being a significant drain on resource, the firm concerned will be required to provide the independent person with full access to its books and records, as well as to make staff available for interview, to allow the inquiry to proceed.

The end product of such inquiries is often a report, published by the company, setting out the independent person's findings and recommendations for remediation. Those findings can sometimes require the payment of significant restitution to affected customers, together with providing a platform for future regulatory investigation should the independent person conclude that individuals have behaved improperly.

12.7.2 A strategy for dealing with concurrent investigations and inquiries is key

Where a company finds itself the subject of, or involved in, multiple concurrent inquiries and investigations, while it will be important to adopt a strategy for dealing with each process separately, the company should not lose sight of the need to look at how the various processes interact.

---

[53] The term "Maxwellisation" takes its name from a case brought in 1974 against what was then the Department for Trade and Industry by the tycoon Robert Maxwell, in which Maxwell argued that he should be given the right to see draft findings made by inspectors appointed under companies legislation before they were finalised and published by the Department.

For example, in 2014 the Co-operative Bank Plc was subject to, or involved in, the following inquiries or investigations:

(a)   the FCA (enforcement investigations into the bank and senior executives);
(b)   the PRA (enforcement investigations into the bank and senior executives);
(c)   the FRC (enforcement investigations into senior executives and auditors);
(d)   an independent review commissioned by the bank of the events leading to its capital shortfall, carried out by Sir Christopher Kelly (the Kelly Review);
(e)   an inquiry by the House of Commons Treasury Committee into the bank's aborted purchase of a number of branches of Lloyds Bank Plc; and
(f)   a review commissioned by the Co-operative Group of its overall governance arrangements, carried out by Lord Myners (the Myners Review).

Each of the inquiries and investigations were carried out under different arrangements, with different timetables, and each process carried with it different powers to compel evidence and witnesses.

Then, in 2018, the Treasury gave a direction to the PRA to establish a *Review of the prudential regulation of the Co-operative Bank plc during the period 2008–2013*.[54] That direction made clear that the PRA review could rely on any conclusion reached by the Kelly Review, the Myners Review and the Treasury Committee review (or any other reports as the investigator considered appropriate).

As a result, when facing multiple reviews and investigations, it will be key for the company and its directors to adopt a strategic approach, not least because a position they adopt in one investigation or inquiry could affect their freedom to adopt a different—or nuanced—position in another forum (and potentially several years in the future).

12.8   Practicalities

12.8.1   *Immediate steps on receiving a notice of appointment*

It is vital that a company receiving a notice of appointment of investigators takes a number of steps immediately on receiving the notice, including:

---

[54] See *https://assets.publishing.service.gov.uk/government/uploads/system/uploads/attachment_data/file/685503/Direction_to_the_Prudential_Regulation_Authority_to_investigate_the_prudential_regulation_of_the_Co-operative_Bank_plc_during_the_period_2008_-_2013.pdf* [Accessed 10 May 2019].

(a) instructing external lawyers to represent it in the investigation;

(b) considering the extent to which—if individuals working within the company are under suspicion, or are themselves the subject of the investigation—any employment and/or disciplinary action ought to be taken;

(c) considering with external counsel the extent to which the company may need to carry out an internal investigation of its own into the events concerned[55];

(d) placing a hold on any routinely-scheduled destruction of documents or other information held by it relating to the subject matter of the investigation;

(e) taking steps to ensure any information relating to the subject matter of the investigation that is not subject to routine destruction is also preserved. This would include ensuring staff do not manually delete relevant documents, should they hold it in electronic systems they have access to (e.g. email software);

(f) considering the extent to which a listed company may have disclosure obligations to the financial markets, and/or to other regulators; and

(g) considering and settling an internal and external communications strategy concerning the investigation.

These issues are considered in more detail below.

12.8.2 Companies and their directors/employees

12.8.2.1 Potential conflicts of interest

One of the first things the directors of the company under investigation must do is to consider whether there is any potential risk of a conflict of interest between the director's own interests and those of the company. If there is such a risk, that will need to be carefully managed. This can be achieved by a conflicted director excluding themselves from the responsibility of managing the company's response to the investigation. If no alternative is available, then the director will need to consider the extent to which that conflict can be mitigated by appointing independent professional advisers.

Any director who does not have such a conflict must take appropriate steps (in conjunction with other non-conflicted directors as needed) to ensure that a director with a conflict does not remain involved in the company's

---

[55] It is important that external counsel are involved in any decision to carry out internal investigative activity. This is for two reasons: first, the question of whether internal investigations benefit from legal privilege is complicated (see above for more detail), and secondly, care is needed to ensure that the internal investigation is carried out in a way that does not undermine the authority's ability to investigate (what the SFO has in the past called "trampling on the crime scene").

response to the investigation. One solution to this is to rely on non-executive directors to perform the role of ensuring that the investigation is properly dealt with from the company's perspective.

12.8.2.2   *Centralising management of the response to the investigation*

The company should consider how it proposes to deal with the investigation. Usually, companies will appoint a board member to have overall responsibility for the investigation and for co-ordinating the various workstreams that will arise.

It will also normally be necessary to establish a central team to deal with the investigation, with a mix of skills and experience potentially involving lawyers, compliance staff and staff with operational experience. The number of staff dealing with the investigation should be kept to a minimum to ensure that confidentiality is maintained and that tight control can be kept of the evidence and other information generated during the course of the investigation. The level of control exerted over the information generated during the investigation may have a direct bearing on whether legal privilege can be claimed over it as the investigation progresses.

12.8.2.3   *Employment law issues arising out of investigations*

In relation to employees or directors who are themselves subjects of the investigation (or in respect of whom the investigating authority has alleged wrongdoing), the company will need to consider whether any disciplinary action ought to be taken against them. These are difficult and delicate issues, which will almost always require employment law advice to be taken.

12.8.2.4   *Directors and Officers (D&O) Liability Cover*

If there is D&O insurance cover in place, the company will need to consider the terms of the policy and whether the insurers should be notified of the investigation. Underwriters and/or the broker may wish to be involved, and it may be necessary or sensible to obtain their consent to the steps that the firm is taking and to inform them regularly of developments.

If there has been substantial loss to the company as a result of, for example, fraud, then the company will need to consider notifying its insurers. Again, this should be done at an early stage.

Instead of, or alongside, D&O coverage a company may have provided an individual director or officer with a corporate indemnification agreement by which the company agrees to pay the individual's legal expenses.

With the increasing regulatory focus on individual accountability, D&O cover is becoming ever more important in allowing individuals subject to regulatory investigation the means to obtain legal advice and defend themselves through the investigation process without incurring significant personal expense. The corollary of this is, however, that insurers (whose approach to dealing with investigations has become increasingly sophisticated) may need to be involved at the outset, and regularly throughout the investigation.

12.8.2.5   Independent legal representation for individuals

Where individuals who are not covered by the D&O policy and/or a corporate indemnity are swept up in the investigation, the company will need to consider the extent to which they may need independent legal representation and whether, in the circumstances, the company may wish to help bear some or all of the cost of such legal representation.

12.8.3   Investigations by external advisers

One matter a company that is subject to investigative activity must consider is the extent to which it wishes to conduct its own investigation into the events that have occurred. This is often important as it allows the company to determine the extent of its potential liability, and to consider availing itself of policies of investigating authorities aimed at reducing penalties for companies which self-report and co-operate with the resulting investigation.

In appropriate cases, therefore, some authorities may be prepared to hold off on their own investigation to allow the company to conduct internal investigations and produce a report to be provided to the authority concerned. Engaging suitably independent and expert external advisers will also be key to ensuring the credibility of the overall process.

When engaging an external adviser, the company will need to consider the extent to which any professional services firm, or law firm, that is routinely instructed by the company, might be said to be actually or potentially conflicted by reason of their prior involvement with the company.

In most cases, however, while the investigating authorities recognise, in theory, the need for the company to understand its potential liability, they generally frown on the company carrying out its own investigation *alongside* any external investigation. This is particularly the case in the criminal context, where the SFO has in the past noted that internal investigations (particularly those that involve interviews of staff) tend to make their own task that much more difficult, because their investigators are not able to access the staff members' first recollection of the events.

One other point to note here is that, if an internal investigation is carried out, the question as to whether any resulting documents benefit from legal professional privilege is fraught with difficulty and will require careful consideration with the firm's legal advisers.

As a result, while some investigative steps will be expected by the investigating authorities as a means of the company forming a judgement about its own position, companies and their directors should tread carefully in considering how any such work should proceed. As such, companies and directors should seek legal advice before carrying out any internal investigation.

The financial services regulators also have the power under FSMA s.166, to appoint a so-called "Skilled Person" to carry out a review at the firm's expense, and supply the results in a report to the regulator. The important point to note here is that this is not a substitute for an enforcement investigation, but a s.166 report which credits the firm with significant remediation activity may convince the regulator that a more formal investigation is not required, and that the matter might better be dealt with in the course of day-to-day supervision.

12.8.4 *Preservation of evidence*

At the very beginning of the investigation, the company must take all possible steps to identify, secure and preserve all the evidence that would be relevant to the investigation. This will include identifying the key individuals who may have the evidence (electronic, or hardcopy) in their possession, and where it might be stored (such individuals are generally referred to as "custodians"). It will also be necessary to establish how far-reaching the problem is within the company, to be able to be sure that all relevant information has been identified and preserved.

In complex, multinational enterprises (and particularly those which may have acquired other entities), this is often a difficult process. Investigating agencies regularly cite with some frustration examples of the disruption caused to an investigative timetable where a company under investigation has "discovered" a new source of evidence (e.g. an unknown, or forgotten, server containing relevant electronic documents) part-way through an investigation. While they are understanding that a company's IT provision may be complex, investigating authorities will expect a company to have looked carefully at its IT infrastructure and identified potential sources of relevant information from the outset.

It is difficult to overstate the complexity of this task for companies. Almost all companies will have a mixture of hardcopy and electronic records, held in various locations, and often on multiple servers. This information will need to be retrieved, preserved, searched and reviewed in order to determine the extent to which it may be relevant to an information requirement provided by the regulator.

This means that—while there are a variety of electronic solutions available from commercial providers to help companies deal with large quantities of information in the context of an investigation (and the advent of machine learning and artificial intelligence is changing the nature of the process all the time), gathering, reviewing and determining the relevance of information held by a company is still a time consuming—and resource intensive—exercise.

12.8.4.1   Hardcopy documents

The company will need to consider what classes of hardcopy document (correspondence, notes, minutes, diaries, internal memoranda, audit documentation and print outs of electronic documents held elsewhere) may have been created and need to be preserved. This involves considering not only files which are available on the premises of the company, but also retrieving any potentially relevant documentation from any physical archiving facility that the company may have, either itself or with a commercial provider of archival services.

Increasingly, executives are keeping hardcopy records of their actions when they move roles, to ensure they have evidence of the actions they took if a regulator opens an investigation. As such, one question for companies is the extent to which the firm will engage with ex-senior staff to request any records they have personally retained (whether in notebooks or print outs), for the purposes of the investigation. Note that in order to preserve a right to require the immediate delivery up of company property and documents provided to a senior executive or director during their period of appointment, it is advisable to include an express delivery up obligation in the service contract and/or letter of appointment.[56]

On occasions, an investigating authority may require the production of original hardcopy documents. As such, while it is routinely the case that original documents are converted to electronic form to aid their production to the investigators, care should be taken to preserve the originals.

12.8.4.2   Electronic records

The amount of electronic data held by institutions has increased exponentially. As such, the most significant task for companies in terms of identifying and preserving relevant information is almost always the question of where the electronic information is stored, which custodians' data ought to be preserved, and over what time period.

---

[56]   *Eurasian Natural Resources Corp Ltd v Judge* [2014] EWHC 3556 (QB).

The key to any electronic records search is to involve IT specialists within the company, who have a detailed knowledge of the company's current IT infrastructure and legacy estate, early in the investigation to ensure the company has a clear view of where relevant electronic records may be stored. Specialist IT support will be required to ensure that records are not lost and relevant devices are effectively dealt with such that the forensic integrity of the data is preserved. The faster this occurs the greater the chance of recovering usable evidence from them.

Emails

Emails often represent by volume the largest category of electronic information that a company under investigation needs to preserve, retrieve and search for relevant documents. Key to this effort will be determining which email custodians hold information relevant to the investigation. Once the relevant custodians have been identified, the company will need to consider—if the custodian is still working at the firm—the extent to which it can take an appropriate copy or copies of all relevant information while still allowing the custodian to make use of the email system for their day to day work, in a scenario where the custodian may not know (possibly because the company is not permitted to tell them) that their emails are relevant to an ongoing investigation.

Document management systems

While the wholesale adoption of electronic document management systems has, in theory at least, made it easier for companies to store the increasingly large volume of electronic information they generate, they pose some potential issues for companies dealing with investigations. Firms will not only need to consider how best to search such systems (e.g. by author, title, date, content), but also the extent to which the way data on those systems is structured may impact on the documents that might be returned. If a firm has moved from one document management system to another, then it may be necessary to conduct searches of legacy systems, or—if data has been ported over from one system to another—to convince the investigating authority that there is no need to do so because all information on the legacy system has been ported to the new system (though this can be a difficult task).

A second issue is the extent to which multiple versions of the same document (e.g. drafts saved on the system) may also need to be disclosed.

In addition, if the system is configured such that documents can be saved outside of it (e.g. on the Desktop) then further more specific searches may be required of individual custodians' devices.

Other forms of communication—chats and instant messaging

In recent years, with the advent of chat rooms and instant messaging, the volume of data that may need to be reviewed has become significant.[57] Chat room data may not be stored by the company, but hosted by one of the various chat room providers. If so, the company will need to review the contract it has with the provider to determine:

(a) the extent to which the external provider retains that information (retention periods may vary depending on the service to which the company subscribes); and

(b) if it is entitled to access the relevant chat rooms and associated chat data (there may be an additional cost).

Instant messaging services, while often hosted within the organisation's own servers, may or not be retained depending on how the system is configured. This should be looked at early on to ensure that any relevant archived instant message strings are included.

Encrypted communications

The advent of highly encrypted communications (e.g. WhatsApp) pose challenges for the investigating authority and the company seeking to provide full disclosure of relevant material to an investigation. Where encrypted communications are carried out on company devices for commercial purposes, the company may come under some pressure to provide these to the investigating authority, if it is able to do so. In doing so, it will need to consider whether the set-up of any company devices, and in particular the back-up arrangements for such devices, mean that the content of those devices could be said to be available to the company, and therefore should be included in any evidence preservation process.

Other devices

The near ubiquitous use of mobile devices such as smartphones and tablets in business presents a number of challenges for investigating authorities and companies alike.

First, the company will need to identify, for each custodian, the extent to which they are using multiple devices to access and store company

---

[57] This was particularly the case in the financial services sector in the Foreign Exchange (FX) manipulation cases, where companies and investigating authorities alike had to contend with large amounts of relatively unstructured data from chat rooms in which FX traders discussed operations in the market. Those particular chat rooms had the added complication of using terminology understood between the individuals concerned, which meant that investigators had to learn the "jargon" in order to make sense of the matters under discussion.

information. The company will then need to consider how it can gain access to the information on those devices. Where the company has provided the device to the custodian for use as part of the custodian's employment, this should be relatively straightforward. However, where an organisation operates a "bring your own device" policy, this may be more complicated, as the device will contain personal information of the custodian as well as the information belonging to the company.

Secondly, investigating authorities regularly have to deal with the issue of legacy devices—particularly in cases where the alleged misconduct or crime spans a number of years. If legacy devices have been retained, either by the custodian concerned or the company—and not properly decommissioned—then they may need to be searched for potentially relevant information. This can be difficult because companies and executives may not even recall that they have retained the device. As such, when dealing with an investigation that spans a number of years, the company will need to consider asking custodians to confirm that they have not retained any old company devices, and requiring them to provide them to it for searching if they have.

12.8.4.3   *Telephones*

Often, companies will have facilities for recording telephone lines, particularly in cases involving the securities industry. Recordings will need to be retrieved and transcribed, potentially from desk telephones and mobile devices (where the latter are recorded). In addition, there may be a need to identify and produce telephone logs, and voicemail messages, as these can be useful evidence of who was speaking to whom and when, even if the detail of what was discussed has not been preserved.

12.8.5   *Issues to consider on providing evidence to the investigating authority*

As set out above, one of the limits on the ability of investigating authorities to require disclosure of information is the fact that in almost all cases the authorities cannot compel the production of material that is subject to legal professional privilege.

When considering what information ought to be provided to the investigating authority in response to an information requirement, the company will need to take care to ensure that it does not inadvertently provide information that is subject to legal privilege. Disclosing such information to the investigating authority risks losing privilege. The law on legal privilege is complex, and the company should take legal advice on the information to be disclosed and the implications for it should legally privileged material be disclosed.

Finally, the company will need to liaise with the investigating authority to determine in what form the authority would like to receive any information disclosed. Some authorities (for example, the SFO) have policies on the method(s) by which data should be provided to them, and indeed the format in which data should be provided.

12.8.6   Other notifications

12.8.6.1   Financial Markets

A company whose securities are listed on a regulated market must also consider the extent to which rules concerning market disclosure may require it to disclose the fact of the investigation. This is a complicated area, and will require the directors of the company concerned to take legal advice. The company may also need to consult with the listing authority to seek its advice on a course of action, particularly if there are market rumours or press speculation as to a potential investigation.

12.8.6.2   Other regulators

A company that is regulated by multiple regulators (both domestically and internationally) must also consider the extent to which any regulatory requirements—for example to be open and co-operative with its regulator) may mean it needs to make another agency aware of an ongoing investigation into it, or any of its employees or officers. In the financial services sector in particular, the UK regulators have taken enforcement action against firms and individuals for failing to inform them of ongoing investigations by overseas regulators.[58] Overlapping regulatory require- ments in this area can be complicated, and tricky to navigate. As such, where there are international regulatory requirements pointing the firm in different directions, the firm should take legal advice as to the implications in each jurisdiction.

12.8.7   Internal and external communications strategy

At the beginning of the investigation, the existence of the investigation may not be publicly known (and the number of individuals within the company who are aware of it may be relatively small). However, from the outset, the company should consider—potentially with the assistance of PR consultants—what it would say, both internally to its own staff and externally to the media, should the fact of the investigation become public.

---

[58] See, e.g. fines levied against two Japanese Banks (and two executives of the banks concerned) by the PRA for a failure to disclose an investigation by the New York Department of Financial Services, at *https://www.bankofengland.co.uk/news/2017/february/pra-imposes-fine-on-the-bank-of-tokyo-mitsubishi-ufj-limited-and-fine-on-mufg-securities-emea-plc* [Accessed 10 May 2019].

While the ultimate decision may be to say as little as possible about the investigation, it is preferable for that decision, and any associated press notices and staff emails, to be settled early in the investigation, rather than seeking to settle those matters at a time when the existence of the investigation is about to enter the public domain.

Chapter 13

Disqualification of Directors

Stephen Robins
South Square, Gray's Inn

13.1   Introduction

The power of the courts to make a disqualification order prohibiting a person from being concerned in the management of a company was first introduced by Companies Act 1928 s.75 on the recommendation of the Greene Committee. The powers of the courts to make disqualification orders were extended incrementally over the years. They are now contained in the Company Directors Disqualification Act 1986 (as amended) (CDDA).

The purpose of the statutory regime for the disqualification of directors has always been perceived as the two-fold objective of the protection of the public from future misconduct and the prevention of the misuse or abuse of the privilege of limited liability.[1]

Although the majority of disqualification orders and undertakings relate to directors of insolvent companies, the fact that a company is solvent and profitable is no bar to disqualification, as it is the conduct of the director which determines whether disqualification is appropriate, not the success or otherwise of the company.

Judicial decisions in disqualification proceedings are highly relevant to a proper understanding of the duties to which directors are subject and the standards of behaviour which the courts expect from them, and it should therefore come as no surprise that a book addressing the subject of directors' duties contains an analysis of this subject matter.

---

[1]   See, e.g. *Atlantic Computers Plc, Re* Unreported, 15 June 1998 per Timothy Lloyd J, as quoted in *Secretary of State for Business, Enterprise and Regulatory Reform v Sullman* [2008] EWHC 3179 (Ch); [2010] B.C.C. 500; [2009] 1 B.C.L.C. 397 per Norris J.

13.2 Grounds of disqualification by the courts

The CDDA provides the statutory basis for the commencement of disqualification proceedings. CDDA s.1 prescribes the scope of the disqualification order which can be made by the court. The CDDA separates those sections which make provision for the basis for a disqualification order into three broad categories:

(a) general misconduct in connection with companies[2];
(b) unfitness to act as a director of a company[3]; and
(c) other cases.[4]

13.2.1 The first category: general misconduct

CDDA s.2 provides for disqualification where a person is convicted of an indictable offence "in connection with the promotion, formation, management, liquidation or striking off of a company, or with the receivership or management of a company's property". The court which convicts the person may make a disqualification order of its own motion.[5]

In the event that the criminal court does not impose a period of disqualification, CDDA s.16(2) provides that an application for a disqualification order may be made by the Secretary of State or the official receiver, or by the liquidator or any past or present member or creditor of any company.

The period of disqualification which the court may impose is dependent upon which court makes the order. Where the disqualification order is made by a court of summary jurisdiction, a period of up to five years may be imposed. In any other case a period of up to 15 years may be imposed.[6]

The principles which the criminal courts apply when determining whether to make a disqualification order and the period of such order have always been consistent with those applied by the civil courts.[7]

CDDA s.3 provides for disqualification of up to five years where a person has been:

---

[2] CDDA ss.2–5.
[3] CDDA ss.6–8.
[4] CDDA ss.8ZA–8ZE, 9A–9E, 10, 11 and 12.
[5] See, e.g. *R. v Georgiou (Christakis)* (1988) 4 B.C.C. 322; (1988) 87 Cr. App. R. 207; (1988) 10 Cr. App. R. (S.) 137; *R. v Goodman (Ivor Michael)* [1993] 2 All E.R. 789; [1992] B.C.C. 625; [1994] 1 B.C.L.C. 349; *R. v Myatt (Martin Leonard)* [2004] EWCA Crim 206; *R. v Scragg (Michael Garett)* [2006] EWCA Crim 2916.
[6] CDDA s.2(3).
[7] *Secretary of State for Trade and Industry v Tjolle* [1998] B.C.C. 282; [1998] 1 B.C.L.C. 333; (1997) 94(24) L.S.G. 31 at 336e–336g.

"persistently in default in relation to provisions of the companies legislation requiring any return, account or other document to be filed with, delivered or sent, or notice of any matter to be given, to the registrar of companies."

CDDA s.3(2) provides that the required persistent default can be conclusively proved if the director is found guilty of three or more defaults in any five-year period.

CDDA s.4 provides that a disqualification order of up to 15 years may be made where in the course of the winding up of a company it appears that the director has been guilty of fraudulent trading under Companies Act 2006 s.993[8] or any other fraud in relation to the company.[9] Disqualification orders may be made in respect of conduct in relation to a solvent company under this section. Where the company is insolvent, the proceedings will likely be brought under CDDA s.6.

CDDA s.5 enables the court to make a disqualification order of up to five years where a person has been convicted of an offence due to:

"a contravention of, or failure to comply with, any provision of the companies legislation requiring a return, account or other document to be filed with, delivered or sent, or notice of any matter to be given, to the registrar of companies (whether the contravention or failure is on the person's own part or on the part of any company)"[10]

and during the five years preceding the conviction the person has had three or more default orders and offences within s.5.[11]

CDDA s.5A enables the court to make a disqualification order where a director has been convicted of a relevant offence abroad in connection with the management of a company "which corresponds to an indictable offence under the law of England and Wales or (as the case may be) an indictable offence under the law of Scotland".[12]

13.2.2 The second category: unfitness to act as a director

CDDA s. 6obliges the court to make a disqualification order if it is satisfied that the defendant's conduct as a director of a company which has become insolvent makes him unfit to be concerned in the management of a company.[13]

---

[8] CDDA s.4(1).
[9] CDDA s.4(2).
[10] CDDA s.5(1).
[11] CDDA s.5(3).
[12] CDDA s.5A(3)(b).
[13] CDDA s.6(1). Where the court is satisfied that unfitness has been established, disqualification is mandatory; the court has no discretion to decline to make an order. The introduction of mandatory disqualification gave effect to a recommendation of the Cork Committee in 1982.

CDDA s.12C sheds light on the concept of "unfitness" by requiring the court to have regard specifically to certain matters specified in CDDA Sch.1. This issue is considered below.

CDDA s.7(1) provides that an application for a mandatory order under s.6 can be made only if it appears to the Secretary of State that it is expedient in the public interest that such an order should be made. The Secretary of State is under a continuing duty to keep the position under review. Proceedings can be brought and continued only if it appears, and continues to appear, to the Secretary of State that it is expedient in the public interest that an order be made.

An application for a mandatory order under CDDA s.6 can only be made by the Secretary of State or, if the Secretary of State so directs in a case where the person against whom the order is sought is or has been a director of a company which is being wound up by the court in England and Wales, by the Official Receiver. As originally enacted, this meant that, if the winding up had been completed and the company dissolved, the application could be made only by the Secretary of State. Accordingly, the words "is being wound up" were amended by the Insolvency Act 2000 to read "is being or has been wound up".

Section 8 of the Act provides for the Secretary of State to make an application for a disqualification order if he believes it to be in the public interest to do so.

The maximum period of disqualification which the court can impose under s.8 is 15 years. There is no need for the company to have become insolvent for a disqualification order to be made under s.8.

13.2.3   *The third category: competition cases and other cases*

Section 9A, which was added by Enterprise Act 2002 s.204(2) and came into force on 20 June 2003, relates to competition law and obliges the court to make a disqualification order against a person, provided that two conditions are satisfied in relation to him.

First, the company of which he is a director must be shown to have committed a breach of competition law.

Secondly, the court must be satisfied that his conduct as a director makes him unfit to be concerned in the management of a company. For the purpose of s.9A, the court is expressly forbidden from considering the matters mentioned in Sch.1. Instead, the court is required to consider:

(a)   whether the director's conduct contributed to the breach of competition law;

(b) whether the director had reasonable grounds to suspect that the conduct of the undertaking constituted the breach and he took no steps to prevent it; and

(c) whether the director did not know but ought to have known that the conduct of the undertaking constituted the breach.

The court is also permitted to have regard to the director's conduct as a director of a company in connection with any other breach of competition law. The maximum period of disqualification under s.9A is 15 years.

CDDA s.10 provides that where a court has made an order under either Insolvency Act 1986 (IA 1986) s.213 or s.214[14] that a person is liable to contribute to the assets of a company, the court may, of its own motion, make a disqualification order of up to 15 years.

CDDA s.11 makes it an offence for an undischarged bankrupt or a person subject to a bankruptcy restrictions order or undertaking or a debt relief restrictions order or undertaking or a moratorium period under a debt relief order "to act as director of a company or directly or indirectly to take part in or be concerned in the promotion, formation or management of a company" without the permission of the court.[15] Whether a defendant has been concerned in the promotion, formation or management of a company will be a question of fact for the jury and will not depend on the defendant's own view of his actions.[16]

This Chapter's limited examination of the law of directors' disqualification will focus on the law and procedure applicable to applications for disqualification orders under CDDA ss.6 and 8 on the grounds of unfitness.

13.3 The purpose of disqualification

The primary purpose of disqualification is the protection of the public.[17] Disqualification proceedings do not amount to a criminal charge.[18]

The protection conferred upon the public by disqualification has two constituent elements:

---

[14] For fraudulent trading and wrongful trading respectively.

[15] CDDA s.11(1).

[16] *R. v Doring (Petra)* [2002] EWCA Crim 1695; [2002] B.C.C. 838; [2002] Crim. L.R. 817.

[17] See, e.g. *Blackspur Group Plc (No.2), Re* [1998] 1 W.L.R. 422; [1998] B.C.C. 11; [1998] 1 B.C.L.C. 676 at 426; *Atlantic Computers Plc, Re* Unreported, 15 June 1998 per Timothy Lloyd J; *Dawes & Henderson (Agencies) Ltd (In Liquidation) (No.2), Re* [2000] B.C.C. 204; [1999] 2 B.C.L.C. 317; (1999) 96(8) L.S.G. 29; *Pantmaenog Timber Co Ltd, Re* [2003] UKHL 49; [2004] 1 A.C. 158; [2003] 3 W.L.R. 767 at [74] and [77]–[79]; *Secretary of State for Business, Enterprise and Regulatory Reform v Sullman* [2008] EWHC 3179 (Ch); [2010] B.C.C. 500; [2009] 1 B.C.L.C. 397 per Norris J.

[18] *R. v Secretary of State for Trade and Industry Ex p. McCormick* [1998] B.C.C. 379; [1998] C.O.D. 160; (1998) 95(10) L.S.G. 27.

(a)   the prohibition imposed upon an unfit director from undertaking a position in the formation, promotion or management of a company without the permission of the court[19]; and

(b)   the deterrent effect of disqualification, which is intended to raise the standards of conduct of company directors generally.[20]

13.4   Territorial limits of the CDDA

The CDDA has extra-territorial effect. CDDA 1986 s.22(2)(b) provides that the word "company" includes any company which may be wound up under IA 1986 Pt V. By virtue of IA 1986 ss.220 and 221, companies incorporated in foreign jurisdictions may be wound up by the English courts.

To wind up a foreign company, the court must be satisfied:

(a)   that the company's centre of main interests is in England and Wales; or

(b)   that the company has an establishment in England and Wales; or

(c)   if the company's centre of main interests is outside the EU, that there is:

(i)   a sufficient connection with the jurisdiction;

(ii)   a potential benefit to creditors; and

(iii) at least one creditor subject to the jurisdiction.

Pursuant to CDDA s.6, the court can make a disqualification order in respect of any person who is or has been a director of a foreign company that may be wound up under IA 1986 Pt V. Similarly, the prohibition in a disqualification order against acting as a director of a company extends to prohibit the disqualified person from undertaking directorships of any company that may be wound up under IA 1986 Pt V.

The court may grant permission to serve disqualification proceedings on defendants out of the jurisdiction.[21] There is nothing to prevent foreign nationals from being made the subject of disqualification proceedings. Extra-territoriality is necessary to ensure that the CDDA is effective in the context of cross-border transactions and communications. Electronic means of communication enable companies to be controlled across borders, and therefore Parliament must be presumed to have intended CDDA s.6 to extend to foreigners who were out of the jurisdiction and to conduct which

---

[19]   *Secretary of State for Trade and Industry v Bannister* [1996] 1 W.L.R. 118; [1996] 1 All E.R. 993; [1995] B.C.C. 1027.

[20]   *Secretary of State for Trade and Industry v Ettinger* [1993] B.C.C. 312; [1993] B.C.L.C. 896 at 899; *Grayan Building Services Ltd (In Liquidation), Re* [1995] Ch. 241; [1995] 3 W.L.R. 1; [1995] B.C.C. 554 at 253G; *Westmid Packaging Services Ltd (No.2), Re* [1998] 2 All E.R. 124; [1998] B.C.C. 836; [1998] 2 B.C.L.C. 646 at 654; *Secretary of State for Trade and Industry v Ball* [1999] 1 B.C.L.C. 286 at 344d.

[21]   Practice Direction para.6.4.

occurred out of the jurisdiction.[22] In exercising its discretion to order service out of the jurisdiction, the court will need to be satisfied that the claimant has a good arguable case against the defendant.

13.5   Procedure

The majority of applications for disqualification are brought under CDDA s.7 for an order under CDDA s.6. Proceedings under CDDA s.7 can be commenced by the Secretary of the State or, in circumstances where the company is being wound up by the court, by the Official Receiver at the Secretary of State's direction.[23]

The application must be made to the court which is winding up the company or, if the company is not being wound up by the court (e.g. because it is in administration or because it is in creditors' voluntary liquidation), to the court which would have jurisdiction to wind it up (or, where the company has been dissolved under IA 1986 Sch.B1 para.84, to the court which would have jurisdiction to wind it up, had it not been dissolved).[24] Proceedings commenced in the wrong court are not invalid, and proceedings commenced in the wrong court may be retained in that court.[25]

13.5.1   *The relevant procedural rules*

The relevant procedural rules for an application for a disqualification order will be determined by the section under which the application for disqualification is made. The sources of the procedural rules for disqualification proceedings are the Practice Direction on Directors' Disqualification Proceedings (the Practice Direction), the Insolvent Companies (Disqualification of Unfit Directors) Proceedings Rules 1987[26] (as amended) (the Disqualification Rules) and the Civil Procedure Rules (CPR). The procedure for disqualification proceedings for orders under CDDA ss.6 and 8 is provided for by both the Disqualification Rules and the Practice Direction.[27] The Disqualification Rules apply the provisions of the CPR to proceedings, except where the provisions of the Disqualification Rules are inconsistent with the CPR,[28] and the application of the CPR is also subject to the application of the appeal and review procedure under r.12.59 (appeals and

---

[22]   *Seagull Manufacturing Co Ltd (No.2), Re* [1994] 1 B.C.L.C. 273.
[23]   CDDA s.7(2).
[24]   CDDA s.6(1) and *Secretary of State for Trade and Industry v Arnold* [2007] EWHC 1933 (Ch); [2008] B.C.C. 119; [2008] 1 B.C.L.C. 581.
[25]   See also *Secretary of State for Trade and Industry v Shakespeare* [2005] B.C.C. 891; [2005] 2 B.C.L.C. 471.
[26]   Insolvent Companies (Disqualification of Unfit Directors) Proceedings Rules 1987 (SI 1987/2023).
[27]   Practice Direction para.1.3.
[28]   Disqualification Rules r.2(1); CPR 2.1(2).

reviews of court orders in corporate insolvency) and r.12.62 (procedure on appeal) of the Insolvency (England and Wales) Rules 2016.[29]

13.5.2   Recommendations to the Secretary of State under CDDA section 7A

In cases where the company is insolvent, it is the office-holder who is likely to discover grounds capable of supporting a finding of unfitness. He or she is the person who will discover the information which the Secretary of State will need to consider when determining whether to commence disqualification proceedings. CDDA s.7A requires the office-holder[30] of an insolvent company to provide a report to the Secretary of State. The Court of Appeal has held that, in proceedings under the CDDA, there is an implied exception to the strict rules of hearsay evidence and opinion evidence and that reports obtained by the Secretary of State pursuant to his statutory powers are admissible in evidence in proceedings under the CDDA.[31]

CDDA s.7A is supplemented by CDDA s.7(4) which enables both the Secretary of State and the Official Receiver, where he is not the office-holder, to require any person to provide such information or documents as the Secretary of State reasonably requires to determine whether to bring proceedings for a disqualification order. The Secretary of State has no absolute right to production of the documents. The court exercises its discretion when determining whether to order a person to comply with the request of the Secretary of State.[32]

The purposes of liquidation, administration and administrative receivership include obtaining information on the conduct of the affairs of the company and of those responsible for it during its trading history. The authorities provide some useful guidance:

---

[29] Insolvency (England and Wales) Rules 2016 (SI 2016/1024). Disqualification Rules r.2(4).

[30] The office-holder will be the official receiver in relation to all companies being wound up by the court. The obligation remains on the official receiver even when his appointment as liquidator is superseded by the appointment of another liquidator. The office-holder will be the liquidator in creditors' voluntary liquidations. In administration and administrative receivership, the office-holder will be the administrator and the administrative receiver respectively.

[31] *Secretary of State for Business, Enterprise and Regulatory Reform v Aaron* [2008] EWCA Civ 1146; [2009] Bus. L.R. 809; [2009] C.P. Rep. 10. See also *Travel & Holiday Clubs, Re* [1967] 1 W.L.R. 711; [1967] 2 All E.R. 606; (1967) 111 S.J. 272; *Armvent, Re* [1975] 1 W.L.R. 1679; [1975] 3 All E.R. 441; (1975) 119 S.J. 845; *St Piran Ltd, Re* [1981] 1 W.L.R. 1300; [1981] 3 All E.R. 270; (1981) 125 S.J. 586; *Rex Williams Leisure Centre Plc, Re* [1994] Ch. 1; [1993] 3 W.L.R. 685; [1993] B.C.C. 79; *Secretary of State for Trade and Industry v Ashcroft (No.1)* [1998] Ch. 71; [1997] 3 W.L.R. 319; [1997] B.C.C. 634 and *Official Receiver v Stojevic* [2007] EWHC 1186 (Ch); [2008] Bus. L.R. 641.

[32] *Lombard Shipping and Forwarding Ltd, Re* [1992] B.C.C. 700; [1993] B.C.L.C. 238 at 245.

(a)   in *Polly Peck International Ex p. The Joint Administrators*,[33] interviews of officers of the company had been conducted under IA 1986 s.236 on the basis that the joint administrators had assured the interviewees that the information would only be used for the purposes of the administration. It was held that disclosure of the transcripts of the interviews to the Secretary of State would be in accordance with the undertaking, as it would be in furtherance of the purposes of the administration;

(b)   in *Westminster Property Management Ltd (No.1), Re*,[34] it was held that the use of statements obtained under IA 1986 s.235 in disqualification proceedings did not necessarily involve a breach of European Convention on Human Rights (ECHR) art.6;

(c)   in *Pantmaenog Timber Co Ltd, Re*,[35] the House of Lords held that the court may make an order under IA 1986 s.236 requiring third parties to disclose documents and provide information to the Official Receiver where the Official Receiver's sole purpose is to obtain evidence for use in the disqualification proceedings; and

(d)   a report compiled by the office-holder will not be subject to legal professional privilege. Therefore, the court can order disclosure of the report to a defendant to disqualification proceedings.[36] In contrast, the working papers of the office-holder or inspector will not be admissible or disclosable.[37]

The Secretary of State is entitled to use information which has come into his possession by means other than the report of the office-holder when determining whether an application for a disqualification order should be made. The Secretary of State will form his own view on the relevant report and is under no obligation to act in accordance with the opinion of the office-holder. The Secretary of State will commence proceedings where he believes that it is in the public interest to do so. The decision of the Secretary of State to commence proceedings is one which, in theory at least, is susceptible to judicial review, but the prospects of succeeding in such an application are likely to be very low.[38]

---

[33]   *Polly Peck International Ex p. The Joint Administrators* [1994] B.C.C. 15.

[34]   *Westminster Property Management Ltd (No.1), Re* [2000] 1 W.L.R. 2230; [2001] B.C.C. 121; [2000] 2 B.C.L.C. 396.

[35]   *Pantmaenog Timber Co Ltd, Re* [2003] UKHL 49; [2004] 1 A.C. 158; [2003] 3 W.L.R. 767.

[36]   In *Secretary of State for Trade and Industry v Baker (No.2)* [1998] Ch. 356; [1998] 2 W.L.R. 667; [1998] B.C.C. 888, Scott V-C held that disclosure of the report was necessary in the interests of fairness and to save costs.

[37]   *Astra Holdings Plc, Re* [1999] B.C.C. 121; [1998] 2 B.C.L.C. 44.

[38]   As displayed by the decision in *Secretary of State for Trade and Industry v Davies (No.1)* [1996] 4 All E.R. 289; [1997] B.C.C. 235; [1997] 2 B.C.L.C. 317.

13.5.3 *Procedure on an application for a disqualification order*

CDDA s.16(1) provides that "a person intending to apply for the making of a disqualification order shall give not less than 10 days' notice of his intention to the person against whom the order is sought".[39]

In previous cases, the courts have had to consider whether this provision is intended to be mandatory or directory. In the event that it were mandatory, the failure to comply with the ten-day notice period would render the proceedings a nullity, whereas the failure to comply with a directory provision would merely constitute a procedural irregularity which the court has a discretion to excuse. In *Secretary of State for Trade and Industry v Langridge*,[40] the Court of Appeal held that failure to give notice was a procedural irregularity and therefore did not render the proceedings a nullity.

The notice does not need to contain any indication of the grounds upon which a disqualification order will be sought; it needs only to state the intention to make an application for a disqualification order.[41] In fact, the notice is unlikely to be of any practical use to the director unless he can show that it is a case of mistaken identity. The respondent should attempt to use this period to obtain legal representation.

Applications for disqualification orders are to be made by the issue of a claim form and the use of CPR Pt 8.[42] All disqualification proceedings are to be allocated to the multi-track.[43]

Upon issuing the claim form or application notice, the claimant will be given a date for the first hearing, such date to be at least eight weeks after the date of issue.[44] At the time of issuing the claim form, the claimant shall file his evidence in support of the application.

There is an obligation on the claimant to set out in the affirmation in support the main parts of the evidence on which he intends to rely, which is

---

[39] The period of ten days is calculated excluding both the date on which the notice is given and the date on which the proceedings are issued. This provision is only applicable to those cases where the application is made to the court with jurisdiction to wind up a company and is not applicable where the court is empowered of its own motion to make a disqualification order or where the application is before a court which does not have jurisdiction to wind up a company: *Cedac, Re* [1991] Ch. 402; [1991] 2 W.L.R. 1343; [1991] B.C.C. 148.

[40] *Secretary of State for Trade and Industry v Langridge* [1991] Ch. 402; [1991] 2 W.L.R. 1343; [1991] B.C.C. 148.

[41] *Surrey Leisure Ltd, Re* [1999] 1 B.C.L.C 731; (1999) 96(6) L.S.G. 33.

[42] Practice Direction para.4.1. CPR Pt 8 is to apply to disqualification applications, subject to the provisions of the Practice Direction and the Disqualification Rules.

[43] Practice Direction para.2. Accordingly, the rules relating to allocation questionnaires and track allocation do not apply.

[44] Practice Direction para.4.3.

all the more important where there are no particulars of claim to identify the key facts upon which the court will be asked to exercise its powers. Fairness to the respondent demands that he be informed not only of the allegations of unfitness but also the essential facts which are to be relied on in support of them. The more serious the allegations made against the director, the more important it is for the case against him to be set out clearly and with adequate particularity. That applies in all cases where serious wrongdoing is alleged, particularly where it is asserted that the director knew his acts were wrongful or improper.[45]

It is for the claimant to effect service of the claim form, and the affidavit evidence upon which he relies,[46] which shall be accompanied by an acknowledgment of service. Service of the claim form by first class post shall be deemed to be effective on the seventh day after posting, unless the contrary is shown.[47]

Upon receipt of the claim form, the defendant should ensure that he files and serves the acknowledgment of service form within 14 days after service of the claim form. This acknowledgment of service form shall state whether:

(a)   he contests the application on the grounds that he was not a director or shadow director of a named company at the time of the conduct which forms the basis of the application, or that he disputes that his conduct was as alleged by the claimant;
(b)   in the case of any conduct which he admits, he disputes that such conduct renders him unfit; and
(c)   while not intending to defend the application for his disqualification, he intends to adduce mitigating factors with a view to reducing the period of disqualification which is to be imposed.[48]

If the defendant fails to file evidence within the applicable time limit and/or within any extension of time granted by the court, the court may make an order that unless the defendant files evidence by a specified date he shall be debarred from filing evidence without the permission of the court. If the defendant then fails to file evidence within the time specified by the debarring order and subject to any further court order, the disqualification application will be determined by way of an uncontested disposal hearing.[49] Within 28 days of service of the claim form upon him, the defendant must file and serve any evidence in opposition to the application upon which he wishes to rely. In the event that the claimant

---

[45]   *Secretary of State for Trade and Industry v Swan* [2003] EWHC 1780 (Ch); [2004] B.C.C. 877; (2003) 100(36) L.S.G. 37.
[46]   All evidence in disqualification proceedings is to be by affidavit, subject to the exception that when the official receiver is a party, his/her evidence may be in the form of a written report.
[47]   Practice Direction para.6.2.
[48]   Practice Direction para.7.1.
[49]   Practice Direction para.11.1.

wishes to put in evidence in reply, such evidence must be filed and served within 14 days after receiving the defendant's evidence. At all times before the first hearing of the application, it is open to the parties to extend the time for service of evidence by written agreement.[50]

At the first hearing of the application, the judge will either determine the case or give directions and adjourn the application. It is advisable to seek all necessary directions at this first hearing, as it is intended that disqualification applications should be determined at the earliest possible date. Furthermore, it will be in the defendant's interests to do so in order to minimise the costs of the proceedings.

On applications under CDDA ss.7 or 8, the court may hear and determine the application summarily on the first hearing of the application, without further notice to the defendant. In the event that this approach is taken by the court, the maximum period of disqualification which may be imposed by the court is five years. In circumstances where the court is of the view that a period in excess of five years would be appropriate, it will adjourn the application to be heard at a later date that will be notified to the defendant.[51] The court will also take the course of adjourning the application where it is of the view that there are questions of law or fact which are not appropriate for summary determination.[52] Where the court adjourns the application, it will also give any further directions for the case management of the application.[53] In contested applications, such directions are likely to include fixing of a pre-trial review of the case after the close of evidence.

13.5.4 Applications under CDDA section 7(2) to commence proceedings for an order under CDDA section 6 out of time

Applications under CDDA s.7 should be brought within three years (formerly two years) after the company became "insolvent" within the meaning ascribed to the term by CDDA s.6(2).[54] When the application is made outside this period, the permission of the court is needed. The application for permission should be made to the court which would have

---

[50] Practice Direction para.8.7.
[51] Disqualification Rules r.7(4)(a).
[52] Disqualification Rules r.7(4)b).
[53] Practice Direction para.9(2).
[54] Where more than one event of insolvency occurs, the two-year period begins to run from the time of the first event: *Tasbian Ltd (No.1), Re* (1989) 5 B.C.C. 729; [1989] B.C.L.C. 720. The case law supports the proposition that the day on which the company became insolvent within s.6(2) is to be included when calculating the relevant period of two years. There is no time limit in relation to applications for orders under ss.2–5, 8 and 10. For the purposes of the CDDA, proceedings to disqualify company directors are "brought" on the day when the request and claim form are received by the court office, rather than on the date that the form was issued by the court: *Secretary of State for Trade and Industry v Vohora* [2007] EWHC 2656 (Ch); [2008] Bus. L.R. 161; [2009] B.C.C. 369.

jurisdiction over the disqualification proceedings under CDDA s.6(3) if permission were to be given and the proposed respondent must be made a party.

The three-year period is not a limitation period, but merely a period during which proceedings can be brought without permission. After the period has expired a defendant director does not acquire immunity from suit. All that occurs is that the Secretary of State needs to surmount an additional hurdle. Thus, in *Secretary of State for Trade and Industry v Davies (No.1)*,[55] Millett LJ said at 298j–299b (referring to the two-year period which applied at that time):

> "I do not find it helpful to describe s.7(2) of the 1986 Act as a limitation provision, or to regard the grant of leave as depriving the respondent of an accrued immunity from suit. The grant of leave is built into the two-year period. Parliament clearly recognised that the two-year period might not be sufficient in every case. Even before the period expires, proceedings cannot be brought unless the Secretary of State has first determined that it is expedient in the public interest that they should be brought; after it has expired, the further requirement is imposed that the leave of the court should be obtained. There are then two preconditions instead of one, but that is all. Once the two-year period has expired, delinquent directors are not immune from disqualification proceedings; they are immune from such proceedings brought without the leave of the court, but that is a very different thing."

The Secretary of State will bear the burden of showing a good reason for the extension of the period. When permission is not obtained prior to the issue of a claim form outside this time limit, the defendant will be entitled to have the proceedings struck out, as the permission must be obtained prospectively, rather than retrospectively.

The case law reveals that the imposition of a limited period for the issue of proceedings by CDDA s.7(2) has two main objectives:

(a)   to enable those who have been directors of insolvent companies to have the ability to organise their affairs once the relevant period has passed free of the risk of future disqualification; and
(b)   to protect the public interest, as it is obviously wrong that a person whom the Secretary of State considers to be unfit to act as a director should be left free to act as one any longer than is necessary.[56]

The discretion of the court under s.7(2) is a wide and unfettered one, subject to the limitation that it must be exercised judicially. Factors which the court will take into account when considering an application to commence

---

[55]   *Secretary of State for Trade and Industry v Davies (No.1)* [1996] 4 All E.R. 289; [1997] B.C.C. 235; [1997] 2 B.C.L.C. 317.
[56]   *Blackspur Group Plc (No.2), Re* [1998] 1 W.L.R. 422; [1998] B.C.C. 11; [1998] 1 B.C.L.C. 676; *Noble Trees Ltd, Re* [1993] B.C.C. 318; [1993] B.C.L.C. 1185 at 1190; *Polly Peck International Plc (In Administration) (No.3), Re* [1993] B.C.C. 890; [1994] 1 B.C.L.C. 574 at 590.

proceedings out of time[57] include the length of the delay,[58] the reasons for the delay,[59] the prejudice caused to the director by the delay[60] and the strength and seriousness of the case against the director (the public protection factor).[61] These factors, although important, are not exhaustive, and all relevant factors will be taken into account. The court will then carry out a balancing exercise to determine whether the grant of permission is appropriate on the facts of the case, and in doing so its discretion is unfettered.[62] The approach described in this paragraph was confirmed in *Instant Access Properties Ltd, Re*,[63] in which Floyd J said:

> "If the evidence passes this threshold, the court embarks on a balancing exercise in which both the gravity of the charge and the court's provisional view of the prospects of the charges being established come into play. At the stage of granting permission, without the benefit of full evidence or cross-examination or detailed submissions, it is extremely difficult for the court to come to a precisely graduated estimate of the prospects of success. Nevertheless, these twin considerations, gravity and prospects of success, are a measure, admittedly an imprecise one, of the public interest in allowing the proceedings to continue. They are inter-related. There is little in the way of public interest in allowing a trivial case to go forward even if there are very good prospects of it being established. Equally the public interest will not be particularly well served by allowing even a very grave allegation to go forward if it appears that it faces really significant difficulties of proof."

ECHR art.6(1), incorporated into English law by the Human Rights Act 1998, provides the right to a fair trial within a reasonable time. The rationale for the reasonable time requirement is that defendants should not be subjected to "prolonged uncertainty and anxiety in learning whether their opponents' claims will be established or not".[64] The relevant question is whether having regard to all the circumstances of the case, the time taken to

---

[57] *Probe Data Systems Ltd (No.3), Re* [1992] B.C.C. 110; [1992] B.C.L.C. 405 at 416.

[58] *Manlon Trading Ltd (Directors: Disqualification), Re* [1996] Ch. 136; [1995] 3 W.L.R. 839; [1995] 4 All E.R. 14 at 23: the public interest in the disqualification of unfit directors does not diminish with the passage of time, but it must be balanced against the right of the director to carry on without the threat of disqualification proceedings for an unreasonable period.

[59] *Secretary of State for Trade and Industry v McTighe (No.1)* [1993] B.C.C. 844; [1994] 2 B.C.L.C. 284: permission was given where the delay was attributable to the conduct of the directors. Where the delay is not due to the conduct of the director, the reasons for such delay should be explained by the Secretary of State.

[60] *Polly Peck International Plc (In Administration) (No.3), Re* [1994] 1 B.C.L.C. 574: illness of the director may, on suitable facts, be taken to represent so serious a prejudice as to bar an extension. The prejudice caused by disqualification proceedings on the director's livelihood may be taken into account. The weakening of the director's evidence with the passage of time may also be taken into account as a form of prejudice.

[61] *Secretary of State for Trade and Industry v Cleland* [1997] B.C.C. 473; [1997] 1 B.C.L.C. 437; *Packaging Direct Ltd, Re* [1994] B.C.C. 213.

[62] The unfettered nature of the discretion is illustrated by *Stormont Ltd, Re* [1997] 1 B.C.L.C. 437, in which the court held that it would be appropriate to give permission in relation to the claim against one of the directors but exercised its discretion to stay the proceedings on the basis of undertakings offered by the director.

[63] *Instant Access Properties Ltd, Re* [2011] EWHC 3022 (Ch); [2012] 1 B.C.L.C. 710.

[64] *Att-Gen's Reference (No.2 of 2001)* [2003] UKHL 68; [2004] 2 A.C. 72; [2004] 2 W.L.R. 1 at [16].

determine the person's rights and obligations was unreasonable.[65] The relevant period will begin at the earliest time at which a person is officially alerted to the likelihood of proceedings against him. Where a delay between the official notification of the likelihood of proceedings and the hearing of the matter is such that the hearing is likely to be unfair, the court or tribunal should dismiss the proceedings.[66]

These principles have been applied in disqualification cases. In *Davies v United Kingdom*,[67] for example, the European Court of Human Rights (ECtHR) held that the state was responsible for the greater part of the five-and-a-half years it took to dispose of the proceedings. In all the circumstances the proceedings had not been pursued with the diligence required by art.6 and the failure to determine the applicant's "civil rights and obligations" within "a reasonable time" amounted to a violation of art.6.

In *Eastaway v United Kingdom*,[68] the disqualification proceedings against the applicant lasted almost nine years. The applicant himself was largely responsible for the last period of some three-and-a-half years because of his unmeritorious application for judicial review to the High Court and appeals to the Court of Appeal and House of Lords. However, the ECtHR held that the state authorities were responsible for a substantial part of the delay prior to that period. Applying the principles that the reasonableness of the length of proceedings was to be assessed in the light of the circumstances of the case and that special diligence was called for in bringing disqualification proceedings to an end expeditiously because of the considerable impact which they had on a company director's reputation and ability to practise his profession, the ECtHR held that the proceedings against the applicant had not been pursued with the diligence required by art.6 and that the failure to determine the applicant's "civil rights and obligations" within "a reasonable time" amounted to a violation of art.6.[69]

13.6 Determining unfitness

Three factors must be present for the court to make an order under s.6:

(a)   the defendant must have been a director of the company;
(b)   the company must have become "insolvent"; and

---

[65] *Porter v Magill* [2001] UKHL 67; [2002] 2 A.C. 357; [2002] 2 W.L.R. 37 at [109].
[66] *Att-Gen's Reference (No.2 of 2001)* [2003] UKHL 68; [2004] 2 A.C. 72; [2004] 2 W.L.R. 1 at [24].
[67] *Davies v United Kingdom* [2005] B.C.C. 401; [2006] 2 B.C.L.C. 351; (2002) 35 E.H.R.R. 29.
[68] *Eastaway v United Kingdom* [2006] 2 B.C.L.C. 361; (2005) 40 E.H.R.R. 17.
[69] See, by way of comparison, *Secretary of State for Trade and Industry v Eastaway* [2003] B.C.C. 520; [2001] 1 B.C.L.C. 653, in which it was held that there had been no breach of the defendant's right to a hearing "within a reasonable time" even though proceedings against him under CDDA s.6 had been on foot for over eight years.

(c)   the defendant's conduct as a director of that company must be shown to have been such as to make him unfit to be concerned in the management of a company.

13.6.1   Who is a director?

The reach of the CDDA extends to apply to:

(a)   directors properly appointed in accordance with the articles of association of the company;
(b)   shadow directors as defined in CDDA s.22(5); and
(c)   de facto directors.

The first category is straightforward and requires no comment; the second and third categories have proved more difficult in their application.

13.6.1.1   Shadow directors

The statutory definition in CDDA s.22(5) provides (in summary) that a shadow director is someone on whose directions and instructions the company's board is accustomed to act, but a person is not deemed a shadow director by reason only that the directors act on advice given by him in a professional capacity. The meaning of the definition of shadow director was considered by the Court of Appeal in *Secretary of State for Trade and Industry v Deverell*,[70] in which Morritt LJ summarised the law in a number of propositions as follows:

(a)   the definition of a shadow director is to be construed in the normal way to give effect to the parliamentary intention ascertainable from the mischief to be dealt with and the words used. In particular, as the purpose of the CDDA is the protection of the public and as the definition is used in other legislative contexts, it should not be strictly construed merely because it also has quasi-penal consequences in the context of the CDDA;
(b)   the purpose of the disqualification legislation is to identify those, other than professional advisers, with real influence in the corporate affairs of the company. But it is not necessary that such influence should be exercised over the whole field of its corporate activities;
(c)   whether any particular communication from the alleged shadow director, whether by words or conduct, is to be classified as a direction or instruction must be objectively ascertained by the court in the light of all the evidence. In that connection it is not necessary to prove the understanding or expectation of either giver or receiver. In many, if

---

[70]   *Secretary of State for Trade and Industry v Deverell* [2001] Ch. 340; [2000] 2 W.L.R. 907; [2000] 2 All E.R. 365. See also *Secretary of State for Trade and Industry v Aviss* [2006] EWHC 1846 (Ch); [2007] B.C.C. 288; [2007] 1 B.C.L.C. 618 and *Instant Access Properties Ltd (in liq) v Rosser* [2018] EWHC 756 (Ch); [2018] B.C.C. 751.

not most, cases it will suffice to prove the communication and its consequence. Evidence of such understanding or expectation may be relevant but it cannot be conclusive. Certainly the label attached by either or both parties then or thereafter cannot be more than a factor in considering whether the communication came within the statutory description of direction or instruction;

(d)   non-professional advice may come within that statutory description. The proviso excepting advice given in a professional capacity appears to assume that advice generally is or may be included. Moreover the concepts of "direction" and "instruction" do not exclude the concept of "advice" for all three share the common feature of "guidance";

(e)   it will, no doubt, be sufficient to show that in the face of "directions or instructions" from the alleged shadow director the properly appointed directors or some of them cast themselves in a subservient role or surrendered their respective discretions. But it is not necessary to do so in all cases. Such a requirement would be to put a gloss on the statutory requirement that the board are "accustomed to act" "in accordance with" such directions or instructions;

(f)   if the directors usually took the advice of the putative shadow director, it is irrelevant that on the occasions when he did not give advice the board did exercise its own discretion; and

(g)   if the board were accustomed to act on the directions or instructions of the putative shadow director it is not necessary to demonstrate that their action was mechanical rather than considered.

13.6.1.2 *De facto directors*

CDDA s.22(4) provides that the definition of the word "director" includes "any person occupying the position of director". This makes clear that the jurisdiction to make a disqualification order extends to a person occupying the position of a director, by whatever name called.

Persons who undertake the functions of directors, even though not formally appointed as such, are called de facto directors or directors in fact. But the authorities are not entirely consistent in defining a de facto director. The critical issue, and the jurisprudential difficulty, is to distinguish a de facto director from someone who acts for, or otherwise in the interests of, a company but is never more than, for example, a mere agent, employee or adviser.

The correct approach is for the court to ask whether the individual in question assumed the status and functions of a company director so as to make himself responsible as if he were a de jure director, i.e. whether he was part of the corporate governing structure.[71] This approach was confirmed by the Supreme Court in *Revenue and Customs Commissioners v Holland*.[72]

The following guidance may be derived from the relevant authorities[73]:

(1)   a de facto director must presume to act as if he were a director;

(2)   he must be, or have been in point of fact, part of the corporate governing structure and participated in directing the affairs of the company in relation to the acts or conduct complained of;

(3)   he must be either the sole person directing the affairs of the company or a substantial or predominant influence and force in so doing as regards the matters of which complaint is made. Influence is not otherwise likely to be sufficient;

(4)   the key indicia is whether the person concerned has undertaken acts or functions such as to suggest that his remit to act in relation to the management of the company is the same as if he were a de jure director;

(5)   the functions he performs and the acts of which complaint is made must be such as could only be undertaken by a director, not ones which could properly be performed by a manager or other employee below board level;

(6)   it is relevant whether the person was held out as a director or claimed or purported to act as such: but that, and/or use of the title, is not a necessary requirement, and even that may not always be sufficient;

(7)   his role may relate to part of the affairs of the company only, so long as that part is the part of which complaint is made;

(8)   lack of accountability to others may be an indicator; so also may the fact of involvement in major decisions;

(9)   the power to intervene to prevent some act on behalf of the company may suffice; and

(10) the person concerned must be someone who was more than a mere agent, employee or advisor.

13.6.1.3   Mutually exclusive concepts?

Formerly, it had been suggested that the two concepts of de facto director and shadow director were mutually exclusive. But the better view is that there is no conceptual difficulty in concluding that a person can be both a shadow director and a de facto director simultaneously. He may, for example, assume the functions of a director as regards one part of the

---

[71]   *Kaytech International Plc, Re* [1999] B.C.C. 390; [1999] 2 B.C.L.C. 351. See also *Secretary of State for Trade and Industry v Hollier* [2006] EWHC 1804 (Ch); [2007] Bus. L.R. 352; [2007] B.C.C. 11 and *Secretary of State v Hall* [2006] EWHC 1995 (Ch); [2009] B.C.C. 190.

[72]   *Revenue and Customs Commissioners v Holland* [2010] UKSC 51; [2010] 1 W.L.R. 2793; [2011] 1 All E.R. 430.

[73]   The propositions are usefully gathered together in *Secretary of State for Business, Innovation and Skills v Chohan* [2013] EWHC 680 (Ch); [2013] Lloyd's Rep. F.C. 351 at [40].

company's activities (say, marketing) and give directions to the board as regards another (say, manufacturing and finance).[74]

Even so, it may still be necessary to distinguish between the two categories in determining the extent of their culpability. Thus, in *Ultraframe (UK) Ltd v Fielding*,[75] Lewison J (as he then was) stated (at [1289]):

> "The indirect influence exerted by a paradigm shadow director who does not directly deal with or claim the right to deal directly with the company's assets will not usually, in my judgment, be enough to impose fiduciary duties upon him; although he will, of course, be subject to those statutory duties and disabilities that the Companies Act creates. The case is the stronger where the shadow director has been acting throughout in furtherance of his own, rather than the company's, interests. However, on the facts of a particular case, the activities of a shadow director may go beyond the mere exertion of indirect influence."

Lewison J went on to stress that the real question is as to the nature of the activities undertaken, and not a label attached to their perpetrator.

13.6.2 *When does a company become insolvent?*

A company becomes "insolvent" for the purposes of CDDA s.7 on the happening of any of the events mentioned in CDDA s.6(2), namely:

(a) the company goes into liquidation at a time when its assets are insufficient for the payment of its debts and other liabilities and the expenses of the winding up;

(b) the company enters administration; or

(c) an administrative receiver of the company is appointed.

The event of insolvency may occur "whether while he was a director or subsequently": CDDA s.6(1)(a). For the purposes of determining whether a liquidation was insolvent:

(a) the assets and liabilities should be valued as at the date of liquidation, and not according to what is subsequently realised;

(b) interest accruing on debts after the liquidation and statutory interest under IA 1986 s.189 is not to be taken into account; and

(c) the "expenses of the winding up" must be construed as if the word "reasonable" were included immediately before the phrase.[76]

---

[74] *Secretary of State for Trade and Industry v Aviss* [2006] EWHC 1846 (Ch); [2007] B.C.C. 288; [2007] 1 B.C.L.C. 618 at [89]. The Supreme Court confirmed in *Revenue and Customs Commissioners v Holland* [2010] UKSC 51 at [91] and [110] that the differences between de facto directors and shadow directors may have been overstated in *Hydrodan (Corby) Ltd, Re* [1994] B.C.C. 161; [1994] 2 B.C.L.C. 180.

[75] *Ultraframe (UK) Ltd v Fielding* [2005] EWHC 1638 (Ch); [2006] F.S.R. 17; [2007] W.T.L.R. 835.

[76] *Gower Enterprises Ltd, Re* [1995] B.C.C. 293; [1995] 2 B.C.L.C. 107.

It will not be open to the director to challenge the validity of the insolvency proceedings, by reason of which the company is deemed to be insolvent, within the disqualification proceedings. The validity of the insolvency proceedings must be determined in other proceedings, pending the outcome of which the disqualification proceedings may be adjourned or stayed.[77]

13.6.3 What is "unfitness"?

In *Sevenoaks Stationers (Retail) Ltd, Re*,[78] Dillon LJ said that the words contained in CDDA s.6:

> "are ordinary words of the English language and they should be simple to apply in most cases. It is important to hold to those words in each case ... [T]he true question to be tried is a question of fact—what used to be pejoratively described in the Chancery division as a jury question."

As Hoffmann LJ put it in *Grayan Building Services Ltd (In Liquidation), Re*,[79] the court must decide whether the conduct in question, "viewed cumulatively and taking into account any extenuating circumstances, has fallen below the standards of probity and competence appropriate for persons fit to be directors of companies". Ordinary commercial mis-judgement is in itself not sufficient to justify disqualification.

CDDA s.12C and Sch.1 provide a non-exhaustive list of guidance on the matters to which the court must "have regard in particular"[80] when assessing whether a respondent is unfit. The matters listed in CDDA Sch.1, to which the court must have regard in particular, include any breach of fiduciary duty extent of responsibility for the insolvency of the company and a failure to comply with the obligations placed on a director by the IA 1986. However, it is clear that the provisions of CDDA s.12C and Sch.1 are not exhaustive and the court can consider any misconduct of the director in deciding whether he is unfit.[81]

---

[77] *Secretary of State for Trade and Industry v Jabble* [1998] B.C.C. 39; [1998] 1 B.C.L.C. 598; (1997) 94(35) L.S.G. 33 at 601.

[78] *Sevenoaks Stationers (Retail) Ltd, Re* [1991] Ch. 164; [1990] 3 W.L.R. 1165; [1990] B.C.C. 765 at 176B–176G.

[79] *Grayan Building Services Ltd (In Liquidation), Re* [1995] Ch. 241; [1995] 3 W.L.R. 1; [1995] B.C.C. 554 at 253E.

[80] CDDA s.9(1). These words and the phrase "conduct in relation to any matter connected with or arising out of the insolvency of that company" in CDDA s.6(2), show that the court may take any misconduct into account: *Secretary of State for Trade and Industry v Ball* [1999] 1 B.C.L.C. 286.

[81] See, e.g. the observations of Neuberger J in *Secretary of State for Trade and Industry v Lubrani (No.2)* [1998] B.C.C. 264; [2001] 1 B.C.L.C. 562 at 568 and Peter Gibson J in *Bath Glass Ltd, Re* (1988) 4 B.C.C. 130 at 133. See also *Secretary of State v Murphy* [2019] EWHC 459 (Ch) at [11].

In each case it will be a question of fact for the court whether the conduct amounts to unfitness. Jonathan Parker J summarised the position in *Secretary of State for Trade and Industry v Baker (No.6)*[82]:

> "In considering the question of unfitness, the respondent's conduct must be evaluated in context—'taken in its setting'... It follows ... that the court will assess the competence or otherwise of the respondent in the context of and by reference to the role in the management of the company which was in fact assigned to him or which he in fact assumed, and by reference to his duties and responsibilities in that role. Thus the existence and extent of any particular duty will depend upon how the particular business is organised and upon what part in the management of that business the respondent could reasonably be expected play (see *Bishopsgate Investment Management Ltd (in liq) v Maxwell (No.2)* [1993] B.C.L.C. 1282 at 1285 per Hoffmann LJ) ... Thus while the requisite standard of competence does not vary according to the nature of the company's business or to the respondent's role in the management of that business—and in that sense it may be said that there is a 'universal standard'—that standard must be applied to the facts of each particular case. Hence to say that the Act envisages a 'universal' standard of competence applicable in all circumstances takes the matter little further since it says nothing about whether the requisite standard has been met in any particular case. What can be said is that the court, whilst taking full account of the demands made upon a respondent by his management role, will recognise incompetence in whatever circumstances and at whatever level of management it occurs, from the chairman of the board down to the most junior director."

Although the determination of whether a director's conduct was such to render him unfit will always be a question of fact, an analysis of the case law discloses the following guidelines:

(a) ordinary commercial mis-judgement is in itself not sufficient to justify disqualification[83] but incompetence "to a very marked degree or a high degree" can amount to unfitness[84];

(b) misconduct by the director which has the consequence of conferring a benefit upon him personally to the detriment of the company is likely to lead to a finding of unfitness. An obvious example is where a director causes a company to enter into a transaction which constitutes a preference within IA 1986 s.239 or a transaction at an undervalue within IA 1986 s.238, the beneficiary of which is the director. In *Funtime Ltd, Re*,[85] for example, a company director who knowingly entered transactions that were improper preferences in favour of himself and his associates was declared to be unfit to be a director;

---

[82] *Secretary of State for Trade and Industry v Baker (No.6)* [2001] B.C.C. 273; [1999] 1 B.C.L.C. 433 at 483g and 484c–484g.

[83] *Lo-Line Electric Motors Ltd, Re* [1988] Ch. 477; [1988] 3 W.L.R. 26; (1988) 4 B.C.C. 415.

[84] *Official Receiver v Ireland* [2002] B.C.C. 428; [2001] 1 B.C.L.C. 547; *Secretary of State for Trade and Industry v Baker (No.6)* [2000] 1 B.C.L.C. 523.

[85] *Funtime Ltd, Re* [2000] 1 B.C.L.C. 247.

(c)   criteria of competence, discipline in complying with the duties regarding records, accounts and returns, and honesty are highly relevant in assessing fitness or unfitness. However, the question for the court is the much broader issue of applying to the facts of the case the standard of conduct laid down by the courts appropriate to a person fit to be a director, that being a question of mixed law and fact. In particular, unfitness by reason of incompetence may be established without proof of a breach of duty. On the other hand, although dishonesty is not the acid test, the court must be very careful before holding that a director is unfit because of conduct that does not amount to a breach of any duty (whether contractual, tortious, statutory or equitable) to anyone, and is not dishonest[86];

(d)   the companies legislation does not impose on directors a statutory duty to ensure that their company does not trade while insolvent; nor does the legislation impose an obligation to ensure that the company does not trade at a loss. Directors may properly take the view that it is in the interests of the company and of its creditors that, although insolvent, the company should continue to trade out of its difficulties. They may properly take the view that it is in the interests of the company and its creditors that some loss-making trade should be accepted in anticipation of future profitability.[87] If, with hindsight, it is clear that this decision was the wrong one, it does not follow automatically that the directors should be disqualified. The evaluation of risk is to some extent a subjective matter[88] ordinary commercial mis-judgement is not in itself sufficient to justify disqualification[89];

(e)   however, causing a company to trade, first, while it is insolvent and, secondly, without a reasonable prospect of meeting creditors' claims is likely to constitute incompetence of sufficient seriousness to grant a disqualification order. But it is important to emphasise that it would usually be necessary for both elements of that test to be satisfied. In general, it is not enough for the company to have been insolvent and for the director to have known it. It must also be shown that he knew or ought to have known that there was no reasonable prospect of meeting creditors' claims[90];

(f)   non-payment of Crown debts is no more serious than a failure to pay other creditors and it cannot be treated as automatic grounds for

---

[86] *Secretary of State for Trade and Industry v Goldberg (No.2)* [2003] EWHC 2843 (Ch); [2004] 1 B.C.L.C. 597.

[87] *Secretary of State for Trade and Industry v Taylor* [1997] 1 W.L.R. 407; [1997] B.C.C. 172; [1997] 1 B.C.L.C. 341.

[88] *Secretary of State for Business Innovation and Skills v Aaron* [2009] EWHC 3263 (Ch) at [39].

[89] *Lo-Line Electric Motors Ltd, Re* [1988] Ch. 477; [1988] 3 W.L.R. 26; (1988) 4 B.C.C. 415 at 486 per Sir Nicolas Browne-Wilkinson V-C.

[90] *Secretary of State v Creegan* [2001] EWCA Civ 1742; [2004] B.C.C. 835; [2002] 1 B.C.L.C. 99 at 101. See also *Secretary of State for Trade and Industry v Gill* [2004] EWHC 933 (Ch); [2006] B.C.C. 725; *Kotonou v Secretary of State for Business, Enterprise and Regulatory Reform* [2010] EWHC 19 (Ch); and *Secretary of State for Business, Innovation and Skills v Akbar* [2017] EWHC 2856 (Ch), [2018] B.C.C. 448.

disqualification. However, in some cases it might be evidence of a policy of unfair discrimination between creditors which would merit disqualification[91];

(g)   a history of repeated failure, whether ignorant or intentional, to comply with the statutory obligations to prepare and file financial statements, annual returns and other statutory documents will usually lead to a finding of unfitness.[92] The principal reason behind the attitude of the court to this type of misconduct is that compliance with the statutory provisions should enable the company to detect and address financial difficulties at an early juncture. The failure to detect such matters at an early stage is likely to have the consequence of increasing losses sustained by creditors;

(h)   directors should be careful before seeking to transfer the assets and goodwill of an ailing company to a new company prior to the ailing company entering into a formal insolvency procedure. Apart from the personal liabilities which can arise out of such facts, it is very likely that the director will be found to be unfit, particularly if the transferee company subsequently becomes insolvent[93]; and

(i)   a director of a company which becomes insolvent is obliged, under the IA 1986, to co-operate with and give assistance to the office-holder appointed over the insolvent company's affairs. This co-operation is essential for the office-holder to be able to identify and recover the company's assets. A repeated failure on the part of a former director to comply with his duty to co-operate is likely to result in a finding of unfitness.[94]

It is no answer for a defendant in disqualification proceedings to assert that he had little or no involvement in the company's business and no real knowledge of its affairs. A director is under a continuing duty to keep himself fully informed about the company's affairs, and this duty will not be satisfied where the director maintains only a negligible actual involvement in the affairs of the company.[95] As long as an individual continues to hold office as a director, he is under a duty to inform himself as to the financial affairs of the company and to play an appropriate role in the management of its business. In the event that a director is not prepared to

---

[91] *Sevenoaks Stationers (Retail) Ltd, Re* [1991] Ch. 164; [1990] 3 W.L.R. 1165; [1991] B.C.L.C. 325; *Verby Print for Advertising Ltd, Re* [1998] B.C.C. 652; [1998] 2 B.C.L.C. 23 at 39; *Official Receiver v Dhaliwall* [2006] 1 B.C.L.C. 285; *Official Receiver v Key* [2009] B.C.C. 11; [2009] 1 B.C.L.C. 22; *Cathie v Secretary of State for Business, Innovation and Skills* [2012] EWCA Civ 739; [2012] B.C.C. 813.

[92] *Secretary of State for Trade and Industry v Ettinger* [1993] B.C.C. 312; [1993] B.C.L.C. 896; *Frewen v Secretary of State* [2002] EWHC 2688 (Ch); [2003] 2 B.C.L.C. 305; *NCG Trading Ltd, Re* [2004] EWHC 3203 (Ch); *Normanton Wells Properties Ltd, Re* [2011] 1 B.C.L.C. 191.

[93] *Keypak Homecare Ltd (No.2), Re* [1990] B.C.C. 117; [1990] B.C.L.C. 440; *Walker v Secretary of State for Trade and Industry* [2003] EWHC 175 (Ch); [2003] 1 B.C.L.C. 363.

[94] *Secretary of State for Trade and Industry v McTighe (No.2)* [1997] B.C.C. 224; [1996] 2 B.C.L.C. 477.

[95] *Wimbledon Village Restaurant Ltd, Re* [1994] B.C.C. 753; *Secretary of State for Trade and Industry v Thornbury* [2007] EWHC 3202 (Ch); [2008] B.C.C. 768; [2008] 1 B.C.L.C. 139; *Secretary of State for Trade and Industry v Hall* [2006] EWHC 1995 (Ch); [2009] B.C.C. 190.

discharge these responsibilities properly, the appropriate course is for him to resign his directorship.[96] There are several cases where a director has, in effect, been disqualified on grounds of complete non-participation, and the courts have made clear repeatedly that a lack of knowledge (or alleged lack of knowledge) will not prevent a finding of unfitness.[97]

A non-executive director will also be under an obligation to inform himself of the affairs of the company, and to read and understand the company's accounts, and enquire as to any difficulties.[98] This approach is necessary to ensure that the practice of appointing respected city figures as directors to improve investor confidence has appropriate safeguards.

Under CDDA Sch.1, the court is required to consider the relative responsibility of the respondent for the defaults of the company. In practice, this will involve both the consideration of each director's involvement in the particular acts relied upon to establish unfitness, and an investigation of the division of work within the company, and the experience and particular expertise of each board member.

The fact that a director has professional advisers who fail to draw attention to the impropriety of transactions might negate a finding of unfitness or be a mitigating factor in the period of disqualification to be imposed. However, any reliance on such advice must be reasonable.[99]

The delegation of certain functions is a necessary element of the affairs of most companies, and directors are clearly entitled to order the company's affairs in this manner. While this is a perfectly reasonable act, the mere act of delegation will not absolve a director from any responsibility for that particular part of the business. When delegating the functions a director will be entitled to trust the competence and integrity of the person to a reasonable extent, in the absence of any facts putting him on inquiry, but he and the other members of the board of directors, will remain responsible for supervising the conduct of the person in fulfilling the delegated duties.[100] The extent of supervision which is necessary will be dependent on the facts of the particular case, and it is likely to be a different standard for executive and non-executive directors.

---

[96] *Dicksmith (Manufacturing) Ltd (In Liquidation), Re* [1999] 2 B.C.L.C. 686.

[97] *Secretary of State for Trade and Industry v Baker (No.6)* [1999] 1 B.C.L.C. 433; *Park House Properties Ltd, Re* [1998] B.C.C. 847; [1997] 2 B.C.L.C. 530; *Secretary of State for Trade and Industry v Harper* [1993] B.C.C. 518 at 526–528; *Secretary of State for Trade and Industry v Thornbury* [2007] EWHC 3202 (Ch); *Official Receiver v Key* [2009] B.C.C. 11; [2009] 1 B.C.L.C. 22.

[98] *Continental Assurance Co of London Plc (In Liquidation) (No.1), Re* [1996] B.C.C. 888; [1997] 1 B.C.L.C. 48; (1996) 93(28) L.S.G. 29.

[99] *Official Receiver v Ireland* [2002] B.C.C. 428; [2001] 1 B.C.L.C. 547.

[100] *Secretary of State for Trade and Industry v Baker (No.6)* [1999] 1 B.C.L.C. 433 at 586e–586f; *Polly Peck International Plc (In Administration) (No.3), Re* [1994] 1 B.C.L.C. 574; *Westmid Packing Services Ltd (No.2), Re* [1998] 2 B.C.L.C. 646.

There are certain duties, however, which cannot be delegated to others. For example, statutory duties such as maintaining proper financial statements, and fiduciary duties cannot be delegated to others. Furthermore, all directors, including non-executive directors need to keep themselves informed of the company's financial position.

A director will not simply be able to assert that another director had responsibility for the area of the business which led to the failure of the company. The board of directors as a whole remains collectively responsible for the supervision of the conduct of the individual director in carrying out the delegated functions.[101] A non-executive director will be able to rely on what he is told by the executive directors, but must ensure that he evaluates the information given in a critical and objective manner.[102]

It is imperative for the less senior directors to question the actions of those more senior to them and not simply be blindly led by an autocratic chairman. The duties to which directors are said to require them to act with "independence and courage".[103] An employee who has been promoted to the board of directors must ensure that he satisfies his responsibility for supervising the conduct of the more senior members of the board. In the event that he is not consulted on, for example, financial matters and the other members of the board refuse to consider the matter at his request, the appropriate course may be to resign unless he remains in office to continue to challenge the conduct of the other directors. If the other directors continue to pay insufficient attention to financial matters, the director may have a duty to inform the non-executive directors of the misconduct, or even the company's auditors.

Regardless of the size or structure of the company in relation to which the conduct alleged to render the director unfit is said to have occurred, the court must decide whether that conduct is such to render the respondent unfit to be concerned in the management of companies in general.[104]

The court is also able to consider the defendant's conduct in relation to other companies when determining whether the defendant is unfit, and such companies need not be insolvent. There is no need for the conduct relied upon in relation to the collateral companies to be the same as or similar to that adduced in relation to the "lead company". The only connection necessary is that the defendant had been a director of the collateral companies and that his conduct as a director of the collateral

---

[101] *Secretary of State for Trade and Industry v Ball* [1999] 1 B.C.L.C. 286 at 346f; *Secretary of State for Trade and Industry v Bairstow* [2004] EWHC 1730 (Ch); [2005] 1 B.C.L.C. 136. See also the general duties of company directors in Companies Act 2006 ss.171–177.

[102] *TLL Realisations Ltd, Re* Unreported 27 November 1998 (upheld on appeal, [2000] B.C.C. 998; [2000] 2 B.C.L.C. 223; (2000) 97(2) L.S.G. 29).

[103] *Secretary of State for Trade and Industry v Ball* [1999] 1 B.C.L.C. 286 at 353g.

[104] *Polly Peck International Plc (In Administration) (No.3), Re* [1994] 1 B.C.L.C. 574.

company tended to show unfitness.[105] The conduct of the defendant in relation to collateral companies will only be looked at cumulatively with those matters in relation to the insolvent company for the purpose of finding additional matters of complaint. The respondent will not be able to set up his conduct as a director in relation to other companies which have been successful in the period running up to his trial in order to prevent a disqualification order being made.[106]

In *Surrey Leisure Ltd, Re*,[107] the Court of Appeal rejected the argument that there could be only one "lead company" in an application for an order under CDDA s.6. The decision was based upon there being no provision in the CDDA which imposed a limit on the number of lead companies on which the applicant for a disqualification order could rely. It was held that it would be inappropriate for the court to impose a maximum on the number of lead companies in these circumstances as it would not advance the cause of public protection, and permitting more than one lead company would not give rise to any unfair procedure.

The burden of proving unfitness lies on the Secretary of State. Although the standard of proof is the civil standard, that is to say on the balance of probabilities, the seriousness of the allegation is reflected in the need for evidence of appropriate cogency to discharge the burden of proof.[108]

13.7   Period of disqualification

In the event that the court finds a director unfit on an application made under CDDA s.6, it is obliged to impose a disqualification period of at least two years. In contrast, where a director is found unfit on an application brought under CDDA s.8, the court can exercise its discretion against making a disqualification order in an appropriate case.

In the leading case of *Sevenoaks Stationers (Retail) Ltd, Re*,[109] the Court of Appeal laid down the following guidelines, dividing the possible 15-year period into three brackets:

(a)   the minimum bracket of two to five years is for those cases where, though disqualification is mandatory, the case is not very serious;
(b)   the middle bracket of six to ten years is for those cases which are serious but do not fall within the top bracket; and

---

[105] *Secretary of State for Trade and Industry v Ivens* [1997] B.C.C. 396; [1997] 2 B.C.L.C. 334.
[106] *Bath Glass Ltd, Re* (1988) 4 B.C.C. 130; [1988] B.C.L.C. 329; *Grayan Building Services Ltd (In Liquidation), Re* [1995] Ch. 241; [1995] 3 W.L.R. 1; [1995] B.C.C. 554.
[107] *Surrey Leisure Ltd, Re* [1999] B.C.C. 847; [1999] 2 B.C.L.C. 457; (1999) 96(32) L.S.G. 31.
[108] *Living Images Ltd, Re* [1996] B.C.C. 112; [1996] 1 B.C.L.C. 348 at 355–356; *H (Minors) (Sexual Abuse: Standard of Proof), Re* [1996] A.C. 563; [1996] 2 W.L.R. 8; [1996] 1 F.L.R. 80 at 586–587.
[109] *Sevenoaks Stationers (Retail) Ltd, Re* [1991] Ch. 164; [1990] 3 W.L.R. 1165; [1990] B.C.C. 765.

(c) the top bracket of over ten years is for particularly serious cases, e.g. where a director who has been disqualified once already is subsequently disqualified again.

The Court of Appeal has stated that it is not appropriate or necessary to perform a detailed comparison with the facts of other cases when determining the period of disqualification.[110] Generally speaking, however, it may be said that cases involving misappropriation are always serious, since creditors will legitimately feel aggrieved at others, particularly those responsible for the management of the company, benefiting at their expense.[111]

When determining the appropriate period of disqualification, the court will take into account any mitigating factors which are present. These factors can either be extenuating circumstances accompanying the misconduct such as reliance on professional advice or an absence of personal gain, or factors which are unconnected to the misconduct such as a low likelihood of re-offending or personal loss in the failure of the company (the former type of mitigating factor will have more weight).

13.8   Disqualification undertakings and the *Carecraft* procedure

The Insolvency Act 2000 (IA 2000) came into force on 2 April 2001. One of the main changes effected by this Act was the amendment of the CDDA so as to permit the Secretary of State to accept disqualification undertakings from directors without the need for a court hearing.[112] This procedure has largely avoided the need for the costly *Carecraft* procedure that the courts had developed previously.[113]

13.8.1   *Disqualification undertakings*

CDDA s.1A as amended provides that in the circumstances specified in CDDA ss.5A, 7, 8 , 8ZC and 8ZE the Secretary of State may accept a "disqualification undertaking". A disqualification undertaking is an undertaking by a person that, for a period specified in the undertaking, the person will not be a director of a company, act as receiver of a company's

---

[110] *Westmid Packaging Services Ltd (No.2), Re* [1998] 2 B.C.L.C. 646.

[111] *Secretary of State for Trade and Industry v Blunt* [2006] B.C.C. 112; [2005] 2 B.C.L.C. 463. See also *City Truck Group Ltd, Re* [2007] EWHC 350 (Ch); [2008] B.C.C. 76; [2007] 2 B.C.L.C. 649 and *Secretary of State for Business, Enterprise and Regulatory Reform v Poulter* [2009] B.C.C. 608. For an example of a lengthy period of disqualification, see *Secretary of State for Business, Innovation and Skills v Chohan* [2013] EWHC 680 (Ch); [2013] Lloyd's Rep. F.C. 351.

[112] The general background history to the introduction of undertakings is set out in the judgment of Chadwick LJ in *Blackspur Group Plc (No.3), Re* [2001] EWCA Civ 1595; [2004] B.C.C. 839; [2002] 2 B.C.L.C. 263.

[113] *Carecraft Construction Co Ltd, Re* [1994] 1 W.L.R. 172; [1993] B.C.C. 336; [1993] B.C.L.C. 1259.

property or in any way, whether directly or indirectly, be concerned or take part in the promotion, formation or management of a company unless (in each case) he has the leave of a court, and will not act as an insolvency practitioner.

The maximum period which may be specified in a disqualification undertaking is 15 years, and the minimum period which may be specified in a disqualification undertaking under ss.7 or 8ZC is two years.[114] Where a disqualification undertaking by a person who is already subject to such an undertaking or to a disqualification order is accepted, the periods specified in those undertakings or (as the case may be) the undertaking and the order are to run concurrently.[115]

In determining whether to accept a disqualification undertaking by any person, the Secretary of State may take account of matters other than criminal convictions notwithstanding that the person may be criminally liable in respect of those matters.[116]

A disqualification undertaking corresponds in terms to the order which the court may make under CDDA s.6 and has the same consequences. The director will be prohibited by the undertaking from acting as a director or as a receiver of a company's property or as an insolvency practitioner for the period stated in the undertaking and any breach of the undertaking during the period of disqualification would constitute a criminal offence under CDDA s.13.

The preliminary considerations are also broadly the same. Most importantly, CDDA s.7(1) requires the Secretary of State to form the view that it is expedient in the public interest that a disqualification order should be made against a person under s.6 before initiating proceedings for such an order. Section 7(2A) of the Act provides as follows:

> "If it appears to the Secretary of State that the conditions mentioned in Section 6(1) are satisfied as respects any person who has offered to give him a disqualification undertaking, he may accept the undertaking if it appears to him that it is expedient in the public interest that he should do so (instead of applying, or proceeding with an application, for a disqualification order)."

The Secretary of State must form the opinion that the conditions specified in s.6(1) are satisfied before becoming entitled to accept a disqualification undertaking. He must therefore apply his mind to the evidence of conduct and unfitness in precisely the same way as the court is required to do when considering an application for a disqualification order. CDDA s.12C(3) has the effect that, in determining whether he may accept a disqualification undertaking from any person, the Secretary of State shall, as respects the

---

[114] CDDA s.1A(2).
[115] CDDA s.1A(3).
[116] CDDA s.1A(4).

person's conduct as a director of any company concerned, have regard in particular to the matters mentioned in CDDA Sch.1. Before the Secretary of State can determine whether it is expedient in the public interest that he should accept the undertaking which is offered, he must first satisfy himself that the necessary basis for disqualification is made out.

The CDDA as amended also contains provisions for the release or modification of any disqualification undertakings that are accepted. CDDA s.1A makes the prohibition contained in the undertaking subject to the leave of the court, s.8A deals with variation of undertakings,[117] and CDDA s.17 sets out the procedure to be followed in cases where application for leave is made. On the hearing of an application for leave for the purposes of s.1(1)(a) or 1A(1)(a), the Secretary of State must appear and call the attention of the court to any matters which seem to him to be relevant, and may himself give evidence or call witnesses.[118]

A director who has given a disqualification undertaking may also apply to the court under s.8A for the period of disqualification to be reduced or for the undertaking to cease to be in force. On an application under s.8A, the applicant is not permitted to challenge any facts recorded in the agreed statement of unfit conduct, unless either some ground was shown which would be sufficient to discharge a private law contract or some ground of public interest was shown which outweighed the importance of holding a party to his agreement.[119] On the hearing of an application under subs.(1), the Secretary of State shall appear and call the attention of the court to any matters which seem to him to be relevant, and may himself give evidence or call witnesses: see CDDA s.8A(2).

The Secretary of State is entitled to refuse to accept a disqualification undertaking if it is not accompanied by an acceptable statement of unfit conduct.[120] He has power to require such a statement and is entitled to refuse to accept a disqualification undertaking if an acceptable statement is not provided.

CDDA s.9B, as inserted by Enterprise Act 2002 s.204(2), provides for "competition disqualification undertakings". It applies where:

(a) the Competition and Markets Authority (CMA) thinks that a company has committed or is committing a breach of competition law; and
(b) the CMA also thinks that a director of that company is unfit to be concerned in the management of a company; and

---

[117] See *Taylor v The Secretary of State for Business, Innovation and Skills* [2016] EWHC 1953 (Ch) for a discussion of this jurisdiction.
[118] CDDA s.17(5).
[119] *Secretary of State for Trade and Industry v Jonkler* [2006] EWHC 135 (Ch); [2006] 2 All E.R. 902; [2006] 2 B.C.L.C. 239.
[120] *Secretary of State for Trade and Industry v Eastaway* [2003] B.C.C. 520; [2001] 1 B.C.L.C. 653.

(c)   the director in question offers to give the CMA a disqualification undertaking.

The CMA has a discretion to accept a disqualification undertaking from the director instead of applying for or proceeding with an application for a disqualification order. The maximum period that may be specified in a disqualification undertaking is 15 years.

13.8.2   *The Carecraft procedure*

Where the parties are able to agree the wording of a statement of unfit conduct but fail to reach agreement in respect of the period of disqualification, the *Carecraft* procedure may be used.

The adoption of the *Carecraft* procedure is dependent upon the parties being able to draft an agreed statement. This statement will be placed before the court, and the court will be requested to exercise its discretion to make an order based only upon the facts in the statement. The use of the procedure is now enshrined in the Practice Direction para.12. The Practice Direction further provides that where the court makes a disqualification order under the *Carecraft* procedure, the *Carecraft* statement should be annexed to the order.

The ultimate discretion as to whether to make an order on a *Carecraft* basis lies with the court, and this gives rise to need for the statement to provide for its status in the event that the court refuses to deal with the application on this basis. This should ensure that any admissions of fact made by the director in the statement cannot be used at the full hearing of the application.

There is no critical time by which a director must agree to the use of the *Carecraft* procedure or otherwise face a full trial of the application for his disqualification. In the interest of costs, however, it will be prudent for the director to determine whether he is amenable to compromising the proceedings by use of the *Carecraft* procedure at the earliest opportunity. To this end, the defendant should prepare his evidence at the earliest possible stage in order to evaluate the relative strengths and weaknesses of the case against him. The Secretary of State will not usually be prepared to enter into negotiations until after he has received the director's affidavit evidence in opposition to his application. It is advisable that all negotiations which are focused upon agreeing a *Carecraft* statement should be conducted on a without prejudice basis. This will ensure that in the event that the parties are unable to reach an agreement, the negotiations will not be available to the court at the full trial of the application.

In addition to setting out those admitted or undisputed facts which are said to justify a finding of unfitness, the *Carecraft* statement should also set out any mitigating circumstances relied upon by the parties. The willingness of the director to adopt the *Carecraft* procedure may, in itself, constitute a mitigating factor.

13.9 Discontinuance of proceedings

The Secretary of State may discontinue disqualification proceedings at any time by filing and serving a notice of discontinuance on each defendant specifying against which defendants the claim is discontinued.[121] The costs incurred by the director in defending the proceedings up to the date of service of the notice will, unless the court otherwise orders, be paid by the Secretary of State.[122] When the director has filed a defence prior to the discontinuance of the proceedings and the Secretary of State seeks to make another claim arising out of the same or substantially the same facts, the Secretary of State will need the permission of the court to make the claim.[123] The fact that a defendant to disqualification proceedings has previously successfully resisted disciplinary proceedings will not necessarily be a bar to the commencement of subsequent disqualification proceedings against him.[124]

13.10 Appeals

A defendant may appeal against a disqualification order on the ground that it should not have been made or on the ground that the period of disqualification is excessive. An appeal may also be made by the Secretary of State on the ground that the period of disqualification is too lenient. An appeal from an order made by a county court judge, or a district judge, or an ICC judge will lie to a single judge of the High Court. Permission to appeal is required. Appeals from a High Court judge will lie to the Court of Appeal. Again, permission is required.

The appeal will be a true appeal rather than a hearing de novo, with the result that the appellate court will not depart from the trial judge's findings of primary fact on the oral evidence of the witnesses unless such finding was perverse. In *Grayan Building Services Ltd (In Liquidation), Re*,[125] Hoffmann LJ explained the general principle in the following terms:

---

[121] CPR Pt 38. In circumstances where any party to the disqualification proceedings has given an undertaking to the court, the Secretary of State will need the permission of the court to discontinue the proceedings.

[122] CPR 38.6.

[123] CPR r.38.7.

[124] *Secretary of State for Trade and Industry v Baker (No.4)* [1999] 1 W.L.R. 1985; [1999] B.C.C. 639; [1999] 1 B.C.L.C. 226.

[125] *Grayan Building Services Ltd (In Liquidation), Re* [1995] Ch. 241; [1995] 3 W.L.R. 1; [1995] B.C.C. 554 at 254.

"The [trial] judge is deciding a question of mixed fact and law, in that he is applying the standard laid by the courts (conduct appropriate to a person fit to be a director) to the facts of the case. It is in principle no different from the decision as to whether someone has been negligent ... On the other hand, the standards applied by the law in differing contexts vary a great deal in precision and generally speaking, the vaguer the standard and the greater the number of factors which the court has to weigh up in deciding whether or not the standards have been met, the more reluctant an appellate court will be to interfere with the trial judge's decision ... I agree with the way in which the matter was put in *Re Hitco 2000 Ltd* [1995] B.C.C. 161: 'Plainly, the appellate court would be very slow indeed to disturb such conclusion as to fitness or unfitness. In many, perhaps most, cases the conclusion will have been so very much assisted and influenced by the oral evidence and demeanour of the director ... that the Appellate Court will be in nowhere near as good a position to form a judgment as to fitness or unfitness than was the trial judge. But there may be cases where there is little or no dispute as to the primary facts and the Appellate Court is in as good a position as the trial judge to form a judgment as to fitness. In such cases the Appellate Court should not shrink from its responsibility to do so, and, if satisfied that the trial judge was wrong, to say so' ..."[126]

Similarly, the actual order or period of disqualification will not be interfered with unless the trial judge can be shown to have erred in principle. In *Deaduck Ltd (In Liquidation), Re*,[127] Neuberger J gave the following guidance in relation to appeals concerned with the length of a period of disqualification:

"In this connection care must be taken before an appellate court interferes with the period of disqualification imposed by an inferior court. To use a term sometimes invoked in connection with criminal appeals, it is normally inappropriate for the appellate court to tinker with the period imposed. Nonetheless, where the appellate court is satisfied that a period of disqualification imposed was too great to a significant extent, or where the appellate court considers that appropriate factors were not or cannot have been taken into account, it is right, indeed, it is only fair on the director concerned, for the appellate court to interfere."[128]

It is possible, in theory, for a disqualified person to seek a stay of the order pending his appeal. However, the courts have repeatedly held that a disqualification order should not be stayed save in exceptional cases and that the correct course of action for the disqualified director will be to apply for permission to act as a director notwithstanding the disqualification, pending the hearing of the appeal.[129]

---

[126] See also *Kotonou v Secretary of State for Business, Enterprise and Regulatory Reform* [2010] EWHC 19 (Ch).

[127] *Deaduck Ltd (In Liquidation), Re* [2000] 1 B.C.L.C. 148.

[128] For an example of a successful appeal against the length of the period of disqualification, see *R. v Randhawa (Charnit)* [2008] EWCA Crim 2599.

[129] See *Secretary of State for Trade and Industry v Bannister* [1996] 1 W.L.R. 118; [1995] B.C.C. 1027; [1995] 2 B.C.L.C. 271 and *Secretary of State for Business, Enterprise and Regulatory Reform v Sainsbury* [2009] EWHC 3456 (Ch).

13.11   The effect of disqualification orders and undertakings

Disqualification orders and undertakings are recorded in a public register kept by the Secretary of State, which also includes details of any relevant permission to act granted by the courts. A disqualified person must resign from any offices which he is prohibited from holding.[130]

13.11.1   The extent of disqualification

CDDA s.1(1) provides that a disqualification order is one that prevents the person subject to the order from acting as a director,[131] liquidator or administrator,[132] a receiver or manager of a company's property,[133] or being directly or indirectly concerned or taking part in the promotion, formation, or management of a company.[134] CDDA s.1 was amended by the IA 2000 to prevent disqualified directors from acting as insolvency practitioners. CDDA s.1A(1), which relates to disqualification undertakings, replicates the provisions of s.1(1) as amended by the IA 2000.

Upon the making of a disqualification order, the court does not have jurisdiction to order that the disqualified person is prohibited only from doing certain of the acts specified in s.1(1); it is an all or nothing situation.[135] There is no jurisdiction to limit a disqualification order to the holding of directorships in a public company.[136] Furthermore, the court does not have jurisdiction to impose additional prohibitions upon the disqualified person.

A company for the purposes of CDDA s.1(1) includes any company which may be wound up under IA 1986 Pt V. As explained above, this has the effect of extending the prohibition to foreign companies susceptible to being wound up here as unregistered companies.

Where a disqualification order is made, the prohibition will apply to companies limited by guarantee and unlimited companies, as well as private and public companies limited by shares.[137] In the case of

---

[130] Articles of association often require a director to resign upon becoming "prohibited by law from being a director".

[131] CDDA s.1(1)(a).

[132] CDDA s.1(1)(b).

[133] CDDA s.1(1)(c).

[134] CDDA s.1(1)(d).

[135] *Gower Enterprises Ltd (No.2), Re* [1995] B.C.C. 1081; [1995] 2 B.C.L.C. 201; *R. v Bramley (Philip Lindsey)* [2004] EWCA Crim 3319.

[136] *R. v Ward (Michael Grainger)* [2001] EWCA Crim 1648; [2002] B.C.C. 953; *Times* 10 August 2001.

[137] This is the effect of CDDA s.22(9).

partnerships, where an insolvent partnership is wound up as an unregistered company under Pt V of the Act, the provisions of ss.1, 1A , 5A, 6–10, 12C, 13–15C, 17, 19(c) and 20 of, and Sch.1 to, the CDDA will apply, with modifications.[138]

The disqualified person will be prohibited from acting as a director regardless of the title he uses, with the result that he will be in breach of the order or undertaking if he is acting as a director even if the title he uses is, for example, "trustee".[139] It is also irrelevant whether the person is a de jure director or a de facto director. Furthermore, disqualification on the grounds of unfitness will result in the person being prohibited from acting as a shadow director in relation to a company.[140] Disqualification will also prevent the person from acting as a director of a building society,[141] a member of the committee of management or officer of an incorporated friendly society,[142] or a director or officer of an NHS foundation trust,[143] among other things.

The other prohibition in CDDA s.1(1) which merits further consideration is that of being directly or indirectly concerned or taking part in the promotion, formation or management of a company. There is no statutory definition for the terms "promotion", "formation" or "management". Interpretation of these terms is left to the courts. The protective purpose of disqualification is likely to result in a liberal interpretation of these words.[144] The concepts of "taking part in" promotion, formation and management and being "concerned in" promotion, formation and management are distinct and either may be satisfied by direct or indirect conduct.[145]

It is likely that any involvement in the internal or external management of a company will constitute a breach of a disqualification order or undertaking. Therefore a person who is unsure whether his proposed conduct would amount to a breach of the terms of disqualification should consider applying to the court for permission to act in such a manner.

An insolvency practitioner who is subject to a disqualification order or undertaking is automatically disqualified from acting as an insolvency practitioner.[146] It is an offence under the IA 1986 to act as an insolvency practitioner without the relevant qualifications.

---

[138] The Insolvent Partnerships Order 1994 (SI 1994/2421) reg.16, and Sch.8.
[139] CDDA s.22(4).
[140] CDDA s.22(4). The term "shadow director" is defined in CDDA s.22(5) as "a person in accordance with whose directions or instructions the directors of the company are accustomed to act (but so that a person is not deemed a shadow director by reason only that the directors act on advice given by him in a professional capacity".
[141] CDDA s.22A.
[142] CDDA s.22B.
[143] CDDA s.22C.
[144] *R. v Campbell (Archibald James)* (1984) 78 Cr. App. R. 95.
[145] *R. v Campbell (Archibald James)* (1984) 78 Cr. App. R. 95.
[146] IA 1986 s.390(4). The effect of this provision is that the impact of the order will be wider

13.11.2 Criminal and civil sanctions

A person who acts in breach of a disqualification order or undertaking is liable to both criminal and civil sanctions.

Criminal sanctions are provided by CDDA s.13, which provides that a person who acts in breach of a disqualification order or undertaking is liable on conviction on indictment, to imprisonment for not more than two years or a fine or both,[147] and on summary conviction to imprisonment for not more than six months or a fine not exceeding the statutory maximum or both.[148] The offence committed by acting in breach of a disqualification order or undertaking is one of strict liability, with the consequence that an honest belief that the acts did not breach the order (or, as the case may be, undertaking) will not be a sustainable defence.[149]

Where a body corporate which is subject to a disqualification order or undertaking acts in contravention of the order or undertaking and it is proved that the offence occurred with the consent or connivance of, or was attributable to any neglect on the part of any director, manager, secretary or other similar officer, or any person purporting to act in such a capacity, he is also guilty of the offence.

Civil sanctions are provided by CDDA s.15, which provides for civil liability in circumstances where a person acts in breach of a disqualification order or undertaking. By virtue of CDDA s.15(1)(a), such a person will be personally liable for all the debts and other liabilities of the company which are incurred at a time when he was involved in the management of the company.[150] Section 15(1)(b) imposes civil liability on others involved in the management of the company who act, or are willing to act, on instructions given by a disqualified person without permission of the court if they know the person to be disqualified. The liability imposed is personal liability for all the debts and other liabilities of the company which are incurred at a time when the person was acting or was willing to act on instructions given by the disqualified person.[151] For this purpose, once it is shown that the person acted, or was willing to act, on the instructions of a person who he knew to be subject to a disqualification order or undertaking, there is a rebuttable presumption that he was willing at any time thereafter to act on any instructions given by the disqualified person.[152]

---

than that envisaged by CDDA s.1(1). The prohibition will extend to acting, e.g. as a provisional liquidator, administrative receiver, trustee in bankruptcy and supervisor of a corporate or individual voluntary arrangement.

[147] CDDA s.13(a).
[148] CDDA s.13(b).
[149] *R. v Brockley (Frank)* [1994] B.C.C. 131; [1994] 1 B.C.L.C. 606; (1994) 99 Cr. App. R. 385.
[150] CDDA s.15(3)(a).
[151] CDDA s.15(3)(b).
[152] CDDA s.15(5).

The liability imposed by s.15 is joint and several liability with the company and any other person who may be personally liable for the company's debts. Those who are appointed directors in place of the disqualified person should be particularly aware of this potential liability. They must ensure that they do not merely act as the nominee for the disqualified person, or act in any way which enables the disqualified person to play a role in the management of the company.

Where a company, acting by a disqualified director, enters into contracts, it is not possible to contend that those contracts are void for illegality; rather, they will be valid and enforceable. This is because the policy underlying CDDA s.11 is the protection of the public from untrustworthy individuals being involved in the management of a limited liability company. The protected class includes those who extended credit to the company. If a company were unable to sue on its contracts, the company's debtor book would be destroyed, and the very persons whom the legislation was designed to protect would thereby be prejudiced.[153]

13.12 Applications for permission to act by a disqualified director

Although a disqualification order or undertaking prohibits the director from engaging in any of the conduct specified in CDDA ss.1A(1) and 1(1), this prohibition is expressly subject to "the leave of the court".[154] This ensures that in appropriate cases a person will not be prevented from acting as a director for the entirety of the period of his disqualification.

The procedure which governs an application for permission to act is found in CDDA s.17. The Practice Direction provides that the application will be made by a Pt 8 Claim Form,[155] or by an application notice in existing disqualification proceedings.[156] If possible the application should be made immediately upon disqualification, or at least within the period before disqualification commences, as this will enable the applicant to request permission to continue to act in the proposed capacity pending the hearing of his application.[157] The respondent to an application for permission will be the person who made the application for the disqualification order.[158]

---

[153] *Hill v Secretary of State for the Environment, Food and Rural Affairs* [2005] EWHC 696 (Ch); [2006] 1 B.C.L.C. 601; [2005] B.P.I.R. 1330.
[154] The disqualification imposed upon an undischarged bankrupt by CDDA s.11(1) and under CDDA s.12(2) is also expressed to take effect "except with leave of the court".
[155] A claim form issued pursuant to CPR Pt 8.
[156] Practice Direction para.17.2.
[157] The evidence in support of the application must be by affidavit: Practice Direction para.19.
[158] In circumstances where the applicant for the disqualification order was not the Secretary of State, the Secretary of State should also be made a respondent to the application. For the

When considering an application for permission, the court will be mindful not to grant permission too freely for fear of undermining either the protection of the public[159] or the deterrent effect served by disqualification.[160] The case law dealing with applications by disqualified directors for permission to act reveals that the court will not usually entertain an application for the prohibition to simply be lifted; rather, the court will normally only grant permission in relation to a specific company or companies.

The applicant will bear the burden of proof in establishing that the case is one in which it is appropriate for the court to give permission. In cases where the court is prepared to give permission, it will only do so subject to conditions which it believes are necessary to give the public sufficient protection.[161] The court is likely, on balance, to be less ready to grant permission to the applicant to act if the disqualification order made against him was in the "higher bracket". The adoption of this approach by the courts reflects the need for protecting the public from the conduct of the individual which justified disqualification in the first place. The cases show that the chances of the application being successful are enhanced where the application relates to a company with which the applicant was involved at the time of disqualification but his conduct in relation to the company did not form part of the disqualification proceedings.

The court will look to all the circumstances of the case when determining whether to give permission, and its discretion is not fettered in any way.[162] The case law reveals that two factors will have an important bearing on the exercise of the court's discretion:

(a) whether there is a need for the applicant to act contrary to the prohibition imposed by CDDA s.1(1); and
(b) whether the public would be adequately protected in the event that the court gives permission.

The applicant will need to address the grounds upon which his original disqualification was based to show that there are sufficient controls in place

---

avoidance of doubt, the Practice Direction para.20.2 provides that in all applications the claim form or application notice and supporting evidence must be served on the Secretary of State.

[159] *Secretary of State for Trade and Industry v Baker (No.5)* [2000] 1 W.L.R. 634; [1999] 1 All E.R. 1017; [1999] B.C.C. 960; *Cunningham v Secretary of State for Trade and Industry* [2004] EWHC 760 (Ch); [2006] 1 B.C.L.C. 1; *Morija Plc, Re* [2007] EWHC 3055 (Ch); [2008] 2 B.C.L.C. 313.

[160] *Tech Textiles Ltd, Re* [1998] 1 B.C.L.C. 259; *Morija Plc, Re* [2007] EWHC 3055 (Ch); [2008] 2 B.C.L.C. 313.

[161] Conditions commonly ordered include the imposition of controls at board level, e.g. by the appointment of an independent accountant as a finance director, an obligation to hold board meetings at monthly intervals, and an obligation to have the monthly management accounts inspected by the auditors.

[162] *Dawes & Henderson (Agencies) Ltd (In Liquidation) (No.2), Re* [2000] B.C.C. 204; [1999] 2 B.C.L.C. 317; (1999) 96(8) L.S.G. 29; *Morija Plc, Re* [2007] EWHC 3055 (Ch); [2008] 2 B.C.L.C. 313.

at the company in respect of which he seeks permission to act as a director, to convince the court that the misconduct is unlikely to occur again. The court will wish to be informed of the financial position of the company to be satisfied that it is trading successfully, to be satisfied that the company has adequate financial controls; to be informed of the risks inherent in the company's business, and that the company is being managed in accordance with the standards prescribed by the relevant legislation and the courts.[163]

In *Secretary of State for Trade and Industry v Baker (No.5)*,[164] for example, Scott V-C heard an application by the former chief executive officer of Barings for permission to act as a non-executive director in respect of three private companies. The application was made prior to the disqualification order made against Mr Norris. There were no allegations of dishonesty or fraudulent impropriety; only allegations of incompetence. Scott V-C granted permission as he held that there was no risk of the recurrence of the defects apparent in Mr Norris's previous conduct. This was especially so in a case where the applicant was not seeking to be given permission to exercise any executive responsibilities in relation to the companies. Permission was therefore given on the condition that Mr Norris remained an unpaid non-executive director and that he be barred from entering into a service contract with the companies. Scott V-C stated:

> "The improprieties which have led to and required the making of a disqualification order must be kept clearly in mind when considering whether a grant of Section 17 leave should be made. If the conduct of a director has been tainted by any dishonesty, if the company in question has been allowed to continue trading while obviously hopelessly insolvent, if a director has been withdrawing from a struggling company excessive amounts by way of remuneration in anticipation of the company's collapse and, in effect, living off the company's creditors, and if a disqualification order were then made, these circumstances would loom very large on any Section 17 application. The court would, I am sure, have in mind the need to protect the public from any repetition of the conduct in question. That conduct, and the protection of the public from it, would have been the major factor requiring the imposition of the disqualification."[165]

He rejected the submission that the applicant had to show a "need" to act as a prerequisite for success, and held that the balancing exercise was between the protection of the public and the desire of the applicant to act as a director.

In *Britannia Homes Centres Ltd, Re*,[166] the registrar's decision to grant leave was overturned on appeal on the grounds that it undermined the effect of

---

[163] Including the numerous requirements imposed by the Companies Act 2006.
[164] *Secretary of State for Trade and Industry v Baker (No.5)* [2000] 1 W.L.R. 634; [1999] B.C.C. 960; [1999] 1 B.C.L.C. 262.
[165] *Secretary of State for Trade and Industry v Baker (No.5)* [2000] 1 W.L.R. 634; [1999] B.C.C. 960; [1999] 1 B.C.L.C. 262 at 265c–265e.
[166] *Britannia Homes Centres Ltd, Re* [2001] 2 B.C.L.C. 63; (2000) 97(26) L.S.G. 36.

the disqualification order. Leave would have meant that the disqualification order had no practical effect whatsoever because the respondent would have been trading in the same way having previously managed a series of one-man companies, all of which had gone into liquidation.

In the event that the applicant is successful, the order of the court granting permission to act, along with any conditions imposed, must be notified to the Secretary of State for entry on the disqualification register. Conditions which will commonly be attached to the grant of permission include the appointment of an independent accountant as a finance director, an obligation to hold regular board meetings, the auditing of monthly management accounts and the removal of the applicant from the company's bank mandate.

13.13 Conclusion

Disqualification is an essential part of the statutory mechanism for the prevention of abuse of limited liability. Directors of companies must ensure that they are fully aware of their duties and that they act in accordance with them. In the event that directors fail to conduct themselves in the required manner, disqualification plays an important role in the protection of the creditors and exists to deter others who hold the office of a director from engaging in similar conduct.

Index